CW01574900

A Companion to Heritage Studies

The *Blackwell Companions to Anthropology* offer a series of comprehensive syntheses of the traditional subdisciplines, primary subjects, and geographic areas of inquiry for the field. Taken together, the series represents both a contemporary survey of anthropology and a cutting edge guide to the emerging research and intellectual trends in the field as a whole.

1. *A Companion to Linguistic Anthropology*, edited by Alessandro Duranti
2. *A Companion to the Anthropology of Politics* edited by David Nugent and Joan Vincent
3. *A Companion to the Anthropology of American Indians*, edited by Thomas Biolsi
4. *A Companion to Psychological Anthropology*, edited by Conerly Casey and Robert B. Edgerton
5. *A Companion to the Anthropology of Japan*, edited by Jennifer Robertson
6. *A Companion to Latin American Anthropology*, edited by Deborah Poole
7. *A Companion to Biological Anthropology*, edited by Clark Larsen
8. *A Companion to the Anthropology of India*, edited by Isabelle Clark-Decès
9. *A Companion to Medical Anthropology*, edited by Merrill Singer and Pamela I. Erickson
10. *A Companion to Cognitive Anthropology*, edited by David B. Kronenfeld, Giovanni Bennardo, Victor de Munck, and Michael D. Fischer
11. *A Companion to Cultural Resource Management*, edited by Thomas King
12. *A Companion to the Anthropology of Education*, edited by Bradley A.U. Levinson and Mica Pollack
13. *A Companion to the Anthropology of the Body and Embodiment*, edited by Frances E. Mascia-Lees
14. *A Companion to Paleopathology*, edited by Anne L. Grauer
15. *A Companion to Folklore*, edited by Regina F. Bendix and Galit Hasan-Rokem
16. *A Companion to Forensic Anthropology*, edited by Dennis Dirkmaat
17. *A Companion to the Anthropology of Europe*, edited by Ullrich Kockel, Máiréad Nic Craith, and Jonas Frykman
18. *A Companion to Border Studies*, edited by Thomas M. Wilson and Hastings Donnan
19. *A Companion to Rock Art*, edited by Jo McDonald and Peter Veth
20. *A Companion to Moral Anthropology*, edited by Didier Fassin
21. *A Companion to Gender Prehistory*, edited by Diane Bolger
22. *A Companion to Organizational Anthropology*, edited by D. Douglas Caulkins and Ann T. Jordan
23. *A Companion to Paleoanthropology*, edited by David R. Begun
24. *A Companion to Chinese Archeology*, edited by Anne P. Underhill
25. *A Companion to the Anthropology of Religion*, edited by Janice Boddy and Michael Lambek
26. *A Companion to Urban Anthropology*, edited by Donald M. Nonini
27. *A Companion to the Anthropology of the Middle East*, edited by Soraya Altorki
28. *A Companion to Heritage Studies,* edited by William Logan, Máiréad Nic Craith and Ullrich Kockel

Forthcoming

A Companion to Oral History, edited by Mark Tebeau
A Companion to Dental Anthropology, edited by Joel D. Irish and G. Richard Scott
A Companion to South Asia in the Past, edited by Gwen Robbins Schug and S.R. Walimbe

A Companion to Heritage Studies

Edited by
William Logan, Máiréad
Nic Craith, and Ullrich Kockel

WILEY Blackwell

This edition first published 2016
© 2016 John Wiley & Sons, Inc.

Registered Office
John Wiley & Sons, Ltd, The Atrium, Southern Gate, Chichester, West Sussex, PO19 8SQ, UK

Editorial Offices
350 Main Street, Malden, MA 02148-5020, USA
9600 Garsington Road, Oxford, OX4 2DQ, UK
The Atrium, Southern Gate, Chichester, West Sussex, PO19 8SQ, UK

For details of our global editorial offices, for customer services, and for information about how to apply for permission to reuse the copyright material in this book, please see our website at: www.wiley.com/wiley-blackwell.

The right of William Logan, Máiréad Nic Craith, and Ullrich Kockel to be identified as the authors of the editorial material in this work has been asserted in accordance with the UK Copyright, Designs and Patents Act 1988.

All rights reserved. No part of this publication may be reproduced, stored in a retrieval system, or transmitted, in any form or by any means, electronic, mechanical, photocopying, recording or otherwise, except as permitted by the UK Copyright, Designs and Patents Act 1988, without the prior permission of the publisher.

Wiley also publishes its books in a variety of electronic formats. Some content that appears in print may not be available in electronic books.

Designations used by companies to distinguish their products are often claimed as trademarks. All brand names and product names used in this book are trade names, service marks, trademarks, or registered trademarks of their respective owners. The publisher is not associated with any product or vendor mentioned in this book.

Limit of Liability/Disclaimer of Warranty: While the publisher and authors have used their best efforts in preparing this book, they make no representations or warranties with respect to the accuracy or completeness of the contents of this book, and specifically disclaim any implied warranties of merchantability or fitness for a particular purpose. It is sold on the understanding that the publisher is not engaged in rendering professional services, and neither the publisher nor the author shall be liable for damages arising herefrom. If professional advice or other expert assistance is required, the services of a competent professional should be sought.

Library of Congress Cataloging-in-Publication Data

A companion to heritage studies / edited by William Logan, Máiréad Nic Craith and Ullrich Kockel.
pages cm. — (Wiley Blackwell companions to anthropology)
Includes bibliographical references and index.
ISBN 978-1-118-48666-5 (hardback)
1. Cultural property. 2. Historic sites. 3. National characteristics. 4. Ethnicity. I. Logan, William, 1948– editor of compilation. II. Nic Craith, Máiréad, editor of compilation. III. Kockel, Ullrich, editor of compilation.
CC135.C535 2015
363.6′9–dc23

2015003598

A catalogue record for this book is available from the British Library.

Cover image: Bamiyan, Afghanistan © Jon Arnold Images Ltd / Alamy ; Tourists on the new bridge over the river Neretva, Mostar, Bosnia and Herzogovina © age fotostock Spain, S.L. / Alamy; Traditional drum-making in Nam Kham, northern Shan State, Myanmar, 2014, photo © W. Logan

Set in 10/12pt Galliard by SPi Global, Pondicherry, India
Printed and bound in Malaysia by Vivar Printing Sdn Bhd

1 2016

We would like to dedicate this book to Tom McGrath, Máiréad's brother, who died unexpectedly while this book was in production.

Contents

List of Figures and Tables

Figures

Tables

Notes on Contributors

George Okello Abungu is Associate Professor of Heritage Studies at the University of Mauritius, fellow of the Stellenbosch Institute for Advanced Studies at the University of Stellenbosch, South Africa, and Visiting Professor of Applied Anthropology, University of Florida. A former director-general of the National Museums of Kenya, he is currently vice-president of ICOM and member of the international jury of the UNESCO Melina Mercouri International Prize for the Safeguard and Management of Cultural Landscapes. He has published widely in the areas of archaeology, heritage, and museology.

Natsuko Akagawa is Lecturer at the Royal Melbourne Institute of Technology University, Australia. She has undertaken heritage projects in Thailand, Vietnam, Japan, China, Macau SAR, and the Netherlands, and was a research fellow at East-West Centre, Hawaii. She is currently vice-president of the ICOMOS International Scientific Committee on Intangible Cultural Heritage. Among her publications is *Heritage Conservation and Japan's Cultural Diplomacy: Heritage, National Identity and National Interest* (2014).

Zeynep Aygen is Professor and chair at the Environmental Studies and Control Discipline, Mimar Sinan Fine Arts University, Istanbul, Turkey. She is a fellow of the Higher Education Academy and member of the Institute of Historic Building Conservation, both in the United Kingdom. Her research explores opportunities for physical and social sustainability in a cross-cultural context through conservation policies and their application.

Melissa F. Baird is Assistant Professor of Anthropology in the Social Sciences Department, Michigan Technological University. Her research seeks to broaden our understanding of global heritage and environmental politics, especially how heritage intersects with indigenous rights and environmental protection.

O. Hugo Benavides is Professor of Anthropology, Latin American and Latino studies, and International Political Economy and Development, Fordham University, New York. He is the editor and author of numerous articles and books on Latin American culture, politics, and history, including *Making Ecuadorian Histories: Four Centuries of Defining Power* (2004).

Kristal Buckley is Lecturer in Cultural Heritage at Deakin University's Cultural Heritage Centre for Asia and the Pacific, Melbourne, Australia. Her interests include evolving forms of global cultural heritage practice, and heritage institutions and knowledge practices. She has been a vice-president of ICOMOS and a member of the ICOMOS delegation to the World Heritage Committee since 2007.

Christina Cameron holds the Canada Research Chair on Built Heritage at the University of Montreal, Canada. She previously served as an executive with Parks Canada for thirty-five years. Involved with World Heritage since 1987, she carries out research on the history of the World Heritage Convention, and directs the World Heritage Oral Archives program.

Gary Campbell is an independent scholar based in Canberra, Australia. He has a background in sociology, political studies, and industrial relations. He is co-editor of the book *Heritage, Labour and the Working Classes*, and has co-authored work with Laurajane Smith on issues of representation and recognition of working-class heritage and de-industrialization.

Benjamin Chan is a member of the Political Science Department at the National University of Singapore. His research interests include humanitarianism, post-conflict reconciliation, and post-disaster relief and reconstruction. He has conducted fieldwork in mainland Southeast Asia and in Central America.

Andrea Connor is a research associate with the Transforming Cultures Research Center at the University of Technology, Sydney. She is a sociocultural researcher working across the fields of heritage studies, cultural geography, museum studies, and cultural studies. She is currently working on a research monograph on the afterlife of monumental things.

Rosemary J. Coombe is the Tier One Canada Research Chair in Law, Communication and Culture at York University, Toronto, Canada. Her work explores the intersection of intellectual property, cultural property, and human rights, with an emphasis on heritage politics, indigenous peoples, governmentalities, and neoliberalism.

Patrick Daly is a senior fellow at the National University of Singapore and a principal investigator at the Earth Observatory of Singapore. His research focuses upon the intersection of heritage and post-disaster/post-conflict recovery and reconstruction. He has conducted fieldwork in the Middle East, the Philippines, Cambodia, and post-tsunami Aceh, Indonesia. He is the co-editor of the *Routledge Handbook of Heritage in Asia* (2011).

Marion Demossier is Professor of French and European studies in the Department of Modern Languages, University of Southampton, England. She is the author of various works on wine producers, wine drinking culture, and wine consumption. She is currently finalising a book on a critical analysis of *terroir* in Burgundy.

Stefan Disko is an ethnologist focusing on human rights and the protection of cultural and natural heritage. He is currently co-editing a book on World Heritage sites and indigenous peoples' rights to be published jointly by the International Work Group for Indigenous Affairs (IWGIA), Forest Peoples Programme, and the Gundjeihmi Aboriginal Corporation.

Maria Economou is Lecturer in Museum Studies at the University of Glasgow, Scotland, and based at the Hunterian Museum and the Humanities Advanced Technology and Information Institute. She has worked at the universities of the Aegean, Manchester, and Oxford (at the Pitt Rivers Museum), and collaborated with cultural heritage institutions around the world, particularly on the use of new technologies for public engagement. She specializes in digital cultural heritage.

Julie Fedor is Lecturer in Modern European History at the University of Melbourne, Australia. She is the author of *Russia and the Cult of State Security* (2011), co-author of *Remembering Katyn* (2012), and co-editor of *Memory and Theory in Eastern Europe* (2013) and *Memory, Conflict and New Media* (2013).

Richard W. Hallett is Professor in the Department of Linguistics, Northeastern Illinois University. He is interested in the discourse(s) of tourism, especially in the social construction of national identity through government-sponsored tourism websites. His research agenda also includes issues in the areas of world Englishes, sociolinguistics, and second-language acquisition.

Benjamin Isakhan is Senior Lecturer in Politics and Policy Studies and Convenor of the Middle East Studies Forum at Deakin University, Australia. Ben is also Adjunct Senior Research Associate in the Department of Politics at the University of Johannesburg, South Africa.

Ullrich Kockel is Professor of Culture and Economy at Heriot-Watt University, Edinburgh, Scotland, Visiting Professor of Social Anthropology at Vytautas Magnus University, Kaunas, Lithuania, and Emeritus Professor of Ethnology at the University of Ulster. He is currently editor-in-chief of the *Anthropological Journal of European Cultures*, a fellow of the UK's Academy of Social Sciences, and a member of the Royal Irish Academy.

Kristin Kuutma is Professor of Cultural Research at the University of Tartu, Estonia. Her research in cultural history and anthropology focuses on disciplinary knowledge production, representation, and critical heritage studies. She has conducted fieldwork and published on policy-making and implementation at the international and local level of UNESCO's Intangible Heritage Convention.

William Logan is Professor Emeritus at Deakin University, Melbourne, Australia, where he was founding director of the Cultural Heritage Center for Asia and the Pacific.

He is a fellow of the Academy of Social Sciences in Australia, and has been president of Australia ICOMOS and a member of the Heritage Council of Victoria. His research focuses on World Heritage, heritage and human rights, and Asian heritage.

Christian Manhart is an art historian and archeologist. Since joining UNESCO in 1987, he has worked on the conservation of heritage sites in Africa and Asia, particularly Afghanistan. He was responsible in the World Heritage Centre for partnerships, communication, and, more recently matters arising in relation to the international conventions of 1954, 1970 and 2001, and the Committee for Restitution of Cultural Property, Museums and Creativity.

Lynn Meskell is Professor of Anthropology and director of the Archaeology Center at Stanford University. Her recent books include *The Nature of Culture: The New South Africa* (2012) and the edited volume *Cosmopolitan Archaeologies* (2009). Her current research focuses on the role of UNESCO in terms of heritage rights, sovereignty, and international politics.

Maurice Mugabowagahunde is a doctoral candidate in African archaeology at University of Bergen, Norway. His research interests include Rwandan prehistory and ethnography. He has previously conducted archeological and ethnographic research in Rwanda for the Institute of National Museums of Rwanda.

Webber Ndoro is a research associate with the Department of Archaeology, University of Cape Town, South Africa, and director of the African World Heritage Fund, based in Johannesburg.

Máiréad Nic Craith is Professor of European Culture and Heritage at Heriot-Watt University, Edinburgh, Scotland, having previously held a chair in the School of Social Sciences and Applied Social Studies at the University of Ulster. A Member of the Royal Irish Academy, she has also been an honorary professor at the University of Exeter, and a DAAD guest professor at the University of Göttingen, Germany.

Gertjan Plets was a researcher on the Altai Project at Ghent University, Belgium, from which he received his doctorate. He joined Stanford University initially as a Belgian American Education Fund (BAEF) fellow, and now holds a three-year research-intensive post-doctoral fellowship at the Stanford Archaeology Center.

Anca Claudia Prodan holds a Ph.D. in Heritage Studies and works as scientific assistant at the UNESCO Chair in Heritage Studies, BTU Cottbus-Senftenberg. Prior to this, she studied in Romania and Germany, obtaining degrees in Anthropology, Philosophy, and World Heritage Studies. Her research interests center on theories and concepts of culture and heritage.

Keir Reeves holds a chair in Australian history at Federation University Australia, Victoria, Australia. He has held teaching and research posts at Monash University and the University of Melbourne. In 2013 he was a visiting fellow at Clare Hall, University of Cambridge, England. His research concentrates on regional development as well as Australian, Asian, and Pacific cultural heritage.

Britta Rudolff holds an interim chair in heritage management at Brandenburg Technical University, Cottbus, Germany, where she is also the managing director of the Institute for Heritage Management. A cultural heritage conservator, with postgraduate qualifications in heritage studies and a doctorate in cultural geography, her focus has been on UNESCO heritage conventions.

Folarin Shyllon read law at King's College, London, and taught at the University of Ibadan, Nigeria, from 1975 to 2005. His teaching and research interests are in cultural property and intellectual property law. He is on the editorial board of the *International Journal of Cultural Property* and *Art Antiquity and Law*, and is chairperson of the Nigeria chapter of UNESCO's Memory of the World Committee.

Neil A. Silberman is an author, historian, and managing partner of Coherit Associates, an international heritage consulting firm. He is an adjunct lecturer in the Department of Anthropology at the University of Massachusetts, and serves as president of the ICOMOS International Committee on Interpretation and Presentation (ICIP). His research interests include interpretation theory, the history of heritage practice, and the politics of commemoration.

Helaine Silverman is Professor in the Department of Anthropology, University of Illinois, Urbana-Champaign, and director of CHAMP (Collaborative for Cultural Heritage Management and Policy). She is especially interested in the cultural politics of heritage production and management, tourism and economic development, and identity and memory. She has conducted research in Peru, Thailand, and England.

Anita Smith is Senior Lecturer responsible for course enhancement in the Faculty of Arts and Education, Deakin University, Melbourne, Australia. As an archeologist, she has been engaged in the UNESCO Pacific World Heritage Programme since 2004. She was a member of Australia's delegation to the World Heritage Committee between 2008 and 2012, and is editor of *World Heritage in a Sea of Islands* (2012).

Laurajane Smith is Professor of Heritage and Museum Studies and head of the Centre for Heritage and Museum Studies, School of Archaeology and Anthropology, Australian National University, Canberra, Australia. She is editor of the *International Journal of Heritage Studies*, co-editor (with William Logan) of Routledge's Key Issues in Cultural Heritage Series, and author of *Uses of Heritage* (2006).

Brenda Trofanenko holds the Canada Research Chair in Education, Culture, and Community at Acadia University in Wolfville, Nova Scotia, Canada. Her research focuses on how public cultural institutions define identity and knowledge through social processes. She is currently conducting research on how youth respond to the collective memories of distressing events.

Ron van Oers held a doctorate from Delft University of Technology, the Netherlands, and had worked at UNESCO's World Heritage Centre in Paris, coordinating various programs including the development of the Recommendation on the Historic Urban Landscape (2011). He was vice-director of the World Heritage Institute of Training and Research for Asia and the Pacific (WHITRAP) in Shanghai, China.

***Editor's note*:** **Dr van Oers** passed away unexpectedly on 28 April 2015 while on a UNESCO mission to Lhasa, Tibet. He made a major contribution to the cultural heritage field and will be greatly missed.

Ona Vileikis is an architect with international experience in World Heritage-related issues such as risk management, monitoring, geographic information systems, heritage documentation, and conservation. She is currently a doctoral researcher at the Raymond Lemaire International Centre for Conservation, University of Leuven, Belgium, working on the monitoring of serial transnational World Heritage issues and the use of geospatial content management systems, focused on the Central Asia Silk Roads.

Ana Filipa Vrdoljak is Professor of Law in the Faculty of Law, University of Technology, Sydney, Australia. She is the author of *International Law, Museums and the Return of Cultural Objects* (2006), editor of *The Cultural Dimension of Human Rights Law* (2013), and joint general editor (with Franceso Francioni) of the Oxford University Press series Cultural Heritage Law and Policy.

Jonathan Webber is Professor at the Institute of European Studies, Jagiellonian University, Kraków, Poland. He specializes in Jewish studies and Holocaust studies, and was a founding member of the International Auschwitz Council, serving on it between 1990 and 2012.

Gamini Wijesuriya has qualifications in architecture, history and historic preservation, and archaeology and heritage management. He was director of conservation in the Sri Lankan Department of Archaeology between 1982 and 1999, and principal regional scientist in the New Zealand Department of Conservation from 2001 to 2004. Moving to ICCROM in Rome in 2004, he played a key role in developing the 2011 World Heritage Capacity Building Strategy.

Tim Winter is Research Professor at the Alfred Deakin Institute for Citizenship and Globalisation, Deakin University, Melbourne, Australia. He has published widely on heritage, development, modernity, urban conservation, and tourism in Asia. He is co-editor of *The Routledge Handbook of Heritage in Asia* (2011), and editor of *Shanghai Expo: An International Forum on the Future of Cities* (2013).

Andrea Witcomb is Professor of Cultural Heritage and Museum Studies and deputy director of the Alfred Deakin Institute for Citizenship and Globalisation at Deakin University, Melbourne, Australia. Her work analyzes how museums and heritage sites create spaces for cross-cultural encounters. Her books include *Reimagining the Museum: Beyond the Mausoleum* (2003) and (with Kylie Message) *Museum Theory* (2015).

Haiming Yan is a sociologist at the Chinese Academy of Cultural Heritage, Beijing, and received his doctorate from the University of Virginia. His research interests include cultural sociology, memory and heritage, and globalization.

Acknowledgements

This volume originated in our desire to address the emergence and nature of the "new heritage studies," which we see as the exploration of cultural heritage as a construct resulting from processes that give present-day significance to elements from the past. Our conception of the volume was rigorously reviewed by Wiley-Blackwell. For their time and patience, we wish especially to thank Rosalie Robertson, the initial commissioning editor, and Ben Thatcher, the project editor at Blackwell.

We wish to say a special thank you to the contributors to this volume. Coming from five continents, these scholars were identified on the basis of their innovative ideas, practical expertise, and international reputation, and invited to contribute to this collaborative, multidisciplinary project in the cultural heritage field. They were a pleasure to work with. As the volume has been peer reviewed at every stage, from the original proposal to its final production, we would also wish to thank everybody who participated in that review process.

While this project was in progress, Máiréad Nic Craith and Ullrich Kockel moved from the University of Ulster in Northern Ireland to Heriot-Watt University in Edinburgh, and William Logan officially retired but was reappointed as emeritus professor attached to the Cultural Heritage Centre for Asia and the Pacific and the Alfred Deakin Research Institute at Deakin University in Melbourne. We would like to thank our colleagues in all three institutions – Deakin University, Heriot-Watt University, and the University of Ulster – for their continued support.

Finally, we would like to make a very special mention of Cristina Clopot and Philip Thomas. Cristina is currently undertaking her Ph.D. at Heriot-Watt University but devoted much time and effort in administering the project. Philip performed the critical copy editing role with an eagle eye for detail. We are very grateful to them both for their enthusiasm and professionalism in the preparation of the materials.

William Logan, Máiréad Nic Craith, and Ullrich Kockel

List of Abbreviations

ACCU	Asia-Pacific Cultural Centre of UNESCO
ACHPR	African Commission on Human and Peoples' Rights
ACHS	Association of Critical Heritage Studies
art.	article
EU	European Union
FPIC	free, prior, and informed consent
GDP	gross domestic product
GIS	geographic information system
GeoCMS	geospatial content management systems
ICCROM	International Centre for the Study of the Preservation and Restoration of Cultural Property
ICOM	International Council of Museums
ICOMOS	International Council on Monuments and Sites
IUCN	International Union for the Conservation of Nature
IWGIA	International Work Group for Indigenous Affairs
MoW	Memory of the World Programme
MDGs	Millennium Development Goals
NGO	non-governmental organization
OHCR	Office of the UN High Commissioner for Human Rights
para.	paragraph
POW	prisoner of war
sec.	section
UN	United Nations
UNCERD	United Nations Committee on the Elimination of Racial Discrimination
UNCESCR	United Nations Committee on Economic Social and Cultural Rights

UNCEHR	United Nations Commission on Human Rights
UNDESA	United Nations Department of Economic and Social Affairs
UNDG	United Nations Development Group
UNEP	United Nations Environment Programme
UNESCO	United Nations Educational, Scientific and Cultural Organization
UNGA	United Nations General Assembly
UN-Habitat	United Nations Human Settlements Programme
UNHRC	United Nations Human Rights Council
UNPFII	United Nations Permanent Forum on Indigenous Issues
UNSC	United Nations Security Council
WHIPCOE	World Heritage Indigenous Peoples Council of Experts
WIPO	World Intellectual Property Organization
WTO	World Trade Organization

CHAPTER 1

The New Heritage Studies: Origins and Evolution, Problems and Prospects

William Logan, Ullrich Kockel, and Máiréad Nic Craith

Heritage and heritage studies have evolved in quite astounding ways over the last sixty years. Nobody could have imagined when the Venice Charter (ICASHB 1964) jump-started the heritage profession in the aftermath of World War II that there would be a veritable heritage boom in the 1990s, and continuing into the twenty-first century. Who would have predicted that so much attention would now be paid to protecting environmental features, material culture, and living traditions from the past, or the vast numbers of community members, policy-makers, practitioners, and scholars engaged in caring for, managing, and studying heritage? Who would have foreseen the explosion of heritage-based cultural tourism, the reconfiguration of heritage as an economic asset, and a World Heritage List comprising of more than a thousand properties spread around the globe?

This volume seeks to investigate the story of expansion in heritage and heritage studies. Containing 37 chapters commissioned from 44 scholars and practitioners from 5 continents, it is designed to provide an up-to-date, international analysis of the field, the steady broadening of the concept of heritage and its social, economic, and political uses, the difficulties that often arise from such uses, and current trends in heritage scholarship. Starting from a position of seeing "heritage" as a mental construct that attributes "significance" to certain places, artifacts, and forms of behavior from the past through processes that are essentially political, we see heritage conservation not merely as a technical or managerial matter but as cultural practice, a form of cultural politics.

A Companion to Heritage Studies, First Edition. Edited by William Logan, Máiréad Nic Craith, and Ullrich Kockel.
© 2016 John Wiley & Sons, Inc. Published 2016 by John Wiley & Sons, Inc.

We are interested in the different extent to which various groups within global, national, and local communities are able to participate in heritage identification, interpretation, and management. Moreover, we want to address the extent to which communities have access to and enjoy heritage once it has been officially recognized, conserved, or safeguarded. This interest inevitably leads to human rights considerations, to developing closer intellectual links with international lawyers and others in the human rights field, and to strengthening both the multidisciplinary nature of heritage studies and what we sees as the critical relationship between theory and practice.

Whether this new vision of heritage studies represents a "paradigm shift" or only the culmination of changes already occurring in the heritage studies field since the late 1980s is an issue we will discuss later. For now, let us go back to the field's origins and interpret its evolution.

Expanding Heritage

When ideas of "heritage" were initially formalized, their focus was on monuments and sites. This was especially the case in Europe, from where these ideas spread across the British, French, and other European empires and the anglophone United States (Nic Craith 2007). Writer-practitioners such as John Ruskin and Nikolaus Pevsner in England, and Eugène Viollet-le-Duc in France, were enormously influential in the early days of heritage identification and protection. From these beginnings, heritage planners around the world have sought to protect broad areas of historic, aesthetic, architectural, or scientific interest. Although there is considerable variation across the world, most countries now attempt to protect, as official policy and through professional practice, a much wider range of features than they did 60 years ago.

It was gradually realized, for instance, that the protection of a monument or building was not in itself enough, and that good conservation work was often being rendered ineffective by unsympathetic developments allowed to occur in front of, beside, behind, or even over heritage buildings. Attention therefore extended to the precincts around major monuments and buildings. A further extension of interest took place in 1962, when André Malraux, then the French minister for culture, first established planning regulations (known as the *loi Malraux*) designed to protect and enhance the historic features of the Marais district of Paris. The English were also expanding their focus at about this time, to take in conservation areas, the first of which were designated in 1967. England now has over 8000 protected areas, including the centers of historic towns and cities, fishing and mining villages, eighteenth- and nineteenth-century suburbs, model housing estates, and historic transport links and their environs, such as stretches of canal (English Heritage n.d.).

At the international level, the World Heritage List established under UNESCO's Convention Concerning the Protection of the World Cultural and Natural Heritage (1972), or as it is commonly known, the World Heritage Convention, now contains a large number of cities inscribed for what the convention calls their Outstanding Universal Value. An Organization of World Heritage Cities, founded in 1993 with headquarters in Quebec City, today brings together 250 cities that are either inscribed or have inscribed sites within them (OWHC 2014). In 1992, the World Heritage Committee added the new category of "cultural landscapes" to the World Heritage system to allow recognition of places presenting a blend of cultural and natural elements. Twenty years later, the landscape concept was translated into urban areas as the "historic urban landscape," blending modern and historic architectural and urban design forms rather than natural and cultural elements, but nevertheless emphasizing, like cultural landscapes, the need for a holistic view of the environment and a sensitive, balanced approach to new human interventions.

Vernacular structures are now seen as being of cultural heritage interest; that is, structures that are not architect-designed but owner- or community-built, using available resources and traditional techniques. So, too, are industrial structures. Publications by Miles Lewis (1977), Paul Oliver (1997), and William Siew Wai Lim and Tan Hock Beng (1998) began to fill in major gaps in the tangible heritage literature. More recently there has been considerable heritage interest internationally in "cultural routes." The Council of Europe in 1987 established a program of European cultural routes that is managed from a specialized institute located in Luxembourg. The program's first initiative is the Santiago de Compostela Route, the famous Christian pilgrimage route of the Middle Ages. In the United States and Canada, efforts have been made to commemorate the Underground Railroad – the route taken by slaves trying to reach freedom before the Civil War – by protecting a series of key sites along its length. In Asia, UNESCO is supporting the Silk Road Project for developing cultural heritage and cultural tourism along the traditional routes of the silk trade between south-eastern Europe and China.

In the international development field, there was a marked shift in the 1990s in the attitude of key agencies such as the World Bank towards cultural heritage. Rather than seeing cultural heritage protection as an obstacle to development, it is now recognized that the two can go hand in hand to bring about more effective programs to raise standards of living in developing countries and elsewhere (Logan 2003: xxi).

Neil Silberman (Chapter 2) explores the evolving heritage conception, and the changing forms and functions of heritage places from their initial validation as national institutions in the early nineteenth century to their multicultural context in the early twenty-first century. He shows that the meanings and values of heritage places are neither static nor inherent, but ascribed by particular social groups choosing to emphasize or ignore particular items or aspects for social and political purposes. Romantic nationalism led to a first "heritage boom" during the emergence of nation-states in nineteenth-century Europe, as commemorative sites and structures were created to serve as tangible evidence of a nation's pedigree, harmonizing the diverse populations of nations into singularly national peoples, or sometimes re-fragmenting them, laying the foundations for new identity claims in the future. Already by the late nineteenth century, accelerating domestic and international tourism engendered a second "heritage boom," albeit differently motivated: the new "heritage tourists," on their quest for historical authenticity and exotic landscapes as means of (however temporary) escape from modern industrial life dominated by economic calculus, contradictorily created the demand that allowed for the commoditization of built heritage as a "cultural resource."

A focus on the built environment is arguably based on a European concept of cultural heritage, which is entirely appropriate for an environment dealing largely with the conservation of buildings made of stone, brick, and other durable materials (Logan 2006). This view of heritage has been frequently criticized. Walled cities, cathedrals, and eye-catching landscape formations like the Giant's Causeway in Northern Ireland heavily dominate the list of European World Heritage sites. This contrasts starkly with the concept of permanency found on other continents. An example of this is the imperial shrine at Ise, Japan. From a Western perspective, this shrine hardly qualifies as "old" since it is rebuilt every twenty years. However, from a Japanese perspective, it is old because it is rebuilt "in exactly the same way – using the same ancient instruments, materials – with each step of the process marked by appropriate ancient rituals" (Sahlins 2002: 9).

Although heritage has for a long time been defined primarily in terms of material objects, as "tangible heritage," there has been a parallel interest in what is nowadays called "intangible heritage," which for most of the past two centuries, however, remained in the shadow of the more prominent heritage of material objects and the built environment. To some extent and in some parts of the world, particularly Europe, North America, and Australia, this reflects the different social and political status of the signified: whereas monuments, works of fine art, castles, and cathedrals materially and visually project and transmit the heritage of the hegemony, folk songs and wisdom, as with many other traditional skills, tend to project and transmit heritage of the lower classes non-materially and orally.

Kristin Kuutma (Chapter 3) traces the emergence of folklore as an academic discipline and its subsequent involvement in cultural policy-making, including the contemporary transition from "folklore" to "intangible cultural heritage," and the discipline's contribution to the international management of heritage regimes. Originating during the period of nation-building, when they formed part of the creation of national cultural heritages, collections of folklore represent past repertoires and practices of mostly pre-industrial (peasant) lifestyles that nowadays often feed various linguistic, ethnic, or other local revival movements. As global power relationships at the turn of the twenty-first century are creating ever-shifting discourses of inclusion and exclusion, rootedness, and rights for possession, a need to identify and safeguard intangible cultural heritage was postulated, leading to the UNESCO Convention for the Safeguarding of the Intangible Cultural Heritage, adopted in 2003, and commonly known as the Intangible Heritage Convention. Although intangible elements had always been included in understanding the significance of heritage places under the World Heritage Convention (1972), this new convention focused on and led to a system for evaluating and safeguarding intangible heritage in its own right.

Heritage in the post-war years was conceived as and called "cultural property," an understanding and terminology that is still found today in relation to some disciplines (e.g. anthropology) and some forms of heritage (e.g. intellectual property). Pertti Anttonen has observed that "the cultural representations that are selected for making heritage-political claims are commonly called traditions, with a special emphasis on their character as cultural properties; that is, representations with an ownership label" (Anttonen 2005: 39). Ownership, lying at the heart of the notion of cultural property, has become a major and growing concern since the second half of the twentieth century. Folarin Shyllon (Chapter 4) considers these concerns, especially in the context of human rights. Access to and enjoyment of cultural heritage is considered to be a fundamental cultural right, a sub-category of human rights (Shaheed 2011). It might be argued that a similar right to intellectual property also exists, but some intellectual property rights do not fit human rights easily because they are economic and commercial rather than social or cultural. Considering cultural heritage as a fundamental human right can raise difficult ethical issues, as different cultures tend to regard their own values as universal and those of others, where they conflict, as culturally contingent. The debate on intellectual and, by extension, cultural property is rather more focused on economic value. As Shyllon points out, some cultural heritage, such as the sites inscribed on UNESCO's World Heritage List, may be regarded as universal property in the wider sense, while intellectual property rights tend to be held as monopolies.

Except from a natural law perspective, values can be seen as being in the mind; this goes even for economic, monetary values, which are the result of negotiations between actors. In contrast, artistic, linguistic, and technical skills can be seen as embodied. As an example of a non-Western approach to intangible heritage, Natsuko Akagawa (Chapter 5) examines the philosophy behind Japanese legislation for safeguarding cultural property. Her analysis highlights the significance of embodiment as a concept for understanding, and dealing with, heritage.

Landscapes of Memory

Recent decades have seen a growing interest across different contexts in how heritage has been embodied in the land (see Gilbert 2010). Perspectives on this vary, from geographical analyses of how hegemonic powers have shaped symbolic landscapes (e.g. Cosgrove 1984) to accounts of indigenous relationships with the land as an animate being and keeper of memory (e.g. Blue Spruce and Thrasher 2008). Associative landscapes now serve as the foundation for official designations of heritage origins, such as the French *terroir* discussed by Marion Demossier (Chapter 6). Involving communities in identifying and managing heritage landscapes and individual sites has become a key concern, moving traditional knowledge systems, their contribution to heritage management, and the need to support them into the spotlight.

However, this concern has not necessarily been recognized in the practice of international heritage programs. With reference to the Pacific islands, Anita Smith (Chapter 7) explores differences in the recognition of traditional knowledge systems in two UNESCO conventions – the World Heritage Convention (1972) and the Intangible Heritage Convention (2003) – and underlines long-standing critiques of the World Heritage system as Eurocentric in its determination of Outstanding Universal Value. In the late 1990s there was an attempt to establish an indigenous body to advise the World Heritage Committee in accordance with the UN Declaration on the Rights of Indigenous Peoples (United Nations 2007). While this initiative failed (see Logan 2013; Meskell 2013a), the call has been renewed in recent years (see Disko, this volume).

Although in public perception issues of land and landscape are particularly associated with indigenous peoples, they also play a major role in other contexts. The application by parts of Burgundy in eastern France for World Heritage status is a case in point. Using an "ethnographic gaze," Marion Demossier (Chapter 6) examines different conceptions of Burgundy as a re-territorialized site, and the construction of its micro-regional *climats* with their historical depth of place as "God-given," naturalized artifacts in the context of global competition, where UNESCO designation is prized for conveying an elite status.

The embodiment of heritage in landscapes of memory also raises issues of the relationships between natural and cultural heritage, and their frequent separation in the practice of heritage management, where different government and non-government bodies are in charge of different types of heritage, and conflicts of interest arise not least from budget constraints and varying lines of responsibility. This can be exacerbated where a designated site stretches across one or more political or administrative boundary.

The Curonian Spit, shared by Lithuania and Russia, is one of only 31 such transnational World Heritage sites where different approaches by the two administrations to environmental issues have been problematic (Armaitienė *et al.* 2007). Moreover, multiple layers of cultural memory affect the site and its contemporary meaning as heritage for different constituencies (Kockel 2012a). Appropriately contextualizing cultural heritages in relation to place and memory has been made difficult by a widespread tendency to treat cultural differences as mere constructs (Kockel and Nic Craith 2015). This is particularly apparent where we are dealing with places of pain and shame.

Not all heritage serves as a reminder of a glorious past (Logan and Reeves 2009). In the Lithuanian national open air museum at Rumšiškės near Kaunas, the extensive display of farm buildings and machinery, as well as the central small town, invoke nineteenth- and early twentieth-century Lithuania, but close to the center there is a clearing in the woods where the time frame is different. Several items, including an earthen yurt and a cattle wagon, commemorate the deportations of thousands of Lithuanians between 1941 and 1953, when they were sent to the Soviet Gulags (Kockel 2015). Jonathan Webber (Chapter 8) seeks to make sense of Auschwitz, designated a UNESCO World Heritage site in 1979, as a heritage site and landscape of memory. Auschwitz means different things to different victim groups in terms of their own histories, but also to other visitors. Emblematic of "undesirable heritage," it is at the same time a powerful symbol, a theatre where multiple memorial events are performed, and a destination for "dark" tourism attracting large numbers of spectators.

Collecting Heritage

Ever since interest in heritage began to develop, the collection of material items and oral testimony has been a central activity aimed at facilitating their preservation. This remains so despite a growing critique of museum and archiving practices. UNESCO's Memory of the World Programme (MoW) is a major initiative for the protection of documentary heritage. However, with the exception of Charlesworth (2010), it has been largely overlooked in academic research, even within the field of heritage studies. Against this background, Anca Claudia Prodan (Chapter 9) attempts to clarify the main features of the program, and to identify points for research. MoW is part of UNESCO's policies aimed at building inclusive knowledge societies. While acknowledging the contribution of MoW in that regard, Prodan argues that in the process of this, the program is reduced to being merely a source of information, and that it needs to be strengthened by being recontextualized within UNESCO's international system of heritage protection.

Artifact collections and the practices employed in accumulating them have come under scrutiny in the context of postcolonial critiques of intercultural relations. In 2002, the British Museum and the Louvre, together with an international group of major museums, issued the Declaration on the Importance and Value of Universal Museums (ICOM 2004) Most of these museums date back to the late eighteenth century, before the period of European imperial expansion, and the declaration has been widely interpreted as an attempt to guard against claims for the repatriation of much of their collections to the countries of origin. Such claims are made not only with regard to indigenous peoples, but extend to Western countries such as Greece, as the case of the Elgin Marbles illustrates. Maurice Mugabowagahunde (Chapter 10) discusses the politics of possession with regard to indigenous heritage in colonial and postcolonial museums, drawing on examples from sub-Saharan Africa, where indigenous peoples find much of their heritage conserved in European museums.

Using and Abusing Heritage

Consistent with the new rhetoric that came into fashion in the 1980s when neoliberal politics gained ground and governments set out to more clearly prioritize support for business organizations and, in Western Europe, to dismantle the welfare state that had emerged after World War II, local culture and heritage have increasingly been harnessed as foundations for social and economic growth. In most instances, this has involved the promotion of some form of "heritage" as a resource, especially for tourism. Consequent reappraisals of local resources created conditions under which the ailing primary sector, especially agriculture and fishing, was seen as something that could be revived as a supplier of raw materials for the production of culinary specialties (Tschofen 2008; see also Demossier, this volume) and other "cultural goods." Increasing emphasis on sustainability has led to the expectation that the utilization of culture will enhance rather than diminish the cultural resource base of a region or sociocultural group, which raises questions about the nature of the heritage "product" and its relation to traditional knowledge and practices (Kockel 2007a).

Socioeconomic Development

Heritage sites are increasingly ascribed with additional purposes beyond their original *raison d'être*, to the extent that they have become an integral part of the "memory industry" (Klein 2000). Connecting past and present, such sites also serve political functions. Brenda Trofanenko (Chapter 11) considers the case of the Grand-Pré National Historic Site, a recently designated UNESCO site in Canada, in the light of these developments. Grand-Pré tells the local story of the Acadian expulsion from Canada in the eighteenth century. With the recent World Heritage site designation, remembrance of the expulsion and interpreted historical narratives are placed alongside claims of Outstanding Universal Value for cultural traditions in the area, while the site is considered a key engine for economic development in a peripheral Canadian province with limited and declining natural resources and a disadvantageous demographic profile. This creates tensions between different expectations, but also raises a critical issue. From a policy-maker's perspective, heritage has several advantages over other resources: it is an omnipresent resource, in the sense that anyone anywhere, regardless of social, political, or economic position, can claim some kind of cultural heritage; and as a postmodern product, heritage is highly flexible and can be readily adapted to changing market conditions (Kockel 2007b). However, developers regarding "culture" and "heritage" as unlimited resources fail to appreciate the limited carrying capacity of any ecological system, including that of local cultures cast as heritage: there comes a point when further exploitation of the resource will destroy its very base. The heritage industry uses "visitor footfall" to measure the danger of overexploitation, mainly with regard to tangible heritage, but this is only one side of the issue. Traditional knowledge and practices also have limits beyond which any further exploitation can become destructive.

Considering a major recent initiative to brand Peru for the tourism market, Helaine Silverman and Richard Hallett (Chapter 12) offer a critical discourse analysis of promotional materials that reveal both a reification of iconic Peruvian material culture into intangible cultural heritage and a shift in the focus of the tourism industry from objects to emotions. The latter have recently come under the spotlight in tourism studies more generally (e.g. Picard and Robinson 2012). The new Peru "brand" exemplifies a tourism product that is about the sensory experience of immersion, which at least appears more immediate than the classic "sightseeing" version of cultural tourism.

Beyond tourism, heritage plays a crucial role in city image-making, and is increasingly being recognized for its potential to contribute to good design in urban areas (Logan 2005; Bristol 2010). Neil Silberman's review of the evolving social role of heritage places (this volume) shows how the categories and constellations of heritage places selected for protection and official commemoration facilitate a unique articulation of a spectrum of (often contradictory) collective memories. This creation of symbolic urban landscapes very much represents hegemonic discourses embodied in the built environment. At a different level, heritage designation often creates problems for those living in the vicinity of listed sites, raising issues of sustainability for both the sites and the communities living at and with them. Tim Winter (Chapter 13) takes the fortieth anniversary of the World Heritage Convention in 2012 as his starting point for an analysis of these challenges. The anniversary was celebrated under the theme of "sustainable development and the role of communities," reflecting recognition of significant problems in this area of governance, as well as the ties between cultural preservation and economic welfare.

Heritage is arguably central to social needs and to the preservation of communities in the face of developments that can compromise, and sometimes destroy, social fabric and community cohesion. Keir Reeves and Gertjan Plets (Chapter 14), examining this wider context of heritage, argue that considering tangible and intangible heritage together offers a valuable way of understanding the relevance of heritage to social needs, and especially to social cohesion.

Digital Heritage

In conventional museums, the focus has been on actual cultural objects from the past, whereas in contemporary exhibitions, the dynamics of the display, facilitated by modern technology and know-how, often take center stage. When visitors later remember the stunning special effects rather than the story behind these, the purpose of the display becomes questionable (Kockel 2007b). And when, as in the Bannockburn Heritage Centre near Stirling, Scotland, which opened to coincide with and celebrate the seven-hundredth anniversary of the famous battle between the English and Scots armies, the visitors are able to change the outcome of the battle in an animated role play, one is left to wonder about the merits of virtual heritage. To what extent is a full-size glass-fiber model of Stonehenge, or a printable 3D scan of a precious metal object, still heritage? And whose heritage is it? In the post-postmodern free-for-all virtual world, any heritage is anybody's. Or is it?

Encounters with heritage sites are increasingly mediated through digital resources, and people use digital means not only to buy and sell heritage items in internet auctions (Hewitt 2007) but to learn about the history of places and objects. The younger generation in particular often experiences heritage in the first instance through digital surrogates.

Maria Economou (Chapter 15) looks at how social interaction around heritage is increasingly transferred to the digital sphere, and how heritage institutions are using digital tools in an effort to open up to diverse communities.

With the advent of technologies like smartphones with integrated high-resolution cameras, the question of ownership, which has been raised in relation to cultural property (see Mugabowagahunde, this volume), is extended to copyright, covering not only the original artifact, but also any copies made of it, or audiovisual recordings of intangible heritage. Folarin Shyllon (this volume) explores the far-reaching implications of treating cultural rights and intellectual property rights as commensurable human rights, an area of growing concern, especially but not only in relation to the commercial exploitation of traditional ecological knowledge through pharmaceutical companies and other economic interests.

The use of heritage can be malign as well as benign (Logan 2007: 42). The concept of heritage was inextricably associated with that of the nation-state as nineteenth-century elites composed interpretations of the past that generated a national consciousness of historical destiny (Nic Craith 2008). Many emerging European nation-states, from Italy to Germany and from Ireland to Finland, drew legitimacy from the formation and transmission of a largely "national" heritage (Crooke 2000). Folklorists, as nation-builders, "mapped" the territory and its people (see Kuutma, this volume). Folklore, seen as expressing the authentic voice of the people, was frequently a tool of resistance through which a colonized or subjugated people reasserted its spiritual heritage and status (Ó Giolláin 2000).

Following the transfer of imperial hegemony from Sweden to Russia in 1809, one of the slogans of the emerging Finnish nationalist movement was, "Swedes we are no longer, Russians we can never become, so let us be Finns!" Probably coined by Johan Snellman, a Stockholm-born philosopher and later a Finnish statesman, the slogan encapsulates the need for a legitimizing discourse of the nation. In the twentieth century, Douglas Hyde (of Anglo-Irish rather than Gaelic Irish background) famously called for the "de-Anglicization" of Ireland. Folklorists rediscovered the nation's voice, and frequently anchored it to a particular territory or cultural landscape (Nic Craith 2008).

In the twentieth century, the geopolitical constellation changed several times. The collapse of the great empires – cataclysmic in the case of Austria-Hungary and Turkey, slower but painful for the British, Dutch, French, and Japanese – enabled small separatist nationalisms to replace integrative imperial projects. In the second half of the twentieth century, this was superseded by the rise of new global powers, first in the binary configuration of the Cold War. The collapse of communism sparked another wave of small separatist nationalisms in former Soviet and allied territories. At the same time, the focus of geopolitics finally shifted away from Europe, except for a recent footnote, where grassroots movements for independence in Scotland and Catalonia signal a shift in political culture that perhaps indicates a new direction for nationalism in the twenty-first century.

Against this background of waxing and waning nationalisms, UNESCO introduced the idea of a global heritage that belongs to all peoples of the world, an idea adopted at least rhetorically by the states that have signed up to its various conventions. However, in practice, designations such as World Heritage or Outstanding Universal Value are abused in much the same way as heritage was in the process of nation-building. China, for example, has framed the concept of World Heritage with national characteristics, transforming it into a nationalistic discursive device, as Haiming Yan (Chapter 16) demonstrates. By creating a set of narratives of World Heritage, the Chinese state has sought to invent a vast nation of China characterized by ethnic cohesion, stability, and solidarity. But China is not alone in this. To some extent, nation-states utilize rather than simply abide by UNESCO discourses (Logan 2001, 2014b).

War and Civil Unrest

In times of war and civil unrest, leading to the often large-scale displacement of people through ethnic cleansing, heritage is often damaged or destroyed, targeted deliberately or becoming collateral damage. Where the tangible heritage of artifacts is displaced along with a people, or historic monuments and sites are preserved amid the surrounding destruction, they can be revalidated, adapted, and repossessed through processes of place-making (Kockel 2012b). It is more difficult to resurrect the intangible heritage that was embodied in those who are killed or uprooted from their cultural context.

Looking at the debates over plans for the Gdańsk Museum of World War II, Julie Fedor (Chapter 17) examines the struggle to define and preserve the heritage of the war in Poland and Russia. Originally conceived partly as a counterweight to the memory projects of the German Centre against Expulsions (see Kockel 2012b), the museum constitutes an ambitious and large-scale memory project aiming to be the first museum in Europe to cover the experiences of both Nazi and Soviet occupations in depth, and help incorporate the East European experience into a broader European memory.

Accommodating a multidimensional wartime past within a museum context has proved difficult (see Webber, this volume). After the collapse of communism, museums in Eastern Europe have often been used for narrating revised "national" stories. In these narratives, a national society locates itself on a trajectory extended as far back in time as possible, thus establishing continuity with a pre-communist past. In some instances, an attempt has been made to tell the "national" story in different ways that try to come to terms with the reality of different cultures coexisting in a particular place.

In spring 2012, the Silesian Museum at Katowice launched a temporary exhibition entitled *Koledzy z platzu* ("Colleagues from the Platz: Parallel Life Stories of Upper Silesians"), employing the life stories of neighbors sharing the same backyard in an Upper Silesian town (Kockel 2015). These neighbors were represented as ordinary people who "did not stand out from the crowd, who – in spite of numerous differences – had a common denominator: their native land" (Muzeum Śląskie 2012). The people represented, born at the turn of the twentieth century, had to contend with consecutive enforced changes of place names, official language, and even citizenship. However, the heritage narrative of the museum claims that they did not develop roots in the cultural traditions of any of the neighboring countries to Upper Silesia. Their story represents an example of a growing discourse of indigeneity that scholars of European culture and heritage find rather disconcerting (Kockel 2010, Straczuk 2012; Kiiskinen 2013).

During conflicts, heritage is often deliberately destroyed for its symbolic value. This became particularly clear during the 1990s in southeastern Europe. Focusing on the iconic Old Bridge in Mostar, Bosnia Herzegovina, destroyed in 1993, Andrea Connor (Chapter 18) considers the politics of heritage destruction and reconstruction. A site of real and imagined "gathering," this 400-year-old footbridge was not only an emblem of the city but a metaphorical conduit for meanings of place and a site of embodied encounter. Reopened 11 years after its destruction as a monument to reconciliation, the "new Old Bridge" gained World Heritage status in 2005. However, cultural expressions once held in common have been recast as "ethnic heritage," making the reconstruction of heritage a contentious and potentially divisive act.

The Middle East has been a major theater of war for some decades, and increasingly so since the invasion of Iraq in 2003, which brought unprecedented destruction to some of the world's most sensitive heritage sites. Drawing lessons for cultural property protection from this experience, Benjamin Isakhan (Chapter 19) details the policies and protocols of the US-dominated coalition toward Iraq's important monuments and museums, and discusses the obstacles and challenges that face the Iraqi government. Updating Isakhan's analysis, it has to be said that the renewed air strikes on Iraq in late 2014 do not bode well for civilian populations ("collateral damage"), their embodied, once living intangible heritage, or their tangible places and artifacts.

The deliberate targeting of heritage for military or non-military destruction can go beyond the material, and involve the destruction of a people's embodied intangible heritage and their cultural identity for the sake of ideology. Christian Manhart (Chapter 20) examines these processes in Afghanistan and Mali, explaining UNESCO's dual mandate to build peace and protect heritage, and the contradictory situations that can arise in the context of war and destruction. While the rebuilt Mostar bridge has been awarded World Heritage status, UNESCO is, for complex reasons, currently not in favor of reconstructing the Bamiyan Buddhas. Whereas the obliteration of the Buddhas was driven by religious fanaticism, the destruction of the Mostar bridge was, on the face of it, ethnically motivated. However, it has been observed that in reporting on the conflict in former Yugoslavia, journalists often referred to "Serbs, Croats, and Muslims," juxtaposing two rival Christian denominations described in ethnic terms with an ethnic group described in religious terms. At the end of the twentieth century, one might have hoped it would be unthinkable – or politically incorrect – to describe a European war in terms of religion.

Cultural obliteration through war and violent unrest may be more spectacular than other forms of the same process, but the long-term consequences of these other forms may arguably run as deep. Centuries of colonization have, for example, left their mark on the cultures of the Andes. Nevertheless, as Hugo Benavides (Chapter 21) argues, the legacies of genocide and ethnocide on the region's native population can be contrasted with creative resistance to such cultural obliteration. Benavides examines how heritage has both supported and subverted hegemonic control and ethnic decimation as native communities and their descendants continue to reinvent and reassess their identities in the face of hegemonic pressures.

Recasting Heritage

When the production and protection of heritage attracts public resources, this works as an incentive to invent and sustain, to produce and reproduce "heritages" that may have little or no basis in tradition. Their legitimacy then derives not from their historicity but from financial calculus (Kockel 2007a). This applies equally to tangible and intangible heritage, although each has its own specific problems in this regard: tangible heritage may require much larger financial outlays for its maintenance and protection; the cost of safeguarding intangible heritage is more difficult to verify. In either case, scarce public resources determine the fact that not every single item deemed worth preserving can actually be supported. At the onset of industrial decline in the North Atlantic sphere, heritage – as part of the service and information sectors – was perceived as a renewable resource ready to be exploited, requiring a small initial investment for good long-term returns. Since then, it has become clear that even heritage has its carrying capacity beyond which maintenance costs are likely to exceed revenue. And searching questions are being asked: What are the costs of heritage protection? Is it economically sustainable? Is heritage a luxury, appropriate in advanced Western postindustrial societies but not in poorer societies? We seem to live in an age in which heritage is ubiquitous (Harrison 2013: 3). Is there too much heritage? Have we gone too far? Is it time to start limiting heritage preservation programs, even the concept itself? And if so, in what ways?

Limiting Heritage

With more than 1000 sites inscribed on UNESCO's World Heritage List at the close of 2014, is there a case for the list to be capped in the light of limited and – in real terms – diminishing funds to sustain them? Is there an unlimited number of places of Outstanding Universal Value, and could we list them all, or are we now listing places of national rather than universal significance? Many sites are running into difficulties for various reasons, not necessarily connected with the sites themselves. The World Heritage Committee at its 2014 meeting studied reports on 150 such properties, and there are 45 properties on the List of World Heritage in Danger (UNESCO 2014a, 2014b). As we are seeing a decline in resources available for heritage preservation, most notably in Western Europe, where funding used to be comparatively generous, Ron van Oers (Chapter 22) contends that the system of cultural heritage conservation and its management is simply not robust enough, having too narrow a base in the educated elite while lacking a sustainable mechanism of financing independent of government funding. One response might be to cut back on heritage protection programs. Van Oers, however, argues that the problem can be addressed by involving a broader range of stakeholders, including policy-makers, local councils, the private sector, and local communities.

Stakeholders need to be open to innovative approaches in order to achieve economic sustainability, which may require the redefinition of what is meant by "heritage." Brenda Trofanenko (this volume) argues that sites seek to achieve various, often conflicting purposes, all for the sake of attracting people by their "universal value," and wonders about the limitations such sites hold with regard to the very purposes they are expected to support – not just in terms of their physical carrying capacity, but as sites of cultural reproduction or distortion. In North Karelia, Finland, for example, there is considerable pride in the musical heritage of the region. The repertoire of events, however, is not based on a celebration of past Karelian music itself, but on the idea of music-making as a heritage characterized by a distinct creativity and originality of the musical material performed; that is, a "tradition of invention" emphasizing continued development rather than the conservation of some unadulterated heritage (Kockel 2007b).

The international cultural discourse underlying UNESCO's heritage initiatives has its roots in the 1920s and 1930s, when the League of Nations fostered ideas of common global heritage and international collaboration. Following its establishment in 1945,

UNESCO led significant progress in these areas, with the founding of several international organizations like the International Council on Monuments and Sites (ICOMOS), and the creation of policy instruments for cultural property, excavations, landscape, and the built environment, among others. Christina Cameron (Chapter 23) argues that, with the benefit of hindsight, those initiatives and the philosophy underpinning them may seem naive. The continuing destruction of historic urban centers and monuments by planners or warlords, and the ongoing dispute over the concept of Outstanding Universal Value, certainly cast doubts on the future viability of the current system. As more countries joined the World Heritage Convention (1972), received notions were challenged. With the Intangible Heritage Convention (2003), a Representative List of the Intangible Cultural Heritage of Humanity was introduced, which is no longer limited by notions of Outstanding Universal Value. The initial objectives with which UNESCO set out in 1945 may not be attainable, and alternatives may be radical and unpalatable in a global cultural and financial climate marked by geopolitical rivalries.

Perhaps we expect too much of UNESCO and the other global heritage bodies. The emphasis on cultural heritage as a resource for development has been questioned by scholars critical of the new governmentalities engendered by heritage regimes (Coombe 2012) and their depoliticizing impacts on communities and other so-called stakeholders. Drawing on anthropological research in indigenous contexts and addressing the role of corporate actors, Rosemary Coombe and Melissa Baird (Chapter 24) argue international heritage institutions face new challenges that will limit any emancipatory expectations we might have as heritage governance is certain to become re-politicized in rights-based struggles on "resource frontiers" (Tsing 2003).

In a situation of limited resources and other opportunities, what kinds of heritage should be protected, and how should we decide what not to protect? The independent expert Farida Shaheed (2011) addressed the issue of limitations to cultural rights in her first report to the UN Human Rights Council. Cultural rights may be limited in certain circumstances, following the principles enshrined in international human rights law. This also applies to the right of access to and practice of cultural heritage, for example where an element of cultural heritage infringes on human rights. Practices that are contrary to human rights cannot be justified by reference to the safeguarding of cultural heritage, diversity, or rights.

There are clearly some dimensions of our own and other people's cultures that we prefer to see disappear, indeed that we might actively seek to wipe out (Logan 2007: 37, 2009: 15). Some have been eradicated in the past, such as social forms like Chinese foot-binding, and economic forms like New World slavery. But what of contemporary heritage elements? Heritage professionals generally baulk at the idea of destroying heritage. Colin Long and Keir Reeves (2009), however, do not walk away from this dilemma in a discussion that has bearing on Auschwitz and Rwanda. Investigating Anlong Veng, Pol Pot's home village in Cambodia, which is becoming a cult site, they argue that the removal of reminders of Pol Pot would have the justifiable effect of "emphasizing above all else the voices of the victims and silencing the perpetrators once and for all" (Long and Reeves 2009: 81).

Human rights are then an obvious starting point for the consideration of limitations that should be imposed on cultural heritage, regardless of resource issues. Human rights treaties are formulated as catalogues of "rights" or claims that individuals or persons belonging to groups such as ethnic minorities and indigenous peoples hold against the state within whose territory they live (Ekern *et al.* 2012: 216). They may be fine on paper, but getting governments to implement those rights is very often extremely difficult. A case in point is the struggle of indigenous peoples to bring implementation of the World Heritage Convention (1972) in line with international standards concerning their rights. Adopted before most other international human rights treaties came in to force – including the International Covenant on Civil and Political Rights (1966) and the International Covenant on Economic, Social and Cultural Rights (1966) – the World Heritage Convention finds itself at odds with international human rights standards as well as other standards and principles developed since the early 1970s. Stefan Disko (Chapter 25) discusses some of the major shortcomings of the convention from an indigenous rights perspective, such as the lack of provisions ensuring that the free, prior, and informed consent of indigenous peoples is obtained before parts of their territories are designated as World Heritage sites.

Another limitation on the effectiveness of heritage programs is raised by George Abungu (Chapter 26) and Webber Ndoro (Chapter 27). Examining the challenges that must be faced by sub-Saharan African heritage practitioners and actors now and in the future, they see the key issue being how to achieve best conservation practice when surrounded by a sea of poverty. Both see the failure of the supposed trickledown effect, in which the benefits of World Heritage inscription and consequent global tourism are meant to flow down to those Africans whose heritage is on show. Ndoro notes that while World Heritage sites can help in supporting job creation, the development of infrastructure and small-scale business ventures, and provide general economic benefits to the national economy, the record is disappointing. Most of the investors at World Heritage sites are foreign tour operators, hotel chains, and airlines, and resentment is growing among local communities that they are missing out on the economic benefits of World Heritage listing. It is understandable that communities and sometimes representative governments turn their backs on heritage in favor of more effective ways of increasing material well-being.

Holistic and Inclusive Heritage

One of the lessons that should have been learnt by government, policy-makers, and heritage practitioners alike over the last 60 years is the need to listen to the voices of local communities. Some governments have been reluctant to take this approach, as have heritage professionals in some countries. In relation to World Heritage places, UNESCO has moved strongly in recent years to engage local and especially indigenous communities in heritage identification and management. It used the Linking Universal and Local Values conference held in Amsterdam in 2003 (de Merode, Smeets, and Westrik 2004) to promote the view that heritage protection does not solely depend on top-down interventions by governments or the expert actions of heritage industry professionals, but must involve local communities (Logan, Langfield, and Nic Craith 2010: 9). UNESCO recognizes that the notion of Outstanding Universal Value at the heart of World Heritage may not always coincide with local ideas about what is significant heritage, and that a reconciliation of the views of locals and UNESCO must be achieved if local communities are to feel a sense of ownership of World Heritage sites, which is a pre-requisite for the sustainability of Outstanding Universal Value.

In other words, respect for and inclusion of traditional knowledge and management practices are fundamental elements of the new, fairer, and more inclusive approach to heritage conservation and heritage studies. Indigenous peoples have learned to use the language of rights effectively, a useful part of their battery of political tactics. We will have to wait longer to see if and how the heritage rights of other ethnic and racial minorities, as well as minorities defined by gender, sexuality, and class, are affected. With good fortune and a lot of effort by these groups and their supporters, there may also be beneficial consequences for these groups (Logan 2014a: 13).

Another important step toward inclusivity lies in reducing the Eurocentric character of the World Heritage system and, more generally, heritage discourse, and acknowledging variations in concepts and practice in other world regions. This has been a long struggle, involving UNESCO and World Heritage Committee initiatives such as the Global Strategy for a Representative, Balanced and Credible World Heritage List (UNESCO 2015), which has been discussed by scholars such as Sophia Labadi (2005, 2013) and Lynn Meskell (2013b). It is taken up in this volume by practitioner-scholars Britta Rudolff and Kristal Buckley (Chapter 35). In their analysis of the World Heritage system and the common perception that it is at a "crossroads," they identify Eurocentrism as one of six key challenges that need to be met.

From Africa, the focus next turns to Asia. Zeynep Aygen and William Logan (Chapter 28) argue that the economic and geopolitical shift towards Asia that is currently being witnessed will inevitably lead to a stronger Asian voice being heard in the heritage field. It follows, they maintain, that more needs to be learnt about Asia's heritage and Asian heritage safeguarding projects. They note that the so-called "Asian century" really started in the late 1980s, and they warn against the danger of overstating the differences between "Asian" and "Western" heritage approaches. In a world of the continuing culture-based conflict, even wars, the need today is to strengthen cross-cultural dialogue, building on the commonalities rather than differences between people.

One of the fundamental ways that Asian heritage practice has influenced the West is in the prominence given to intangible heritage. The tradition of Western heritage practice, starting with Ruskin and Viollet-le-Duc and enshrined in the Venice Charter (ICASHB 1964), focused largely on the tangible until the Japanese opened the way for the Nara Document on Authenticity (ICOMOS 1994), UNESCO following suit with the Intangible Heritage Convention (2003). This is not to say that the intangible was and is not vitally important in the cultural life of the West or other non-Asian parts of the world. Indeed, while it may be true that "Asian heritage is valued for its spiritual significance rather than historical or material significance" (Chapagain 2013: 12), Western people have always placed great store in the "living" and "embodied" heritage of religion and spiritualism, festivals and markets, and associated cultural contexts – even if Western heritage practice did not.

There remains much room for Western heritage practice to embrace the intangible, both as a feature giving value to the tangible heritage of places and artifacts, and as a form of heritage in its own right. Máiréad Nic Craith and Ullrich Kockel (Chapter 29) explore the ways in which Westerners think about places. They see a greater complexity developing in the understanding of the built environment over the past two decades or so, and a rising concern to protect the "sense of place" or *genius loci*. This new emphasis on the cultural significance of place partly emanated from the Australia ICOMOS Burra Charter (1979, with subsequent revisions; see Australia ICOMOS 2013) and was accompanied by a values-driven approach to conservation and management, the purpose of which was not to preserve the physical fabric of a place for its own sake but to maintain the values embodied in a place (Avrami, Mason, and de la Torre 2000: 7). Such values are intrinsically intangible, and this being so, Nic Craith and Kockel conclude that UNESCO and other governmental heritage agencies would do well to consider bringing their separate tangible and intangible heritage systems together.

In Chapter 30 Laurajane Smith and Gary Campbell explore another intangible dimension of heritage, on this occasion within the context of museums. Starting with the assertion Smith made in her important book *Uses of Heritage* (2006), that heritage was an embodied cultural performance of meaning-making, they seek to remedy the lack of recognition of affect and emotion as "essential constitutive elements of heritage-making." This had been noted earlier by Laurajane Smith and Emma Waterton (2009: 49), likening this failure as "an elephant in the room" of heritage studies and its museum studies sub-branch. The chapter concludes that heritage and museum visitors' experiences, rather than being merely learning experiences, can only be explained if the emotional aspects of their visit are taken into account, and that it is therefore essential to understand how emotions work if the staging and experience of heritage and museums are to be more effective.

As Smith and Campbell note, there has been a growing interest in emotion and affect in recent heritage studies literature. One scholar contributing to this is Andrea Witcomb (Chapter 31), who provides a case study of memories and memorialization of the Thai–Burma Railway, built during World War II. This is heritage as performance, focusing on remembering and forgetting, story-telling, religion, and festivals. But it is more than a descriptive case study: it seeks to move beyond the conventional discussion of heritage as a site of ideological productions reflecting hegemonic interests to recognize that heritage also "embodies far more localized, personal, emotional, and affective relationships." Witcomb argues that emotion plays a fundamental role in expressions of heritage, and in impacting on people's understanding of their sense of self in relation to others. In other forums such an argument can provide the basis for strengthening communities that are suffering from macro-economic restructuring, unemployment, and demographic change. In this chapter, however, Witcomb focuses on the moments of encounter between various individual and sets of actors from different cultures involved in remembering and memorializing – performative practices that she sees as producing a form of heritage practice in its own right.

The Ethics of Heritage

Andrea Witcomb is right in arguing that it is time to move on from case studies of contestation over heritage and of heritage's links with the ideology of regimes in power. Heritage is, of course, never apolitical or in any way neutral, and, as has been earlier discussed, it has all too often been used as a means of welding populations together to prop up regimes, to support ethnic cleansing, and to justify hostilities against neighboring states. But heritage is no longer seen as just something actually or allegedly inherited from the past and used for a narrow political purpose. It is increasingly recognized as a dynamic evolving interplay of multiple factors touching all aspects of contemporary human life.

Our understanding of heritage and interventions to safeguard it require the establishment of an ethical basis. Witcomb's analysis of cross-cultural encounters in the Thai–Burma Railway case draws upon theories about the politics of identity, but it also emphasizes the importance of taking a cosmopolitan ethical stance. This is argued further by Lynn Meskell (Chapter 32), who explores the notions of rights and responsibilities that are central to cosmopolitanism as a set of ethical and philosophical beliefs.

Meskell explains that cosmopolitanism holds that we are all citizens of the world and have responsibilities to others. As heritage is acquiring a role in global movements of conservation, post-conflict restoration, indigenous rights, and sustainable development, Meskell asks how cosmopolitanism might prepare us for the challenge of the past being drawn into contemporary struggles for recognition and self-determination. As heritage experts, these obligations may entail addressing the political and economic damage wrought by past regimes, improving community livelihoods, or confronting transnational corporations.

Kwame Appiah (2006) focuses on the key issue of reciprocity – that is, of showing how and why human rights should continue to be supported, but also of articulating the view that there is a reciprocal set of duties that humans have toward each other and their physical and cultural environment. He challenges heritage practitioners and scholars to shift our focus away from nations and peoples and to focus instead on the individuals who create (and pay for) the things that are valued today and who will benefit from experiencing them (Appiah 2006: 122). His cosmopolitan perspective is "to ask what system of international rules about objects of this sort will respect the many legitimate human interests at stake" (Appiah 2006: 126–27). A cosmopolitan approach to heritage practice and scholarship also requires that respect is given to the heritage of others as you would have your own heritage respected. This applies to the heritage of indigenous peoples, other minority groups, and national neighbors. Heritage as a cultural process might thus be re-envisioned as a path to mutual understanding and respect, peace and security (Logan 2010, 2012a).

It may not be so simple, however, as Patrick Daly and Benjamin Chan (Chapter 33) show. They turn our attention to the role of heritage in post-conflict situations, drawing on their research into post-Khmer Rouge Cambodia and post-World War II Japan. They warn that while there is considerable potential for heritage to be a useful tool for supporting political reconciliation and stability, it seems that the achievement of stability and peace may be facilitated at the expense of the victims of conflict who are denied both justice and healing. They see post-conflict situations as "complicated, messy, and unique, with conflicting narratives, agendas, and various levels of empowered stakeholders," making it extraordinarily difficult to construct a consensus around what is needed and how to do it. Denis Byrne also sees great potential for heritage studies to foster empathy with the past experiences of others, but notes that this requires a "sophisticated understanding of how objects become imbued with affect and how they transmit it" (Byrne 2013: 596).

Perhaps heritage can be used to build cross-cultural and transnational dialogue so that conflicts are minimized or avoided in the first place. In some cases, breaking down nationalist narratives might help, as might giving fuller recognition to the hybridity of diasporic heritages (Eng 2011). Strengthening cross-cultural dialogue underlies the creation of UNESCO, and its World Heritage program could give a stronger priority to activities focused on dialogue creation (Logan 2010). These might include, for example, transnational inscriptions and developing new strategies for interpreting sites in more cross-culturally sensitive ways. Ona Vileikis (Chapter 34) takes up this notion, using her experience in the Central Asian Silk Roads World Heritage nomination process as a case study. She finds that transparent collaboration and sharing information, practices, and expertise has proven to be a valuable step towards strengthening transnational dialogue. The five countries involved so far – Kazakhstan, Kyrgyzstan, Tajikistan, Turkmenistan, and Uzbekistan – used consultation workshops and meetings in preparation of the nomination strategy, as well as established networks at institutional and governmental levels, that have an ongoing role in capacity-building, raising necessary funds and awareness, as well as providing technical assistance.

The New Heritage Studies: Paradigms and Challenges

The story outlined above portrays heritage practice and heritage studies as vastly transfigured over the last sixty years, most of the difference in conceptions, philosophies, and approaches occurring since the late 1980s and early 1990s. Senior members of the profession such as Gustavo Araoz, currently ICOMOS president, and many academics have referred to this transfiguration as "a new paradigm" (e.g. Araoz 2011; Silberman 2013). Gregory Ashworth (1997) proposed two paradigms: conservation as preservation, and conservation as heritage. Even one of the current authors, William Logan (2012b: 10), has used the term paradigm, although referring to a future when heritage conservation develops into a human rights-based cultural practice.

Paradigm Change

Has there been a paradigm change? In the strict sense of the word, as coined by Thomas Kuhn (1962), probably not, although the term has come to be used in common parlance whenever we want to describe a pronounced change in direction of the way we see the world around us. Certainly massive change has occurred over the decades, but it has been evolutionary rather than revolutionary, the latter marking paradigm shifts according to Kuhn; it has thus built on the past rather than swept it all aside. Technical and managerial research and publications continue to make their valuable contribution to the field alongside the new heritage studies.

Indeed, some scholars are calling for even more change, and use revolutionary language to do so. An Association of Critical Heritage Studies (ACHS) was formed in 2012, with a preliminary manifesto calling for heritage studies to be changed "from the ground up" (ACHS 2011). Designed as a "provocation," the ACHS's manifesto seeks much that in this volume has been envisaged under the name "new heritage studies," as the following extract shows:

> Heritage is, as much as anything, a political act and we need to ask serious questions about the power relations that "heritage" has all too often been invoked to sustain. Nationalism, imperialism, colonialism, cultural elitism, Western triumphalism, social exclusion based on class and ethnicity, and the fetishising of expert knowledge have all exerted strong influences on how heritage is used, defined and managed. We argue that a truly critical heritage studies will ask many uncomfortable questions of traditional ways of thinking about and doing heritage, and that the interests of the marginalised and excluded will be brought to the forefront when posing these questions. (ACHS 2011)

Other heritage scholars have reacted to the ACHS manifesto, with some debate emerging in a special issue of the *International Journal of Heritage Studies* in September 2013. One of the concerns raised there by Witcomb and Buckley (2013) is that the ACHS, if it adheres to its manifesto, is likely to deepen the already existing gulf between theory and practice, scholars and practitioners.

Practical Implementation Challenges

We should not underestimate the difficulty of achieving effective change, and we need closer collaboration between scholars and practitioners so that the "new heritage studies" can better influence practice while keeping its feet on the ground where practitioners operate. William Logan (2012b: 241) has previously described the difficulties in relation to the World Heritage system, noting that while it may be possible to tweak the Operational Guidelines for the Implementation of the World Heritage Convention, this may not be enough.[1] UNESCO is an international governmental organization relying on its Member States – or those that have become States Parties to the World Heritage Convention (1972) – to cooperate on their own accord in the World Heritage mission. States Parties will always make World Heritage decisions that suit their national interests. Even the United States, one of the instigators of the World Heritage Convention, and, as Diane Barthel-Bouchier (2013: 38) observes, usually an upholder of the values of universalism, human progress, and rationality, is causing difficulties. Its current refusal to pay its financial contribution to UNESCO is causing the organization to scale back its activities rather than embark upon new initiatives (Erlanger 2011). The heritage profession can also be resistant to change with its entrenched attitudes in many countries, its tight networks, and its gate-keeping actions.

In this difficult context, and mindful of the criticism, overload, and pessimism facing UNESCO, the World Heritage Centre and the Advisory Bodies, perhaps ICOMOS in particular, Britta Rudolff and Kristal Buckley (Chapter 35) ask what it might mean to consider "alternative" futures for the World Heritage system. They want to go beyond the small incremental changes to the Operational Guidelines and changes to inscription and other processes through "upstreaming" that are already contemplated, and they note that revising the World Heritage Convention (1972) is extremely unlikely. It seems to them that the best approach is to focus on possible future enhancements in relation to the intended purposes of the convention, and to push for a further evolution in heritage concepts and mechanisms. This leads Rudolff and Buckley to identify six interrelated problems where focused reform could deliver significant, "alternative," and better futures for the World Heritage system: (1) the problem of Eurocentrism; (2) the problem of inflation and overload; (3) the reduction of credibility; (4) the problem of inclusion; (5) the nature/culture divide; and (6) the problem of conservation. Cautiously optimistic, they conclude that the most significant potential outcome that explorations of "alternative" futures can achieve is to give direction and stimulus to those presently active to carry on working towards their common goals as established by the World Heritage Convention while striving to improve and innovate.

Ana Filipa Vrdoljak (Chapter 36) and William Logan and Gamini Wijesuriya (Chapter 37) deal with two other challenging areas for implementing change: the legal field on the one hand, and education, training, and capacity-building on the other. Vrdoljak outlines the multilateral instruments that make up the contemporary international legal framework for the protection of cultural heritage, noting that more than half were adopted in the decades after the end of the Cold War. She observes that these recent treaties have profoundly broadened the definition of what is being protected and the range of stakeholders attracting rights and obligations. The inclusion of intangible heritage complicates matters, as do the extension of rights holders beyond states and the redefinition of the role of states. Existing legal concerns have been exacerbated and new challenges opened up. She warns against UNESCO adding yet more specialist legal instruments, and argues instead for the development of a framework instrument that would provide an overarching set of principles inspired by developments in human rights and environmental law, and by which all of UNESCO's existing heritage instruments must be interpreted. The Council of Europe's Framework Convention on the Value of Cultural Heritage for Society (2005), commonly known as the Faro Convention, offers UNESCO a model to follow. Such an approach, Vrdoljak concludes, would help promote a more holistic approach to cultural heritage, facilitating effective involvement of a broad range of stakeholders at all levels in its protection.

Something similar was needed, and in fact has been established, in the case of education, training, and capacity-building. A World Heritage Strategy for Capacity Building (UNESCO 2011) was adopted by the World Heritage Committee at its thirty-fifth session in 2011, and a program to achieve its objectives is being undertaken by its developers – UNESCO, through the World Heritage Centre, and the three Advisory Bodies (ICCROM, ICOMOS, IUCN). In line with the holistic approach taken by the World Heritage Convention (1972), the capacity-building strategy covers both cultural and natural heritage. It focuses on capacity-building, a concept that subsumes the education and training of individual practitioners, but extends beyond practitioners to cover the wider audience that is, or should be, engaged in the heritage conservation process. The capacity-building strategy recognizes that capacity in fact resides in practitioners, institutions, communities, and their networks, that these are effectively different audiences, and that capacity-building activities are needed involving different learning areas and a diverse range of pedagogical approaches.

Logan and Wijesuriya particularly focus on how the capacity-building strategy reflects the broader and more critical conception of heritage that has emerged. They pick up some of the concerns outlined in Ekern *et al.* (2012: 221), regarding the limitations faced by practitioners in dealing with the political character of their interventions, particularly in relation to minority and marginalized peoples. It is critically important to understand the broader economic, political, and social context in which they are operating. Practitioners need to recognize that there can be many motives behind official heritage interventions, that such action is sometimes made primarily to achieve political goals, and that this can undermine rather than strengthen cultural diversity, cultural identity, and human rights. The shift towards a more critical approach to both heritage practice and heritage studies encourages educators, scholars, and practitioners to consider the human rights implications of conservation interventions, and to devise ways in which local people, especially indigenous peoples and ethnic minorities, can be empowered to play a meaningful role in determining how their heritage is identified and managed. Practitioners in the field thus need new skills in facilitating small group discussions, conflict resolution, and in listening patiently and respectfully rather than assuming their specialist training gives them ready-made answers.

Much of the discussion in Logan and Wijesuriya's chapter – as indeed in the volume as a whole – is focused on World Heritage and the global heritage agencies. This is not unreasonable, given the richness of discourse at the global level and the way in which ideas developed at the global level flow down to influence heritage practice and scholarship at national and local levels. There is also profitable interaction between these levels, the flow of ideas often originating at the national or local level – the "periphery" (Logan 2001) – and moving out to affect and sometimes become incorporated by the global. Heritage thinking, like heritage management, cannot be solely top-down; we need to listen to local voices expressing "heritage from below" (Robertson 2012) and their claim to heritage rights. Denis Byrne argues in relation to Southeast Asian

Buddhist societies that, without taking into consideration popular beliefs and associated practices, we are "poorly positioned to enact conservation policies and programs at the local level" (Byrne 2011: 3). George Abungu sums up the matter in his chapter on African heritage issues in this volume, when he concludes: "Practitioners who care about the future of heritage have an obligation to change the fundamentals of the practice to fit into the current world of high expectations and compelling rights." The obligation, we should add, applies equally to new heritage studies scholars, educators, and capacity-builders.

Logan and Wijesuriya end their chapter with the admonition that efforts should not be directed exclusively towards World Heritage. The needs of nationally and locally significant heritage, or, indeed, intangible heritage as well as heritage places and artifact collections in museums and galleries, must not be neglected. The World Heritage Convention puts the overall aim of heritage conservation clearly as "to give the cultural and natural heritage a function in the life of the community."[2]

We agree that this applies to heritage at all levels – to enable people to better understand, have access to, and enjoy their heritage in ways they choose. This is probably the greatest challenge for policy-makers, practitioners, scholars, educators, trainers, capacity-builders, and communities themselves – globally, nationally, and locally.

Notes

1 The Operational Guidelines for the Implementation of the World Heritage Convention is a document first adopted by the World Heritage Committee in 1977 and contains precise criteria for the inscription of properties on the World Heritage List and for the provision of international assistance under the World Heritage Fund. The document has been revised by the committee numerous times to reflect new concepts, knowledge or experiences, the most recent revision dating from July 2013 (see UNESCO 2013).

2 World Heritage Convention (1972), art. 5.

References

Legislation

Convention Concerning the Protection of the World Cultural and Natural Heritage (World Heritage Convention) (UNESCO, 1972). Available at: http://whc.unesco.org/archive/convention-en.pdf (accessed March 19, 2015).

Convention for the Safeguarding of the Intangible Cultural Heritage (Intangible Heritage Convention) (UNESCO, 2003). Available at: http://unesdoc.unesco.org/images/0013/001325/132540e.pdf (accessed March 19, 2015).

Framework Convention on the Value of Cultural Heritage for Society (Faro Convention) (Council of Europe, 2005). Available at: http://conventions.coe.int/Treaty/en/Treaties/Html/199.htm (accessed March 19, 2015).

International Covenant on Civil and Political Rights (United Nations, 1966). Available at: http://www.ohchr.org/Documents/ProfessionalInterest/ccpr.pdf (accessed March 19, 2015).

International Covenant on Economic, Social and Cultural Rights (United Nations, 1966). Available at: http://www.ohchr.org/Documents/ProfessionalInterest/cescr.pdf (accessed March 19, 2015).

Other Works

ACHS (Association of Critical Heritage Studies) (2011) Manifesto. Available at: http://archanth.anu.edu.au/heritage-museum-studies/association-critical-heritage-studies (accessed October 1, 2014).

Anttonen, P. (2005) *Tradition through Modernity: Postmodernism and the Nation-State in Folklore Scholarship*. Helsinki: Finnish Literature Society.

Appiah, K.A. (2006) *Cosmopolitanism: Ethics in a World of Strangers*. New York: Norton.

Araoz, G. (2011) Preserving Heritage Places under a New Paradigm. *Journal of Cultural Heritage Management and Sustainable Development*, 1 (1), 55–60.

Armaitienė, A., Boldyrev, V., Povilanskas, R., and Taminskas, J. (2007) Integrated Shoreline Management and Tourism Development on the Cross-Border World Heritage Site: A Case Study from the Curonian Spit (Lithuania/Russia). *Journal of Coastal Conservation*, 11 (1), 13–22.

Ashworth, G.J. (1997) Conservation as Preservation or Conservation as Heritage: Two Paradigms and Two Answers. *Built Environment*, 23 (2), 92–102.

Australia ICOMOS (2013) Charter for the Conservation of Places of Cultural Significance (Burra Charter), revised version. Available at: http://australia.icomos.org/wp-content/uploads/The-Burra-Charter-2013-Adopted-31.10.2013.pdf (accessed June 29, 2014).

Avrami, E., Mason, R., and de la Torre, M. (2000) Report on Research. In *Values and Heritage Conservation*. Los Angeles: Getty Conservation Institute, pp. 3–11.

Barthel-Bouchier, D. (2013) *Cultural Heritage and the Challenge of Sustainability*. Walnut Creek, CA: Left Coast Press.

Blue Spruce, D., and Thrasher, T. (eds) (2008) *The Land Has Memory: Indigenous Knowledge, Native Landscapes, and the National Museum of the American Indian*. Chapel Hill, NC: University of North Carolina Press/Museum of the American Indian/Smithsonian Institution.

Bristol, G. (2010) Rendered Invisible: Urban Planning. In M. Langfield, W. Logan, and M. Nic Craith (eds), *Cultural Diversity, Heritage and Human Rights: Intersections in Theory and Practice*. London: Routledge, pp. 117–134.

Byrne, D. (2011) Thinking About Popular Religion and Heritage. In J.N. Miksic, G.Y. Goh, and S. O'Connor (eds), *Rethinking Cultural Resource Management in Southeast Asia: Preservation, Development, and Neglect*. London: Anthem, pp. 3–14.

Byrne, D. (2013) Love and Loss in the 1960s. *International Journal of Heritage Studies*, 19 (6), 596–609.

Chapagain, N.K. (2013) Introduction: Contexts and Concerns in Asian Heritage Management. In K.D. Silva and N.K. Chapagain (eds), *Asian Heritage Management: Contexts, Concerns, and Prospects*. London: Routledge, pp. 1–29.

Charlesworth, H. (2010) Human Rights and the Unesco Memory of the World Programme. In M. Langfield, W. Logan, and M. Nic Craith (eds), *Cultural Diversity, Heritage and Human Rights: Intersections in Theory and Practice*, London: Routledge, pp. 21–30.

Coombe, R. (2012) Managing Cultural Heritage as Neoliberal Governmentality. In R. Bendix, A. Eggert, and A. Peselmann (eds), *Heritage Regimes and the State*. Göttingen: Universitätsverlag Göttingen, pp. 375–387.

Cosgrove, D. (1984) *Social Formation and Symbolic Landscape*. Madison: University of Wisconsin Press.

Crooke, E. (2000) *Politics, Archaeology and the Creation of a National Museum in Ireland: An Expression of National Life*. Dublin: Irish Academic Press.

De Merode, E., Smeets, R, and Westrik, C (eds) (2004) *Linking Universal and Local Values: Managing a Sustainable Future for World Heritage*. World Heritage Papers 13. Paris: UNESCO World Heritage Centre. Available at: http://whc.unesco.org/documents/publi_wh_papers_13_en.pdf (accessed February 15, 2015).

Ekern, S., Logan, W., Sauge, B., and Sinding-Larsen, A. (2012) Human Rights and World Heritage: Preserving Our Common Dignity through Rights-Based Approaches to Site Management. *International Journal of Heritage Studies*, 18 (3), 213–225.

Eng, I. (2011) Unsettling the National: Heritage and Diaspora. In H. Anheier and Y.R. Isar (eds), *Heritage, Memory and Identity*. London: Sage, pp. 82–94.

English Heritage (n.d.) Conservation Areas. Available at: https://www.english-heritage.org.uk/caring/listing/local/conservation-areas/ (accessed October 5, 2014).

Erlanger, S. (2011) Cutting off Unesco, US May Endanger Programs in Iraq. *New York Times*, November 16. Available at: http://www.nytimes.com/2011/11/17/world/middleeast/cutting-off-unesco-us-may-put-iraq-programs-at-risk.html?_r=0 (accessed September 30, 2014).

Gilbert, J. (2010) Custodians of the Land: Indigenous Peoples, Human Rights and Cultural Integrity. In M. Langfield, W. Logan, and M. Nic Craith (eds), *Cultural Diversity, Heritage and Human Rights: Intersections in Theory and Practice*. London: Routledge, pp. 31–44.

Harrison, R. (2013) *Heritage: Critical Approaches*. London: Routledge.

Hewitt, B. (2007) Heritage as a Commodity: Are We Devaluing Our Heritage by Making It Available to The Highest Bidder via the Internet? In U. Kockel and M. Nic Craith (eds), *Cultural Heritages as Reflexive Traditions*. Basingstoke: Palgrave, pp. 194–208.

ICASHB (International Congress of Architects and Specialists of Historic Buildings) (1964) International Charter for the Conservation and Restoration of Monuments and Sites (Venice Charter). Available at: http://www.icomos.org/charters/venice_e.pdf (accessed March 9, 2015).

ICOM (2004) Declaration on the Importance and Value of Universal Museums. *ICOM News*, 1, 5.

ICOMOS (1994) The Nara Document on Authenticity. Available at: www.icomos.org/charters/nara-e.pdf (accessed September 25, 2014).

Kiiskinen, K. (2013) *Bordering with Culture(s): Europeanization and Cultural Agency at the External Borders of the European Union*. Turku: University of Turku.

Klein, K. (2000) On the Emergence of Memory in Historical Discourse. *Representations*, special issue 69, 127–150.

Kockel, U. (2007a) Reflexive Traditions and Heritage Production. In U. Kockel and M. Nic Craith (eds), *Cultural Heritages as Reflexive Traditions*. Basingstoke: Palgrave, pp. 19–33.

Kockel, U. (2007b) Heritage versus Tradition: Cultural Resources for a New Europe? In M. Demossier (ed.), *The European Puzzle: The Political Structuring of Cultural Identities at a Time of Transition*. Oxford: Berghahn, pp. 85–101.

Kockel, U. (2010) *Re-Visioning Europe: Frontiers, Place Identities and Journeys in Debetable Lands*. Basingstoke: Palgrave.

Kockel, U. (2012a) Borders, European Integration and UNESCO World Heritage: A Case Study of the Curonian Spit. In A. Peselmann, A. Eggert, and R. Bendix (eds), *Heritage Regimes and the State*. Göttingen: Universitätsverlag Göttingen, pp. 227–246.

Kockel, U. (2012b) Toward an Ethnoecology of Place and Displacement. In U. Kockel, M. Nic Craith, and J. Frykman (eds), *Blackwell Companion to the Anthropology of Europe*. Malden, MA: Wiley-Blackwell, pp. 551–571.

Kockel, U. (2015) Re-placing Europe: An Ethnological Perspective on Frontiers and Migrants. In C. Whitehead, R. Mason, and S. Eckersley (eds), *Museums, Migration and Identity in Europe: Peoples, Places, Identities*. Aldershot: Ashgate, pp. 81–100.

Kockel, U., and Nic Craith, M. (2015) Hybride Ethnologien des Eigenen, Anderen und Dritten: Toposophische Erkundungen am Beispiel der Pfälzer in Irland. In F. Jacobs and I. Keller (eds), *Das Reine und das Vermischte: Festschrift für Elka Tschernokoshewa*. Münster: Waxmann, pp. 73–95.

Kuhn, T. (1962) *The Structure of Scientific Revolutions*. Chicago: University of Chicago Press.

Labadi, S. (2005) A Review of the Global Strategy for a Balanced, Representative and Credible World Heritage List, 1994–2004. *Conservation and Management of Archaeological Sites*, 7, 89–102.

Labadi, S. (2013) *UNESCO, Cultural Heritage and Outstanding Universal Value*. Walnut Creek, CA: AltaMira Press.

Lewis, M. (1977) *Victorian Primitive*. Melbourne: Greenhouse.

Lim, W.S.W. and Beng, T.H. (1998) *Contemporary Vernacular: Evoking Traditions in Asian Architecture*. Singapore: Select Books.

Logan, W. (2001) Globalizing Heritage: World Heritage as a Manifestation of Modernism and Challenges from the Periphery. In D. Jones (ed.), *Twentieth Century Heritage – Our Recent Cultural Legacy: 2001 Australian ICOMOS National Conference*. Adelaide: School of Architecture, University of Adelaide, pp. 51–57.

Logan, W. (2003) *The Disappearing "Asian" City: Protecting Asia's Urban Heritage in a Globalizing World*. Hong Kong: Oxford University Press.

Logan, W. (2005) The Cultural Role of Capital Cities: Hanoi and Hue, Vietnam. *Pacific Affairs*, 78 (4), 559–575.

Logan, W. (2006) Needs for Heritage Education at Universities. Paper presented at an international symposium on "Heritage Education – Capacity Building in Heritage Management," Brandenburg University of Technology, Cottbus, Germany, June 14–18.

Logan, W. (2007) Closing Pandora's Box: Human Rights Conundrums in Cultural Heritage Practice. In H. Silverman and D. Fairchild Ruggles (eds), *Cultural Heritage and Human Rights*. New York: Springer, pp. 33–52.

Logan, W. (2009) Playing the Devil's Advocate: Protecting Intangible Cultural Heritage and the Infringement of Human Rights, *Historic Environment*, 22 (3), 14–18.

Logan, W. (2010) Heritage and Dialogue: Using Heritage Conservation to Strengthen the Defences of Peace. In *Proceedings of the World Universities Congress, Canakkale 18 Mart University, Canakkale, Turkey, 20–24 October 2010*, Vol. 2. Canakkale: Canakkale 18 Mart University:, pp. 1440–1448.

Logan, W. (2012a) States, Governance and the Politics of Culture: World Heritage Places in Asia. In P. Daly and T. Winter (eds), *The Routledge Handbook of Heritage in Asia*. London: Routledge; pp. 113–128.

Logan, W. (2012b) Cultural Diversity, Cultural Heritage and Human Rights: Towards Heritage Management as Human Rights-Based Cultural Practice. *International Journal of Heritage Studies*, 18 (3), 231–244.

Logan, W. (2013) Australia, Indigenous Peoples and World Heritage from Kakadu to Cape York: State Party Behaviour under the World Heritage Convention. *Journal of Social Archaeology*, 13 (2), 153–176.

Logan, W. (2014a) Heritage Rights: Avoidance and Reinforcement. *Heritage and Society*, 7 (2), 1–15.

Logan, W. (2014b) Making the Most of Heritage in Hanoi, Vietnam. *Historic Environment*, 26 (3), 62–72.

Logan, W., Langfield, M., and Nic Craith, M. (2010) Intersecting Concepts and Practices. In M. Langfield, W. Logan, and M. Nic Craith (eds), *Cultural Diversity, Heritage and Human Rights: Intersections in Theory and Practice*. London: Routledge, pp. 3–20.

Logan, W., and Reeves. K. (eds) (2009) *Places of Pain and Shame: Dealing with "Difficult" Heritage*. London: Routledge.

Long, C., and Reeves, K. (2009) "Dig a Hole and Bury the Past in It": Reconciliation and the Heritage of Genocide in Cambodia. In W. Logan and K. Reeves (eds), *Places of Pain and Shame: Dealing with "Difficult" Heritage*. London: Routledge, pp. 68–81.

Meskell, L.M. (2013a) UNESCO and the Fate of the World Heritage Indigenous Peoples Council of Experts (WHIPCOE). *International Journal of Cultural Property*, 20 (2), 155–174.

Meskell, L.M. (2013b) UNESCO's World Heritage Convention at 40: Challenging the Economic and Political Order of International Heritage Conservation. *Current Anthropology*, 54 (4), 483–494.

Muzeum Śląskie (2012) Colleagues from the Platz: Parallel Life Stories of Upper Silesians. Available at: http://www.muzeumslaskie.pl/en/colleagues-from-the-platz-parallel-life-stories-of-upper-silesians.php> (accessed July 29, 2012).

Nic Craith, M. (2007) Cultural Heritages: Process, Power, Commodification. In U. Kockel and M. Nic Craith (eds), *Cultural Heritages as Reflexive Traditions*. Basingstoke: Palgrave, pp. 1–19.

Nic Craith, M. (2008) Intangible Cultural Heritages: The Challenges for Europe. *Anthropological Journal of European Cultures*, 17 (1), 54–73.

Ó Giolláin, D. (2000) *Locating Irish Folklore: Tradition, Modernity, Identity*. Cork: Cork University Press.

Oliver, P. (ed.) (1997) *Encyclopedia of Vernacular Architecture of the World*, 3 vols. Cambridge: Cambridge University Press.

OWHC (Organization of World Heritage Cities) (2014) Introduction to the OWHC. Available at: http://www.ovpm.org/en/presentation (accessed October 5, 2014).

Picard, D., and Robinson, M. (eds) (2012) *Emotion in Motion: Tourism, Affect and Transformation*. Aldershot: Ashgate.

Robertson, I.J.M. (2012) *Heritage from Below*. Farnham: Ashgate.

Sahlins, M. (2002) *Waiting for Foucault, Still*. Chicago: Prickly Paradigm Press.

Shaheed, F (2011) Report of the Independent Expert in the Field of Cultural Rights, Farida Shaheed. Human Rights Council Seventeenth Session Agenda Item 3. UNHRC document A/HRC/17/38. Available at: http://www.unesco.org/new/fileadmin/MULTIMEDIA/HQ/CLT/images/Report%20of%20Farida%20Shaheed.pdf (accessed February 14, 2015).

Silberman, N. (2013) Heritage Interpretation as Public Discourse: Towards a New Paradigm. In M.-T. Albert, R. Bernecker, and B. Rudolff (eds), *Understanding Heritage*. Berlin: De Gruyter, pp. 21–33.

Smith, L. (2006) *Uses of Heritage*. London: Routledge.

Smith, L., and Waterton, E. (2009) *Heritage, Communities and Archaeology*. London: Duckworth.

Straczuk, J. (2012) Local Practices of European Identity on the New Eastern Borders of the EU. In U. Kockel, M. Nic Craith, and J. Frykman (eds), *Blackwell Companion to the Anthropology of Europe*. Malden, MA: Wiley-Blackwell, pp. 199–211.

Tschofen, B. (2008) Of the Taste of Regions: Culinary Practice, European Policy and Spatial Culture – A Research Outline. *Anthropological Journal of European Cultures*, 17 (1), 24–53.

Tsing, A. (2003) Natural Resources and Capitalist Frontiers. *Economic and Political Weekly*, 38 (48), 5100–5106.

UNESCO (2011) World Heritage Strategy for Capacity Building. Document WHC-11/35. COM/9B. Available at: http://whc.unesco.org/archive/2011/whc11-35com-9Be.pdf (accessed August 27, 2014).

UNESCO (2013) Operational Guidelines for the Implementation of the World Heritage Convention. Available at: http://whc.unesco.org/en/guidelines/ (accessed February 15, 2015).

UNESCO (2014a) List of World Heritage in Danger. Available at: http://whc.unesco.org/en/danger/ (accessed September 30, 2014).

UNESCO (2014b) State of Conservation (SOC). Available at: http://whc.unesco.org/pg.cfm?cid=171&l=en&&action=list&soc_start=2014&soc_end=2014&&maxrows=150 (accessed September 30, 2014).

UNESCO (2015) Global Strategy. Available at: http://whc.unesco.org/en/globalstrategy/ (accessed February 15, 2015).

United Nations (2007) Declaration on the Rights of Indigenous Peoples (UNDRIP). Document A/RES/61/295. Available at: http://www.un-documents.net/a61r295.htm (accessed March 19, 2015).

Witcomb, A., and Buckley, K. (2013) Engaging in the Future of "Critical Heritage Studies": Looking Back in Order to Look Forward. *International Journal of Heritage Studies*, 19 (6), 562–578.

PART I Expanding Heritage

CHAPTER 2

Heritage Places: Evolving Conceptions and Changing Forms

Neil A. Silberman

The Australia ICOMOS Charter for Places of Cultural Significance, better known as the Burra Charter, has long been recognized as an international standard for the management of heritage places (e.g. Zancheti *et al.* 2009). Yet its text offers clear evidence of just how difficult an exact definition of "heritage places" can be. Equating "cultural heritage places" with "places of cultural significance" (Australia ICOMOS 2013: pmbl.), the Burra Charter defines "place" as "a geographically defined area" that "may include elements, objects, spaces and views" (Australia ICOMOS 2013: art. 1.1). Further noting that "place may have tangible and intangible dimensions," Burra conflates divergent notions of space and place, referring both to an objectively measurable, bounded area of the earth's surface and to subjective, qualitative perceptions such as "sacred mountain," "busy street," or "home." These subjective perceptions are of an entirely different character than either measurement or typological categories (Manzo 2005), and it is not quite clear if, or even how, the two categories mesh. Furthermore, the Burra Charter's definition of "cultural significance" is equally expansive, encompassing "aesthetic, historic, scientific, social, or spiritual value for past, present, or future generations" that is "embodied in the place itself, its fabric, setting, use, associations, meanings, records, related places and related objects" (Australia ICOMOS 2013: art. 1.2). As an additional complicating factor, the charter adds that "[p]laces may have a range of values for different individuals or groups" (Australia ICOMOS 2013: art. 1.2).

A Companion to Heritage Studies, First Edition. Edited by William Logan, Máiréad Nic Craith, and Ullrich Kockel.
© 2016 John Wiley & Sons, Inc. Published 2016 by John Wiley & Sons, Inc.

How can such sweeping, all-inclusive definitions – attempting to cover all material, immaterial, objective, and subjective aspects of heritage places – possibly capture their irreducible essence? How can we identify the distinctive characteristic of heritage places without endlessly extending the list of specific material forms and subjective associations a heritage place may possess? At a time when officially recognized heritage types are splintering into distinct regional, ethnic, and religious variants (Ashworth, Graham, and Tunbridge 2007), when the UNESCO World Heritage List has exceeded a thousand inscribed properties all said to possess Outstanding Universal Value (UNESCO 2014), when the possession and control of cultural heritage resources have become symbols of political legitimacy,[1] no single physical definition of a heritage place seems capable of capturing the thoroughly fragmented reality of cultural heritage in the twenty-first century. Thus focusing on process, rather than object, may be a more useful approach. I will argue in the following pages that a heritage place can be best understood as any physical structure, archaeological feature, or landscape that serves as a stimulus for collective and individual memory and historical associations. Indeed, ascriptions of heritage significance can be fixed on almost any place or locus of past human activity – from the Athenian acropolis (e.g. Loukaki 1997) to a Brazilian fishing village (Correia, Carlos, and Rocha 2013: 59–63), to the residence of the King of Rock 'n' Roll (Marling 1996). It is the evocative relationship of present to past that makes a heritage place significant, not anything inherent to the type or date of the site itself. Thus there are countless inaccessible and unpromoted medieval structures, archeological ruins, and celebrity homes that offer no emotional connection in the public psyche, and, despite their typological potential to be considered worthy of commemoration, are accordingly not considered heritage places except in the most general and most abstract sense (Baillie, Chatzoglou, and Taha 2010).

At the same time, it is important to recognize that heritage places, once officially or informally identified as such, do not necessarily last forever. Quite apart from physical deterioration, changing tastes, values, and shifting generational affinities and attachments can result in the neglect or abandonment of once venerated or respected places,[2] and can likewise give rise to the sudden "heritagization" of places that possessed no such significance before (Franck and Paxson 2013). This chapter will trace the evolving social role of heritage places, from their initial roles as sites for pilgrimage and ritual to their formalization as national institutions the early nineteenth century, to their multicultural context in the early twenty-first century. The chapter will argue that the significance of heritage places is neither static nor inherent in their physical components, and their definition and classification should focus on their roles in confirming or contesting the values attributed to them by particular social groups. Indeed, the categories and constellations of heritage places chosen for official commemoration offer a unique articulation of each era's spectrum of (often contradictory) collective memories. Heritages places can thus be defined – without reference to their specific components – as focal points of reflection, commemoration, and debate about the values of the past in contemporary society.

Touching Eternity: Heritage Places as Tokens of Faith

More than a century ago, Alois Riegl, the great fin de siècle Austrian art historian, famously recognized what had become by his time "a modern cult of monuments" (Riegl 1903). Noting that in former times, monuments primarily served "for the specific purpose of keeping particular human deeds and destinies ... alive and present in the consciousness of future generations," he asserted that the "erection and maintenance of such 'deliberate' monuments has all but come to a halt" (Riegl 1996: 69). Writing just a few years before thousands of "deliberate" monuments to the dead of World War I would once again spring up to express the grief of villages, towns, and city squares across Europe, Riegl was nonetheless correct in noting that at the turn of the twentieth century, an epoch-making shift in public commemoration had occurred. For in marked contrast to earlier times when heritage was a shared concern of the community, professionals (like Riegl himself) were now entrusted as members of government-appointed national commissions to designate official monuments that, according to their expert opinion, bore outstanding historical or artistic significance. It might even be fair to say that in earlier ages the whole world was a heritage site.

For many ancient, rural, and indigenous peoples, wisdom indeed "sat in places," with significant features of the landscape bearing visual witness to ancestors' exploits, ancient battles, and boundaries, and the earthly traces of cosmic creation myths (Basso 1996). The entire landscape was an evocative historical record. Scattered allusions in the Hebrew Bible to such geographical curiosities as a pillar of salt in the southern Dead Sea region (Gen. 19:26), the twelve large stones rising above the surface of the Jordan River near Jericho (Josh. 4:9), and the "great heap of stones" in the hill country near Ai (Josh. 7:26), were each associated with famous events of the Israelite tradition. Yet the identification of these places was not motivated by haphazard antiquarian curiosity. Similar to the famous landmarks of Egypt mentioned by Herodotus in the fifth century BC (Baragwanath and de Bakker 2012) and those in Greece described by Pausanias in the second century AD (Alcock, Cherry, and Elsner 2001), these ancient "heritage places" were symbolic verifications of much wider religio-historical narratives, in which the each physical landmark was used to substantiate the whole. This attempt at the validation of historico-theological belief systems through the selective description of heritage places continued for centuries, and indeed endures up to the present day (Lewis 2012).

Another important element of veneration was added to religiously inspired heritage places when the cult of relics arose in most major world religions (Tambiah 2013). Significant sites and features of the landscape not only provided tangible evidence of sacred events and personalities, they also offered a medium for physical contact with the divine. Peter Brown's vivid description of the logic of the early Christian cult of saints (Brown 2009) also applied to other religions: the places where holy men and women had walked, the scenes of their martyrdom or spiritual triumphs, even the reliquaries and shrines that contained their earthly remains and possessions, offered a means of direct communication with the grace-giving sources of their faith. That eternal realm of communion was not necessarily otherworldly, but could, as the humanists of the Renaissance would show, also exist in a remote golden age of beauty, prosperity, and wisdom: the classical epoch of Greece and Rome.

And so heritage as we know it was born as a new kind of spiritual veneration, in reaction to the reaction to the increasingly rigid medieval theological and earthly regimes. Cyriac of Ancona, among of the first of the Renaissance antiquarians, traveled widely throughout the eastern Mediterranean in the fifteenth century, studying, drawing, and describing long ignored and neglected classical remains. Yet his was not merely a search for information, but a quest for communion. When asked by a priest why he so tirelessly sought out areas of half-buried ruins, sarcophagi, and ancient Latin inscriptions – which we would today unhesitatingly call heritage places – Cyriac replied that he had a higher calling: to bring the dead back to life (Belozerskaya 2009: 42). That belief, that somehow material relics from the past could reveal transcendent truths about human existence, would remain a central motivation of archaeology and the study of cultural heritage. Whether it was Winckelmann's theory of aesthetic development, through its endless cycles of rise, flowering, and decay (Potts 2000), or Christian Thomson's neat scheme of universal technological development across the millennia through raw materials of stone, bronze, and iron (Eskildsen 2012), heritage places were becoming sites of ideological or spiritual reflection about transcendent patterns of human destiny. As will be described below, the cult of the nation would become the most widespread observances at heritage places all over the world. Yet the element of personal communion with archaeological remains, architectural ruins, and natural landmarks still endures at heritage places with both ancient and modern spiritual associations like Stonehenge, the Pyramids, the Old City of Jerusalem, Uluru, Machu Picchu, and even the UFO cultists' Area 51 (Timothy and Olsen 2006; Battaglia 2006). Thus one social process that can characterize a heritage place is the quest for tangible contact with a transcendent metaphysical belief. Such feelings still resonate in even local settings where a powerful need for ruins (Jackson 1980) offers a sense of psychic intimacy with distant eras and vast expanses of human history, bolstering our own sense of mortality with at least a fleeting encounter with timelessness.

Belonging to a Nation: Heritage Places as Objects of State Power

One of the primary rationales for a more precise definition of "heritage places" is legal rather than theoretical; in modern nation-states, the official designation of heritage places brings with it a variety of benefits, tax incentives, responsibilities, and legal restrictions that affect its status as a special class of property (e.g. Phelan 1993; Bendix, Eggert, and Peselmann 2012; Pickard 2012). Whether owned by the state, or protected by the state against destruction or undesirable changes by their private owners, legally recognized monuments, archaeological sites, historic districts, and cultural landscapes have become the objects of international conventions, protracted bi-national legal battles, and criminal prosecutions within individual states (Forrest 2010). Oversight of material and intangible elements of collective memory – at least those officially recognized as having national significance – is a recognized prerogative of sovereignty in the modern system of nation-states (Pavoni 2012). Like the regulation of the exploitation or conservation of natural resources deemed vital to a nation's security, the development or protection of heritage places is seen as an unalienable national right. Although the properties on the ever-expanding UNESCO World Heritage List are recognized as possessing Outstanding Universal Value as the patrimony of all humanity, the individual States Parties to the World Heritage Convention (1972) still retain full legal sovereignty over their listed World Heritage sites (Atherton and Atherton 1995).

How did the state come to be the legal custodian of a certain class of designated heritage places? Here too the social process, rather than the material fabric, provided the underlying rationale. As mentioned earlier, the cult of relic-bearing heritage places gradually expanded; the eighteenth-century classical antiquarians and the three-age archaeologists who succeeded the earlier pilgrims thought in terms of grand, universalist schemata, in which particular miraculous events, aesthetic developments, and technological advances were arranged as grand narratives of human history. Yet as the Age of Kings and the Age of Reason gave way to an era of competing nation-states, a new kind of heritage narrative arose. Simultaneously universal and particular, it recognized the nation as the culmination of a succession of earlier forms of communal organization, in which each people's unique character could be expressed. Each emerging nation saw itself as unique and eternal; the qualities most prized in the present were perceived in the monuments and heritage places of the past (cf. Silberman 1989, 1996). The civic narrative taught in government schools and displayed in the galleries of national museums were also enacted in public pageants that re-enacted the evolving embodiments of national genius – from Prehistory, through the Bronze Age and Iron Age, through increasingly complex social organization and artistic achievements, to their ultimate fulfillment in the form of a nation-state. Gradually, individual heritage places that were informally identified by antiquarians and romantic nationalists as national symbols (e.g. Dietler 1994; Hutchinson 2012; Silberman 2013) were regularly incorporated into national heritage registers and bureaucratically administered by national monuments services or culture ministries (e.g. Munasinghe 2005). The official lists of protected heritage cumulatively represented the national narrative – and thus public visits to government-protected heritage places and historic landmarks essentially became civic rituals, with each site reaffirming, *pars pro toto*, the validity of the entire national narrative (see e.g. Bodnar 1991).

As long as the nation-state defined itself through its homogeneity of language, culture, cuisine, and national costume, the network of official heritage places had resonance with the vast majority of citizens. "Heritage place" had a distinct connotation as a site of ethno-national commemoration, a place where loyalty to the nation-state was literally or symbolically mobilized.[3] However, this close association between a sequence of distinctive heritage places with perceived ethnic characteristics often led to the twin evils of extending territorial claims to encompass adjoining areas containing "national" heritage places (e.g. Silverman 2011), and ignoring or neglecting heritage places within national boundaries that do not illustrate the accepted national narrative (Waterton 2009). The civic significance of commemorative heritage places is thus exclusionary by nature, even, as will be shown, when formerly marginalized indigenous or minority ethnic groups begin to officialize their own set of heritage places as symbols of communal identity.

Escaping from Everyday Routines: Heritage Places as Entertainment Venues

From the time of Pausanias's *Description of Greece* to the Baedeckers, Blue Guides, and Lonely Planet volumes of more modern times, public visitation to heritage places has been conditioned by an implicit quality quite distinct from the spiritual significance of sites or their relevance to national epics. The aesthetic quality of the remains, the ease with which they can be reached, and – not least important – the quality of the local cuisine and nearby accommodation, have always been important components of the character of a heritage place. Yet until the rise of mass tourism in Europe and the Mediterranean in the nineteenth century with the advent of railroads and, perhaps even more important, steamships (Armstrong and Williams 2005), and with the further individualization of family tourism in the United States with the construction of long-distance highways and the spread of automobile ownership (Rugh 2008), a large class of heritage places were transformed from sober places of reflection and awe to entertainment venues.

There had always been informal commercial activity surrounding famous heritage places, but it was only with the rise of the great World Expositions that the practice of gawking at antiquities became a holiday pursuit. From the display of the massive Nineveh reliefs and sculptures at the 1851 Crystal Palace Exhibition (Malley 2012) to the traditional Japanese village at the 1893 Columbian Exposition (Stone 2011), to the full scale reproduction of Jerusalem's Old City at the St Louis World's Fair in 1904, reproductions of cultural heritage sites (Çelik 1992) became highly visible symbols of the Western imperial conquest of time as well as resources and space. Gradually, heritage places themselves were remade. At first a perimeter fence, a simple ticket booth, and a few identifying signposts were all the infrastructure needed. But as guided coach tours and family auto vacations encountered a greater variety of roadside diversions, the design of heritage places gradually grew more complex, adding a standard set of amenities: parking lots, visitor centers, cafeterias, rest rooms, and souvenir shops. A new architectural form gradually crystallized, transforming at least one possible definition of a heritage place. Borrowing design principles from the world's fairs and the theme parks that were by the 1950s becoming so successful, heritage places became tourist attractions offering a standardized narrative read by the feet – from the parking lot, through the ticket booth, along carefully demarcated interpretive paths, through the cafeteria and gift shop, and out to the parking lot again (Silberman 2007). The *experience* of visiting a heritage place, rather than the knowledge and particular facts and figures presented there, became its primary value.

Indeed, as public budgets for monuments services and culture ministries steadily declined with the worldwide rise of neoliberal austerity policies, independent income generation or privatization became a crucial factor in the management of many heritage places, despite their sometimes adverse effects (Palumbo 2006). Especially with the added attractions of multimedia visitor centers, immersive virtual environments, and interactive interpretive installations eagerly supplied by a growing industry of IT heritage designers and funded by government agencies and international development agencies, heritage places and revitalized historic centers were reconceptualized as productive centers that would stimulate local economies (cf. Bandarin, Hosagrahar, and Albernaz 2011).

In cases where visitation soars, physical conservation usually suffers – leading to extraordinary measures to limit visitor traffic or substantially raise admission fees (Russo 2002). Likewise, the necessity to generate revenue from heritage places imposes a practical constraint on interpretation – only sanitized, museumized representations of the past's unpleasantness and horror can be permitted lest potential visitors be driven away (Waitt 2000). In this sense, heritage places can be seen as holiday venues whose most threatening competitors are not other heritage places, but other entertainment attractions that provide welcome weekend or vacation relief from the daily grind. And for the members of local communities whose economic underdevelopment often serves as the main reason for investment in the often costly design and management of such heritage places, the heritage place often loses its distinctly local significance or historical value, becoming just another workplace in a service industry designed to appeal to consumers from the outside.

Asserting Independence: Heritage Places as Symbolic Resistance

Postcolonial independence and civil rights movements have given rise to yet another meaning to the term "heritage place." As mentioned above, the creation of "officialized" heritage places by national governments gave voice to homogenized mainstream heritage narratives while marginalizing or ignoring the heritage perspectives of indigenous peoples and ethnic minorities (see e.g. Buciek and Juul 2008; Litter 2008; Robertson 2008; Smith 2008). Yet the eventual recognition of indigenous rights and the legitimation of the cultural (if not always fully political) autonomy of regional communities and ethnic minorities led to the identification of certain heritage places as proud symbols of independence from the long-dominant majority elites (Silberman 2010). Yet the primary difference with what I have called "neo-nationalist heritage" from its predecessors was that it was aimed in the first place to separate rather than unite. Heritage self-definition was a declaration of independence from a formally united (however unjust and unequal) society. And therein lies the cruel irony of this stage of the evolution of heritage places – a neologism that had its origins, as noted in the earlier discussion of the Burra Charter, in the notion that all heritage perspectives and values should be recognized. In encouraging acceptance and respect for the historical assertions and authenticity standards of all polities and peoples (cf. Larsen 1995), the inevitability of direct ideological conflict over twice- or thrice-claimed heritage places – most recently Ayohda, Bamiyan, Preah Vihear, and Timbuktu, for example (Ratnagar 2004; Flood 2002; Williams 2011; O'Dell 2013) – produced yet more bloodshed and conflict as new oppositions arose to claim their place on the heritage landscape, shattering the usefulness of heritage as a community-building tool.

In such situations of conflicting claims defended by violence and destruction, heritage places took on yet another meaning, symbolizing the fragmentation of pre-existing memory communities rather than the congealing of new collectivities. The irony is, however, that new heritage activists followed the same pattern as earlier imperial and colonial elites. The power to declare unilateral significance, to craft self-justifying historical narratives, and to exclude rivals and despised subordinates from "true" membership in the community became prerogatives of new postcolonial political elites.

I cannot conclude this survey of twenty-first century heritage fragmentation without also mentioning the use of heritage places as sites of conscience and foci of diasporic identity, in which traditional geographical and national commemorative understandings of heritage places simply do not apply. The transformation of places of mass murder, enslavement, exploitation, and inhumanity to formal heritage sites (with the infrastructure of modern heritage interpretation, but designed to encourage moral reflection) offers a sobering counterpoint to the use of heritage places as platforms for partisanship or as simple entertainment venues (Sevcenko 2010). And in an era of massive demographic shifts through rural-to-urban migration, undocumented workers from poorer nations seeking employment in developed economies, or the forced displacement of ethnic minorities, we can often see nativist reactions that decry the perceived disintegration of formerly homogenous nations (e.g. Vogelaar and Hale 2013) – and the inward turn of diasporic communities themselves (e.g. Agnew 2005). These twenty-first century variations in the significance and social role of heritage places make it clear that a better understanding of the dynamic process of heritage place-making – rather than a single comprehensive definition – must be sought.

Grasping for Meaning: Heritage Places as Reactions to Change

Heritage places can variously or even simultaneously be sites of conflict, identity, entertainment, patriotism, ideology, and reflection. None is necessarily more important or constitutive than the rest. The new social networks being created through indigenous and "bottom-up" approaches to the establishment of heritage places stand alongside and almost always intertwine with the web of relationships that earlier concepts of heritage places inspired. The concepts of authenticity and significance that underlie the range of meanings reflect the self-perceptions of communities and individuals and are oriented at least as much toward the present and the future as the past. Heritage places should therefore be seen as stages for a kind of performative action, in the expression of a value or a sense of identity, whose subjectivity and ephemerality contradicts the very notion of the "timelessness" of cultural heritage. Gustavo Araoz has redefined the heritage place, not as a material relic with a single unchanging meaning, but rather as a "vessel of value" (Araoz 2011). Araoz rightly asserts that over the past two centuries,

> the modern heritage conservation movement developed under the assumption that values rested mostly, if not entirely on … material form. The philosophy of conservation and its resulting doctrinal foundation, the protective legislation, the identification and official registration processes, and the methodological framework and professional protocols for intervening in heritage places are all fixated on the protection of the material vessels that carry the value. (Araoz 2011: 58)

It is now time to recognize the centrality of values in establishing that this or that landscape feature is a heritage place. Indeed, the heritage place of the twenty-first century potentially contains all the values that have been associated with sites of memory and commemoration over the centuries, yet it is also the stage on which or imaginings of the future are born. As David Lowenthal (2006) has eloquently noted, our appreciation of the past through heritage places requires a creative sense of imagination that is uncannily parallel to our visions of the distant future. To have no vision of the past beyond a static conception of a particular material form of a historic structure is to have no sense of the trajectory of time. The significance of heritage places is neither static nor inherent in their material components; authenticity and significance are ascribed to them by social groups, whose composition and self-perceptions change with time. These groups selectively highlight or ignore various elements of material and intangible heritage, to defend their social rank, express their hopes for the future, or historicize their political goals.

As we have seen, the categories and constellations of heritage places chosen for protection and commemoration throughout the centuries embody each era's spectrum of (often contradictory) collective memories. We should thus begin to see heritage places as cultural phenomena rather than things. Though the conservation of the physical vessels that are assumed to contain the values handed down to us from earlier eras is an essential responsibility, we must not lose sight of the nature of those values themselves. Good or bad, noble or immoral, they are projections of a society's ever-changing collective psyche, foci of nostalgic reflection that are always stimulated and decisively shaped by present hopes and fears. In that sense, our primary task in understanding the nature of heritage places is to distinguish the various projections of collective memory from the inherited landscapes, monuments, and landmarks that serve as the "screens" on which they are shown.

Notes

1 For a description and critique, see Nilsson Stutz (2013).
2 For the case of Cold War sites in the United States, see Wiener (2012).
3 Among countless case studies, see Azaryahu and Kellerman-Barrett (1999), Ranger (2004), Yan and Bramwell (2008), and Hamilakis (2009).

References

Legislation

Convention Concerning the Protection of the World Cultural and Natural Heritage (World Heritage Convention) (UNESCO, 1972). Available at: http://whc.unesco.org/archive/convention-en.pdf (accessed March 19, 2015).

Other Works

Agnew, V. (2005) *Diaspora, Memory and Identity: A Search for Home*. Toronto: University of Toronto Press.

Alcock, S.E, Cherry, J.F., and Elsner, J. (2001) *Pausanias: Travel and Memory in Roman Greece*. Oxford: Oxford University Press.

Araoz, G.F. (2011) Preserving Heritage Places under a New Paradigm. *Journal of Cultural Heritage Management and Sustainable Development*, 1 (1), 55–60.

Armstrong, J., and Williams, D. (2005) The Steamboat and Popular Tourism. *Journal of Transport History*, 26 (1), 61–77.

Ashworth, G.J., Graham, B.J., and Tunbridge, J.E. (2007) *Pluralising Pasts: Heritage, Identity and Place in Multicultural Societies*. London: Pluto Press.

Atherton, T.-A., and Atherton, T.C. (1995) The Power and the Glory: National Sovereignty and the World Heritage Convention. *Australian Law Journal*, 69, 631–649.

Australia ICOMOS (2013) Charter for Places of Cultural Significance (Burra Charter), revised version. Available at: http://australia.icomos.org/wp-content/uploads/The-Burra-Charter-2013-Adopted-31.10.2013.pdf (accessed June 29, 2014).

Azaryahu, M., and Kellerman-Barrett, A. (1999) Symbolic Places of National History and Revival: A Study in Zionist Mythical Geography. *Transactions of the Institute of British Geographers*, 24 (1), 109–123.

Baillie, B., Chatzoglou, A., and Taha, S. (2010) Packaging the Past. *Heritage and Society*, 3 (1), 51–71.

Bandarin, F., Hosagrahar, J., and Albernaz, F.S. (2011) Why Development Needs Culture. *Journal of Cultural Heritage Management and Sustainable Development*, 1 (1), 15–25.

Baragwanath, E., and de Bakker, M. (2012) *Myth, Truth, and Narrative in Herodotus*. Oxford: Oxford University Press.

Basso, K.H. (1996) *Wisdom Sits in Places: Landscape and Language among the Western Apache*. Albuquerque: University of New Mexico Press.

Battaglia, D. (2006) *E.T. Culture: Anthropology in Outerspaces*. Durham, NC: Duke University Press.

Belozerskaya, M. (2009) *To Wake the Dead: A Renaissance Merchant and the Birth of Archaeology*. New York: Norton.

Bendix, R., Eggert, A., and Peselmann, A. (2012) *Heritage Regimes and the State*. Göttingen: Universitätsverlag.

Bodnar, J.E. (1991) *Remaking America: Public Memory, Commemoration, and Patriotism in the Twentieth Century*. Princeton: Princeton University Press.

Brown, P. (2009) *The Cult of the Saints: Its Rise and Function in Latin Christianity*. Chicago: University of Chicago Press.

Buciek, K., and Juul, K. (2008) "We Are Here, Yet We Are Not Here": The Heritage of Excluded Groups. In B.J. Graham and P. Howard (eds), *The Ashgate Research Companion to Heritage and Identity*. Aldershot: Ashgate Publishing, pp. 105–124.

Çelik, Z. (1992) *Displaying the Orient: Architecture of Islam at Nineteenth-Century World's Fairs*. Berkeley: University of California Press.

Correia, M., Carlos, G., and Rocha, S. (2013) *Vernacular Heritage and Earthen Architecture*. Boca Raton: CRC Press.

Dietler, M. (1994) "Our Ancestors the Gauls": Archaeology, Ethnic Nationalism, and the Manipulation of Celtic Identity in Modern Europe. *American Anthropologist*, 96 (3), 584–605.

Eskildsen, K.R. (2012) The Language of Objects: Christian Jürgensen Thomsen's Science of the Past. *Isis*, 103 (1), 24–53.

Flood, F.B. (2002) Between Cult and Culture: Bamiyan, Islamic Iconoclasm, and the Museum. *Art Bulletin*, 84 (4), 641–659.

Forrest, C. (2010) *International Law and the Protection of Cultural Heritage*. London: Routledge.

Franck, K., and Paxson, L. (2013) Transforming Public Space into Sites for Mourning or Free Expression. In K. Franck and Q. Stevens (eds), *Loose Space: Possibility and Diversity in Urban Life*. London: Routledge, pp. 132–153.

Hamilakis, Y. (2009) *The Nation and Its Ruins: Antiquity, Archaeology, and National Imagination in Greece*. New York: Oxford University Press.

Hutchinson, J. (2012) *Dynamics of Cultural Nationalism: The Gaelic Revival and the Creation of the Irish Nation State*. London: Routledge.

Jackson, J.B. (1980) *The Necessity for Ruins: And Other Topics*. Amherst: University of Massachusetts Press.

Larsen, K.E. (1995) *Nara Conference on Authenticity in Relation to the World Heritage Convention*. Trondheim: Tapir Publishers.

Lewis, J.R. (2012) Excavating Tradition: Alternative Archaeologies as Legitimation Strategies. *Numen*, 59 (2/3), 202–221.

Litter, J. (2008) Heritage and "Race." In B.J. Graham and P. Howard (eds), *The Ashgate Research Companion to Heritage and Identity*. Aldershot: Ashgate Publishing, pp. 89–104.

Loukaki, A. (1997) Whose Genius Loci? Contrasting Interpretations of the "Sacred Rock of the Athenian Acropolis." *Annals of the Association of American Geographers*, 87 (2), 306–329.

Lowenthal, D. (2006) Stewarding the Future. *Norsk Geografisk Tidsskrift*, 60 (1), 15–23.

Malley, S. (2012) Nineveh 1851: An Archaeography. *Journal of Literature and Science*, 5 (1), 23–37.

Manzo, L.C. (2005) For Better or Worse: Exploring Multiple Dimensions of Place Meaning. *Journal of Environmental Psychology*, 25 (1), 67–86.

Marling, K.A. (1996) *Graceland: Going Home with Elvis*. Cambridge, MA: Harvard University Press.

Munasinghe, H. (2005) The Politics of the Past: Constructing a National Identity through Heritage Conservation. *International Journal of Heritage Studies*, 11 (3), 251–260.

Nilsson Stutz, L. (2013) Claims to the Past: A Critical View of the Arguments Driving Repatriation of Cultural Heritage and Their Role in Contemporary Identity Politics. *Journal of Intervention and Statebuilding*, 7 (2), 170–195.

O'Dell, E.J. (2013) Waging War on the Dead: The Necropolitics of Sufi Shrine Destruction in Mali. *Archaeologies*, 9 (3), 506–525.

Palumbo, G. (2006) Privatization of State-Owned Cultural Heritage. In *Of the Past, for the Future: Integrating Archaeology and Conservation*. Proceedings of the Conservation Theme at the Fifth World Archaeological Congress, Washington, DC, June 22–26, 2003, Los Angeles: Getty Publications, pp. 35–39.

Pavoni, R. (2012) Sovereign Immunity and the Enforcement of International Cultural Property Law. Available at: http://papers.ssrn.com/sol3/papers.cfm?abstract_id=2244798 (accessed June 29, 2014).

Phelan, M. (1993) Synopsis of the Laws Protecting Our Cultural Heritage. *New England Law Review*, 28, 63–108.
Pickard, R. (2012) *Policy and Law in Heritage Conservation*. London: Taylor and Francis.
Potts, A. (2000) *Flesh and the Ideal: Winckelmann and the Origins of Art History*. New Haven: Yale University Press.
Ranger, T. (2004) Nationalist Historiography, Patriotic History and the History of the Nation: The Struggle over the Past in Zimbabwe. *Journal of Southern African Studies*, 30 (2), 215–234.
Ratnagar, S. (2004) Archaeology at the Heart of a Political Confrontation: The Case of Ayodhya. *Current Anthropology*, 45 (2), 239–259.
Riegl, A. (1903) *Moderne Denkmalkultus: sein Wesen und seine Entstehung*. Vienna: W. Braumüller.
Riegl, A. (1996) The Modern Cult of Monuments: Its Essence and Development. In N.S. Price, K.M. Talley, and A.M. Vaccaro (eds), *Historical and Philosophical Issues in the Conservation of Cultural Heritage*. Malibu: Getty Publications, pp. 69–93.
Robertson, I.J.M. (2008) Heritage from Below: Class, Social Protest and Resistance. In B.J. Graham and P. Howard (eds), *The Ashgate Research Companion to Heritage and Identity*. Aldershot: Ashgate Publishing, pp. 143–158.
Rugh, S.S. (2008) *Are We There Yet? The Golden Age of American Family Vacations*. Lawrence: University Press of Kansas.
Russo, A.P. (2002) The "Vicious Circle" of Tourism Development in Heritage Cities. *Annals of Tourism Research*, 29 (1), 165–182.
Sevcenko, L. (2010) Sites of Conscience: New Approaches to Conflicted Memory. *Museum International*, 62 (1/2), 20–25.
Silberman, N.A. (1989) *Between Past and Present: Archaeology, Ideology, and Nationalism in the Modern Middle East*. New York: Henry Holt.
Silberman, N.A. (1996) Promised Lands and Chosen Peoples: The Politics and Poetics of Archaeological Narrative. In P. Kohl and C. Fawcett (eds) *Nationalism, Politics, and the Practice of Archaeology*. Cambridge: Cambridge University Press, pp. 249–262.
Silberman, N.A. (2007) Sustainable Heritage? Public Archaeological Interpretation and the Marketed Past. In Y. Hamilakis and P. Duke (eds), *Archaeology and Capitalism: From Ethics to Politics*. Walnut Creek, CA: Left Coast Press, pp. 179–193.
Silberman, N.A. (2010) Validation, Resistance, and Exclusion: Neo-Nationalist Cultural Heritage in a Globalized World. Available at: http://works.bepress.com/cgi/viewcontent.cgi?article=1033&context=neil_silberman (accessed January 12, 2015).
Silberman, N.A. (2013) The Tyranny of Narrative History, Heritage, and Hatred in the Modern Middle East. *Journal of Eastern Mediterranean Archaeology and Heritage Studies*, 1 (2), 175–184.
Silverman, H. (2011) Border Wars: The Ongoing Temple Dispute between Thailand and Cambodia and UNESCO's World Heritage List. *International Journal of Heritage Studies*, 17 (1), 1–21.
Smith, L. (2008) Heritage, Gender and Identity. In B.J. Graham and P. Howard (eds), *The Ashgate Research Companion to Heritage and Identity*. Aldershot: Ashgate Publishing, pp. 159–180.
Stone, L.A. (2011) The Japanese Village and Deer Park. *Studies in the History of Gardens and Designed Landscapes*, 31 (3), 216–227.
Tambiah, S.J. (2013) The Charisma of Saints, Amulets, and Tomb Shrines. In F. Aulino, M. Goheen, and S.J. Tambiah (eds), *Radical Egalitarianism: Local Realities, Global Relations*. New York: Fordham University Press, pp. 15–50.
Timothy, D., and Olsen, D. (2006) *Tourism, Religion and Spiritual Journeys*. London: Routledge.
UNESCO (2014) Twenty Six New Properties Added to World Heritage List at Doha Meeting. UNESCO World Heritage Centre. Available at: http://whc.unesco.org/en/news/1162 (accessed June 29, 2014).
Vogelaar, A.E., and Hale, B.W. (2013) Constituting Swiss Heritage: Discourse and the Management of "Invasive Species". *International Journal of Tourism Anthropology*, 3 (2), 130–149.
Waitt, G. (2000) Consuming Heritage: Perceived Historical Authenticity. *Annals of Tourism Research*, 27 (4), 835–862.

Waterton, E. (2009) Sights of Sites: Picturing Heritage, Power and Exclusion. *Journal of Heritage Tourism*, 4 (1), 37–56.

Wiener, J. (2012) *How We Forgot the Cold War: A Historical Journey across America*. Berkeley: University of California Press.

Williams, T. (2011) The Curious Tale of Preah Vihear: The Process and Value of World Heritage Nomination. *Conservation and Management of Archaeological Sites*, 13 (1), 1–7.

Yan, H., and Bramwell, B. (2008) Cultural Tourism, Ceremony and the State in China. *Annals of Tourism Research*, 35 (4), 969–989.

Zancheti, S.M., Hidaka, L.T.F., Ribeiro, C., and Aguiar, B. (2009) Judgement and Validation in the Burra Charter Process: Introducing Feedback in Assessing the Cultural Significance of Heritage Sites. *City and Time*, 4 (2), 47–53.

CHAPTER 3 From Folklore to Intangible Heritage

Kristin Kuutma

> What's in a name? That which we call a rose,
> By any other name would smell as sweet.
>
> —Shakespeare, *Romeo and Juliet*

The word "folklore" stands for many things – it often marks poetry, sayings, myths, songs, but also dances, music, customs, and festivals. What appears essential is the representational category assigned to each denotation. Yet representation implies interests, which in turn relate to particular epistemologies. This chapter will trace briefly an intellectual history, from the early study of folklore to current international endeavors to safeguard intangible cultural heritage. The latter were established by the UNESCO Masterpieces of the Oral and Intangible Heritage of Humanity program introduced in 2000, and even more so by the Convention for the Safeguarding of the Intangible Cultural Heritage (2003), which affects the field substantially. My study combines disciplinary history with critical analysis of the uses to which changing ideas were put. It also brings out the (in)stability of concepts which intrigued me in the first place and led me to write this piece. I have been puzzled by the significant rejection of the term "folklore," which has occurred particularly among English-language users, though a similar transition appears noticeable in other languages. If "(intangible) cultural heritage" carries more weight and presumably alternative power, does it also entail an ontological shift to "a brave new world"? Or is this just semantic quibbling?

A Companion to Heritage Studies, First Edition. Edited by William Logan, Máiréad Nic Craith, and Ullrich Kockel.
© 2016 John Wiley & Sons, Inc. Published 2016 by John Wiley & Sons, Inc.

The disciplinary change and renaming that has taken place in all corners of the world should not be underestimated, because an international concept as "folklore" or "intangible cultural heritage" can become instrumental in local contexts. William Thoms coined the English term "folklore" in the mid 1800s, designating the collected remnants of past traditional performances and practices that had been referred to as "popular antiquities". "Folklore" then became of growing scholarly interest, and similar designations appeared in several languages, borrowed or translated with simultaneous knowledge transfer. However, did the term concern existing organic objects toward which measures can be taken, or was it a product of (cultural) identification? What about the aura of falseness or negative connotations which were attached to it in some contexts? Interestingly, Barbara Kirshenblatt-Gimblett (1998) announced "folklore's crisis" already two decades ago in her presidential address to the American Folklore Society, signaling a long debate over naming in the United States.

In this chapter, I analyze the impact of an epistemological identification that occurred with the rise of folklore studies and look at the emergence of a field while not singling out the object in the process. In differentiating folklore as an object from the scholarly study of it, I recognize the scholarly endeavor's inherent relation to history. In order to understand the transformation from (documenting) folklore to the rise of the intangible, my aim is to position folklore studies between scholarship, society and the polity. Though a recent comprehensive *Companion to Folklore* (Bendix and Hasan-Rokem 2012) provides an insightful global perspective on the matter, one should also consider earlier seminal works that situated folklore studies in a wider intellectual context (e.g., Anttonen 2005; Bendix 1997; Feintuch 2003) and other groundbreaking analyses that focused on a single country (Wilson 1976; Herzfeld 1982; Zumwalt 1988; Ó Giolláin 2000). Oft-cited critical work introducing particular regions or periods (Paredes and Bauman 1972; Oinas 1978; Dow and Lixfeld 1986; Bausinger 1990; Abrahams 1993) complemented historical overviews of a more descriptive nature (e.g. Cocchiara 1981; Dundes 1999). For the sake of brevity, I refer only to a few works published in English. The earlier contextualization of folklore studies in heritage discourse dates back to the 1990s (see Kirshenblatt-Gimblett 1995), while conceptual concerns were prominent mostly within the UNESCO framework (Seitel 2001; Aikawa 2004). It could be argued that after Hemme, Tauschek, and Bendix (2007), the number of edited volumes with this disciplinary focus has increased notably.

I have discerned three particular phases in the transformation from folklore to intangible cultural heritage when thinking about the period from the nineteenth to the twenty-first century: identification and mapping; institutionalization and networking; translation and knowledge transfer. While it would be difficult to tell an all-encompassing global story in the limited space available, I shall resort to exemplary cases that illuminate these three phases. In order to explain the paradigm shifts involved, I shall situate folklore within history, geography, and research traditions more consistently in Estonia. This will enable me to represent different aspects of the usage and significance of folklore in a post-imperial Eastern European country where international heritage initiatives have found remarkable resonance.

Identification and Mapping

In the initial phase of identifying folklore, scholars manifested a general interest in the topic, and this coincided with the broader trend of modernization and a profound sociocultural transition for rural populations that deemed previous lifestyles and repertoires obsolete. The conceptualization of folklore included an immanent textual imperative from the start – the process of defining the object of interest was related to the urge for preservation, of retaining a record of folklore in its many forms; that is, collecting. Consequently, collecting also involved an interest in mapping in order to discover the geographic and cultural territories of those involved.

From the nineteenth century, the historical development of folklore studies dovetailed with the complexities of burgeoning nationalism. This was particularly significant in European countries where the nation-building process coincided with the extensive collecting of verbal lore. Collecting folklore was aimed at representing past repertoires and practices, celebrating mostly pre-industrial (peasant) lifestyles. The cultural philosophy of the European Enlightenment designated rural peasants as generators of the national spirit that needed to be ascertained to find its symbolic core in the profound reformulation of the nation-state. Following the lead of German-speaking scholars who found inspiration in Herder's belief that the inner qualities of the nation could be detected in folk poetry and epic, the idea of peasants as retainers of ancient popular creativity spread widely. Likewise, Romantic interest in popular repertoires drew on recognizing the significance of the language of peasants.

These agendas combined two ideologies that depended on documenting and collecting verbal expressions of the rural lower social classes. It was believed that peasants had retained archaic traits of creative genius and/or primeval linguistic affinities that gave rise to national-historical narratives (Leerssen 2006). Those poetic accounts had to be collected among the peasant folk. These were sought to testify to the origin of the nation and to symbolize its descent, which became instrumental in creating national pride. The alignment of folklore with language, land, and the idea of the nation were characteristic of emergent elites. On the one hand, this reflected a political environment where the middle classes sought to "assert political power in the face of international, cosmopolitan domination that was related to the general process of social change" (Abrahams 1993: 8–9). On the other hand, the geopolitical cause of nationalism distinguished between the agenda of unification and separatism (Leerssen 2006: 175). A particular transformation unfolded among oppressed peoples for whom a first dictionary, grammar, or collection of folksong might have been their first declaration of independence. Such achievements marked revolutionary moments in the marginal corners of Europe, where collections of folklore involved the collation of oral fragments to compile a coherent national narrative. Those were often complemented with archeological findings and the accumulation of peasant artifacts that were meant to represent an age-old (unrecognized) history and singular expression. And this generated impressive collections. In the nineteenth century, Estonia was a distinct Baltic province in the contested northwestern border of the Russian Empire. Its first initiatives in the field of folklore were related to an interest in the (poetic) repertoires and practices of the *undeutsch* peasant serfs on behalf of the German-speaking upper-class clergy and intellectuals. Upwardly mobile native Estonians soon took active part in the process thanks to edifying programs and social mobilization (see Kuutma 2005).

Romanticizing rural folk coincided with the modernization and gradual social change that accelerated by the end of the nineteenth century (cf. Anttonen 2005). The new contexts of possibly corrupt urban environments caused by emergent socioeconomic and industrial change were perceived as a threat to innocence, myth, and age-old tradition. Ironically, the increasing urbanization of Europe was a cosmopolitan trend that went against ethno-national ideas; whereas, folklore has been diagnosed as always "out of step with its time and surroundings" (Kirshenblatt-Gimblett 1998: 297). The transition to modernity that prompted the "discovery" of folklore rested on a perceived contrast between societies with dominant authority and those with emergent forms of social organization. But both considered folklore as in decline, and thus retained an interest in folk traditions (Bauman 1992: 30–31).

Institutionalization and Networking

Collecting folklore was organized by the urban cultural elite and was part of the nation-building process. This worked toward civil recognition of emergent citizenship in modern states, and was aimed at distinguishing the identities of previously suppressed ethnic groups in the dominant empires of Europe, not least in its central and eastern part. The creation of national-historical epic narratives begot a "complementary interest in carrying out linguistic and textual inventories" (Leerssen 2006: 199). The flourishing study of folklore denoted also the gradual development of a scholarly approach to systematizing the amassed collections. In the nineteenth and early twentieth century, this was usually not the initiative of a single state, but it presented an international exchange and scholarly networking of truly wide-reaching impact. New organizations were founded to gather together those interested in folklore within the same language regions. The cherished founding figures of these large collections were often in close correspondence or scholarly exchange with colleagues in close or remote countries.

In England, folklore indicated survivals in a civilized society. Specifically, it referred to survivals of repertoires and expressions whose origins lay in earlier stages of cultural evolution. In Ireland, folklore was perceived as a vehicle of spoken language with significance in current politics (see Ó Giolláin 2000). The establishment of organizations for the revival of the Irish language sustained the Celtic imaginary and worked towards the "Gaelicization of folklore" (Ó Giolláin 2000: 114). In the 1920s, the Folklore of Ireland Society was founded. The next decade saw the establishing of the Irish Folklore Institute and the Irish Folklore Commission, which guaranteed government finance for researchers and collectors, the product of whose work increased accordingly. The initiatives of folklore collecting and research were directly influenced by interaction with Scandinavian folklorists, who also provided formal training in the field. A long-established national culture like England had no ideological need for folklore and directed its anthropological gaze towards its colonies. Sweden also had a former empire; nevertheless, it felt marginalized and sought to reinforce its national self-image by collecting folklore; in 1873, the Nordic Museum was founded, and in 1912 an academic chair in folklore was established (Kvideland and Sehmsdorf 1989: 4).

The Nordic cooperation had a crucial impact in the field, both regionally and globally. This was particularly prominent in the establishment of a transnational research network of Folklore Fellows in 1907 that organized publications, networks, and scholarly meetings. This regional, collaborative initiative survived until the end of the 1950s, when the Nordic Institute of Folklore was founded. Frequent conferences also took place whose agendas reflected international (rather than merely trans-Atlantic) disciplinary developments. In the 1960s, genre analysis questioned the terminology used in the discipline. In the 1970s, an interpretation of cultural history as "oral tradition" shifted to critical fieldwork and performance studies (Kvideland and Sehmsdorf 1989).

Eventually, this led to expert-level cooperation between the Nordic Institute of Folklore, UNESCO and the World Intellectual Property Organization (WIPO) (see Sherkin 2001).

The oldest folklore archives of scholarly societies were founded in the 1830s in Finland, and the first professorship in the discipline was established there in 1900. Finnish folklore scholarship has had an enormous impact in Estonia over the past two centuries, providing inspiration for societies and publications, being involved in joint ventures, creating the theoretical basis for research and assisting with facilities for training. The Finnish lower-class vernacular belonged to the same Finno-Ugric language group as Estonian. Collections of folklore in Estonian exceeded a million pages, forming the basis for an emerging national identity, and the archives of these volumes followed the Finnish model. It is also significant to point out that it was essential to translate all the terminology used in folklore and ethnological studies into the vernacular in Estonia as part of the national intellectual program that emerged from out of the shadow of German and Russian domination.

The academic field of folklore studies thrived and became institutionalized in many countries in the first half of the twentieth century, but the prevailing epistemologies related to survivalism and evolutionism. This took a complicated twist when the lore of rural hinterlands was imagined to contain residues of lost glories that could be drawn on for reconstructing the past. Studies made positivist claims for scientific rigor when the philological direction in folklore studies focused on taxonomies and the systematization of foundational mythologies that tacitly sustained chronological and territorial imaginaries. Questions of distribution and efforts at mapping the dissemination of folklore became a prominent exercise of inventorying. The historico-geographic method developed comparative classification to specify shared origins and migration.

Furthermore, state-sponsored folklore studies were instrumental in the archaicization and exoticization that nourished the image of the purity of national culture. This was supposed to be preserved in rural settings, and provided material for the construction and development of nationalist, separatist, populist, and localist ideologies across Europe (Bausinger 1990; Wilson 1976; Herzfeld 1982; Cocchiara 1981). Peasant origins, regional diversity, and popular folk traditions responded to urbanization, industrialization, mechanization, and "perceived" cultural homogenization. Instead, folk music and dance were put on display in urban settings and festivals to propagate national pride, demonstrate "native exotics," or promote tourism (see Peer 1998).

Knowledge Transfer and Manipulation

From the 1930s onward, folklore gradually became subject to political manipulation, with relevant studies maintaining pretensions of national and racial purity. At the same time, this phase involved a popular dissemination of the results of folklore research. Academic pursuits paralleled social interest in rural practices and facilitated this knowledge transfer.

Totalitarian ideologies such as Nazism and fascism sought romantic representations of the national soul in the lore of the morally pure peasantry. Meanwhile, the urban environment was associated with the corruption of national virtues. The Nazi regime acquired legitimacy through the ideological and methodological foundations of scholarly works produced in the field of folklore studies, and infamously employed them in German-speaking countries (Dow and Lixfeld 1994). These political abuses of folklore helped the regime to justify violent atrocities in Germany. Unsurprisingly, this led to calls for the abolition of the field and the term *Volkskunde* after World War II. As a result, the discipline has reinvented itself entirely and been sensitive to manipulative politics (see Bendix 1997). In Italy, the fascist regime actively supported folklore research with an aim at consolidating national unity. Yet the notion of purity was incongruously reaffirmed in the policy of banning the foreign word *folklore* in 1933, which was substituted by *popolaresca* (Ó Giolláin 2000: 84). Similarly, military regimes with nationalist and imperial ambitions that ruled in southwestern parts of Europe (such as France, Spain, and Portugal) discredited the term 'folklore' owing to the historical takeover of the field by the repressive Vichy, Franco, and Salazar regimes (see Thiesse 1999). Consequently, in these countries, *folklore/folclore* appears outdated, referring to an amateurish approach to the field. In Latin America, intellectuals criticize folklore as being associated with official, politically manipulated notions of heritage and public display of folk arts (see Canclini 1993).

Under the Soviet regime, folklore was abused for propaganda purposes, and the work of folklorists was bent to communist political ideology. Folklorist research was directed at the propagation of Soviet cultural ideology and political education according to Communist Party guidelines. Folklore, either discovered or fabricated, had to be made consistent with the ideology and objectives of the Soviet state. Collective cultural practices – especially music, dance, and costume – were subjugated to government planning and censorship in order to conform to so-called progressive folk traditions. Soviet cultural and administrative models were applied across communist Eastern Europe. Estonia was incorporated into the Soviet regime after World War II. However, collecting folklore was suppressed to a degree, while intellectual interest in representations of pre-industrial past were not censored. Due to sociopolitical circumstances, peasant cultural expression, its current residues, and archived collections became idealized as a haven of non-Soviet Estonian identity.

In the context of multinational federations such as Yugoslavia and the Soviet Union, the political manipulation of representations of past or modern folk culture practices was geared towards a unifying image. Paradoxically, the political appropriation of folk culture ultimately had the opposite effect. By recognizing "native" representations of the past, communist elites sought to provide popular support for their regimes, twisting nationalist narratives and symbols together with folkloric cultural traditions (see Verdery 1995). Instead, the strengthening of local and regional attachments challenged wider allegiances. Folklore performances and initiatives for cultural revival were used for maintaining and engendering anti-Soviet sentiment. This use of folklore-related performative occasions gave rise to the "folklore movement" in Estonia and other Baltic countries in the 1970s and, in particular, the 1980s. People began to manifest their ethnic identities within the state-sponsored framework of folk culture. The conceptual shift that had occurred was especially clear when the loan word *folkloor/folklora/folkloras* was substituted for previously used vernacular terms.

Translation and Knowledge Transfer

In terms of origins and historical practice, the identification and study of folklore is a European endeavor reflecting essentially Eurocentric interests. However, the geographic confinement of folklore studies has never been exclusive. For example, recordings of local vernacular practices and mythologies appeared in the first written documents of European travelers in Latin America. These demonstrated relevant projects in a colonial context. Nevertheless, an interest in folklore as a sociopolitical project was exported to other parts of the world and took seminal shape in places where there were aspirations for building the modern nation-state. This is the case in late nineteenth-century Brazil. Major efforts in the sphere of cultural practices were undertaken to overcome the influence of colonial history by reinforcing particular identity representations. The first collections of popular song (*cantos populares*) date from the 1880s. The interest of Brazilian folklorists gradually focused on traditional music, which could be posited as quintessentially Brazilian in contrast to oral literature in Portuguese – the language of the colonizer (Ó Giolláin 2000: 90). The middle of the twentieth century saw two decades of a "folklore movement" that united intellectuals with the purpose of uniting a vast country. Ethnomusicological studies were seen to reflect music and poetry that could mediate vernacular interpretations and modernity-induced tensions between rural and urban settings. Folklore was seen as a popular, subaltern public sphere, separate from the bourgeois sphere that had been shaped by print media. In sum, oral tradition could "spread information, inform opinion and motivate action or create feelings of solidarity" (Ó Giolláin 2000: 93). It was assigned a role in development plans which were, however, overturned by the military coup in 1964. This put an end to populist initiatives (see Ortiz 2002).

From the very beginning, folklore studies have struggled with the perpetual question of oral tradition's relation – or subordination – to published (written) texts. The latter are explicitly connected with "high culture," and the difference between these and oral tradition resonates with social hierarchies, particularly in non-Western contexts. In India, for example, oral tradition is based on an age-old dissemination of texts. The earliest literary texts of the Indo-Europeans are the Vedas, a classic example of oral poetry in the phonocentric context where the spoken word is prominent. Folk versions of epic poetry have been presented in performance styles including song, recitation, dance, shadow puppetry, and painted scrolls. In the context of colonial rule, British administrators collected local knowledge and folklore with the purpose of gaining a better grasp of their subjects. Simultaneously, missionaries had an evangelical purpose. During the post-independent period, academic institutions studied folklore in search of elements of national identity to be found in legends, myths, and epics.

At the end of the nineteenth century, Japan was going through an accelerated process of modernization. Folklore studies emerged thanks to dedicated intellectuals who were inspired by similar undertakings in Europe, and who devoted their lives to the collection and study of popular repertoires (Kunio Yanagita, for example). They also established relevant societies (see Schnell and Hashimoto 2003). In this context, local definitions of "folk" and folklore studies served the needs of nationalist mobilization. However, artistic expression depended historically on the distinction between elite and commoner. Folklore studies or "nativist ethnology" grew into a localized form of scholarship that was used for community enactment and reconstructive purposes, and which was seen, for example, in the impact of Yanagita's folktale publications on popular thinking, or the hiring of folklorists by local municipalities to plan and implement museum projects (Schnell and Hashimoto 2003: 190). The recording of rural lifestyles in the early twentieth century spurred a revitalization movement in response to reform and emergent industrial transformation (see Harootunian 2000). Nevertheless, Japanese folklore studies contested Euro-American imaginaries and supported a kind of ethnic nationalism that promoted Japanese cultural uniqueness. The sociopolitical significance of "folkism" clearly held the "natural" union of the nationalist agenda in the inter-war period when the idyllic image of rural villages with rice fields and the veneration of ancestors was co-opted by nationalist ideologues to foster unity among the people and allegiance to the state and the emperor (Harootunian 2000; Schnell and Hashimoto 2003). Indeed, these studies had an enormous impact on popular thinking, which took a new turn in the period of economic growth from the 1960s onward when public interest in local culture flourished.

China is a country with a highly developed literary culture and artistic traditions. The organized study of folklore by Chinese scholars started in the early twentieth century in response to European and Japanese inspiration, which followed the "historical-geographic" school in search of ancient continuities (see Zhang 2013). Folklore collections started with songs, and they recognized the diverse, multiethnic composition of China, with a tendency to exoticize minorities. Due to the complexities of the past century and the multitude of ethnic minorities, the agenda of striving toward unity and developing a single national culture were extensively influenced by Confucianism, the Chinese writing system and historical textual imperatives, the tradition of a massive, centralized bureaucracy, and the recent epoch of Chinese Maoist Marxism (see Liu 1995). Folklore scholarship aimed to simultaneously present the uniqueness of the origin and expression of Chinese culture, and to promote national unity. After 1949, and particularly during the Cultural Revolution, stories and folksongs were reinterpreted and reworked to align with Communist Party politics. Since the 1980s, the China Folklore Society has sought to build folklore studies with Chinese characteristics. These were accompanied by widespread preservation initiatives with an instrumental use of local culture in economic development (see Zhang 2013). In Chinese, the vernacular term for folklore is relatively encompassing, so that it lends itself well to recent intangible heritage initiatives.

These brief sketches of currents in national traditions of folklore studies fail to do justice to the complexities of particular histories. However, the main goal of my account is to point out general tendencies observable in the activities of identifying and collecting folklore that reflect local responses to broad international developments. While these tendencies may be characteristic of European settings, they are not limited to a single geopolitical region, or a particular moment in history. The establishing of archives and museums, and the establishment of depositories of past repertories, cultural practices, and artifacts has inherently served the purpose of creating national cultural heritages. The elements of cultural expression are perceived as being representative symbols of the past, serving to signify the continuity of ancient cultural traditions – an idea which is paradoxically a modern cultural phenomenon. Archaic phenomena are publicly displayed and engaged for representational purposes and transformed into ethnic or national symbols.

A Change of Paradigm

European folklore studies crossed the Atlantic with lasting consequences, eventually shaping disciplinary research on both sides of the ocean. In 1888, the American Folklore Society was founded, and it is still going strong today as a prominent scholarly organization in the field. However, it is particularly in the United States that the most influential paradigm change in the discipline occurred, influenced by postcolonial and postmodern critiques in the late twentieth century. Intellectual and research developments in the United States initiated not only a disciplinary transformation that led to changes in research in Europe, for they also created a profound conceptual shift leading to a break in the intersecting frames of modernity, colonialism, and nationalism, thus confronting disciplinary provincialism, with shattering results. This was a period of general epistemological revision regarding the conditions of knowledge production. A postcolonial crisis in disciplinarity was induced by reflexive investigations into historical research practices, and this eventually brought about disciplinary changes (Fabian 2001: 80). In addition, the turn to social engagement and the recognition of agency in social practices led to scholarly involvement in cultural policy-making. This coincided with a larger shift in research paradigms, from the analysis of structures to sociocultural processes.

American folklorists began to critically reflect on their particular knowledge format and on knowledge transfer as a result of the social changes of the 1960s and 1970s. Folklorists delved into their own disciplinary history in order to view critically the Eurocentric process of folklore collection, the prevailing fixation on the textual product, or the "metadiscursive" distortions arising from performance to print (see Briggs and Shuman 1993). They questioned the treatment of "native exotics" as the "other," and problematized the social basis of "the folk." And folklore itself became reinterpreted as a communicative process (Ben-Amos 1972; Zumwalt 1988; Abrahams 1993). Concurrent "postmodern disciplinary boundary crossings" (Briggs 2008: 97) infused folkloristics with analytic perspectives from anthropology, communications, and sociolinguistics that injected new life into genre, repertoire, community, and transmission. Critiques also suggested additional scrutiny of contextual constraints and of the notion of performance (see Bauman 1977). Scholars in the United States left behind the essentialist assumptions of cultural givens to be recovered and preserved. They drew on Marxist, feminist, postcolonial, and other critical modes in their reinterpretation of the previously conditioned "neutral and objective examinations of cultural production into objects of critical inquiry" (Briggs 2008: 96) and questioned agendas of representation. This brought about a reformulation of tradition as a selective, interpretive construction symbolically constituted in the present. Thus in the United States, the focus and rationale transformed folklore into the study of expressive interactions, and the discipline began to investigate a process of communication based on in-group knowledge, rather than a celebratory symbol of the national past.

This caused a reflexive and painful self-examination that recognized the inability of the discipline to connect to the contemporary since it was obsessed with a "poetics of disappearance" (Kirshenblatt-Gimblett 1998: 305). This retrospective stance deconstructed the ontological and epistemological grounds of both the discipline and its object of study. The subsequent debates surrounding the denomination of the discipline in the face of eroding institutional support for academic programs brought about changes, and new designations were created to describe scholarly endeavors, such as studies of "oral tradition" or "expressive culture" (e.g. Feintuch 2003). Interestingly, the identification of "folklore's crisis" and debates about its denomination were concurrent with the paradigm shift in the UNESCO framework. In fact, Kirshenblatt-Gimblett, possibly inspired by Fabian, pointed out this link quite early on, and suggested that the field "should be converted into the critical study of 'heritage'" (Kirshenblatt-Gimblett 1998: 284). With the object and focus of study changed, it became necessary to change the term used to refer to it.

Folklore Overboard with a Paradigm Preserved

This conceptual shift spilled over into the international scene, but it also reflected new, growing global tendencies. The gradual decomposition of colonial rule brought about the resignification of both cultural practices and interest in them. This caused innovative moves in public policy-making in the field of culture in combination with a wider reaction to globalization and concomitant economic processes. Political manipulation and the nationalist abuse of cultural expression were then recognized. Simultaneously, the general empowerment of non-European cultures and the foregrounding of indigenous concerns took place as the previously "voiceless" contributed to complex debates about cultural property rights. The constraints of modernization and the presumably detrimental effects of globalization led to international initiatives of cultural protection, like UNESCO conventions and WIPO programs.

At the beginning, "folklore" stood as a valid and publicly accepted term in the policy-making and legislative arenas. This is particularly the case concerning copyright issues in relation to folklore, and folklorists have been prominently involved in debates of these, starting with the Nordic Institute of Folklore analysis from 1975 (Sherkin 2001: 44). For the WIPO, folklore continues to exist prominently as an element in regulative ownership debates (cf. Hafstein 2004). In the early 1970s, the "intangible" was first registered in a folklore format as a counterpart to monuments, sites, and landscapes that became recognized under the protective program of the World Heritage Convention (1972). However, due to prevailing academic currents of cultural deconstruction and the spread of sociopolitical criticism, the foundational premise of the field and the term that referred to it had changed profoundly, especially due to international interaction and networking. Another factor for assisting the process of erosion was the expediency of universality which requires not only cultural but also lexical translation. The different national, regional, or semantic connotations clashed and became contested. The term folklore had first been coined and its denotation became fixed in a world where the past was a constant, but under the augmenting globally-interdependent circumstance those denotations had become fluid.

When US scholars adopted the deconstructive stance that "all folklore is made, not found," they perceived folklorists to have carried out "folklorization" by being engaged in the process of the "identification and designation" of cultural expressions (Kirshenblatt-Gimblett 1995: 369; 1998: 305). Thus, the scholarly production of folklore had involved the identification of a research object in Anglo-American academic parlance. Yet the commercial and political abuse of folklore had been part of disciplinary self-reflection for decades, besides its tacit commoditization. However, in the Romance-language sphere, the use of folklore in hegemonic strategies or the state appropriation of cultural artifacts and repertoires has altered their connotations to such an extent that scholarly approaches as well as public discourse now refer rather exclusively to *traditions populaires*. This is the case in France, for example. If derivatives of the English term "folklore" are used, these carry deliberate and negative implications that signal the misuse and transformation of cultural expressions (see e.g. Khaznadar 2011).

Other factors also increased the growing global feeling of uncertainty and instability. Another rupture that affected the field was the disintegration of the Soviet Union and the re-establishment of claims for independent (or reconfirmed) identities by a multitude of Eastern and Central European nations. From their perspective, the concept of folklore had been (and continued to be) highly instrumental in grounding the origins and manifestation of cultural ethno-identities. There existed a direct channel for justifying regionally bounded, historically rooted practices, and using expressive displays as a valorizing representation of national culture. In this context, folklore continued to denote music, dance, costume, crafts and festivals, while poetic and narrative repertoires tacitly drew upon the vast collections housed in archives and museums. With an upsurge of alternative identities and sociocultural reinvention in the post-Soviet context, vernacular designations borrowing the English term "folklore" signaled a break from the recent exploitation of so-called official folk culture.

Still, the gradual erosion of the concept of folklore in the arena of cultural politics is traceable in the documents of global initiatives. In 1989, UNESCO adopted its Recommendation on the Safeguarding of Traditional Culture and Folklore, which in French is referred to *la culture traditionelle et populaire* (UNESCO 1989). The multilingual debates – often originating in French-speaking circles (Gruzinski 1993; also Aikawa 2004: 146) – inside UNESCO in the 1990s gradually distanced themselves from folklore in search of a substitute, presumably to do away with nationalist agendas and the term's pejorative political implications. The relatively extensive deliberations at the time made a serious (if not idealistic) attempt at being all-inclusive and considerate towards a global recognition of different voices, and empowered the representation of diversity (see Seitel 2001). The model of the World Heritage Convention (1972) brought the concept of "heritage" unavoidably center stage. Thus, initial shifts toward "traditional and popular culture" were substituted by "oral heritage" and "intangible heritage" (Seitel 2001: 302). It should be pointed out here that the group of English-speaking experts closely involved in policy design was not unanimous in this. Indeed, a number of them still stood behind the broad interpretation of the term "folklore" and urged that it be retained (see e.g. McCann *et al.* 2001: 60).

The contribution of Anglo-American scholars to the renaming of the discipline and policy-making becomes particularly poignant when considering the distancing of English-speaking states from international initiatives in policy-making for safeguarding the intangible. Indeed, I should point out that at present none of them has ratified the Intangible Heritage Convention (2003),[1] whereas the countries discussed in the foregoing have all done so. Besides, local interpretations of the new term have created recurrent "translation" problems. In fact, difficulties in that respect appear to be universal when all languages – including English – require an additional explanation that verbalizes a justification of this new "knowledge format" with instrumental political implications. In many languages this concept is a new, relatively technical coinage that tacitly carries reference to ownership while often ascribing construction to its counterpart, the tangible. Additional explanation is required by giving a definition of what it encompasses, but also when spelling out its difference from the previous terms or significations used. In this respect, Japan, China, and India have been particularly successful, and Brazil has played a significant role in the policy-making process. However, the expertise of scholars has been undermined by the intervention of public and political bodies. In Estonia, cultural policy-making has been quite substantially redirected towards intangible heritage, whereas the term "folklore" continues to exist particularly in an academic context. The two also appear non-reflexively interchangeable.

It remains problematic to what extent the terminological shift from folklore to cultural heritage has actually denoted a conceptual shift. Again, cultural carryover or knowledge transfer and applied local knowledge formats differ from country to country, depending a lot on disciplinary and research histories and current policies. Nevertheless, what is observable are processes of listing, mapping, and identifying repertoires, practices, and worldviews with the aim of celebration and preservation. The emergence of "intangible cultural heritage" as an overarching and instrumental designation has transferred from international policy-making to the academic sphere and public imaginaries as a powerful asset and an intervention. It builds upon the cultural politics of inclusion and exclusion, of rootedness and rights of possession. Having enhanced the public presentation of heritage, as well as the construction of hierarchies of experience, the concept of heritage is a resonant and politically implicated tool that moved outside the academic scene to become visible to the general public, becoming an instrument of political arbitration and social engineering (see Kuutma 2012).

In sum, the process described seems circular. The transformation I have traced above with respect to "intangible cultural heritage" involved initiatives against the prescriptive or national(ist) agendas of folklore, but in reality the new format involves instrumental acts of identifying, mapping, and celebrating which closely resemble those of a century ago. There lingers an intellectual and existential paradox: we cannot consciously "safeguard" anything before we name it, fixing it in time and, consequently, losing its dynamism. Regardless of well-intentioned acts of valorization, the act of conceptualization and the identification of a discipline unavoidably constitutes turning it into something else.

Acknowledgements

This chapter is based on research supported by the European Regional Development Fund (Centre of Excellence in Cultural Theory) and by the Estonian Ministry of Education and Research (institutional research funding grant IUT34–32).

Note

1 The following observations are based on fieldwork at the Intangible Cultural Heritage Convention (2003) and related meetings from 2005 to the present.

References

Legislation

Convention Concerning the Protection of the World Cultural and Natural Heritage (World Heritage Convention) (UNESCO, 1972). Available at: http://whc.unesco.org/archive/convention-en.pdf (accessed March 19, 2015).

Convention for the Safeguarding of the Intangible Cultural Heritage (Intangible Heritage Convention) (UNESCO, 2003). Available at: http://unesdoc.unesco.org/images/0013/001325/132540e.pdf (accessed March 19, 2015).

Other Works

Abrahams, R.D. (1993) Phantoms of Romantic Nationalism in Folkloristics. *Journal of American Folklore*, 106 (419), 3–37.

Aikawa, N. (2004) An Historical Overview of the Preparation of the UNESCO International Convention for the Safeguarding of Intangible Cultural Heritage. *Museum International*, 56 (1/2), 137–149.

Anttonen, P.J. (2005) *Tradition through Modernity: Postmodernism and the Nation-State in Folklore Scholarship*. Helsinki: Finnish Literature Society.

Bauman, R. (1977) *Verbal Art as Performance*. Newbury, MA: Rowley House.

Bauman, R. (ed.) (1992) *Folklore, Cultural Performances, and Popular Entertainments: A Communications-Centered Handbook*. New York: Oxford University Press.

Bausinger, H. (1990 [1961]) *Folk Culture in a World of Technology*, trans. E. Dettmer. Bloomington: Indiana University Press.

Ben-Amos, D. (1972) Toward a Definition of Folklore in Context. In A. Parades and R. Bauman (eds), *Toward New Perspectives in Folklore*. Austin: University of Texas Press, pp. 3–15.

Bendix, R. (1997) *In Search of Authenticity: The Formation of Folklore Studies*. Madison: University of Wisconsin Press.

Bendix, R.F., and Hasan-Rokem, G. (eds) (2012) *A Companion to Folklore*. Oxford: Wiley-Blackwell.

Briggs, C.L. (2008) Disciplining Folkloristics. *Journal of Folklore Research*, 45 (1), 91–105.

Briggs, C., and Shuman, A. (eds) (1993) Theorizing Folklore: Toward New Perspectives on the Politics of Culture. *Western Folklore*, 52 (2–4), 109–134.

Canclini, N.G. (1993) *Transforming Modernity: Popular Culture in Mexico*. Austin: University of Texas Press.

Cocchiara, G. (1981 [1952]) *The History of Folklore in Europe*. Philadelphia: Institute for the Study of Human Issues.

Dow, J.R., and Lixfeld, H. (eds) (1986) *German Volkskunde: A Decade of Theoretical Confrontation, Debate, and Reorientation 1967–1977*. Bloomington: Indiana University Press.

Dow, J.R., and Lixfeld, H. (eds) (1994) *The Nazification of an Academic Discipline: Folklore in the Third Reich*. Bloomington: Indiana University Press.

Dundes, A. (ed.) (1999) *International Folkloristics: Classic Contributions by the Founders of Folklore*. Lanham, MD: Rowan and Littlefield.

Fabian, J. (2001) Ethnology and History. In *Anthropology with an Attitude: Critical Essays*. Stanford, CA: Stanford University Press, pp. 70–86.

Feintuch, B. (ed.) (2003) *Eight Words for the Study of Expressive Culture*. Urbana: University of Illinois Press.

Gruzinski, S. (1993) Sauvegarde du patrimoine immatériel: bilan et nouvelles perspectives. Working Paper. Paris: Centre national de la recherche scientifque.

Hafstein, V. (2004) The Politics of Origins: Collective Creation Revisited. *Journal of American Folklore*, 117 (465), 300–315.

Harootunian, H.D. (2000) *Overcome by Modernity: History, Culture, and Community in Interwar Japan*. Princeton: Princeton University Press.

Hemme, D., Tauschek, M., and Bendix, R. (eds) (2007) *Prädikat "Heritage": Wertschöpfungen aus kulturellen Ressourcen*. Berlin: LIT.

Herzfeld, M. (1982) *Ours Once More: Folklore, Ideology, and the Making of Modern Greece*. Austin: University of Texas Press.

Khaznadar, C. (2011) Avant-propos. La relation de la France au patrimoine culturel immatériel. In C. Hottin (ed.), *Le patrimoine culturel immaterial: premières expériences en France*. Paris: Maison des cultures du monde, pp. 11–23.

Kirshenblatt-Gimblett, B. (1995) Theorizing Heritage. *Ethnomusicology*, 39, 367–380.

Kirshenblatt-Gimblett, B. (1998) Folklore's Crisis. *Journal of American Folklore*, 111, 281–327.

Kuutma, K. (2005) Introduction: Constructing a Disciplinary History. In K. Kuutma and T. Jaago (eds), *Studies in Estonian Folkloristics and Ethnology: A Reader and Reflexive History*. Tartu: Tartu University Press, pp. 9–15.

Kuutma, K. (2012) Between Arbitration and Engineering: Concepts and Contingencies in the Shaping of Heritage Regimes. In R.F. Bendix, A. Eggert, and A. Peselmann (eds), *Heritage Regimes and the State*. Göttingen: Universitätsverlag Göttingen, pp. 21–36.

Kvideland, R., and Sehmsdorf, H.K. (eds) (1989) *Nordic Folklore: Recent Studies*. Bloomington: Indiana University Press.

Leerssen, J. (2006) *National Thought in Europe: A Cultural History*. Amsterdam: Amsterdam University Press.

Liu, L.H. (1995) *Translingual Practice: Literature, National Culture, and Translated Modernity – China 1900–1937*. Stanford, CA: Stanford University Press.

McCann, A., *et al.* (2001) The *Recommendation* Ten Years On: Towards a Critical Analysis. In P. Seitel (ed.), *Safeguarding Traditional Cultures: A Global Assessment*. Washington: Center for Folklife and Cultural Heritage, Smithsonian Institution, pp. 57–61.

Oinas, F. (ed.) (1978) *Folklore, Nationalism, and Politics*. Columbus, OH: Slavica.

Ortiz, R. (2002) Latin American Modernity. In E. Ben-Rafael and Y. Sternberg (eds), *Identity, Culture and Globalization*. Leiden: Brill, pp. 121–130.

Ó'Giolláin, D. (2000) *Locating Irish Folklore: Tradition, Modernity, Identity*. Cork: Cork University Press.

Paredes, A., and Bauman, R. (eds) (1972) *Toward New Perspectives in Folklore*. Austin: University of Texas Press.

Peer, S. (1998) *France on Display: Peasants, Provincials, and Folklore in the 1937 Paris World Fair*. Albany: State University of New York Press.

Schnell, S., and Hashimoto, H. (2003) Revitalizing Japanese Folklore. *Asian Folklore Studies*, 62 (2), 106–113.

Seitel, P. (ed.) (2001) *Safeguarding Traditional Cultures: A Global Assessment*. Washington: Center for Folklife and Cultural Heritage, Smithsonian Institution.

Sherkin, S. (2001) A Historical Study on the Preparation of the 1989 *Recommendation on the Safeguarding of Traditional Culture and Folklore*. In P. Seitel (ed.), *Safeguarding Traditional Cultures: A Global Assessment*. Washington: Center for Folklife and Cultural Heritage, Smithsonian Institution, pp. 42–56.

Thiesse, A.M. (1999) *La Création des identités nationales: Europe XVIIIe–XXe siècle*. Paris: Seuil.

UNESCO (1989) Recommendation on the Safeguarding of Traditional Culture and Folklore. Available at: http://www.unesco.org/culture/ich/index.php?meeting_id=00313 (accessed January 30, 2014).

Verdery, K. (1995) *National Ideology under Socialism: Identity and Cultural Politics in Ceausescu's Romania*. Berkeley: University of California Press.

Wilson, W. (1976) *Folklore and Nationalism in Modern Finland*. Bloomington: Indiana University Press.

Zhang, J. (2013) Folklore Studies in China and the China Folklore Society: A Brief Introduction. *AFS Review: Essays*. Available at: http://www.afsnet.org/news/113754/ (accessed January 30, 2014).

Zumwalt, R.L. (1988) *American Folklore Scholarship: A Dialogue of Dissent*. Bloomington: Indiana University Press.

CHAPTER 4

Cultural Heritage and Intellectual Property: Convergence, Divergence, and Interface

Folarin Shyllon

Some Definitions

What Is Cultural Heritage?

Cultural heritage is the legacy of physical artifacts and intangible attributes of a group or society that are inherited from past generations, maintained in the present and bestowed for the benefit of future generations. It is those things and traditions that express the way of life and thought of a particular society, and which are evidence of its intellectual and spiritual achievements. The term "heritage" embodies the notion of inheritance and handing on, and the duty to preserve and protect. Having at one time referred exclusively to the monumental remains of cultures, heritage as a concept has gradually come to include new categories such as intangible, ethnographic, or industrial heritage (Prott and O'Keefe 1992: 307). There are three types of heritage: tangible, intangible, and natural. The first two are clearly recognized as cultural, although some heritage people argue that seeing some parts of nature as "heritage" is a cultural process.

Tangible Heritage

Tangible cultural heritage includes buildings and historic places, monuments, books, works of art, and artifacts that are considered worthy of preservation for the future. The emphasis is on the pre-eminence of the thing or object. For example, the

A Companion to Heritage Studies, First Edition. Edited by William Logan, Máiréad Nic Craith, and Ullrich Kockel.
© 2016 John Wiley & Sons, Inc. Published 2016 by John Wiley & Sons, Inc.

Convention for the Protection of Cultural Property in the Event of Armed Conflict (1954), commonly known as the Hague Convention, refers to "movable and immovable property of great importance to the cultural heritage of every people."[1] The UNESCO Convention on the Means of Prohibiting and Preventing the Illicit Import, Export and Transfer of Ownership of Cultural Property (1970) emphasizes property "specifically designated by each State as being of importance."[2] The UNESCO Convention Concerning the Protection of the World Cultural and Natural Heritage (1972) mentions things, objects and natural sites "of outstanding universal value."[3] Natural heritage includes landscapes, the natural environment, and flora and fauna.

Between Tangible and Intangible Heritage

Intangible cultural heritage is the opposite of tangible cultural heritage. It is non-physical and therefore not touchable except in its tangible expressions. "A basket is a song made visible", as a Native American saying has it. Intangible cultural heritage includes traditions, folklore, language, rituals, songs, music, social practices, and drama. The three conventions already mentioned of 1954, 1970, and 1972 are all concerned with tangible heritage. But the neglect of intangible heritage could not last. In 1982, UNESCO adopted the Model Provisions for National Laws on the Protection of Expressions of Folklore against Illicit Exploitation and Other Forms of Prejudicial Action (UNESCO 1982). This was followed seven years later by UNESCO's adoption of the Recommendation on the Safeguarding of Traditional Culture and Folklore (UNESCO 1989). And in 2003, the Convention for the Safeguarding of the Intangible Cultural Heritage was adopted.

What Is Intellectual Property?

There are three kinds of property: (a) property consisting of movable things, such as a wristwatch or an automobile; (b) immovable property, namely, land and things permanently fixed on it, such as houses; and (c) intellectual property, such as creations of the human mind and human intellect. Because it is a product of the human intellect, this kind of property is called "intellectual" property (WIPO 1988: 3).

As with cultural heritage, there are various types of intellectual property. Intellectual property is usually divided into two branches, namely "industrial" property and "copyright." Patents, registered designs, and trademarks are referred to as industrial property rights, because they are associated with industry and commerce. Copyright relates to artistic creations, such as poems, novels, music, paintings, and cinematographic works. It is the addition of copyright and related rights to industrial property that constitutes the modern scope of intellectual property.

Convergence

Both cultural heritage and intellectual property are creations of the mind that have economic value, being species of property. Since the end of World War II, UNESCO has taken the initiative through its standard-setting instruments (that is, conventions) to highlight the convergence and interface between cultural heritage and intellectual property. In Article 1 of the Universal Copyright Convention (1952), each contracting state undertakes to provide for the adequate and effective protection of the rights of authors and other copyright proprietors in literary, scientific, and artistic works, including written, musical, dramatic, and cinematographic works, and paintings, engravings, and sculpture. In spite of this early foray into the symbiotic relationship between cultural heritage and intellectual property, the early UNESCO conventions on cultural heritage focused on tangible heritage.

The divorce between tangible and intangible was bound to end sooner or later, for as Dawson Munjeri aptly put it, "Intangible heritage provided the larger framework within which tangible heritage could take its shape and significance" (Munjeri 2004: 18). Or as the International Council on Monuments and Sites (ICOMOS) elegantly put it, "intangible heritage must be made incarnate in tangible manifestations" (Munjeri 2004: 18).

Joint work on the matter by the World Intellectual Property Organization (WIPO) and UNESCO resulted in the Model Provisions for National Laws on the Protection of Expressions of Folklore against Illicit Exploitation and Other Prejudicial Actions (UNESCO 1982). In 1993, UNESCO launched the Living Human Treasures program. Meanwhile, concern for the recognition of the similarity between folklore and copyright was the inspiration for UNESCO's Guidelines for Establishment of the National "Living Human Treasures" System (UNESCO 2002). In 1998, UNESCO furthered the profile of intangible heritage by establishing the biennial Proclamation of Masterpieces of the Oral and Intangible Heritage of Humanity. In addition, WIPO has now established an Intergovernmental Committee on Intellectual Property and Genetic Resources, Traditional Knowledge and Folklore as an international forum for debate and dialogue concerning the interplay between intellectual property, traditional knowledge, traditional cultural expressions (folklore), and genetic resources.

The Convention Establishing the World Intellectual Property Organization (1968), concluded in Stockholm, states that "intellectual property shall include rights relating to, inter alia, 'literary, artistic and scientific works,' and 'performances of performing artists'."[4] We see here the recognition of intellectual property as cultural property, with the inclusion of literary and artistic works, and performances of performing artists. Likewise, the UNESCO Intangible Heritage Convention (2003) accepts intangible heritage as intellectual property with the provision that "intangible cultural heritage," as defined in Article 1, "is manifested inter alia in the following domains: oral traditions and expressions, including language as a vehicle of the intangible cultural heritage; performing arts; social practices, rituals and festive events."[5]

The overlap between cultural heritage and intellectual property is also evident in their both being regarded as a human right. Cultural rights and intellectual property rights are recognized as human rights in the Universal Declaration of Human Rights (1948), which provides that:

> Everyone has the right freely to participate in the cultural life of the community, to enjoy the arts and to share in scientific advancement and its benefits … [and] [e]veryone has the right to the protection of the moral and material interests resulting from any scientific, literary or artistic production of which he is the author. (United Nations 1948: art. 27)

These rights are further emphasized by Article 15 of the International Covenant on Economic, Social and Cultural Rights (1966), Article 19 of the International Covenant on Civil and Political Rights (1966), the Vienna Declaration and Program of Action (WCHR 1993), and other international and regional instruments.

In 1998, both UNESCO and WIPO marked the fiftieth anniversary of the UDHR. WIPO in collaboration with the United Nations Office of the High Commissioner for Human Rights (OHCHR) organized a panel discussion in Geneva on intellectual property and human rights. UNESCO for its part published the book *Cultural Rights and Wrongs* (Niec 1998). Intellectual property rights have in recent years become identified with human rights and cultural heritage rights. In the same year, Michael Brown published his seminal paper on the relationship between culture and copyright (Brown 1998). This was followed a few years later by another excellent article concerned with copyrighting the past by George Nicholas and Kelly Bannister (2004). This was soon followed by the publication of an Oxford Legal Studies Research Paper on cultural heritage and human rights (Ziegler 2007), an article by Peter Yu on intellectual property and human rights (Yu 2007), and a discussion of the legal aspects of cultural heritage and intellectual property rights by Reno Hilty (2009), managing director of the Max Planck Institute for Intellectual Property and Competition Law in Munich. Hilty admits that there is inadequate legal protection of cultural heritage, an issue to which we shall return.

Some cultural heritage, like folklore and traditional knowledge, can be copied, patented, and trademarked. Owners of intellectual property rights are conferred with exclusive rights to their property. Indigenous and traditional communities are now also claiming exclusive rights to their symbols and marks, though this trend has been influenced by the misuse and abuse of their culture. They are also of course influenced by the desire to get adequate compensation for the commercial use of their brands and brand names. After a long drawn-out struggle with Starbucks, Ethiopia succeeded in getting Starbucks to acknowledge Ethiopian ownership of popular coffee designations such as Yirgacheffe, Harrar, and Sidamo, regardless of whether or not they are registered (ICTSD 2007).

Both cultural property and intellectual property in their artistic expressions are susceptible to being "passed off." The forgeries of works of art of "great masters" are well known. The same practice can be seen at least with regard to the Benin bronzes and other artifacts plundered in 1897 by the British. Fakes of these objects are now appearing on the international art market. What makes this a veritable enterprise is that the various guilds that had been producing these artifacts since the fifteenth century are still in place today in Benin. With regard to trademarks, another Benin example can be cited. In 1977, when it hosted the second Festival of Black and African Arts and Civilization (FESTAC '77), Nigeria asked the British Museum for the loan of the Queen Idia mask, which the British Museum declined. The Nigerian authorities simply asked a member of the particular guild to produce a replica, which became the symbol – trademark – of FESTAC '77.

In one respect, intellectual property – specifically copyright – reinforces cultural heritage. As WIPO has convincingly argued, copyright protection is above all one of the means of promoting, enriching, and disseminating national cultural heritage. A country's development depends to a very great extent on the creativity of its people, and the encouragement of individual creativity and its dissemination is a sine qua non of progress (WIPO 2004: 41). The two systems are related and compatible. Enforcing the two concepts, however, can lead to some tension. Cultural heritage in the form of traditional knowledge is often criticized by Western commentators opposed to the idea of its legal protection because of the secrecy aspect that is often involved. Indeed, Brown (1998: 195) asserts that secrecy and the strict control of knowledge contradict the political ideal of liberal democracies. Rosemary Coombe (1998: 208), in her pungent comment on this aspect of Brown's article, has reminded us that trade secrets, corporate confidentiality arrangements, and the fiduciary obligations of employees have long been important means of maintaining the value of intangibles in industries and family firms in capitalist democracies. On the contrary, therefore, rather than being a source of divergence, the secrecy aspect of some traditional knowledge is in accord with the industrial world's requirements. Coombe went on to highlight the fact that by using the idiom of "property," many indigenous people may simply be taking the initial and necessary step of insisting upon a leveling of the playing field before working out the details of particular contractual arrangements. And as Willow Powers (1998: 212) suggested, there is no reason why traditional communities should not argue these issues in the same courts and in the same manner as all other parties to this dialogue.

Divergence

The economic and commercial motivation for enforcing intellectual property rights cannot be denied. While it is right to state that economic considerations form the main bedrock upon which intellectual property rights rest, it is equally true that cultural objects and cultural property sometimes have economic value, and sometimes very considerable value. Nonetheless, in terms of UNESCO conventions, cultural objects and property could be "the cultural heritage of all mankind." Thus whereas cultural heritage is universal, intellectual property is not. Cultural heritage has universal beneficiaries, whereas intellectual property has an individual beneficiary, or, in the case of joint authors or intellectual property rights owned by a company or collective, group beneficiaries.

Intellectual property rights are territorial in character and of limited duration.[6] The grant of an exclusive right to the owner of an intellectual property confers a monopoly to utilize the grant during the term of the patent, copyright or design right in the country where the grant is issued. Cultural heritage is eternal and everlasting. Even though copyright has expired with regards to the symphonies of Beethoven and novels of Dickens, they remain part of the cultural heritage not only of Germany and Britain, but of humanity. It also means that the same creation of the human intellect may be copyright material today, while tomorrow it is cultural heritage.

Whereas intellectual property is subject to national treatment which is discriminatory, cultural heritage has no boundary. Items on the World Heritage List or on the International Memory of the World Register have no boundary, and belong to humanity. Indeed, the various definitions of cultural heritage emphasize age, longevity, and universality. To cite just one example, the Hague Convention (1954) provides that for the purpose of the convention, "cultural property shall cover, irrespective of origin or ownership: (a) movable or immovable property of great importance to the cultural heritage of every people."[7]

Interface

Both intellectual property and cultural heritage are property, sometimes of the same species and sometimes not. Objects of intellectual property are creations of the human mind, the human intellect. Since real property is the combination of land and any improvement to or on the land (through the creation of the human intellect), it means that it can also in part or by extension be intellectual property. For example, the creator of a painting on the wall of a building is the copyright owner of that painting. If the building is in London, and has one of the famous blue plaques on it, such as "Charles Dickens once lived here," it may be a cultural monument. An author who has written a work has personal property in it as well as copyright. Property is also classified into tangible (such as monuments, that is, cultural heritage) and intangible (copyright, patents and trademarks, that is, intellectual property). The latter is controlled by intellectual property laws.

The interface between intellectual property and cultural heritage can be pushed further. The authors of visual arts are protected by national copyright laws as a branch of intellectual property. These national laws were not made to protect the art work (cultural property, objects, and heritage) itself; rather, they seek to protect the moral and economic rights of the author by conferring exclusive rights on the owners of those rights. Cultural objects (heritage) are more than simple goods; indeed, many states now classify their cultural property and heritage (antiquities) as non-tradable goods (*res extra commercium*), which cannot be sold and are not subject to acquisitive prescription.

Two Hundred Years Late: Emerging from Imperial Shadows

Although the two concepts of intellectual property and cultural heritage are related as we have demonstrated, the linkage did not manifest itself in treaty-making discourse until well into the second half of the twentieth century. They seemed to develop along parallel routes, as was the case with tangible and intangible heritage highlighted earlier. This led Hilty to conclude, "It is not accidental – but characteristic – that this desideratum [the campaign to protect traditional knowledge via intellectual property rights] originated with an enormous delay of more than two centuries compared to the establishment of intellectual property rights" (Hilty 2009: 768).

There are reasons for this delay. Between the fifteenth and nineteenth century, European powers like Britain, France, Germany, Italy, Portugal, Spain, and the Netherlands ruled the world. Western norms, rules, and laws prevailed. By the eighteenth century, with the slave trade in full swing, followed by colonial subjugation, African and Asian countries could not mount any challenge to the predominant rules and laws of European powers. In any event, in the nineteenth and twentieth centuries, the European colonial powers simply made their laws applicable to their subjugated territories (Kunz-Hallstein 1982: 690). The Paris Convention for the Protection of Industrial Property of 1883 was concluded on the eve of the 1884/85 Berlin Conference, which was convened by Otto von Bismarck, first chancellor of Germany, at the request of Portugal. The Berlin Conference regulated colonization and trade in Africa until the 1960s. Elsewhere in the world, the Age of Empire held sway. It may therefore not be accidental that the partitioning of Africa occurred on the very eve of the first international treaty concerning intellectual property. As soon as the wind of change brought independence to Africa, and Africans, like other Third World peoples, had a voice and vote in the community of nations, no time was lost in seeking redress and restitution. In this connection, and while not digressing, it should be recalled that on the issue of cultural objects and property expropriated during the colonial era, the twelve states that sponsored the first United Nations General Assembly resolution on cultural property – the Restitution of Works of Art to Countries Victims of Expropriation (UNGA 1973) – were all African.

Another reason for the long delay has been captured by Ralph Oman (1997). As long as indigenous and traditional communities were shielded from the prying eyes of the outside world, their expressions of folklore remained safe. But once technology and communication made easy access possible, the traditional knowledge of once isolated communities was copied and extensively exploited outside of their communities and countries of origin, without any remuneration or other advantages flowing back to those countries. Meanwhile, Oman observed, "the interpretive performers, the village bards, the travelling troubadours, and the wandering minstrels, who have created these original variations of works derived from traditions with deep roots in the culture, get neither credit, nor money, nor protection for their creative expression" (Oman 1997: 3–4).

Oman's point can be illustrated with the case of the Maasai of Kenya and Tanzania.[8] As a BBC news article recently pointed out, "a Maasai warrior or a Maasai woman adorned with beads [is] one of the most powerful images of tribal Africa." According to Light Years IP, a US NGO which specializes in securing intellectual property rights for developing countries, over 80 companies around the world are currently using either the Maasai image or name. These include: a range of accessories called Maasai made for Land Rover; Maasai Barefoot Technology, which makes specialty trainers; the Maasai line of the high-end fashion house Louis Vuitton, which includes beach towels, hats, and scarves. Echoing Oman, Isaac ole Tialolo, a Maasai elder and chairman of the Maasai Intellectual Property Initiative, told the BBC, "We all know that we have been exploited by people who just come around, take our pictures and benefit from it." If the Maasai brand were owned by a corporation, it is estimated that it would be worth more than $10m a year (Anon. 2013).

Specifically, in the area of intellectual property, in 1976 the Tunis model law on copyright for developing countries was adopted by a committee of governmental experts, convened by the Tunisian government in Tunis with the assistance of WIPO and UNESCO. The Tunis model law provides specific protection for works of national folklore. Such works need not be fixed in material form in order to receive protection, which is without limitation in time. It was followed by UNESCO's Model Provisions for National Laws on the Protection of Expressions of Folklore against Illicit Exploitation and Other Forms of Prejudicial Action (UNESCO 1982).

A number of participants at the meeting that adopted the model provisions stressed that international measures would be indispensable for extending the protection of expressions of folklore of a given country beyond the borders of the country concerned. WIPO and UNESCO acted accordingly when they jointly convened a group of experts on the international protection of expressions of folklore by intellectual property law, which met in December 1984. While there was a general recognition of the need for international protection of expressions of folklore, the great majority of the participants considered it premature to establish an international treaty in view of insufficient national experience, particularly in the implementation of the model provisions (WIPO 2004: 60).

Cultural Heritage and Collective Intellectual Property Rights

Reno Hilty has argued, "we cannot regard the legal protection of indigenous resources or traditional knowledge just as a further branch of intellectual property rights, so to speak, as an example of the general trend of a permanent broadening field of law" (Hilty 2009: 768). But the trend is for the legal protection of cultural heritage as intellectual property. The broadening of traditional intellectual property concepts has been going apace in recent years – witness the protection of computer software.

Be that as it may, several states already provide specific legal protection of traditional cultural expressions as intellectual property in their national laws or regulations, usually within their copyright legislation. What also makes Hilty's argument untenable is that a number of companies have already acquired trademarks for use of the Maasai name or image. Is it therefore fair and proper to deny the Maasai the possibility of trademarking their identity when free loaders, so to speak, are availing themselves? "Brand Maasai" is therefore not a really outlandish idea. As Carlo Severi has pointed out, in a response to Brown's article, everybody is committed, at least in Europe, to the preservation of the cultural heritage of a nation:

> If the Italian or French governments have the right to prevent, for instance, a Michelangelo or a Chardin from being commercialized on the international market, one does not see why the American Indians should not be keen to protect their own techniques, religious beliefs, traditional narratives, and works of art. (Severi 1998: 215)

In 1992, a Coca-Cola advertisement published first in an Italian newspaper caused uproar in Greece because it included a manipulated photograph of the Parthenon with its columns refashioned as Coca-Cola bottles. Much of the Greek press and several public commentators and politicians condemned the "sacrilege" committed on the country's national symbol, the ownership rights of which are seen belonging firmly to Greece (Hamilakis and Yalouri 1996: 120). Archeological artifacts and sites have long served as symbols of national identity. When Rhodesia gained independence in 1980 and became Zimbabwe, it took its new name from an archeological site and chose as its national symbol a carved soapstone bird from the site. Thus archeological sites, assert Nicholas and Bannister (2004: 332), constitute the major physical manifestation of cultural heritage of all human societies – they are not only cultural heritage but intellectual creations.

Even the World Bank appears interested in the idea of cultural heritage and collective intellectual property rights. Juliana Santilli has convincingly argued for the emergence of a legal regime for "collective intellectual property rights":

> The creation of such a legal regime adequate for the protection of collective traditional knowledge has to be based on the concept of legal pluralism and the recognition of the legal diversity existing in traditional societies. In order to understand the essential elements of such a regime, it is necessary to accept a plurality of legal systems, recognizing that our society is pluralistic and has parallel legal systems manifest in the customary laws of local communities. (Santilli 2006: 2, paragraph breaks elided)

One might also note the Intellectual Property Issues in Cultural Heritage Project (IPinCH). This is an international, multidisciplinary research project examining intellectual-property-related issues that are emerging within the realm of heritage, especially those affecting indigenous peoples. There are also two exciting initiatives promoting the idea of cultural heritage as intellectual property in Africa. They are Light Years IP and the African IP Trust, and both have achieved modest gains from their efforts. Light Years IP was the first NGO in this field, and in fact the midwife of African IP Trust. Light Years IP specializes in a niche – but growing – area of development policy and strategy, known as intellectual property value capture. It has been involved in two high profile cases of struggling to secure for Africans intellectual property rights for their products and traditional cultural practices. In the case of Ethiopia, Starbucks believed they could obtain a trademark for Sidamo, an old Ethiopian strain of coffee (from the Sidamo area of Ethiopia) simply because Starbucks were the first to file an application for it under trademark law. Light Years IP, alongside Ethiopian intellectual property office, challenged Starbucks and worked hard to secure Ethiopian ownership of the named coffee. One outcome of this struggle is the Ethiopian Coffee Trademarking and Licensing Initiative. This has helped Ethiopia to differentiate Ethiopian coffee from coffees from other countries, which strengthened the confidence and bargaining position of the country's coffee growers and exporters (see ECTLI 2004; LYIP n.d.).

Light Years IP has also teamed up with Maasai elders and designed a project called the Maasai Intellectual Property Initiative, which seeks redress for the Maasai. It is aimed at helping the Maasai secure licenses and trademarks, reduce the offensive use of their name and image, and return income to the Maasai for the benefit of the community. The recently founded African IP Trust has taken on the Maasai Intellectual Property Initiative as one of its first causes. Santilli (2006) suggests that sharing benefits from traditional cultural resources can be in the form of, among others, profit-sharing, royalty payments, access to and transfer of technologies, the licensing of products and processes, the capacity-building of human resources, the payment of collection and bio-prospecting fees for samples of biological and genetic material, and the payment of fees for research.[9]

All this shows that the policy of cultural heritage protection through intellectual property law is now widespread. Moreover, it is now too late to worry that "attempts to legally protect intangible goods as such … risk conflicting with common intellectual property principles" (Hilty 2009: 776). Besides, this is what has been happening, at least lately. An example is the legal protection of computer software, even when there is no unanimity about whether to protect it as a copyright or patent. As acts of national sovereignty, countries have protected these intangible goods. Brown is not in favor of "a radical expansion of intellectual property laws" (Brown 1998: 205). If what has happened with regard to software is not a radical expansion of intellectual property laws, then what is? What Light Years IP is doing is using the West's intellectual property rights and asking for their radical expansion, as this is the best way to prevent and preempt outsiders using the same laws to the disadvantage of traditional communities.

The legal and non-legal protection of traditional knowledge and cultural heritage has started and is gathering momentum. This should be so. The appropriation and commoditization of traditional knowledge without financial and technological benefits accruing to indigenous communities have gone on long enough. After all, computer technology and biogenetic engineering have led to the gradual broadening and expansion of traditional intellectual property law to accommodate these forms of knowledge (Nicholas and Bannister 2004: 328).

Human Rights for Cultural Heritage and Intellectual Property

The treatment of cultural heritage and intellectual property as members of the human rights family has increased over the last thirty years. The menu is now three-dimensional. Three powerful concepts or perhaps ideologies are conflated and interfaced. There are those who advocate the primacy of human rights over intellectual property rights. They therefore urge the legal protection of traditional cultural resources (TCRs) and traditional knowledge (TK). On the other hand, purists have frowned at the dilution of traditional intellectual property rights. But the dilution has been going on almost from the beginning. Once authors of joint works are recognized, group rights were recognized in order to enforce the individual rights of the authors in a group. Furthermore, anonymous authors have copyright. Again this appears to be a recognition of group rights. One of the great objections to granting intellectual property rights to traditional cultural resources is its anonymity.

This reluctance or opposition appears to be based on the fear of dilution – the nightmare of warping Western ideas of law. But warping is what has been happening lately, with computer software being accommodated as copyright or patent, or both. The lack of unanimity as to the vehicle of protection has not prevented a ring fence being erected. Intellectual property rights have thus been continuously expanding, and the protection of TCRs should therefore be included in this expansion (Yu 2007: 1149). Why is it that TCRs cannot be accommodated if it has happened in the case of joint and anonymous authors, and computer software?

When someone takes a picture of a Maasai in their regalia to use in the promotion of their goods, they are, one would say in response to Brown (2008), copyrighting culture. The article about the Maasai mentioned earlier tells how a Maasai some 20 years ago smashed the camera of a tourist who took their picture without asking for permission. The Maasai person certainly did not accept that they were in the public domain (see Anon. 2013). This single incident illustrates the human rights aspect of cultural heritage and intellectual property, and the intertwining of the concepts. Had their camera not been broken, the photographer of the Maasai would be the copyright owner of the photograph, but without due regard being taken to the feeling of the subject of the photograph, since the copyright owner of the photograph is the photographer and not the subject. The individual who smashed the camera is now the chair of Maasai Intellectual Property Initiative and is determined to trademark brand Maasai.

An expert in international intellectual property law told the BBC that the Maasai will have a difficult time establishing their "cultural property mark": "They are on a sticky wicket with the law." Why? This is due to the fact that "a number of companies have already got trademarks for use of the Maasai name or image" (Anon. 2013). Here we come face to face with the double standards of the debate. The Maasai individual is expropriated from intellectual property rights inherent to them. Their cultural identity means nothing in the international intellectual property regime. You cannot approbate, that is, use the Maasai as a trademark because she is in the public domain, in one instance, and reprobate in another that she is not in the public domain and therefore cannot have trademark in her being. This is why, as Frantzeska Papadopoulou (2011: 307) has observed, a skeptical to fully negative view prevails regarding the World Trade Organization (WTO) and the Agreement on Trade-Related Aspects of Intellectual Property Rights (TRIPS) (1994). The report of the UN Commission on Human Rights went so far as to state that the WTO is "a veritable nightmare" for certain sectors of humanity, in that TRIPS in some ways encourages, or has the side effect of, human rights violations. As the Draft Declaration on the Rights of Indigenous Peoples asserted:

> Indigenous peoples are entitled to the recognition of the full ownership, control and protection of their cultural and intellectual property. They have the right to special measures to control, develop and protect their sciences, technologies and cultural manifestations, including human and other genetic resources, seeds, medicines, knowledge of the properties of fauna and flora, oral tradition, literatures, designs and visual and performing arts. (UNCHR 1994: art. 29)

Helfer (2003: 47–48) has accurately identified the two approaches to human rights and intellectual property interface. The first approach views human rights and intellectual property as being in fundamental conflict. This is exemplified in the idea that the Maasai cannot have a "cultural property mark." The second approach sees both areas of law as concerned with the same fundamental question: defining the appropriate scope of private monopoly power that gives authors and inventors a sufficient incentive to create and innovate, while ensuring that the consuming public has adequate access to the fruits of their efforts. This is exemplified in initiatives like Light Years IP. Helfer (2003: 47–48) urges the WTO and WIPO to promote the integration of legal rules governing the same broad subject matter. Such integration will also allow national and international lawmakers and NGOs to turn to the more pressing task of defining the interface of human rights and intellectual property with coherent, consistent, and balanced legal norms that enhance both individual rights and global economic welfare. Likewise, Peter Yu (2007: 1149) is in no doubt that the successful development of a human rights framework for intellectual property will not only offer individuals the well-deserved protection of their moral and material interests in intellectual creations, but also will allow states to harness the intellectual property system to protect human dignity and respect, as well as to promote the full realization of their important human rights. Paterson and Karjala conclude that, "traditional concepts of Western law – contract, privacy, trade secret, and trademarks – can take us a long way in the desired direction" (Paterson and Karjala 2003/4: 669). Ziegler has also concluded that there is plenty of "soft law" reflecting the tendency of cultural heritage protection to move towards the rights of people as a new generation of cultural rights (Ziegler 2007: 15).

Enshrining human rights as aspects of cultural heritage and intellectual property is emerging; indeed, in some respects one can say that it has emerged. Definitions can take care of the grey areas: what to include and what to exclude. All multilateral treaties are compromises, the outcome of balancing processes. Accommodation should replace resistance, and compromise should take the place of conflict. It is not all or nothing, and by the same token it should not be nothing at all.

Notes

1 Hague Convention (1954), art. 1a.
2 UNESCO Convention (1970), art.1.
3 World Heritage Convention (1972), art. 1.
4 WIPO Convention (1968), art. 2.viii.
5 Intangible Heritage Convention (2003), art. 1.2.
6 The territorial aspect of intellectual property rights is, however, ameliorated through treaties like the Paris Convention for the Protection of Industrial Property (1883) and the Berne Convention for the Protection of Literary and Artistic Works (1886), whereby through the doctrine of national treatment, each country grants the same protection to nationals of other member states that it grants to its own nationals.
7 Hague Convention (1954), art. 1.
8 The Maasai are an indigenous people, numbering approximately 2 to 3 million across present-day Kenya and Tanzania. They are also one of the most familiar of African peoples on account of their dress and physical appearance.
9 Hilty similarly advocated the licensing option. He also advocated factual means to help the countries concerned learn how to utilize, exploit, trade, and market their own resources and

knowledge, and also to learn how to behave in the global market, in particular to learn how to deal with industries in developed countries (Hilty 2009: 770). This is precisely what Light Years IP has been doing. To cite one example, it has held workshops on intellectual property value capture in numerous locations in Africa.

References

Legislation

Agreement on Trade-Related Aspects of Intellectual Property Rights (TRIPS) (World Trade Organization, 1994). Available at: https://www.wto.org/English/docs_e/legal_e/27-trips.pdf (accessed March 19, 2015).

Berne Convention for the Protection of Literary and Artistic Works (1886). Available at: http://www.wipo.int/treaties/en/text.jsp?file_id=283698 (accessed March 19, 2015).

Convention Concerning the Protection of the World Cultural and Natural Heritage (World Heritage Convention) (UNESCO, 1972). Available at: http://whc.unesco.org/archive/convention-en.pdf (accessed March 19, 2015).

Convention Establishing the World Intellectual Property Organization (WIPO Convention) (United Nations, 1968). Available at: http://www.wipo.int/treaties/en/text.jsp?file_id=283854 (accessed March 19, 2015).

Convention for the Protection of Cultural Property in the Event of Armed Conflict (Hague Convention) (UNESCO, 1954). Available at: http://unesdoc.unesco.org/images/0008/000824/082464mb.pdf (accessed March 19, 2015).

Convention for the Safeguarding of the Intangible Cultural Heritage (Intangible Heritage Convention) (UNESCO, 2003). Available at: http://unesdoc.unesco.org/images/0013/001325/132540e.pdf (accessed March 19, 2015).

Convention on the Means of Prohibiting and Preventing the Illicit Import, Export and Transfer of Ownership of Cultural Property (UNESCO Convention) (UNESCO, 1970). Available at: http://unesdoc.unesco.org/images/0013/001333/133378mo.pdf (accessed March 19, 2015).

International Covenant on Civil and Political Rights (United Nations, 1966). Available at: http://www.ohchr.org/Documents/ProfessionalInterest/ccpr.pdf (accessed March 19, 2015).

International Covenant on Economic, Social and Cultural Rights (United Nations, 1966). Available at: http://www.ohchr.org/Documents/ProfessionalInterest/cescr.pdf (accessed March 19, 2015).

Paris Convention for the Protection of Industrial Property (1883). Available at: http://www.wipo.int/treaties/en/text.jsp?file_id=288514 (accessed March 19, 2015).

Universal Copyright Convention (UNESCO, 1952). Available at: http://portal.unesco.org/en/ev.php-URL_ID=15381&URL_DO=DO_TOPIC&URL_SECTION=201.html (accessed March 19, 2015).

Other Works

Anon. (2013) Brand Maasai: Why Nomads Might Trademark Their Name. *BBC News Magazine*. Available at: htpp://www.bbc.co.uk/news/magazine-22617001?print=true (accessed May 28, 2013).

Brown, M. (1998) Can Culture be Copyrighted? *Current Anthropology*, 39 (3), 193–222.

Coombe, R. (1998) Comment on M. Brown, "Can Culture be Copyrighted?" *Current Anthropology*, 39 (3), 207–209.

ECTLI (2004) Ethiopian Coffee Trademarking and Licensing Initiative. Available at: http://www.pegnet.ifn-kiel.de/research/grants/results/arslan_ethiopia (accessed January 4, 2014).

Hamilakis, Y., and Yalouri, E. (1996) Archaeology as Symbolic Capital in Modern Greek Society. *Antiquity*, 70, 117–129.

Helfer, L. (2003) Human Rights and Intellectual Property: Conflict or Coexistence? *Minnesota Intellectual Property Review*, 5, 47–61.

Hilty, R. (2009) Legal Protection of Cultural Heritage in a World of Intellectual Property Rights. In W. Waldeck, M. Pyrmont, R. Adelman, J. Brauneis, J. Drexl, and R. Nack (eds), *Patents and Technological Progress in a Globalized World: Liber Amicorum Joseph Straus*. Berlin: Springer, pp. 763–779.

ICTSD (International Centre for Trade and Sustainable Development) (2007) Ethiopia and Starbucks Reach Coffee Agreement. *Bridges Trade BioRes*, 7 (13), July 6. Available at: http://ictsd.org/i/news/biores/9121/ (accessed January 4, 2014).

Kunz-Hallstein, H. (1982) Recent Trends in Copyright Legislation of Developing Countries. *International Review of Industrial Property and Copyright Law*, 13 (6), 689–703.

LYIP (Light Years IP) (n.d.) Ethiopian Fine Coffee Initiative. Available at: http://lightyearsip.net/projects/ethiopiancoffee/ (accessed January 4, 2014).

Munjeri, D. (2004) Tangible and Intangible Heritage: From Difference to Convergence. *International Museums*, 56 (1/2), 12–19.

Nicholas, G., and Bannister, K. (2004) Copyrighting the Past? Emerging Intellectual Property Rights Issues in Archaeology. *Current Anthropology*, 45, 327–350.

Niec, H. (ed.) (1998) *Cultural Rights and Wrongs*. Paris: UNESCO.

Oman, R. (1997) Folkloric Treasures: The Next Academic Frontier. *American Bar Association Section of Intellectual Property Law Newsletter*, 15 (4), 3–4.

Papadopoulou, F. (2011) TRIPS and Human Rights. In A. Kur and M. Levine (eds), *Intellectual Property Rights in a Fair World Trade System: Proposals for Reform of TRIPS*. Cheltenham: Edward Elgar Publishing, pp. 262–307.

Paterson, R., and Karjala, D. (2003/4). Looking Beyond Intellectual Property in Resolving Protection of the Intangible Cultural Heritage of Indigenous Peoples. *Cardozo Journal of International and Comparative Law*, 11, 633–670.

Powers, W. (1998) Comment on M. Brown, "Can Culture be Copyrighted?" *Current Anthropology*, 39 (3), 212.

Prott, L., and O'Keefe, P. (1992) "Cultural Heritage" or "Cultural Property." *International Journal of Cultural Property*, 1, 1307–1320.

Santilli, J. (2006) Cultural Heritage and Collective Intellectual Property Rights. World Bank IK Notes No. 95. Available at: https://openknowledge.worldbank.org/bitsream/handle/10986/10728/370790/AFROCollectiveOIPOiknt9501/PUBLIC1.pdf?sequence=1 (accessed January 4, 2014).

Severi, C. (1998) Comment on M. Brown, "Can Culture be Copyrighted?" *Current Anthropology*, 39 (3), 215.

UNCHR (1994) *Draft Declaration on the Rights of Indigenous Peoples*. UN document E/CN.4/Sub.2/1994/2/Add.1. Geneva: UNCHR.

UNESCO (1982) Model Provisions for National Laws on the Protection of Expressions of Folklore against Illicit Exploitation and Other Forms of Prejudicial Action. Available at: http://unesdoc.unesco.org/images/0006/000684/068457mb.pdf (accessed March 6, 2015).

UNESCO (1989) Recommendation on the Safeguarding of Traditional Culture and Folklore. Records of the General Conference Twenty-fifth Session Paris, 17 October to 16 November 1989. Annex I, pp.238–243. Available at: http://unesdoc.unesco.org/images/0008/000846/084696e.pdf#page=242 (accessed March 6, 2015).

UNESCO (2002 [1996]) Guidelines for Establishment of the National "Living Human Treasures" System. Available at: http://www.unesco.org/new/fileadmin/MULTIMEDIA/FIELD/Apia/pdf/00031-EN.pdf (accessed March 6, 2015).

UNGA (1973) Restitution of Works of Art to Countries Victims of Expropriation. Resolution 3187. Available at: http://www.unesco.org/culture/laws/pdf/UNGA_resolution3187.pdf (accessed March 6, 2015).

United Nations (1948) Universal Declaration of Human Rights. UNGA Resolution 217 A (III). Available at: http://www.un.org/en/documents/udhr/ (accessed March 19, 2015).

WCHR (World Conference on Human Rights) (1993) Vienna Declaration and Program of Action. Available at: http://www.ohchr.org/Documents/ProfessionalInterest/vienna.pdf (accessed March 6, 2015).

WIPO (1988) *Background Reading Material on Intellectual Property*. Geneva: World Intellectual Property Organization. Available at: ftp://ftp.wipo.int/pub/library/ebooks/wipopublications/wipo_pub_659(e).pdf (accessed March 6, 2015).

WIPO (2004) *WIPO Intellectual Property Handbook*. WIPO Publication No. 489 (E). Geneva: World Intellectual Property Organization. Available at: http://www.wipo.int/edocs/pubdocs/en/intproperty/489/wipo_pub_489.pdf (accessed March 6, 2015).

Yu, P. (2007) Reconceptualizing Intellectual Property Interests in a Human Rights Framework. *University of California Davis Law Review*, 40, 1039–1149.

Ziegler, K. (2007) Cultural Heritage and Human Rights. Oxford Legal Studies Research Paper No. 26/2007. Available at: http://papers.ssrn.com/sol3/papers.cfm?abstract_id=1002620 (accessed March 6, 2015).

CHAPTER 5

Intangible Heritage and Embodiment: Japan's Influence on Global Heritage Discourse

Natsuko Akagawa

While the idea of intangible heritage has now become generally accepted as an integral element in global heritage discourse, when it comes to practice, clearly defining what is understood as intangible cultural heritage and how the UNESCO protocols for safeguarding intangible cultural heritage are to be implemented remains challenging. This chapter aims to contribute to a better understanding of the history and philosophy that underpin the concept of intangible heritage. In this chapter I trace its evolution to recover the original meaning of the concept. In particular, the chapter highlights how, based on a long tradition of safeguarding heritage, Japan has led the way in the practice of intangible heritage conservation and influenced conservation policy generally.

It is generally understood that the current interest in intangible heritage today owes much to the Nara Document on Authenticity (ICOMOS 1994). This statement on heritage can be regarded as an important turning point in the evolution of heritage discourse. It questioned dominant assumptions concerning the criteria for what constitutes "authenticity" in assessing heritage value and, in so doing, emphasized the importance of recognizing cultural diversity. It has often been interpreted as recognition within Western-dominated discourse of the differences in approach to heritage between "East" and "West." This in turn opened the way for recognizing the importance of intangible heritage and the development of an international convention to safeguard it.

In the evolution of this discourse, the notion of intangible heritage has typically been discussed in conjunction with examples drawn from Japanese policy and practice. The core argument of Japanese conservation philosophy is that skill, which is embodied in

A Companion to Heritage Studies, First Edition. Edited by William Logan, Máiréad Nic Craith, and Ullrich Kockel.
© 2016 John Wiley & Sons, Inc. Published 2016 by John Wiley & Sons, Inc.

a person, is integral to the process of creation and/or construction, and therefore is crucial to a consideration of a structure's "authenticity." For Japanese heritage practitioners, this implies that without replicating the element of skill that has been transmitted from generation to generation, the authenticity of a built form, or creative expression, cannot be maintained. Only when a skill that is embodied in a person is passed on and embodied in another is the succession born. This is a different point of view from the traditional idea of authenticity as it has been understood in the West, which has tended to focus on what we actually see – the material form – and which placed less, if any, importance on the skill that was involved in creating the form we see today. The notion of "embodiment" is therefore an implicit and crucial element in the criteria applied to heritage in the Japanese context, whether "tangible" or "intangible."

This chapter begins by tracing the origins of the UNESCO Convention for the Safeguarding of the Intangible Cultural Heritage (2003), on which the Nara Conference on Authenticity (ICOMOS 1994) is generally recognized as having been influential. I then trace the historical background of the intangible heritage concept as it evolved in Japan's heritage conservation movement from the time of the Meiji Restoration (1868). At this time, a focus on heritage through legislation and determined attempts to raise public awareness of its national significance became a vital element in Japanese national identity formation. This shows that, in part, Japan's concern to revisit the question of what constituted Japanese identity was a response to its confrontation with the West. Faced with negative Western assumptions about the East, and with not being seen as an equal on the international stage, Japan sought to demonstrate its sophistication as a modern country through a display of the strength of its culture, in particular of its craft skill and technology. It is in this context, the chapter suggests, that craft skill reinforced by the Mingei movement, along with the concept of *mukei* or "non-form," came to be considered a highly significant symbol of national identity that was deeply embedded in the meaning of places, objects, and people. The chapter concludes by reflecting on more recent debates concerning the significance of the notion of "embodiment" and its application to the practice of safeguarding intangible heritage.

The International Convention on Intangible Heritage in Context

Although in many ways the Nara Conference on Authenticity held in 1994 marked a significant turning point in heritage discourse, a concern for what has come to be referred to in the English language as "intangible heritage" or "intangible cultural heritage" can be traced back to at least 1971.[1] The Nara conference was, however, important in drawing together debates that had been developing over the course of the 1970s and 1980s regarding the nature of heritage and its conservation. It confirmed the view that had emerged amongst heritage practitioners that a more holistic and global approach needed to be taken with regard to heritage conservation, one that recognized cultural diversity by respecting the role of community, the traditional custodians of heritage. In this process, as will be shown, the Japanese national system for safeguarding intangible heritage became an influential reference point.

While the first UNESCO Convention Concerning the Protection of the World Cultural and Natural Heritage (1972), or as it is commonly known, the World Heritage Convention, had enshrined long-established national protocols protecting the significance of physical monuments, it had gradually become recognized that "folklore" was also a definable cultural manifestation of world significance worthy of protection. Folklore was defined as including a range of items including song and dance, literature, theatre, as well as folk craft objects, rituals, and practices. Lacking the physical presence of monuments, however, presented a major difficulty in developing measures for assessing such heritage. In 1971, the UNESCO Secretariat took the first tentative steps in defining appropriate guidelines by preparing a document entitled Possibility of Establishing an International Instrument for the Protection of Folklore (UNESCO 1971; see also Sherkin 1999).

The difficulty of developing measures for assessing such heritage, however, undoubtedly explains why it was not until 1989 that a first attempt to construct a framework for addressing this challenge saw the light of day. The UNESCO Recommendation on the Safeguarding of Traditional Culture and Folklore (UNESCO 1989) was adopted, as Aikawa recalled, only "[a]fter sixteen years of a long, arduous, and costly process" (Aikawa 1999: 13). It represented "the first international standard-setting instrument for the protection of traditional culture and folklore" and was the first document that set out the parameters of what we now call intangible cultural heritage (Aikawa 1999: 13).

The origins of the 1989 set of recommendations can be found in the decision by UNESCO in 1982 to set up an international directive for the protection of folklore. In that year, jointly with the World Intellectual Property Organization (WIPO), UNESCO ratified the Model Provisions for National Laws on the Protection of Expressions of Folklore against Illicit and Other Forms of Prejudicial Action (UNESCO 1982). The focus at this stage was on intellectual property issues relating to folklore, and ways of ensuring the protection of folklore through copyright law. However, by the time of UNESCO's first governmental expert meeting in Paris convened later in 1982 to address more overall aspects of folklore, interest in the question had shifted considerably. The aim of that meeting was to define and identify measures to safeguard the continued existence of folklore, its development, and the means of protecting its authenticity from distortion. Samantha Sherkin, a consultant working for Intangible Cultural Heritage Unit at UNESCO, notes that it was during this meeting that for the first time a firm definition of "folklore" was established (Sherkin 1999: 47–48).

In 1985, at the twenty-third session of the UNESCO General Conference, it was decided that the new instrument for the protection of folklore would be a "recommendation" rather than a "convention." A "recommendation" takes the form of a general principle as determined by the General Conference which Member States are free to implement by whatever means they select, legislative or otherwise. It is therefore a more flexible instrument while still carrying the authority of the General Conference. In addition, "recommendation" requires only a simple majority to be accepted, whereas for a convention to be adopted, a two-thirds majority is required.

An important event setting the stage for the Nara Conference took place in 1993 when UNESCO held a conference at its Paris headquarters, funded by the newly established Japanese Funds-in-Trust for the Preservation and Promotion of the Intangible Cultural Heritage (Aikawa 1999: 14). It was here that UNESCO first officially introduced the term "intangible cultural heritage" for a new program it had introduced in 1991, replacing the earlier term, "non-physical cultural heritage." The conference also prepared guidelines for the Intangible Cultural Heritage program. The outcome of the conference (see UNESCO 1993) was a motion for a greater awareness of intangible heritage and the communities who were its creators and bearers.

Participants at the 1993 conference had emphasized the need for traditional cultures to be revitalized by encouraging adaptation to the contemporary world. To implement this key consideration, the conference elucidated a series of key principles for the forthcoming Intangible Cultural Heritage program (Aikawa 1999: 14–15):

- not to crystallize intangible cultural heritage, whose fundamental characteristic was seen as permanently evolving;
- not to take intangible heritage out of its original context, as, for example, "folklorization" did;
- to be aware of the obstacles threatening the survival of intangible cultural heritage;
- to give greater emphasis to the intangible heritage of hybrid cultures, which develop in urban areas;
- to employ a different methodology for intangible cultural heritage than that adopted for tangible cultural heritage.

In the short-term, the conference decided to give priority to music, dance, theatre, oral traditions, and languages (UNESCO 1993: Annex VII, 4–16). Under this program, UNESCO inaugurated five pilot projects in five continents in 1993 (see UNESCO 1993: Annex I, 2). In the same year, following a proposal by the Republic of Korea (South Korea), UNESCO instigated the Living Human Treasures program. As Pai (2013) has noted, South Korea already had a well-developed heritage system, a legacy of Japanese colonization, which included identification of craft and craft traditions. As a first stage of this new program, there was a decision to conduct an initial survey of national systems to ascertain whether any country had already established an instrument for the official recognition of people who possessed traditional skills. This confirmed that, besides Japan and South Korea, Thailand and the Philippines also had been successfully implementing ways to recognize traditional craft workers. Based on these initial survey results, an agreement was reached to: establish legislation to protect intangible heritage; identify the possessors of relevant know-how; formulate a national register of the types of intangible heritage to be protected; and prepare a roster of potential candidates for inclusion on the list of national Living Human Treasures (Aikawa 1999: 25). This was followed up in the second half of the 1990s, by eight regional seminars to consider how the previously drawn-up recommendations (see UNESCO 1989) could be applied in different regions of the world.

This overview makes clear that in the course of the 1980s and 1990s, attitudes to heritage changed considerably. As Aikawa (1999) has pointed out, some of the factors that led to promoting the idea of protecting traditional folk culture were the rise in the number of ethnic groups attaining independence after the end of the Cold War, as well as the movement in Latin America commemorating the five-hundredth anniversary of the encounter with Europe. As a result, the expression of local identity through traditional cultures increasingly became a matter of worldwide interest. Equally, as Herb Stovel has pointed out, there was a growing desire to find "universal principles which lie at the essence of our conservation endeavours, without trivializing the cultural expressions or denying the cultural values of non-central, non-conforming communities or groups" (Stovel 1995a: xxxvi). Undoubtedly the rise of Asia, in particular the post-war resurgence of Japan as a leading economic power amongst OECD nations and the intellectual critique of Western cultural imperialism also played a role in universalizing heritage values. This required a "re-examin[ation of] basic assumptions in a context in which heritage conservation can be seen to have a truly global importance, and be guided by truly global precepts" (Stovel 1995b: 394). The Nara conference that resulted in the Nara Document on Authenticity (ICOMOS 1994) was in many ways the outcome of this long gestation.

In 1994, 45 leading conservation experts from 26 countries met in the historic former Japanese capital of Nara. There, they aimed to "clarify the application of the 'test of authenticity' to World Heritage nomination by revising and extending the definition of the various aspects of authenticity" (Larsen 1995: xi). The concept of authenticity was a key element of the Operational Guidelines (UNESCO 2013) adopted by the existing World Heritage Convention in the 1970s. This comprised of four aspects: design, material, workmanship, and setting. Partly because the notion of heritage had been broadened in the intervening period, and partly because of the increasing difficulty being experienced in applying the concept universally, there was now a felt need for review. The well-developed system of Japanese heritage conservation "often unfairly seen by the West as paying little or no respect to historical materials" (Larsen 1995: xii) provided an exemplary case for urgently reviewing existing global protocols with regard to these criteria.

That Japan played an active role in promoting the concept of intangible heritage and in formulating this new framework for heritage conservation was not only due to the fact that Japan had had in place a legal instrument for the recognition of intangible heritage since 1950. It was also motivated by Japanese dissatisfaction with the limitations of the existing World Heritage Convention (1972). Its strongly voiced criticism during earlier discussions had been instrumental in ensuring that the Nara Document on Authenticity (ICOMOS 1994) recognized the importance of the intangible aspect of tangible heritage, such as craftsmanship, rather than merely the physical authenticity of materials. Before examining the next stage in the development of international discourse on intangible heritage that eventually led to the adoption of the 2003 convention, it is important to understand what Japanese concerns had been and why it sought to prominently intervene in the global debate on heritage.

Japan and the Safeguarding of Its Intangible Heritage: Modernization, Heritage, and National Identity

As in the West, a concern for heritage emerged in Japan in the context of modern nation-building. For Japan, the quest for defining "national character" was not only a response to rapid modernization and industrialization, but also a response to its confrontation with the West following Japan's opening up to the rest of the world under the Meiji Restoration. As one of the few countries in Asia during the age of European imperialism to systematically develop national legislation to protect its artworks and monuments, the question of what constituted Japanese identity took on particular importance (Pyle 1971: 8).

With the end of seclusion and the growing influence of the West, the Japanese became increasingly conscious of the uniqueness of their own culture. The "high culture" that had evolved during the long period of stable, centralized government that characterized the preceding Edo period (1603–1868), during which Japan had formally isolated itself from the West, came to be regarded as epitomizing Japanese culture (see e.g. Marks 2010; Reeve 2005; Forrer 1988). It is in this context that craft skill came to be considered as a highly significant symbolic form of national identity deeply embedded in the meaning of places and people. From this developed a specifically Japanese approach to heritage that centered on the national importance of the transmission of the skills, values, and ideas embodied in physical heritage.

Very early in the Meiji era, Japan had begun to present itself at international exhibitions in ways that challenged the international status quo. Japan first exhibited a collection of decorative arts at the Paris International Exhibition in 1867 and soon thereafter at the Vienna International Exhibition in 1873. In the West, these early exhibitions of Japanese arts and crafts, as well as exhibitions of Japanese art throughout the West, generated remarkable interest. It produced a veritable fashion in the West of what became known as *japonisme*, with objects eagerly collected by the well-to-do. It was also immensely influential on the Arts and Crafts movements developing in the West at the same time (Watanabe 1991: 94–98). Exhibitions increasingly became arenas for demonstrating political prowess, and Japan exploited such opportunities to directly challenge Western imperialist and Orientalist conceptions of the Orient.

At home, international interest in Japanese craft skill as demonstrated at international expositions helped consolidate a sense of pride in national identity. It encouraged government initiatives domestically to provide support for the development and maintenance of these important national occupations. In 1885, the Japanese government established a Department of Industrial Craft at Tokyo Imperial University, and in 1890 the Imperial Technical Staff Scheme was established to protect the crafts unique to Japan. Subsequently, Japan's successes in the First Sino-Japanese War (1894–1895) and the Russo-Japanese War (1904–1905) reinforced her image as a world power and the prevailing force in the Far East.

After World War I, Japanese national identity came to be associated with the broader identity of Asianism. Now recognized as a world power with intimate knowledge of Asian civilization, Japan saw itself as playing a major role in contributing to world culture (Lincicome 1999: 353). This found direct expression in Japan's active policy of imperial expansion before World War II, and heavily influenced the politics and philosophical debates of the time. But Japan's presentation of itself abroad continued to be premised on an internal process of definition of what could be termed its sense of cultural nationalism based on the "distinctiveness of the cultural community" (Yoshino 1992: 1).

As part of its national heritage protection and definition of national identity, Japanese archeologists, museum curators, and national heritage officials also began to systematically identify and conserve both monumental and cultural objects in colonial Korea, perceived by Japanese authorities as the historical pathway from which modern day Japan evolved (Pai 2013). This, as mentioned above, formed the basis of South Korea's postwar development of a systematic heritage safeguarding program.

By the early twentieth century this sense of national identity came to be extensively represented in academic writing and promoted by the state through instruments such as the national education system, which exercised tight control over curricula and textbooks (Lincicome 1999: 341). Whether "generated by her fears and anxieties of the outside world" (Matsumoto 1971: 53) or by the "reactionary, escapist or anti-modern [response] integral to the experience of modernization" (Brett 1996: 26), a concern for safeguarding past traditions represented a self-conscious attempt to differentiate itself from the West. Internally, what Hobsbawm (1983) has identified as "the invention of tradition" formed an important element in developing a strong sense of cultural nationalism. In this context, folk crafts, symbolically and economically, formed a significant role in the quest to unify the nation radiating from urban centers.

Government initiatives in the late nineteenth century and growing interest abroad gave rise in the early twentieth century to the Mingei movement. *Mingei* literally means "people's art," more commonly translated as "folk-crafts." The Mingei movement in Japan, which came after the Arts and Crafts movement in Europe, held aims similar to those of its Western counterpart. In Europe the movement had emerged in a reaction to the increasing impact of industrialization and mass-production. Inspired by the writing of John Ruskin (1819–1900) and the activities of William Morris (1834–1896) and the Arts and Crafts Exhibition Society they founded in London in 1887, similar movements, such as the Wiener Werkstätte established in Vienna in 1903 or the Deutsche Werkbund founded in Munich in 1907, were established on the continent to foster and safeguard the traditions of arts and crafts in response to the impact of industrialization and mass production (Sembach 1996).

In Japan, the Mingei movement found its inspiration in the writing of Yanagi Soetsu (1889–1961) (Moeran 1989: 139; 1981: 87; Kikuchi 1997: 39). In the 1920s, Yanagi, a philosopher, applied the term *mingei* to things that were functional, "unpretentious," and used in people's everyday lives. In their "pure" and "simple" form they incorporated what he considered a concept of supreme beauty. These were hand-made folk-crafts made for ordinary use, produced by unknown craft workers who worked in groups, free of a sense of ego and of the desire to be famous or rich, merely working to earn their daily bread. He argued that *mingei* was characterized by communal tradition and not by the individuality of the craft worker. He believed that the categorization of "art" should not be associated with the work of these individual creators because their work should be "unassuming," the work of "non-individuality" in the service of tradition (Yanagi 1946: 14).

The Mingei movement developed a nationwide campaign for the revival of folk-crafts, its members united and inspired by a sense of cultural nationalism. The movement led to the establishment of a Folk Craft Museum, where objects regarded as truly *mingei* could be exhibited, and where a "standard of beauty" could be established (Yanagi 1936: 3). It also led to the development of another influential but short-lived craft society, Mukei, that emerged in the mid 1920s. Their adherents extended the idea of craft and promoted the concept of "non-form" (without form), that held that every form should be freely expressed. Founded by Takamura Toyochika, a metal craftsman, its promoters argued that the importance of craft work lies in its use value, that is its functionality. Since, however, this was dependent on the subjective view of users, the creators of craft works were also required to consider the aesthetics of the form (Takamura 1927).

Reflecting this popularization of traditional Japanese crafts and the increasing attention given to the importance of craft skill and of craft as industry, the Japanese government established training venues. In 1921 it established the Tokyo School of Industrial Craft, and in 1928 the Institute for Industrial Craft, under the auspices of the Ministry of Commerce and Industry. Craft thus came to be recognized as something lying between art and industry and, as Hida has suggested, the creators of industrial craft could be seen as the producer of tradition (Hida 2004). The dilemma facing craft promoters, however, was that, because of the intrinsic functionality of craft, its aesthetic quality was often overlooked. Amongst craft workers and aficionados of Japanese craft in Japan, on the other hand, the functionality of craft came to be seen as the core element of a "craft," its form as intrinsic to its aesthetic dimension, and, together with its creators, as embodying traditional values and skills.

In the aftermath of World War II, concern for heritage emerged as a central preoccupation in Japan's post-war reconstruction, taking up the ideas and activities that had emerged in the 1920s and 1930s. In 1950, the Law for the Protection of Cultural Properties (hereafter the Cultural Properties Law) consolidated previous heritage conservation laws that had accumulated since the Meiji period. In response to the devastation wrought by the war, it focused prominently on the category of *mukei bunkazai* – "non-form cultural properties", or, as it has become known, intangible heritage. The Cultural Properties Law focused on protecting those items of *mukei bunkazai* "that require support of the government or else will disappear."[2] Providing a new comprehensive legal mechanism for heritage protection, the Cultural Properties Law was widely publicized in the media, with newspaper articles detailing the development of a heritage conservation system in Japan and urging citizens to take pride in, and participate in the protection of, heritage and traditions that were under threat.

In 1954 the Cultural Properties Law was revised, and extended to include "holders of important intangible cultural heritage," or "living human treasures" (*ningen kokuho*), to protect the crafts skills unique to Japan. This endorsed a principle first introduced in 1890 with the establishment of the Imperial Technical Staff Scheme designed to train craft workers in traditional craft techniques. Along with this, the 1954 act also inaugurated the notion of "folk materials," a system for documenting intangible folk materials which now became part of the broader Japanese system of heritage conservation. This was aimed at providing more emphasis on protecting the cultural forms and skills of common people, and also to prevent these forms and skills from disappearing. It thus provided "a great opportunity to revive the confidence of the Japanese and strengthen the spirit of independence, to nurture the love of one's hometown and correct the meaning of love for the nation within the individual" (cited by Kida 2011: 36). As important as these initiatives were in the context of post war national reconstruction, by the 1960s and 1970s, government promotion of "Japan's living treasures" (*ningen kokuho*) and of *mingei* had reached their peak. The notion expressed in the catchy term *ningen kokuho* was heavily promoted to the general public through the media and cultural organizations.

In 1975, heritage legislation was again revised to now include "folk cultural properties" and two new categories, namely "preservation districts for groups of traditional buildings" and the "protection of conservation techniques for cultural properties" (ACA 2013). This provided the basis for the Furusato Program initiated in 1988. *Furusato*, literally means "old village," "native place" or "hometown," and the program paid particular attention to the conservation and appreciation of traditional village structures. The program included conservation and reconstruction of old vernacular architecture, and supporting villagers committed to maintaining or revitalizing rural landscapes. It came at the peak of Japan's economic boom and was aimed at generating popular support for the heritage that appeared to be rapidly disappearing from the Japanese countryside. Its explicit aim was to engage people's sense of nostalgia about a remembered rural past, and to use visual confirmation of the past to satisfy a sense of nostalgia and longing for people's imagined hometown. Robertson points out that a *furusato-zukuri* project represented "both an acknowledgement of change, insofar as it constitutes a reaction to post-war changes, and an attempt to control change by restoring a sense of socio-cultural continuity with respect to that which is perceived to verge on the discontinuous" (Robertson 1988: 511–12). As such, *furusato* revitalization projects have tried to compensate for the anxiety Japanese people felt over the loss of their past. It also represented yet another relevant concept in understanding the Japanese emphasis on the intangible elements of heritage. In 2004, folk techniques became subject to protection, a safeguard mechanism for cultural landscapes was established, and the existing registration system was revised (ACA 2013).

As this summary of Japan's century-long history of concern for the safeguarding of traditional techniques and crafts indicates, a central focus has been on the importance given to the recognition of the craft skills that were seen to be embodied in the execution, form, and function of traditional crafts and the natural environment. While the Japanese interest in heritage conservation has evident parallels with earlier Western movements, the focus of heritage conservation in the West, in large part due to Ruskin's influence, had increasingly been directed towards "authenticity" in material terms. This focus is seen in the Venice Charter:

> Imbued with a message from the past, the historic monuments of generations of people remain to the present day as living witnesses of their age-old traditions. People are becoming more and more conscious of the unity of human values and regard ancient monuments as a common heritage. The common responsibility to safeguard them for future generations is recognized. It is our duty to hand them on in the full richness of their authenticity. (ICASHB 1964: preamble)

As Japan began to engage in Western-dominated international discourses on heritage during the 1980s, it became increasingly dissatisfied with the privileging of the built form and assumptions concerning authenticity, and it sought to inject its own perceptions into these debates. Backed by evidence of its well-established and detailed national heritage system with its strong focus on artisanship, the Japanese input had a decisive impact on the course of the heritage debate in the 1990s. This began in earnest when Japan co-hosted the ICOMOS international conference on authenticity with the support and cooperation of international experts, and which subsequently formulated the Nara Document on Authenticity (ICOMOS 1994; see also Akagawa 2014).

Constructing the Intangible Cultural Heritage Convention of 2003

It was agreed at the thirty-first session of the General Conference of UNESCO held in August 2001 that at its next session it would consider a draft international convention on intangible cultural heritage and a possible set of regulations governing its implementation (UNESCO 2001a, 2001b). The first session of drafting the new convention defined intangible heritage as:

> the practices and representations – together with their necessary knowledge, skills, instruments, objects, artefacts and places – that are recognized by communities and individuals as their intangible cultural heritage, and are consistent with universally accepted principles of human rights, equity, sustainability, and mutual respect between cultural communities. This intangible cultural heritage is constantly recreated by communities in

> response to their environment and historical conditions of existence, and provides them with a sense of continuity and identity, thus promoting cultural diversity and human creativity [the cultural diversity and creativity of humanity]. (UNESCO 2002: art. 2, original brackets)

The "practices and representations" of intangible cultural heritage were listed as covering four types: forms of oral expression; the performing arts; social practices, rituals, festive events; and knowledge and practices about nature (UNESCO 2002). After this meeting, the first preliminary draft (see UNESCO 2002) underwent a series of amendments, and in the final draft of the convention, a fifth category – "expressions, knowledge, skills and traditional craftsmanship" – was added. In the final version of the Convention for the Safeguarding of the Intangible Cultural Heritage (2003), or the Intangible Heritage Convention, as it is commonly known, intangible heritage is defined as "the practices, representations, expressions, knowledge, skills – as well as the instruments, objects, artefacts and cultural spaces associated therewith – that communities, groups and, in some cases, individuals recognise as part of their cultural heritage."[3] This is manifested, among other places, in the following domains:

- oral traditions and expressions, including language as a vehicle of intangible cultural heritage;
- performing arts;
- social practices, rituals, and festive events;
- knowledge and practices concerning nature and the universe;
- traditional craftsmanship.

Significantly, while the original idea for the Intangible Heritage Convention (2003) had emphasized the preservation of oral traditions, endangered languages, and forms of cultural expression, in particular those of minorities and indigenous peoples (UNESCO 1997), the final convention emphasized the need to safeguard "living" intangible heritage. This in practice was understood to mean, "if choices have to be made, preference will have to be given to safeguarding measures in situ, that is within the habitat of the communities concerned, rather than to representations outside the context of the community of the traditional enactors" (Smeets 2004).

The intention of the Intangible Heritage Convention (2003), then, was to attempt to accommodate the complexity of intangible heritage in different parts of the world, as well as the different conservation mechanisms of Member States. The notion of "safeguarding" in the convention was understood to cover a wide range of conservation measures including "the identification, documentation, research, preservation, protection, promotion, enhancement, transmission, particularly through formal and non-formal education, as well as the revitalization of the various aspects of such heritage."[4] Comparing the successive drafts, it can be seen that this scope was extended from the first draft in 2002, where safeguarding only included "the identification, documentation, protection, promotion, transmission and revitalisation of aspects of such heritage" (UNESCO 2002).

Numerous meetings and seminars were held to promote the Intangible Heritage Convention (2003) after its adoption, focusing on key aspects of its implementation dealing with inventorization, including the establishment of a representative list of intangible cultural heritage of humanity,[5] a list of intangible cultural heritage in need of urgent safeguarding,[6] and the development of inventories at the national level.[7] In this aspect, Japan, working through the Asia-Pacific Cultural Centre for UNESCO (ACCU), was particularly active disseminating its own experience in developing inventories and systems for the protection of intangible heritage. Between 2005 and 2009 Japan hosted nine ACCU expert and training meetings and seminars to develop skills, guidelines, and protocols for implementing the Intangible Heritage Convention. But even though it had played a key role in developing and promoting the convention, and in ensuring this new international system reflected some of its own well-established principles and practices, Japan, too, faced a number of challenges in implementing it. In the first place, the Intangible Heritage Convention has a wider scope than the three categories of intangible heritage that had been developed in Japan: intangible cultural properties, intangible folk cultural properties, and preservation techniques for cultural properties (Akagawa 2014). Secondly, in contrast to the Japanese national system, the convention focused on the role of community. It encourages communities to play a key role in safeguarding intangible heritage, including respecting their right to revitalize cultural heritage by innovation and re-creation. Under the Japanese national system, however, cultural heritage remains very much a matter of national government, which tends to favor heritage that fits the national narrative (Kawada 1999). The question of community initiative is unclear, and local community tradition that does not fit the national legal framework may not be recognized.

For other States Parties, political considerations have also played a role. For some, the Intangible Heritage Convention (2003) appeared to raise difficult political questions. In 2003, while 120 States Parties voted for its adoption and none voted against, eight abstained. Although each of these countries has its own heritage and indigenous peoples policies and approaches, Koïchi Matsuura nevertheless suggested that the abstentions of the United States, Canada, Australia, New Zealand, and Denmark could have been motivated by concerns that the Intangible Heritage Convention might have unacceptable implications for policies related to their indigenous inhabitants (Matsuura 2006: 3). Since then, Denmark has signed the convention, while the United States has indicated its intention to do so.

Another difficulty related to the Intangible Heritage Convention (2003) with political implications has arisen in relation to the development of national inventories. As Member States develop their lists, items most clearly recognized nationally, and most closely associated with dominant images of the nation, are typically listed first. However, where traditional cultural boundaries overlap modern political ones, the potential exists for unseemly competition and conflict in relation to claims of ownership. A prominent recent case involves the claim by Malaysia to own the heritage of batik, which is hotly disputed by neighboring Indonesia.

Consideration of cultural diversity has also highlighted political concerns related to human rights and in relation to intangible heritage. This is a particularly important and potentially contentious issue which, Logan (2007) predicts, will place limits on recognizing and listing intangible heritage. With respect to human rights, permanent body mutilation (such as female genital circumcision and foot binding) and permanent body-deforming adornment (such as tattoos, and the neck-rings of the Karen hill tribes of Thailand) are clearly problematic. The castration of young male singers in Europe to maintain their particular style of singing also would clearly no longer be acceptable. To address these kind of concerns, the Intangible Heritage Convention (2003) does emphasize that its activities are subject "to existing international human rights instruments, in particular to the Universal Declaration on Human Rights of 1948, the International Covenant on Economic, Social and Cultural Rights of 1966, and the International Covenant on Civil and Political Rights of 1966."[8] More broadly, some community or national festivities may also become subject to international sanction. One example would be the tradition of Sinterklaas in the Netherlands. This apparently innocent family tradition, which involves a white bishop character assisted by Zwarte Pieten, or "Black Peters," is seen by some as a form of racism or as continuing to condone the practices of slavery and colonialism (Anon. 2013). There are signs that such criticisms are already having an effect of modifying its celebration, as well as eliciting strong denials of imputed racism. In recent years, male genital circumcision practiced by some religious groups has also been debated (O'Neill 2012; Guilliatt 2012).

Problematizing Intangible Heritage

Of more immediate significance, perhaps, is the ongoing debate about the meaning of intangible heritage, and many publications on the topic address themselves primarily to questions of definition. Since the Intangible Heritage Convention (2003) was adopted, questions about its meaning and scope, and of the criteria and methods of application of the principles of intangible heritage, have become vastly more complex. UNESCO itself continues to devote many pages of its website to explanation and discussion of the convention. Two issues in particular have been at the centre of intense discussion: the question of what constitutes "intangibility," and how this is to be assessed.

Even before the Intangible Heritage Convention came into force in 2006, during a number of conferences and expert meetings, representatives of Member States drew attention to several crucial problems. Early criticism of the original text focused on the question of selection. After heated debate among intergovernmental experts, the original criteria of "outstanding" was changed to "representative" in order to avoid injecting comparative value into intangible heritage. The initial approach, Smeets suggested, "was considered discriminatory" (Smeets 2004: 144). It was argued that if a potential candidate for the intangible heritage list was equally important to others, it should be nominated as well, so that there should not be any basis for possible discrimination. In fact, as Hafstein has noted, "In the final text of the Convention, the provisions for the Representative List are vague enough to postpone this debate until the present time when state parties are beginning to revisit it" (Hafstein 2009: 93).

Related to this were questions about criteria for the process of evaluation when it came to inventorying and listing. Under the World Heritage Convention (1972), nominations are required to meet specific qualifying conditions related to authenticity and integrity, and "once things are on the List, these qualifying conditions also become the conditions for protection, and therefore a necessary part of management" (Stovel 2004). The Intangible Heritage Convention (2003), by contrast, provided little detail about the measures required to be undertaken to safeguard intangible heritage elements and their ongoing management. Instead, the major emphasis was on the development of intergovernmental political frameworks to safeguard intangible heritage. To help overcome this perceived problem, operational Directives for Implementation of the Intangible Heritage Convention were drawn up (see UNESCO 2012), somewhat equivalent to the Operational Guidelines for the World Heritage Convention (see UNESCO 2013).

More intractable, however, has been the debate surrounding the very notion of "intangible." In part this has been a philosophical debate, for which UNESCO itself has been partly responsible. Many writers on the subject quote an explanation originally published on the UNESCO website, "What is Intangible Cultural Heritage?" (UNESCO 2015). For example, John Collins cites a UNESCO website that asserts, "The depository of this heritage is the human mind, the human body being the main instrument for its enactment, or – literally – embodiment" (Collins 2011: 122). This interpretation has focused the discussion about what constitutes intangible heritage on the meaning of, and the means of assessing, "embodiment," and its relationship to tangible heritage. Taking this original definition, Ruggles and Silverman, following Logan (2007: 33), have concluded that intangible heritage is "heritage that is embodied in people rather than in inanimate objects" and to be found in their "practices, representations, expressions, knowledge, skills" (Ruggles and Silverman 2009: 1). Others, such as Bredekamp (2004) and Kim also consider "instruments, objects, artefacts and cultural spaces" as "tangible embodiments of intangible ideas and practices" (Kim 2004: 18). However, the content of the UNESCO website has been renewed, and at the time of writing (2014), the word, "embodiment" is no longer used.

Reflections: Heritage and Embodiment

The range of understandings incorporated in the notion of intangible heritage and embodiment is far broader than that originally adopted in the Intangible Heritage Convention (2003). Smith's assertion that "all heritage is intangible" (Smith 2006: 3) or Bredekamp's suggestion that heritage places and artifacts are the "tangible embodiments of intangible ideas and practices" (Bredekamp 2004) also indicate that the relationship between tangible and intangible heritage is now recognized as being much more complex than previously thought. Increasingly, the view has been that, alongside any intrinsic value heritage may have, ultimately meaning resides in the "intangible" relationships it provides between people and things. Taylor (2015) in a recent article further dissects this question by drawing a distinction between "intangible value" and "intangible embodiment." The former refers to the "associations and qualities that people find important," while the latter refers to heritage "without continuous physical embodiment … that communicates value and discourse" (Taylor 2015: 74). Without examining in detail his theoretical model, for Taylor "embodiment" becomes the central element of both tangible and intangible heritage in that both can be regarded as "communicative and social practice" (Taylor 2015: 66). In his conceptualization, heritage, tangible or otherwise, "embodies" a message which is "encoded" by its "creators and consumers" (Taylor 2015: 74). This implies that heritage needs to be understood as "the 'event' that happens or takes place when a [heritage site] and discourse [the message relating to value and meaning] meet, when the message is embodied in the medium" (Taylor 2015: 74). At the same time, however, just as Ruskin's emphasis on the materiality of built heritage influenced generations of Western heritage practice (Taylor 2015: 67), the definition of such "meaning," when officially inscribed, can have a stultifying impact on intangible heritage. This has been observed, for instance, in Japan, where, as Siegenthaler notes with regard to Japan's *ningen kokuho* and the "commercialization and commodification of Japan's architectural heritage," the official celebration of heritage value "threatens to privilege a particular version of tradition over all other versions … as well as ruling out more obvious forms of innovation altogether" (Siegenthaler 1999: 13).

In certain respects, this argument brings us back, however, to the roots of the contemporary heritage debate which, as suggested earlier, can be found at least implicitly in both East and West. It also helps dispose of the rather artificial distinction between "intangible" and "tangible" heritage, since both embody meaning. Moreover, while the concept of "authenticity" remains central to both, since it relates to the ability of the medium to deliver the message, their materiality and meaning are open to change and manipulation. Their meaning is also open to manipulation and power struggles, as well as the danger of ossification and irrelevance. Amanda Kearney, reflecting the concerns of Brown (2005) in considering indigenous efforts to take control of their heritage, has extended this perspective in what she calls a phenomenological approach, which "views heritage as an embedded concept that cannot be disengaged from the world and the people around it while establishing distinguishing links between the perceptual subject [human beings] and their distinct and owned perceptual objects [heritage]" (Kearney 2009: 211). In the context of Kearney's argument, this has a particular relevance in recognizing the holistic nature of indigenous cultural expression "rooted in the spiritual health, culture and language of [a] people and way of life" (Longley Cochran, cited in Kearney 2009: 217). While perhaps an increasingly abstract notion in modern society, the principle equally applies there, and Kirshenblatt-Gimblett concludes more generally that "intangible heritage is not only embodied, but also inseparable from the material and social worlds of persons" (Kirshenblatt-Gimblett 2004: 59).

It can be said that the Intangible Heritage Convention (2003) is still in the early stage of its evolution and its associated operational directives need further development. Although these guidelines aimed at providing the criteria for inscription were adopted in 2008 and revised in 2010, they still do not clearly explain how intangible heritage should be assessed. This remains a challenge to those in UNESCO and elsewhere who wish to see the Intangible Heritage Convention succeed in safeguarding the intangible heritage of humanity.

What has become increasingly recognized as a result of the re-evaluation of what constitutes heritage is that heritage involves a relationship between the creator of an object or a place or creative expression, and the one who experiences it. It refers to the experience of that relationship. What gives meaning to that experience is what we do not see but what is nevertheless embodied as the core value of the heritage to be transmitted. This everyday understanding of heritage has sometimes been lost in arcane debates and efforts to define abstract measures of evaluation. Although the Japanese national system has its limitations, the addition of "intangibility" to the lexicon of heritage discourse has nevertheless immensely enriched our understanding of it, not only by ascribing heritage value to "immaterial" heritage, but more fundamentally in deepening our understanding of this important dimension of our lives. It has emphasized the arbitrary division between tangible natural and cultural heritage on the one hand, and intangible heritage on the other, a division that Kirschenblatt-Gimblett sees as "not without its history and logic" (Kirschenblatt-Gimblett 2004: 59). Ultimately, by emphasizing the dependence of heritage on the relationship between preceptor and perceived, the notion of embodiment that the concept of intangible heritage highlights the fact that heritage is a living process, and thus constantly evolving. This again goes back to the initial discussion on authenticity which led to the paradigm shift enabling the acknowledgment of cultural diversity.

Notes

1 In this chapter, I use the term intangible heritage throughout, as all intangible heritage is considered to be cultural.
2 Cultural Properties Law (1950, revised 1954), art. 67.
3 Intangible Heritage Convention (2003), art. 2.
4 Intangible Heritage Convention (2003), art. 2.3.
5 Intangible Heritage Convention (2003), art. 16.
6 Intangible Heritage Convention (2003), art. 17.
7 Intangible Heritage Convention (2003), art. 12.
8 Intangible Heritage Convention (2003), preamble.

References

Legislation

Convention Concerning the Protection of the World Cultural and Natural Heritage (World Heritage Convention) (UNESCO, 1972). Available at: http://whc.unesco.org/archive/convention-en.pdf (accessed March 19, 2015).

Convention for the Safeguarding of the Intangible Cultural Heritage (Intangible Heritage Convention) (UNESCO, 2003). Available at: http://unesdoc.unesco.org/images/0013/001325/132540e.pdf (accessed March 19, 2015).

Law for the Protection of Cultural Properties (Cultural Properties Law) (Government of Japan, 1950, revised 1954). Available at: http://www.unesco.org/culture/natlaws/media/pdf/japan/japan_lawprotectionculturalproperty_engtof.pdf (accessed March 19, 2015).

Other Works

ACA (Agency of Cultural Affairs) (2013) *Cultural Properties for Future Generations: Outline of the Cultural Administration of Japan*. Tokyo: ACA.

Aikawa, N. (1999) The UNESCO Recommendation on the Safeguarding of Traditional Culture and Folklore (1989): Actions Undertaken by UNESCO for Its Implementation. Paper presented at the conference A Global Assessment of the 1989 Recommendation on the Safeguarding of Traditional Culture and Folklore: Local Empowerment and International Cooperation, Washington, June 27–30, 1999.

Akagawa, N. (2014) *Heritage Conservation and Japan's Cultural Diplomacy: Heritage, National Identity and National Interest*. London: Routledge.

Anon. (2013) Is Zwarte Piet Racism? *Economist*, November 2. Available at: http://www.economist.com/news/europe/21588960-debate-holiday-tradition-exposes-racial-attitudes-zwarte-piet-racism (accessed July 30, 2014).

Bredekamp, H.C.J. (2004) Transforming Representations of Intangible Heritage at Iziko Museums. Paper presented at the session Museums and Living Heritage, ICOM General Conference, Seoul, October 2–8, 2004.

Brett, D. (1996) *The Construction of Heritage*. Cork: Cork University Press.

Brown, M.F. (2005) Heritage Trouble: Recent Work on the Protection of Intangible Cultural Property. *International Journal of Cultural Property*, 12 (1), 40–61.

Collins, J.F. (2011) Culture, Content, and the Enclosure of Human Being: UNESCO's "Intangible" Heritage in the New Millennium. *Radical History Review*, 109, 121–135.

Forrer, M. (1988) *Hokusai: Mountains and Water, Flowers and Birds*. New York: Prestel Publishing.

Guilliatt, R. (2012) The First Cut. *The Australian*, August 25. Available at: http://www.theaustralian.com.au/news/features/the-first-cut/story-e6frg8h6-1226454065974?nk=a7202754a5f05e90d1ecdc7e08588331 (accessed July 15, 2014).

Hafstein, V. (2009) Intangible Heritage as a List: From Masterpieces to Representation. In L. Smith and N. Akagawa (eds), *Intangible Heritage*. London: Routledge. pp. 93–111.

Hida, T. (2004) 工芸家「伝統」の生産者 [Craftspersons: producers of tradition]. Tokyo: Bigakusyuppan.

Hobsbawm, E.J. (1983) Introduction: Inventing Traditions. In E.J. Hobsbawm and T.O. Ranger (eds), *The Invention of Tradition*. Cambridge: Cambridge University Press, pp. 1–14.

ICASHB (International Congress of Architects and Specialists of Historic Buildings) (1964) International Charter for the Conservation and Restoration of Monuments and Sites (Venice Charter). Available at: http://www.icomos.org/charters/venice_e.pdf (accessed March 9, 2015).

ICOMOS (1994) Nara Document on Authenticity. Available at: http://www.icomos.org/charters/nara-e.pdf (accessed August 6, 2014).

Kawada, J. (1999) How to Promote Incentives for Cultural Heritage Practitioners. Unpublished paper presented at the conference A Global Assessment of the 1989 Recommendation on the Safeguarding of Traditional Culture and Folklore: Local Empowerment and International Cooperation, Washington, June 27–30, 1999.

Kearney, A. (2009) Intangible Cultural Heritage: Global Awareness and Local Interest. In L. Smith and A. Natsuko (eds), *Intangible Heritage*. London: Routledge. pp. 209–226.

Kida, T. (2011) 伝統工芸と倣作:草創期の日本伝統工芸展の模索 [Traditional craft and reproduction]. *Kenkyukiyo*, 15, 23–46.

Kikuchi, Y. (1997) Hybridity and the Oriental Orientalism of “Mingei” Theory. *Journal of Design History*, 10 (4), 343–354.

Kim, H. (2004) Intangible Heritage and Museum Actions. *ICOM News*, 4, 18–20.

Kirshenblatt-Gimblett, B. (2004) Intangible Heritage as Metacultural Production. *Museum International*, 56 (1/2), 52–65.

Larsen, K.E. (1995) Preface. In J.I. Jokilehto and K.E. Larsen (eds), *Nara Conference on Authenticity in Relation to the World Heritage Convention, Nara, Japan, 1-6 November 1994, Proceedings*. Paris: UNESCO World Heritage Centre, pp. xi–xiii.

Lincicome, M.E. (1999) Nationalism, Imperialism, and the International Education Movement in Early Twentieth-Century Japan. *Journal of Asian Studies*, 58 (2), 338–360.

Logan, W.S. (2007) Closing Pandora’s Box: Human Rights Conundrums in Cultural Heritage Protection. In H. Silverman and D.F. Ruggles (eds), *Cultural Heritage and Human Rights*. New York: Springer, pp. 33–52.

Marks, A. (2010) *Japanese Woodblock Prints: Artists, Publishers, and Masterworks, 1680–1900*. North Clarendon, VT: Tuttle Publishing.

Matsumoto, S. (1971) The Significance of Nationalism in Modern Japanese Thought: Some Theoretical Problems. *Journal of Asian Studies*, 31 (1), 49–56.

Matsuura, K. (2006) 無形文化遺産の保護に関する条約の発効を記念して [To celebrate the bringing into force of the Convention on the Protection of Intangible Cultural Heritage]. *Asia-Pacific Cultural Centre for UNESCO Newsletter*, April 5.

Moeran, B.D. (1981) Yanagi Muneyoshi and the Japanese Folk Craft Movement. *Asian Folklore Studies*, 40 (1), 87–99.

Moeran, B.D. (1989) Bernard Leach and the Japanese Folk Craft Movement: The Formative Years. *Journal of Design History*, 2 (2/3), 139–144.

O’Neill, B. (2012) The Circumcision Wars. Available at: http://www.abc.net.au/news/2012-09-17/oneil-the-circumcision-wars/4264406 (accessed July 15, 2014).

Pai, H.I. (2013) *Heritage Management in Korea and Japan: The Politics of Antiquity and Identity*. Seattle: University of Washington Press.

Pyle, K.B. (1971) Introduction: Some Recent Approaches to Japanese Nationalism. *Journal of Asian Studies*, 31 (1), 5–16.

Reeve, J. (2005) *Japanese Art in Detail.* London: British Library Press.

Robertson, J. (1988) Furusato Japan: The Culture and Politics of Nostalgia. *International Journal of Politics, Culture, and Society*, 1 (4), 494–518.

Ruggles, D.F., and Silverman, H. (2009) From Tangible to Intangible Heritage. In H. Silverman and D.F. Ruggles (eds), *Intangible Heritage Embodied.* New York: Springer, pp. 1–14.

Sembach, K.J. (1996) *Jugendstil: Die Utopie der Versöhnung.* London: Taschen.

Sherkin, S. (1999) A Historical Study on the Preparation of the 1989 Recommendation on the Safeguarding of Traditional Culture and Folklore. In P. Sietel (ed.), *Safeguarding Traditional Cultures: A Global Assessment of the 1989 Recommendation on the Safeguarding of Traditional Culture and Folklore.* Washington: Center for Folklife and Cultural Heritage, Smithsonian Institution, pp. 42–56. Available at: http://www.folklife.si.edu/resources/Unesco/index.htm (accessed March 24, 2015).

Siegenthaler, P. (1999). The Ningen Kokuhô: A New Symbol for the Japanese Nation. *Andon: Shedding Light on Japanese Art,* 62, 3–16.

Smeets, R. (2004) Intangible Cultural Heritage and Its Link to Tangible Cultural and Natural Heritage. Paper presented at the Okinawa International Forum, Utaki in Okinawa and Sacred Spaces in Asia: Community Development and Cultural Heritage, Okinawa, March 23–27, 2004.

Smith, L. (2006) *Uses of Heritage.* New York: Routledge.

Stovel, H. (1995a) Working towards the Nara Document. In K.E. Larsen (ed.), *Nara Conference on Authenticity in Relation to the World Heritage Convention, Nara, 1–6 November 1994.* Paris: UNESCO World Heritage Centre, pp. xxxiii–xxxvi.

Stovel (1995b) Consideration in Framing the Authenticity Question for Conservation. In K.E. Larsen (ed.), *Nara Conference on Authenticity in Relation to the World Heritage Convention, Nara, 1–6 November 1994.* Paris: UNESCO World Heritage Centre, pp. 393–398.

Stovel, H. (2004) The World Heritage Convention and the Convention for Intangible Cultural Heritage: Implications for Protection of Living Heritage at the Local Level. Paper presented at the Okinawa International Forum, Utaki in Okinawa and Sacred Spaces in Asia: Community Development and Cultural Heritage, Okinawa, March 23–27.

Takamura, T. (1927) 工芸美術の鑑賞と実用性 [Appreciation of kougei art and practical use]. *Bijyutushinron*, 2 (2).

Taylor, J. (2015) Embodiment Unbound: Moving Beyond Divisions in the Understanding and Practice of Heritage Conservation. *Studies in Conservation*, 60 (1), 65–77.

UNESCO (1971) Possibility of Establishing an International Instrument for the Protection of Folklore. Document B/EC/IX/11-IGC/XR.1/15. Paris: UNESCO.

UNESCO (1982) Model Provisions for National Laws on the Protection of Expressions of Folklore against Illicit and Other Forms of Prejudicial Action. Available at: http://unesdoc.unesco.org/images/0006/000684/068457mb.pdf (accessed March 23, 2015).

UNESCO (1989) Recommendation on the Safeguarding of Traditional Culture and Folklore. Available at: http://unesdoc.unesco.org/images/0008/000846/084696e.pdf#page=242 (accessed March 23, 2015).

UNESCO (1993) International Consultation on the New Perspectives for UNESCO's Programme: The Intangible Cultural Heritage. Report. Document CLT/ACL/93/IH/01. Available at: http://unesdoc.unesco.org/images/0014/001432/143226eo.pdf (accessed March 23, 2015).

UNESCO (1997) Recommendations by the Executive Board on the Draft Programme and Budget for 1998–99. Document 29 C/6. Available at: http://unesdoc.unesco.org/images/0011/001100/110016E.pdf (accessed March 23, 2015).

UNESCO (2001a) Report on the Preliminary Study on the Advisability of Regulating Internationally, through a New Standard-Setting Instrument, the Protection of Traditional Culture and Folklore. Document 161 EX/15. Available at: whc.unesco.org/document/9473 (accessed March 23, 2015).

UNESCO (2001b) Preparation of a New International Standard-Setting Instrument for the Safeguarding of the Intangible Cultural Heritage. Document 31 C/43. Available at: http://unesdoc.unesco.org/images/0012/001234/123437e.pdf (accessed March 23, 2015).

UNESCO (2002) First Preliminary Draft of An International Convention for the Safeguarding of the Intangible Cultural Heritage. Document CLT-2002/CONF.203/3. Available at: www.unesco.org/culture/ich/doc/src/04548-EN.doc (accessed March 23, 2015).

UNESCO (2012) Operational Directives for the Implementation of the Convention of the Safeguarding of the Intangible Heritage. Available at: http://www.unesco.org/culture/ich/en/directives (accessed March 23, 2015).

UNESCO (2013) Operational Guidelines for the Implementation of the World Heritage Convention. Available at: http://whc.unesco.org/en/guidelines/ (accessed March 23, 2015).

UNESCO (2015) What is Intangible Cultural Heritage. Available at: http://www.unesco.org/culture/ich/index.php?lg=en&pg=00002 (accessed March 10 2015).

Watanabe, T. (1991) *High Victorian Japonisme*. Bern: Peter Lang.

Yanagi, S. (1936) 民芸の使命 [Mission of Mingei]. *Kougei*, 70, 1–6.

Yanagi, S. (1946) 民芸運動は何を起工したか [What has the Folk Craft Movement achieved?]. *Kougei*, 115, 1–22.

Yoshino, K. (1992) *Cultural Nationalism in Contemporary Japan: A Sociological Enquiry*. London: Routledge.

CHAPTER 6

The Politics of Heritage in the Land of Food and Wine

Marion Demossier

Introduction

In November 2013, the annual conference of the American Anthropological Association in Chicago organized a session entitled "Edible Identities: Exploring Food and Food Ways as Cultural Heritage," illustrating the emergence of a new sub-field of research in food studies. It followed the publication in 2011 of a special issue of the online journal *Aofood* (*Anthropology of Food*) devoted to "food heritage," or *patrimoines alimentaires* as the French define it. On both sides of the Atlantic, scholars have embraced an innovative and interdisciplinary approach to food and have engaged in a productive debate with the concept of food heritage, recasting food "as a vehicle to express and shape interactions between humans" (Pottier 1996: 303). In their editorial introduction to the special issue of *Aofood*, Jacinthe Bessière and Laurence Tibère argue that the promotion of food heritage in contemporary France appears as a "societal issue," a space for mobilizing projects which contributes to the construction of cultural identities and to the dynamics of territorial development against the landscape of a global economic crisis (Bessière and Tibère 2011). This way of thinking and of using heritage seems unsurprising from a French perspective, the self-appointed land of food and wine, where the concept of culinary heritage was first coined and instrumentalized in the 1980s (Demossier 2000).

Yet the concept of food heritage has now spread further in anthropological circles as part of the development of both food and heritage studies at a global level. This fascinating

A Companion to Heritage Studies, First Edition. Edited by William Logan, Máiréad Nic Craith, and Ullrich Kockel.
© 2016 John Wiley & Sons, Inc. Published 2016 by John Wiley & Sons, Inc.

cross-fertilization of two traditionally separate fields of research opens the door to new areas of enquiry. By locating the anthropology of food heritage at the crossroads of the study of society, food production, and consumption, as well as the politics of scaling, new sets of questions have come to the fore focusing on contested anthropological concepts such as nostalgia, authenticity, territorial identities, tradition, political economy, and innovation. By the politics of scaling, I mean the contextual specificity of political processes and the mechanisms through which localities are differentially incorporated into larger scales of social, economic, and political life. But it is also about how specific localities incorporate broader processes and values into their global story to maintain the permanence of the fit between place, people, and culture. All these constitute the bedrock of our modern, complex, and fluid societies, against which individuals and groups seek to identify, negotiate, and root themselves in the face of major economic upheavals.

Like my colleague, Jean-Louis Tornatore, I have always felt uncomfortable with the idea of transforming daily pleasures into heritage goods. "It is one thing to enjoy cooking up little dishes at home or among friends, but making a cultural trait out of this pleasure, duly circumscribed and labeled as such, could be seen as one more step towards the reification of culture" (Tornatore 2012: 341). One of the most striking examples of this reification is the rather vague concept of the "Gastronomic Meal of the French" (GMF), which was officially inscribed by UNESCO as intangible cultural heritage in November 2010, instead of "French Gastronomy," which had originally been planned (Tornatore 2012). Tornatore reminds us of the role of each individual state in their "take" on heritage. Examining the heritage process behind GMF, Tornatore argues that the project was able to gather national and group interests around a common concept, while a certain degree of compromise was necessary to emphasize the anthropological dimension – an emphasis on cultural practices and rituals – of the application supported by the main expert, the historian Julia Csergo. The paradox is that the adjustments that were made to fit the UNESCO Convention for the Safeguarding of the Intangible Cultural Heritage (2003) were based on Csergo's militant perspective towards the cultural and symbolic dimension of food habits, while the politics of intangible cultural heritage could also be read as a form of the rehabilitation of folklore. Tornatore (2012: 360) concludes that allowing two traditions (folklore and anthropology), which in France are usually seen as irreconcilable, to share the field in this application opened up the Pandora's box of heritage. Yet as we shall see, French heritage initiatives have developed in a far more complex way than Tornatore's analysis might suggest.

Recent French initiatives to win UNESCO World Heritage status for a wide range of sites, landscapes, and objects have to be read against the ways in which States Parties can exploit UNESCO conventions in imaginative ways to suit their own purposes. The development and ratification of the UNESCO Intangible Heritage Convention (2003), which broadened the scope of heritage as defined by the earlier Convention Concerning the Protection of the World Cultural and Natural Heritage (1972) by embodying "a particular understanding and conceptualization of the nature of both cultural and natural heritage" (Smith and Akagawa 2009: 1), has been highly significant. By exploiting in different ways the systems, language, and definitions of culture and nature attached to the conventions of 1972 and 2003, States Parties and local heritage actors have creatively combined different heritage registers to put together convincing cases of "shared heritage." Moreover, in the case discussed in this chapter, the scope of the UNESCO application goes further by integrating many different heritage dimensions, including wine from historical landscapes (the historical cultural landscape of the Tokaj wine region in Hungary), to cultural sites (Piedmont, Italy) and touristic wine routes (Spain). In 2013, the ancient traditional Georgian wine-making method of *kvevri* was inscribed on the Representative List of the Intangible Cultural Heritage of Humanity. It is this broader context that formed the background of some of the discussions behind the UNESCO application discussed in this chapter, as well as debates about food heritage and authenticity (Barrey and Teil 2011).

Food heritage found its concrete expression at a time when UNESCO had begun to institutionally designate the food and cuisine of several European, Middle Eastern, and Latin American countries as intangible cultural heritage. The notion of intangible cultural heritage was first introduced in 2000 in UNESCO's Proclamation of Masterpieces of the Oral and Intangible Heritage of Humanity (1998) as a way of addressing the criticism of its tendency to legitimize a particular Western – if not Western European – perception of heritage in terms of both policy and practice (Smith and Akagawa 2009: 1). This rise of heritage certification corresponded with the broader movement which has affected our societies since the 1980s. As I have argued elsewhere (Demossier 2000), food heritage has become a political tool for the construction of identity in a context of Europeanization and globalization. From Mexico to Kyoto, initiatives have recast national, regional, and local identities through the recognition of food heritage, which is defined in a new political context of rescaling and heritagization. This food heritage fever forms part of an attempt to respond to societal concerns and insecurity attached to modern consumption, but also to feed a wealthy segment of our societies. It also underlines issues of economic development and new forms of post-productivist agricultural adaptation.

In this context, France, which has long dominated European agricultural policies, offers a particularly interesting example of how heritage could be used to suit local purposes. But what constitutes the study of food heritage in the land of food and wine? Could it be read as just another political and economic attempt to secure France's position in the world? Or is it an attempt to engage with processes of globalization in a more active and entrepreneurial fashion? The study of food heritage is thus linked to new theoretical perspectives which problematize heritage as "essentially a political idea" (Fairclough *et al.* 2008: 36).

This chapter discusses how pre-existing local, regional and state efforts to conserve emblematic "objects" or "places" instrumentalize the conventions governing UNESCO definitions of heritage to suit their own political and economic purposes. By focusing on the example of the recent application for UNESCO World Heritage status of Burgundy and its wines , I discuss the ways in which heritage has been used in a creative fashion and constructed at local level by specific groups with different agendas. If the regional wine elites use heritage as a means of defining specific micro-professional identities to counter globalization, the project also forms part of a wider process of global recognition affecting most established wine regions (Champagne is Burgundy's principal competitor) in their claim for singularity. It is also part of both a local tourism strategy, and a shift towards more ecologically defined viticulture. Through my own involvement in the scientific side of the World Heritage bid from 2008 onwards, I question the ways in which these various agendas coalesce and, in some cases, clash or hide structural tensions. I also seek to engage critically with different conceptions of Burgundy as a reterritorialized site, and the construction of its *climats* – parcels of land dedicated to a precisely delimited vineyard, known by that name for hundreds of years, and therefore denoting a precise plot, subsoil, exposure, and microclimate – as "God given" and naturalized artifacts in the context of a global competition for excellence. Moreover, I argue that Burgundy's decision in 2006 to apply for World Heritage status seeks to secure a global seal of approval for a unique local space and culture, and to reposition itself as the original model of *terroir*. The first part of the chapter will define food heritage and the anthropological contribution to the debate. The second part of the chapter engages with the ways in which heritage is used by different groups to promote their own agendas and to "make do" rather than simply protect traditional products.

Defining Food Heritage

When defining food heritage, it is interesting to question the juxtaposition of the two terms, "food" and "heritage," which refer to, on the one hand, "any substance that can be metabolized by an organism to give energy and build tissue" (Fernandes 2006: 979), and on the other, to "a modern practice that redefines as valuable and worthy of protection vernacular practices and traditional products that would otherwise disappear because they cannot compete against modernized lifestyles and mass produced consumer goods" (Welz 2012: 361). Seeking to turn food into a monument or heritage good is clearly problematic, but, as Welz (2012: 361) recalls, from the very beginning of human history, food has always incorporated both the organic and the cultural, entailing biological as well as symbolic properties. Food is above all a source of symbolic representation for various other aspects of life (Fernandes 2006: 980). It is never simply food, and is endlessly symbolic and meaningful, as well as valuable because it motivates action (Paxton 2010: 445). It is easy to see why it offers an ideal and idealistic blueprint for the construction of heritage commodities and identity processes. To sum up, food and foodways have become the object of a politics of commodity heritage which seeks to transform them into "objects of trade and exhibition" (Herzfeld 2004: 196), but also aims at materializing and even, in some cases, fossilizing them. Moreover, heritage recognition contributes to the production of singularity in the global political economy, and therefore carries huge economic implications.

The respective fields of heritage studies and food studies are both growing areas of research characterized by increasing fragmentation, interdisciplinarity, and cross-fertilization. Food heritage covers a wide range of socioeconomic realities from the local product labeled as traditional, consumed locally, and preserved within the locality, to the relaunch of local foodstuffs by young entrepreneurs. In addition, the term heritage can be applied to the preservation of foodstuffs, productive sites, or traditional know-how by seeking UNESCO World Heritage status. At the core of the revival of food heritage, *terroir* plays a central role. Several publications have recently come to the fore dealing either with the concept of *terroir* and its complex expansion (Trubek 2008; Paxton 2010; Demossier 2012) or, more generally, with processes of cultural or ethnic identification, including boundaries of inclusion/exclusion in heritage terms (Grasseni 2011). Bessière and Tibère (2011) differentiate in this growing literature two distinct research themes. The first deals with the understanding of food heritage processes and, in particular, the dynamics of making these processes "theirs," while the second area focuses on the impact of recognition on territorial development with, for example, tourism (Bessière 1998) or issues of food standardization (Grasseni 2011; Vitrolles 2011). What all these publications have in common is the attempt to understand how food and foodways offer a platform to negotiate and mediate socioeconomic and cultural change by using local resources and refashioning them at different levels of the politics of scaling and of heritagization (Micoud 2004).

In this growing literature, *terroir* as a concept epitomizes in its deployment both the process of heritagization and group identification, illustrating the protection and recognition of food and also wine within the new global landscape of consumption. It is also above all a useful ethnographic vignette to question issues of identification and socioeconomic change at the interface between the local and the global. Moreover, *terroir* is used to allow actors to engage with their own controversies (Latour 2005; Candea 2011). The *terroir* controversy is one of those debates revealing the division between nature and culture, illustrating the constant renegotiation between science and human culture.

From the 1930s onwards, French viticulture came to be dominated by the ideology of *terroir*, which was constructed upon a complex combination of viticulture and wine-making practices, and agro-climatic factors which give wines a particular taste, or *terroir typicité*. For scientists who are unable to reduce it to a stable list of determining factors, *terroir* is an unfounded notion, an imaginary social construction, and an economic barrier. Producers, on the other hand, along with the wider distribution network of *terroir* wines, consider *terroir* as a real object, although one whose manifestations cannot be evaluated using the same procedures as those of scientists. Over the years, *terroir* has become increasingly contested, and both consumers and producers have questioned its foundations (Barrey and Teil 2011), while the concept itself has expanded at a global level.

The broader political and institutional context has therefore provided an impetus to food heritage and territorial development. The process of legal recognition played a major role in the expansion of the concept of *terroir* at the European level. During the 1990s in particular, the French idea of *terroir* spread throughout the European Union (EU), which enabled traditional foodstuffs and products to compete in a specific niche market and thus boost economic rural development. Through AOC (*Appellation d'origine contrôlée*) legislation, colloquial environmental space (*terroir*) thus became jurisdictional space (*territoire*) (Gade 2004: 849). The European Community and EU regulations of 1992 and 2006 created international property rights which cover a rising proportion of the world trade in foodstuffs, and have created major tensions within the World Trade Organization (Pratt 2009: 290; also Barham 2003).[1] It is clear that the role of *terroir* has been instrumental in defining or reshaping local and territorial identities as part of the process of European integration. It has also provided the basis for the "*terroir* story" by giving it international and legal recognition. The *terroir* story has by the same token increasingly become articulated in the United States (Paxton 2010; Trubek and Bowen 2008) and elsewhere.

Through this multi-scalar deployment of *terroir*, the "glocal" dimension of food heritage appears to play an important role in reconfiguring territories along the lines of complex processes of territorialization. As Grasseni argues, "a glocal side of reinvention may involve new strategies of self-reinvention and novel readings of local histories," and "within circuits of heritagization, food is being rediscovered and reinvented: both as a means of local development and as a bearer of collective territorial identities" (Grasseni 2011: 2). In my ethnographic study of Burgundy, far from being an attempt to secure UNESCO approval for a unique unchanging physical space and culture, the Burgundian bid is, in reality, the latest example of professional and economic competition, and forms part of a process of constant reinvention.

For Burgundy, claiming to be different means redefining some of its most prominent local references in the global arena, such as that of *terroir* linking place to taste, by fossilizing and historicizing the site of production, which is presented as authentic, stable, and trustworthy. As I will argue, heritagization can even go further, as heritage strategies could be more about "making do" rather than preserving (Berliner 2012) by imposing a certain idea of *terroir* seen as "natural" and authentic.

Anthropological Expertise and the Politics of Scaling

Anthropology, more than any other discipline, has been central to discussions of tradition, authenticity, innovation, and other similar concepts related to food and heritage. The anthropological study of food today has matured enough to serve as a vehicle for examining larger and varied problems of theory and research methods (Mintz and Du Bois 2002: 100). An anthropological approach advocates investigations that utilize different perspectives to contribute to our understanding of the social world by complicating simplicities (Kuutma 2012: 33). These different perspectives may be expressed not only by various groups of producers sharing contrasted interests in relation to their products, or by institutions and political groups which seek to drive specific agendas, but also by individuals who have an extensive knowledge of the society they live in and, as a result, aim to constantly move the goalposts in relation to a set of local issues increasingly defined in a global context. The pioneering work of Laurence Bérard and Philippe Marchenay has shed some light on the complexities and ambiguities of the process of safeguarding and preserving while also adapting and maintaining specific products seen as traditional by local communities. More recently, sociologists have also joined the field of food heritage studies, adopting a more distant perspective and less ethnographically rooted analysis (Barrey and Teil 2011).

What comes to the fore in this emerging area of research is the type of heritage recognition involved in the process. Several commentators have recently pointed out the importance of state heritage regimes (see e.g. Bendix, Eggert, and Peselmann 2012) or the making of heritage through the use of new heritage categories (Heinich 2012). Less attention has been given to these processes in relation to food heritage. The majority of the research conducted has taken place either in the United States or the EU in relation to specific products and their institutionalization in the economic market. Very few studies have focused on the process of UNESCO listing (Tornatore 2012) or, more broadly, on the use of heritage and its impact in the broadest sense of the term. These processes, however, refer to different kinds of heritage, and the ambiguities between the different listings under which heritage is coined and used by social actors in a differentiated fashion. For example, in her work on Alpine cheese, Christina Grasseni (2011) argues that a certain amount of standardization of traditional food systems is required in order to offer local products at a global scale. Defining global heritage as the intersection between what Richard Wilk calls the "global structure of common difference" (Wilk 1995: 60) and the "global hierarchy of values" as theorized by Herzfeld (2004), she observes that the heritage dimension of Alpine cheese is illuminated by the fact that, here as elsewhere, ecology is not natural but situated, and that heritage value is acknowledged as part of a politics of negotiation that entails notions of classification and quality.

My own contribution to the study of Burgundy and its claim to UNESCO World Heritage status provides an example of the process of using different heritage categories to negotiate local and global interests. The Burgundy project is supported by both the French Ministry of Culture and the Ministry of Environment, illustrating broader concerns about ecological and environmental issues. The project was put together by the region of Burgundy, the department of Côte d'Or, the towns of Beaune and Dijon, the Bureau Interprofessionel des Vins de Bourgogne and the Confrérie des Chevaliers du Tastevin. The owner of the Domaine de la Romanée Conti is the president of the association established to campaign for UNESCO recognition, and most of the meetings have taken place under his leadership. By using the *climat* argument (defined as a historical geo-system, and sounding highly ecological), the association introduces a new set of values and meanings around *terroir*, which embrace international environmental preoccupations and ensure that the heritage factor will add further value to the place and the product. In several accounts, Burgundy innovates through its repackaging of *terroir* and its innovative reading of heritage categories. In other ways, it reinvents the wheel by just embracing the new global hierarchy of values (Herzfeld 2004).

As a result, the bid has been carefully crafted around the long historical legacy of *terroir* and the natural qualities of the site. The nomination dossier (AICVB and Grahal 2012, 2013) proposes that the *climats de Bourgogne* be inscribed on the World Heritage List as a "cultural site" and not as a landscape. A "cultural site" is understood as "works of man or the combined works of nature and man and areas including archeological sites which are of outstanding universal value from the historical, aesthetic, ethnological or anthropological point of view."[2] The choice of "cultural site" as the heritage category can be explained by the wish to establish a distinctive and singular application compared to Champagne or other viticultural and heritage objects. The dossier argues that "the exceptionality is based on the material character of these plots which refer back to a culture of taste diversity" (AICVB and Grahal 2013: 64). To date, UNESCO has given heritage status to nine cultural landscapes where viticulture plays a role, and three where there is a mixture of cultural and natural elements, but where viticulture is present (Lüginbuhl 2009). I myself made the mistake at the beginning of the project of confusing landscape and site, and was quickly reminded of the relevant category. Moreover, the geographer appointed to work on the *climats de Bourgogne* dossier, who is an expert in wine landscapes, argued that the idea of Outstanding Universal Value in the World Heritage Convention (1972) defines *climats* not as "landscapes" but as "cultural sites." According to his interpretation, which emphasizes the private nature of the goods, "they are not considered as landscapes, but as a localized set of plots, that is to say material goods that are identifiable in space and clearly delineated" (Lüginbuhl 2009: 2). The plots can thus be identified through the taste of products grown on them. Distinct ecologies of production generate distinctive sensory qualities in handcrafted agricultural products (Paxton 2010: 444), and here the *climats* epitomize remarkably well the concept of *terroir* seen as ecologies of production.

At the core of the application for World Heritage status is the uniqueness and exceptionality of the site, which arguably determines some of the logic behind the application, especially in terms of the heritage categories listed. The dossier cited above has served as the foundation for the rationale of the choice of categories. As the dossier combines historical, natural, and geological elements, as well as historical buildings and towns, including the legacy of the legal denomination of origin which is territorially defined, the concept of "site" has imposed itself. The work of the geographer and his years of experience as an expert on UNESCO viticultural heritage sites have helped to create a narrative about *climats de Bourgogne*. His intellectual contribution as a human geographer has been central in building the case alongside that of the local geologist and archaeologist from the University of Dijon, who edited the conference proceedings of the scientific committee (Garcia 2010). World Heritage inscription criteria (iii) and (v) have been employed to support the application, which emphasizes the uniqueness of a cultural tradition or civilization which is living or which has disappeared (criterion iii), and which is an outstanding example of a traditional human settlement, land-use, or sea-use which is representative of a culture (or cultures), or human interaction with the environment, especially when it has become vulnerable under the impact of irreversible change (criterion v).[3] On the basis of what the dossier defines as a "coherent" geo-system transmitted over generations, and the accumulation of techno-scientific knowledge attached to local viticulture, the *climats* are seen by the regional wine elites and the scientific committee as unique cultural sites. For individual communities, *climats* provide a reference to place and time, and act as markers of excellence, quality, and diversity both in geological and human terms.[4]

Distinction and Heritage: A Claim for Authenticity and Ecology

Unlike the GMF, the *climats de Bourgogne* dossier has distinctively avoided the trap of using either folklore or anthropology as the backbone of its application (see AICVB and Grahal 2012, 2013). The GMF has been criticized by scholars for proposing a rehabilitation of folklore through food culture (Tornatore 2012). Neither word has been used during the various sessions of the scientific committee I have attended. Likewise my own contribution as a social anthropologist appointed to provide the "sociological" dimension has been limited to a report and a short publication. Most of the application has carefully focused on the geographic and historical dimension of the site, including its monumental architecture and landscape. The intangible dimension of heritage has been in the background during a number of high-profile meetings, but it has been left there despite my numerous attempts to engage with it. First and foremost, *climats* are about a place, its history, and the soil. The Pandora's box of heritage in the case of Burgundy has been opened in a precise and unique fashion. Heritage valorization represents not only a fashionable trend, but also social, economic, and political determination (Bessière 1998: 32). The regional and local levels have been central in terms of the state heritage regime, for it is they who have translated and adapted UNESCO conventions to fit their own purposes (Tornatore 2012: 346), and their "take" on it is what determined the nature of the dossier.

The uniqueness of the site as constructed by local actors moves the focus away from the product – wine – to put emphasis on the material, "natural," "authentic," "ecological" element of wine production, the *climats.* In the current context of growing concern for alcohol consumption, this makes perfect sense. It seeks to create a stronger and different identification between peoples and places (Tilley 2006: 14). As products, however, become increasingly simple to replicate, so authenticity gains new value. In relation to wine, authenticity makes a difference that counts (Barrey and Teil 2011). Here, authenticity is seen as a way of using heritage as a strategy to singularize *terroir* through the *climats* presented, and through the constant work and "repeated acts" which establish relationships between the site and the visitors. The UNESCO bid aims to transform the collective, cultural, and regional identity into a monumental and emblematic site of reference for world viticulture. The intimate features of locality are used to rework understandings of the global or the world beyond (Tilley 2006: 25). In this context, the *climats* offer a new reading of *terroir* suggesting a text characterized by the binaries uniqueness/diversity and singularity/plurality, which will be read differently by each individual and have different meanings for different groups of individuals. As Bessière (1998: 28) argues, historical context, origins, and roots are the most important conditions of a successful heritage market.

The project will challenge the economic reading associated with the outdated AOC system, which is increasingly criticized by both consumers and producers (Teil 2011; Barrey and Teil 2011). Burgundy argues very strongly for a clearer identification between the place and the product at a time when food security debates and issues of authenticity question the concept of origin in food production. Rather than being a product that only a minority can afford, the idea of *climat* locates its provenance and source with a clear mental image of the place and the plots of land from which it comes. The uniqueness of one *climat* is constructed in parallel to the extreme diversity of 1247 others, and to the reading of more than 100 AOCs, all located in a single site. The visual dimension is telling, and instrumental to the construction of this new reading. The organization of photographic exhibitions, the series of conferences on the *climats*, and the publications accompanying the application (AICVB and Grahal 2012, 2013) all contribute to this process. The *Marche des Climats*, attended by more than 3000 people, was held at the same time as the ratification of a territorial charter, and is another example of the strategies put in place to enhance the visibility of the place.[5] Another event was organized in 2013 concerning local quarries and how the diversity of the local geological landscape resonates with the diversity of local taste in wine, a traditional and historical theme of local culture. Another recent initiative targeting local schools and children, explaining to them the local landscape and its wines, is part of this new reframing of local wine culture, as is the renaming of the local wine festival, once the Saint-Vincent *tournante* but now the Saint-Vincent *tournante des climats*.

These new activities could be interpreted as a more democratic and more collective sharing of the place, which was traditionally dichotomized and segregated in terms of its social functions and uses, or even in terms of perceptions. The grand narrative constructed around the *climats* was, however, tacitly and consensually accepted by all the experts around the table. Yet most of the people from Dijon interviewed by *Le Monde* in 2012 did not know what *climats* meant (Neiman 2012). *Climats* was used neither by the local population nor by wine-growers, and it is conspicuous by its absence from the historical record. On the rare occasions it was mentioned before the UNESCO bid, it was in scholarly literature, as one of the historians on the scientific committee noted. My objection that *climats* had no basis in local culture was ignored, and since then there has been a veritable propaganda campaign to sell the idea of *climats* to both Burgundians and the wider world.

"Make Do" rather than Preserve

Heritage is traditionally concerned with those special places and landscapes that are worth preserving and generally unchanged for the benefit of future generations (Holtorf, cited by Schofield 2008: 18). Nostalgic discourses and practices underlie the fields of heritage and tourism (Berliner 2012: 770), and the global world of wine is structured on them. In his study of the fabric of heritage in Luang Prabang, David Berliner draws our attention to the creative nature of heritagization. Heritage recognition creates aesthetic forms, historical narratives, the politics of transmission, and more generally, new social configurations (Berliner 2012: 771). This is clearly evident in the case of the *climats* even at this stage of the application. The application focuses on identifying, safeguarding, protecting, and delineating the *climats*, while at the same time imposing a shift in the ways the local landscape has evolved. Part of the application includes managing local resources in a more sustainable way, imposing a more ecologically driven viticulture, conserving grape varieties, and going back to a "golden age" where the vineyard was ploughed by horse traction and the grapes were picked by hand. Kate Clark (2008: 82) has argued that heritage involves a powerful drive for social sustainability, but also for economic competition.

The work of Heather Paxton (2010) on American artisan cheeses offers another compelling example of how heritage could be used for different purposes and in different ways in the same locale. She argues that *terroir*, the taste of place, is being adapted by US cheese producers to reveal the range of values – agrarian, environmental, social, and gastronomic – that they believe constitute their cheese, and distinguish artisanal from mass-produced goods. She goes further by discussing how a few producers see themselves as makers of "reverse engineering terroir" cheeses that create place through environmental stewardship and rural economic revitalization. Her case studies, despite being radically different from the French and European examples I have looked at, resonate with certain issues in the discussion of *climats* in the dossier. Heritage recognition is equally about creating a model for practice and about "trying to be" (Paxton 2010: 446), or "drawing meaningful lines of connection among people, culture and landscape to invest rural places anew with affective significance and material relevance" (Paxton 2010: 445). As with the case of Burgundy, *terroir* is being reframed as a prescriptive category (*climats*) for thoughtful action (more ecologically driven), for bringing-into-being from the ground up places where some wish to live and others to visit (Paxton 2010: 445). These strategies are part of a broader global significance given to being-in-location. They are also driven by specific groups of producers who are often either the most educated or successful. That does not mean that they will be followed.

If these cheese producers share some features with their French viticultural counterparts, they differ, however, regarding debates surrounding economic and political dimensions. According to Latour (1995), heritage seeks in the case of the *climats* to "make do." In the case of the *climats* of Burgundy, *terroir* is not sufficient anymore to produce a different category of quality products; the *climats* are proposed by the local community as new "actants" (Latour 1995) consolidating the distinctiveness of Burgundy wine and ensuring that a sense of isomorphism between culture and space prevails at the local level. By using the term *climats*, the different agendas found here – environmental, societal, economic, and political – create a continuity which is now revealed and used by local actors to protect the integrity of the site. Yet collective engagement with that agenda is far from being consensual, and it has been described as "elitist" by local wine-growers. Cultural sociology shows that myth and narrative are elemental meaning-making structures that form the basis of social life (Woodward 2012: 671). But what comes first are the material interlinkages of person and object rather than questions of meaning, narrative, and interpretation (Woodward 2012: 686). The *climats* of Burgundy offer a unique and distinct relationship between the product, the place, and the producer by identifying and guaranteeing the authentic and "natural" origin of the product. As one of my informers put it:

> This is the *génie Bourguignon*![6] Generations of work in the vineyards by wine-growers who have accumulated a wealth of experience, which each generation has benefited from, but has also improved through constant refinements previously brought by empirical knowledge and today by science.

With the *climats de Bourgogne* dossier, a new type of micro-biopolitics is progressively emerging wherein authenticity is been increasingly contested where wines are concerned (Barrey and Teil 2011).

Conclusion

If Burgundy's UNESCO Word Heritage status application is successful, it will enhance and consolidate the identification between product and place of what is already defined as the *lien au lieu* (link to a location). By drinking a Puligny-Montrachet, one will be able to visualize precisely on the map the origin of the product. This strategy, which is similar to that developed in the luxury-goods industry, emerges at a time when fraud is commonplace. That is why, in the current global wine market, where all the traditional divisions in terms of viticultural practice and wine definitions seem to blur under the pressure of standardization and homogenization, authenticity becomes a crucial area for differentiation (Barrey and Teil 2011). For Burgundy, making a difference that counts means re-enacting some of the global references linking place to taste by fossilizing and historicizing the site of production, which is presented as stable and trustworthy. Rather than competing with New World Chardonnay and Pinot Noir, it seeks to reinforce its image as the place of origin of distinct elite products, with its Montrachet or Clos de Vougeot having a very different historic, geographic, and cultural resonance associated with its *climats*. Interestingly enough, what was once associated with Burgundian wines – an unreliable quantity and quality of production, changing according to the annual climatic cycle – now becomes an advantage.

Cultural landscapes and cultural sites are constructed; that is to say, they derive meaning, and often even their physical form, from the actions and imaginations of people in society. Rather than building a case around the contested concept of *terroir*, Burgundy has carefully crafted an application which endorses *climats* as a more "natural, authentic and historical" term based upon a coherent geo-system in the modern sense of the combination of archaeology and geography. Through the concept of *climats* and its deployment in tourist and cultural media, Burgundy seeks to create and impose a "universal" way of seeing Burgundy wines, proposing a more democratic consumption of these "distinction" commodities normally consumed by a small and tiny section of the world population. It also seeks to create a prescriptive category for thoughtful action (Paxton 2010: 445) by mobilizing professionals around key values, such as authenticity, "natural," and more ecologically sustainable viticultural practices. Viticulture, more than any other type of agriculture, has traditionally required phytosanitary treatments. Yet it is difficult to estimate to what extent the application for World Heritage status, if successful, will transform local environmental issues, which have often been ignored. The collective nature of the enterprise remains a decisive factor in the long-term success of Burgundy's *climats* strategy.

Much depends on the ways in which different interest groups take hold of the power potentially inherent in this new discourse. Careful research is now necessary to understand the gradations of social control that emerge when a cultural product or a site is transformed into a heritage commodity with vast economic and social implications (Smith and Akagawa 2009: 264). The anthropologist has the right to remain skeptical about it. As we have seen, heritage is an arena for documenting and fostering a critical understanding of the nature of late-modern competitive practices. This is where anthropology could come back into the equation. (Smith and Akagawa 2009: 264), but it needs to keep its objective and distanced "take" on things such as heritage commodities. Anthropology is, after all, a science of critique and not a contributor to myth-making.

Notes

1 The regulations mentioned concern the legal certification of the designated origins of agricultural products and foodstuffs. See Council Regulation (EEC) No. 2081/92 and No. 2082/92, both of 1992. These European Community laws were later replaced by European Union laws, Council Regulation (EEC) No. 509/2006 and No. 510/2006, both of 2006.
2 World Heritage Convention (1972), art. 1.3.
3 These criteria are taken from UNESCO (2013: para. 77).
4 These points are emphasized in the dossier (AICVB and Grahal 2012, 2013).
5 In support of Burgundy's application for World Heritage status, on April 8, 2011, 53 people signed a charter, committing themselves to ensuring that the land will be managed with respect for its "exceptional universal value." For more information about the heritage management of the site, see http://www.climats-bourgogne.com/fr/mediatheque/charte-territoriale-des-climats-du-vignoble-de-bourgogne-7.php (accessed July 16, 2014).
6 The "genius" of Burgundy is often evoked by local actors to describe the creativity of producers and the quality of their products.

References

Legislation

Convention Concerning the Protection of the World Cultural and Natural Heritage (World Heritage Convention) (UNESCO, 1972). Available at: http://whc.unesco.org/archive/convention-en.pdf (accessed March 19, 2015).

Convention for the Safeguarding of the Intangible Cultural Heritage (Intangible Heritage Convention) (UNESCO, 2003). Available at: http://unesdoc.unesco.org/images/0013/001325/132540e.pdf (accessed March 19, 2015).

Council Regulation (EEC) No. 2081/92 On the Protection of Geographical Indications and Designations of Origin for Agricultural Products and Foodstuffs (European Community, 1992). Available at: http://eur-lex.europa.eu/legal-content/EN/TXT/PDF/?uri=CELEX:31992R2081&from=EN (accessed March 20, 2015).

Council Regulation (EEC) No. 2082/92 On Certificates of Specific Character for Agricultural Products and Foodstuffs (European Community, 1992). Available at: http://eur-lex.europa.eu/legal-content/EN/TXT/PDF/?uri=CELEX:31992R2082&from=EN (accessed March 20, 2015).

Council Regulation (EEC) No. 509/2006 On Agricultural Products and Foodstuffs (European Union, 2006). Available at: http://eur-lex.europa.eu/legal-content/EN/TXT/PDF/?uri=CELEX:32006R0509&from=en (accessed March 20, 2015).

Council Regulation (EEC) No. 510/2006 On the Protection of Geographical Indications and Designations of Origin for Agricultural Products and Foodstuffs (European Union, 2006). Available at: http://eur-lex.europa.eu/legal-content/EN/TXT/PDF/?uri=CELEX:32006R0510&from=en (accessed March 20, 2015).

Other Works

AICVB and Grahal (Association pour l'inscription des climats du vignoble de Bourgogne and Grahal SARL) (2012) *Les climats du vignoble de Bourgogne: dossier de candidature à l'inscription sur las liste du patrimoine mondial de l'UNESCO*, Vol. 1. Available at: http://www.climats-bourgogne.com/fichiers/Candidature_Climats_TOME1.pdf (accessed March 9, 2015).

AICVB and Grahal (2013) *Les climats du vignoble de Bourgogne: dossier de candidature à l'inscription sur las liste du patrimoine mondial de l'UNESCO*, Vol. 2. Available at: http://www.climats-bourgogne.com/fichiers/Candidature_Climats_TOME2.pdf (accessed March 9, 2015).

Barham, E. (2003) Translating Terroir: The Global Challenge of French AOC Labeling. *Journal of Rural Studies*, 9, 127–138.

Barrey, S., and Teil, G. (2011) Faire la preuve de l'"authenticité" du patrimoine alimentaire Le cas des vins de terroir. *Anthropology of Food*. Available at: http://aof.revues.org/6783 (accessed January 9, 2014).

Bendix, R., Eggert, A., and Peselmann, A. (eds) (2012) *Heritage Regimes and the State*. Göttingen: Universitätsverlag Göttingen.

Berliner, D. (2012) Multiple Nostalgias: The Fabric of Heritage in Luang Prabang (Lao PDR), *Journal of the Royal Anthropological Institute*, 18, 769–786.

Bessière, J. (1998) Local Development and Heritage: Traditional Food and Cuisine as a Tourist Attraction in Rural Areas. *Sociologia Ruralis*, 38 (1), 21–34.

Bessière, J., and Tibère, L. (2011) Editorial: Patrimoines Alimentaires. *Anthropology of Food*. Available at: http://aof.revues.org/6758 (accessed January 9, 2014).

Candea, M. (2011) "Our Division of the Universe": Making Space for the Non-Political in the Anthropology of Politics. *Current Anthropology*, 52 (3), 309–334.

Clark, K. (2008) Only Connect: Sustainable Development and Cultural Heritage. In G. Fairclough, R. Harrison, J.H. Jameson, and J. Schofield (eds), *The Heritage Reader*. London: Routledge, pp. 82–98.

Demossier, M. (2000) Culinary Heritage and Produits de Terroir in France: Food for Thought. In S. Blowen, M. Demossier, and J. Picard (eds), *Recollections of France: Memories, Identities and Heritage in Contemporary France*. Oxford: Berghahn, pp. 141–153.

Demossier, M. (2012) The Europeanization of Terroir: Consuming Place, Tradition and Authenticity. In R. Friedman and M. Thiel (eds), *European Identity and Culture: Narratives of Transnational Belonging*. Farnham: Ashgate, pp. 119–136.

Fairclough, G., Harrison, R., Jameson, J.H., and Schofield, J. (eds) (2008) *The Heritage Reader*. London: Routledge.

Fernandes, L. (2006) Food. In H. Birx (ed.), *Encyclopedia of Anthropology*. Thousand Oaks, CA: Sage Publications, pp. 979–981.

Gade, D.W. (2004) Tradition, Territory, and Terroir in French Viniculture: Cassis, France, and Appellation Contrôlée. *Annals of the Association of American Geographers*, 94 (4), 848–867.

Garcia, J.P. (ed.) (2010) *Les "climats" du vignoble de Bourgogne comme patrimoine mondial de l'humanité*. Dijon: Editions Universitaires de Dijon.

Grasseni, C. (2011) Re-inventing Food: Alpine Cheese in the Age of Globalisation. *Anthropology of Food*. Available at: http://aof.revues.org/6819 (accessed January 9, 2014).

Heinich, N. (2012) *La fabrique du patrimoine*, 4th edn. Paris: Editions de la Maison des Sciences de l'Homme.

Herzfeld, M. (2004) *The Body Impolitic: Artisans and Artifice in the Global Hierarchy of Value*. Chicago: University of Chicago Press.

Kuutma, K. (2012) Between Arbitration and Engineering: Concepts and Contingencies in the Shaping of Heritage Regimes. In R. Bendix, A. Eggert, and A. Peselmann (eds), *Heritage Regimes and the State*. Göttingen: Universitätsverlag Göttingen, pp. 21–38.

Latour, B. (2005) From Realpolitik to Dingpolitik, or How to Make Things Public. In B. Latour and P. Weibel (eds), *Making Things Public: Atmospheres of Democracy*. Cambridge, MA: MIT Press, pp. 14–43.

Lüginbuhl, Y. (2009) Rapport climats de Bourgogne. Internal report prepared for the Association pour l'inscription des climats du vignoble de Bourgogne.

Micoud, A. (2004) Des patrimoines aux territoires durables: Ethnologie et écologie dans les campagnes françaises. *Ethnologie française*, 2, (37), 13–22.

Mintz, S., and Du Bois, C. (2002) The Anthropology of Food and Eating. *Annual Review of Anthropology*, 31, 99–119.

Neiman, O (2012) Climats de Bourgogne à l'Unesco: tout ce que vous avez toujours voulu savoir. *Le Monde* blog post, July 16. Available at: http://missglouglou.blog.lemonde.fr/2012/07/ (accessed March 12, 2015).

Paxton, H. (2010) Locating Value in Artisan Cheese: Reverse-Engineering Terroir for New World Landscapes. *American Anthropologist*, 112 (3), 442–455.

Pottier, J. (1996) Food. In A. Barnard, and J. Spencer (eds), *Encyclopedia of Social and Cultural Anthropology*. London: Routledge, pp 238–241.

Pratt, J. (2007) Food Values: The Local and the Authentic. *Critique of Anthropology*, 27 (3), 285–300.

Schofield, J. (2008) Heritage Management, Theory and Practice. In G. Fairclough, R. Harrison, J.H. Jameson, and J. Schofield (eds), *The Heritage Reader*. London: Routledge, pp.15–31.

Smith, L., and Akawaga, N. (eds) (2009) *Intangible Heritage*, London: Routledge.

Teil, G. (2011) No Such Thing as Terroir? Objectivities and the Regime of Existence of Objects. *Science, Technology and Human Values*, 37 (5), 478–505.

Tilley, C. (2006) Introduction: Identity, Place, Landscape and Heritage. *Journal of Material Culture*, 11 (1), 7–32.

Tornatore, J.-L. (2012) Anthropology's Payback: "The Gastronomic Meal of the French," the Ethnographic Elements of a Heritage Distinction. In R. Bendix, A. Eggert, and A. Peselmann (eds), *Heritage Regimes and the State*. Göttingen: Universitätsverlag Göttingen, pp. 341–365.

Trubek, A. (2008) *The Taste of Place: A Cultural Journey into Terroir*. Berkeley: University of California Press.

Trubek, A., and Bowen, S. (2008) Creating the Taste of Place in the United States: Can We Learn from the French? *GeoJournal* 73, 23–30.

UNESCO (2013) Operational Guidelines for the Implementation of the World Heritage Convention. Document WHC.13/01. Available at: http://whc.unesco.org/archive/opguide 13-en.pdf (accessed March 12, 2015).

Vitrolles, D. (2011) When Geographical Indication Conflicts with Food Heritage Protection: The Case of Serrano Cheese from Rio Grande do Sul, Brazil. *Anthropology of Food*. Available at: http://aof.revues.org/6809 (accessed January 9, 2014).

Welz, G. (2012) The Diversity of European Food Cultures. In U. Kockel, M. Nic Craith, and J. Frykman (eds), *A Companion to the Anthropology of Europe*. Chichester: Wiley-Blackwell, pp. 355–372.

Wilk, R. (1995) Learning to Be Local in Belize: Global Systems of Common Difference. In D. Miller (ed.), *Worlds Apart: Modernity through the Prism of the Local*. London: Routledge, pp. 110–133.

Woodward, I. (2012) Consumption as Cultural Interpretation: Taste, Performativity and Navigating the Forest of Objects. In J.C. Alexander, R. Jacobs, and P. Smith. (eds), *The Oxford Handbook of Cultural Sociology*. Oxford: Oxford University Press, pp. 671–697.

CHAPTER 7

(Re)visioning the Ma'ohi Landscape of Marae Taputapuatea, French Polynesia: World Heritage and Indigenous Knowledge Systems in the Pacific Islands

Anita Smith

Introduction

On the fortieth anniversary of the World Heritage Convention in 2012, participants at an expert workshop on the World Heritage Convention and indigenous peoples called on the World Heritage Committee to give full and effective participation to indigenous peoples in World Heritage processes (IWGIA 2012). The concerns of participants centered on two interrelated issues. Firstly, many World Heritage sites are situated within land traditionally owned by indigenous peoples, and this has significant ramifications for the human rights and self-determined development of those indigenous peoples. Secondly, World Heritage processes do not give adequate voice to indigenous peoples in the evaluation of World Heritage nominations and associated reporting mechanisms, thereby exacerbating the significant under-representation of indigenous values on the World Heritage List.

The number of World Heritage sites in which outstanding universal value is indigenous value continues to be very low, despite initiatives such as the introduction of

A Companion to Heritage Studies, First Edition. Edited by William Logan, Máiréad Nic Craith, and Ullrich Kockel.
© 2016 John Wiley & Sons, Inc. Published 2016 by John Wiley & Sons, Inc.

cultural landscape as a category of World Heritage sites in 1993 (Titchen 1996) and the capacity-building programs under the global strategy for a balanced and credible World Heritage List (Smith 2012). As Meskell (2013: 191) and others have argued, the involvement of indigenous peoples in World Heritage sites continues to be primarily as "stakeholders" rather than drivers of the nomination dossiers or state-of-conservation reports prepared by States Parties and brought before the World Heritage Committee.

As I discuss in this chapter, unlike the experience of many indigenous peoples, among Pacific island nations, the majority of the population is indigenous and, as customary landowners, communities have a strong voice in the World Heritage process at local and national levels.[1] For over a decade, governments and communities in the Pacific islands have been supported by the World Heritage Committee to develop nominations, resulting in a significant increase in the number of Pacific World Heritage sites. However, while representation of the Pacific region on the World Heritage List has increased, this has not come about due to an increased consideration of indigenous values or understandings of place, land, or seascapes through traditional or customary knowledge systems as being of outstanding universal value, suggesting the need for the further interrogation of factors that may underlie the continuing under-representation of indigenous values on the World Heritage List.

In 2010, the government of French Polynesia requested that Na Papa E Va'u, a local community organization on the island of Ra'iatea, oversee the development of the World Heritage nomination of the sacred site of Marae Taputapuatea. The transnational heritage values of the site for Polynesian communities across the Pacific were well known prior to inclusion of the site on France's Tentative List of World Heritage properties, but Na Papa E Va'u emphasized that the custodianship of the local community must also be recognized in the World Heritage nomination, and has insisted that management of the site is based on local traditional knowledge and protocol in relation to access and use of the site (Smith 2010). This knowledge, recorded over a four-year period, now informs not only the management of the site but also the justification of the outstanding universal value of the property as an expression of Ma'ohi (Central Polynesian) history, culture, and identity.

In this chapter, Marae Taputapuatea is presented as a case study of the extraordinary potential contribution of local traditional knowledge to understanding the values of World Heritage sites, even where the indigenous significance of the place is widely recognized. This has particular resonance for the Pacific region because of the central role traditional knowledge systems continue to have in structuring relationships to land, resources, and people (Nemani 2011), but it also provides insights into the processes of nomination that may hinder the recognition of indigenous knowledge systems on the World Heritage List in general.

Traditional Knowledge and Its Protection in the Pacific Islands

The World Intellectual Property Organization (WIPO) defines traditional knowledge as "knowledge, know-how, skills and practices that are developed, sustained and passed on from generation to generation within a community, often forming part of its cultural or spiritual identity" (WIPO n.d.). That is, traditional knowledge is differentiated from other forms of knowledge in being associated with a particular community, passed on within that community, and seen by that community as an essential element of the collective cultural identity of the community, differentiating it from other communities.

In the Pacific islands, traditional knowledge systems encompass an extraordinary diversity of cultural knowledge associated with indigenous communities, who make up over 80 percent of the population across the region. Systems of traditional knowledge incorporate:

> technical insights and detailed observations of natural, social and spiritual phenomena, which in turn are used to validate what is important in life – what sustains people and what connects them to particular places and spaces, and is crucial to their identity. Spirituality, or the sacred, is fundamental – people are the carriers of the lifeblood of future generations and have complex responsibilities to their physical environment and other living things. (Du Plessis and Fairbairn-Dunlop 2009: 110–11)

These relationships between people and land are sustained by the strength of continuing traditional or customary systems of land tenure. Unlike many other indigenous communities, Pacific islanders do not comprise minority nations within a larger state, but live in autonomous nation-states. Communities within these nation-states may have a common sense of national identity, but their cultural identity is defined by their genealogical connections to a particular place and to communities elsewhere, on other islands and sometimes over vast distances. The islands are rich with ancestral stories explaining connectedness, movement between islands, relationships between people and communities, totems exemplifying peoples' bond with the environment, and elaborate rituals and ceremonies (Nemani 2011: 11). This intangible cultural heritage underpins the cultural diversity of Pacific island communities, and structures relationships to place, access to resources, social interaction, and community decision-making. The landscapes and seascapes of the region are patterned by these highly complex and diverse cultural practices.

Solomon Islands anthropologist David Gegeo (2001: 213) explains that within the indigenous epistemology of the Kwara'ae community, of which he is a member, place is also an expression of traditional knowledge and has a set of characteristics that he argues may more broadly define indigeneity.[2] Being Kwara'ae means place is a physical location but also genealogy, the location of one's kin both in the present and reaching backward and forward in time; place is having land or the unconditional right to access land in Kwara'ae through genealogy and marriage, and the unquestioned position based on genealogy and marriage from which one may speak to important issues in Kwara'ae. Place, he describes, is also native fluency in language and the assumption that one is knowledgeable about Kwara'ae. Place means obligations and responsibilities and shared Kwara'ae perspectives, and having a Kwara'ae cultural framework (Gegeo 2001: 493–95).

Gegeo's description of place as a complex network of Kwara'ae relationships, responsibilities, and understandings are echoed by Ralph Regenvanu, previously director of the Vanuatu Kaljoral Senta, who identified the two key characteristics of Pacific cultures as being that they are contemporary societies that demonstrate a high level of cultural continuity with previous generations, and societies in which the "tangible elements of the culture are but a small sub-set of the intangible elements, which are all-encompassing" (Regenvanu, quoted in Galla 2008: 15).

The development and implementation of national and regional measures to protect traditional knowledge and promote cultural industries reflects the importance of traditional knowledge for the social, environmental, and economic well-being of communities in the region. Many community projects are recording local traditional knowledge or intangible heritage as a means of protecting this cultural knowledge. For example, the elders of Atafu Atoll of the tiny island nation of Tokelau have recorded their knowledge of their marine environments and their traditional techniques for exploiting them for the benefit of their children and grandchildren (Hooper and Tinielu 2012: v). Other projects look to traditional resource strategies as a basis for communities to respond to ecological and socio-economic changes through sustainable resources use (Veitayaki 2005; Hviding 2006), or to meet the challenges of specific environmental impacts, most notably climate change and associated sea-level rise (UNESCO and ICHCAP 2013).

Projects such as these are supported by several key regional policy and guidance documents and legal frameworks for the protection or safeguarding of the traditional knowledge or intangible cultural heritage of the region. In 2002, the Secretariat of the Pacific Community (SPC), the intergovernmental agency overseeing cultural development of the Pacific islands nations, produced the landmark draft model law for the protection of traditional knowledge and expressions of culture that establishes statutory rights for traditional owners of traditional knowledge and expressions of culture (SPC *et al.* 2008). Eight Pacific island nations are signatories to UNESCO's Convention for the Safeguarding of the Intangible Cultural Heritage (2003). Assisting them to implement the convention, the SPC has developed an intangible cultural heritage "mapping toolkit" (Nemani 2011), specifically designed to enable communities to independently research, collect, collate, and archive their intangible cultural heritage for current and future generations. The toolkit recognizes a symbiotic relationship between intangible and tangible cultural heritage (Nemani 2011: 11), but protection of the tangible is enabled through the protection of traditional knowledge.

World Heritage Values in the Pacific

In 2004, the World Heritage Committee initiated the World Heritage – Pacific 2009 Programme to build the capacity of Pacific nations to implement the World Heritage Convention (1972), and to develop nominations and address the region's under-representation on the World Heritage List (Smith 2012). The value placed on traditional knowledge as shaping and giving value to the tangible heritage of the region was evident from initial discussions to establish the Pacific World Heritage program in 1997, at which representatives of the Pacific island nations noted:

> the inseparable connection between the outstanding seascapes and landscapes in the Pacific islands which are woven together by rich histories, oral and life traditions of the Pacific island peoples ... [and] bound through voyaging, kinship, trade and other relationships ... The natural diversity of the region is paralleled by an extraordinary richness of cultural heritage expressed in thousands of different languages, and distinct cultural traditions ... [T]he region contains powerful spiritually valued natural features and cultural places rather than an extensive range of monuments and human built permanent features. These places are related to the origins of peoples, the land and sea, and other sacred stories. (UNESCO 1997)

Ten years later this was reiterated in a statement to the World Heritage Committee in which the Pacific island nations stated, "Our heritage is holistic, embracing all life, both tangible and intangible, and is understood through our cultural traditions" (UNESCO 2007, Annex 1: 8). Since 2004, the number of World Heritage sites in the independent Pacific island states has increased from one to six. Two further sites in the region have also been inscribed, one in Hawaii (by the United States) and one in New Caledonia (by France). In total, these include four cultural sites, two mixed sites (cultural and natural), and two natural sites.[3] This increase in the representation of the region on the World Heritage List is a substantial achievement for Pacific island governments and the World Heritage Committee. However, in relation to being a representation of the outstanding cultural heritage of Pacific island peoples as expressed in the above statements, the picture is not as clear.

All four natural sites – the Lagoons of New Caledonia (2008), the Phoenix Islands Protected Area, Kiribati (2010), Rock Islands Southern Lagoon, Palau (2012) and Papahānaumokuākea, Hawaii (2010) – are seascapes inscribed for their outstanding marine biodiversity, their natural phenomena (with the exception of Papahānaumokuākea), and/or aesthetic values. In three of the cultural sites, "outstanding universal value" is reflected in archaeological evidence that is explained within well-known global narratives. At the Kuk Early Agricultural Site in Papua New Guinea (2008), archeological evidence testifies to the early and independent development of agriculture in Melanesia. The Bikini Atoll Nuclear Test Site in the Marshall Islands (2010) is an outstanding example of a nuclear test site, and testimony to the birth of the Cold War and the "nuclear era" that dominated global politics in the second part of the twentieth century. The archeological evidence of rock art, cave deposits, burials, and abandoned stone villages of the Rock Islands Southern Lagoon, Palau (2012), is described as testimony to small island communities and their harvesting of marine resources over some three millennia, and illustrative of the intersection of the consequences of climate change, population growth, and subsistence behavior on a society living in a marginal marine environment. Levuka Historical Port Town, Fiji (2013), is a Pacific port town landscape inscribed for its built and landscape heritage, reflecting a combination of colonial settlement typologies and local building traditions, and exhibiting the important interchange of human values and cultural contact in the Pacific during the process of European maritime expansion during the nineteenth century.

At only two of the World Heritage sites in the Pacific, Chief Roi Mata's Domain in Vanuatu (2008) and the mixed site of Papahānaumokuākea in Hawaii, are indigenous knowledge systems referred to in the listing statement. The burial place of Chief Roi Mata within the World Heritage site of Chief Roi Mata's Domain has also been the subject of substantial archeological excavation and analysis, but unlike the aforementioned sites, the outstanding universal value of the site is as an example of a landscape representative of Pacific chiefly systems evidenced in the association of the landscape with the ancestral chief, Roi Mata. The continuing customary knowledge of and respect for Roi Mata in this place underpins the authenticity of the site, and the connection between Pacific people and their places from the past and into the future.

The cultural values of the vast seascape of Papahānaumokuākea northwest of the Hawaiian Islands are also supported by archeological evidence, notably the remains of *heiau* (stone temples or shrines) on some of the remote islands of the site. *Heiau* are associated with living traditions of Native Hawaiians and testimony to the strong cultural affiliation between Hawaii, Tahiti, and the Marquesas, celebrating the natural abundance of Papahānaumokuākea and its association with sacred realms of life and death. Like Chief Roi Mata's Domain, oral traditions are the principal evidence for traditional cultural associations of the land and seascape, and in Papahānaumokuākea these traditions reflect the cultural connections of Hawaiians with their ancestral homeland in Central Polynesia.

All the World Heritage properties in the independent Pacific island nations recognize local customary knowledge and land tenure in the management of the property. However, with the exception of Chief Roi Mata's Domain, an indigenous understanding of place such as that articulated by representatives of the Pacific island states in 1997 (see above) is yet to lead the selection or nomination of a place of potential outstanding universal value.

The choice made by Pacific governments to nominate these sites as their first World Heritage sites was informed by each site having been the subject of international research that could provide the information, rationale, and expertise to enable the nominations to be developed with the limited resources and short time frames of assistance through the World Heritage Fund (UNESCO 2012, Annex 8). Unlike most European countries, almost none of the Pacific island states had (or have) established national processes for the identification and protection of heritage places, particularly cultural heritage places that would have provided a foundation upon which to identify outstanding representative examples of Pacific heritage sites. In many of the Pacific nations – with the notable exception of Vanuatu – the World Heritage program has led the development of national heritage policy and legislation, specifically for the protection of places. While Pacific island communities may clearly and strongly articulate their heritage values as being reflected in the land and sea, customary land and sea tenure, storied places, and cultural practices, there are only very limited national or regional studies or inventories of heritage places or sites. Where these exist, they are primarily focused on archeological sites or built heritage.

The "cherry-picking" of iconic sites for World Heritage nomination is not unusual, and many of these sites have iconic status because they are exceptional and worthy of inscription. However, although iconic or unusual sites may reduce regional underrepresentation on the World Heritage List, their inscription does not automatically lead to a list that is representative of cultural diversity.

Transnational Values and the International Significance of Marae Taputapuatea

The decision of France through the government of French Polynesia to support the development of a nomination for Marae Taputapuatea on the island of Ra'iatea provided the opportunity for a place of indigenous significance for Polynesian communities across the region to be recognized as being of outstanding universal value.

It was in the Opoa Valley on the southeast coast of Ra'iatea Island that Ta'aroa, father of the Polynesian gods and creator of all things, is said to have first entered the earth creating Havai'i (Ra'iatea), the Polynesian homeland (Henry 1928). On the shore at the entrance to the valley, at Matahira-i-te-ra'i Point, stands Marae Taputapuatea, a monumental stone platform with an *ahu* (altar) of enormous upright coral slabs running the length of its eastern edge. Marae Taputapuatea is the centre of a complex of ceremonial stone structures including other *marae*, notably Marae Hauviri, on which Tamatoa high chiefs of Ra'iatea were invested at the time of European contact in the late eighteenth century. This complex is the heart of the cultural landscape of the Opoa

Figure 7.1 Marae Taputapuatea, Ra'iatea Island, French Polynesia. Source: photograph by Anita Smith.

Valley as defined by the *paripari fenua*, a traditional oration for the land that describes the natural elements of the landscape of the valley from the mountain Te-a'etapu to the Te Ava Mo'a, the sacred pass through the reef opposite Matahira-i-te-ra'i.

It was through Te Ava Mo'a that Polynesian navigators are said to have steered their great voyaging canoes (*va'a*) when departing for, and returning from, islands as distant as the Cook Islands, Hawaii and Aotearoa/New Zealand (Henry 1928: 123). Ra'iatea is acknowledged as the ancestral homeland by Polynesian communities in Central Polynesia, Hawaii, the Cook Islands, Rotuma, and Aotearoa/New Zealand.

Marae Taputapuatea is the largest and most famous of the *marae* monumental stone and coral structures found throughout central Polynesia. The central Polynesian *marae* are akin in function if not materials to the *marae* of Māori in Aotearoa/New Zealand, the *heiau* of indigenous Hawaiians, and *ahu* of Rapanui/Easter Island, and attest to the common origin, history, and culture, of East Polynesian peoples. *Marae* are *tapu*, or sacred places, that express the essence of traditional Polynesian culture, the relationships of people to each other, to their gods, and to the land and the sea that are maintained through rituals associated with the *marae* (Eddowes 1991). For nearly a century, *marae* have been the subject of systematic archeological research that has analyzed their age and variability in form, function, material, and method of construction as evidence of the evolution of Polynesian societies, tracing the patterns of interaction between Polynesian communities over time (Wallin 1993).

The fame of Marae Taputapuatea flows from an enormous wealth of documented oral traditions and European observations of Polynesia from the late eighteenth century onwards, including the journals and images of early European explorers such as Wallis, Bougainville, Cook, and Boenechea (see Salmon 2009). Other sources include the journals and letters of missionaries who began arriving in 1797 (e.g. Ellis 1829), and the memoirs of indigenous commentators and historians such as the Ari'i Tamai (Adams 1947), Marau Taaroa (Taaroa 1971), and Teura Henry (1928; see also Handy 1930). This extraordinary body of evidence attests to the pre-eminence of Marae Taputapuatea as a ceremonial center and navigational reference point from at least the sixteenth century, when Opoa Valley became the center for the worship of 'Oro, god of war and fertility. Associated with the worship of 'Oro were the Arioi, a cult of skilled navigators who carried images of the 'Oro and stones from Marae Taputapuatea on their voyages to spread the worship of the god from island to island, establishing new *marae* dedicated to 'Oro in the Society Islands, Cook Island, Aotearoa/New Zealand and Hawaii (Salmon 2009: 22–32). Tupaia, the famous Polynesian navigator who accompanied Captain Cook on the voyage from Tahiti to Aotearoa/New Zealand in 1769, was a priest of 'Oro from Opoa (Salmon 2009: 204–5).

In more recent times, the traditional significance of Marae Taputapuatea as a voyaging center and homeland of Polynesian communities has acquired new meaning with the revitalization of traditional navigation and voyaging in the Pacific. In 1976, the *Hokule'a*, a replica of a Polynesian voyaging canoe, demonstrated for the first time that it was possible for Polynesians to have voyaged across the vast distances of Polynesia using only traditional navigation methods, by sailing from Hawaii to Opoa to be greeted on arrival at Marae Taputapuatea (PVS n.d.). This and subsequent voyages are highly symbolic in the revitalization of Polynesian languages, cultural traditions of navigation and voyaging, and associated ceremonies on Marae Taputapuatea that are re-establishing the ancestral linkages between the communities of Ma'ohi (Central Polynesia), Maoli (Hawaii), Māori (Aotearoa/New Zealand), and Rapanui/Easter Island, who have been separated by national borders and the languages of colonial powers.

The Tentative List submission for the cultural landscape of Marae Taputapuatea describes the potential outstanding universal value of the site as being:

- the traditional indigenous significance of Marae Taputapuatea and the Opoa Valley for Polynesian peoples;
- the ethnohistoric significance of Taputapuatea Marae as a place of encounter between indigenous and European people and their societies in the late 18th Century;
- the archaeological and architectural significance of the Marae as a distinct form of monumental architecture representative of Eastern Polynesian society that in its various forms reflects the shared origin and history of Polynesian peoples and the evolution of their unique social societies (UNESCO 2010).

Notwithstanding issues of protection and management, the site clearly has the potential to demonstrate the outstanding universal value required for inscription on the World Heritage List.

The Traditional Knowledge of Papa Maraehau

In 2010, the government of French Polynesia gave responsibility for community awareness of and support for a World Heritage nomination to Na Papa E Va'u ("The eight kings"), a local Opoa community organization under the guidance of several indigenous elders. Over the previous decade, Na Pap E Va'u had revitalized and promoted traditional protocol associated with Marae Taputapuatea led by the key knowledge holder and orator for the Marae, Romy Tavaeari'i, known to all as Papa Maraehau. In anticipation of the inclusion of the site on France's Tentative List of World Heritage sites, Na Pap E Va'u enlisted my support in a project to record this traditional knowledge as a basis for developing a management plan for the site that would be based on local community stewardship. Our initial task was to develop with Papa Maraehau a set of protocols to guide access to and use of Marae Taputapuatea that would respect the traditional significance of the site and meet the requirements of the World Heritage Committee.

According to Papa Maraehau, he was born in Opoa in 1945. As a youth he learnt from two elders, Tehaarama and Tapuvahine, many stories about places and events in the valley, the history of Marae Taputapuatea, and the origins and relationships of the ancestors. As children, these elders had, along with many others in Opoa, resisted French domination following the 1880 annexation of Tahiti by retreating to caves in

Figure 7.2 Romy Tavaeari'i, "Papa Maraehau," at Marae Taputapuatea, November 2007. Source: photograph by Anita Smith.

the mountains at the head the valley for about a decade. It was during this time they had been taught this knowledge.

During five fieldwork seasons between 2009 and 2012, Papa Maraehau slowly and carefully told us many stories of the history of Opoa. He wished to share this and to have it recorded as a systematic and complete body of knowledge, one that he considers is essential to fully appreciate and respect Marae Taputapuatea. He insisted that the stories must be told and recorded as a genealogy that expresses the relationships between people, events, and places or features in the valley through time. The stories were recorded in the indigenous Ma'ohi language of French Polynesia and subsequently translated into French and English.

Most of these stories, or at least elements of them, are familiar in Polynesia, at least to scholars of Ma'ohi culture, and versions of a number of the stories are included in the accounts of early Polynesians in the late eighteenth and nineteenth centuries noted above (see esp. Henry 1928; Handy 1930; Emory 1933, n.d.). However, in listening to and transcribing the words of Papa Maraehau, anthropologist Timiri Hopuu and archeologist Martine Ratimassamy, both of the Department of Culture, French Polynesia, have commented that this is the first time they have heard these stories in this form, that is, linked together chronologically and spatially with events, people, and concepts specifically associated with places or features in the valley.[4]

This highly complex history describes three main phases in the history of the Ma'ohi people: a foundation phase, a consolidation phase, and the final phase of the appearance of the Ari'i Nui, or high chiefs, encountered by Europeans in the late eighteenth century. Each phase is associated with a period of construction of Marae Taputapuatea, and characterized by a cyclical pattern of exploration through voyaging and expansion, including the creation of communities elsewhere and external linkages with communities on other islands, followed by contraction (in the two earlier phases). This is illuminated by specific stories of individuals who by their actions create these cycles. The phases end or begin with the destruction and rebuilding of Marae Taputapuatea and other structures at Matahira-i-te-ra'i. Marae Taputapuatea assumes its current name only in the third and final phase, when it was expanded to take on its current form. Other locations and features within the Opoa Valley and surrounding valleys and coast are prominent in different stories, especially in relation to episodes in the lives of heroes and ancestors, noted for their food or plant resources, or natural events such as the tsunami that destroyed the first *marae*.

The stories link the origin of the world in the first footsteps of Ta'aroa to the appearance of the Ma'ohi people, the social changes that gave rise to the first *marae* constructed at Matahira-i-te-ra'i, through to the time of recorded genealogies for the *marae*, the construction of the great Marae Taputapuatea and the time of the Tamatoa high chiefs of Ra'iatea. Through the commentaries of Papa Maraehau, this detailed and complex history of Marae Taputapuatea and the Opoa Valley becomes a history of the Ma'ohi people and an explanation of the significance of key concepts in Ma'ohi culture, such as personal sacrifice so that others may survive. The stories also explain how these concepts are reflected in the symbolic form of the *marae* and the associated cultural practices, including current protocol around access and use of the site.

Most importantly in relation to the World Heritage nomination for Marae Taputapuatea and the Opoa Valley, this knowledge illuminates the associative and evolving cultural landscape of the valley through directly associating events, people, natural resources, and changing environments with places and features in the valley, and especially with extant features, platforms, and locations on Matahira-i-te-ra'i. This traditional knowledge has been used in conjunction with the digital modeling of the landscape of the Opoa Valley to create a layered cultural and conceptual map illustrating the changing relationships of people and events to places in the valley over time. The knowledge of Papa Maraehau fills in the boundary of the associative landscape, described in the *paripari fenua*, with a traditional history that reveals the richness of the valley as a representation of Ma'ohi culture and identity. In doing so, this history shifts arguments for the Outstanding Universal Value of the valley away from Marae Taputapuatea as emblematic of the cult of 'Oro, the struggles for power of Ari'i Nui, and the exoticism of the European accounts of the contact era, to a more egalitarian understanding of the social and economic life that underpins the cultural practices associated with *marae*. This supports arguments for World Heritage List inscription based on transnational values, but also an argument for the Outstanding Universal Value of the valley as an associative cultural landscape representative of Ma'ohi people.

In this sense, the cultural landscape of the Opoa Valley may be more appropriately considered an "ancestral landscape" (Kawharu 2009). This, Merata Kawharu argues, better describes Māori associative landscapes such as Tongariro National Park in Aotearoa/New Zealand because it emphasizes the centrality of ancestors as original trustees of the land, and the centrality of trusteeship values guiding present and future generations. She defines such landscapes "as part of a network of places and areas that were created or used by gods, mythological heroes, ancestors and their descendants" (Kawharu 2009: 322), emphasizing the inseparable connection of the ancestors and their descendants, past and present, and the role of customary owners in ensuring that knowledge and relationships to land are passed on within the cultural context in which traditional cultural knowledge was and is created.

Papa Maraehau stresses that the traditional knowledge he has shared is inseparable from Marae Taputapuatea and the local tradition of custodianship of the site and the valley. The traditional knowledge is "the place itself" (Gegeo 2001: 213), the significance of the place being maintained through the knowledge that is passed on in the community. This relationship is maintained and expressed through the protocols and cultural practices associated with access to and respect for Marae Taputapuatea and the Ma'ohi cultural traditions it embodies. When completed, the management plan for the site will enshrine local community custodianship and responsibility for culturally appropriate management practices that will ensure that the link between Marae Taputapuatea, the Opoa Valley, and the knowledge associated with them continues and evolves as a living tradition.[5]

Conclusion

The transnational values of Marae Taputapuatea and the Opoa Valley express the historical connections of East Polynesian communities, and attest to the immense significance of the site as representative of the unique heritage of the Pacific region. Alongside these transnational values, the associative cultural landscape of Opoa Valley may also now be regarded as reflecting an indigenous knowledge system that bears exceptional testimony to the culture and history of the Ma'ohi people, giving great depth, nuance, and authenticity to the transnational values of Marae Taputapuatea.

An equivalent relationship between international and local community values does not directly inform the Outstanding Universal Value of potential World Heritage sites in general, as is clear in relation to many of the Pacific World Heritage sites discussed.

Places may be of international significance for distinctly different reasons to those for which they are valued by local communities. The Bikini Atoll Nuclear Test Site is, by way of example, of significance to Bikini Islanders as the homeland to which they are unable to return as a consequence of the nuclear tests. However, if, as Gegeo (2001: 213) argues, "place" for indigenous communities is both tangible and intangible, the complex network of relationships, responsibilities, and language that are shared by a community, then it is precisely these "local" values – or traditional knowledge systems – that must be recognized as of Outstanding Universal Value if indigenous peoples and communities are to have their heritage represented on the World Heritage List. The inscription of properties such as Uluru Kata Tjuta (Australia), Tongariro National Park (Aotearoa/New Zealand), and Chief Roi Mata's Domain (Vanuatu) as indigenous cultural landscapes demonstrates that this is possible within the current system, but the number of such inscriptions remains low (Smith 2013).

The creation of an indigenous advisory body to the World Heritage Committee may facilitate the inscription of properties and assist in ensuring the rights of indigenous communities are respected by the World Heritage system. The challenge will be to assist indigenous communities wishing to engage in World Heritage processes to undertake the nomination of places they consider of potential Outstanding Universal Value and the research required to demonstrate this, and, within the requirements of the World Heritage Committee, to communicate their values in their own way. In the words of Tumu Te Heu Heu, paramount chief of the Ngati Tuwharetoa Māori tribe and chair of the World Heritage Committee in 2007, indigenous communities need to have the opportunity to share through World Heritage processes the way in which they "traditionally see, feel and listen to the Universe" (Te Heu Heu, Kawharu, and Tuheiava 2012: 10).

Notes

1 The fourteen self-governing Pacific island nations referred to in this chapter are Fiji, Nauru, Tonga, Samoa, Niue, Papua New Guinea, Kiribati, Cook Islands, Tuvalu, Vanuatu, Solomon Islands, Republic of the Marshall Islands, the Federated States of Micronesia, and Palau.
2 The word "(re)visioning" in the title of this chapter is used with reference to David Gegeo's paper, in which he argues for the (re)visioning of place as an expression of traditional knowledge systems within indigenous epistemologies (Gegeo 2001).
3 All data and description of the Outstanding Universal Value of World Heritage properties discussed in this chapter are compiled from information available on the World Heritage Centre website: http://whc.unesco.org.
4 Timiri Hopuu and Martine Ratimassamy, personal communication, Opoa, February 2012.
5 A World Heritage nomination and management plan for the "The Sacred Site of Taputapuatea Marae/TePo, Valley of Opoa" is under development by GIE Océanide, New Caledonia.

References

Legislation

Convention Concerning the Protection of the World Cultural and Natural Heritage (World Heritage Convention) (UNESCO, 1972). Available at: http://whc.unesco.org/archive/convention-en.pdf (accessed March 19, 2015).

Convention for the Safeguarding of the Intangible Cultural Heritage (Intangible Heritage Convention) (UNESCO, 2003). Available at: http://unesdoc.unesco.org/images/0013/001325/132540e.pdf (accessed March 19, 2015).

Other Works

Adams, H.B. (1947) *Tahiti: Memoirs of Arii Tamai*, ed. R. Spiller. New York: Scholars' Facsimile.

Du Plessis, R., and Fairbairn-Dunlop, P. (2009) Ethics of Knowledge Production: Pacific Challenges. *International Social Science Journal*, 60 (195), 109–114.

Eddowes, M. (1991) Ethnohistorical Perspectives on the Marae of the Society Islands: The Sociology of Use. M.A. dissertation. Auckland: Department of Anthropology, University of Auckland.

Ellis, W. (1829) *Polynesian Researches during a Residence of Nearly Eight Years in the Society and Sandwich Islands*, Vols. 1 and 2. London: Henry G. Bohn.

Emory, K.P. (1933) *Stone Remains in the Society Islands*. Honolulu: Bernice P. Bishop Museum.

Emory, K.P. (n.d.) "Traditional History of Maraes in the Society Islands". Unpublished MS. Honolulu: Bernice P. Bishop Museum Archive.

Galla, A. (2008) The First Voice in Heritage Conservation. *International Journal of Intangible Heritage*, 3, 10–25.

Gegeo, D. (2001) Cultural Rupture and Indigeneity: The Challenge of (Re)visioning "Place" in the Pacific. *Contemporary Pacific*, 13 (2), 491–550.

Handy, E.S. (1930) *History and Culture in the Society Islands*. Honolulu: Bernice P. Bishop Museum.

Henry, T. (1928) *Ancient Tahiti*. Honolulu: Bernice P. Bishop Museum.

Hooper, A., and Tinielu, I. (eds) (2012) *Echoes at Fishermen's Rock: Traditional Tokelau Fishing*. Paris: UNESCO.

Hviding, E. (2006) Knowing and Managing Biodiversity in the Pacific islands: Challenges of Conservation in the Marovo Lagoon. *International Social Science Journal*, 58 (1), 69–85.

IWGIA (2012) World Heritage and Indigenous Peoples – A Call To Action. Available at: http://www.iwgia.org/news/search-news?news_id=678 (accessed February 20, 2014).

Kawharu, M. (2009) Ancestral Landscapes and World Heritage from a Māori Viewpoint. *Journal of the Polynesian Society*, 118 (4), 317–338.

Meskell, L. (2013) UNESCO and the Fate of the World Heritage Indigenous Peoples Council of Experts (WHIPCOE). *International Journal of Cultural Property*, 20, 155–174.

Nemani, S. (2011) *Pacific Intangible Heritage Mapping Toolkit*. Noumea: Secretariat of the Pacific Community.

PVS (Polynesian Voyaging Society) (n.d.) Hawaiian Voyaging Traditions. Available at: http://pvs.kcc.hawaii.edu/ike/kalai_waa/kane_building_hokulea.html (accessed February 20, 2014).

Salmon, A. (2009) *Aphrodite's Island: The European Discovery of Tahiti*. Auckland: Viking.

Smith, A. (2010) Archaeology, Local History and Community in French Polynesia. *World Archaeology*, 42 (3), 367–380.

Smith, A. (2013) People and their Environments: Do Cultural and Natural Value Intersect in the Cultural Landscapes on the World Heritage List? In J. Webb, D. Frankel, and S. Lawrence (eds), *Archaeology in Environment and Technology: Intersections and Transformation*. London: Routledge, pp. 181–204.

Smith. A. (ed.) (2012) *World Heritage in a Sea of Islands: The Pacific 2009 Program*. Paris: UNESCO World Heritage Centre.

SPC *et al.* (Secretariat of the Pacific Community, Pacific Islands Forum Secretariat, and UNESCO Pacific Regional Office) (2008 [2002]) *Pacific Regional Framework for the Protection of Traditional Knowledge and Expressions of Culture*. Noumea: Secretariat of the Pacific Community.

Taaroa, M. (1971) *Memoires de Marau Taaroa, dernière reine de Tahiti*, trans. A.T. Pomare. Paris: Musée de l'Homme.

Te Heu Heu, T., Kawharu, M., and Tuheiava, R. (2012) Introduction: World Heritage and Indigeneity. *World Heritage Review*, 62, 10–14.

Titchen, S. (1996) On the Construction of "Outstanding Universal Value": Some Comments on the Implementation of the 1972 UNESCO World Heritage Convention. *Conservation and Management of Archaeological Sites*, 1, 235–242.

UNESCO (1997) Identification of World Heritage Properties in the Pacific: Findings and Recommendations. First Global Strategy Meeting for the Pacific, Suva, Fiji, 15–18 July 1997. Document WHC-97/ CONF.208/INF.8. Paris: UNESCO.

UNESCO (2007) Appeal to the World Heritage Committee from Pacific Island State Parties. Document WHC-07/31.COM/11C. Available at: http://whc.unesco.org/en/sessions/31COM/documents/ (accessed February 22, 2015).

UNESCO (2010) Tentative List of France Submitted to the World Heritage Committee. Available at: http://whc.unesco.org/en/tentativelists/5568/ (accessed February 22, 2015).

UNESCO (2012) Operational Guidelines to the World Heritage Convention. Paris: UNESCO World Heritage Centre. Available at: http://whc.unesco.org/en/guidelines/ (accessed February 22, 2015).

UNESCO and ICHCAP (2013) Traditional Knowledge for Adapting to Climate Change: Safeguarding Intangible Cultural Heritage in the Pacific. Apia, Samoa: UNESCO Office for the Pacific States.

Veitayaki, J. (2005) Fisheries Resource-Use Culture in Fiji and its Implications. In A. Hooper (ed.), *Culture and Sustainable Development in the Pacific*. Canberra: Australian National University Press, pp. 116–130.

Wallin, P. (1993) *Ceremonial Stone Structures: The Archaeology and Ethnohistory of the Marae Complex in the Society Islands, French Polynesia*. Uppsala: Societas Archaeological Upsaliensis.

WIPO (n.d.). Traditional Knowledge. Available at: http://www.wipo.int/tk/en/tk/ (accessed February 22, 2015).

CHAPTER 8

The Kingdom of Death as a Heritage Site: Making Sense of Auschwitz

Jonathan Webber

The Historical Background

In the early summer of 1940, some nine months after the German invasion of Poland which marked the outbreak of World War II, a Nazi concentration camp was established near the town of Oświęcim, in the southwest of the country. It was intended principally for the incarceration of ethnic Poles considered to be opponents of the occupation. Following the German attack on the USSR a year later, large numbers of Soviet prisoners of war were sent to this camp. Six months after that, in the early spring of 1942, the Germans began to send huge transports of Jews to the camp from across the whole of German-occupied Europe. Known to the world as Auschwitz (the German name for the town), the camp then functioned as a vast depot for prisoners of many different national and ethnic origins, whom the Germans either exploited as slave labor for their war economy, housing them principally in three very large labor camps, or, if they were deemed unfit for work, simply murdered them on a massive scale. As key elements of this systematic, centrally planned murder operation, aimed primarily at the Jews of Europe, four large gas chambers were installed in a new sub-camp at Auschwitz-Birkenau, which opened in the spring of 1943, about two miles away from the original camp. There Jews were murdered, principally by gassing, their corpses were incinerated in crematoria, and their ashes scattered. By the time Auschwitz was liberated, by the Red Army on January 27, 1945, about one million Jews had been murdered there, of whom about 40 percent had been deported from Hungary in the spring and early

A Companion to Heritage Studies, First Edition. Edited by William Logan, Máiréad Nic Craith, and Ullrich Kockel.
© 2016 John Wiley & Sons, Inc. Published 2016 by John Wiley & Sons, Inc.

summer of 1944. The other 60 percent came from just about every occupied country in Europe, including Jews from Norway in the north, and from the Greek islands in the south. Auschwitz was not only the largest German concentration camp and the single largest place of Jewish victimhood during the Holocaust, but also the most international. There were many survivors, and so there are many testimonies about it, including some that became particularly well known, for example the books by the Italian Jew Primo Levi and the Hungarian Jew Elie Wiesel. In addition to the one million Jewish deaths, which account for about 92 percent of the total number of human beings murdered in Auschwitz, the other 8 per cent included about 75,000 ethnic Poles, 20,000 Sinti and Roma (Gypsies), 15,000 Soviet prisoners of war, as well as smaller groups of petty German criminals, homosexuals, and Jehovah's Witnesses.[1] It is estimated that about 185,000 Jewish children were murdered in Auschwitz (Gutman and Berenbaum 1994: 417); if nothing else, the mass murder of children defines this clearly as genocide.

The Germans established several other major camps in Poland for the purpose of mass murder – such as Treblinka (870,000 victims), Bełżec (600,000), Sobibór (250,000), and Chełmno (320,000)[2] – but almost nothing physically remains of those camps, as they were systematically dismantled after they were finished with, in order to conceal the evidence of the crimes committed. At Auschwitz, however, the Red Army arrived before the camp could be dismantled: the gas chambers in Birkenau had been blown up with explosives, but much else remained – including prisoner barracks, watch-towers, electrified barbed-wire fencing, the railway tracks leading directly to the gas chambers, and the monumental entry gates, along with large quantities of prisoners' personal belongings. Shortly after the war, the Polish government declared these two sites a memorial, and in 1947 a state museum was established, covering both former camps. Many of the barracks in the base camp were converted into indoor exhibition spaces, and in 1967, a major monument was erected in Birkenau, which was preserved as an open-air museum, with a handful of smaller monuments at places the museum considered of special importance. By this time the museum had become a stable, multifunctional institution dedicated not only to the memorialization of Auschwitz victims but also to scholarship and public education – with a library, research archive, staff of historians, scholarly journal, and dozens of guides. In 1979, UNESCO placed the Auschwitz museum on its World Heritage List, stating that, "by virtue of its activities, the Museum makes an important contribution to the struggle for world peace and security" (cited in Huener 2003: 230). Commemorative ceremonies have been regularly held since the museum was established, especially on the anniversary of the liberation on January 27, often attracting Polish and foreign delegations, which include senior politicians and heads of state as well as Auschwitz survivors. The Auschwitz site has become a major tourist destination, and to this day there are very large numbers of visitors both Polish and from all over the world: more than one million visitors have been coming annually since 2007.[3]

The prime purpose of the Polish government in 1947 in declaring the Auschwitz site a museum and war memorial, which would preserve the remains of the camp and develop its didactic exhibitions, was that it should stand as a key symbol of the brutality suffered by Poles during the German occupation.[4] In parallel, however, over the decades, Auschwitz steadily came to be seen by Jews throughout the world as the key symbol of the Holocaust, although under the Polish communist government little was done *in situ* to emphasize Jewish victimhood there. After 1989, following the collapse of communist rule in Poland, the Auschwitz museum found itself having to reposition the meaning of its composite heritage and re-specify the packaging of the site; it remained under government control, and did not become an independent museum.

To assist in the negotiation of the necessary changes, the Polish government immediately appointed a new body, the International Auschwitz Council, to act in an advisory capacity to the museum's director and the Polish Ministry of Culture, which was responsible for the site. In fact, the messages and "lessons" of Auschwitz, as presented by the museum, had been constantly undergoing change during the communist period, depending on shifts in the ideological stance of central government in Warsaw vis-à-vis the meaning of World War II in official Polish national history. In one sense, the museum was thus accustomed to being responsive to new ways of understanding the history of Auschwitz – but the task of the present-day generation of addressing the subject in the context of the new democratic Poland poses many difficulties.

Making sense of Auschwitz has proved to be deeply complex, because its multilayered and multidimensional past has proved hard to accommodate within a museum context, not to mention the very idea of museologizing the setting of industrialized mass murder and presenting it as "heritage." UNESCO's recognition of Auschwitz as part of its World Heritage List, a register that focuses on the grand and the beautiful, was provocative, to say the least. The nominating documents of 1979 identified the Outstanding Universal Value of the Auschwitz site in terms of its status as "an irrefutable and concrete witness to one of the greatest crimes which has been perpetrated against humanity" (cited in Huener 2003: 230). This was evidently not seen as a contradiction in terms, but rather that a global view of the most outstanding examples of our collective cultural heritage must also include a place of exceptional cruelty and depravity, highlighting the human capacity to inflict suffering and brutality. Or maybe it can also be understood as drawing attention to something more profound – that it is precisely in focusing on crimes "against humanity" and contemplating the very denial of human dignity in that "kingdom of death" that we can perhaps come closer to a more noble definition of cultural heritage, one which stands perhaps as a beacon, challenging humanity to restate, restore, and maintain its universal values, and the morality, ethics, and respect for others that were so utterly denied in Auschwitz. In that sense, Auschwitz does indeed stand for grand ideas, most notably of course the "struggle for world peace and security." Although that vision of a "world heritage" certainly continues to this day to inspire the keynote speeches delivered at the site's major ceremonies, in practice everyday remembrance has broken down into smaller pieces, making room for much more limited and competing perspectives, deriving from the ethnic mosaic of the victims and respective groups of survivors and memory-makers. Auschwitz heritage is thus at the same time both universal and particularist, dissonant and contested. The purpose of this chapter is to offer an introduction to some of these issues.[5]

Making Sense of Auschwitz: The Challenges of a Dissonant, Contested Heritage

For many educators today, the meaning of Auschwitz is comparatively straightforward and uncontroversial. They see Auschwitz as best understood in a universalist, humanist frame of reference – in particular, that it has an emblematic role to remind the world of the importance of human rights and of the dangers of intolerance, fascism, xenophobia, and state-sponsored violence in general. In that sense, the immense scale of the appalling atrocities committed at the Auschwitz concentration camp is to be read in the context of the capacity of humanity to undertake genocide; and so in this view Auschwitz can and indeed should be bracketed together with other instances of genocide elsewhere in the world – before, during, and after World War II. For example, at the opening of the Auschwitz museum in 1947, the Polish Prime Minister Józef Cyrankiewicz (who had himself been a political prisoner in the camp) made a speech declaring that the tragedy of the millions who were murdered there was a warning and a demonstration to the entire world, with (as he put it) the great battle cry, "Never Again!" (Huener 2003: 50). The phrase "Never Again!" entered the language, and became a slogan, widely used elsewhere. It was echoed nearly fifty years later, when the Bangladesh Liberation War Museum was set up in Dhaka in 1996. Its trustees put out a fundraising appeal indicating that they were committing themselves to "the movement of 'Never Again' to violence, atrocities, crimes against humanity and violation of human rights" (cited in Mookherjee 2011: 72). In her analysis of this museum on the other side of the world, Mookherjee (2011: 80, 87–88) indeed refers to the way in which descriptions of genocides in different instances draw on each other, and that there is a transnational cross-referencing of historical atrocities, an "intertextuality and intercitationality" of globally recognizable, cosmopolitan instances of genocide. Maybe, in so doing, this decontextualizes the specificity of each case, as she points out, but on the other hand, it enables them all to be located within broader debates and a broader understanding. In fact, there is substantial interest nowadays in the broad category: memorial museums commemorating atrocities have sprung up all over the world in recent years (Williams 2007), and the growth of this "dark tourism" (Lennon and Foley 2010) would seem to suggest that it relates to a major preoccupation of post-modernity – probably because of the evidence provided by atrocities for the collapse of the Enlightenment project, although Macdonald proposes that it functions today almost as a talismanic activity; that is, to avoid bad history being repeated (Macdonald 2009: 169).

The attempt to universalize the meaning of Auschwitz, and locate it within a broad frame of reference, was certainly a central part of the intention of the founders of the museum during its early years (1947 to 1954). In line with the Stalinist ideology of the Polish state current at the time, the museum's exhibitions and speeches at commemorative events there emphasized that what Auschwitz essentially stood for was socialist heroism and the need for solidarity with all those across the world dedicated to world peace in the ongoing communist struggle against fascists and international imperialists. In the interests of presenting Auschwitz within this context, the regime sent an official commission in 1950 to inspect what was being done there. Its report referred to the museum's exhibitions including a succession of "un-Marxist errors of interpretation," such as the specificity of Germans as the perpetrators of the crimes at Auschwitz (Huener 2003: 99–103). In this early post-war Polish construction of the symbolic meaning of Auschwitz, the specificity of Jewish victimhood was marginalized; to have identified Jews as having constituted more than 90 percent of the victims would have been to clutter, if not to obfuscate, the cultural and political message; it was an inconvenient irrelevance best left to one side.

After the death of Stalin in 1953, the Auschwitz museum moved towards a far less universalist understanding of its historical importance. Auschwitz became instead the central site of Polish commemoration of World War II, financed by central government (with special funds for conservation needs). A new permanent exhibition installed in 1955, on the tenth anniversary of the liberation, thus put the focus on Polish national martyrdom, whilst continuing to marginalize Jewish victimhood; hence Birkenau (which was deemed to symbolize the latter) was neglected, given no exhibition space, and left "to speak for itself," although in fact it slowly became totally overgrown with vegetation. What instead was emphasized was the museologized presentation of Block 11 in the base camp as the key site where Polish political prisoners, resistance fighters, and patriots were tortured and executed. The courtyard outside Block 11, where the executions (by shooting) took place, became – and indeed remains – the main destination for Polish pilgrims to Auschwitz to lay wreaths, recite prayers, and celebrate the Roman Catholic mass. Polish survivors remembered Block 11 as the "block of death," and indeed the museum long ago placed a large sign with those words over its entrance. Of special significance in Block 11 is the cell where Maksymilian Kolbe, the Franciscan priest who gave his life for another prisoner, was confined. Canonized in 1982, Kolbe's self-sacrifice, suffering and death have been part of Auschwitz commemorative ritual since the early post-war years. His former cell is visited by Catholic pilgrims from Poland and abroad. His death was that of a martyred saint, and was treated in the Polish patriotic political narrative of Auschwitz as that of a true hero.

Meanwhile, Auschwitz was becoming for the Jewish world a symbol of the Holocaust, and *only* the Holocaust. The popular Jewish collective memory of the Holocaust has been derived substantially from the memoirs and filmic testimonies of Jewish survivors, facilitating a focus on the victims, not the perpetrators. Interestingly, the Israeli case against Adolf Eichmann in Jerusalem in 1961 was built on eyewitness testimony (unlike the Nuremberg trials of 1945/46, which were conducted by the prosecutors on the basis of documents), and witnesses were deliberately chosen from a wide range of backgrounds and occupations, to emphasize the fact that the catastrophe had fallen on the entire Jewish nation (Wieviorka 1999: 133–36). Given the central role of the Eichmann trial in opening Jewish minds (not only in Israel) to previously suppressed public discussion of the Holocaust, this emphasis on survivors is noteworthy, and it continues to the present day. Survivors from Poland also spread the idea that, given their common experience of anti-Semitism in pre-war and post-war Poland, Poles must have shared the responsibility for what happened at Auschwitz. Why else (according to this view) was Auschwitz located in Poland? To this day, most Jews are simply unaware of the details of the German occupation of Poland – for example, that there was no Polish quisling government in collaboration with the Germans (unlike the situation in some other German-occupied countries), or that the "Polish concentration camps" (as they are still commonly referred to by Jews) were thus not under Polish command, let alone that Auschwitz was originally opened for the incarceration of ethnic Polish political prisoners, or that 100,000 non-Jews were also murdered in Auschwitz, of whom 75,000 were ethnic Poles. Jewish visitors to the Auschwitz museum have thus found themselves alienated from much of what they see there, although in recent years the newly retrained museum guides do indeed provide a well-balanced narrative – even if the permanent main exhibition, largely inherited from what was installed in 1955, still provides relatively little on the subject of the Holocaust as such. A long-overdue new permanent exhibition is still on the drawing board.

Auschwitz represents for Jews the immensity of the Holocaust, a catastrophe completely without parallel. It represents the near-total destruction of an entire civilization across virtually the whole European continent. For several centuries, the center of the Jewish world had been in Europe, particularly in Poland: about 90 percent of the Jews of the world lived in Europe in the middle of the nineteenth century, although because of emigration (principally to the United States) the amount had dropped to about

60 percent by 1939 (DellaPergola 1994: 62). The sheer horror and brutality with which Jews were uprooted from their homes and taken away to be murdered defy normal language, normal categories of explanation – and most Jews report an overpowering sense of numbness after a visit to Auschwitz. If Auschwitz is the symbol of the Holocaust, for Jews it is a symbol of the incomprehensible anti-Semitism that rendered the living Jewish world in literally thousands of towns and villages an ever-present absence.

None of that, of course, can be seen at Auschwitz today. For Jewish visitors, the world that was destroyed is entirely in their imagination, or it is to be heard from the Holocaust survivors whom they routinely bring with them to the place. Nor, unlike what Auschwitz has been made to mean for Poles, is there much by way of heroism here. The artifacts on display in the glass showcases of the Auschwitz museum, such as the mounds of women's hair, worn-out shoes or twisted spectacles, are perfectly powerful as representations of loss and absence – but they are pathetic and banal, "the collected debris of a destroyed civilization" (as James Young puts it), forcing us to recall the victims as the Germans have remembered them to us (Young 1993: 132). They reveal nothing of the vitality or spirituality of the ancient civilization that the Jews first brought with them to Europe and then developed there over many centuries. Given the secular, racist ideology of the Nazis, it is barely meaningful even to refer to Jewish victimhood during the Holocaust as a case of martyrdom. Maybe there were some exceptional cases – appropriate examples from Auschwitz of courageous Jewish spirituality and commitment to the faith are commonly cited in Orthodox Jewish literature (see e.g. Rosenbaum 1976) – but in the main they were not suffering and dying for any higher good, and certainly (unlike the Polish resistance fighters) did not meet their deaths as a result of any conscious choice of that kind.[6]

The two cases, then – the Polish case and the Jewish case – are not at all symmetrical. How can the Auschwitz museum hope to represent them both in a single master narrative? The short answer is that it cannot. An approach grounded in a universalist human rights framework can certainly make good headway, but Jews do not usually see it that way at all. What Auschwitz tends to symbolize for Jews is not so much humanity's inhumanity, but rather humanity's inhumanity to the Jews. For many Jews, visiting Auschwitz is not a tourist experience at all – it is to visit the real place where so many of their family members were actually murdered. Auschwitz is what happened to their family, and the traumatic realization that they themselves, or their parents or grandparents, could have ended up there as well. What Auschwitz is made to symbolize for present-day Jews is the constant, nightmarish reminder of where even some relatively simple anti-Semitic incident can lead. Week in, week out, throughout the year, the Auschwitz museum today is visited by large groups of Israeli soldiers, Israeli teenagers, and Jewish schoolchildren from around the world, whose educators and guides see it as their duty to emphasize Jewish victimhood, to explain how Europe stopped functioning as the major home for the Jews of the world, and to elaborate in a nationalist fashion how this role is fulfilled nowadays by the state of Israel. For the past 25 years, there has been a major annual event in spring at the Auschwitz museum, on a date in the Jewish calendar fixed long ago by the Israeli parliament as Holocaust Remembrance Day (not January 27). Known as the March of the Living, the event now attracts about 10,000 teenage Jewish participants from around the world, waving Israeli flags, singing "Am Yisrael Chai" ("The Jewish People Lives On"), and listening to speeches that emphasize "Jewish victory over Nazism" and "the triumph of life over death"; that is, post-Holocaust Jewish survival and, in particular, post-Holocaust Jewish achievements in the state of Israel (Sheramy 2007).

From what has been indicated above, it follows that neither Poles nor Jews are encouraged today to place Auschwitz in a broad frame of reference or to see its universalist messages as constituting its central significance. On the contrary, what seems to present itself as the common denominator of these two very different sets of messages and "lessons" is a sense of patriotism – their own respective patriotism, of course, in the context of their very different ethnic and political histories. Both the Polish national martyrdom narrative and the Jewish triumphant survivalist narrative leave each other out of the account.

Post-1989: New Challenges, New Negotiations

Prior to 1989, the Auschwitz museum followed the wording of the 1947 Polish act of parliament in describing its mission as being to commemorate "the martyrdom of the Polish nation and other nations," a phrase which was stated in prominent signage on the site; and the main monument in Birkenau (prominently located at the end of the railway tracks, between two of the former gas chambers) identified the identity of the Auschwitz victims simply as amounting to 4 million, a figure which it also used in its publications as late as 1985 (e.g. Piper 1985: 132).

In 1989 there began the complex and tortuous processes of change. In 1991 the same museum historian acknowledged that the figure of 4 million (which had derived from Soviet, American, and other sources at the Nuremberg trials) was a major distortion, admitting that he himself (amongst many others) had used it (Piper 1991: 61, n.41). The presentation of the new figures, which showed (amongst other things) that Polish victimhood at Auschwitz – substantial though it was, at 75,000 – was merely 8 percent of the total, clearly demanded the negotiation of quite a new approach. There was in any case quite a new political context: Poland had been occupied and divided up between three European empires throughout the whole of the nineteenth century, and so finally, in 1989, it was once again an independent country, for the first time in 200 years (other than the short interwar period of 1918–39). Polish national culture began to be reformulated, and amongst many new trends (including the development of close Polish political relations with Israel), the most spectacular change has been a rapid growth of interest in the role of the Jews in Polish national history and culture (they had been 10 percent of the pre-war population, and as high as 30 percent in many of the large cities, including Warsaw). The subject had been repressed under communism – it was Poland's "difficult heritage" (Macdonald 2009) – but now the public, especially young people, began to demand access to it and ethical reflection about it.[7]

With the support of the International Auschwitz Council – half of whose members are Jewish, and whose Polish chairman, Władysław Bartoszewski, had himself been awarded "Righteous Gentile" status by Yad Vashem (Israel's Holocaust museum and remembrance authority in Jerusalem) for his courageous support for Jews during the war – the Auschwitz museum began to open itself up to outside influences. The annual March of the Living, for example, would have been unthinkable much before 1989, but has now become an established feature of the museum's memorial landscape; and collaboration between the museum and Yad Vashem, for example in reciprocal access to archives or the training of guides, has developed exponentially: the interpretation of Auschwitz is in other words also being undertaken in places far removed from its location. Birkenau has been cleaned up, and the vegetation has been cut down. It is no longer un-interpreted: a fine new exhibition in the restored former "sauna" building there focuses explicitly on Jewish victimhood, and since 1995 the limited signage in Birkenau (formerly including Russian and German) has been significantly expanded, and now appears just in three languages – Polish, English, and Hebrew. It is a major statement of new realities. Polish martyrdom is still there, of course, but it has receded in prominence (the old Polish signs defining the museum's mission and identity dating from 1947 have been removed, as has the sign outside Block 11 announcing the "block of death"). The International Auschwitz Council found a new text for the inscriptions at the main monument in Birkenau, not only giving the new figure for the total number of victims ("about 1.5 million") but also stating that they were "mainly Jews from various countries of Europe." Not a word here about Poles.[8]

This new post-1989 preoccupation with finding ways to incorporate the Jewish narrative at Auschwitz has in practice pushed the idea of cosmopolitan genocide even further away. It seems, in fact, that although there are glimpses of the language of universal human rights (especially at the main commemorative ceremonies), there can never in practice be a single history of Auschwitz, nor can the remembrance of Auschwitz ever be a unified phenomenon. Unfortunately, more or less at the very moment when the Jewish narrative was beginning to make its appearance at Auschwitz, a major controversy erupted over the presence of a Carmelite convent. It had been established in 1984 in an unused building adjacent to the base camp. Jewish leaders, conscious that the Auschwitz site was not only "de-Judaized" but now being overtly "Christianized," demanded its removal. The debate, which was well publicized internationally, lasted several years, and at times it became quite hostile, arousing pain and anger on both sides, where both Jewish anti-Polish stereotypes and Polish anti-Jewish stereotypes emerged in public statements. What was at stake was the stewardship of the Auschwitz memory in relation to a highly contested sense of moral ownership. Eventually an agreement was negotiated (to disallow all places of worship and religious symbols at the Auschwitz site), and in 1992 the convent was relocated to a new purpose-built building a very short distance away, but outside the borders of the museum.[9] Understandable it may have been, but it was an astonishing act of withdrawal.

One might have thought that religion would have been ideally suited to convey a sense of the overpowering mystery of Auschwitz, or the moral and ethical dilemmas of all the categories of population caught up in the events – perpetrators, bystanders, victims, and rescuers – as well as the dilemmas of present-day remembrances. Instead of retreating, religion could perhaps have had a more proactive role in Auschwitz memorialization, especially in those areas where it has well-developed expertise, such as in providing rituals that mourn human suffering and loss, or in promoting healing, the universalist aspects of peace and reconciliation, and the spiritual and moral repair of the world, based on a sense of hope for the future. In practice, interfaith dialogue (respecting others by encouraging them to speak and listening to what they say) has since 1992 been undertaken elsewhere, at the Center for Dialog and Prayer in buildings adjacent to the new convent – near the museum but not part of the official Auschwitz site itself.

It should be added that the authenticity of this location is blurred: the museum itself is far from occupying the 40 square kilometers of the historical Auschwitz *Interessengebiet* (special zone); it is very considerably smaller than that (Auschwitz III, for example, is not part of the museum at all), and in that sense it is a representation that is a historical misrepresentation – a "dark site" that has been abbreviated as part of the commoditization process (Lennon and Foley 2010: 49–50, 166–67).[10] Moving the convent away from the camp was a rhetorical device, negotiated for symbolic purposes – for example, to provide the practical possibility of delineating between reverential and non-reverential spaces (Lennon and Foley 2010: 106) – rather than as an act made in the interests of historical truth. Indeed, similar but less publicized disputes have arisen over the use of other sites near the museum, such as the development of a supermarket and a nightclub. The International Auschwitz Council also had to deal with a request from Elie Wiesel in 1996 to remove all the white-painted wooden crosses and Stars of David that had been planted in the 1980s by a Polish youth group in a remote part of Birkenau (a field of ashes). It agreed to the request (though not unanimously), and consequently there was a vociferous protest amongst Catholic Poles which again brought the issues into the media spotlight. The whole question of the moral ownership of Auschwitz remains contested, and still comes to the surface from time to time.

Multiple Narratives and Alternative Histories

Just as there was a "mosaic" of victims, so too is there a "mosaic" of memories. It was very common during World War II that places of mass murder were used by the Germans for different groups of victims (Sinti and Roma were often taken to Jewish cemeteries to be shot), and Auschwitz was no exception. In historical terms, the result is that many places of mass murder encompassed complex sequences of events and may often carry a number of quite different meanings. Auschwitz is an exceptionally complex example of this, especially since it has come to symbolize not only the collective horrors of the Holocaust and Polish national martyrdom, but also the suffering of other groups with whom neither Jews nor Poles necessarily feel any close sense of identification. The fact that members of these groups were murdered in the same place does not in itself provide them with a sense of shared destiny; on the contrary, each group tends to see its experience as unique to itself and to its own history. It is obvious that Jews, Poles, Germans, Russians, and Sinti and Roma contextualize Auschwitz differently, in terms of the positioning of Auschwitz within their own ethnic and national histories. They all have different stereotypes, different contours of memory, and different rites of remembrance which relate to their own long-term ethnic and national experiences, and also to their respective cultural differences, in terms of which they go about making sense of the past more generally.

These differences have for a long time been essentialized and institutionalized at the Auschwitz museum. The exhibitions there are, significantly, of two types. The main exhibition, in several barracks, attempts a universal history of Auschwitz: it explains how prisoners arriving at Auschwitz were "selected" by the SS doctors either for immediate death in the gas chambers, estimated at the horrific figure of 865,000 people (Piper 1991: 93), or, alternatively, if they were considered able-bodied, to be used as slave labor. The exhibition presents a detailed but generalized, largely de-ethnicized description of both the murder process at the gas chambers and the rigors of everyday life for the registered prisoners in the labor camp. However, in addition to the main exhibition is another type of exhibition entirely, consisting of a series of about a dozen "national" exhibitions (which together are three or four times larger than the main exhibition) and housed in a number of other barracks. Ostensibly the museum is here giving the opportunity to various European associations of former Auschwitz prisoners (or other relevant agencies) to give their own Auschwitz narratives; and indeed each of them clearly presents a different museological perspective on the importance of Auschwitz in their own particular national circumstances during World War II. Through these national exhibitions, which have for some time included a Jewish exhibition (updated by Yad Vashem in 2013) and more recently a Sinti and Roma exhibition, visitors who have enough time to view all the displays can absorb the idea that there is in fact a specifically Hungarian narrative of Auschwitz, a specifically Dutch narrative, an Italian narrative, a French narrative, and so on. These narratives are all structured quite differently, telling quite different stories, identifying quite different heroes and villains, displaying quite different photographs, and in general demonstrating the very different ways that Auschwitz heritage is to be understood.

These two types of exhibition coexist at Auschwitz as "alternative pasts" (Lennon and Foley 2010: 162) – one of more universal character, the other of very decidedly particularist character. Although it is perfectly true that the Nazis arrested non-Jewish communists from many European countries and deported them to Auschwitz, the overwhelming majority of people deported from those countries were Jews, and were deported to Auschwitz only because they were Jews – and not because of any criminal charges as such, as was the case with the Polish political prisoners accused of anti-Nazi activity or other "asocial" behavior. Jews came to Auschwitz as families, even as whole communities; the "criminals" came as individuals. Representing Auschwitz victimhood on the basis of nationality was originally motivated partly to emphasize the Polish communist idea of the international reach of imperialist fascism, but it had the added advantage that the overwhelmingly Jewish character of Auschwitz victimhood could be suitably concealed behind an international façade. The museum's official guidebooks in communist times certainly listed Jews – but as one "nationality" among more than twenty – and so indeed the main monument at Birkenau replicated this by having plaques in all the relevant European languages, including Hebrew and Yiddish – and more recently Ladino, the native language of many of the Jews from Greece, of whom about 55,000 were deported to Auschwitz (Piper 1991: 78).

In short, the museum has backed away from imposing across the site a single master narrative, for example on the subject of genocide. In practice, however, it offers multiple perspectives on the story it has to tell. It certainly is not at all made clear at the museum whose history should prevail, in whose history Auschwitz is or should be located, or whose memory it belongs to. German history? Jewish history? Polish history? European history? World history? It is an ethical dilemma. The museum exhibitions make no explicit attempt to encourage visitors even to ask these questions, although implicitly it does suggest that Auschwitz belongs to all of these, and more. The Holocaust is both a Jewish catastrophe and a universal catastrophe at the same time; the challenge is for the memorialization of it to look both ways simultaneously.

As if Auschwitz history is not complicated enough as it is, a further difficulty arises when one considers that the survivors of the camp who wrote memoirs, and so contributed to the collective memory of the place, would not necessarily have shared the same experiences. An "Auschwitz survivor" does not mean someone who survived the gas chamber (that simply did not happen), but rather a prisoner who survived the labor camps at Auschwitz. In addition to three very large labor camps – the original or base camp (Auschwitz I), Birkenau (Auschwitz II), and Monowitz (Auschwitz III) – there were as many as forty much smaller auxiliary camps, for anything between a few dozen and several thousand slave laborers. It is hard to generalize their experiences. As Jonathan Huener puts it:

> While one prisoner worked in the fishery of a nearby auxiliary camp, another laid railroad ties; while one prisoner never saw … Auschwitz I, another never left it; and while many prisoners may never have seen the gas chambers and crematoria at Birkenau, the majority of Jews deported there saw nothing else. (Huener 2003: 9)

Certainly all prisoners suffered from poor housing, inadequate diet, exhausting labor, and interminably long open-air roll calls (in all weathers), all of which led (as intended) to a high mortality rate. But the system of prisoner administration was designed to discourage solidarity among the prisoners; on the contrary, the intention was to breed rivalries, fears, and resentments among them. There was a definite hierarchy among the prisoners, with Jews at the bottom and Germans (German criminals) at the top. Moreover, each individual work unit had its own foreman, known as a *kapo*, who would routinely not only be given special privileges but also unlimited power over the members of their unit, including beatings, even fatal ones. Conditions for the prisoners thus varied enormously, according to their work assignment and location, relations with their *kapos*, and especially by their national or "racial" status, which was clearly signaled by different colored triangles on the prisoner uniforms they were obliged to wear. Some jobs were relatively "easy" (such as indoor clerical or administrative work, including the sorting of personal belongings brought by deportees). Some, meanwhile, were particularly gruesome, such as the work of the Sonderkommando, Jewish prisoners who were ordered to service the gas chambers and crematoria – for example, cleaning the gas chambers of feces, blood, and urine after each batch of gassing, cutting the hair off female corpses, examining all corpses for gold teeth, rings, and earrings, and then carrying the corpses to the crematoria ovens where they would be incinerated.

The special case of the Sonderkommando, who (other than the victims themselves) really did see the apparatus of genocide close up, makes it particularly clear that there is no single master narrative of the Auschwitz prisoner experience. An important point follows from this. It is obviously impossible to remember or memorialize all the different individual experiences of well over one million people who were deported to Auschwitz, and yet, at the commemorative ceremonies, it is the survivors who are the guests of honor and describe their experiences. To think of them in such contexts as "typical" or suitably representative may well be to miss the point. All Auschwitz memories, different as they may be from each other, may have something to say, even if they may be historically unreliable and subject to change over time; they can all contribute something to the multilayered, multidimensional knowledge of the subject.[11] After all, one cannot assume that all Jews or all Hungarians or all Poles saw the same Auschwitz. They didn't.

To take the Jewish case here: a self-consciously Zionist approach to the collective Jewish memory of the Holocaust tends to emphasize ancient ethnic and religious hatreds, in other words to locate the Holocaust in the context of a long history of European anti-Semitism, pogroms, and anti-Jewish violence. But other models are also possible, and can be found in some of the personal memoirs of survivors – those for example which would stress warm memories of a pre-war world where the Jews lived happily in their diaspora environments, in relatively peaceful coexistence. So the genocide is then understood as the "politics" that came not from the inside but from the outside (for example, Nazi propaganda about Jewish Bolshevism); this is what brought about the fundamental shift in attitude, causing their neighbors to turn against them. These two rival models are of course over-generalized, but interestingly enough they can both be found as explanatory memory formulae in other instances of genocide.[12] Certainly it is clear from survivor accounts that Jews collectively hold in their heads more than one broad narrative structure of what happened – after all, like any minority group, European Jews possess multiple identities in terms of their sense of belonging to the majority societies in which they live. But the Nazis were not the slightest interested in those cultural nuances that had previously mattered to Jews – all Jews, without exception, were to be deported and murdered. They all met each other, as one people, in the gas chambers of Auschwitz. But in terms of internal Jewish history, there is no one "Jewish memory of the Holocaust" as regards its relationship with what had gone before.

What is to be found at Auschwitz today are thus three kinds of memory and alternative histories – the bland "historical facts" (assembled by the scholar-specialists, and purveyed by the museum's exhibitions and guides), the different national histories (essentialized, if not also politicized), and the personal memories of survivors (relied upon at the commemorative ritual events, even if conventional political messages and quasi-universalist slogans are superimposed on what they have to say). The coexistence of these disparate messages is an uneasy one. Contesting the pedagogic credentials of the scholar-specialists, tour leaders of Jewish groups from Israel, particularly youth groups, have made every effort to refuse the services of the museum's guides (otherwise obligatory for all groups); and after much negotiation, a compromise agreement was reached in recent years to permit the survivors and Jewish educators who accompany such groups to give their speeches after the museum's guides have given their own explanations at particular points along the visitor route. The realities presented by the survivors are quite different from what the guides have to say: they derive from their experiences and their personal emotions. In any case, they would not at the time have known the broader historical facts, let alone the centrally planned schemes of the perpetrators. But the solution here parallels the Israeli approach: Yad Vashem in Jerusalem made it a priority in its new exhibition (of 2005) to represent the Holocaust through ninety well-documented individual stories of victims and survivors, in order to bring a very personal encounter between the story and the storytellers (Williams 2007: 7, 33). Meanwhile what persists at Auschwitz are the contradictions and paradoxes.

Contradictions and Paradoxes

Perhaps the clearest evidence for the contradictions and paradoxes embedded in the Auschwitz memory is to be found in the physical appearance of the site today. There is much for the visitor to see which seems to confirm its authenticity as historical heritage, even if the barbed wire is not original, and the gas chamber in the base camp was heavily (and somewhat clumsily) reconstructed. There are also buildings which are in ruins, most notably the four main gas chambers in Birkenau. They genuinely belong, as ruins, to the wartime Auschwitz history: the ruins of one of them, gas chamber and crematorium number 4, mark the success of the prisoner uprising there of October 1944 (see note 6). The other three gas chambers were blown up by the Germans, in an attempt to conceal the evidence of their crimes as the Red Army was approaching, but they undertook that operation too late and too hastily; the ruins of the three gas chambers are still present on the site to this day. Furthermore, a very large number of the barracks in the labor camp in Birkenau are also in ruins, but for quite different reasons – after the war they were simply dismantled by locals seeking building materials, or (because the museum had neither the funds nor the political will to restore them, given that Birkenau was seen as largely non-Polish in its historical importance) they slowly collapsed over the course of time; the majority of them vanished.

The existence of these four kinds of ruin, side by side, confuses the issues. It is a multidimensionality not all of which is relevant to the story the museum now wants to tell; and so, in an effort to renew its credibility as the guardian of this heritage, the museum has in recent years launched a major international fundraising appeal to restore the ruined barracks and prevent further deterioration, although what precisely should be done with the ruins of the gas chambers is by no means self-evident.[13] Still, the question remains whether all these surviving realia really do appropriately represent Auschwitz as the authentic historical epicenter of evil, or whether the need for the tourist gaze regarding these visual exotica should not be taken as decisive. What difference would it make to the meaning of the site if the ruins slowly sank quietly into the ground? After all, no original structures remain at all of the death camp at Bełżec – does this mean that once the physical realities are gone, its meaning vanishes also?[14] What actually is Auschwitz, then? In one sense it is obviously a cemetery, probably the largest cemetery known to humanity. But of course Auschwitz heritage is atrocity heritage; the site was never intended or treated as a cemetery. So Auschwitz is a cemetery, but at the same time it is not a cemetery.

It is questions and uncertainties such as these which give an indication of how fundamentally subversive are the issues relating both to the original genocide and how it is to be memorialized. If the present-day appearance of the Auschwitz site is important simply for educational purposes – to document the basic facts of what happened at Auschwitz, and then to teach new generations moral and political lessons about the horrors of that past history, which must be avoided in the future – then the apparatus of the evil, as represented in the surviving buildings and other structures erected on the orders of the perpetrators, clearly take priority. After all, UNESCO's definition of the Outstanding Universal Value of the World Heritage to be found at Auschwitz was in terms of its being "an irrefutable and concrete witness to one of the greatest crimes which has been perpetrated against humanity." In other words, the focus, in heritage terms, is on the crime. But what about the suffering of the victims, and in particular the remembrance of the dead? Can that objective also find its architectural representation on the site, or does that (once again) clutter the image? Can the museum effectively do both? In addition to erecting numerous weatherproof information stands (some of them bearing wartime photos taken by the SS, to give visitors a sense of how the place looked at the height of the massive deportations from Hungary in 1944), the museum decided to install a handful of discreet black granite tombstones, with simple memorial inscriptions, in some key places in Birkenau (behind the ruins of the gas chambers and the ponds of ashes, for example) – but there is no current intention to reserve at least part of the site for the installation of, say, one million such tombstones. In the interests of pursuing an "educational" mission, the site does not allow for the Auschwitz dead to have their individual tombstones; the families of the victims must remember them elsewhere.

Auschwitz education must present the facts accessibly, but in so doing it often suffers similarly from the temptation to oversimplify and cut out inconvenient issues. The celebrated description by the Auschwitz survivor Primo Levi of what he called a moral and ethical "grey zone" (Levi 1989: 22–51) – with reference, for example, to the Sonderkommando prisoners at Auschwitz who were simultaneously victims as well as being collaborators with the perpetrators, and who therefore may in some sense be said to have shared some moral culpability for the mass murders there – is a constant reminder of the philosophical problems in finding a suitable way of telling the story of what happened in Auschwitz. Genocide is a world that is turned upside down, where ordinary peacetime morality, or normal social relations across boundaries between social groups, can no longer be relied upon. But the museological focus (also found in many Holocaust museums across the world) on "the evidence of the crime," using familiar photographs, alongside the documents and other displayed artifacts, probably ends up over-domesticating the telling of the story – in contrast with the complex theoretical and historiographic challenges of presenting Auschwitz as a fundamentally subversive reality, including its incomprehensibility and unrepresentability. To convey the "historical facts" in smooth documentary style, with neat, coherent, and conceptually unproblematized descriptions, cannot really do justice to the enormity of the place. Auschwitz is not to be explained according to the usual conventions of understanding the past. Over-domesticating a comprehension of genocidal violence may miss the point. If, as it is said by so many nowadays, the reality of Auschwitz should change the way we think about the world, we have not really begun to make sense of it unless we learn how to reassess how we retell the story of the tragedy.[15] How far, for example, should a dignified silence dominate its landscape, and how far should all the different voices be accommodated?

There is no "final solution" to these problems. The Auschwitz site is characterized by numerous contradictions – as an emblematic site of "undesirable heritage," it is simultaneously a symbol, a cemetery, a pilgrimage site, a museum, a theater for the enactment of multiple memorial events, and a place of "dark tourism" that continues to attract huge numbers of visitors. The incorporation of these entangled, dissonant attributes is constantly being contested and renegotiated.

Contemplated from afar, Auschwitz is a convenient shorthand symbol. Encountered close-up, however, it not a symbol, it is a real place. For example, tourists tend to speak about visiting "Auschwitz" rather than visiting "the Auschwitz museum," as if in some sense the site is still so totally authentic that it possesses its original character, whatever that may be. They can say that they are visiting "Auschwitz" because of the simultaneities: Auschwitz is both a symbol and not a symbol at the same time. But what is the "real" Auschwitz, and where is it physically? Is it to be found in Birkenau's wide open spaces and ruins, where so much has disappeared, or is it in the many different museum exhibitions inside the well-maintained, freshly repainted brick-built barracks of the original camp of Auschwitz I? Is it a problem that Auschwitz I seems so relatively sanitized, even aestheticized? Maybe for some it is, but the truth is that different people in any case move through the place seeing it through different mental landscapes, depending for example on their ethnic background, whether they are relatives of people who were deported and murdered there, how much education and what kind of education they already have about Auschwitz, or whether they are students of political history or pilgrims wishing to meditate or say prayers in memory of the dead. For many foreign Jewish visitors, the name "Auschwitz" may be profoundly part of their consciousness, but its status does not depend on its existence in real space at all. They can ignore the physical surroundings if they find that it is of no intrinsic interest to them; like many other aspects of present-day Poland, those realities are not what they have come to see or to experience. Like all pilgrims everywhere, they see things which are not physically there and not even signposted, and they ignore many things which are actually there and which *are* signposted. It is not possible to generalize whether they find it comforting to see the huge crowds of visitors from around the world (reinforcing the Jewish desire that the Auschwitz story is universally known), or whether, on the contrary, they are lost in their own thoughts and so ignore others and make no effort to interact with them.

Whilst such different mental landscapes among the visitors may thus coexist synchronically, at any one moment in time, especially during the height of the tourist season in midsummer, the existence of such multidimensionality is best witnessed diachronically, at the annual large-scale commemoration ceremonies that are held successively on the main anniversaries – both those held in the enclosed courtyard of Block 11 or in the large space adjacent to the main monument in Birkenau. At such times, Auschwitz becomes a theatrical stage set for the performance of quite different, quite specific imagined meanings and associated rituals. The rhetorical power of such events gains its immediacy from the realization among the participants that the "real" Auschwitz today is indeed a theater for the enactment of memory. In historical terms, the key landmark event (other than the political rallies that were held in the early years after the war) was the visit of the Polish-born Pope John-Paul II in 1979. After a brief stop at Block 11, he arrived in Birkenau, to be greeted by a vast crowd, estimated at 300,000 people: an altar and gigantic cross had been specially erected, transforming the site into a public Christian setting suitable for his celebration of the Mass. The homily which he delivered there stressed Poland's wartime sacrifice, which he framed as an integral part of the conscience of contemporary humanity and the Christian commitment to human rights; but he also specifically paid homage to Jewish suffering at Auschwitz, very possibly the first public figure to do so at a major ceremony there. The presence, authority, and personal magnetism of a Polish pope clearly made a profound impression, and although it would be ten years before Poland emerged from communist rule, this event probably laid the foundations for the democratic internationalization of Auschwitz as a memorial site that has occurred since 1989.[16] Important ceremonies, attended by numerous heads of state and Auschwitz survivors in the presence of massive crowds, were held in Birkenau in 1995 to mark the fiftieth anniversary of the liberation of Auschwitz, and again for the sixtieth anniversary in 2005. These were of course secular, civic rituals, where instead of Christian symbols huge overhead television screens dominated the scene. Much smaller events held nowadays, integral elements of this internationalization process encouraged and negotiated by the International Auschwitz Council, include the annual March of the Living event for Jewish youth, and a high-profile visit by the Israeli parliament (involving half of its members) that was held on January 27, 2014. In all these cases, the same space at Birkenau, offering an exceptionally powerful architectural environment at the main monument there, alongside the railway tracks and the ruins of the gas chambers and crematoria, is perfectly "real"; but its elements become used as theatrical props for quite different occasions, quite different cultural enactments of the imagined meanings of the Auschwitz memory. The setting "explains" and animates the various theatrical performances, permitting the unpacking of the historical imagination in the public space.

Conclusion

In reviewing the multidimensionality, contradictions, and paradoxes of present-day Auschwitz, and thinking about the future of Auschwitz, what emerges is not at all a stable, coherent picture, but rather, as befits a place of such complex heritage, a jumble of many different styles of meaning from many different sources – a colorful collage blending together reality, dreams, memories, and political visions of all kinds. The ideas are often tangled and chaotic, without any evident need for chronological sequence. On the contrary, past, present, and future coexist here unselfconsciously. In approaching the relevance of the past, there is no boundary of any importance between the historical and the contemporary. Episodic, disconnected moments from the historical facts, survivor memories, and national histories are linked up with subsequent competing political or spiritual messages that claim an integrated view. In one sense it is simply disorder, reflecting the basic truth that Auschwitz memory is divided and fragmented. In another sense, when looked at in this way, it is an extremely potent mixture, allowing in a sense of the subversive character both of the genocide itself and its aftermath. Inasmuch as the genocide tore the previous world to pieces, it is not inappropriate that the memory is pieced together from the fragments that were left behind. There is no single narrative, nor a holistic outlook on what happened. Building up a multifaceted picture of Auschwitz out of those fragments and partial views parallels its status as simultaneously being a symbol, a cemetery, a pilgrimage site, a museum, a theater, and a place of "dark" tourism. It is inclusive of all of these. There is not, and probably never can be, just one single authority to whom Auschwitz morally belongs. The Auschwitz memory needs to address many issues at once – both the local and the universal; both the specific and the more general; both one's neighbor and those who are far away; both the names of the particular individuals who are known to have perished, and also an understanding of the wider historical processes which brought about the catastrophe; both the empirical facts of the deliberate, systematic, and planned rationality of mass murder, and also a making sense, in the perspective of the victims, of the fundamental incomprehensibility and meaninglessness of Auschwitz and the entire genocidal enterprise. The Auschwitz memorial site is thus in this sense a very strange place – and, in terms of its mission, understandably so.

What "Never Again" must surely mean is the commitment to restore moral decency and ethical integrity to humanity, in a context also of intercultural respect and dialogue. Learning from the horrors of the evil and inhumanity of what happened at Auschwitz means to take on such a commitment. Perhaps it is yet another of those paradoxes, but maybe it is through contact with the kingdom of death that people can find the meaning of life.

Notes

1 The figures given here are based on the landmark, authoritative study by Franciszek Piper (1991), then head of the Auschwitz museum's historical research department, which also analyses the many different estimates that were then in circulation. Piper estimates that about 200,000 people survived Auschwitz (Piper 1991: 92) – an extraordinarily high figure (certainly when compared to other death camps), although it includes prisoners who were transferred to other camps and may not have survived the war; but it does help explain the high number of survivor testimonies.

2 These figures have been used for a long time and can be found in respective entries in Gutman (1990). Recent research, however, suggests they are most probably all in need of downward revision.

3 Visitor figures reached 1,430,000 in 2012 – a record number since the museum was established in 1947 – though they dipped slightly in 2013 (to 1,330,000). The majority are foreigners (Polish visitors account for only about 30 percent of the total), indicating that visitor interest in Auschwitz is far from waning (for details of these figures, see the museum reports on the Auschwitz museum website: www.auschwitz.org, last accessed January 29, 2014). Particularly during the midsummer tourist high season, the museum is packed with people – contrary to some popular images of Auschwitz as a lonely, desolate place (a stereotype that may be encouraged by present-day photos focusing on such features as the symbolic entry gates, but which do not show the crowds of visitors).

4 For a full account of Polish government intentions at that time, see e.g. Huener (2003: 48–58, 76–78).

5 It has not been possible here to cite (let alone analyze) the vast literature which now exists on the history of Auschwitz, or a similarly vast literature of survivor memoirs. On the history of Auschwitz, an important source is Długoborski and Piper (2000), an encyclopedic, fully indexed, five-volume work covering the following themes: the establishment and organization of the camp (vol. 1), conditions of the life and work of prisoners in the labor camp (vol. 2), mass murder (vol. 3), the resistance movement (vol. 4), and an epilogue (vol. 5). The fifth volume, covering the liquidation of the camp and some of the post-war trials, includes a 50 page bibliography and a 100 page, day-by-day "calendar of the most important events" in the history of Auschwitz. A leading one-volume survey, though with a slightly wider brief, is Gutman and Berenbaum (1994). Much of the material in the present chapter is based on my own fieldwork at the Auschwitz museum over a number of years, although excellent sources for this material can also be found in Young (1993: 128–54) and the equally magisterial Van Pelt and Dwork (1996: 354–78).

6 Young mothers accompanying small children and who refused to be separated from them when the children were sent to the gas chamber should, however, be included in the category of those who made conscious choices. One important Auschwitz event also ought to be noted: an uprising in October 1944 led by the Jewish prisoners of the Sonderkommando, which succeeded in destroying one of the gas chambers in Birkenau using gunpowder that had been smuggled into the camp (Gutman 1990: 115–16). They were all executed.

7 For a good overview of this reformulation of national identity in post-communist Poland, see Mach (2007).

8 On the history of the negotiation of this new inscription, see Webber (1993).

9 For a detailed description of the episode, see e.g. Young (1993: 144–50) and Klein (2001). For a discussion by scholars and theologians in a spirit of dialogue, see Rittner and Roth (1991). See also Webber (2006).

10 Hence there are certainly buildings belonging to the history of Auschwitz, but are outside the museum's boundaries surrounding Auschwitz I and Birkenau. They have for decades been used for different purposes – most notably the *Lagererweiterung* (camp extension), used as barracks for the Polish army and as low-income housing, the villa occupied by the camp's commandant Rudolf Höss, today used as an ordinary dwelling, and the *Kommandantur* at Birkenau, used since 1983 as the local village church. The exclusion of the *Lagererweiterung* is particularly serious: as Van Pelt and Dwork note, "A misconstruction of history begins right in the parking lot: visitors think they have arrived at the periphery of Auschwitz I; in fact, they are already in the middle of the camp as it existed in 1945" (Van Pelt and Dwork 1996: 359–60).

11 The survivor turned professional historian Saul Friedländer puts the point powerfully: "An individual voice suddenly arising in the course of an ordinary historical narrative of events [such as the Holocaust] … can … pierce the … smugness of scholarly detachment and 'objectivity'. Such a disruptive function would hardly be necessary in a history of the price of wheat on the eve of the French Revolution, but it is essential to the historical representation of mass extermination" (quoted in Hayes and Roth 2010: 405, 424).

12 See for example Sorabji (2006) on variant local memories of the war in Bosnia in the 1990s.

13 For a discussion of the conservation challenges facing the museum, see Marszałek (2004).

14 In fact a major new monument, covering the whole of the site, was erected there in 2004.

15 For example, as Williams puts it, how do the "causes" of the Holocaust make such extreme outcomes rational or explicable? Genocide is often described as "inhuman" – but that is a kind of linguistic surrender (Williams 2007: 157). For a book-length study of these issues, in the light of recent critical philosophy of history, see Stone (2003).

16 For a detailed report of the pope's visit, see Huener (2003: 212–25).

References

DellaPergola, S. (1994) An Overview of the Demographic Trends of European Jewry. In J. Webber (ed.), *Jewish Identities in the New Europe*. London: Littman Library of Jewish Civilization, pp. 57–73.

Długoborski, W., and Piper, F. (eds) (2000) *Auschwitz 1940–1945: Central Issues in the History of the Camp*, 5 vols., trans. W. Brand. Oświęcim: Auschwitz-Birkenau State Museum.

Gutman, I. (ed.) (1990) *Encyclopedia of the Holocaust*, 2 vols. New York: Macmillan.

Gutman, Y., and Berenbaum, M. (eds) (1994) *Anatomy of the Auschwitz Death Camp*. Bloomington: Indiana University Press.

Hayes, P., and Roth, J.K. (eds) (2010) *The Oxford Handbook of Holocaust Studies*. Oxford: Oxford University Press.

Huener, J. (2003) *Auschwitz, Poland, and the Politics of Commemoration, 1945–1979*. Athens: Ohio University Press.

Klein, E. (2001) *The Battle for Auschwitz: Catholic–Jewish Relations under Strain*. London: Vallentine Mitchell.

Lennon, J., and Foley, M. (2010 [2000]). *Dark Tourism*. Andover: Cengage Learning.

Levi, P. (1989 [1986]). *The Drowned and the Saved*, trans. R. Rosenthal. London: Penguin.

Macdonald, S. (2009) *Difficult Heritage: Negotiating the Nazi Past in Nuremberg and Beyond*. London: Routledge.

Mach, Z. (2007) Constructing Identities in a Post-Communist Society: Ethnic, National, and European. In D.F. Bryceson, J. Okely, and J. Webber (eds), *Identity and Networks: Fashioning Gender and Ethnicity across Cultures*. Oxford: Berghahn Books, pp. 54–72.

Marszałek, K. (ed.) (2004) *Preserving for the Future: Material from an International Preservation Conference, Oświęcim, June 23–25, 2003*. Oświęcim: Auschwitz-Birkenau State Museum.

Mookherjee, N. (2011) "Never Again": Aesthetics of "Genocidal" Cosmopolitanism and the Bangladesh Liberation War Museum. *Journal of the Royal Anthropological Institute*, special issue, S71–S91.

Piper, F. (1985) Extermination. In Auschwitz State Museum (ed.), *Auschwitz: Nazi Extermination Camp*, 2nd edn. Warsaw: Interpress, pp. 87–132.

Piper, F. (1991) Estimating the Number of Deportees to and Victims of the Auschwitz-Birkenau Camp. *Yad Vashem Studies*, 21, 49–103.

Rittner, C., and Roth, J.K. (eds) (1991) *Memory Offended: The Auschwitz Convent Controversy*. New York: Praeger.

Rosenbaum, I.J. (1976) *The Holocaust and Halakhah*. Brooklyn, NY: Ktav.

Sheramy, R. (2007) From Auschwitz to Jerusalem: Re-enacting Jewish History on the March of the Living. *Polin: Studies in Polish Jewry*, 19, 307–325.

Sorabji, C. (2006) Managing Memories in Post-War Sarajevo: Individuals, Bad Memories, and New Wars. *Journal of the Royal Anthropological Institute*, 12 (1), 1–18.

Stone, D. (2003) *Constructing the Holocaust: A Study in Historiography*. London: Vallentine Mitchell.

Van Pelt, R.J., and Dwork, D. (1996). *Auschwitz: 1270 to the Present*. New Haven: Yale University Press.

Webber, J. (1993) Creating a New Inscription for the Memorial at Auschwitz-Birkenau: A Short Chapter in the Mythologization of the Holocaust. In J. Davies and I. Wollaston (eds), *The Sociology of Sacred Texts*. Sheffield: Sheffield Academic Press, pp. 45–58.

Webber, J. (2006) Memory, Religion, and Conflict at Auschwitz: A Manifesto. In O.B. Stier and J.S. Landres (eds), *Religion, Violence, Memory and Place*. Bloomington: Indiana University Press, pp. 51–70.

Wieviorka, A. (1999) From Survivor to Witness: Voices from the Shoah, trans. J. Winter. In J. Winter and E. Sivan (eds), *War and Remembrance in the Twentieth Century*. Cambridge: Cambridge University Press, pp. 125–141.

Williams, P. (2007) *Memorial Museums: The Global Rush to Commemorate Atrocities*. Oxford: Berg.

Young, J.E. (1993) *The Texture of Memory: Holocaust Memorials and Meaning*. New Haven: Yale University Press.

CHAPTER 9 The Memory of the World and its Hidden Facets

Anca Claudia Prodan

Introduction

The movie *The Wizard of Oz*, the court case of Nelson Mandela, the Benz patent, the Bayeux tapestry: what do these artifacts, so different from each other, have in common? At first glance, they seem to have nothing in common. After all, what relationship could exist between an American movie, a South African court case, a German motor patent, and a tapestry discovered in France? These are very different items, from very different times and places, but they do have something in common: they belong to the UNESCO Memory of the World Programme (MoW), which has brought them together by declaring them all valuable as part of the heritage of humanity. MoW is a 1992 initiative of UNESCO concerned with so-called "documentary heritage." It is considered complementary with other heritage-related initiatives, namely the UNESCO Convention Concerning the Protection of the World Cultural and Natural Heritage, or World Heritage Convention (1972), and the Convention for the Safeguarding of the Intangible Cultural Heritage, or Intangible Heritage Convention (2003), together offering a comprehensive framework for the protection of different facets of heritage.

A review of the literature shows that for different authors MoW means different things. Often a focus is placed on the International Memory of the World Register (e.g. Robertson-von Trotha and Hauser 2010; Charlesworth 2010), this being the equivalent of the World Heritage List and the Representative List of the Intangible Cultural Heritage for documents. In other cases, such as in some reports of its leading bodies, MoW is presented as a program centering on the "preservation of information" (UNESCO 2006). In still other cases, it is said that the key objectives of MoW are the preservation of, and access to, documents (UNESCO 2008). Indeed, MoW incorporates all these aspects; yet none of them represents the essence of MoW, which rests on the

A Companion to Heritage Studies, First Edition. Edited by William Logan, Máiréad Nic Craith, and Ullrich Kockel.
© 2016 John Wiley & Sons, Inc. Published 2016 by John Wiley & Sons, Inc.

view that documentary heritage is a heritage of humanity. The International MoW Register is considered the most visible aspect of the program (Edmondson 2002: 4); nevertheless, it is just a tool towards a different end. Information preservation falls under the scope of MoW; however, MoW is concerned with documentary heritage, and there are important differences between this concept and that of information. Finally, preservation and access, although key objectives, are not the key purpose of MoW. These are the mission of libraries and archives, and MoW was not intended to simply duplicate these activities but to complement them with awareness-raising measures and encourage partnerships and cooperation activities.

Preservation, access, and the International MoW Register are important, but they are only objectives or tools for implementing the MoW. The key purpose of MoW arises from its underlying philosophy constructed around the concept of heritage of humanity, which conditions all actions directed at documentary heritage, including preservation and access. Clarifying the underlying philosophy of MoW is the aim of the present chapter, and it seeks to enhance the understanding of the relevance of MoW in the context of international heritage protection. To this end, the notion of the heritage of humanity is employed, as it properly captures the essence and thus uniqueness of MoW. The chapter commences by introducing the program, explaining its position in the UNESCO structure, and emphasizing why MoW cannot be reduced to preservation, access, or the International MoW Register. Consequently, the notion of the heritage of humanity is introduced, along with its implications in the context of MoW. For illustration, two key aspects of MoW – structure and strategy – are presented in order to point out the relevance of MoW as a heritage initiative, complementing others such as the World Heritage Convention (1972) and the Intangible Cultural Heritage Convention (2003). Finally, the key points raised are reiterated, emphasizing the need to take the underlying philosophy as a starting point in order to understand the relevance of MoW in international heritage protection.

The UNESCO Memory of the World Programme

Tracing the roots of MoW, we come to learn that this program was established to complement the efforts of libraries and archives. Having the collection and preservation of documents as their core activities, these institutions were the ones to observe that documents around the world could disappear forever if urgent measures were not taken. The risks are both natural and man-made. Documents suffer from physical decay, being composed of natural and synthetic materials. Often due to lack of resources, libraries and archives are not able to take all necessary measures to ensure preservation, and documents are also at risk due to natural disasters affecting the buildings in which they are housed. Additionally, documents are endangered due to man-made causes, ranging from neglect caused by lack of awareness regarding the manifold relevance of documents, to looting, illegal trading, and intentional destruction, as illustrated by book-burning or the destruction of libraries during wars. In fact, it was the destruction of the National Library of Sarajevo in 1992 that led to the conviction that the efforts of libraries and archives were not enough, and that additional measures to safeguard valuable documents around the world were necessary. Consequently, the international community represented by UNESCO established MoW as a large-scale mobilization effort to positively change mindsets regarding the relevance of documents and their preservation, and accessibility needs, by promoting a comprehensive and global perspective on documents as heritage (UNESCO 1998). The aim to positively change mindsets about documents is characteristic of MoW, this being what differentiates it from the activities of libraries, archives, and other institutions concerned with preservation and the accessibility of documents (UNESCO 1998).

MoW takes a very broad view in its definition of document, seeing it as that which records something, and approaches it as a unity between the informational content and the physical carrier of the information (Edmondson 2002). Both may be very diverse in the context of MoW, covering documents in any kind of media ranging from paper to digital carriers, including less usual media such as tapestry, and in terms of content featuring themes as diverse as the examples given at the beginning of this chapter. In order to illustrate the manifold significance of documents, MoW selects out of a wide variety those which it deems unique, irreplaceable and of world significance (Edmondson 2002). These documents are declared documentary heritage and raised above their informational value to the level of the heritage of humanity. With this, MoW is clearly a heritage initiative, and thus more than a program concerned with the preservation and accessibility of information. However, this aspect is somehow overshadowed by the position of MoW in the UNESCO structure.

MoW is carried out under the Communication and Information Programme sector of UNESCO, under the Knowledge Societies Division, unlike the World Heritage Convention (1972) and Intangible Heritage Convention (2003), which belong to the Culture Programme sector. This has implications. Each of the five UNESCO sectors is driven by its specific overarching objective, in the Communication and Information sector this being the building of inclusive knowledge societies, whereas in the Culture sector it is the fostering of cultural diversity, intercultural dialogue, and a culture of peace. Due to its position in the Communication and Information sector, MoW is sometimes presented as a contribution to knowledge societies (Souter 2010) or to programs centering on information, such as the Information for All Programme. Indeed, MoW may represent a contribution in this regard, but this perspective does not seem to facilitate the visibility of MoW especially among heritage initiatives, with which it is considered complementary.[1] However, by relying on the notion of heritage, MoW can be placed in line with heritage initiatives, rather than being framed around the notion of information, the latter also being misleading as regards its scope. The explanation below illustrates this argument.

As already stated, for MoW a document is defined as a unity between an informational content and the physical carrier on which it resides (Edmondson 2002). However, the notion of document has subtle meanings, as pointed out by Feather, who distinguishes two understandings; that is, document as artifact and document as information carrier:

> As an artefact, a document in any format is a physical object, part of whose interest lies in its information content. As an information carrier, a document is a device for storing and transmitting its contents and the format is of interest only to the extent that it contributes to, or inhibits, that objective. (Feather 2004: 4–5)

Following this distinction, and considering the definition of document by MoW, it can be said that MoW approaches a document as an artifact rather than simply as an information carrier. Pointing out this distinction is important for yet another reason.

According to Feather (2004: 4–5), this distinction guides preservation, with the focus falling either on the document as a whole, including the carrier, or only on the informational content. The same distinction can be found in MoW in the general guidelines, which is the key instrument for its implementation.[2] In the preliminary draft of potential guidelines (Arnoult 1993), it is specified that we must differentiate between information and its physical support. Either the information is significant, for example due to its linguistic interest; or its physical support is significant, due to its aesthetic values. Consequently, at least two forms of heritage exist: "either the emphasis is laid on the content … or … on the nature of the object (the materials of which it is composed, for instance)" (Arnoult 1993: 2–3). Nevertheless, the development and spread of digital technology in recent years has had an important influence on this conceptualization, and consequently on MoW, as evidenced by a chronological analysis of how the guidelines developed.

The preliminary draft guidelines note that the development of audiovisual media has led to a decrease in the aesthetic value of the carriers, and also a tendency to attach heritage value to information alone (Arnoult 1993: 4). Indeed, an illustrated manuscript is more likely to be considered as having aesthetic values than a computer disk. The preliminary draft guidelines further remark in the case of computer disks that, "the heritage value of these supports resides in … their capacity for stocking vast quantities of information in a small place" (Arnoult 1993: 4). This statement is perhaps not self-explanatory, implying that more storage capacity means more heritage value. However, the purpose of citing this statement is neither to criticize nor explain it, but to illustrate that in the beginning of MoW's existence, at least an attempt existed to consider the potential heritage value of digital carriers. This has now changed, with attention largely paid to content (UNESCO 2011). As an explanation given in one of the most recent documents for the implementation of MoW illustrates, in the case of digital documents, "the carrier, although necessary to physically hold the information, is of lesser, and often of no importance in the context of Memory of the World" (UNESCO 2011). As opposed to the previous definition, here MoW seems to approach documents as information carriers. The trigger of this change is the process of technological obsolescence, meaning that software and hardware rapidly fall into disuse as new ones develop, which makes older digital documents incompatible with newer technologies in a matter of just a few years. This renders transferring the content from one carrier to another necessary in order for the content to be preserved (UNESCO 2011). True as this may be, it triggers a concern with content at the expense of the carrier, implying a reduction of documents to information (content). It also results in ignoring the carrier's potential relevance as heritage and emphasizing its instrumental value in making content accessible.

The shift in perspective from document as unity of content and carrier to document as carrier of content is present not only in MoW but broadly in libraries and archives. In libraries and archives this shift is said to indicate the replacement of the notion of document with information as a basic unit of analysis (Hjørland 2000). Some consider it a disadvantage, as it reduces the understanding of documents to their content while ignoring other dimensions, such as their social aspects (e.g. Hjørland 2000; Frohmann 2004). With MoW it also seems to have disadvantages not just because it draws attention away from the potential value of the digital carrier, but also because it does not reflect the core philosophy of MoW. Without ignoring the fact that MoW belongs structurally to the Communication and Information sector, or its potential contribution and link to information-related initiatives, in order to properly understand MoW it is useful to recontextualize it as part of the heritage of humanity. First, this concept is explained and then its implications for MoW are discussed.

The Heritage of Humanity

The concept of the heritage of humanity – also known as the common heritage of humanity or mankind, universal heritage, and so forth – is a component of nearly all UNESCO standard-setting instruments for culture, but also of numerous UN conventions, and it can be approached in different ways. Often being part of convention preambles, it can be seen as a philosophical statement, illustrating a vision about certain resources whose value is not confined by national or other borders; they are of "humanity." Other UNESCO documents speak about the common heritage of humanity as a human right and about the duty to protect it (UNESCO 1982). If it is called the "common heritage of humanity" or "common heritage of mankind," then the reference can be to its use as a principle of law. In the case of some UN conventions related to international spaces, such as the UN Convention on the Law of the Sea (1982), that principle acts as a legal regime triggering binding implications, such as non-appropriation and non-sovereignty over resources found in the high seas (Wolfrum 1983), which belong to no one in particular yet equally to all. According to scholars of law (e.g. von Schorlemer 1992; Francioni 2004), the heritage of humanity can act as principle of law also in the case of cultural resources. Perhaps with the exception of public-domain works, cultural resources are already in somebody's ownership; therefore, the concept triggers slightly different implications, not applying to the juridical statute of the resource. In the case of cultural resources, it implies the idea of trusteeship or the principle of stewardship, in that, despite ownership rights not being affected, owners still turn into stewards or trustees who must preserve the heritage, not for themselves but rather for a second beneficiary, which is humanity (von Schorlemer 1992: 564–66; Francioni 2004; Forrest 2006). For some this offers good opportunities in the context of heritage protection, because even if ownership disputes arise, they should not affect the need to serve the interests of humanity (Forrest 2006).

One element seems inseparable from the concept of the heritage of humanity whenever it is invoked, namely the benefit of humanity. In international law, humanity may refer to all states (signatories to a legal instrument), to different forms of human associations, or to all individuals (cf. Forrest 2006; Wolfrum 1983). Despite these different understandings, scholars agree that relating humanity to heritage at least indicates that future generations have to be taken into account (Wolfrum 1983, Schorlemer 1992; Forrest 2006). Consequently, the notion of humanity has a temporal dimension represented by future generations. However, it also has a spatial dimension represented by present generations, regardless of geographical location, with the notion of humanity covering all individuals or states. This aspect arises from the international character of these instruments, drafted by an international organization that aims at no less than building peace in the minds of men and women, and driven by ethical principles as those enshrined in the UNESCO Constitution. According to this understanding of humanity, having to address the interests of both present and future generations, the preservation of the heritage of humanity can also be said to have a spatial and a temporal dimension, which has practical implications for how activities directed at it should be carried out – that is, always for the benefit of humanity. In-depth study of the concept in standard-setting instruments allows us to list a few principles arising from the requirement that resources of the heritage of humanity should be used for the benefit of humanity. These can be grouped according to the spatial and temporal dimension of the notion of humanity.

In its spatial dimension, the benefit of humanity triggers principles such as intragenerational equity, solidarity, and cooperation. For example, not all countries have the same capacity to "benefit" from the heritage of humanity because they lack the technology to access it (von Schorlemer 1992: 573). Thus, principles of solidarity and cooperation come in because, at an international level, countries are expected to assist each other in ensuring that the heritage of humanity is equitably shared by all, and that all countries contribute to its protection, given that the heritage of humanity is not just a right but a duty. Given countries' different capacities, a related principle emerges, namely the "principle of common but differentiated responsibility." The principle is considered to have evolved from the notion of the common heritage of mankind and implies that states have a common responsibility for a global problem, yet that there is a need to consider the different circumstances, and particularly each state's contribution to a problem as well as its means and capacity to solve it (CISDL 2002). Given the differences between countries' capacities and means for heritage protection, the cultural heritage of humanity represents a common but differentiated responsibility, as it arises from international cooperation measures stipulated in most UNESCO legal tools for culture or heritage, for example the World Heritage Convention (1972), where the duty of the international community to cooperate to protect World Heritage is explicitly stated.

In its temporal dimension, the benefit of humanity triggers the principles of intergenerational equity and sustainability. For example, some UNESCO standard-setting tools emphasize that "present generations may use the common heritage of humankind, as defined in international law, provided that this does not entail compromising it irreversibly" (UNESCO 1997: art. 8). This is similar to the idea of sustainability popularized by the Brundtland Report in an environmental context (see WCED 1987). Related to this is the "precautionary principle," which triggers the need to protect humans and the environment against uncertain but scientifically plausible risks by taking anticipatory measures (COMEST 2005: 14). Applying the precautionary principle in a cultural context, Throsby suggests that certain resources may have value that is not yet recognized, but whose loss could lead to a future loss of opportunities. Therefore, applying the precautionary principle implies keeping options open by avoiding decisions that could lead to the permanent loss of an item, including heritage (Throsby 2004: 43–44).

All the principles discussed above as deriving from the status of the heritage of humanity are also relevant and present in the context of MoW, although it is only a program, not having legal implications as standard-setting instruments have. The Charter on the Preservation of Digital Heritage (UNESCO 2003) is the only normative instrument under the auspices of MoW, being its offshoot, but it focuses only on one specific type of documents, namely digital ones, and its purpose is to encourage the development of policies and legal frameworks for this type of documentary heritage.[3] However, regardless of whether they have legal implications, all activities undertaken by UNESCO are underpinned by its global ethics of moral solidarity, justice, and fairness. This vision is well reflected in MoW, giving it its unique profile, which sets it apart from initiatives concerned with the preservation of, and access to, information, as those carried out by libraries and archives.

The Documentary Heritage of Humanity

That MoW takes the concept of the heritage of humanity as a starting point is explicit in the following statement:

> The Memory of the World Programme proceeds on the assumption that some items, collections, holdings or fonds of documentary heritage are part of the inheritance of the world, in the same way as are sites of outstanding universal value listed in the UNESCO World Heritage List. Their significance is deemed to transcend the boundaries of time and culture, and they should be preserved for present and future generations and made accessible to all peoples of the world in some form. (Edmondson 2002: 5)

The implications triggered by the notion of the heritage of humanity are evident in MoW in several regards. First a general overview is provided, and then focus is placed more closely on the MoW structure and strategy, which illustrate the existence of these implications in mechanisms for its implementation. This will also point out how using the heritage of humanity as a lens opens up new views and understandings of MoW.

The ethics of UNESCO is reflected in the implications triggered by the concept of the heritage of humanity in its spatial and temporal dimensions. These are present in the mission statement of MoW, which states it intends to provide both universal and permanent access to documentary heritage (Edmondson 2002: 6). On the one hand, universal access can be considered a reference to present generations and the spatial dimension of preservation, because access to documentary heritage is considered the right of all without discrimination. Moreover, it implies the need for intra-generational equity. This principle is reflected in the general guidelines in various respects: regarding the need to ensure a balanced geographical representation of documentary heritage on the International MoW Register; the acknowledgement that not all people have equal access to the internet and the need for complementary measures to ensure equal access; the acknowledgment that communities differ in their capacity to protect documentary heritage; or the statement that cooperation at different levels is essential (Edmondson 2002). These statements bring to mind the principles of equity, solidarity, and cooperation, and common but differentiated responsibility. On the other hand, the mission statement of MoW speaks about permanent access, which can be considered a reference to future generations and the temporal dimension of preservation, access being also considered the right of future generations. This principle is well reflected in the general guidelines, as for example in the recognition that demands for short-term access should not compromise long-term access; or the remark that conserving an original means that no information is lost and that all future options remain open (Edmondson 2002). These bring to mind the principle of sustainability and the precautionary principle. Accordingly, the principles deriving from the concept of heritage of humanity can be considered guiding principles of MoW. Moreover, they illustrate that MoW was drawn up with a certain philosophy in mind, and this is definitely one constructed on the idea of a heritage of humanity. This is evident also in its structure and strategy.

Unlike other heritage initiatives, MoW has a three-tier structure, being implemented at international, regional, and national levels. The structure of MoW is not only unique but also very flexible, being able to accommodate the diversity of the world's cultures and their documentary heritage expressions. At an international level, MoW is led by the International Advisory Committee, composed of 14 members, and supported by five subsidiary bodies – the Bureau, the Sub-Committee on Technology, the Marketing Sub-Committee, the Register Sub-Committee, and the Sub-Committee on Education and Research – and a Secretariat provided by the Knowledge Societies Division. Here it is necessary to remark that, unlike the case of the heritage conventions, whose leading bodies are representatives of States Parties, in MoW they comprise individuals appointed in their personal capacity as experts.

At a national level, MoW is implemented through national MoW committees, or UNESCO national commissions where the former do not exist, their setting up not being mandatory. Here it is worth pointing out that there is acknowledgment of different national policies, specific situations and practices of each country, this being reflected in the status of National Committees as autonomous entities, with their own terms of reference and rules of procedure (Edmondson 2002: 32). At a regional level, MoW recommends the setting up of regional committees, which represent cooperative structures beyond the national level, composed of people from two or more countries (Edmondson 2002: 33). In MoW, national and regional committees are considered of high relevance (Edmondson 2002: 32), but regional committees especially offer possibilities to accommodate the implications arising from the concept of the heritage of humanity. Currently there are three regional committees – Asia and the Pacific; Latin America and the Caribbean; and Africa – grouped around UNESCO regional offices. However, committees do not have to be formed based on geopolitical considerations but on different criteria, such as shared culture or shared interests (Edmondson 2002: 33). Such committees do not exist today, but the presence of these measures indicates the flexibility and inclusiveness existing in the MoW structure, which is not based solely on political considerations, and which is able to accommodate the implications deriving from the heritage of humanity. Regional committees are a key mechanism for international cooperation, being able to set up cross-border projects and activities, and supporting the endeavors of individual countries as well as of national institutions and organizations. Moreover, regional committees are relevant because they provide an inclusive mechanism that considers challenges regarding the protection of the documentary heritage of minorities or subcultures. These are not always recognized by governments at the national level, but they can make recourse to, and rely on the activities of, regional committees, these being supranational structures (Edmondson 2002: 20).

To this, one can add further cooperation mechanisms, including NGOs and professional associations such as the International Federation of Library Associations and Institutions or the International Council of Archives, committees having the freedom to delegate roles to such institutions (Edmondson 2002: 33). These examples are an expression of the idea of a heritage of humanity, strongly advocating equity, solidarity, and cooperation at different levels, and giving MoW an important role in international heritage protection that enforces the mission of UNESCO in creating mechanisms for peace-building, moral solidarity, and international cooperation and understanding.

The implications of the heritage of humanity are evident also in the strategy of MoW. To a certain extent, the advantages of the three-tier structure are present also in the strategy, given the existence of MoW registers at all three levels – not just at the international level, as is the case of the World Heritage Convention (1972) and Intangible Heritage Convention (2003). Again, this is a unique feature of MoW, providing a multifaceted mechanism for heritage protection that is not present in other heritage initiatives. Australia's PANDORA web archive, which is a rare example of documentary heritage in digital form existing currently on MoW registers, provides an illustration. PANDORA was inscribed on the Australian National MoW Register in 2004. In MoW, an item may exist simultaneously on several registers; thus, PANDORA was later also submitted for the international register. However, it was not accepted, the reasons for this rejection including that PANDORA was not unique in terms of content (UNESCO 2005), despite the fact that its nominators did not place heritage value on the content. The justification for inscription clearly explained that "PANDORA has aesthetic significance, given that it preserves the appearance and functionality (the 'look and feel') of publications and websites, as well as their intellectual content" (UNESCO 2004). In the field of libraries and archives, the notion of preserving the "look and feel" means that the document should be preserved as an artifact, a unity between carrier and content, not simply as an information carrier (Rothenberg 1999). In the case of PANDORA, this indicates that the value of the documents belonging to it lies also in the carrier, not the content. Another important consideration was that PANDORA, being created soon after the emergence of the World Wide Web, is significant as "a record of the early years of this new and revolutionary publication and communication medium" (UNESCO 2004). As indicated by this statement, the relevance here does not lie in what was written in the documents, but rather in the fact that they are evidence of a major change in the field of communication. However, the value of this nomination lies perhaps also in that it was proposed "to highlight that information in digital formats is as important as any other to our cultural and documentary history and needs to be preserved" (UNESCO 2004).

Despite the reasons for rejection at the international level, the strategies existing at different levels enable MoW to apply alternative mechanisms that still allow it to fulfill its mission, PANDORA being protected today at a national level under the Australian MoW Register. The existence of registers at international, regional, and national levels allows addressing the benefit of humanity, as it represents a mechanism that can accommodate a diversity of situations, international standards being sometimes too rigid in this regard. It should also be added that, unlike other heritage initiatives, in MoW not just States Parties but any kind of organization and even individuals can submit nominations, which is another illustration of its flexibility and inclusiveness.

Mechanisms deriving from the heritage of humanity are theoretically present, but they are not necessarily followed in practice. A recent survey on the implementation of MoW at national level (UNESCO 2012) shows that it is mainly (but not solely) countries from Europe and North America that have less interest in MoW because the field is well developed there, with protective legislation in place and a society aware of the value of documentary heritage (UNESCO 2012: 48). Despite having inscribed items on the International MoW Register, these countries consider MoW a duplication of practices already existing at national level. They seem to equate the program with the International MoW Register, revealing a narrow understanding that ignores the requirements arising from the concept of the heritage of humanity, at least in two regards: on the one hand, in terms of the duties of cooperation which should exist between countries, and would require the moral obligation to support other countries in achieving a similar level of protection; on the other hand, in terms of the duties to develop joint activities at the regional level, which are an acknowledgement of the fact that the protection of documentary heritage is a collective effort, exceeding geopolitical boundaries. These countries, although well aware and informed about the requirements of document preservation, seem to be less aware of those surrounding the documentary heritage of humanity, and which provide MoW with a unique profile and a special relevance in the field of heritage protection, and perhaps beyond.

The examples given above were meant to point out that the international significance of MoW lies in its ability to accommodate local and cultural variations, and in its potential to address the benefit of humanity in its temporal and spatial dimensions. MoW is neither simply a program for the preservation and accessibility of information, nor simply a register. It is a source of solidarity, cooperation, and equity, a mechanism that encourages responsible behavior, and thus an indispensable component of international heritage protection. However, this perspective requires taking the concept of the heritage of humanity as a starting point, and implementing MoW in a way that addresses the principles arising from the need to consider the benefit of humanity. Without this, MoW could indeed be seen as just a duplication of the activities of libraries and archives, or merely a contribution to information-related initiatives.

Conclusions

Starting from the argument that in order to comprehend the scope and central message of the Memory of the World Programme (MoW) it is first necessary to understand its underlying philosophy, the aim of this chapter has been to present some features that can be considered to give MoW its unique profile among initiatives concerned with the preservation and accessibility of information. To this end a few known and less known facets of MoW were presented. Some aspects are better known, such as the International MoW Register and the fact that MoW deals with the preservation of documents. Others, such as the potential of MoW in terms of the requirements triggered by the concept of the heritage of humanity, are less known, being present in theory but not reflected in how MoW has evolved and is implemented. It should be acknowledged that there are some exceptions, for example the UNESCO Bangkok office, which has proposed a so-called common heritage methodology to promote the World Heritage Convention (1972), the Intangible Heritage Convention (2003), and MoW together, or a 2011 MoW conference organized in Warsaw, which attempted to establish links between these heritage programs. But MoW has not really followed the line of the heritage of humanity in its development. Rather, it seems to have focused mainly on access and preservation, the International MoW Register, and increasingly the notion of (digital) information. Without denying the relation existing between MoW and information-related initiatives, this chapter has attempted to argue that contextualizing MoW among other heritage initiatives, and thus as part of what UNESCO calls the heritage of humanity, is exactly what gives MoW its unique profile. To demonstrate this, a modest illustration was given to show that using the heritage of humanity as a lens through which to look at the Memory of the World Programme may change its potential in the field of heritage protection, and give a different direction to how it can be conceptualized and implemented.

There is not space in this chapter for more than a brief discussion and a few examples to illustrate how the concept of the heritage of humanity may give MoW a profile that goes beyond its role in preservation and access. Without specifically mentioning the concept of the heritage of humanity, there are a few scholars who do see MoW as having a broader role, at least in theory. Charlesworth (2010) argues that MoW has strong human rights foundations, but that addressing them in practice would give MoW a different focus, such as being more responsive to the documentary heritage of minorities, or to the discriminatory aspects existing in any selection process based on the notion of significance. Robertson-von Trotha and Hauser (2010) argue that MoW can be a source of intercultural education, but that addressing this in practice requires providing contextual information and ensuring multilingual access to inscribed documentary heritage, this currently not being the case. As these examples reveal, supporting the argument advanced in this chapter, the role of MoW can and should go beyond the preservation and accessibility of information. My preference is for using the concept of the heritage of humanity to guide the way forward. The concept is already part and parcel of MoW but, while lying at the program's roots, it remains well hidden. It has, however, the potential to stretch into and shape all aspects of MoW. For that reason, reconceptualizing the relevance of MoW in international heritage protection may offer a useful starting point.

Notes

1 There has been an ongoing discussion since the inception of MoW to either find ways to link it with the other heritage programs or move it to the UNESCO Culture Sector. At the time of writing, MoW continues to belong to the Communication and Information Sector.

2 A preliminary draft for potential guidelines was prepared by Jean-Marie Arnoult in 1993 (Arnoult 1993). The first official guidelines were written in 1995. They were updated in 2002, and this is the version used today. Additionally, in 2011 the so-called Register Companion was drafted as an addition to the guidelines to support the preparation of nominations (UNESCO 2011).

3 The thirty-seventh session of the general conference of UNESCO requested the preparation of a draft recommendation on preservation and access to documentary heritage, the drafting of this normative instrument now being in progress.

References

Legislation

Convention Concerning the Protection of the World Cultural and Natural Heritage (World Heritage Convention) (UNESCO, 1972). Available at: http://whc.unesco.org/archive/convention-en.pdf (accessed March 19, 2015).

Convention for the Safeguarding of the Intangible Cultural Heritage (Intangible Heritage Convention) (UNESCO, 2003). Available at: http://unesdoc.unesco.org/images/0013/001325/132540e.pdf (accessed March 19, 2015).

Convention on the Law of the Sea (United Nations, 1982). Available at: http://www.un.org/depts/los/convention_agreements/texts/unclos/unclos_e.pdf (accessed March 19, 2015).

Other Works

Arnoult, J.-M. (1993) Memory of the World Programme: Suggested Guidelines for the Protection of Endangered Manuscripts and Archives. Document PGI-93/WS/14. Available at: http://unesdoc.unesco.org/images/0009/000962/096263eb.pdf (accessed July 12, 2014).

Charlesworth, H. (2010) Human Right and the UNESCO Memory of the World Programme. In W. Logan, M. Langfield, and M. Nic Craith (eds.), *Cultural Diversity, Heritage and Human Rights: Intersections in Theory and Practice.* London: Routledge, pp. 21–30.

CISDL (Center for International Sustainable Development Law) (2002) The Principle of Common but Differentiated Responsibilities: Origins and Scope. Legal brief prepared for the World Summit on Sustainable Development 2002, Johannesburg, August 26. Available at: http://cisdl.org/public/docs/news/brief_common.pdf (accessed July 12, 2014).

COMEST (World Commission on the Ethics of Scientific Knowledge and Technology) (2005) The PrecautionaryPrinciple.Availableat:http://unesdoc.unesco.org/images/0013/001395/139578e.pdf (accessed January 27, 2014).

Edmondson, R. (2002) Memory of the World: General Guidelines to Safeguard Documentary Heritage. UNESCO document CII-95/WS-11rev. Available at: http://unesdoc.unesco.org/images/0012/001256/125637e.pdf (accessed July 14, 2014).

Feather, J. (2004) Introduction: Principles and Policies. In J. Feather (ed.), *Managing Preservation for Libraries and Archives: Current Practice and Future Developments.* Aldershot: Ashgate, pp. 1–26.

Francioni, F. (2004) Beyond State Sovereignty. *Michigan Journal of International Law*, 4 (25), 1209–1229.

Forrest, C. (2006) Angkor Wat: The Common Heritage of Humankind? An International Law Perspective. Paper presented at UNESCO Conference, University of Sydney, July 17–22. Available at: http://www.conferences.arts.usyd.edu.au/viewpaper.php?id=527&print=1&cf=9 (accessed April 20, 2013).

Frohmann, B. (2004) Documentation Redux: Prolegomenon to (Another) Philosophy of Information. *Library Trends*, 3 (52), 387–407.

Hjørland, B. (2000) Documents, Memory Institutions and Information Science. *Journal of Documentation*, 1 (56), 27–41.

Robertson-von Trotha, C., and Hauser, R. (2010) UNESCO and Digitalized Heritage: New Heritage, New Challenges. In D. Offenhäusser, W.C. Zimmerli, and M.-T. Albert (eds), *World Heritage and Cultural Diversity Challenges for University Education.* Bonn: German Commission for UNESCO, pp. 69–78.

Rothenberg, J. (1999) *Avoiding Technological Quicksand: Finding a Viable Technical Foundation for Digital Preservation.* Washington: Council on Library and Information Resources.

Souter, D. (2010) Towards Inclusive Knowledge Societies: A Review of UNESCO's Action in Implementing the WSIS Outcome. UNESCO document CI/INF/2010/RP/1. Available at: http://unesdoc.unesco.org/images/0018/001878/187832e.pdf (accessed September 15, 2011).

Throsby, D. (2004) Sweetness and Light? Cultural Diversity in the Contemporary Global Economy. In J.-M. Baer, A. Klamer, D. Throsby, and I.P. Laleye (eds), *Cultural Diversity.* London: British Council, pp. 40–53.

UNESCO (1982) UNESCO and Peoples' Rights, Conclusions of the International Symposium of Experts on Rights of Solidarity and Peoples' Rights, Republic of San Marino, 4–8 October 1982. Document SS-82/WS/61. Available at: http://unesdoc.unesco.org/images/0005/000522/052250eb.pdf (accessed March 6, 2015).

UNESCO (1997) Declaration on the Responsibilities of the Present Generations towards Future Generations. Available at: http://www.unesco.org/cpp/uk/declarations/generations.pdf (accessed March 19, 2015).

UNESCO (1998) Report of the First Meeting of the Bureau of the International Advisory Committee of the "Memory of the World" Programme, London, United Kingdom, 4–5 September 1998. Available at: http://www.unesco.org/new/fileadmin/MULTIMEDIA/HQ/CI/CI/pdf/mow/mow_bureau_meeting_1998_final_report_en.pdf (accessed June 25, 2014).

UNESCO (2003) Charter on the Preservation of Digital Heritage. Available at: http://unesdoc.unesco.org/images/0013/001331/133171e.pdf#page=80 (accessed March 19, 2015).

UNESCO (2004) Nomination Form "PANDORA, Australia's Web Archive": Nomination Form Submitted by Australia to the International Memory of the World Register. Ref No. 2004–28. Available at: http://portal.unesco.org/ci/en//ev.php-URL_ID=18001&URL_DO=DO_TOPIC&URL_SECTION=201.html (accessed November 7, 2012).

UNESCO (2005) Report of the Third Meeting of the Register Sub-Committee of the International Advisory Committee of the "Memory of the World" Programme, Paris, 21 March 2005. Available at: http://www.unesco.org/new/fileadmin/MULTIMEDIA/HQ/CI/CI/pdf/mow/mow_2nd_3rd_register_sub_committee_final_report_en.pdf (accessed June 25, 2014).

UNESCO (2006) Report of the Ninth Meeting of the Sub-Committee on Technology of the International Advisory Committee of the "Memory of the World" Programme, Mexico City, 7–8 September, 2006. Available at: http://www.unesco.org/new/fileadmin/MULTIMEDIA/HQ/CI/CI/pdf/mow/mow_9th_technical_sub_committee_final_report_en.pdf (accessed March 6, 2015).

UNESCO (2008) Report of the Tenth Meeting of the Sub-Committee on Technology of the International Advisory Committee of the "Memory of the World" Programme, Egypt, 20–21 November, 2008. Available at: http://www.unesco.org/new/fileadmin/MULTIMEDIA/HQ/CI/CI/pdf/mow/mow_10th_technical_sub_committee_final_report_en.pdf (accessed March 6, 2015).

UNESCO (2011) Memory of the World Register Companion. Official Website of the Memory of the World Programme. Available at: http://www.unesco.org/new/fileadmin/MULTIMEDIA/HQ/CI/CI/pdf/mow/Register%20Companion.pdf (accessed November 10, 2013).

UNESCO (2012) Implementation of UNESCO Memory of the World Programme at National Level, Survey Results. Available at: http://www.unesco.org/new/fileadmin/MULTIMEDIA/HQ/CI/CI/pdf/mow/latvian_survey_results_on_national_registers_en.pdf (accessed November 10, 2013).

von Schorlemer, S. (1992) *Internationaler Kulturgüterschutz: Ansätze zur Prävention im Frieden sowie im bewaffneten Konflikt.* Berlin: Duncker and Humblot.

Wolfrum, R. (1983) The Principle of the Common Heritage of Mankind. *Zeitschrift für ausländisches öffentliches Recht und Völkerrecht*, 43, 312–337.

WCED (World Commission on Environment and Development) (1987) *Our Common Future.* Oxford: Oxford University Press.

CHAPTER 10

African Indigenous Heritage in Colonial and Postcolonial Museums: The Case of the Batwa of Africa's Great Lakes Region

Maurice Mugabowagahunde

Museums and Indigenous People

Generally, people visit museums as places to learn about culture through objects, labels, exhibition notes, and display of artifacts (Kelly 2001: 2; Brown 2009: 148). Some of the material exhibited in museums belongs to indigenous peoples, and their identity as culture is frequently presented at the museums through the anonymous voice of museum authority, which is most of the time not indigenous (Trofanenko 2006: 311). During the colonial era in Africa, and elsewhere, most museum texts were written by non-indigenous people, and focused upon negatively perceived aspects of their culture, such as cannibalism and sorcery, and described indigenous peoples using racist language (Brown 2009: 150). An important question is: How can indigenous communities benefit financially from their cultural material being displayed in both Western and local museums? More importantly: How can these materials be presented according to indigenous culture?

Collecting both anthropological and archeological materials was very popular in the nineteenth century among the European colonial powers that controlled countries in Africa and Asia. Evidence of newly discovered cultures ended up in public and private

A Companion to Heritage Studies, First Edition. Edited by William Logan, Máiréad Nic Craith, and Ullrich Kockel.
© 2016 John Wiley & Sons, Inc. Published 2016 by John Wiley & Sons, Inc.

collections (Ostergard, Tubin, and Dikirr 2006: 313; Orford 2011: 1). Subsequently, in the postcolonial period, the trade in cultural objects has flourished, despite laws prohibiting the exportation of antiquities, especially in Africa (Orford 2011: 11). Many objects have been removed forcibly and exported illegally. The most cited example in Africa is Nigeria, from where, in 2010, the Nok terra-cottas were smuggled to France (Eyo 2010: 3). Many of these objects have considerable cultural and spiritual significance. Others include remains of indigenous ancestors that are held in Western museums in Europe and America.

In these Western museums, most indigenous heritage is displayed in ethnographic collections, and visitors expect to rely on the curatorial expertise of museum staff in learning about different concerns regarding indigenous heritage, since in most cases there is an absence of indigenous groups in museum's projects (Trofanenko 2006: 309). The materiality and physical presence of indigenous objects within these museums provide the public with perceived access to understanding the indigenous world and, more specifically, indigenous culture.

As a prestigious public space where valued objects are held to embody essential forms of evidence, ethnology museums' displays of indigenous objects serve to capture the fascination of viewing another culture. This stems from a central historical principle, the belief that one could capture, display, and teach something fundamental about culture through objects (Trofanenko 2006: 310). Museum exhibitions that focus on indigenous peoples, however, are constantly accused of failing to present indigenous peoples as having dynamic and living cultures (Pilcher and Vermeylen 2008: 2). This chapter discusses how for the last few years there has been much discussion concerning the repatriation of indigenous peoples' heritage material conserved in different Western museums. It takes examples from the Batwa pygmies of the Great Lakes region of Africa, a community whose heritage is either misrepresented or not represented at all in museums.

Batwa Pygmies, or the Contested Indigenous in the Great Lakes of Africa

In Africa, the term "indigenous" as a legal and rights concept has two different meanings with reference to international law and norms. In the first instance, it refers to Africans who were colonized by Europe and subsequently regained sovereignty through the decolonization process. In this usage, the African state's sovereignty arises from its legitimate representation of "indigenous" people liberated from colonial rule (Crawhall 2008: 4). The second use of the term "indigenous" refers to the more recent legal and indigenous rights terminology in Africa, and in many other places in the world. Since 1995, the term has come to apply to first-settled peoples who experienced various forms of discrimination within Africa. These peoples for the most part practice a subsistence economy different from the national norm, usually involving hunting and gathering or transhumant/nomadic pastoralism (Biesbrouck, Elders, and Rossell 1999). The African Commission on Human and Peoples' Rights debated the applicability of the term "indigenous" in the African context, and in 2003 produced a report recognizing the importance of redress and rights for these communities (ACHPR 2005).

An example of this second use of the term "indigenous" is that of pygmies, forest-based hunter-gatherer communities living in the tropical rainforests of the Great Lakes region of Central Africa. Pygmies are economically distinct from their Bantu and other farming neighbors (Crawhall 2008), and have been designated by anthropologists as people who exhibit an average height of less than 1.5 meters (Ndahinda 2011: 216). The term "pygmies" itself is used by some organizations and researchers, but is widely considered pejorative (Lewis 2001: 5; Ndahinda 2011: 217), and some researchers prefer to use "Central African foragers" instead of "pygmies" (e.g. Crawhall 2008).

One such group is the Batwa of Rwanda, Burundi, Uganda, and the eastern portion of the Democratic Republic of Congo.[1] Today it is estimated that less than 7,000 Batwa still have access to forest resources (Lewis 2006: 3). During the pre-colonial era, agriculturalists and pastoralists deforested large parts of the Great Lakes region, taking large parts of the most fertile areas for farming and herding (Ndahinda 2011: 218). Before the colonial period, some Batwa, for example in Rwanda, served in the court as entertainers,[2] potters and even as royal bodyguards (Kagabo and Mudandagizi 1974: 83; Crawhall 2008; Lewis 2001: 9). During the colonial period, most Batwa were ignored, and economically marginalized (Kagabo and Mudandagizi 1974: 79), and since the independence not much has been done by different governments to improve the Batwa's worsening conditions (Ndahinda 2011: 234).

In Rwanda, the Batwa[3] population live throughout the country, and current estimates put their population at somewhere between 25,000 and 35,000 people out of a total population of around 11,000,000; they thus comprise 0.3 per cent of the total population (Lewis 2001: 5; Wessendorf 2011: 432; Ndahinda 2011: 216). They have a distinct culture, often associated with their folkloric and traditional dances, and the intonation of their specific language, and according to some historians, they were the first occupants of the Great Lakes (Lewis 2001: 7; Ndahinda 2011: 218). Despite being numerically insignificant in Rwanda today, the Batwa's historic role as the first people of this area makes them a fundamental constituent of Rwandan society and culture (Lewis 2006: 3).

Prior to 1973, when national parks were created in Rwanda, the Batwa lived mainly from hunting and gathering in the country's natural forests (Lewis 2001: 27; Wessendorf 2011: 432), but they now constitute the poorest and most marginalized group in Rwanda (Lewis 2001: 29). Statistics from 2004 clearly illustrate this. For example, in 2004, 77 percent of the Batwa were unable to read, write, or count, less than 1 percent had completed secondary education, and none had completed higher education. Some 47 percent of Batwa families had no farmland; 95 percent of them produced pottery, though their clay products were sold at less than the cost of production; 85 percent barely even ate once a day; and more than 46 percent of Batwa families lived in grass huts (Wessendorf 2011: 432).[4] In addition, their complete lack of representation in previous governance structures has been a great problem (Lewis 2001: 12; Wessendorf 2011: 432).

In Rwanda, pottery became synonymous with the Batwa, because they made pots that every Rwandan household required (Kagabo and Mudandagizi 1974: 78; Lewis 2001: 11). Batwa claimed that up until the 1970s pottery provided a small but dependable income. In the 1970s, industrially produced goods such as jerricans, basins, bowls, and plates became widely popular. This competition forced Batwa to keep their prices static and attractively cheap (Lewis 2001: 6; 2006: 4).

According to Kagabo and Mudandagizi (1974: 84), Batwa were subjected to abuse, discrimination, and exploitation by their neighbors (see also Ndahinda 2011: 216). For example, many non-Batwa will not eat or drink with them, will not allow them to approach

Figure 10.1 Today in Rwanda, the majority of Batwa are still potters. Source: photo by Maurice Mugabowagahunde.

too closely, to sit near them, or touch cooking, eating, and drinking implements. Their communities are segregated from other groups, and they are forced to live on the boundaries of population centers, or on marginal land unwanted by others. It is often claimed that even in pre-colonial times Batwa could not intermarry with, or drink from the same cup as, members of the other ethnic groups (Ndahinda 2011: 227).

Despite being "the fountain of civilization" (Ndahinda 2011: 224) – the first in the land, the inventors of fire, teachers about habitats, wise healers with medicinal plants, sometimes even the first metallurgists and, on occasion, the first farmers – negative stereotypes have also been attributed to them, like the claims that Batwa are backward, childish, dirty, ignorant, thieving, immoral, and stupid (Lewis 2006: 5). In myths and chiefly rituals in Africa's Great Lakes region, the Batwa's hunting life is portrayed as decadent, immoral, and depraved, and as a people they are stereotyped as not fully human or socialized beings. Indeed, today their rights as first inhabitants are conveniently denied (Lewis 2006: 7).

Thus, the Rwandan government still does not recognize the indigenous or minority identity of the Batwa (Lewis 2001: 31), even though the government voted in favor of the UN Declaration on the Rights of Indigenous People (United Nations 2007) (Wessendorf 2011: 433). Early studies of tropical Africa tend to agree on the fact that Batwa were the first inhabitants of the region, but theories about African migrations and human settlement in the Great Lakes are now being challenged (Ndahinda 2011: 221). One of the main arguments here concerns the highly complex clan system. Clans brought together Hutu, Tutsi, and Batwa, despite the fact that, like families and lineages, clans were said to be initially descent-based (Ndahinda 2011: 226; Ostergard, Tubin, and Dikirr 2006: 319). The other point is that inhabitants of the country spoke the same language, except for intonation, which may vary from region to region, and shared a common culture at the time of the colonial encounter (Kagabo and Mudandagizi 1974: 76), and that basically Batwa, Hutu, and Tutsi were simply social categories and not ethnic groups (Twagiramutara 1989: 94). In fact, all ethnic identification has been banned since the 1994 genocide and civil war (Tiemessen 2004: 68).

Because of this unwillingness to identify people by ethnic group, there is no specific law in Rwanda to promote or protect Batwa rights (Lewis 2001: 11). However, indigenous rights advocates might argue that non-recognition of indigenous rights is a violation by Rwanda of internationally recognized norms, and Rwanda has been encouraged to recognize and protect Batwa as an indigenous people (Ndahinda 2011: 251).

We should note, however, that during the colonial era and the time immediately following independence, theories about the separate identities, origins, and successive migratory waves of Batwa, Hutu, and Tutsi in Rwanda were central to the reconstruction of the history of the country. Observations on, and measurement of, physical characteristics of members of each group were common at the time (e.g. Hiernaux 1968: 46). On the other hand, Batwa are often referred to as Abasangwabutaka (Ndahinda 2011: 224), literally "people found on earth, or on the land", meaning the original inhabitants of the land. In other words, they are recognized as autochthonous or indigenous people of the country. Designation as indigenous in the vernacular seems to give credence to, if not to be the foundation of, contemporary indigenous claims under evolving international legal frameworks.

Despite their marginalization, in 1991 the Batwa succeeded in setting up their first representative organization (Lewis 2006: 21). The Association pour la promotion des Batwa (APB) was founded in Rwanda to promote Batwa rights, and to assist Batwa to improve their standard of living (Lewis 2001: 6). The APB has been described as the first autonomous "pygmy" association in Africa (Ndahinda 2011: 236). Now known as the Communauté des Potiers du Rwanda (Rwandan Potters' Community), the organization aims to promote, protect, and sustainably develop Batwa interests in Rwanda (Ndahinda 2011: 239; Wessendorf 2011: 435).

During the 1994 genocide in Rwanda, when Hutu extremists turned against their Tutsi co-nationals, Batwa in many areas were threatened and killed by the Interahamwe, a Hutu paramilitary organization which was responsible for the genocide. Batwa were also used by the Interahamwe to rape women, especially at roadblocks (Lewis 2006: 11). At the end of the genocide, many Batwa around the country found themselves imprisoned (Lewis 2001: 26). At the moment, neither the museums nor the genocide memorials mention the difficulties that Batwa communities experienced during this period.

Batwa Heritage and Great Lakes Museums

In Africa's Great Lakes region, the museum concept is still new. The Uganda Museum was established in 1908 (May 2013: 13), some twenty odd years before Congo's Musée National de Kinshasa, founded in 1930 (Konaré and O'Byrne 1995: 1). But it was not until 1947 that the Institute of National Museums of Rwanda (INMR) was created. In the beginning, local people in the region did not visit museums, considering them to be the expensive tourist places, or houses of fetishes. For example, in Uganda, museums were called *Enyuma y'amayembe*, or "houses of fetishes," because of the ritual objects conserved there (May 2013: 13). Now views are changing. Statistics from the region show that the number of nationals visiting museums has grown considerably (e.g. INMR 2007), and the number of museums in postcolonial nations and among indigenous, or Fourth World communities is rapidly increasing (Herle 1997: 65).

In Rwanda's museums and genocide memorials, attention has focused on Hutu and Tutsi relations (Lewis 2001: 3), with the result that the Batwa remain invisible in accounts of the events. However, during the genocide, Batwa were extremely vulnerable, and far from invisible. Thus, during Rwanda's 1994 genocide and civil war, Batwa communities were targeted all over Rwanda, and many of them were murdered (Lewis 2006: 8). According to Lewis (2001: 27), one third of the Batwa perished during the conflict.

According to census estimates, some 937,000 died in the genocide in Rwanda (Lewis 2006: 2). Although less than 1 percent of Rwanda's population, it is estimated that 30 percent of Rwanda's Batwa died or were killed during the genocide and the ensuing war (Lewis 2006: 2; Crawhall 2008). This human tragedy remains ignored by most of the public, because local museums and genocide memorials do not mention it. Members of the Batwa community have been on the margin of society to the extent that most social studies of the region hardly spare more than a few paragraphs, if any, for this group.

On the other hand, in 2008, the INMR decided to change the text in its exhibition, the aim being to follow the new government's policy regarding ethnic issues in the country. Thus, according to the policy of "Rwandanness" (Kanimba and Van Pee 2008: 6) – or *Ndi umunyarwanda* ("we all are Rwandans") in Kinyarwanda – Hutu, Tutsi, and Batwa are the same people. This was the reason all texts with ethnic identification were removed from museums, and thus cultural material that used to be described as belonging to Batwa is now described as belonging to all Rwandans.

This denial of ethnicity in Rwanda means that the cultural ownership of indigenous Batwa objects is also being denied. This shows that being indigenous, and the ownership of cultural property, is not just an issue involving the West versus the Global South, but can also be an internal issue in once colonized countries.

With the policy of "Rwandanness," all Rwandans are called to visit museums in order to learn from the rich information on Rwandan history and culture disseminated there (Kanimba and Van Pee 2008), and recent statistics show that the number of Rwandans visiting museums has increased. However, whilst the Batwa community I visited in June 2013 in Kinigi, northern Rwanda, knew about the genocide museums, it did not know anything about other museums, and they have no idea about what is displayed in them. This is mainly due to the fact that Batwa people, as mentioned above, are generally not educated, have no access to new technologies and media such as the internet, and museum programs do not involve them. Because of their poverty, they also cannot afford to pay for museum tickets to visit their property exhibited there.

On the other hand, members of this community I interviewed have no idea where their cultural materials are conserved. They cite their lack of education as the cause, and ask the government to help them track down these materials. They also ask the government to see how revenues produced by these materials can be used to improve the Batwa people's social conditions.

When I asked them what these materials would be, their answer was that these materials would be different types of pottery, musical instruments, and products from hunting as well as hunting equipment. Some of these materials were taken by colonizers during the colonial period, while others were even taken after independence. However, there has been no specific study to identify and locate these materials. A study to rectify this situation is therefore needed.

Cultural Heritage Policy and Indigenous Rights in Rwanda

The real meaning and significance of indigenous rights in a situation such as Rwanda is always buried in confusing discourses. Thus, according to a document about cultural heritage policy written by Rwanda's Ministry of Sport and Culture in 2006, before the colonial era Rwanda was unquestionably a nation-state with a people sharing the same religious beliefs, the same traditions and customs, and speaking the same language, Kinyarwanda; in short, Rwanda was culturally uniform. However, in order to consolidate their power, colonizers and missionaries destroyed the identity and collective memory of Rwandans (MINISPOC 2008: 4; Ndahinda 2011: 247).

Currently, Rwanda's cultural heritage is governed by a 1939 law on the protection of sites, monuments, and production of indigenous art (MINISPOC 2008: 13). This text needs to be updated. Furthermore, the Rwandan Constitution stipulates that the government is obliged to ensure preservation of its cultural heritage, memorials, and sites of genocide. It also requires the government to establish mechanisms for the return of Rwanda's cultural property kept abroad. The government is also encouraged to collaborate with different institutions like UNESCO to fight against theft, looting, and the illegal import and export of cultural property, which may involve archeological sites, public and private collections, religious buildings, and cultural institutions like museums.

An example to illustrate the need of updating laws governing Rwanda's cultural heritage concerns the royal remains kept at the ethnographic museum in Huye. Two graves of former Rwandan kings and one of a former queen mother were excavated in the 1960s (Kanimba and Van Pee 2008: 50). These remains were initially displayed in the museum, but under the pressure from Inteko izirikana – an association of Rwandan elders which wishes to revive and educate people in Rwandan cultural values – who argued that the display was against Rwandan culture, the remains were removed from public display.[5] They are now kept in the museum's reserve collection, and only researchers have access to them.

More research on Rwandan cultural property kept abroad is also needed. Thus, even if the Ministry of Sport and Culture talks about repatriation, no studies have been conducted so far to identify and locate these materials. However, the recent exhibition of Rwandan musical instruments at the Musée Royal de l'Afrique Centrale in Tervuren, Belgium, shows that items of this kind are held by Western museums (Gansemans and Nkulikiyinka 2012).

Give Me What Is Mine: African Indigenous People and the Politics of Repatriation

Besides Batwa cultural material, many other cultural objects from African, Asian, and Latin American countries were stolen or illegally taken from their place of origin (Abungu 2004: 5; Gabriel 2006: 1). For Africa, the main example cited is of Benin, where in 1897 a British expeditionary force destroyed the royal palace, now in Nigeria, home to tens of thousands of works of art in wood, ivory, and bronze. These were the private property of the *oba* (king) of Benin (Gabriel 2006: 1). The king was deposed and his palace burnt down. Much of his collection of bronze and ivory was seized as the spoils of war, and ended up in private collections and public museums, such as the British Museum in London (Orford 2011: 3; Ostergard, Tubin, and Dikirr 2006: 314).

The problem now is that museums in the West are claiming that the Benin pieces and other indigenous material they have were all bought on the art market, and therefore have been legitimately acquired (Schuster 2004: 5). But for Africans, purchases of stolen goods are not legitimate transactions (Opoku 2007: 4). Some of these works are now, apart from their spiritual and cultural value, highly regarded and extremely valuable (Ostergard, Tubin, and Dikirr 2006: 322), worth millions of dollars (Orford 2011: 3). Indeed, the British Museum has sold some Benin bronzes to the Nigerians, and one can imagine how Nigerians felt after being obliged to buy back goods previously stolen from them (Orford 2011: 3). A less-well-known example is the attack by the British in 1874 on Kumasi, Gold Coast (Ghana), where British soldiers ransacked the town and took everything in gold they could find (Opoku 2007: 1). Most African countries have been victims of similar actions regarding their cultural heritage at the time of European colonization.

In the Great Lakes region, Batwa communities are asking for the repatriation of their property, but it is still difficult to know where these materials are held. One example of cultural material stolen in this region, however, comes from the Bunyoro kingdom of Uganda, where King Salomon Gafabusa Iguru is asking for the return of his royal regalia. He has asked the Ugandan government to support his demand that Britain return his royal throne, which was confiscated by Colonel Colville, a colonial agent, in 1894. According to the king, this throne is kept at the Pitt Rivers Museum, Oxford, and the king claims he saw it during a visit to the museum in 2013 (Mugerwa 2014). He also accuses this museum of financially benefiting from the throne. However, the Pitts Rivers Museum denies holding the said throne.

Regarding human remains, one example is that of Saartjie Baartman (1789–1815), a Khoekhoe domestic worker taken to England in 1810, where she was exhibited to the public in a cage for the amusement of paying crowds (Verna 2011: 7). She died in 1815, and her remains were exhibited in various museums in Europe. After the fall of apartheid, President Nelson Mandela raised the issue of Baartman's repatriation to South Africa, and her remains were returned home in 2002. She was buried on the bank of the Gamtoos River the same year.

There has been a lot of discussion about the repatriation and reburial of indigenous skeletons held in museums and other collections (e.g. Layton 1989; Ostergard, Tubin, and Dikirr 2006: 313). From the museums' perspective, the human remains should be retained in institutional collections because they have scientific value (Layton 1989: 3; Lane 1996: 3). Thus they have the potential to provide anthropologists with historical data about such things as disease, diet, social practices, population movement, and human evolution. For example, the use of prehistoric human remains has helped in the study of syphilis (Verna 2011: 13). However, indigenous communities have responded that many of these remains have laid unused for decades, and if there are claims regarding their scientific value, it is for the scientific community to prove this (Verna 2011: 13).

Currently some museums, libraries, and universities, under pressure from indigenous movements (Pilcher and Vermeylen 2008: 2), are taking measures for the repatriation or restitution of cultural property (Schuster 2004: 5; Pannell 1994: 19).[6] Nevertheless, the practice is still debated among researchers (e.g. Brown 2009: 161; Orford 2011: 2; Shyllon 2000). Thus calls to repatriate indigenous cultural objects from Western museum collections have become an important issue for museums in recent years.

The main reason indigenous people want their heritage back, apart from it being their right, is the way these objects are presented in Western museums. Much of the property removed from indigenous people, especially in Africa, was not treated by them as a piece of art for individual enjoyment as it would be in the West (Gabriel 2006: 3; Lane 1996: 5). Rather, these items were part of the spiritual, cultural, and material property connected to the land of different groups on the continent (Brown 2009: 160). Such artifacts tell the story of the journeys of different nations, and when museums present them purely for their aesthetic qualities, they decontextualize them and silence the many stories that give them meaning (Gabriel 2006: 2). The issue is not only about the physical removal of objects from indigenous people, but also the change in the context of their use.

Indigenous groups, especially those of North America, Oceania, and Australia, frequently complain that public display of objects held to be sacred, and which would not usually be displayed for everybody to see, violates their cultural rules and vitiates the objects' power (Gabriel 2006: 2; Brown 2009: 152). This means people are reluctant to go to museums as they feel that they do not want to see their culture denigrated and sometimes portrayed as low down on the hierarchy of cultural evolution (Gabriel 2006: 3).

According to Opoku (2007: 6), people who are against repatriation argue that most indigenous communities have corrupt leadership, and that unless indigenous communities get their own house in order there is a risk that repatriated objects may be mistreated or stolen and re-sold to collectors. They cite the example of the Democratic Republic of the Congo (Gabriel 2006: 2), where collections have disappeared and entered the illegal international art market. Here museums have been degraded or destroyed, there is no money to look after them, and few people care about them. Those in favor of repatriation, however, say that this is an insulting argument, an act of intimidation aimed at dissuading all African, Asian, and Latin American states from making claims for the repatriation of stolen or illegally exported cultural objects (Gabriel 2006: 3).

The debate is also about the responsibility of museums to ensure respect for indigenous peoples' rights (Pilcher and Vermeylen 2008: 1; Brown 2009: 152). Some indigenous communities have recently argued that while museums in general collect and preserve objects, they do not address or serve the needs of the people among whom the materials originated (Verna 2011: 6). They accuse museums of being united in their determination not to return objects to their rightful owners, the indigenous peoples (Opoku 2007: 2).

Researchers against repatriation suggest that Western museums should hold these objects for the whole world, and that anybody who wants to come and see them and study them is welcome (Gabriel 2006: 1). For them, the only way forward is for indigenous people in the diaspora to be more involved in how objects are displayed and represented in Western museums (Gabriel 2006: 3; Brown 2009: 162).

Thus, since the 1980s, many Western museums have involved indigenous scholars in their exhibitions (Verna 2011: 15; Brown 2009: 158; Herle 1997: 66). The involvement is also extended to the collection, interpretation, and representation of materials, as well as to research and educational programs, and at the same time museums benefit from the experience and knowledge of these scholars. However, some researchers would argue that no matter how good the intention is, the participation of indigenous people in these activities does not in any way change the question of the illegality and the illegitimacy of the acquisition of these cultural objects (Opoku 2007: 5; Pilcher and Vermeylen 2008: 1). The collaboration between museum researchers and indigenous communities is being observed in archeological research as well (Ferris 2003: 175). Because of this relationship between museums and indigenous groups, for the last two decades the number of members of indigenous groups visiting Western museums has increased (Herle 1997: 66).

In Australia, for example, museums have worked closely with indigenous communities for many years to assist them in achieving their own cultural objectives, and supported small museums established by these communities, called "keeping places" (Kelly 2001: 1). "Keeping places" are established by indigenous people in their local area to house repatriated artifacts, host exhibitions, conduct education and research programs whilst also providing employment and a meeting place. An analysis conducted by Kelly (2001: 4) found that "keeping places" were being set up for two reasons: firstly, to meet the needs of indigenous communities, and secondly, to promote reconciliation through understanding. Increasing numbers of communities are now thinking about establishing "keeping places" in their local area (Kelly 2001: 4).

Another suggestion would be the use of "cyber-museology" or "online museums," transforming the act of exhibiting ethnographic objects accompanied by text and graphics into an act of cyber-discourse that allows indigenous people to become involved in their own history through their own voices and gestures (Pilcher and Vermeylen 2008: 4). This is particularly the case since some indigenous people are using technologies such as the internet as a new medium through which they can recuperate their histories, land rights, knowledge, and cultural heritage.

Sharing copies, images, or audio recordings of original material held by repositories, including museums, is another suggestion (Brown 2009: 153). The problem is that indigenous people judge this insufficient and demand that all information held by these repositories be repatriated to the source communities. They want complete control over the material, regardless of competing claims by those who currently hold it, be they folklorist, ethnographer, photographer, or missionary. They have suggested the voluntary repatriation of all artifacts held by the former colonial powers to the descendants of their original owners. However, they are aware that it is uncommon for museums to return objects when there is no legal obligation to do so (Opoku 2007: 4).

Currently, especially in the United States and Canada, there is a move toward indigenous self-representation, with native communities running their own museums (Brown 2009: 154). These institutions are managed by an emerging indigenous elite, and are likely to enjoy a high level of local participation, and serve as catalysts for cultural renewal and collective pride. They also offer a laboratory for innovative collaboration between anthropologists and indigenous communities.

In the meantime, the Declaration on the Importance and Value of Universal Museums was signed on 10 December 2002 by leading museums of Europe and North America (see ICOM 2004). According to this, objects acquired, whether by purchase or gift, have over time become part of the museums that have cared for them, and by extension part of the heritage of the nations which house them. The directors of these museums even argued that these objects gained notoriety because they are displayed in these "universal museums" (Schuster 2004: 5). This declaration was criticized by some researchers, who think that it is "imperialistic" (Gabriel 2006: 1; Opoku 2007: 2–3) and that it was signed because of the fear that if large scale repatriation were to take place, then many Western museums would be left with hardly any collections at all (Abungu 2004: 5). For others (e.g. Mugerwa 2014) it was because of the financial benefits these materials generate for these museums.

I would, however, say that in the museum world, indigenous rights have considerably improved, compared with the late nineteenth and early twentieth century, when exhibitions were mainly based on assumptions of cultural superiority. Such assumptions are now rightly contested (Brown 2009: 149). For example, the American Association of Museum Directors now recommends that art museums enter into "good faith" negotiations with groups who believe that sacred objects in museum collections deserve special treatment (Brown 2009: 150). More broadly, museums are under increasing pressure to consult with indigenous communities when planning exhibitions in which such communities are deemed to have a moral stake. Museums understand now that they must produce their exhibitions with the full involvement of the indigenous communities they propose to represent, and that they must involve them in all aspects of their development (Brown 2009: 159).

Conclusion

The example of the Batwa of the Great Lakes region of Central Africa showed us that the problem of indigenous people and the appropriation of their property is not an issue concerning relations between the North and the South, but also relations between postcolonial nation-states and minority (and sometimes marginalized) groups who live within their boundaries. Museums in this region need to involve more Batwa and other minority groups in their daily activities, and national legislation needs updating regarding the protection of their cultural heritage. Museums also need to recognize Batwa rights to their cultural property, as well as ensure that financial benefits they obtain from this cultural property is used in part to support Batwa communities. Education is a key issue, and improvements in education are needed for the Batwa to understand their rights and enable them to protest when their heritage is misrepresented or misused by museums.

On the other hand, the argument made by some Western museums that indigenous objects in their possession now belong to "world culture," and are best kept in the West because museums in Africa or other poor countries do not have adequate security, has to be revisited (Ostergard, Tubin, and Dikirr 2006: 322), especially when one considers the problems people from poor countries now have in entering Europe and United States. It is now very hard for some indigenous people to visit a Western museum to see their cultural objects held there. Some indigenous people, such as the Batwa, do not even know where their lost property is being held. As I understand it, the repatriation of these materials, especially to African countries, would promote tourism since people would have to come to Africa to see them in their original context (see also Gabriel 2006: 1). Besides, it would be just as legitimate to send these materials back to the people who created them and who understand how they should be treated with respect.

Acknowledgements

I would like to thank John Giblin of the British Museum in London for his constructive comments on an earlier draft of this chapter.

Notes

1 According to Lewis, the term "Batwa" has the same meaning as the term "pygmy" (Lewis 2001: 5).
2 Although generally marginalized, Batwa were unanimously known for their dancing and artistic ability.
3 In Rwanda, the name Batwa refers to the least known of the three "ethnic groups" that make up the Rwandan population – the others being Hutu, and Tutsi – although the term "ethnic group" should be used with caution here since there are still persistent disagreements over its use in the country.
4 In November 2010, the Rwandan government began a program to destroy straw huts throughout the country. The government's justification for this was that all people in Rwanda must live in modern houses (e.g. Rutareka 2011).
5 Misago Kanimba, former director of Rwanda's museums, personal communication, 2007.
6 For example, in 2013 the Museum of Medical History in Berlin returned 33 skulls and skeletons to members of tribes from the Torres Strait, between Australia and Papua New Guinea.

References

Abungu, G. (2004) The Declaration: A Contested Issue. *ICOM News*, 1, 5–7.

ACHPR (African Commission on Human and Peoples' Rights) (2005). *Report of the African Commission's Working Group of Experts on Indigenous Populations/Communities.* Copenhagen: International Working Group on Indigenous Affairs. Available at: http: //www.iwgia.org/iwgia_files_publications_files/African_Commission_book.pdf (accessed January 28, 2014).

Biesbrouck, K., Elders, S., and Rossel, G. (eds) (1999) *Central African Hunter-Gatherers in a Multidisciplinary Perspective: Challenging Elusiveness.* Leiden: Universiteit Leiden.

Brown, F.M. (2009) Exhibiting Indigenous Heritage in the Age of Cultural Property. In J. Cuno (ed.), *Whose Culture? The Promise of Museums and the Debate over Antiquities.* Princeton: Princeton University Press, pp. 147–165.

Crawhall, N. (2008) *Heritage Education for Sustainable Development: Dialogue with Indigenous Communities in Africa.* Paris: UNESCO.

Eyo, E. (2010) *From Shrines to Showcases: Masterpieces of Nigerian Art.* Abuja: Ministry of Information and Communication.

Ferris, N. (2003) Between Colonial and Indigenous Archaeologies: Legal and Extra-legal Ownership of the Archaeological Past in North America. *Canadian Journal of Archaeology*, 27 (2), 154–190.

Gabriel, D. (2006). Stealing History: The Great Debate on the Repatriation of African Cultural Property. Available at: http://deborahgabriel.com/wp-content/uploads/2010/05/Stealing-history-the-great-debate-on-the-repatriation-of-African-cultural-property.pdf (accessed January 31, 2014).

Gansemans, J., and Nkulikiyinka, J.B. (2012) *Les instruments de musique du Rwanda.* Tervuren: Musée Royal de l'Afrique Centrale.

Herle, A. (1997) Museums, Politics and Representation. *Journal of Museum Ethnography*, 9, 65–78.

Hiernaux, J. (1968) Bodily Shape Differentiation of Ethnic Groups and of the Sexes through Growth. *Human Biology*, 40 (1), 44–62.

ICOM (2004) Declaration on the Importance and Value of Universal Museums. *ICOM News*, 1, 5.

INMR (Institute of National Museums of Rwanda) (2007) *Le Musée National du Rwanda (1995–2006): Douze ans d'exercice après le Genocide*. Butare: Musée National du Rwanda.

Kagabo, J., and Mudandagizi, V. (1974) Complainte des gens de l'argile. *Cahiers d'Etudes Africaines*, 14 (53), 75–87.

Kanimba, M., and Van Pee, L. (2008) *Rwanda and its Cultural Heritage: Past and Present*. Butare: Institute of National Museums of Rwanda.

Kelly, L. (2001) Policy, Practice and Partnerships: Museums, Indigenous Communities and Evaluation. Available at: http: //www.ou.edu/cls/online/lstd5790house/pdf/unit1_kelly.pdf (accessed February 18, 2014).

Konaré, A.O., and O'Byrne, P. (1995) *Création du Musée National de Kinshasa*. Paris: UNESCO.

Lane, P. (1996) Breaking the Mould? Exhibiting Khoisan in Southern African Museums. *Anthropology Today*, 12 (5), 3–10.

Layton, R. (ed.). (1989) *Conflict in the Archaeology of Living Traditions*. London: Unwin Hyman.

Lewis, J. (2001) *Les pygmées batwa de la region des Grands Lacs*. London: Minority Rights Group International.

Lewis, J. (2006) The Twa Pygmies: Rwanda's Ignored People. In S.C. Abega and P.B. Logo (eds), *La marginalisation des pygmées d'Afrique Centrale*. Langres: Maisonneuve et Larose, pp. 79–105.

May, E. (2013) *Architecture and Urban Planning in Kampala: An Exhibition at the Uganda Museum*. Kampala: Uganda Museum.

MINISPOC (Ministry of Sport and Culture) (2008) *Policy on Cultural Heritage*. Kigali: MINISPOC.

Mugerwa, F. (2014) Bunyoro Wants UK to Return Stolen Throne. Available at: http://www.monitor.co.ug/News/National/Bunyoro-wants-UK-to-return-stolen-throne/-/688334/2244398/-/10qkxvv/-/index.html (accessed April 6, 2014).

Ndahinda, F.M. (2011) *Indigenousness in Africa: A Contested Legal Framework for Empowerment of "Marginalized" Communities*. The Hague: T.M.C. Asser Press.

Opoku, K. (2007) Benin Exhibition: Some Reflections on Repatriation of Stolen or Illegally Exported Cultural Goods. Available at: http: //www.afrikanet.info/archiv1/index.php?option=com_content&task=view&id=627&Itemid=120 (accessed March 2, 2014).

Orford, T. (2011) "Sending It Back": The Role of Law and the Cultural Patrimony Debate. Available at: https: //www.yumpu.com/en/document/view/20149742/sending-it-back-by-toby-orford-artright (accessed February 14, 2014).

Ostergard, L.R., Tubin, M.R., and Dikirr, P. (2006) Between the Sacred and the Secular: Indigenous Intellectual Property, International Markets and the Modern African State. *Journal of Modern African Studies*, 44 (2), 309–333.

Pannell, S. (1994) Mabo and Museums: "The Indigenous (Re)Appropriation of Indigenous Things'. *Oceania*, 65 (1), 18–39.

Pilcher, J., and Vermeylen, S. (2008) From Loss of Objects to Recovered Meanings: Online Museums and Indigenous Cultural Heritage. *M/C Journal*, 11 (6), 1–26.

Rutareka, A. (2011) Nyakatsi Eradication Moves 125,000 People into Decent Housing. Available at: http: //focus.rw/wp/2011/05/nyakatsi-eradication-moves-125000-people-into-decent-housing/ (accessed January 24, 2014).

Schuster, P.K. (2004) The Treasures of World Culture in the Public Museum. *ICOM News*, 1, 4–5.

Shyllon, F. (2000) The Recovery of Cultural Objects by African States through the UNESCO and UNIDROIT Conventions and the Role of Arbitration. *Uniform Law Review*, 2, 219–241.

Tiemessen, A.E. (2004) After Arusha: Gacaca Justice in Post-Genocide Rwanda. *African Studies Quarterly*, 8 (1), 57–76.

Trofanenko, B. (2006) Displayed Objects, Indigenous Identities, and Public Pedagogy. *Anthropology and Education Quarterly*, 37 (4), 309–327.

Twagiramutara, P. (1989) Archaeological and Anthropological Hypotheses Concerning the Origin of Ethnic Divisions in Sub-Saharan Africa. In R. Layton (ed.), *Conflict in the Archaeology of Living Traditions.* London: Unwin Hyman, pp. 88–95.

United Nations (2007) Declaration on the Rights of Indigenous Peoples (UNDRIP). Document A/RES/61/295. Available at: http://www.un-documents.net/a61r295.htm (accessed March 19, 2015).

Verna, M. (ed.). (2011) *Museums and the Repatriation of Indigenous Human Remains.* Montreal: McGill University.

Wessendorf, K. (2011) *The Indigenous World.* Copenhagen: International Working Group in Indigenous Affairs.

PART II Using and Abusing Heritage

CHAPTER 11

Valuing the Past, or, Untangling the Social, Political, and Economic Importance of Cultural Heritage Sites

Brenda Trofanenko

As heritage sites continue to protect valuable objects and creations, they are increasingly assigned additional purposes. Not only are they considered to have moved beyond a caring directive to become firmly placed in what Kerwin Lee Klein has called the "memory industry" (Klein 2000: 27), they are also considered to be elements influencing the economic development of local, national, and international markets. As places where such purposes have been increasingly "investigated," "interrogated," and "problematized" over the past two decades, the challenges facing such sites include navigating through various public expectations and institutional mandates. Serving to connect the past with the present, such sites (especially those that are state-supported) also serve political functions that support the state and the state's mandates including advancing tourism, migration, and economic development.

In the case of the Grand-Pré National Historic Site (GPNHS) in the Province of Nova Scotia, Canada, a UNESCO site designated in 2012 and run under the auspices of Parks Canada, questions about the economic, social, and political functions such a site serves have highlighted a spectrum of tensions. To be certain, the significance or "outstanding universal value" ascribed to the "Landscape of Grand-Pré" by the UNESCO designation serves to witness the vibrant Acadian farming practices and

A Companion to Heritage Studies, First Edition. Edited by William Logan, Máiréad Nic Craith, and Ullrich Kockel.
© 2016 John Wiley & Sons, Inc. Published 2016 by John Wiley & Sons, Inc.

settlements of the seventeenth century that remain obvious in the area today. Indirectly, the designation tells not only of the Acadian expulsion from Canada in the eighteenth century that has held little interest beyond the Acadian community, but also that it remains a *lieu de mémoire*, an

> iconic place of remembrance of the Acadian diaspora, dispersed by the Grand Dérangement … Its [marshland] landscape and archaeological remains are testimony to the values of a culture of pioneers able to create their own territory, whilst living in harmony with the native Mi'kmaq people. Its memorial constructions form the centre of the symbolic re-appropriation of the land of their origins by the Acadians, in the 20th century, in a spirit of peace and cultural sharing with the English-speaking community. (UNESCO 2012: 193)

The site also serves as a reminder of the Acadian expulsion from Nova Scotia, which is an often forgotten episode of Canadian history. It is a symbol of the reappropriation of Grand-Pré by the Acadian people, a memorial site including a memorial chapel, historic gardens, and monuments, and a tourism site to bolster the Nova Scotia's tourist industry, which serves as a major revenue producer. The UNESCO designation of the site enhances the opportunity to remember the long-standing presence of Acadians and their communal contributions, which may bring about not only feelings of pride but also about estrangement and identification pivotal to the Acadian historic experience without necessarily seeking to bolster economic revenues.

There are competing interest groups that consider the GPNHS a site which, simultaneously, affirms Acadian identity, serves as an economic boost to the provincial tourism industry, and is an example of government collaboration. These groups comprise the Acadian community, the federal and provincial governments and local businesses. They remain in conflict about the nature and extent of impact on the GPNHS site and the purposes the site is to serve. This chapter aims to show, using a case study, how heritage sites such as the GPNHS hold competing mandates, including that of a memorial site and a tourist site, and to make good those wrongs committed in the past to local peoples, all with the focus of drawing people to an area claiming to hold universal value. A significant issue here concerns understanding that the designation of a place like Grand-Pré as a "national historic site" needs to be considered within the political climate of local, national, and international communities. This chapter investigates how management of the site seeks to balance the tensions around the site's purpose in order to maintain support from all stakeholders.

The Exceptionality of Grand-Pré

Situated on the banks of a rise on Old Post Road, Hortonville, Nova Scotia, is a small area designated as a park and identified by Parks Canada as "the Landscape of Grand-Pré." Largely barren, and dotted with several benches, flags, maps, and plaques, the site overlooks local vineyards and wineries, orchards of apple and other upland crops, and thousands of acres of cultivated marshland located in the continuous villages of Grand-Pré, North Grand-Pré, and Hortonville. It also overlooks the GPNHS, with the notable steeple of a church visible amongst the trees. It is easy to note the distinct landscape and farming patterns below, regardless of the maps highlighting the distinct land-use patterns. In the distance, visitors can see the Minas Basin and the site where Acadians were systematically gathered together and expelled from Canada. The park offers a point from which to see the expanse of the dyke system credited to the Acadians, which "bears exceptional testimony to a traditional farming settlement … still in use today," and gives the viewer a vantage point from which to see out over Grand-Pré (the geographical locale), "the iconic place of remembrance of the Acadian diaspora, dispersed by the Grand Dérangement."[1]

Beyond the "Landscape of Grand-Pré" site and the GPNHS, the area is of local, provincial, and global relevance, notably regarding the robust farming community and wine industry. Acadians established themselves in the Grand-Pré area following an exodus from Port Royal in the western part of Nova Scotia in the late 1680s. Grand-Pré provided the Acadians with more stable and suitable marshes, located in the Minas Basin along the Bay of Fundy. The Acadian settlement of Grand-Pré transformed the marsh areas into fertile agricultural land through employing their own system of dykes and drainage (Bleakney 2004: 4). By building dykes along tidal rivers and modifying the landscape, they created fertile marshlands that remain evident today. Although reasons for the Acadian relocation from the westernmost area of the province to Grand-Pré remain much debated, British authorities were behind the forced movement of the Acadian population (the event known as the Grand Dérangement) between 1755 and 1763, when they were forced to go to other colonies in North America, primarily along the eastern seaboard of the United States, and to Louisiana. Within five years of their initial expulsion from Grand-Pré, Acadians were systematically expelled from the present-day Canadian provinces of Nova Scotia, New Brunswick, and Prince Edward Island (LeBlanc 2003: 44). The expulsion of the Acadians was followed by a settlement

Figure 11.1 View of Grand-Pré and the Grand-Pré National Historic Site. Source: photo by Brenda Trofanenko.

plan for English-speaking New England Planters, brought in to occupy the farmland established by the Acadians.

Several events occurred after the Grand Dérangement that drew attention to Grand-Pré. Henry Longfellow's poem *Evangeline*, published in 1847, was the basis of increased public recognition of the deportation from Grand-Pré, as well as the established repopulation of the area (LeBlanc 2003: 64). In the nineteenth century, Acadians who returned to the area asserted their distinct identity by adopting national symbols such as a flag (the French flag with a gold star), an anthem ("Ave Maris Stella") and a decision-making body (the Société nationale de l'Assomption, the precursor of today's Société nationale de l'Acadie). Beyond the GPNHS building proper, a memorial chapel, gardens, and several monuments including a statue of Evangeline (an Acadian girl, who was a key figure in Longfellow's poem, who searches for her lost love set during the time of the Grand Dérangement) affirm UNESCO's statement regarding the Outstanding Universal Value of the site that such material elements provide a "symbolic re-appropriation" of a collective Acadian identity (LeBlanc 2003: 176–77).

But the history of the GPNHS is more complex and multifaceted, for it is not simply a designated UNESCO site supported by Parks Canada and local, provincial, and federal governments. On June 30, 2012, after five years of planning, the GPNHS was recognized as having outstanding universal value because of its natural significance, because of the evidence of long-standing agricultural techniques, and because of it being a symbol of the resilience of the Acadian people. The broad political involvement of three levels of government not only provided a stamp of authority legitimizing the existence of an Acadian memorial site that serves as a heritage tourism destination, but also serves to show support from various government levels for an historical event involving an identified group of people.

At the local level, a personal cause aided the establishment of the GPNHS. In 1907, John Fredric Herbin, whose mother was Acadian, led a campaign to have the site of Grand-Pré preserved as a memorial. He bought land, selling it eventually to the Dominion Atlantic Railway (DAR) on the condition that the lands be deeded to Acadians so that the site would become preserved as a memorial. They maintained the grounds until 1921, when possession was transferred to the provincial Société nationale de l'Assomption branch, who erected the memorial church.[2] The DAR eventually sold the land to the Canadian federal government in 1957. Parks Canada, the Canadian government-supported parks service, took over the operation of the park and designated it a Canadian National Historic Site in 1961. Parks Canada state that the purpose of the site is to:

> Commemorate the Acadians of the Minas Basin and the expulsion of the Acadians from their ancestral homeland; to protect for all time the memorial landmarks, cultural resources, ornamental gardens and physical environment that make up the special atmosphere and nature of the park; and to encourage public understanding, appreciation and enjoyment of the Acadian historical heritage. (Parks Canada 1985)

A visitor reception and interpretation center was established in 2003 that continues to feature exhibits about the history of Grand-Pré and Acadia, as well as a video presentation of the Acadian deportation. In addition, there is an administrative area, art gallery, and gift shop. In 2004, Parks Canada along with the Friends of Grand-Pré, an estabished community group, added the site to Canada's Tentative List of potential future World Heritage sites.

More than being solely a site supported by various levels of government to broker revenue through tourism, the GPNHS serves to show that "heritage stewardship [is] a shared responsibility" and that "all Nova Scotians have a role to play in preserving, protecting, and promoting our heritage as a shared responsibility (DTCH 2008: 9). Although the very idea of heritage has been questioned by some (e.g. Smith 2006: 11), it is both the tangible and intangible elements of the Acadian past that have established an Acadian identity (along with a particular historical narrative) at the GPNHS. The church, visitor center, monuments, and gardens help construct an Acadian identity in numerous ways. The multiple elements of that identity, specifically Acadian nationality, class, culture, and other community ideals (including a continued commitment to their historical contributions to the area) are being advanced through various political, economic, and social processes.

The focus of the GPNHS is on how Acadian identity, culture, and history can be advanced, protected, legitimated, and commemorated. As an institution considered both a "memory institution" (Crane 2000) and a *lieu de mémoire* (Nora 1989), it not

Figure 11.2 Evangeline statue and memorial church. Source: photo by Brenda Trofanenko.

only presents a historical narrative, but moves from "the historical to be remembered and the remembered to be commemorative" (Nora 1989: 626). Nora has importantly gone further in recognizing that sites of memory do not simply arise out of lived experiences, but rather have to be created. The various expectations served by Grand-Pré allow it to act as a vehicle for any number of identity projects, one being nationalism and the sense of belonging through memory. As Smith (1999) and Anderson (2006) note, memory has occupied a central role in nation-building projects since the global spread of nationalism from the late nineteenth century onward. Using the language of invention and imagination, stories, images, and symbols are utilized to illustrate a nation, a national history, and an affirmed identity that continues on in contemporary society. At Grand-Pré this has taken two main forms. First, the site continues to valorize and reify the traditional Acadian cultural practices that distinguish it as a nation from its proximal neighbors (the Planters) and similar groups (Mi'kmaq). In nationalist discourse and cultural politics, these practices take the form of the implicit memory of the nation and cultural routines that distinguishes an "us" from "them," or in the instance of Grand-Pré, Acadians from non-Acadians. Second, the site is used by those who seek to advance the idea of a distinct nation, and who utilize historical narratives to present a strong explicit collective story.

The relationship between history and nation-building is commonly discussed in various disciplines. Within academic history, various historical tropes have been used to produce particular narratives about states as nations. In realizing the limits of their discipline, some academic historians have reflected on how particular and partial historical narratives advance the nation as an imperial project of nation-building. This theoretical shift has prompted historians to re-examine the insular historical narratives that have formed the basis of their discipline. By insisting on the implicit and explicit political purposes that any narrative holds, historians have questioned the relationship history has with nation-building and territorially bounded nation-states.[3]

Yet there remains a paradoxical purpose of history. As Suny has noted, history "as a discipline helped to constitute the nation, even as the nation determined the categories in which history was written and the purpose it was to serve" (Suny 2000: 589). As the GPNHS shows, Acadian history remains a critical and central organizing concept. The creation and maintenance of an Acadian national identity focuses on one particular historical event – the Grand Dérangement, the expulsion of Acadians from Grand-Pré to other areas in the Atlantic provinces, the east of the United States, and south as far as Louisiana and beyond. The expulsion provides, as Sheila Andrew notes, a "very strong and unifying and leveling historical experience" that can be utilized for establishing a distinct national identity (Andrew 1996: 9–10). Of interest here is how history continues to do the work of imagining the nation through the sensibilities of memory and remembrance by affirming particular historical narratives, which have, as Ernest Renan noted more than a century ago, "forgotten things and have gotten history wrong" (Renan 1996: 41).

Although the initial work to establish the site began as a local effort years before what Winter (2006) has called the "memory boom," the remembrance and commemoration of Acadian history and culture have come to comprise a large collective global project that draws Acadians from beyond the immediate area. Instead of solely advancing local collective memory, the site provides a conventional history, narrative expositions, and didactic representations. It seems fair to say that the church, the monuments, exhibitions, and landscapes have played a significant role in the conventional history, narratives, and exhibition representations. As a *lieu de mémoire*, the GPNHS utilizes these and other elements to ensure that the remembrance of Acadian life is foregrounded in the understanding of their history. The Acadian flag is flown, visitors to the site wear the gold star that adorns the flag, the national anthem is played and sung, and interpreters dress in replicas of the garb Acadians wore in the late eighteenth and early nineteenth centuries.

This physical embodiment as cultural performance is, as Connerton (1989) has argued, central to a process of memory where physically incorporated practices are conceived of as "tradition." In a more recent work, Connerton (2009) explores how societal changes in how we remember and commemorate the past influences what and how we are able to remember past events and what they come to mean. Memory depends on stability and social processes central to a specific place. In this case, the GPNHS provides a foundation upon which the remembrance of Acadian history and culture can be built and shared.

Certainly, as a site of memory where the past is crystallized, a particular version of the past is sanctioned through the elements comprising the site. As is to be expected, the Acadian version of the past is acknowledged and presented in a struggle for recognition and affirmation of their resilience and persecution. What is at stake in their representations is not the past for its own sake but the past as it holds value and importance in the present. History, like remembrance, is a selective process. The history of conflicts and human rights violations relies on specific readings of the past. The role of historical figures, events, and the materiality and cultural lives of artifacts are utilized to construct a particular narrative. What occurs at the GPNHS is not necessarily the study of the past – of Acadian history as an object of inquiry as such – but rather how this Acadian history is remembered.

The focus on Acadian history in the area was not always prevalent and widely accepted by the community but gave way at points to multiple narratives and foci. In the 1960s, the museum included New England Planter artifacts in addition to British colonial objects that highlight the area's bicultural heritage. This bicultural identity followed the federal focus of Canada as a bicultural and bilingual state, but resulted in increasing "public dissatisfaction" about mixing Acadian and Planter culture, which was "designed to create a reflective and commemorative atmosphere to recall the story of the deported Acadians" (Parks Canada 1985: 11, 2). As with many other sites established in Canada during the late nineteenth and early twentieth centuries and built on "imperialist assumptions" that venerated British colonial rule resulting from conquest and expansion, there was a move towards eliminating narratives of British supremacy (Ricketts 1996). Yet narratives of British supremacy (specifically in the multimedia historical presentation) and Acadian resilience maintained today provide an intriguing and unsettling contradiction. They offer a counter-narrative to a standard historic trope, but it assumes replacing one narrative with another for a better understanding of past injustices committed against the Acadians.

As a *lieu de mémoire*, it is also a geographic place intended to commemorate an Acadian past. While the historical narrative has been established, commemoration is an ongoing process through which the idea and ideal of place is recognized both as local and as global. As James Opp and John Walsh acknowledge, "the 'local' is a fluid and uncertain category, reminding us that, despite the claims of planners, architects, and other spatial engineers, the production of place is always unfinished and uneven" (Opp and Walsh 2010: 7). Considering it as a process speaks directly to how geography is wrapped up in issues of power, language, and ideology. Grand-Pré as a geographic locale is positioned between the material and the immaterial, between the physical space of the site and the process through which the site has become a commemorative place. The geographic aspect – the establishment of Grand-Pré as both a physical place and a space in which commemoration is set – is articulated as a place and location that matters to national identity, and lies at the core of Acadian identity.

The Economics of Tourism

Even as the GPNHS continues to serve the function established for it by Parks Canada over the last fifty years, the more recent UNESCO designation supports an additional function beyond advancing and supporting the Acadian narrative of identity formation. As an institution situated in Nova Scotia, it also seeks to provide a financial return in a province with a higher than national average unemployment rate, limited employment opportunities, and a continuous net loss of individuals relocating to other Canadian provinces. Nova Scotia is one of the country's three maritime provinces, and the most populous province of Atlantic Canada. Including Cape Breton and some 3800 coastal islands, Nova Scotia is the second-smallest province of Canada (21,300 square miles), and its Department of Tourism portrays the province as a place of scenic beauty and rich heritage, framing it as a desirable maritime travel destination and highlighting its unique, and welcoming, travel opportunities: "Explore our breathtaking shores – from towering cliffs and long peaceful beaches to picturesque bays and charming villages. There is no shortage of ways to discover our renowned hospitality and charm" (DTCH 2009a). Such messages have made Nova Scotia both an international tourist destination and a place for out-of-province visits for Canadians. With a total population of 940,000, and faced with continuous out-migration and loss of population, Nova Scotia has traditionally depended upon a resource-based economy (fishing, agriculture, and exports of both). A long-term and continuous economic downturn facing the province, due in part to its dependence on these resources, has long positioned the province as one that is economically disadvantaged in relationship to other parts of Canada. With an average income of CAN$38,000 per year, Nova Scotians' average earnings are lower than the national average (CAN$47,000) and almost half of that of Alberta, a more economically enriched province. Being considered a "have not" province, Nova Scotia continually advances various economic development plans, including tourism, as it seeks to engage in projects and programs to tap the flow of capital in order to maintain economic and social stability (DoF 2010).

The increasing focus on tourism, and particularly heritage tourism, draws on the history of the area, its continued strong ties to the Commonwealth, its geographic diversity, and the perceived resilience of the ancestors who settled the land, tropes commonly drawn on by the province's tourism department:

> The past is present every day in Nova Scotia. Explore the fishing town of Lunenburg. Relive a day in the life of 1744 in the Fortress of Louisburg, the largest reconstruction of its kind in North America. Pass through the immigration sheds of Pier 21 National Historic Site in Halifax where over a million immigrants, troops, war brides, and evacuee children started their new lives. Experience Halifax's role as a principal naval station in the British Empire. (DTCH 2009b)

This explicit focus on Nova Scotia's place in Canadian history and the establishment of the nation situates many heritage sites on the supply side of tourism. Various sites in Nova Scotia are highlighted as being significant in terms of nation-building, as well as being sites of authentic historical events. It is obvious that the province's efforts to draw more tourists to Nova Scotia are aimed at not only verifying historical narratives of both the nation and the province, for they also utilize such narratives as a tourist draw. The promotion of local historical sites and the strengthening of the relationship between these and national identity is certainly a stated aim of the province's tourist industry, but the relationship is open to question.

Tourism currently plays a significant role in the economy of Nova Scotia. As an industry, it directly employs approximately 33,000 people with and a CAN$520 million annual payroll (DTCH 2004). Tourism in Nova Scotia has declined since 2004 with the decline being attributed to various economic factors including high fuel prices and a strong Canadian dollar (Macleod 2008: 252). The strategy by which the province seeks to increase tourism and its associated monetary gains is clearly highlighted in its advertising campaigns. While the provincial government promotes sites as worthy of visiting in their public promotional material, local communities are more cognizant of the values of heritage sites within their local area.

The Annapolis Valley region, located on the western shore of the Nova Scotia peninsula, is home to various tourist destinations that are historical, scientific, or culturally focused, including the GPNHS. A significant but declining amount of tourist activity can be attributed to the Annapolis Valley region. While tourism has annually increased by approximately 2 percent in Nova Scotia since 2003, the Annapolis Valley has witnessed a 13 percent decrease over the same time period (Macleod 2008: 251–53), and the GPNHS has suffered similar negative trends. The site was also considered an essential engine for economic development in a province that has limited economic resources and a declining population. Except for 2004, when the Annual Acadian Congress led to a large increase in the number of visitors to the site, there has been a consistent decline in visitors. It is believed that the World Heritage site designation will reverse this trend, producing a positive economic impact on the local economy (George 2013). However, in 2008, Parks Canada voiced its own concerns that fewer Canadians were visiting and interacting with national protected heritage sites. It pointed out that the cultural makeup of the country was much more multicultural than a mix of First Nations, English, and French inhabitants, and that the majority of Canadians lived in urban areas (Parks Canada, cited in Macleod 2008: 7–8).

If history serves as an example, the increase in economic returns on UNESCO-designated sites may not hold the key to the economic advancement of local and provincial economies. It is too early to tell whether the new designation of the GPNHS as a UNESCO World Heritage site of Outstanding Universal Value will draw significant numbers of visitors. The provincial government has provided support for tourism promotion efforts aimed at preserving natural and cultural heritage resources. In order to do this, the province has supported efforts to have both the Joggins Fossil Cliffs (which contain fossils preserved in their natural environmental contexts) and Old Town Lunenburg (considered the best surviving example of a planned British colonial settlement) designated as World Heritage sites. While such a designation does not guarantee any significant economic gain, this did not impede the financial support of various governments. In the successful bid for Grand-Pré, three levels of government contributed a total of CAN$1.3 million to a project that would see the area receive recognition as a worldwide cultural treasure. The successful bid would, the government believed, raise awareness of its significance and the value of other cultural sites in Nova Scotia, and in turn make the province a desirable tourist destination.

It is often thought that a UNESCO designation will bring a community together to celebrate the significance and value that is ascribed to a site (Goeldner, McIntosh, and Ritchie 1995). This is not necessarily the case in every instance. As Campbell noted in reference to the UNESCO designation of Old Town Lunenburg, "there is a potential for a hierarchy or rivalry between local history and international significance, between community memory and external expectations, between a specific place and local artifacts and a generally accessible heritage" (Campbell 2008: 2). Despite various public comments and concerns about the designation of the GPNHS as a World Heritage site with Outstanding Universal Value, specifically its historical agricultural significance, the purpose of the World Heritage nomination process was to highlight the site and its various features as symbols of Acadian identity and history (GoC 2011: 28).

An Uncommon Union

For many, the designation of the GPNHS as a World Heritage site affirms Acadian identity by designating the park as significant beyond local, provincial, and national realms. While UNESCO's recognition of the site's outstanding universal value does not speak explicitly about the French–English tensions that brought about the Acadian expulsion, it does speak to cultural sharing between the various local communities. This sharing has not been without issue.

History imbues the past with coherence and purpose. Much has been made within the academic community about presenting the history of subaltern groups and individuals to capture the diasporic, cultural, social, and political histories that further our understanding of the past. The GPNHS introduces these elements through the notion of recognition, either through an historical narrative or ensuring memory and remembrance. Focusing on the way recognition often frames how the public and particular groups imagine cultural identity as supporting (or not) their history, or ensuring an obvious and unambiguous identity, the GPNHS demonstrates its essential role in strengthening a communal form of social knowledge and memory that connects personal experiences to a past event. But the GPNHS is not solely about the development of a collective identity, for it also concerns enhancing individual experiences. In other words, public reactions and responses to what is presented at the GPNHS help explore critical relationships between individuals and groups, defining an individual and communal identity and the degree of personal engagement with local and national histories.

Heritage sites like the GPNHS, with its multiple roles and purposes, indicate the complex and shifting issues that are driven by political and economic tensions linking local communities, including the Acadians and Planters, different government levels involved and their expectations, and the Acadian diaspora to the American colonies, France, Haiti, and French Guiana. Like other heritage sites, it attempts to fulfill particular goals, both ideological (serving as a beacon of Acadian history, identity, and retribution) and commercial (increasing tourism and affirming Outstanding Universal

Value). By ensuring that the site remains relevant to its various attending and interested publics, the GPNHS is faced with tensions that may not, and perhaps should not, be resolved. The reasons individuals may or may not attend the site is as varied as the demographics they represent. The issue, then, is to realize how the differing purposes any institution serves has both an immediate and long-term implicit and explicit expectation. To consider the GPNHS as a site from which to understand the tensions underlying issues of memory, history, economic development, tourism, and identity, to name but a few, may result in a continued examination of such sites and their degree of success or not relative to various ideologies and purposes. The academic community needs to explore the relationship between the social, economic, and political purposes of heritage tourism, and discuss how the tensions define what purpose sites such as the GPNHS serve.

It is perhaps too early to gauge the impact that the UNESCO designation has had on the GPNHS and on the tourism industry in Nova Scotia. What is clear is that there is a concerted effort by the local, provincial, and federal governments along with the Acadian community to utilize the site as a vessel through which to augment the tourist industry while advancing knowledge of the Acadian history and experience. By drawing more tourists, whether Acadian or non-Acadian, the Acadian community has their heritage and history told in a sanctioned site authorized by Parks Canada and put in place for public consumption. The government involvement through Parks Canada makes the Acadian contribution to the area more politically manageable (although not necessarily acceptable). One of the issues facing the GPNHS is how its associations with the Acadian community, the various levels of government, and the public have made it difficult to know exactly how such a site seeks to achieve its general mandate while retaining support from various stakeholders. For the Acadian people, the site may not tell enough of the variety of Acadian experiences, whereas for the local community, it may tell too much of Acadian history at the expense of other groups, notably the Planters and Mi'kmaq. For the local and provincial governments, it may provide a vessel for economic development through tourism. For the federal government, it may not advance Canada's multicultural character.

The case study discussed here exemplifies both local and global challenges for a number of stakeholders, and their reactions toward an established heritage site. In this area of Acadian settlement, the principal aim of the community beyond the GPNHS is to ensure increased public awareness of the Acadian historic contribution to the area's present-day geography and the continuing Acadian cultural identity that survived the expulsion. The response to the established narrative can exacerbate the division of cultural groups within the immediate community. A key problem is that the Acadian community tends to consider the site as dedicated solely to the Acadian nation, its identity, and commemoration of its past. The fundamental issue, then, facing heritage sites such as the GPNHS is reconciling its commoditization as a federally supported National Heritage Site having UNESCO designation with the Acadian nation's desire to provide a narrative and celebration of their past. As the commemoration of Acadia continues, the relationship between the social, political, and economic importance ascribed to the GPNHS by various agencies and community groups will implicitly and explicitly impact those beyond the immediate geographic area with a greater awareness of the entanglements of heritage sites and federal support.

Notes

1 "The Landscape of Grand-Pré: Inscribed on the World Heritage List in 2012." Parks Canada press release, June 30, 2012. Available at: http://www.pc.gc.ca/APPS/CP-NR/release_e.asp?bgid=1657&andor1=bg (accessed March 25, 2015).
2 The Société mutuelle de l'Assomption was a national society initially established in the United States in 1903 to support Acadians by improving their socioeconomic conditions.
3 See Gagné (2013) for an example particular to the Acadians and Grand-Pré.

References

Anderson, B. (2006) *Imagined Communities: Reflections on the Origin and Spread of Nationalism*, rev. edn. London: Verso.

Andrew, S.M. (1996) *The Development of Elites in Acadian New Brunswick, 1861–1881*. Montreal: McGill-Queen's University Press.

Bleakney, J.S. (2004) *Sods, Sail, and Spades: The Acadians at Grand-Pré and Their Dykeland Legacy*. Montreal: McGill-Queen's University Press.

Campbell, C. (2008) Global Expectations, Local Pressures: Some Dilemmas of a World Heritage Site. *Journal of the Royal Nova Scotia Historical Society*, 11 (1), 1–18.

Connerton, P. (1989) *How Societies Remember*. Cambridge: Cambridge University Press.

Connerton, P. (2009) *How Modernity Forgets*. Cambridge: Cambridge University Press.

Crane, S. (2000) *Museums and Memory*. Stanford: Stanford University Press.

DoF (Department of Finance) (2010) Nova Scotia Economic Indicators. Report. Halifax: Province of Nova Scotia. Available at: http://novascotia.ca/finance/pushlish/ei/hsei201308.pdf (accessed August 20, 2014).

DTCH (Department of Tourism, Culture, and Heritage) (2004) Nova Scotia Long-Term Marketing Plan: Executive Summary. Briefing paper. Halifax: Province of Nova Scotia.

DTCH (2008) A Treasured Past, A Precious Future: A Heritage Strategy for Nova Scotia, 2008–2013. Briefing paper. Halifax: Province of Nova Scotia.

DTCH (2009a) About Nova Scotia. Report. Available at: http://novascotia.com/en/home/aboutnovascotia/default.aspx (accessed February 11, 2014).

DTCH (2009b) About Nova Scotia: History and Heritage. Report. Halifax: Province of Nova Scotia. Available at: http://novascotia.com/en/home/aboutnovascotia/historyheritage/default.aspx (accessed February 11, 2014).

Gagné, M. (2013) "Memorial Constructions": Representations of Identity in the Design of the Grand-Pré National Historic Site, 1907–Present. *Acadiensis*, 42 (1), 67–99.

George, E. W. (2013) World Heritage, Tourism Destination and Agricultural Landscape: The Case of Grand Pre, Nova Scotia, Canada. *Journal of Resources and Ecology*, 4 (3), 275–284.

GoC (Government of Canada) (2011) World Heritage Nomination Proposal for the Landscape of Grand Pré, Nova Scotia, Canada. Report. Available at: http://whc.unesco.org/uploads/nominations/1404.pdf (accessed February 9, 2014).

Goeldner, C.R., McIntosh, R.W., and Ritchie, J.R. (1995) *Tourism: Principles, Practices, Philosophies*, 7th edn. New York: Wiley.

Klein, K.L. (2000) On the Emergence of Memory in Historical Discourse. *Representations*, special issue, 69, 127–150.

LeBlanc, B. (2003) *Postcards from Acadie*. Kentville, NS: Gaspereau Press.

Macleod, E.L. (2008) Words Apart: Performing Linguistic and Cultural Diversity in Cheticamp, Nova Scotia. Ph.D. dissertation. Amherst: University of Massachusetts.

Nora, P. (1989) Between Memory and History: Les Lieux de Mémoire. *Representations*, 26 (1), 7–24.

Opp, J., and Walsh, J. (2010) *Placing Memory and Remembering Place in Canada*. Vancouver: University of British Columbia Press.
Parks Canada (1985) Parks Canada Guiding Principles and Operational Policies: Activities Policy. Briefing paper. Available at: http://www.pc.gc.ca/eng/docs/pc/poli/princip/sec2/part2a/part2a6.aspx (accessed February 9, 2014).
Parks Canada (2008).
Renan, E. (1996 [1882]) What Is a Nation? In G. Eley and R. Suny (ed.), *Becoming National: A Reader*. Oxford: Oxford University Press, pp. 41–55.
Ricketts, S. (1996) Cultural Selection and National Identity: Establishing Historic Sites in a National Framework. *Public Historian*, 18 (3), pp. 23–41.
Smith, A. (1999) *Myths and Memories of a Nation*. Oxford: Oxford University Press.
Smith, L. (2006) *Uses of Heritage*. London: Routledge.
Suny, R. (2000) History and the Making of Nations. In Z. Gitelman (ed.), *Cultures and Nations of Central and Eastern Europe*. Cambridge, MA: Harvard University Press, pp. 569–589.
UNESCO (2012) Decisions Adopted by the World Heritage Committee at Its 36th Session, Saint-Petersburg, 24 June–6 July. Report. Available at: http://who.unesco.org/en/decisions/4798 (accessed February 11, 2014).
Winter, J. (2006) *Remembering War: The Great War Between Memory and History in the Twentieth Century*. New Haven: Yale University Press.

CHAPTER 12

Cultural Heritage under the Gaze of International Tourism Marketing Campaigns

Helaine Silverman and Richard W. Hallett

Introduction

This chapter is concerned with the role of cultural heritage imagery in the international campaigns of national tourism agencies. We privilege this topic because a country's touristic self-promotion may be the most direct, obvious window into its dominant national narrative of identity. We take as our point of departure Barbara O'Connor's statement that "cultural and national identities [are] constructed from the representations which certain people both inside and outside our culture produce for us" (O'Connor 1993: 68–69). The study of international tourism campaigns importantly reveals the tension between these emic and etic representations. State agencies charged with designing tourism campaigns highlight that which they regard as the most indicative and desirable about the country. But, independently, the potential tourist has access to a vast array of representations in multiple media that generate a tourism imaginary (Salazar 2012). These representations may be variously, even subversively, interpreted (e.g. Russell 2006; Waterton and Watson 2010a, 2010b; see also Walsh 1992).

International tourism campaigns attempt to entice foreign tourists to visit a distant land. As media, the adverts of these tourism campaigns have "the discursive power … to

A Companion to Heritage Studies, First Edition. Edited by William Logan, Máiréad Nic Craith, and Ullrich Kockel.
© 2016 John Wiley & Sons, Inc. Published 2016 by John Wiley & Sons, Inc.

enable spectators to witness distant realities and events otherwise unavailable to them" (Chouliaraki 2008: 686). Typically, the campaigns showcase cultural features of some antiquity (tangible: such as built environments, sites, monuments) or pedigree (intangible: such as traditional practices), as well as the natural environment (scenery, fauna, flora). Exciting contemporary celebrations, cosmopolitan cities, and events may also represent the national image in these campaigns (think of Brazil and the 2014 World Cup and 2016 Olympics). International tourism campaigns commoditize their country's culture (and nature) as a product to be exploited. Of course, the commoditization of culture is well known, whether in the form of identity (e.g. Comaroff and Comaroff 2009), heritage (e.g. AlSayyad 2001; Silberman 2013), the arts (e.g. Graburn 1976; Phillips and Steiner 1999), the archaeological past (e.g. Rowan and Baram 2004; Di Giovine 2009), historic city centers (e.g. Licciardi and Amirtahmasebi 2012), or entire countries (Anholt 1998; Dinnie 2008). At issue is how this commoditization is accomplished. Critical discourse analysis (CDA) enables us to peer into the process.

As a form of economic discourse – as well as of advertising and promotional culture – tourism is one of Bloomaert and Bulcaen's (2000) top ten preferred topics in CDA. CDA is a useful tool for the analysis of tourist materials, even when the discourse examined is more visual than oral or written (Hallett and Kaplan-Weinger 2010; Thurlow and Jaworski 2010). CDA is especially useful to understand "how and why a particular discourse is being used" (Waterton 2013: 66). The use of CDA expands traditional content analysis, creating "more critical, richer and complex interpretations of representations" (Pritchard and Morgan 2001: 172). Studies by Emma Waterton and Steve Watson (Waterton 2010, 2013; Waterton, Smith, and Campbell 2006; Waterton and Watson 2010b; Watson and Waterton 2010), in particular, have demonstrated the appropriateness of CDA in identifying the discursive construction of cultural heritage (see also Smith 2006) and tourism, including the political, social, and cultural work discourses do, and also their ambiguities and contradictions.

Two recent international tourism campaigns, one produced by India and the other by Peru, are especially worthwhile vantage points for considering cultural heritage from the perspective of the discourse of tourism advertising because both countries are exceptionally rich in tangible and intangible cultural resources. The new campaigns, created by India's Ministry of Tourism and Peru's PromPerú (the Commission for the Promotion of Peru for Exports [International Commerce] and Tourism), mobilize culture (and nature) to be consumed by the voracious global tourism industry, and to promote the nation-brand worldwide (Anholt 1998).

In this chapter, we employ CDA to achieve a deep reading of particular products of the Peruvian and Indian international tourism campaigns: their recent internet videos. We deconstruct the process of enchantment (Selwyn 2007) by which these videos attempt to seduce us and turn us into consumers of their products. And through CDA, we identify what the respective national tourism agencies selectively represent as their key tourism resources. Our study has two striking conclusions: first, both videos downplay the monumental heritage for which Peru and India are famous; second – and to our surprise, given the uniqueness of each country – the narratives produced through these internet videos are largely interchangeable.

Heritage Inconsequence

Incredible India 2009–2011

In 2002, India's Ministry of Tourism contracted Ogilvy and Mather, a major international advertising firm, to produce a worldwide campaign that would dramatically increase tourism, and thus generate significant revenue for the country.[1] Recognizing that India at the time lacked "common branding" or a "clear, precise message" (Kant 2009: 4), the task set before Ogilvy and Mather was to produce an exciting and unmistakable country image. The product of their effort was a brilliant worldwide campaign called Incredible India, comprised of a clever logo (actually, Incredible !ndia), an exceptionally creative series of print advertisements, and subsequently an appealing internet video we refer to as *Incredible India 2009–2011*.[2]

Incredible India 2009–2011 is constructed around an exuberant young man who travels alone through a fascinating land. His story unfolds in two minutes and thirty seconds, and is told through his adventures amidst India's magnificent natural scenery, indigenous animals, and exotic people and their customs. He bathes an elephant and travels by camel, horse-drawn carriage, train, and motorcycle. He camps on snow-capped mountains, treks through the desert, and swims in rivers and oceans. He tries native dance, enjoys local food, and participates in festivals. The only words we hear are when the traveler says *bahut accha*, Hindi for "very good." As Hallett (2011) notes, such use of an indigenous language appears to have no other purpose in tourism advertising than to exoticize the "other." At the end of the video, the young man sits next to a red mailbox along a rural road penning a postcard. The tag line, "Incredible India," is sung, verbalizing the two-word message he has written. He drops the postcard into the mailbox and then walks away, glancing back at the camera.

Perú 2012

At the same time that India's Ministry of Tourism was creating the Incredible India campaign, PromPerú undertook a similar initiative to brand the country as an enthralling destination, relying first on the creativity of JWT and then Futurebrand as its international consultants. The result was an international campaign whose slogan and imagery have evolved through several print versions over the past decade, and more recently in internet videos (Silverman 2015). The current PromPerú overall campaign is called "Empire of Hidden Treasures." We refer to its principal internet video as *Perú 2012*.[3]

Perú 2012 was created to promote the Peru nation-brand. The three-minute video begins with a prosperous mid-forties-ish businessman seated in his ultra-modern office in the year 2032. He receives a package containing a flash drive on which is a video he recorded during his trip to Peru as a young man twenty years earlier. The younger self, with Machu Picchu in the background, addresses his mature self. The action quickly moves through the country, and everywhere the young man reminds his older self of the many wonderful adventures he had in Peru's stunning natural environment and while engaging directly with ordinary Peruvian people. He narrates these intimate experiences with what are actually tourism pitches: "Remember when we were travelers, not tourists"; "And we were drawn by curiosity, not a book"; "We didn't have to make plans to have a good night"; "Remember, we always had time to make friends"; "Life is a series of events and it all depends on how we live them." After many scenes across Peru's desert coast, towering highlands, and verdant jungle, the retrospective travelogue ends with the young man once again at Machu Picchu, where he appeals to the emotion and nostalgia of his older self, saying, "Wherever you are in twenty years, remember when you came to Peru." Then the action shifts back to the businessman in his office. He has been enchanted by what he has seen and re-assesses his priorities. He places a call to his wife and asks her if she has ever been to Peru, suggesting that he will return to Peru with her and have another experience of personal renewal and personal discovery. The video then cuts away to PromPerú's new logo of the single word Perú, and the tag line of the campaign is spoken: "Whatever you need is now in Peru."[4]

Comparison and Discussion

Predictably, the videos present each country as unique. As Roland Robertson has observed, "we appear to live in a world in which the expectation of uniqueness has become increasingly institutionalized and globally widespread" (Robertson 1995: 28). Yet because the tourism industry is a global business with a particular repertoire of discursive tools, notwithstanding the obvious differences between Peru and India, *Incredible India 2009–2011* and *Perú 2012* independently deploy what is basically the same script, the same narrative structure, and the same communicative tropes. Only the setting varies. Below we summarize our comparison of the key narrative elements in the scripts of the two videos.

Incredible India 2009–2011 and *Perú 2012* are compelling video productions that have gone viral on the internet. They are part of the commoditized visual culture of the international tourism industry, and present market-tested tourism enticements. The videos offer up their country's culture to tourism. Importantly, *culture* in these videos is not "heritage" in the sense of the academic field, and even less as the specific official heritage that UNESCO elevates to World Heritage or Intangible Cultural Heritage status. Given that Peru has 11 spectacular World Heritage sites and India has a resplendent group of 30 inscribed properties, not to mention their several dozen Tentative

Table 12.1 Comparison of the key narrative elements in the scripts of *Incredible India 2009–2011* and *Perú 2012*.

Script	*India*	*Peru*
A young man as protagonist: independent traveler	yes	yes
He travels by foot, motorcycle and train	yes	yes
Shows exceptional variety of the natural environment	yes	yes
He engages this natural environment, swims, climbs, camps, etc.	yes	yes
He eats street food with enthusiasm	yes	yes
Shows many kinds of traditional cultural practices	yes	yes
He interacts with local people in their vernacular and religious activities	yes	yes
Depicts the young man as curious and contemplative about experiences	yes	yes
Shows characteristic animals (*surprisingly, not one llama appears in the Peru program*)	yes	no
Shows the premier cultural heritage site of the country (*but see below*)	yes	yes
Verbal narration	no	yes
Traditional music as the background for the video	yes	no
Ends with the tag line and logo for the campaign	yes	yes

List candidates and almost countless other fascinating, important, photogenic examples of built environments, it is notable that cultural heritage sites do not drive the action in *Incredible India 2009–2011* or *Perú 2012*. They do not feature in the videos, apart from when Machu Picchu appears as a quick backdrop to bookend the Peruvian video, and the Taj Mahal is barely glimpsed in the distance in the Indian video. The cultural heritage of Peru and India – particularly the monumental heritage of "the past" – is inconsequential in these new internet-based tourism campaigns. Their focus is "traditions" (life in daily and celebratory form), "novelties" (spontaneous tourist-initiated insertions into daily life), and nature. A diverse and predominantly vernacular package of appealing cultural and natural images sells India and Peru in *Incredible India 2009–2011* and *Perú 2012* rather than "official" heritage. In terms of international tourism marketing, it does not matter in these campaigns whether or not the featured attractions encompass the heritage domains that are managed by heritage professionals and studied by heritage scholars. As Rosemary Coombe argues:

> Heritage regimes are increasingly neoliberal in obvious and not so obvious ways. Certainly we are witnessing a new dominance of market ideologies in heritage management and in its means of "valuation" with an increasing emphasis on *investment* in cultural resources and human capital so as to yield economic returns, adding value to them so as to encourage tourism, foster foreign direct investment, encourage product differentiation, and promote new commodifications. (Coombe 2012: 378, original emphasis)

These two videos exemplify the well-known tension in globalization between homogeneity and heterogeneity, especially in the domain of tourism (see e.g. Robinson and Picard 2006: 34–36). The intent of the campaigns is to create "difference," and thereby generate the desire for visitation (Cohen 1979). As Waterton and Watson observe, the "representative and performative accretions of place imagery … differentiate destinations according to the market position and their 'target audiences'" (Waterton and Watson 2010b: 11) But the similarity between the internet video campaigns for two such different countries is startling in their blithe conundrum of marketed *placefulness* – "the territorial imaginary of the nation-state" (Appadurai 2008: 345) – achieved through an interchangeable *placelessness*; that is, a generic tourism imaginary that generates *exoticlandia*: elaborately costumed natives, curious customs, dramatic geography, unfamiliar architectural forms, telluric religious rituals, animals that do not roam the Western landscape, and so forth. Featuring two of the world's most culturally rich and scenically beautiful countries, the videos portray Peru's and India's diversity and uniqueness while reducing them to interchangeable marketing clichés.[5] They offer traditions reified for public consumption, and remove their respective countries from the rapid modernization both are undergoing. They also hide disquieting poverty in their visual scripts.[6]

From Heritage Tourism to Emotional Tourism

Neither *Incredible India 2009–2011* nor *Perú 2012* is a documentary. They are mini movies telling a story about a young man's adventure. The videos stimulate "powerful bodily sensations … [which] are experienced as existing beyond the corrosion of commercialism" (Lindholm 2008: 48), hence suggesting that in Peru and India the tourist will experience a cultural, personal, and performative authenticity (see Knudsen and Waade 2010) of intercultural engagement that will transcend the crass commercialism and commoditization of mass tourism.

Although the local, non-professional actors in these videos are "real people," their actions in the videos have been scripted and directed by the film-makers hired by India's Ministry of Tourism and by PromPerú. And while the scenes of indigenous cultural performance resemble those that actually take place out of the camera's eye, the videos produce rather than record actual events and the interactions that would comprise them. Thus, that which appears to the tourist to be "backstage" is, in fact, "frontstage" (MacCannell 1976). Yet the videos suggest to the potential tourist that it will be possible to have these same "authentic" experiences on their trip.

Earlier versions of Peru's and India's nationally organized tourism campaigns were conceived much more within the traditional, distanced, object-oriented parameters of cultural heritage tourism, and they put the potential tourist in the invisible position of passive observer. The new internet travelogues locate the tourist squarely in the action. They market up-close journeys of personal experience and self-discovery. Applying Noel Salazar to our case, "Prospective tourists are invited to imagine themselves in a paradisiacal environment, a vanished Eden, where the local landscape and population are to be consumed through observation, embodied sensation and imagination" (Salazar 2012: 866). *Incredible India 2009–2011* and *Perú 2012* are all about sensory experience – embodied tourism – coincidentally paralleling the new academic attention to emotion in tourism (e.g. Picard and Robinson 2012). The videos are selling everything one can discover and experience (Salazar 2012: 866) to fulfill oneself. "Whatever you need is now in Peru," says the narrator at the end of *Perú 2012*. The print version of "Empire of Hidden Treasures" has the tag line: "Don't Watch the Movie. Live It For Real!" Similarly, the 2012 re-launch of *Incredible India* is conceived as "Find What You Seek,"[7] conveying the same promise of emotional satisfaction. As a result, the targeting of major monuments of the cultural heritage landscape is unnecessary. Instead, the tourist is now the connoisseur of self-generated experiences, experiences that do not require expert interpretive mediation by purveyors of an authorized heritage discourse (see Smith 2006) because "cultural heritage sites" are not being promoted in the videos. Bear in mind, though, that in *Incredible India 2009–2011* and *Perú 2012* it is still the state that defines exploitable resources (e.g. Smith 2006) – they just do not conform to the official heritage canon.

Thus, the destination country's advertising is not promoting cultural heritage tourism in its "classical" sense (see e.g. Timothy and Boyd 2003; Timothy and Nyaupane 2009; Watson and Waterton 2010; Timothy 2011; Staiff, Bushell, and Watson 2013) but, rather, experiential tourism (e.g. Cohen 1979, 2004; Wang 2000: 46–71). This marketing approach opens far more of these countries to exploration, but, consequently, also to intrusion by tourists. Problematically, the transgressive tourism depicted in the two videos – the outsider's insertion of self into domains of community sociality – is presented as unproblematic in both videos. Communities will need to determine their own boundaries and the exchange value of experience.

Of course, we do not suggest that the communities represented in the videos are "pristine" or that the locals lack agency, as Bruner (2001) argued in his critique of Urry's (1990) original formulation of the tourist gaze. Moreover, as Beck has indicated with his concept of globality, "we have been living for a long time in a world society, in the sense that the notion of closed spaces has become illusory" (Beck 1999: 10).

Appadurai (1996), among others, has highlighted interconnecting cultural flows across the globe in his various "scapes." But the empowerment of the individual, especially male,[8] tourist to participate at will in any and all aspects of daily life in the *Incredible India 2009–2011* and *Perú 2012* travelogues suggests a one-way transculturality that, as any anthropologist working in a foreign society will attest, is not so easily and rapidly achieved.[9]

Tourism Imaginaries

The two campaigns analyzed in this chapter exemplify the concept of "tourism imaginary," that is, the "socially transmitted representational assemblages that interact with people's personal imaginings [that] are used as meaning-making and world-shaping devices" (Salazar 2012: 864). Those "personal imaginings" are informed by a range of media: books (e.g. Robinson and Andersen 2011), photographs (Robinson and Picard 2009), art (e.g. Howard 2003), film, TV, and, most recently, the internet (e.g. Crouch, Jackson, and Thompson 2005). As Lean. Staiff, and Waterton (2014) note, imagination – informed by multiple sources – has long been associated with travel and tourism. In practice, imagination blurs the boundaries between our everyday lives and the idea of travel (Lean, Staiff, and Waterton 2014). *Perú 2012* and *Incredible India 2009–2011* give us (or are intended to give us) a vicarious sense of being there.

Global tourism enables the worldwide expansion and reproduction of "an assemblage of technologies, texts, images, [and] social practices" (Urry and Larsen 2011: 28). Tourists carry their imaginings and assemblages "in their minds" when they travel to their chosen destination (Nielsen 2010: 53) – even though they are not necessarily aware of all of them. Part of the assemblage or cultural baggage that is carried into the foreign destination is the "place-notion" shaped by the tourism industry's deployment of processes of enchantment (Selwyn 2007), which are accomplished through word and image, in effect a textual attitude (Said 1979) that shapes and predisposes the tourist toward the destination long before arrival. As a cultural technology of seeing that transcends Urry's (1990) gaze, tourism campaigns normalize and instantiate a visual culture underwritten by abundant preconceived and unconceived ideas about distant peoples and places. Robinson and Picard observe that "these are idealized images, designed to emphasize the exotic and overlain with the values of the tourist generating nations" (Robinson and Picard 2006: 33).

We see this clearly in *Perú 2012* and *Incredible India 2009–2011*. The tourism imaginaries enabled by India's and Peru's official agencies arise out of antecedent constructions of these places as exotic and timeless (Lutz and Collins 1993; Fabian 2002), where asymmetrical relations of power, hierarchy, and hegemony have been complicit in the ideological and structural realities behind the appealing stereotypes marketed to the tourist (Salazar 2012: 865). These stereotypes are packaged as "seductive images and discourses about peoples and places" (Salazar 2012: 865). But rather than Said's (1979) Orientalist fantasies, projected by Europeans onto their colonial subjects, in *Perú 2012* and *Incredible India 2009–2011* it is national governments that are exoticizing *themselves* for consumption.

Perú 2012 and *Incredible India 2009-2011* are narratives (Bruner 2005: 19–23) of place, people, and experience. Comprised of images and ideas, they "travel easily" (Salazar 2012: 868) in today's interconnected world. But there can be complications, as suggested by the word play in the titles of two classic works in the anthropology of tourism, *Touring Cultures* (Rojek and Urry 1997) and *Culture on Tour* (Bruner 2005), among many others addressing the complexities of tourism. These narratives operate within the larger metanarrative or master narrative about "discovery, adventure, global intercultural relations" (Leite and Graburn 2009: 46). As such, these narratives are part of the tourism imaginary of Peru and India. Importantly, "tourism imaginaries do not float around spontaneously and independently; rather they 'travel' in space and time through well-established conduits" (Salazar 2012: 868; see also O'Connor 1993: 68–69). In addition to print and performative conduits (guidebooks, print advertising, literature, music, movies, art, the internet, and so forth), these conduits are political and economic. Tourism is promoted not just for benign global citizenship, it has significant political and economic dimensions – as well as implicating other issues. This point is made in a recent editorial in the *Economist* that faults India for its lack of a "strategic culture," arguing that it is not deploying its soft power (Nye 1990), including its cultural richness, to become and assert itself as a truly "great power" (Anon. 2013).[10]

Conclusions

Watson and Waterton observe that heritage tourism is "often characterized by a partial, and sometimes misleading, collection of images selected for display" (Watson and Waterton 2010: 85). As we have said, the official internet videos for Peru's and India's new international tourism-promoting campaigns do not market their wealth of cultural heritage and monumental sites for tourism. The *Perú 2012* and *Incredible India 2009–2011* videos manifest a deliberate inattention to the archeologically and historically endowed landscapes of Peru and India. Instead, they offer the potential tourist a visually stimulating, action-filled, interculturally engaging exploration of the two countries. Each country's tourism marketing agency has produced an easily comprehended script using a set of highly recognizable markers – stereotypes if you will – that readily identify the countries, and thus brand them in a global circuit of commoditization. The elements thus deployed are commoditized as products in the competitive arena of the tourism industry. Vernacular culture in the two tourism campaigns discussed performs its "expedient" function (see Yúdice 2003) as an exploitable resource for PromPerú and the Indian Ministry of Culture.

In both *Incredible India 2009–2011* and *Perú 2012* we see ecotourism (by definition, active) and cultural tourism (typically more educational in nature and leisurely in pace). The type of cultural tourism shown in the videos is exploration – albeit superficial – of the rich vernacular life of India and Peru. The tourist eagerly seeks intercultural experiences. He is curious, engaged, and alone. Thus, this is deeply personal tourism. Predictably, the videos show a positive response amongst those into whose lives he intrudes.

The other kind of cultural tourism we might have expected to see in the two videos would have been focused on the built grandeur of Peru and India. But the tourist is not shown moving from one stunning ancient or historic locale to another. And this observation raises an interesting issue. For as much as countries, particularly developing countries, seek World Heritage List inscriptions (primarily for prestige and for economic development around tourism), and considering that the antecedent print tourism campaigns of both countries featured monumental sites quite prominently, these new tourism promotional videos clearly demonstrate the shift in tourism marketing. The scripts of *Incredible India 2009–2011* and *Perú 2012* present the tourist encounter with monumental heritage as manifestly secondary in importance to the experience of self and the "other" during travel. Moreover, our analysis reveals that the government tourism agencies of Peru and India construct the "destination brand" by reverting to externally generated cultural stereotypes that have long characterized these two countries.

The international tourism campaigns of Peru and India considered in this chapter obligate us to ask why countries invest so much money, personnel, time, and political capital in achieving UNESCO inscription of tangible heritage when their national tourism agencies do not exploit their World Heritage sites in their showcase internet videos. There would seem to be a disconnect. It is all the more puzzling because tourism promotion appears to have overtaken site preservation as a major goal of inscription on the World Heritage List.[11] Bear in mind that this chapter addresses the international campaigns of national tourism agencies. Domestic and foreign private travel agencies do indeed promote the archeological wonders and historic sites of these countries. We do not have a definitive answer concerning national tourism agencies, but the phenomenon merits more attention and we look forward to expanding our study to the international campaigns of other countries that, like Peru and India, are best known for their cultural heritage sites.

Although the UNESCO designation elevates the objects and subjects of its gaze to "outstanding" and "universal" status, it also appropriates and influences. Tentatively, we hypothesize that it is to the advantage of state tourism agencies *not* to emphasize UNESCO-sanctified World Heritage and the Intangible Cultural Heritage of humanity because UNESCO's "property of humankind" ideology deterritorializes and re-territorializes that which countries covet for themselves. Unencumbered by a concern for international management norms, PromPerú and the Indian Ministry of Tourism are free to market their places and peoples as they wish. Whereas "heritage representations … minimize the possibility that objects might be understood beyond their material presence and apparent intrinsic value" (Watson and Waterton 2010: 95), PromPerú and the Indian Ministry of Tourism have gone one step further: they have diminished tangible heritage as a focus of tourism in favor of readily achieved personal experiences with the people who embody local culture. The international tourism campaigns we have analyzed here are a fascinating illustration of the interlinked, parallel, and divergent courses in which culture and heritage operate today.

Notes

1 For the previous decade, India's share of international tourism had remained at a static 0.38 percent of the world market (Kant 2009: 4). As a result of the *Incredible India* campaign, India's share of international tourism increased, but only to 0.64 percent of the world market in 2011. Its rank in world tourist arrivals was 38 in 2011.

2 *Incredible India 2009–2011*. Available at: http://www.youtube.com/watch?v=rNWeBVBqo2c (accessed November 13, 2012).

3 *Perú 2012* [English version]. Previously available at: http://www.youtube.com/watch?v=QqQZG_nLtqA (last accessed February 6, 2013). Spanish: vimeo.com/50361191.

4 The letter 'p' of the Perú logo is shaped using a spiral for the curved element of the letter. It is meaningful for Peruvians as revealed in interviews conducted by Helaine Silverman, being widely identified as referencing the pre-Columbian past (although there are different interpretations as to which ancient culture is appropriated in the design). It appears to be quite appealing to foreigners to judge by its popularity on tee-shirts purchased by them. To see the logo, type "promperu" into your browser (with or without the accent) and multiple images of the logo will appear. The preference for red and white references the Peruvian flag.

5 We call attention to a recent print advert in *Travel + Leisure*, November 2013, showing a tented desert fantasy in Peru that has never existed, and that channels make-believe Arabian nights in an Abu Dhabi advert in the same issue.

6 In the case of *Perú 2012*, we see schoolchildren on a soccer field in the high mountains, but the camera and script do not come in for a "close-up" such that the viewer would see their chapped faces, worn clothes, runny noses, toilet-less homes, bare school rooms, and so forth.

7 Available at: http://shinesquad.me/2012/11/07/incredible-india-new-tourism-campaign-find-what-you-seek-and-go-beyond/ (accessed December 22, 2013).

8 The protagonist in both of the video campaigns is male. Given that independent travel moves the script, we assume the gendering of the campaigns implicitly argues that solo women do not or should not undertake this kind of travel or engage in these experiences. That impression, however, is contradicted by a newer version of the *Incredible India* video (available at: http://www.youtube.com/watch?v=zB8PwkXkvHE) that features a "twenty-seven-ish" woman, although her gender does not become apparent until 33 seconds into the 3 minute video, and she is not a stereotypically feminine protagonist in appearance or action. We assume that this 2012 production was created to capture the 50 percent female segment of the potential tourist market, but are curious to know if its success has been assessed. Regardless, we continue to note the absence of the Taj Mahal and India's built heritage overall in this newer version of *Incredible India* and its greater emphasis on adventure tourism. The female version shares with its male prototype a script dominated by interpersonal intercultural interaction.

9 See Lindholm (2008: 39–41) for an especially interesting comment.

10 In the context of the *Economist* article, we must wonder if the essentialisms of *Incredible India* are the best strategy with which India can deploy its cultural wealth to its advantage. On the other hand, its tourism potential appears to be unlimited and can positively impact development, indeed sustainable development (understood as economic and social).

11 There has been a recent series of alliances between major international tourism agencies and major international institutions of heritage management. In 2005, Expedia and the United Nations Foundation launched the World Heritage Alliance "to promote sustainable tourism and awareness of World Heritage sites and communities around the world. This partnership believes conscientious travelers can contribute directly to nature conservation, historic preservation, and poverty reduction through sustainable tourism." In 2009 UNESCO was delighted to announce its partnership with TripAdvisor to "mobilize support to preserve natural and cultural sites inscribed on its [UNESCO's] World Heritage List." TripAdvisor pledged up to $1.5 million for the next two years "to help UNESCO's World Heritage Centre monitor the conservation of the [then] 890 natural and cultural sites inscribed on the World Heritage List" (UN News Centre, October 23, 2009). And since 1995, American Express has supported the watch list of endangered sites of the World Monuments Fund (WMF). It also participates in a Partners in Preservation program with WMF, and it has contributed substantially to WMF's program at Preah Khan, a major temple at Angkor, which is a World Heritage site and premier tourist destination. See http://www.unfoundation.org/news-and-media/press-releases/2005-1997/2005/expedia-and-unf-launch-WHA.html (accessed August 6, 2013); http://www.wmf.org/partners/americanexpress/ (accessed August 6, 2013); http://www.youtube.com/watch?v=9mcA1-3pJaE (accessed December 21, 2013).

References

AlSayyad, N. (ed.) (2001) *Consuming Tradition, Manufacturing Heritage*. London: Routledge.

Anholt, S. (1998) Nation-Brands of the Twenty-First Century. *Journal of Brand Management*, 5 (6), 395–406.

Anon. (2013) Can India Become a Great Power? *Economist*, March 30. Available at: http://www.economist.com/news/leaders/21574511-indias-lack-strategic-culture-hobbles-its-ambition-be-force-world-can-india (accessed March 5, 2015).

Appadurai, A. (1996) *Modernity at Large*. Minneapolis: University of Minnesota Press.

Appadurai, A. (2008) Sovereignty without Territoriality: Notes for a Postnational Geography. In S.M. Low and D. Lawrence-Zuñiga (eds), *The Anthropology of Space and Place*. Malden, MA: Blackwell, pp. 337–349.

Beck, U. (1999) *What Is Globalization?* Cambridge: Polity Press.

Bloomaert, J., and Bulcaen, C. (2000) Critical Discourse Analysis. *Annual Review of Anthropology*, 29, 447–466.

Bruner, E.M. (2001) The Maasai and the Lion King. *American Ethnologist*, 28 (4), 881–908.

Bruner, E.M. (2005) *Culture on Tour*. Chicago: University of Chicago Press.

Chouliaraki, L. (2008) Discourse Analysis. In T. Bennett and J. Frow (eds), *The Sage Handbook of Cultural Analysis*. London: Sage, 674–697.

Cohen, E. (1979) A Phenomenology of Tourism Experiences. *Sociology*, 13, 179–201.

Cohen, E. (2004) *Contemporary Tourism: Diversity and Change*. London: Elsevier.

Comaroff, J.L, and Comaroff, J. (2009) *Ethnicity, Inc*. Chicago: University of Chicago Press.

Coombe, R. (2012) Managing Cultural Heritage as Neoliberal Governmentality. In R. Bendix, A. Eggert, and A. Peselmann (eds), *Heritage Regimes and the State*. Göttingen: Universitätsverlag Göttingen, pp. 375–387.

Crouch, D., Jackson, R., and Thompson, F. (eds) (2005) *The Media and the Tourist Imagination: Converging Cultures*. New York: Routledge.

Di Giovine, M.A. (2009) *The Heritage-scape: UNESCO, World Heritage, and Tourism*. Lanham, MD: Lexington Books.

Dinnie, K. (2008) *Nation Branding: Concepts, Issues, Practice*. Amsterdam: Elsevier.

Fabian, J. (2002) *Time and the Other: How Anthropology Makes Its Object*. New York: Columbia University Press.

Graburn, N. (ed.) (1976) *Ethnic and Tourist Arts: Cultural Expressions from the Fourth World*. Berkeley: University of California Press.

Hallett, R.W. (2011) "Hafa Adai … Means Hello!" Written Banal Codeswitching on Tourism Websites. *Journal of Tourism and Cultural Change*, 9 (4), 286–297.

Hallett, R.W., and Kaplan-Weinger, J. (2010) *Official Tourism Websites: A Discourse Analysis Perspective*. Bristol: Channel View Publications.

Howard, P. (2003) Artists as Drivers of the Tour Bus: Landscape Painting as a Spur to Tourism. In D. Crouch and N. Lübben (eds), *Visual Culture and Tourism*. Oxford: Berg, pp. 109–123.

Kant, A. (2009) *Branding India: An Incredible Story*. Noida: Collins Business.

Knudsen, B.T., and Waade, A.M. (2010) Performative Authenticity in Tourism and Spatial Experience: Rethinking the Relations between Travel, Place and Emotion. In B.T. Knudsen and A.M. Waade (eds), *Re-inventing Authenticity: Tourism, Place and Emotion*. Bristol: Channel View Publications, pp. 1–19.

Lean, G., Staiff, R., and Waterton, E. (eds) (2014) *Travel and Imagination*. Farnham: Ashgate.

Leite, N., and Graburn, N. (2009) Anthropological Interventions in Tourism Studies. In T. Jamal and M. Robinson (eds), *The Sage Handbook of Tourism Studies*. Los Angeles: Sage, pp. 35–64.

Licciardi, G., and Amirtahmasebi, R. (eds) (2012) *The Economics of Uniqueness: Investing in Historic City Cores and Cultural Heritage Assets for Sustainable Development*. Washington: World Bank.

Lindholm, C. (2008) *Culture and Authenticity*. Malden, MA: Blackwell.
Lutz, C.A., and Collins, J.L. (1993) *Reading National Geographic*. Chicago: University of Chicago Press.
MacCannell, D. (1976) *The Tourist: A New Theory of the Leisure Class*. Berkeley: University of California Press.
Nielsen, N.K. (2010) "The Summer We All Went to Keuruu": Intensity and the Topographication of Identity. In B.T. Knudsen and A.M. Waade (eds), *Re-inventing Authenticity: Tourism, Place and Emotions*. Bristol: Channel View Publications, pp. 52–65.
Nye, J.S. (1990) Soft Power. *Foreign Policy*, 80, 153–171.
O'Connor, B. (1993) Myths and Mirrors: Tourism and Cultural Identity. In B. O'Connor and M.G. Cronin (eds), *Tourism in Ireland: A Critical Analysis*. Cork: Cork University Press, pp. 68–85.
Phillips, R.B., and Steiner, C.B. (eds) (1999) *Unpacking Culture: Art and Commodity in Colonial and Postcolonial Worlds*. Berkeley: University of California Press.
Picard, D., and Robinson, M. (eds) (2012) *Emotion in Motion: Tourism, Affect and Transformation*. Farnham: Ashgate.
Pritchard, A., and Morgan, N.J. (2001) Culture, Identity and Tourism Representation: Marketing Cymru or Wales? *Tourism Management*, 22, 167–179.
Robertson, R. (1995) Glocalization: Time–Space and Homogeneity–Heterogeneity. In M. Featherstone, S. Lash, and R. Robertson (eds), *Global Modernities*. London: Sage, pp. 25–44.
Robinson, M., and Andersen, H.-C. (eds) (2011) *Literature and Tourism: Essays in the Reading and Writing of Tourism*. Andover: Cengage Learning.
Robinson, M., and Picard, D. (2006) *Tourism, Culture and Sustainable Development*. Paris: UNESCO.
Robinson, M, and Picard, D. (eds) (2009) *The Framed World: Tourism, Tourists and Photography*. Farnham: Ashgate.
Rojek, C., and Urry, J. (1997) *Touring Cultures: Transformations of Travel and Theory*. London: Routledge.
Rowan, Y., and Baram, U. (eds) (2004) *Marketing Heritage: Archaeology and the Consumption of the Past*. Walnut Creek, CA: AltaMira.
Russell, I. (ed.) (2006) *Images, Representations and Heritage*. New York: Springer.
Said, E. (1979) *Orientalism*. New York: Vintage Books.
Salazar, N.B. (2012) Tourism Imaginaries: A Conceptual Approach. *Annals of Tourism Research*, 39 (2), 863–882.
Selwyn, T. (2007) The Political Economy of Enchantment: Formations in the Anthropology of Tourism. *Suomen Antropologi*, 32 (2), 48–70.
Silberman, N. (2013) Discourses of Development: Narratives of Cultural Heritage as an Economic Resource. In R. Staiff, R. Bushell, and S. Watson (eds), *Heritage and Tourism: Place, Encounter, Engagement*. London: Routledge, pp. 213–225.
Silverman, H. (2015) Branding Peru: Cultural Heritage and Popular Culture in the Marketing Strategy of PromPerú. In M. Robinson and H. Silverman (eds), *Encounters with Popular Pasts: Cultural Heritage and Popular Culture*. New York: Springer, pp. 131–148.
Smith, L. (2006) *Uses of Heritage*. London: Routledge.
Staiff, R., Bushell, R., and Watson, S. (eds) (2013) *Heritage and Tourism: Place, Encounter, Engagement*. London: Routledge.
Thurlow, C., and Jaworski, A. (2010) *Tourism Discourse: Language and Global Mobility*. New York: Palgrave Macmillan.
Timothy D.J. (2011) *Cultural Heritage and Tourism*. Bristol: Channel View Publications.
Timothy, D.J., and Boyd, S.W. (2003) *Heritage Tourism*. Harlow: PrenticeHall/Pearson Education.
Timothy, D.J., and Nyaupane, G. (2009) *Cultural Heritage Tourism in the Developing World*. London: Routledge.

Urry, J. (1990) *The Tourist Gaze.* London: Sage.
Urry, J., and Larsen, J. (2011) *The Tourist Gaze 3.0.* Los Angeles: Sage.
Walsh, K. (1992) *The Representation of the Past: Museums and Heritage in the Post-Modern World.* London: Routledge.
Wang, N. (2000) *Tourism and Modernity: A Sociological Analysis.* Amsterdam: Pergamon.
Waterton, E. (2010) *Politics, Policy and the Discourses of Heritage in Britain.* Basingstoke: Palgrave Macmillan.
Waterton, E. (2013) Heritage Tourism and its Representation. In R. Staiff, R. Bushell, and S. Watson (eds), *Heritage and Tourism: Place, Encounter, Engagement.* London: Routledge, pp. 64–84.
Waterton, E., Smith, L., and Campbell, G. (2006) The Utility of Discourse Analysis to Heritage Studies: The Burra Charter and Social Inclusion. *International Journal of Heritage Studies*, 12 (4), 339–355.
Waterton, E., and Watson, S. (eds) (2010a) *Culture, Heritage and Representation: Perspectives on Visuality and the Past.* Farnham: Ashgate.
Waterton, E., and Watson, S. (2010b) Introduction: A Visual Heritage. In E. Waterton and S. Watson (eds), *Culture, Heritage and Representation: Perspectives on Visuality and the Past.* Farnham: Ashgate, pp. 1–18.
Watson, S., and Waterton, E. (2010) Reading the Visual: Representation and Narrative in the Construction of Heritage. *Material Culture Review*, 71, 84–97.
Yúdice, G. (2003) *The Expediency of Culture: Uses of Culture in the Global Era.* Durham, NC: Duke University Press.

CHAPTER 13

Heritagescaping and the Aesthetics of Refuge: Challenges to Urban Sustainability

Tim Winter

The year 2012 marked the fortieth anniversary of UNESCO's Convention Concerning the Protection of the World Cultural and Natural Heritage, or World Heritage Convention. Regarded by many as a hugely successful project, World Heritage has provided a framework for safeguarding a wide array of historic built environments. The choice of "sustainable development and the role of communities" as the theme of the fortieth anniversary was, however, recognition of the significant problems and challenges this arena of cultural and spatial governance has created for those living in and around listed sites. Cities have proved particularly challenging, and resistant to prescriptive modeling at the level of international policy. Evictions, punitive legislation, rising living costs, and loss of community are the now familiar by-products of world heritage that continue to go undocumented and ignored.

Against this backdrop, this chapter traces recent developments and trends surrounding urban heritage conservation, highlighting recent turns towards community-driven approaches and discourses of sustainability. It then raises the issue of gentrification, with a particular focus on where such problems take on critical importance: small-scale urban environments. Focusing on Galle in Sri Lanka, the final part of the chapter explores the emergence of a form of "heritagescaping" oriented by an aesthetics of solitude, tranquility, and quiet comfort. In offering a contribution towards debates around urban sustainability and the role of heritage therein, it is argued that such processes present significant obstacles to the development of more community-based, culturally sustainable forms of heritage conservation.

A Companion to Heritage Studies, First Edition. Edited by William Logan, Máiréad Nic Craith, and Ullrich Kockel.
© 2016 John Wiley & Sons, Inc. Published 2016 by John Wiley & Sons, Inc.

Addressing the Community

Recent years have seen important leaps in the attention paid to community-related issues. Long neglected in the field of international conservation, a profession largely oriented by a scientistic materialism, the sociopolitical dynamics associated with conserving historic places are now increasingly orienting heritage management programs. It is common for international organizations and their legal, technical, and bureaucratic structures to both provide leadership for and lag behind their national and localized equivalents. This has been the case in the area of community-related issues in the heritage conservation field, as most visibly evident in UNESCO's marking of the fortieth anniversary in 2012 of its flagship heritage convention via the theme of World Heritage Convention and Sustainable Development: The Role of Local Communities. Likewise, the International Council on Monuments and Sites (ICOMOS) chose the theme of Heritage and Landscape as Human Values for its 2014 general assembly in Florence, Italy. The value of "traditional knowledge" was proposed as one of the priorities of the conference in recognition of the need to both foster and respond to "bottom-up" approaches to conservation management. Moreover, considerable effort has been made around the introduction of rights-based approaches to conservation in an effort to make the sector more people-focused. From 2011 onward, a joint initiative between ICOMOS, the International Union for the Conservation of Nature (IUCN), the International Centre for the Study of the Preservation and Restoration of Cultural Property (ICCROM) and the World Heritage Centre in Paris drew on human rights policy and legislation to construct a working group titled Our Common Dignity (ICOMOS 2011). An initial workshop conducted in Oslo, Norway, led to a special issue of the *International Journal of Heritage Studies* in 2012 (Ekern *et al.* 2012). The key outcome of this initiative has been a more substantiated articulation of the concepts of cultural rights, and rights-based approaches in relation to the management of heritage landscapes, with particular attention paid to issues like development and tourism at World Heritage sites.

It is a shift toward more humanist approaches to conservation that has in large part taken its cues from the international declarations and legislation created in the 1990s and early 2000s around intangible cultural heritage, most notably the UNESCO Universal Declaration on Cultural Diversity (UNESCO 2001), and the follow up Convention for the Safeguarding of the Intangible Cultural Heritage (2003). In unison, these initiatives drew upon the Universal Declaration of Human Rights (United Nations 1948), the International Covenant on Economic, Social and Cultural Rights (1966) and the International Covenant on Civil and Political Rights (1966) as their foundational documents. The Intangible Heritage Convention (2003) recognized the need to counterbalance the power of the state in contexts where culture acts as a mediator of state–citizen relations. It thus emphasized the importance of the community as an entity with political rights and as a space of political action.

Given the evolving nature of these paradigms and their associated discourses, considerable disagreement and ambiguity remains over what value rights-based approaches offer, how they can be enacted or the actual conceptual and practical bases upon which cultural heritage and human rights intersect. One issue that has proved particularly thorny has been the convergence of rights associated with the preservation of culture and those associated with economic development and poverty alleviation. Indeed, stepping back from the language of rights-based approaches, what we have seen since the 1990s is a broad-based reversal of the separation of culture and development that characterized much of the international heritage policy of the second half of the twentieth century. Timothy Mitchell's work on Egypt in the 1950s (Mitchell 2002) is particularly revealing here. As Timothy and Nyaupane (2008) note, where previously culture was seen as an obstacle to development and societal modernization, organizations such as the World Bank were instrumental in creating programs and policies that sought synergies and harmonious goals. Accordingly, Radcliffe (2006) suggests that a distinct cultural turn has been discernible in the international development industry, most tangibly in the state-based and non-governmental aid sector, but much remains to be done (see also Radcliffe and Laurie 2006). Those cultural heritage policy-makers who have taken an interest in more productively addressing the ties between culture and development have also often found themselves entangled in the politics of indigeneity (Canessa 2008; Engle 2010).

Of course, such developments have occurred concurrently with the widespread ascendancy of sustainability discourses. It is widely suggested that a key watershed moment of "sustainability" as an international buzzword was the United Nations Conference on Environment and Development, held in Rio de Janeiro in 1992 (Hirsch and Warren 2002; Scoones 2007). The conference enabled sustainability to move out from its original home in ecology into a number of other sectors. Such cross-sector usage has created confusion, semantic instability, and in some cases a malaise around what the term actually means or refers to. As Scoones notes, sustainability operates as a "boundary term," promising mediation between sectors and ideas that might otherwise be disconnected (Scoones 2007: 589). A number of overlapping tracts of sustainability have thus formed, depending on the agendas at hand and the context, namely environmental sustainability, social sustainability, and more recently the language of cultural sustainability. Broadly speaking, each of these is guided by two core principles. First, sustainability pivots around the idea of extraction from a finite source without incurring its depletion for future generations. And second is an advocacy for the sustainable and the creation of the self-sustaining, whether it be biodiverse environments, traditional cultural practices, programs of poverty reduction, national economies, or bureaucratic institutions.

Depending on the context, the balance in emphasis between these two principles shifts. For example, within a paradigm of ecological conservation, the overarching concern is the preservation of the finite resource, and the promotion of management strategies that avoid depletion. Within the "development sector," however, sustainability typically pivots around sustaining economic growth or the social indices of development such as education, health, or physical infrastructure. Since the 1990s, effort has been given to ensuring that the environmental, social, and cultural are compatible and mutually attainable, with the terms "harmonious" or "synergies" profusely used in the project planning of civil society organizations around the world, particularly in the aid industry. The Millennium Development Goals also contributed significantly to the integration and reconciliation of divergent or discordant approaches to sustainability. As these come to be replaced by the post-2015 development agenda, sustainable development remains the core guiding principle, with greater emphasis placed on culture than previously.

Elsewhere, since the early 1990s onward, countless ecotourism and cultural tourism initiatives have been established, proclaiming mutually compatible goals, whereby socio-economic development both sustains and is sustained by programs targeting environment and cultural conservation. All too often though, ambiguity and contradiction takes hold as notions of sustainability slide between vastly different spatial and temporal scales. The language of sustainability shifts between the local, national, and planetary, and stretches between short-term and glacial time frames. As a consequence, projects targeting sustainable development defined in socioeconomic terms all too often have a detrimental impact on the sustainability of their localized environments, both cultural and natural.

The language of communities has proved pivotal here, and, as Waterton and Smith (2010) point out, it is all too often invoked unproblematically in ways that represent different groups and their interests via overly homogeneous, reductive categories. Indeed – and in large part because of this – the language of synergies has remained expedient, enabling detractors of modernization and economic growth to be brought into the fold, such that concerns for the "local" are now discussed and treated as integral to wider progress-oriented goals. As a result, organizations responsible for the conservation of cultural heritage are now drawn into an array of broader, politically, and ethically loaded spheres, including tourism, urban planning, international aid, poverty reduction, and other areas that draw upon ideas of sustainability as a guiding principle.

But as culture has come to be increasingly framed as a development asset, the actual definition of what heritage is, tangible or intangible, often goes unquestioned. Broad proclamations of the synergies between economic and cultural sustainability are based around the ties between community welfare and a nexus of heritage conservation and development. This has been particularly the case for urban environments, where the material culture of the past is surrounded by, and thus simultaneously threatened by and dependent upon, residential communities. In recognition of the need to better address the complex intersections between heritage, development, and sustainability in urban contexts, bodies such as ICOMOS and UNESCO have looked to develop the more expansive conceptual and policy category of "historic urban landscape" (Bandarin and van Oers 2012). This has proved critical for the successful management of those urban environments that lie within the World Heritage system, which all too often face the problems of tourism development, gentrification, and land speculation. Small, discrete historic cities have proved particularly challenging, their fragile social and cultural environments being susceptible to dramatic transformation by new economies and the rapid domination of one particular industry such as tourism. Unlike bigger cities, which possess a resilience that comes from scale and the presence of multi-sector economies, the dynamics of economic development that have come to surround heritage in recent decades have often proved critical for smaller urban environments. Dubrovnik, Pisa, and Santiago de Compostela are among the many illustrative examples that could be cited here. Given their small scale, the communities of these places have proved especially vulnerable to the impacts and consequences of gentrification, as we shall see.

Urban Futures, and the View from Asia

For the first time in history, more than half of the world's population now lives in urban areas. Today, 80 percent of the global energy output comes from cities; they contribute around 60 percent of the world's green-house gas emissions, and produce almost three-quarters of all waste. The global trend of urbanization is set to continue, but cities in different regions of the world face dramatically different futures. For Europe, North America, and Latin America, more than 70 percent of the population currently reside in cities. As a result, many cities in the developed world will actually experience a gradual decline in population. By contrast, however, over the coming four decades the so-called "developing economies" will account for 95 percent of urban population growth.

According to UN-Habitat, 5 million people a month are currently relocating to cities in developing countries. Across Africa and Asia, nearly two-thirds of the population still resides outside cities. Predictions of sustained rural–urban mobility, however, indicate that both regions will see a 50:50 balance between rural and urban areas in the coming decades (UN-Habitat 2008). Asia remains one the fastest urbanizing regions in the world and, given that another 1.25 billion people are expected to be born in the region in the coming decade or so, this situation is likely to continue. Of the 140 new "large" cities that emerged across the world after 1990, more than three-quarters were in Asia (UN-Habitat 2008). China stands out as the key driving force of this staggering trend, as Thomas Campanella pointed out recently: "China has built more housing in the last twenty five years than any nation in history" (Campanella 2008: 286). Megacities such as Shanghai help explain this growth. The city expanded from a population of 7 million in 1970, to 8 million in 1990, but then accelerated rapidly under a national program of economic liberalization to over 16 million by 2010 (UN-Habitat 2010: 13). It is expected that the city will be home to around 22 million people by 2020 (UN-Habitat 2010: 15).

In unison, scholars such as Robinson (2006), Roy (2011), and Edensor and Jayne (2012) have thus suggested that the academic study of cities and the urban environments needs to decenter the West, which, to date, has been privileged as the site of theory generation. They call for an analytical shift toward the parts of the world where contemporary urbanization is taking place. For example, Jennifer Robinson (2006) critically challenged the geography of urban knowledge, wherein cities in the First World are the spaces around which theories and policies are formed, with those situated in the Third World approached as sites of application and problem solving. Elsewhere she has also argued that our "understandings of city-ness have come to rest on the (usually unstated) experiences of a relatively small group of (mostly Western) cities" (Robinson 2002: 531). The sustained attention given to the emergence of so-called world cities – New York, Paris, London, and Tokyo – and their network affect (Sassen 2002) has meant smaller, less spectacular urban environments have all too often been left off the map. Accordingly, she argues all cities should be regarded as ordinary, with the overly static categories of "developing world" or "global city" discarded. This would enable an "urban theory that draws inspiration from the complexity and diversity of city life, and from urban experiences and urban scholarship across a wide range of different kinds of cities" (Robinson 2006: 13).

There is much to be gained from pursuing similar pathways in the study of urban heritage. As I have highlighted at length elsewhere, the analysis of urban heritage and its conservation privileges the West as the site of historical development and contemporary innovation, with regions outside commonly understood as either imitative, alternative or an extension of Western praxis (Winter 2013, 2014). In the case of Asia, it goes without saying that processes of socioeconomic growth and urban development will continue to vary considerably given the region's political, social, and geographic diversity. Nonetheless, fewer and fewer communities will lie outside, and thus remain untouched, by modernization and industrial and post-industrial forms of development. As others have observed, the widespread reorientation of national economies towards tertiary sectors means the cultural past is being enmeshed in ever more complex social relations. Throughout Asia, dramatic transformations have occurred in the way the material legacies of previous generations have been approached by planners, bureaucrats, architects, and so forth. Back in 2002, the contributors to Logan (2002) outlined the multitude of challenges associated with strengthening a heritage conservation ethos within fast changing urban contexts in Asia. As essays on Hong Kong, Phnom Penh, and

Hanoi illustrated, questions of how to deal with difficult histories of colonial rule or conflict all needed to be tackled within the contexts of rapid heritage loss and destruction. Since then the destruction of historic urban areas in Asia has continued, with the past all too often seen by planning authorities or states as incompatible with their visions for the future. The cities of Beijing and Shanghai provide cases in point, where the hosting of the Olympics and World Expo in 2008 and 2010, respectively, involved the extensive demolition of traditional neighborhoods or *hutong*. In both instances, as elsewhere in Asia, the speed of economic growth means the most valuable asset to be traded has been the land itself, rather than the architecture that sits on it.

But with development-related destruction has come a turn towards re-envisaging the cultural past, both material and intangible, as an asset for urban development. Staying with China, cultural- and creative-sector industries have become important drivers of urban regeneration since the late 1990s, and have enabled Shanghai, Beijing, and other regional cities to position themselves competitively at both the national and international level. As Kong and O'Connor (2009) illustrated, the emergence of these new "creative economies" led to the transformation of industrial buildings into art-district, heritage precincts, with Moganshan Road and District 798 among the various examples that could be cited here (see Figure 13.1). Through adaptive reuse, once-vacant factories and

Figure 13.1 Industrial warehouses transformed into heritage/art precinct District 798, Beijing. Source: photo by Tim Winter.

warehouses now house artist studios and galleries, along with the restaurants, cafés, shops, and apartments familiar to many inner cities. With such processes part of a global trend, museums, historic waterfronts, historic properties, and urban public spaces across Asia have come to be preserved, recognized, and redeveloped as urban heritage. Cities, both large and small, across the region promote their "unique" heritage in an effort to attract tourists, business travelers, and expatriates. But away from the extended metropolitan regions of Jakarta, Shanghai, and Tokyo, perhaps the greatest transformations relative to scale have occurred in the region's smaller urban environments. Here, "heritagescaping" has been a powerful force, such that discrete historic urban spaces have witnessed profound economic, social and physical change. In towns like Galle in Sri Lanka, Melaka in Malaysia, and Pingyao in China, designation as a World Heritage site has been a catalyst for colossal change. Much of this stems from the arrival of large-scale tourism, as numerous scholars have noted and critically examined over the years (Du Cros and Lee 2007; Henderson 2004; UNESCO 2004; Wang 2008). Taken together, these and other studies of the region illustrate how the historic built environment is now absorbed into development trajectories which explicitly utilize and advance the new cultural economies of urban heritage. The following section explores such themes in greater detail, and picks up some of the forces and factors that are driving the transformation of the region's more vulnerable urban environments through a focus on Galle in Sri Lanka.

Coffee Table Architecture and Urban Gentrification

From among the various issues and challenges associated with urban sustainability, the issue I wish to focus on here relates to the intersections between heritage designation and the symbolic economies that now surround discrete historic urban environments and resultant processes of gentrification. Throughout much of Asia, the quest to preserve historic cities via the World Heritage system has been accompanied by the emergence of more popular modes of heritagescaping; ones that create social dynamics that run counter to the process of sustaining communities and a bottom up, people-centered approach to preservation. To illustrate this, attention is given to recent developments at Galle Fort in Sri Lanka.

In 2009, after more than 25 years of violence and armed conflict, Sri Lanka's civil war came to an end. The eventual defeat of the Liberation Tigers of Tamil Eelam (LTTE, or Tamil Tigers as they were more commonly known) heralded a transition toward greater stability and national reconciliation. Whilst international criticism of President Mahinda Rajapaksa during the closing years of the war continued afterwards, not least for his role in the creation of an estimated 300,000 internally displaced people, the country's transition toward an era of peace naturally led to an increase in confidence. Trade and foreign direct investment increased, and the surging economy of the capital Colombo led to a rapid escalation in real-estate prices and land speculation. Somewhat surprisingly, the small, walled city of Galle in the south of the country experienced similar economic developments, with property prices surging in the immediate aftermath of the war. Pivotal to this was the construction of a new highway between Colombo and Galle, the E01, which opened in December 2011. The vast majority of the funds required for the highway stemmed from the new forms of international aid now flowing into the country. As the war came to an end, Sri Lanka's "traditional donors," the United States and

European Union, and the influence they enjoyed, began to be replaced by bilateral aid from around the region (Sengupta 2008). China had dramatically increased its assistance to the country from the mid 2000s onwards, such that a portfolio of aid programs reached nearly US$1 billion in 2008, a fivefold increase on the previous year – a significant landmark in that China now eclipsed Japan as Sri Lanka's largest donor. Much of this money went to upgrading infrastructure, such as roads, airports, and power-production facilities. Sri Lanka's coastline also became the source of much activity as the country transitioned towards peace. In what has now become a familiar story around the Indian Ocean, China provided technical and financial assistance for the construction of deep-water ports on the east and south sides of the island. The long-standing geopolitical unease of the region meant that India, not surprisingly, also stepped up its commitment to the country over that same period.

This post-war transition and the resultant changes in the political economy delivered rapid transformation to the small urban landscape of Galle. Simultaneous to the construction of the E01 highway were plans for the redevelopment of the roads, drainage, and public spaces located inside the walls of Galle Fort (Figure 13.2). Listed as a World Heritage site in 1988, the historical fort saw little development over the years spanning the civil war. In the wake of the damage caused by the 2004 tsunami, a number of buildings needed to be repaired, with the majority of the work carried out by the Archaeological Survey of Sri Lanka. However, in the years following the cessation of military activity in the country, things began to change rapidly. Sri Lanka has long been a favored tourist destination for Europeans. With the return of peace, the tourism industry began to increase, with the most notable growth being among independent travelers. Throughout the war, the backpacker market remained resilient, along with the high-end-resort market. But the end of the civil war also enabled travel agents and smaller hotels to

Figure 13.2 Restoration of housing in Galle Fort. Source: photo by Tim Winter.

productively market the country again as the quintessential island paradise, renowned for its cuisine, fertile landscapes, and tropical beaches. Whilst different parts of the island had experienced inbound tourism since the mid to late nineteenth century onward, the key area to benefit initially from the uptake in international interest this time round was the south of the island, primarily its coastline. Given the Tamil Tigers had previously occupied the north of the country, the south was, not surprisingly, seen as the safest region, with a number of coastal destinations building on existing tourism infrastructures. As a World Heritage site, and celebrated venue for international cricket matches, Galle looked to build on its existing familiarity with inbound tourism.

Across the south of the country, from 2010 onwards, greater political stability, combined with a change in government policy concerning overseas investment, triggered a boom in the country's property market. As investors flooded in, houses and land along the coast surged in value over a few short years. The historic significance of Galle, combined with its transport links to Colombo, meant properties located inside the fort soon fetched a premium, and continued to rise in value over subsequent years. As a discrete walled city, Galle Fort held the promise of becoming a destination known for its cultural and culinary attractions, and renowned for its "charming" atmosphere, comparable to other historic urban environments in Southeast Asia such as Luang Prabang in Laos, Hoi An in Vietnam, and Penang in Malaysia. Accordingly, after 2010, a number of restaurants, cafés, and boutique hotels opened inside the walls, the majority of which involved the renovation of existing buildings. Accompanying this was a rapid increase in the number of domestic properties bought by those either living in Colombo or overseas. Wealthy Sri Lankans were not alone in seeing Galle Fort as a strong investment opportunity, with investors from India, the United Kingdom, Germany, Italy, and France being among those to buy property in the initial post-conflict period. Beyond those purchasing property to build boutique hotels, the walled city was seen as an ideal place for creating a "second home," combining historical interest and nearby pristine beaches. By 2012, two Galle-based real-estate agents estimated that property prices inside the walled city were on a par with housing in the most expensive neighborhoods of Colombo, making them among the highest prices per square meter in the country.[1]

In interpreting this process, I would suggest that Galle has seen the emergence of a form of heritagescaping characterized by certain architectural discourses and comfort aesthetics. Since the mid 2000s, a plethora of coffee-table books have been published "celebrating" the traditional architectural forms of the island. Going by such titles as *Living in Sri Lanka* (Bunbury and Fennell 2006) and *Sri Lanka Style: Tropical Design and Architecture* (Daswatte and Sansoni 2006), these books draw on an abundance of full-color imagery supported by a narrative text that discusses the design choices, furniture, and furnishings of carefully selected domestic spaces. Whilst far from unique to Sri Lanka, claims of a distinctive architectural tradition are based around an island way of living and iconic architects, most notably Geoffrey Bawa. As an architect who practiced throughout the second half of the twentieth century, Bawa achieved widespread international recognition for his hotels, civic buildings, and domestic spaces, which together constituted both a distinct architectural form for a newly independent Sri Lanka and a style more broadly known as "tropical modernism" (Robson 2007). It is an architectural legacy that informs the representation of desirable, aspirational architecture located within the walls of Galle Fort today. The fort is captured by a semiotic framing that speaks of solitude, individuality, comfort, seclusion, and a retreat from hectic, noisy public spaces. Crucially here, such private spaces of domestic dwelling are deliberately disconnected from the public spaces found beyond their physical boundaries, heightening the sense of seclusion and privacy. Interviews with real estate agents and property owners conducted in 2012 confirmed such framings were central concerns for the majority of those wishing to buy and renovate second homes inside the fort. Kasuni, a local resident confirmed:

> Four houses along this street have been sold in the past year. The owners are all from overseas, from England and Australia, I think. They have spent so much money restoring the houses. It's all very traditional style, lots of wood, old bricks. Old furniture. They like to do things differently to Sri Lankans, very interesting. They seem nice, but we never really see them, they keep themselves to themselves.

Whilst accurate cadastral records for the fort are not publicly available, by early 2012 it was apparent that a large number of individual properties had been purchased by non-residents. Across the old city, houses were undergoing renovation, with a number of buildings only retaining their outer façades, as the images below indicate (Figures 13.3 and 13.4). Staff members at the fort's heritage management office confirmed they were unsure of the plans for many of the houses being renovated, and had little power to stop or regulate construction. Underpinning this form of gentrification is a particular heritage aesthetic, one that revolves around a highly stylized form of architectural heritage oriented by comfort, luxury, and privacy, as noted above. But in order to fully appreciate the aesthetic drivers of this transformation of an historic urban area into a gentrified heritagescape, it is necessary to locate places like Galle in their wider regional and historical context.

Figure 13.3 Restoration of housing in Galle Fort. Source: photo by Tim Winter.

Figure 13.4 Reconstruction of public infrastructure inside Galle Fort. Source: photo by Tim Winter.

The military and psychological boundaries between enclosure and safety, as found in the walled architecture of Galle, are highly porous. Fortifications, isolated peninsulas, and mountaintops are among the physical characteristics that provided the *raison d'être* for many of Asia's small, historic settlements. Whether for political, monastic, or military purposes, settlements such as Luang Prabang and Vieng Xai in Laos, Intramuros in the Philippines, and Bogor in Indonesia have long been associated with withdrawal, refuge, or sanctuary. What we see in Galle today is a continuation of these processes, mobilized under the banner of heritage. For those with the financial means, buying a second home and using it as a space of leisure often stems from a desire to retreat, escape, and seek refuge from everyday life elsewhere. The re-establishment of Sri Lanka as a tourism destination has delivered greater levels of convenience for international travelers. Today, major metropolitan regions such as Bangkok, Delhi, Singapore, and Kuala Lumpur are all less than a four-hour flight from Colombo, and a significant proportion of the recent buyers of Galle's housing reside in these cities.[2] With its population of a few hundred residents, Galle Fort offers a distinct contrast to the millions of people and chaos of Asia's largest cities. The key point to note here then is how a mode of "Sri Lankan living" has emerged, one that invokes and relies upon a particular architectural aesthetic that is highly stylized as local heritage, and symbolically coded with notions of luxury, tranquility, and refuge. Whilst the intersections between this popular heritage-framing and the criteria for national and World Heritage site classification are rarely acknowledged or conceptually articulated, they are clearly discernible, with each arena being mutually constitutive of the other in both oblique and direct ways.

Conclusion

The significance of the trend in Galle's transformation is only fully apparent once we situate such stylized architectural heritagescaping within the context of the debates discussed here concerning urban sustainability, the recognized need to embrace residential community groups, and so forth. Clearly, Galle exemplifies a trend that runs counter to the desire to see heritage conservation as a force of engagement and participation. This highly aestheticized form of gentrification not only leads to the displacement of existing residents and the loss of community relations associated with that, but also creates a new sociospatial dynamic oriented by peace, solitude, and very limited engagement. Crucially, over time such heritagescaping also provides the platform for a new service economy, one that caters to both second-homers and tourists. The vast majority of these new residents in Galle Fort do not speak Sinhalese, meaning that the economy of the walled fort is also undergoing another form of transformation as businesses are established with staff who speak English, Korean, Chinese, or Thai. It is a trend that pays little attention to ideas of cultural or social sustainability, and that, at best, seeks its heritage credentials in the narrow realm of material authenticity.

The aesthetics of gentrification of Galle Fort are far from unique, and have their parallels in many other historic settlements around the world facing similar challenges. Departing from the more familiar themes of tourism, and urban planning, the chapter has sought to investigate the more nebulous, subtle dynamics by which a nexus can form for urban World Heritage site around a symbolic economy oriented by ideas of refuge, sanctuary, and comfort, and ever increasing levels of personal mobility. It is suggested that such processes hold important implications for sustaining both the material fabric and the sociocultural vibrancy of urban environments over the longer term. The issue of displacement, for example, remains a real challenge in the fast developing cities of Asia. For many small urban environments vulnerable to rapid and wholesale change, both in Asia and beyond, it is highly likely this problem will remain a key issue for the foreseeable future. The themes highlighted here illustrate why greater attention needs to be paid to the intersections between the formal recognition of these small historic urban environments as significant heritage sites and the more popular framings that heavily influence how such spaces are being conserved and restored. As we have seen, it is a trend that presents considerable obstacles for those concerned with initiating more sustainable, community-driven heritage conservation paradigms.

Acknowledgements

The research for this chapter was supported under the Australian Research Council's Discovery scheme, "The Role of Cultural Heritage in Conflict Transformation Societies" (DP1094533).

Notes

1 This information comes from interviews conducted in Galle in January 2012.
2 Information from interviews with real-estate agents located in Galle and with local residents, January 2012.

References

Legislation

Convention Concerning the Protection of the World Cultural and Natural Heritage (World Heritage Convention) (UNESCO, 1972). Available at: http://whc.unesco.org/archive/convention-en.pdf (accessed March 19, 2015).

Convention for the Safeguarding of the Intangible Cultural Heritage (Intangible Heritage Convention) (UNESCO, 2003). Available at: http://unesdoc.unesco.org/images/0013/001325/132540e.pdf (accessed March 19, 2015).

International Covenant on Civil and Political Rights (United Nations, 1966). Available at: http://www.ohchr.org/Documents/ProfessionalInterest/ccpr.pdf (accessed March 19, 2015).

International Covenant on Economic, Social and Cultural Rights (United Nations, 1966). Available at: http://www.ohchr.org/Documents/ProfessionalInterest/cescr.pdf (accessed March 19, 2015).

Other Works

Bandarin, F., and van Oers, R. (2012) *The Historic Urban Landscape: Managing Heritage in an Urban Century*. Chichester: Wiley-Blackwell.

Bunbury, T., and Fennell, J. (2006) *Living in Sri Lanka*. New York: Thames and Hudson.

Campanella, T.J. (2008) *The Concrete Dragon: China's Urban Revolution and What It Means for the World*. New York: Princeton Architectural Press.

Canessa, A. (2008) The Past Is Not Another Country: Exploring Indigenous Histories in Bolivia. *History and Anthropology*, 19 (4), 353–369.

Daswatte, C., and Sansoni, D. (2006) *Sri Lanka Style: Tropical Design and Architecture*. Singapore: Periplus.

Du Cros, H., and Lee, Y.S.F. (2007) *Cultural Heritage Management in China: Preserving the Cities of the Pearl River Delta*. London: Routledge.

Edensor, T., and Jayne, M. (eds) (2012) *Urban Theory Beyond the West: A World of Cities*. London: Routledge.

Ekern, S., Logan, W., Sauge, B., and Sinding-Larsen, A. (2012) Human Rights and World Heritage: Preserving Our Common Dignity through Rights-Based Approaches to Site Management. *International Journal of Heritage Studies*, 18 (3), 213–225.

Engle, K. (2010) *The Elusive Promise of Indigenous Development: Rights, Culture, Strategy*. Durham, NC: Duke University Press.

Henderson, J. (2004) Tourism and Postcolonialism: Contested Discourses, Identities and Representations. In M. Hall and H. Tucker (eds), *Tourism and British Colonial Heritage in Malaysia and Singapore*. London: Routledge. pp. 113–125.

Hirsch, P., and Warren, C. (2002) Introduction: Through the Environmental Looking Glass. In P. Hirsch and C. Warren (eds), *The Politics of Environment in Southeast Asia: Resources and Resistance*. London: Routledge, pp. 1–25.

ICOMOS (2011) Our Common Dignity: Towards Rights-Based World Heritage Management. Available at: http://www.icomos.no/cms/content/view/142/56/lang.english (accessed March 14, 2014).

Kong, L., and O'Connor, J. (2009) *Creative Economies, Creative Cities: Asian-European Perspectives*. New York: Springer.

Logan, W. (ed.) (2002) *The Disappearing "Asian" City: Protecting Asia's Urban Heritage in a Globalizing World*. Hong Kong: Oxford University Press.

Mitchell, T. (2002) *Rule of Experts: Egypt, Techno-politics, Modernity*. Berkeley: University of California Press.

Radcliffe, S. (ed.) (2006) *Culture and Development in a Globalizing World: Geographies, Actors, and Paradigms*. London: Routledge.

Radcliffe, S.A., and Laurie, N. (2006) Culture and Development: Taking Culture Seriously in Development for Andean Indigenous People. *Environment and Planning D: Society and Space*, 24, 231–248.

Robinson, J. (2002) Global and World Cities: A View from off the Map. *International Journal of Urban and Regional Research*, 26 (3), 531–554.

Robinson, J. (2006) *Ordinary Cities: Between Modernity and Development*. Abingdon: Routledge.

Robson, D. (2007) *Beyond Bawa*. London: Thames and Hudson.

Roy, A. (2011) Postcolonial Urbanism: Speed, Hysteria, Mass Dreams. In A. Roy and A. Ong (eds), *Worlding Cities: Asian Experiments and the Art of Being Global*. Chichester: Wiley-Blackwell, pp. 307–335.

Sassen, S. (2002) *Global Networks, Linked Cities*. London: Routledge.

Scoones, I. (2007) Sustainability. *Development in Practice*, 17 (4/5), 589–596.

Sengupta, S. (2008) Take Aid from China and Take a Pass on Human Rights. *New York Times*, March 9. Available at: http://www.nytimes.com/2008/03/09/weekinreview/09sengupta.html (accessed March 10, 2014).

Timothy, D.J., and Nyaupane, G.P. (2008) *Cultural Heritage and Tourism in the Developing World*. London: Routledge.

UNESCO (2001) Universal Declaration on Cultural Diversity. Document A/RES/66/154. Available at: http://unesdoc.unesco.org/images/0012/001246/124687e.pdf#page=67 (accessed March 19, 2015).

UNESCO (2004) *The Effects of Tourism on Culture and the Environment in Asia and the Pacific: Tourism and Heritage Site Management in Luang Prabang, Lao PDR*. IMPACT series. Bangkok: UNESCO Bangkok and University of Hawaii. Available at: www.tu.ac.th/org/socadm/actppr/pdf/publication4.pdf (accessed February 22, 2015).

UN-Habitat (2008) *The State of the World's Cities 2008/2009: Harmonious Cities*. London: Earthscan.

UN-Habitat (2010) *Urban World: A New Chapter in Urban Development*. Valencia: UN-Habitat. Available at: http://www.mirror.unhabitat.org/pmss/getElectronicVersion.aspx?nr=2960&alt=1 (accessed February 22, 2015).

United Nations (1948) Universal Declaration of Human Rights. Resolution 217 A (III). Available at: http://www.un.org/en/documents/udhr/ (accessed March 19, 2015).

Wang, S. (2008) A Mirror with Two Sides: Heritage Development and Urban Conservation in the Ancient City of Pingyao, China. *Historic Environment*, 21 (3), 22–26.

Waterton, E., and Smith, L. (2010) The Recognition and Misrecognition of Community Heritage. *International Journal of Heritage Studies*, 16 (1), 4–15.

Winter, T. (2013) Clarifying the Critical in Critical Heritage Studies. *International Journal of Heritage Studies*, 19 (6), 532–545.

Winter, T. (2014) Heritage Studies and the Privileging of Theory. *International Journal of Heritage Studies*, 20 (6), 556–572.

CHAPTER 14

Cultural Heritage as a Strategy for Social Needs and Community Identity

Keir Reeves and Gertjan Plets

Our past is woven into the fabric of our present; our awareness of the past is constitutive of our sense of identity and contemporary community. This chapter examines how heritage may be interwoven with strategies to meet social needs in the context of attempts to preserve a sense of community. We wish to pose a question: Is it that heritage is itself a social need, and ultimately without heritage there can be no society? The need to engage in practices of community preservation through heritage is a feeling that can arise in the face of contemporary development trends that are often perceived as compromising the social fabric.

In this chapter we contend that any critically engaged conceptualization of heritage in the opening decades of the twenty-first century is best achieved by seeing heritage as an integral part of a broader set of cultural, social, political, and economic practices. We position heritage not merely as a deliberate sociopolitical practice, but also as one of the many everyday and often unconscious strategies employed in the process of addressing social needs. Because social needs play out at different levels in society, and different social institutions are involved, heritage is similarly ideally understood and tackled through in-depth ethnography and bottom-up management and policy-framework approaches.

In our discussion we appraise how community memory and heritage intersect to provide an important locus of social cohesion and self-esteem, both social needs that lie at the basis of social practice. This is often difficult to measure, but is of immense significance for maintaining sustainable communities and stability. Drawing on existing theories in psychology and sociology, the key objective of our discussion is to position social needs as a complementary analytic tool through an examination of a diverse range of examples. These are investigated to show how heritage plays out in sustaining regional communities,

A Companion to Heritage Studies, First Edition. Edited by William Logan, Máiréad Nic Craith, and Ullrich Kockel.
© 2016 John Wiley & Sons, Inc. Published 2016 by John Wiley & Sons, Inc.

preserving the cultural life and practices of indigenous communities, and maintaining self-esteem. Through this effort we seek to add food for thought and fresh theoretical perspectives to the broader field of heritage studies, an area of enquiry where there is still a lot of scope for additional theorization (Waterton and Watson 2013).

Discussions of heritage in the context of social needs are grounded in a theoretical and methodological discussion that emphasizes the importance of heritage in constructions of community cohesion and identity, and as a bedrock requirement for community and societal harmony. A plethora of previous studies have emphasized that heritage is often used to cultivate cohesion and self-esteem. However, we contend that the use of the past for community cohesion and membership is more than merely a selectively produced discourse. The past is imbued with social structures and dynamics – what Bourdieu (1990) termed "doxa," historically engrained pre-reflexive and intuitive knowledge structures that influence social practice without social actors being consciously aware of it. This approach emphasizes heritage as social action corresponding to the social needs of a given locus, operating in everyday life and constantly reproduced by the reality of that locus. Accordingly, we argue that cultural heritage is best understood as both an unconscious organically grown practice and also an intentional selective enterprise that is inherent in any social context or societal group. Our approach emerges from the volume editors' contention that it is best to consider "heritage as a construct resulting from processes that give present-day significance and value to elements from the past." Through appraising the interrelation between heritage and social needs, we contribute to international conversations about policy responses for ameliorating social needs by promoting good heritage policy and practice.

Social Needs and Human Motivation

From a theoretical perspective, any discussion of the emergence of heritage in the context of social needs begins with a discussion of psychologist Abraham Maslow's widely influential hierarchy of human needs. Maslow's work (Maslow 1943) forms the baseline of a vast amount of research in the field of psychology and sociology on human action and motivation. Drawing on work that focuses on the socially dependent nature of heritage, we contend that applying basic theoretical frameworks from outside the field of heritage studies is necessary in order to understand all the entangled processes and parameters underlying cultural heritage discourses. The main cornerstone of Maslow's theory is that hierarchically organized needs are the most important driving forces behind the human motivation that produces practice and action (see Figure 14.1). These needs – physiological, safety, love, belonging, esteem, and self-actualization – are seen as the main driving forces of human motivation and decision-making. According to Maslow, a person or group only becomes aware of a particular need once a human need lower in the hierarchy has been fulfilled.

Drawing on the work of William James (1962) and Michael Mathes (1981), William Huitt (2007) argues that Maslow's categorization of human needs can be divided into three levels of human needs: material (physiological, safety), social (sense of belonging, esteem), and spiritual (self-actualization). Regarding social needs, Huitt (2007) emphasizes that group membership and esteem/respect are important as humans require a basic sense of belonging to and being accepted by social groups. Another social need identified by Maslow is esteem, a need to feel respected and valued by others.

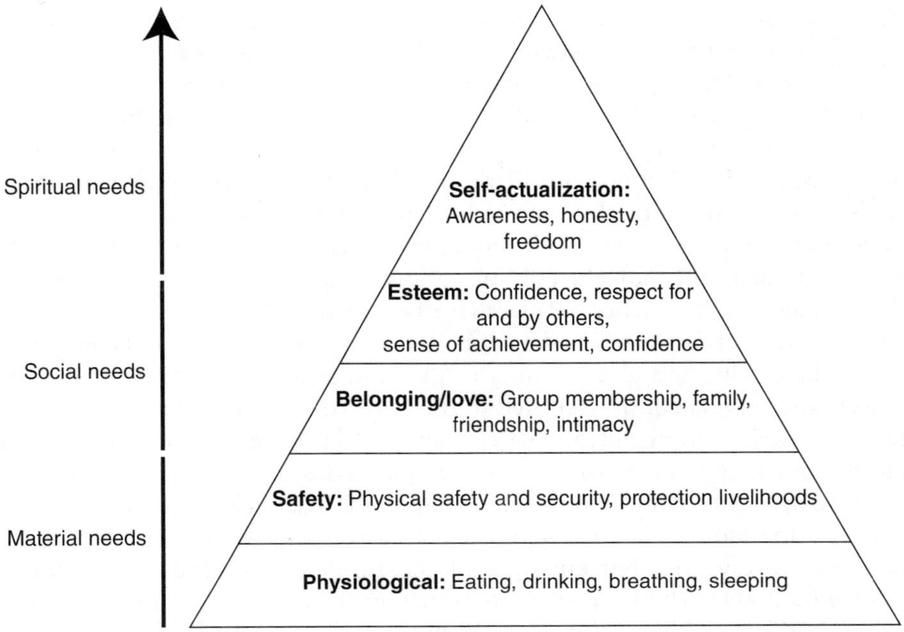

Figure 14.1 Maslow's hierarchy of social needs. Source: adapted from Huitt (2007) and Maslow (1943).

It is closely interconnected with the concept of legitimation, and it is essential to take up a role in the social arena. As many studies of heritage and cultural memory suggest, cultural heritage is a vehicle for belonging, for group membership, as well as social and cultural legitimation. Accordingly, any discussion of heritage as a social need is complemented by allied themes of heritage and human rights, and the role of cultural heritage in sustainable livelihoods (Graham and Howard 2008; Kohl 1998; Halbwachs 1992; Smith 2006). Cultural heritage is a basic need that is both sociologically and psychologically constituted. In this chapter we will further explore these cornerstones of heritage and argue for a sociologically and psychologically grounded approach to heritage.

Later critics of Maslow, including, for example, Geert Hofstede (1984), observed that his appraisal of human needs, and especially his hierarchical arrangement of these, is to a large extent too ethnocentric and functionalist. Although this critique is persuasive in its assertion that Maslow's work indeed reflects (already outdated) American values (Hofstede 2001), drawing on the broad application of his framework, we argue that, applying a cultural-relativist position, Maslow's and Huitt's conceptualization of social needs is a type of cultural form that is constituted though local practices and heterogeneous in nature (Collier and Ong 2004). Similarly, informed by Sharon Macdonald's identification of difficult heritage as a "global assemblage" (Macdonald 2009: 187–92), we argue that, in its most general sense, the centrality of cultural heritage to maintaining social needs, or more specifically the sense of belonging and legitimation, is a global one with different regional and local manifestations. Drawing on our research in the Pacific, Asia, Europe, Australia, New Zealand, and North America, we explore the idea of heritage as a social need and source of community identity with a view to foster future discussion of this research area. This global perspective does not mean that we approach heritage as a universal phenomenon that can be understood through a single teleological law-like framework that can be generically applied throughout the world. By analyzing specific case studies, we aim to explore "social needs" as a useful analytic tool for understanding how heritage is locally constituted and constantly in the making. We strongly apprehend heritage vis-à-vis social needs through a cultural relativist framework; that is, as a cultural practice that is constantly created through the dialectic between the structures of the social environment, the individual dispositions of social agents, and the characteristics of the heritage object, practice, or place (see Bourdieu 1990; Giddens 1984).

Clearly, heritage is in the first instance about contemporary people and communities, and how these value and give meaning to the past. How people read the past, both selectively and spontaneously, is related to their everyday practice, needs, beliefs, value systems, political environment, and social context. As has been widely noted, the main "sources" in heritage studies are not, for example, archeological objects but the actual people who make meaning of the past and interpret the materiality of those archeological objects. Furthermore, the methodologies deployed should not be, for example, archeological excavations but ethnographic fieldwork (Macdonald 2013; Hollowell and Nicholas 2009). The locus of study is neither the site, nor the repository of the museum, but instead the community. During a session of the 2012 meeting of the Australian Anthropological Society entitled "Cultural Heritage in a Material World," the chair Annie Ross rightly stated that the term "cultural heritage" has moved closer towards that of "culture." By emphasizing the "cultural" aspect of "cultural heritage," greater attention is given to how present communities perceive and use heritage. Through analyzing cultural heritage as a sociocultural discourse, we do not examine the past but the cultural processes, worldview, historical trajectory, and social arena of involved agents – including the particular sociocultural needs of a group.

One of the core principles of culture, and in turn heritage, is that it is not stable. Instead, culture is constantly reproduced and revised in relation to both internal and external changes and perceived needs. Cultural heritage as a socioculturally driven valuation similarly changes in relation to the evolving social arena, and its interplay with human agency (Ashworth, Graham, and Tunbridge 2007: 3; Davison 2008; Smith 2006; Tilley 2006).

Three decades ago, Fredrik Barth explored variations in cosmological traditions and rites amongst adjacent Mountain Ok communities of Papua New Guinea, all of which were isolated and non-literate. Interestingly, these indigenous communities, who shared similar languages, material culture, and ecological conditions, had striking differences (some hardly reconcilable) in their communal rites and ceremonies (Barth 1987: 1–9). Breaking with traditional anthropological theory about culture and tradition, Barth argues that all culture is constantly reproduced, and consequently undergoes inevitable change. Based on his comparative research, Barth explains cultural variation and reasons for change through the inherent nuances between different human agencies that constitute creativity, which on its own springs from its interplay with the social arena (Barth 1987: 74–82). Following Barth's stance towards cultural change and sociocultural expressions, one could state that, to paraphrase Barth, heritages are also constantly in the making, as too is the nature of social needs and interests that define cultural heritage practice. Thus, as with any social practice, change is inevitable, presenting heritage practitioners with a paradox: how to respond accordingly to the heritage of the future and the future of what is now considered heritage. What is remembered by a group today may have lost its meaning or be forgotten 20 years later.

As the French cultural historian Pierre Nora observed, "memory is by nature multiple and yet specific; collective, plural, and yet individual" (Nora 1989: 9). In Nora's "new history" (*nouvelle histoire*), culture and in turn community memories are central. Because of the centrality of cultural heritage in the formation of a sense of community, it is appropriate that it is not only conceptualized as a strategy to address needs, but also as a core social need (Ashworth, Graham, and Tunbridge 2007; Graham and Howard 2008: 1; Smith 2006: 80–82). This theoretically driven approach to heritage as a social need abuts more traditional heritage regimes, which are grounded in codified built-heritage processes and driven by a response to development pressures and the heritage conservation implications of local, regional, and national government planning frameworks. This situation is understandable as the bulk of heritage practice continues to occur in the heritage management of the built environment.

Heritage and Belonging

As a number of scholars have shown, both across space and time, historical consciousness and the veneration of the past have played and continue to play a decisive role in negotiating, maintaining, and creating group identity, "ethnic" difference, national prestige, claiming land or justifying nationalistic claims (see e.g. Habermas 1993; Kohl 1998; Lowenthal 1998; Péporté *et al.* 2010; Schnirelmann 1996; Trigger 1984, 1989). This is especially the case during episodes where ethnic boundaries have to be maintained or renegotiated in response to societal changes (including postcolonial episodes during the 1960s and 1970s, and the collapse of the Soviet Union in the early 1990s), when references to the past are an important resource for the revitalization, creation, and consolidation of a national identity, and creating a combined sense of otherness and sameness. Ultimately heritage is integral in constructing a feeling of group membership (Eriksen 2001: 267). It creates a feeling of familiarity, enrichment, escape, and legitimacy of a community's sociocultural interests in the present.

The integral role of heritage as a touchstone for community unity and social cohesion has underpinned recent state-formation initiatives such as the Regional Assistance Mission to the Solomon Islands (RAMSI). This mission was designed to bring about social reintegration in Solomon Islander society in the wake of the 1999 violence that resulted in systemic societal breakdown (events known in Solomon Islands pidgin as the "tension"). RAMSI was a deliberate and legitimate attempt to use cultural heritage as an instrument of social policy to facilitate community harmony. At the core of RAMSI's use of cultural heritage as a means of (re)constructing national identity was an emphasis on Solomon Islanders' roles as combatants and non-combatants in one of the bloodiest conflicts of the Pacific theater during World War II. Accordingly, the role of heritage commemoration and historical recognition were viewed as a key part of cultural memory and, in a sense, national identity. The role of heritage in identity politics is important given recent societal breakdown in the Solomon Islands. The significance of cultural heritage, both in terms of indigenous custom and the historical role of Solomon Islanders in the Allied war effort, is a key social need in the present rather than a luxury at a remove from other key social needs. Interestingly, President Obama's recent endorsement of a commemorative memorial in Honiara dedicated to the role played by Solomon Islanders in support of the Allies during World War II suggests a new understanding that enhances the role of Pacific islanders during the war (Kwai 2013: 112). The point made by Pacific cultural heritage practitioners and researchers about the significance of Solomon Islanders' role in the Pacific war and their enduring memories of the war is persuasive (White and Lindstrom 1990).[1]

Similarly, Lynn Meskell (2012) observes the centrality of cultural heritage (both material and intangible) in constructing redemptive reconciliation narratives for the fractured Rainbow Nation vision of post-apartheid South Africa in the decades following the release of Nelson Mandela from Robben Island prison in 1994, and his presidency leading a government of national unity in 1994. For Meskell, heritage stands not at a remove for settling key social issues of national priority but as a constituent social need. In this respect, cultural heritage serves as a device whereby contemporary cultural heritage practice is effectively a form of social practice where acknowledgement of the significance of indigenous cultural heritage is central to understanding these communities.

In Vanuatu, the role of cultural heritage as a foundation block of social organization and identity is similarly best understood as a key social need. The myth and legend of Chief Roi Mata is a source of cultural unity, identity, and community belonging in Vanuatu, and the case of Chief Roi Mata's Domain provides a valuable insight into the way that cultural heritage is a social need. Closer interpretation of Chief Roi Mata's Domain, now a World Heritage site, reveals the centrality of place as a community touchstone and a site of nation formation in a country which is an archipelago with 50 official languages and diverse cultures, which achieved independence from Britain and France as recently as 1980. The views of the paramount chief of Efate about Chief Roi Mata's Domain reveals the crucial role of heritage as a social need. He deliberately spoke on this matter, saying that the *land bilong Roi Mata* ("the land belongs to Roi Mata"). Tellingly, not all of Chief Roi Mata's Domain is included in the current World Heritage site inscription. The paramount chief also pointed out that for him cultural heritage in Vanuatu was not a case of privileging the "blackbirding" of Chief Roi Mata's Domain (which is widely acknowledged as a foundation narrative for the community and symbol of national identity in the present day),[2] but instead it was all of these cultural heritage issues because each are part of *kulja bilong, me holdem taet* (lit. "my culture I'm holding it close"). Significantly, the paramount chief emphasized the centrality of cultural heritage in the construction of identity, and unambiguously linked it to Ni-Vanuatu identity in the present day.[3] For Ni-Vanuatu, Chief Roi Mata's Domain is a foundational cultural heritage narrative that underpins constructions of national unity in the present day (Cheer, Reeves, and Laing 2013; Spriggs 1997; Trau 2012). That is to say, for many Ni-Vanuatu, heritage is a core social need, not a peripheral matter at a remove from other equally pressing development imperatives and the more visible baseline issues the country faces, including the impact of climate change as well as medical and social needs.

Heritage Conflicts: Negotiating Legitimacy and Esteem

Considering heritage as a socially constituted social need that is of intrinsic importance to a sense of group membership and self-esteem provides us with a fresh way to interpret and mediate heritage conflicts. This approach includes, for example, emphasizing community cohesion, connections between community and the land, and in some cases human rights. Such conflicts are often very politically and emotionally loaded, especially in multicultural contexts where heritage struggles are framed within a broader social struggle between different groups for recognition, empowerment, and sociocultural stability. Because of the political dimension of heritage, conflicts over ownership are very often primarily understood as power-related issues, where control over heritage is linked with broader control in society. In this regard, Chief Roi Mata's Domain is unequalled. A group's use of heritage for external legitimation can have a power-related dimension, but it should also be approached as a desire for respect and esteem, providing confidence to societies to overcome uncertainty. Thus, political actors that respond to ownership conflicts, or deploy cultural heritage in their rhetoric, not only do this to challenge or maintain existing power relations, but also to meet broader needs related to respect and esteem. Drawing on a case study from post-Soviet Russia, we will show how heritage objects – and overcoming ownership disputes – can also function as a type of cultural resource in periods of uncertainty and unprecedented structural change, effectively responding to social needs such as self-esteem, dignity, and legitimation.[4]

In 1993, a mummy of a 2500-year-old female was unearthed in the Altai Republic in Russia. As a result of being buried in permanently frozen ground, the body was especially well preserved, and tattoos were still visible on it; this, along with the numerous grave goods found, meant that the find was viewed as both a scientific treasure and an imaginative cultural object. Archeologists called her the "ice maiden," and together with other finds excavated in the 1990s, she symbolized a revival of scientific research into frozen burials and the survival of the archaeology of protohistory in a period where science in Russia was under severe pressure. The finds and subsequent interdisciplinary research not only resulted in both national and international publishing opportunities, ensuring international collaboration and large amounts of funding. Those who discovered the body were also awarded the highly prestigious State Prize of the Russian Federation (*Gosudarstvennaya Premiya Rossiyskoy Federatsii*) by President Vladimir Putin. The indigenous Altaians, on the other hand, named her the "Altai Princess," and she was understood to be the mythical ancestress of all Altaians, and an embodiment of Altaian cultural values. Drawing on their animist indigenous worldview, requests were made to repatriate the Altai Princess as a prerequisite to restoring the relationship between the people and the land. Indigenous requests were refused, and the ensuing situation rapidly resulted in a sociocultural conflict dominating regional elections and political debate. Clearly the need to control the past is related to the interest of both sides maintaining their respective image and standing in the social arena. This situation is consistent with the popular idea that objects from the past are potential authoritative resources (Lowenthal 1998: x).

Importantly, the Altai Princess was discovered shortly after the collapse of the Soviet Union. For many in the region, this was a period characterized, on the one hand, by political collapse, social instability, and a lack of prospects (Buyandelgeriyn 2007; Halemba 2006), and on the other by an ethno-cultural revival which saw indigenous people and minorities rediscover, reinvent, and reclaim their culture. It fostered a desire to understand heritage in a social context that emphasized broader social and cultural legitimation (Balzer 1999; Buyandelgeriyn 2007; Kaplonski 2004). The Altai Princess as an object of cultural heritage not only embodied Altaian cultural values, but the struggle over her ownership was also related to the broader social needs of the post-Soviet Altaians. Depicted as the ancestress of all Altaians by the indigenous intelligentsia, the polemic surrounding the Altai Princess helped Altaians to overcome the artificial ethnic labels they acquired during the Soviet era, and helped initiate a sense of Altaian cultural identity. Importantly, requesting repatriation also led Altaian community leaders to demand broader recognition for Altaians in the newly founded Russian Federation. This process also led to external recognition of the specific cultural traits that characterizes the Altaian relationship with the dead and their homeland. The extensive use of the Altai Princess during national festivities (see Figure 14.2) was driven by coverage in the popular media, which sought to constitute a sense of a unified Altaian culture. It was an event that emphasized a glorious past, ultimately providing Altaians with a sense of cultural pride, inspiration, and the desire to overcome the difficult realities of the post-Soviet 1990s. This was a somewhat ironic process as Altaian culture was itself a Soviet creation.

At the same time, the struggle of archeologists for *their* heritage can also be linked to a perceived need for external social recognition and respect. During the Soviet era, science and scientific achievement held a central position in Soviet official ideology. Being openly anti-religious, the Communist Party promoted scientific education and political enlightenment (Smolkin-Rothrock 2013), ensuring that scientists, including archeologists, held a respected position in Russian society (Graham 1993). With the

Figure 14.2 Altaian girl dressed up as the Altai Princess during the biennial El-Oiuyn national festival. Source: © http://www.cheinesh.ru/.

breakdown of the Soviet Union, archeologists encountered a radically changed social arena, with shrinking financial and political resources. Furthermore, broader pluralism within society deconstructed the official ideology where science and scientific advancement was promoted. As such, opposition among archeologists to repatriation and defending archeological stewardship can be linked with the archeological community's broader need to maintain a particular respected position and legitimacy vis-à-vis objects that are understood as an integral part of their own heritage.

Heritage as a Social Need in an Institutionalized Environment

Heritage needs to be a pluralistic concept that responds to social change and wider needs. This inclusive process is diametrically opposed to the perceived needs of national governments to straightjacket heritage into taxonomic categories such as intangible heritage, cultural landscapes, and archeological heritage. Throughout the world, governments have made major efforts to find a balance between a plurality of heritages that recognize the significance of heritage as a social need, and in turn the role of heritage as a policy instrument. However, in most of these nations, because of their determined planning regime, heritage is highly institutionalized and a singular discourse prevails, at the expense of the intangible and social imperatives of heritage. Laurajane Smith (2006) calls this particular discourse the "authorised heritage discourse", which "constitutes and legitimizes what heritage is within a certain society," but "also defines who has the ability to speak for and about the nature and meaning of heritage" (Smith 2006: 26). Clearly any discussion of heritage as a social need, or indeed as an integral part of human rights, or more broadly as an overtly politically practice, will disagree with "authorized heritage discourse." In most cases, this official discourse is institutionalized in the legislative framework of a nation or administrative entity, and determines whose value system is more admissible. The value system and ethos underlying this discourse furthermore defines who are the privileged stewards over the past, and validates certain understandings of heritage at the expense of others.

Ultimately, heritage comprises a key social need of cultural life and practice, and is part of community identity throughout the world. However, in most cases, even beyond the heritage sector, official agencies will always privilege expert knowledge because its underlying epistemological framework correlates with that of institutionalized agencies (Ross *et al.* 2011). This means that context-dependent management based on dialogue and empathy is difficult and time-consuming (we often forget that heritage is not the top priority of governments, and often it is quite low in terms of policy agendas). This ultimately makes key stakeholders – including, for instance, archeologists, architects, civil servants, urban planners and human geographers – both the legislators and interpreters of the past. Moreover, providing these people and groups with institutional authority further reinforces their social, professional, and political authority. This ultimately creates the assumption that their value system is the right one, and does not enable scientists to reflect on their own ideals and practices, and their broader social needs. This magnifies epistemological and institutional barriers (Ross *et al.* 2011) between experts and other less privileged groups, making it difficult for those people that are not culturally and politically engaged, and do not speak the authorized language of science and bureaucracy, to challenge official conceptualizations of the past (Smith and Jackson 2006: 313–22;

Smith 2008). In the end, governments are not responding to the broader social needs of the public, and instead respond to historically privileged social needs.

Conclusion

Contemporary development trends can compromise, and ultimately destroy, cultural heritage, the social fabric, and community cohesion. In this chapter we have examined how heritage is fundamentally connected with human strategies to realize social needs in the context of preserving contemporary communities. From our examination of heritage frameworks, policy dialogues, and country-specific examples, it is clear that those who control the interpretation of heritage control heritage narratives, and this matters materially. In the context of early twenty-first century processes of development, then, it is vital that heritage narratives emphasize social needs and the facilitation of community identity. This may be obvious in the developing world, but it is also a globally relevant phenomena where social needs, sustaining community, and the preservation of place are all integral aspects of community identity.

While this chapter necessarily began with a theoretical discussion advocating an expansion of Maslow's hierarchy of needs to incorporate cultural heritage, it emerges that heritage as a social need poses a philosophical challenge to existing heritage institutions, frameworks, and policy. We wish to close with the following thoughts on the idea of heritage as a fundamental social need in the context of broader discussions in the field of heritage studies. If, as we assert, heritage is a fundamental social need and driver of cultural identity, then this understanding must fundamentally underscore a contemporary understanding and appreciation of heritage that emphasizes the interwoven issues of cultural identity, human rights, resource allocation, and intangible heritage. All of these are required as the basis for future attempts to foster pluralistic heritage values during the first half of the twenty-first century.

Acknowledgements

The authors wish to thank the following and acknowledge their contribution to the development of this chapter: Joseph Cheer (Monash University), the Vanuatu Cultural Centre, Jolanta Nowak (Federation University, Australia), Antoinette Dillon, Kirsty Marshall, the Altai Project research team based at Ghent University, Belgium, and the McDonald Institute for Archaeology at the University of Cambridge, UK. The research on which this chapter is based was supported by funding from the Australian Research Council, the Monash Fellowship Scheme of the Faculty of Arts, Monash University, and the Visiting Fellowship scheme of Clare Hall, University of Cambridge.

Notes

1 For a broader discussion of heritage issues in relation to the Pacific theater of World War II, see Smith (2012).
2 Blackbirding was a process of coercing Pacific islanders onto ships, often by deceit, to work on the sugarcane plantations of Queensland and Fiji.

3 The people of Vanuatu are known as Ni-Vanuatu. The language spoken in the quotes, Bislama, is a Western Pacific pidgin English and also the national language of Vanuatu.

4 For additional material regarding this case, see Plets (2013) and Plets *et al.* (2013).

References

Ashworth, G.J., Graham, B., and Tunbridge, J.E. (2007) *Pluralising Pasts: Heritage, Identity and Place in Multicultural Societies.* London: Pluto Press.

Balzer, M.M. (1999) *The Tenacity of Ethnicity: A Siberian Saga in Global Perspective.* Princeton: Princeton University Press.

Barth, F. (1987) *Cosmologies in the Making: A Generative Approach to Cultural Variation in Inner Guinea.* Cambridge: Cambridge University Press.

Bourdieu, P. (1990) *The Logic of Practice.* Cambridge: Polity Press.

Buyandelgeriyn, M. (2007) Dealing with Uncertainty: Shamans, Marginal Capitalism, and the Remaking of History. *American Ethnologist*, 34 (1), 127–147.

Cheer, J.M., Reeves, K.J., and Laing, J.H. (2013) Tourism and Traditional Culture: Land Diving in Vanuatu. *Annals of Tourism Research*, 43, 435–455.

Collier, S.J., and Ong, A. (2004) Global Assemblages, Anthropological Problems. In A. Ong and S.J. Collier (eds), *Global Assemblages: Technology, Politics, and Ethics as Anthropological Problems.* Oxford: Blackwell, pp. 3–22.

Davison, G. (2008) Heritage: From Patrimony to Pastiche. In G. Fairclough, R. Harrison, J. H. Jameson, and J. Schofield (eds), *The Heritage Reader.* London: Routledge, pp. 31–41.

Eriksen, T.H. (2001) *Small Places, Large Issues: An Introduction to Social and Cultural Anthropology.* London: Pluto Press.

Giddens, A. (1984) *The Constitution of Society.* Cambridge: Polity Press.

Graham, B., and Howard, P. (2008) Heritage and Identity. In B. Graham and P. Howard (eds), *The Ashgate Research Companion to Heritage and Identity.* Burlington, VA: Ashgate Publishing, pp. 1–15.

Graham, L. (1993) *Science in Russia and the Soviet Union: A Short History.* Cambridge: Cambridge University Press.

Habermas, J. (1993) Struggles for Recognition in Constitutional States. *European Journal of Philosophy*, 1 (2), 128–155.

Halbwachs, M. (1992) *On Collective Memory.* Chicago: University of Chicago Press.

Halemba, A. (2006) *The Telengits of Southern Siberia: Landscape, Religion and Knowledge in Motion.* Leiden: Brill.

Hofstede, G (1984) The Cultural Relativity of the Quality of Life Concept. *Academy of Management Review*, 9 (3), 389–398.

Hofstede, G. (2001) *Culture's Consequences: Comparing Values, Behaviors, Institutions and Organizations across Nations.* London: Sage.

Hollowell, J., and Nicholas, G. (2009) Using Ethnographic Methods to Articulate Community-Based Conceptions of Cultural Heritage Management. *Public Archaeology*, 8 (2/3), 141–160.

Huitt, W. (2007) Maslow's Hierarchy of Needs. Educational Psychology Interactive. Available at: http://www.edpsycinteractive.org/topics/conation/maslow.html (accessed February 10, 2014).

James, W. (1962 [1892]) *Psychology: Briefer Course.* New York: Collier.

Kaplonski, C. (2004) *Truth, History and Politics in Mongolia: The Memory of Heroes.* London: Routledge Curzon.

Kohl, P. (1998) Nationalism and Archaeology: On the Constructions of Nations and the Reconstructions of the Remote Past. *Annual Review of Anthropology*, 27, 223–246.

Kwai, A.A. (2013) Islanders in the Second World War: A Solomon Islander Perspective. M.A. dissertation. Canberra: Australian National University.

Lowenthal, D. (1998) *The Heritage Crusade and the Spoils of History.* Cambridge: Cambridge University Press.

Macdonald, S. (2009) *Difficult Heritage.* London: Routledge.

Macdonald, S. (2013) *Memorylands: Heritage and Identity in Europe Today.* London: Routledge

Maslow, A.H. (1943) A Theory of Human Motivation. *Psychological Review*, 50 (4), 370–396.

Mathes, E. (1981) Maslow's Hierarchy of Needs as a Guide for Living. *Journal of Humanistic Psychology*, 21, 69–72.

Meskell, L. (2012) *The Nature of Heritage: The New South Africa.* Chichester: Wiley-Blackwell.

Nora, P. (1989) Between Memory and History: Les lieux de mémoire. *Representations*, special issue, 26, 7–24.

Péporté, P., Kmec, S., Majerus, B., and Margue, M. (2010) *Inventing Luxembourg: Representations of the Past, Space and Language from the Nineteenth to the Twenty-First Century.* Leiden: Brill.

Plets, G. (2013) Heritages in the Making: Social Embodiment of Cultural Heritage Objects and Places in the Multicultural Altai Republic. Ph.D. dissertation. Ghent: Ghent University.

Plets, G., Konstantinov, N., Soenov, V., and Robinson, E. (2013) Repatriation, Doxa, and Contested Heritages: The Return of the Altai Princess in an International Perspective. *Anthropology and Archaeology of Eurasia*, 52 (2), 73–100.

Ross, A., Sherman, K.P., Snodgrass, J., Delcore, H., and Sherman, R. (2011) *Indigenous Peoples and the Collaborative Stewardship of Nature: Knowledge Binds and Institutional Conflicts.* Walnut Creek, CA: Left Coast Press.

Schnirelmann, V. (1996) *Who Gets the Past? Competition for Ancestors among Non-Russian Intellectuals in Russia.* Washington: Woodrow Wilson Center Press.

Smith, A. (ed.) (2012) *World Heritage in a Sea of Islands: The Pacific 2009 Program.* Paris: UNESCO World Heritage Centre.

Smith, C., and Jackson, G. (2006) Decolonizing Indigenous Archaeology: Developments from Down Under. *American Indian Quarterly*, 30 (3/4), 311–349.

Smith, L. (2006) *Uses of Heritage.* New York: Routledge.

Smith, L. (2008) Towards a Theoretical Framework for Archaeological Heritage Management. In G. Fairclough, R. Harrison, J.H. Jameson, and J. Schofield (eds), *The Heritage Reader.* London: Routledge, pp. 62–74.

Smolkin-Rothrock, V. (2013) The Ticket to the Soviet Soul: Science, Religion, and the Spiritual Crisis of Late Soviet Atheism. *Russian Review*, 73 (April), 171–197.

Spriggs, M. (1997) *The Island Melanesians.* Oxford: Blackwell.

Tilley, C. (2006) Introduction: Identity, Place, Landscape and Heritage. *Journal of Material Culture*, 11 (1), 7–32.

Trau, A.M. (2012) The Glocalisation of World Heritage at Chief Roi Mata's Domain, Vanuatu. *Historic Environment*, 24 (3), 4–11.

Trigger, B. (1984) Alternative Archaeologies: Nationalist, Colonialist, Imperialist. *Man*, 19 (3), 335–370.

Trigger, B. (1989) *A History of Archaeological Thought.* Cambridge: Cambridge University Press.

Waterton, E., and Watson, S. (2013) Framing Theory: Towards a Critical Imagination in Heritage Studies. *International Journal of Heritage Studies*, 19 (6), 546–561.

White, G., and Lindstrom, L. (1990) *Island Encounters: Black and White Memories of the Pacific War.* Washington: Smithsonian Institution Press.

CHAPTER 15 Heritage in the Digital Age

Maria Economou

Heritage has always been important, but in an increasingly globalized world, our understanding and attitude towards cultural heritage is shaping our sense of place and context more than ever before. Over the last few years, the use of new technologies has grown exponentially, permeating every aspect of our lives. It has consequently also affected the way different communities around the world experience heritage, whether their own or that of other cultures. People are increasingly encountering sites and monuments and learning about the past through digital media, in the form of virtual reconstructions, digital representation of artifacts, online videos, and so on. This is particularly the case for younger generations, for which the first experience of cultural heritage is often through a digital surrogate that shapes their understanding and perception.

The expansion of Web 2.0, the increasing use of smartphones, and the demand for almost constant access to the internet also mean that social interaction with other visitors or staff at heritage sites, as well as the face-to-face discussions about heritage, are increasingly transferred to the digital sphere, whether in the form of discussion forums, computer gaming, or the sharing of photos, videos, experiences, and opinions via social networks. Digital media in all its different forms, such as the multitude of social networking tools that Web 2.0 encompasses (including blogs, podcasts, RSS feeds, Flickr, YouTube), the mobile apps designed for individual use, virtual reality, online games with heritage themes, digital collections, and interactive kiosk applications in exhibitions, all offer new possibilities for heritage organizations to interact with their

A Companion to Heritage Studies, First Edition. Edited by William Logan, Máiréad Nic Craith, and Ullrich Kockel.
© 2016 John Wiley & Sons, Inc. Published 2016 by John Wiley & Sons, Inc.

visitors (both on-site and off-site), but raise also a number of challenges and important issues which this chapter examines.

Heritage institutions have been experimenting with these tools as part of their efforts at greater democratization, opening up to diverse communities and inviting different viewpoints and interpretations of their sites and collections. But have these hopes actually materialized in practice? What is gained and what is lost when heritage is experienced via digital surrogates? What are the main characteristics of this new way of communication? What is the profile of these virtual visitors, their motivations, and the way they interact with heritage content? Should these communications be controlled and moderated, and if so, by whom? Should curators intervene in this free and democratic exchange of information?

The chapter examines applications included under the term "digital heritage," and uses a range of examples to discuss the theoretical issues that are related to the growing area of digital heritage practices. The term "applications" is used in the chapter to refer to all types of digital technology as it is applied to the cultural heritage field, while "apps" refers specifically to programs designed to run on a smartphone or tablet. As with all kinds of interpretation of heritage, the different types of digital heritage applications that have been developed over the last few decades reveal more about our own contemporary views and interpretation of the past than about past societies themselves. For this reason, it is very useful to examine the developments in this area over the last few years, and see what approaches have been taken, what the underlying assumptions are, and where gaps exist.

At the same time, it is interesting to observe how the use of different digital tools has not only allowed the collection and processing of heritage data, but also reshaped the traditional humanities questions we ask. Digital technologies are now being used for capturing data (such as geophysical surveys and laser scanning), modeling (such as geographic information systems), and engaging with different audiences (either through mobile devices, gaming, virtual or augmented reality) in various contexts, such as schools, cultural tourism, museum visits, and life-long learning.

But this is a process that works both ways: not only have digital technologies affected the management and understanding of heritage, but the wider heritage interpretation issues also have an effect on how digital tools are being employed. For example, questions regarding the global and local management of heritage sites, the ethics of public archaeology and of archeologists or other specialists as stewards of heritage, and the representation of multiple interest groups are only some of the issues of the bigger heritage picture which affects how digital applications are being used and in which direction. But first, it is useful to examine the potential of digital media tools, and the ways that these have influenced cultural heritage practices.

The Potential of Digital Technologies

The digital revolution has made our world smaller, making distant cultures and sites more accessible than ever. High resolution images, 3D models, and video recordings provide multiple views of heritage sites from around the world, with immersive applications giving users the feeling of actually being there. As the technology improves, the quality of the digitized images, visualization techniques, 3D scanning (and more recently, also 3D printing and laser cutting) enable the accurate capturing and representation of information at different scales, from minute details of the decoration of a fragment to large-scale models that show the location of different finds over a large area, or the replication (in the case of 3D printing) of objects, buildings, or sites.

Heritage is our link to past cultures and societies, and this, by definition, involves complex interrelationships and phenomena. The use of digital tools can help specialists and professionals organize the large amount of data involved in the scientific investigation and recording of the past, but they can also make these more understandable to a wide audience. For example, digital devices (increasingly transportable and mobile) are being used in excavations to capture information and record socioeconomic changes over time. Virtual exhibitions and interactive games can help diverse user groups, often with little or no prior knowledge of the subject, understand the interpretations of specialists. The combination of different digital media – from moving images to sound, graphic diagrams, and maps and programming tools – which place the user in an active role can be very powerful in the learning process when used appropriately.

Digital resources can be used to help prepare a visit to a heritage site and make it more understandable and enjoyable, or be accessed after a visit once curiosity has been triggered to help visitors build on it, making connections with other sites and providing context, thus allowing deeper and longer-term engagement. Digital technologies are also increasingly being used during heritage visits, whether visiting with family and friends or as part of an organized group, such as in the context of a school trip. There is a growing number of mobile apps and services for cultural tourism, providing suggestions and trails to follow according to the user's location, interests, and previous choices. Increasingly, the use of social media is also helping different audiences personalize this digital heritage material, share it with different communities and make it their own, blurring the boundaries between the public and personal spheres.

By providing different types of interaction with heritage material, it is hoped that digital applications promote an understanding of heritage, as well as encouraging users to value and appreciate heritage. This is ultimately the best long-term investment for the preservation of heritage. In many cases, it is hoped that by using the power of the medium, you can attract users to the message, particularly younger ones. Thus, providing attractive digital heritage applications that encourage understanding and appreciation of heritage will hopefully create citizens who will help preserve heritage and fight against its destruction.

It is very difficult to assess to what extent these strategies have been successful and effective in encouraging a new appreciation of heritage. They have often made us redefine our views of the past and look at it in new ways, but in some cases advanced digital tools have just put a modern sophisticated look on very traditional and conservative interpretations of the past, projecting contemporary biases regarding past societies. It is worth examining these issues in practice by looking at some of the main digital applications used in the digital heritage field to get a clearer picture of the specific manifestations that have taken place, and the different perspectives that have been followed.

Digital Heritage Applications

Virtual and Augmented Reality

Virtual reality (VR) has been used in the cultural heritage field to describe a variety of applications usually related with highly visual, immersive, 3D environments. The use of VR applications in cultural heritage has followed a wider trend for the creation of experiences, trying to give to the user the feeling of being there. For example, the Foundation of the Hellenic World in Athens, Greece, was one of the early adopters of VR for heritage purposes. It experimented with different systems, like the CAVE environment Kivotos – an immersive virtual reality ten-foot cube, where projectors are directed onto five of the walls, creating a 3D experience that can be shared by a group of up to ten people – and the VR theatre Tholos – with a semi-circular projection surface and a capacity of 130 people. Meanwhile, its various in-house productions are shown at its Hellenic Cosmos Cultural Centre, ranging from *The Workshop of Phidias in Olympia* and *A Journey to Ancient Miletus* (the city in Asia Minor) to *An Interactive Tour at the Ancient Agora of Athens* (Sideris 2008).

All these applications use the idea of recreating environments which represent other worlds, and they employ the metaphor of "traveling" to describe visitors interactions through space and time. In the case of augmented reality (AR), rather than immersing the user in a whole simulated world (as is usually the case with virtual reality), it superimposes and adds simulated elements to existing aspects of the physical world. These digital supplementary elements can take various forms, such as sound, video, graphics, or data related to geographical positioning, often combined to enhance users' perception of their surrounding reality. There is a lot of activity in this direction by mobile app designers, and several cultural heritage institutions are taking advantage of AR's potential to offer a personalized experience in users' natural environments (Economou and Meintani 2011). The Museum of London, for example, was one of the early adopters, creating the Streetmuseum app, which uses the museum's historic photographic collections of London to allow users wandering around the British capital to point and click with their smartphone at a monument or street scene of their choice to see a view of the same scene from the past (Ellis 2010).

Other pioneers of this technology in the cultural sector include the Stedelijk Museum in Amsterdam, which used AR both in and outside the building, for example to install digitally created 3D artworks in a local park (see Schavemaker *et al.* 2011), and the San Francisco Exploratorium, which turned an evening event into a surreal AR playground. In 2011, the British Museum also started exploring AR's potential in museum education, running a series of experimental projects that allowed them to push the boundaries of the technology and evaluate its benefits in learning programs. Their experience confirmed that, "AR – although technically still immature – has both the unique ability to engage visitors and [lead to] quantifiable learning outcomes" (Mannion 2011).

AR allows heritage institutions to reuse their digitized collections and reposition them on all possible locations in the urban realm on the small personal screens that people carry with them all the time. It also allows organizations to engage in conversation with their audience, as AR links up easily with social media. Through AR, heritage organizations can reach a new audience, usually early technology adopters, and encourage an interest in art that might lead to an actual visit. AR can assist heritage institutions to tell stories about their collections, sites, and exhibitions, enhancing the visitor's experience.

Geographic Information Systems and 3D Modeling

Geographic information systems (GISs) are being used in the cultural heritage sector to record information about sites and findings across space and time, but also to record complex socioeconomic data and relate them to location. As was predicted in the

1990s, GIS technologies have become an integral part of archeological practice, in interpreting and understanding the socioeconomic structure of the past (Harris and Lock 1995). GIS is also used to help in the preservation of heritage, as climate change and growing populations place the world's heritage under increasing threat. For example, GIS modeling has been used to identify threats to coastal cultural heritage from climate change and land use on Santa Cruz Island in California (Reeder, Rick, and Elandson 2012). In this case, a GIS model of cultural resource vulnerability was used to identify areas and specific sites that are under the greatest threat, building on existing environmental risk indices. This can be adapted to different sites, and can be used to take steps to efficiently and effectively collect information before the coastline disappears by using powerful datasets and technologies that are now widely available. GIS modeling was also used to identify areas of archeological interest, such as the location of possible Macedonian tombs in northern Greece, combining archeological data, geographical factors, geospatial data, and predictive modeling (Balla *et al.* 2014).

In some cases, GIS is being combined with 3D models to assist in the documentation and analysis of heritage sites. The use of 3D modeling in cultural heritage has grown in popularity due to the increasing availability of suitable capturing technology that is specifically designed for heritage objects that often vary in scale, materials, and complexity in surface and shape. There is also an increase in the capabilities of hardware and software to process, store, and visualize models, as well as a growing demand by different heritage users who use 3D visualizations for conservation, restoration, interpretation, and education purposes (Pavlidis *et al.* 2007; Manferdini and Remondino 2012).

3D modeling has been used to create both reality-based representations of existing objects or sites, and reconstructed versions in order to test hypotheses by archeologists and other researchers studying the past, and to present the results in an appealing and understandable way to the public. An example of a collaborative multidisciplinary project working in this area is MayArch3D, which integrates 2D and 3D data, along with models of different size and resolution, in a geodata infrastructure with web-based, interactive features for the analysis and visualization of the ancient Mayan kingdom and UNESCO World Heritage site of Copan in the Honduras (von Schwerin *et al.* 2012). Using these technologies, it is possible to document, georeference, virtually combine, and analyze on one platform information and objects that are housed in disparate collections around the world according to international data-sharing and data-security standards.

The diverse possibilities of 3D model creation in cultural heritage, but also in general cultural heritage documentation, visualization, and analysis, usually result in collections of very heterogeneous types of data for a single cultural site, with different resolutions, accuracy, surface properties, coordinate systems, and so on. As this can prove challenging for large heritage sites regarding resource management, research, and educational outreach, it is important to properly organize and facilitate access to all these models and the corresponding metadata. This is increasingly carried out with web-based solutions, with 3D models used as the intuitive graphical user interface to allow users access to all relevant data (Auer *et al.* 2014). An advantage of GIS and WebGIS is the concentration in a central unified environment of all relevant data from different sources, and their visualization on maps, which can be particularly useful to represent natural and cultural heritage data in a user-friendly way, and connected to tourism applications for capacity-building and the awareness-raising of visitors (Ruoss 2013).

An issue that arises not only with the use of GIS but also in general with the use of all kinds of models, reconstructions, and computer-based visualizations of cultural heritage has to do with the accuracy of the data and the level of confidence of the researcher who proposes a specific interpretation. The increasing concern about the need to document and make transparent this process, reconciling heritage visualization with the agreed norms of scientific research internationally, particularly the standards of argument and evidence, led to the initial conception of the London Charter for the Computer-Based Visualization of Cultural Heritage in 2006 (see LCI 2009), and later the Seville Principles (IFVA 2010), which proposes specific guidelines for the implementation of the London Charter for the archeological community. The London Charter reflects the agreement of the scientific and heritage community on internationally recognized principles that should inform best practice for the documentation and use of computer-based heritage visualizations by researchers, educators, cultural heritage organizations, and other interested bodies across disciplines, and it is now widely recognized as the de facto benchmark according to which heritage visualization processes and outputs should be held accountable (Denard 2012). Initiatives of this kind also help to counterbalance how believable some of the 3D and VR models can be to the end viewer, even when based on very sketchy data, and make clearer which parts of virtual visualizations are based on evidence (and of what type), and which on conjecture.

Mobile Apps

The huge expansion of cell/mobile phone ownership and usage over the last few years, with over 7 billion global SIM subscriptions in 2014, representing 97 percent of the world population, a global average of 1.8 SIM cards per unique subscriber and 3.6 billion unique cell/mobile-phone subscribers (GSMA 2015: 6), has also affected developments in the cultural heritage field. The creation of mobile apps with cultural content is rapidly expanding, with several heritage institutions, companies, and researchers around the world experimenting with their potential, particularly their advanced computing abilities, location awareness, and connectivity. As museums and heritage organizations continuously explore new strategies for communicating with current and potential audiences, one of the most attractive features of mobile technologies is that they open up the possibility for reaching new audiences through a personal device they have chosen and are familiar with, not only during their visit, but also before and after the visit, wherever the user chooses to be (Economou and Meintani 2011).

The ability of cell/mobile phones to be used in conditions and at an environment of the users' choice opens up new possibilities for the communication of cultural content to support engagement with heritage and learning at different levels, as well as establishing a link between the heritage organization and its users that can extend beyond marketing purposes. Apart from this one-to-one connection, the easy use of social networking via mobile devices also allows for the creation of communities and networking among diverse user groups themselves. As smartphone and tablet use continues to grow – with over 2.6 billion smartphone connections in 2014 and 5.9 billion predicted by 2020; and adoption rates which have already reached 60 percent of the connection base of cell/mobile-phone users in the developed world, ranging from 51 percent in Europe to 71 percent in North America at the end of 2014 (GMSA 2015: 13–15) – mobile apps and sites have become powerful tools for heritage organizations in their effort to reach new audiences and communicate in new ways.

Heritage mobile apps include the AR apps mentioned above. An early application in this area includes the EU-funded Archeoguide IST project, which aimed at providing a personalized electronic guide and tour assistant to cultural site visitors, and offered AR reconstructions using as an example the archeological site of Olympia in Greece (Vlahakis *et al.* 2001). More recently, mobile heritage apps have explored the potential of digital storytelling via anthropomorphic guides to historic sites presented through users' mobile devices (Lombardo and Damiano 2012). Influenced by the wider trend for more active participation, rather than passive consumption, at heritage sites, these apps explore the use of storytelling for encouraging more active engagement.

Apart from guides, mobile heritage apps have also explored the use of virtual exhibitions. These bring together digital multimedia objects which are linked by a common theme or some shared characteristics, thus providing a new experience for the user. They can serve as a learning tool, promote heritage sites and collections, provide access to a large number of artifacts without any conservation risk, including inaccessible collections and sites, and be available over a long period of time, even after an exhibition has finished. Virtual mobile exhibitions can also offer added value by providing the opportunity to access culturally rich content directly from users' smartphones, offering them the freedom to browse the content according to their own personal preferences, allowing them to save and reuse the content for their own purposes, and providing them with the flexibility to make connections with other virtual exhibitions or sites (Ciurea, Zamfiroiu, and Grosu 2014).

Another approach in mobile heritage apps has been the use of games to support informal learning in heritage contexts. A crucial aspect of heritage visiting is social interaction, either with the group of visitors of whom one is a part, or with the other visitors one encounters. Whom we go with and whom we meet once we get to a heritage site ultimately affects what we get out of the visit. For this reason it is important that mobile games do not break up the social dynamics of the visit but support group interaction. Very often these follow the paradigm of a treasure hunt, with players trying to find the answers by following clues either indoors or outdoors. As games, and not only mobile ones, have been used widely in cultural heritage, it is worth examining them more carefully.

Gaming in Digital Heritage

Serious games, as the games designed with educational objectives are often called, have been used in different contexts in cultural heritage, and have been designed for various platforms following different philosophies and design approaches. They have been designed for the formal learning context of the classroom for learners of various ages and levels, but also for informal learning environments such as at home, for tourist travel or during heritage visits. Unlike games designed for informal contexts at home, those designed for public spaces installed in heritage sites or museum exhibition galleries need to be very intuitive and usually shorter in duration. In some public setups, multiplayer interaction is supported with multiple controls for different players, but the technological solutions are usually expensive and complex, as are, for example, interactive tables in exhibitions. Another type of heritage game uses the idea of a virtual exhibition, often combining objects from disparate locations (such as the *Discover Babylon* game), or allowing the user to personalize the experience. Heritage sites frequently put up on their websites games of this type to encourage users to visit and engage with the collections and exhibition themes.

When evaluating game effectiveness, Mortara *et al.* (2014) identified two main factors: an attractive and meaningful environment, and an intuitive and appropriate interaction paradigm. They indicated that cultural heritage settings are particularly suited to affective games:

> Empathy with a game character and plot may be very helpful for understanding historical events, different cultures, other people's feelings, problems, and behaviours, on the one hand, and the beauty and value of nature, architecture, art and heritage, on the other one. This persuasive approach should clearly be combined with the rigour of the scientific method, which is a balance not easy to achieve, not only in games. (Mortara *et al.* 2014: 324)

Social Media

A range of social media applications have been used in conjunction with most of the digital heritage applications mentioned above. The move from curated and professionally managed sites towards a more open and democratic attitude to heritage that encourages the participation and co-creation of user groups and communities (Russo and Watkins 2007) made Web 2.0 applications popular as these encourage the exchange of ideas and the creation of online communities of users over various networks. As Graham Fairclough writes, "social media starts by offering a way to 'widen the audience', 'reach new constituencies' but it ends by changing heritage and by asking everyone to participate in its construction, encouraging openness not closure of interpretation and valuation, making flux, uncertainty and doubt critical" (Fairclough 2012: xvi). Our participatory culture encompasses not only online interactions and virtual experiences, but allows us also to attach digital data to artifacts in the real world, thus interweaving physical object, places, and activities, and augmenting them with social data and connectivity (Giaccardi 2012).

Crowdsourcing

One aspect of social media is crowdsourcing, the use of which has rapidly spread in the cultural sector over the last few years. Crowdsourcing involves cultural heritage institutions asking online communities to perform specific tasks that they advertise through an open call, such as correcting the mistakes in texts produced by OCR technologies or tagging paintings with descriptive metadata. Oomen and Aroyo (2011) identify different types of crowdsourcing initiatives: correction and transcription, contextualization (such as writing wiki pages about objects), complementing the collection (such as when seeking objects for an online exhibition), classification (such as the social tagging of collections), co-curation and crowdfunding. Two key issues that affect crowdsourcing initiatives in the heritage sector are the ability to attract a large number of users, and the quality of data that users provide. Heritage organizations and researchers have been investigating different ways to attract users to crowdsourcing projects, such as using games or offering rewards. Similarly, they have also been exploring techniques for ensuring data quality, such as using the community itself to check the authenticity of data or applying technological solutions such as filtering.

An example of a highly successful crowdsourcing project is Your Paintings, a joint initiative between the BBC, the Public Catalogue Foundation (a charity set up to create a complete record of the United Kingdom's national collection of oil, tempera, and acrylic paintings, and make this accessible to the public), and participating collections and museums from across the United Kingdom.[1] The project harnesses the power of a large number of volunteers to improve access by tagging (that is, cataloguing by subject matter) the entire collection of over 200,000 oil paintings in Britain's national collection. As a result of the project, a searchable web site was created showing the entire collection of publicly owned oil paintings across the United Kingdom. This was linked to the art historical information database, with data enhanced through the Your Paintings Tagger program, which allowed users to search not only by artist and collection but also by type of paintings and by subject matter. Volunteer taggers from around the world helped to catalogue the paintings online by subject matter by looking at the paintings in detail, generating subject classifications for each work, and supplying keyword information, including information about people, places, and events shown in the paintings. Special algorithms were then used to ensure a high level of data reliability by calculating which tags are likely to be the most accurate. This is a good example not only of the power of crowdsourcing for democratizing and improving access to art, and helping to educate and entertain users in the process, but also of the importance of partnerships and collaboration in this field, as it shows how a small charity working on behalf of the museum sector and the United Kingdom's national public service broadcaster, which runs the most popular British website in the world, worked together to achieve enormous audience engagement.

Intangible Heritage

Increasing importance has been placed over recent years on the preservation and interpretation of intangible heritage, as previous efforts tended to focus more on tangible sites and collections. The International Council of Museums (ICOM), UNESCO, and similar bodies at the national and international level have brought to the fore the importance of studying and preserving all that intangible heritage encompasses, that is, oral traditions, customs, value systems, skills, traditional dances, diets, performances, and general unique features that communities and groups recognize as part of their cultural heritage and which are passed on from one generation to the next. For example, in 2003 UNESCO adopted the Convention for the Safeguarding of the Intangible Cultural Heritage, while ICOM developed the Shanghai Charter on museums, intangible heritage and globalization in 2002 (ICOM 2002), and devoted its general conference in Seoul in 2004 to the theme of museums and intangible heritage. Increasing urbanization, expanding technological and engineering developments, and globalization have, over recent decades, placed intangible heritage under threat, and made the need to record and protect it more urgent. In this process, digital technologies have been used extensively to digitize diverse materials and capture them in audio or video form, together with the appropriate metadata and related documentation. There are numerous worldwide initiatives in this area, including Europeana, the large European Commission-funded aggregator, which brings together digital material on Europe's cultural heritage (including intangible kinds) in a variety of forms, the Digital Intangible Heritage of Asia (DIHA) group, and the Intangible Cultural Heritage Database of the Asia-Pacific Cultural Centre of UNESCO. The large number of digitization initiatives and programs currently underway highlight the need for digitization strategies at regional, national, and a more global level (Ross and Economou 1998), and raise questions about the kind of material that is digitized and about access to resources for digitization.

In the case of intangible heritage, the circulation of related material through online videos and electronic lists also raises issues about the relationship between original performance and its documentation and mediated recreation. It also leads to concerns about the danger of "fossilizing" the past and outdated heritage practices, rather than supporting change and renewal, which is at the core of living expressions (Pietrobruno 2014). What is the effect of digitally recording and subsequently circulating on the web living heritage, which by its nature is constantly changing and often spontaneous? Does this have the effect of freezing what should not be frozen? Or can the digital environment accommodate continuous transformations and conflicting heritage narratives, including both official heritage narratives as well as divergent representations and user-generated content by various groups?

Intangible heritage digitization programs, like all heritage digitization programs, are creating digital resources which are the building blocks of research, learning, management, cultural tourism, and the general understanding and appreciation of heritage. These digital resources are often used to create interpretative and "edutainment" applications related to heritage. However, it is not the tools or the digital assets themselves which are causing concerns, but rather the use that these are being put to. Who is producing them and towards what means? In what way are these being used and by whom? These are broader issues related to digital heritage that need to be carefully examined.

Discussion

In most countries, cultural heritage is not seen as a priority for national development unless its relationship with economic activities, social values, and local development is made evident (Ruoss 2013). Effective use of digital technologies in the cultural sector can help in this direction, supporting the sustainable use of heritage as an essential engine for economic development.

The variety of applications discussed in this chapter show the multiple ways in which digital technologies have supported the recording, analysis, and management of cultural heritage around the world. This has ultimately assisted in its preservation and interpretation, encouraging understanding and appreciation of the past by diverse audiences. Despite concerns that the use of digital technologies might undermine the need to conserve the "real thing," all the widely accepted related guidelines and recommended practice from heritage organizations and professional bodies advocate the use of digital technologies to improve access to and the understanding of sites and collections, but *not* as a long-term preservation tool that could ever replace the need for preserving the physical original (see LoC n.d.). The NINCH guide to good practice in the digital representation and management of cultural heritage materials states clearly that "digitization of analog materials is not a substitute for investment in their conservation and preservation, but can assist the preservation of the original" (HATII and NINCH 1998: 33). With the rapid increase of "born-digital" heritage materials, that is, materials that originate in digital form, there are also concerns about the appropriate management and preservation of digital heritage assets so that they do not become obsolete and inaccessible (see UNESCO and UBC 2013). Apart from digitization, social media are increasingly used by heritage organizations, such as English Heritage and the National Trust in the UK, in their plans to involve communities much more than before in the stewardship of the natural and built environment.

Our encounter with cultural heritage and the way we are experiencing it is changing because of the expansion of digital media. The examination of digital heritage shows that the journey has not always been smooth and uneventful. As with all heritage applications, the digital endeavors of the last few decades have brought important issues to the fore, and showed how our understanding of the past is shaped by our contemporary biases and context. Some of these issues have to do with the rigor and honesty with which heritage data are recorded and analyzed, but also with what is recorded and what is omitted in our interpretative digital models. Other issues relate to the visitor experience and how the engagement with the virtual world relates to the physical experience of heritage.

One of the most important overarching issues of this discussion, however, is that digital technology is not simply an innocent tool in our effort to record and understand the past, for it inevitably affects and shapes drastically how we experience cultural heritage. As the various digital technologies applied in this field have matured, but also as the socioeconomic developments of the last few years have changed the way we view ourselves, others, and the past, there has been a shift away from the admiration of the technical wizardry of these tools and the realistic representation of the models and reconstructions they produce toward a more critical use of digital heritage applications by communities and stakeholders, encouraging the re-examination and open reinterpretation of heritage.

We are currently focusing less on the realistic representation of the natural and cultural environment in the digital domain, and are becoming more critical about issues regarding the ownership, value, authenticity, and identity of digital heritage. The availability of digital cultural content that is open for reinterpretation and reuse should make us rethink these issues in new ways. In an increasingly globalized world, there is greater emphasis on the use of digital media by local communities interpreting their own places and practices, within a context of greater mobility. The spread of the internet has brought to the fore stronger than ever before the potential for global connectivity and the need to cater for international audiences, while also serving and being adaptable to local or personal preferences. This has also implications for regional, national, and wider digital heritage strategies:

> Policies for digital access to heritage need to address questions about how online heritage can be at the same time owned (cared for, nurtured and interpreted) by [national] communities and also be accessible for a global audience in order to help benefit international tourism, environmental stewardship and cultural diplomacy. (FA and CT 2010: 14)

In order for heritage organizations and custodians to maintain contact with diverse audiences and ensure that heritage remains relevant in a rapidly changing world, it is necessary to examine openly the questions that digital heritage brings up, and invite user communities to participate in this continuous process of reinterpretation and mutual exchange.

Note

1 More information on Your Paintings is available at: http://www.bbc.co.uk/arts/yourpaintings/ (accessed July 20, 2014).

References

Legislation

Convention for the Safeguarding of the Intangible Cultural Heritage (Intangible Heritage Convention) (UNESCO, 2003). Available at: http://unesdoc.unesco.org/images/0013/001325/132540e.pdf (accessed March 19, 2015).

Other Works

Auer, M., Agugiaro, G., Billen, N., Loos, L., and Zipf, A. (2014) Web-Based Visualization and Query of Semantically Segmented Multiresolution 3D Models in the Field of Cultural Heritage. *ISPRS Annals of the Photogrammetry, Remote Sensing and Spatial Information Sciences*, II-5, 33–39.

Balla, A., Pavlogeorgatos, G., Tsiafakis, D., and Pavlidis, G. (2014) Efficient Predictive Modelling for Archaeological Research. *Mediterranean Archaeology and Archaeometry*, 14 (1), 119–129.

Ciurea, C., Zamfiroiu, A., and Grosu, A. (2014) Implementing Mobile Virtual Exhibition to Increase Cultural Heritage Visibility. *Informatica Economică*, 18 (2), 24–31.

Denard, H.D. (2012) A New Introduction to the London Charter. In A. Bentkowska-Kafel, D. Baker, and H. Denard (eds), *Paradata and Transparency in Virtual Heritage*. London: Ashgate, pp. 57–71.

Economou, M., and Meintani, E. (2011) Promising Beginnings? Evaluating Museum Mobile Phone Apps. In L. Ciolfi, K. Scott, and S. Barbieri (eds), *Rethinking Technology in Museums: Emerging Experiences*. Limerick: University of Limerick, pp. 87–101.

Ellis, M. (2010) Streetmuseum: QandA with Museum of London. *Electronic Museum*. Available at: http://electronicmuseum.org.uk/2010/06/01/streetmuseum-qa-with-vicky-lee-museum-of-london/ (accessed July 20, 2014).

FA and CT (Flow Associates and Collections Trust) (2010) *Mapping the Use of Digital Technologies in the Heritage Sector*. London: Heritage Lottery Fund. Available at: http://www.hlf.org.uk/mapping-use-digital-technologies-heritage-sector (accessed March 20, 2015).

Fairclough, G. (2012) Others: A Prologue. In E. Giaccardi (ed.), *Heritage and Social Media: Understanding Heritage in a Participatory Culture*. New York: Routledge, pp. xiv–xvii.

Giaccardi, E. (2012) Introduction. In E. Giaccardi (ed.), *Heritage and Social Media: Understanding Heritage in a Participatory Culture*. New York: Routledge, pp. 1–10.

GSMA (Group Speciale Mobile Association) (2015) The Mobile Economy. Report. Available at: http://www.gsmamobileeconomy.com/GSMA_Global_Mobile_Economy_Report_2015.pdf (accessed March 17, 2015).

Harris, T.M., and Lock, G.R. (1995) Toward an Evaluation of GIS in European Archaeology: The Past, Present and Future of Theory and Applications. In G. Lock and Z. Stančič (eds), *GIS and Archaeology: A European Perspective*. London: Taylor and Francis, pp. 349–365.

HATII and NINCH (Humanities Advanced Technology and Information Institute, University of Glasgow, and National Initiative for a Networked Cultural Heritage) (1998) The NINCH Guide to Good Practice in the Digital Representation and Management of Cultural Heritage Material. Available at: http://www.nyu.edu/its/pubs/pdfs/NINCH_Guide_to_Good_Practice.pdf (accessed August 4, 2014).

ICOM (2002) Shanghai Charter. Available at: http://archives.icom.museum/shanghai_charter.html (accessed March 23, 2015).

IFVA (International Forum of Virtual Archaeology) (2010) The Seville Principles: International Principles of Virtual Archaeology. Available at: http://www.arqueologiavirtual.com/carta/wp-content/uploads/2012/03/BORRADOR-FINAL-FINAL-DRAFT.pdf (accessed March 23, 2015).

LCI (London Charter Initiative) (2009) London Charter for the Computer-Based Visualization of Cultural Heritage, version 2.1. Available at: http://www.londoncharter.org/fileadmin/templates/main/docs/london_charter_2_1_en.pdf (accessed March 23, 2015).

LoC (Library of Congress) (n.d.) Preservation Guidelines for Digitizing Library Materials. Available at: http://www.loc.gov/preservation/care/scan.html (accessed August 4, 2014).

Lombardo, V., and Damiano, R. (2012) Storytelling on Mobile Devices for Cultural Heritage. *New Review of Hypermedia and Multimedia*, 18 (1/2), 11–35.

Manferdini, A.M., Remondino, F. (2012) A Review of Reality-Based 3D Model Generation, Segmentation and Web-Based Visualization Methods. *International Journal of Heritage in the Digital Era*, 1 (1), 103–123.

Mannion, S. (2011) British Museum – Augmented Reality: Beyond the Hype. *Museum iD*. Available at: http://www.museum-id.com/idea-detail.asp?id=336 (accessed July 20, 2014).

Mortara, M., Catalano, C.E., Bellotti, F., Fiucci, G., Hour-Panchetti, M., and Petridis, P. (2014) Learning Cultural Heritage by Serious Games. *Journal of Cultural Heritage*, 15 (3), 318–325.

Oomen, J., and Aroyo, L. (2011) Crowdsourcing in the Cultural Heritage Domain: Opportunities and Challenges. In J. Kjeldskov and J. Paay (eds), *Proceedings of the 5th International Conference on Communities and Technologies*. New York: ACM, pp. 138–149.

Pavlidis, G., Koutsoudis, A., Arnaoutoglou, F., Tsioukas, V., Chamzas, C. (2007) Methods for 3D Digitization of Cultural Heritage. *Journal of Cultural Heritage*, 8 (1), 93–98.

Pietrobruno, S. (2014) Between Narratives and Lists: Performing Digital Intangible Heritage through Global Media. *International Journal of Heritage Studies*, 20 (7/8), 742–759.

Reeder, L.A., Rick, T.C., and Elandson, J.M. (2012) Our Disappearing Past: A GIS Analysis of the Vulnerability of Coastal Archaeological Resources in California's Santa Barbara Channel Region. *Journal of Coastal Conservation*, 16(2), 187–197.

Ross, S., and Economou, M. (1998) Information and Communications Technology in the Cultural Sector: The Need for National Strategies. *DLib Magazine* 4 (6). Available at: http://www.dlib.org/dlib/june98/06ross.html (accessed March 20, 2015).

Ruoss, E. (2013) GIS as a Tool for Cultural Heritage Management. In E. Ruoss and L. Alfarè (eds), *Sustainable Tourism as a Driving Force for Cultural Heritage Sites Development: Planning, Managing and Monitoring Cultural Heritage Sites in South East Europe*. Rome: National Research Council of Italy and CHERPLAN. Available at: https://www.researchgate.net/publication/236256617_GIS_as_Tool_for_Cultural_Heritage_Management (accessed July 23, 2014).

Russo, A. and Watkins, J. (2007) Digital Cultural Communication: Audience and Remediation. In F. Cameron and S. Kenderdine (eds), *Theorizing Digital Cultural Heritage: A Critical Discourse*. Cambridge, MA: MIT Press, pp. 149–164.

Schavemaker, M., Stork, P., Wils, H., *et al.* (2011) Augmented Reality and the Museum Experience. In J. Trant and D. Bearman (eds), *Museums and the Web: 2011 Proceedings*. Toronto: Archives and Museum Informatics. Available at: http://www.museumsandtheweb.com/mw2011/programs/augmented_reality_and_the_museum_experience.html (accessed July 20, 2014).

Sideris, A. (2008) Recontextualised Antiquity: Interpretative VR Visualization of Ancient Art and Architecture. In T.A. Mikropoulos and N.M. Papachristos (eds), *Proceedings: International Symposium on "Information and Communication Technologies in Cultural Heritage," October 16–18, 2008*. Ioannina: University of Ioannina, pp. 159–176.

UNESCO and UBC (University of British Columbia) (2013) Vancouver Declaration on Digitization and Preservation. Available at: http://www.unesco.org/new/en/communication-and-information/resources/news-and-in-focus-articles/all-news/news/unesco_releases_vancouver_declaration_on_digitization_and_preservation/ (accessed August 4, 2014).

Vlahakis, V., Karigiannis, J., Tsotros, M., Gounaris, M., Almeida, L., Stricker, D., Glue, T., Christou, I.T., Carlucci, R., Ioannidis, N. (2001) ARCHEOGUIDE: First Results of an Augmented Reality, Mobile Computing System in Cultural Heritage Sites. In D. Arnold, A. Chalmers, D. Fellner (eds) *Proceedings of the Conference on Virtual Reality, Archaeology and Virtual Heritage (VAST 2001), Athens, Greece, November 28–30, 2001.* New York: ACM, pp. 131–140.

Von Schwerin, J., Richards-Rissetto, H., Remondino, F., Agugiaro, G., Girardi, G. (2012) The MayaArch3D Project: A 3D WebGIS for Analyzing Ancient Architecture and Landscapes. *Literary and Linguistic Computing, special issue*, 28 (4), 736–753.

CHAPTER 16

World Heritage and National Hegemony: The Discursive Formation of Chinese Political Authority

Haiming Yan

A Nation's Preoccupation with World Heritage

On June 24, 2011, the World Heritage Committee of UNESCO added the West Lake Cultural Landscape of Hangzhou to the World Heritage List, claiming that it is a "perfect fusion between man and nature" (UNESCO 2011). In China, the news inspired nationwide excitement and celebrations. Immediately after the designation, thousands of Chinese people used Weibo – the most popular Chinese mini-blog site, the equivalent of Twitter – to circulate the news. Hundreds of media reports about the designation came out the next day. The celebrations were even emotional: the deputy mayor of the city of Hangzhou, Zhang Jianting, broke into tears.

These events represent a microcosm of the larger picture of China's World Heritage. Since its ratification in 1985 of the Convention Concerning the Protection of the World Cultural and Natural Heritage, or World Heritage Convention (1972), China has been remarkably preoccupied with this new concept. By 2013, 45 sites in China had been added to the World Heritage List, with a further 48 currently on the Tentative List; this means that, among all UNESCO States Parties, China has the second largest number of properties on the first list, and it has the most on the second. *Shenyi*, the Chinese term for "World Heritage application," has been a key term in recent years, producing 21.1 million Google search results by the end of 2013.[1] Even small towns

A Companion to Heritage Studies, First Edition. Edited by William Logan, Máiréad Nic Craith, and Ullrich Kockel.
© 2016 John Wiley & Sons, Inc. Published 2016 by John Wiley & Sons, Inc.

that are barely known to people in their own provinces have announced their intention to compete for World Heritage site status. In 2004, the small ancient town of Qikou, located on the shore of the Yellow River, hosted the International Symposium on the Protection of Ancient Architecture in Qikou, which suggested that the ultimate goal of the preservation project was to get Qikou placed on the World Heritage List.

In addition to the statistics and activities, the rhetoric of World Heritage reveals a nationalist dimension. In 2004, South Korea nominated a local tradition, *Ganjeung Danojie* – a local festival of mountain worship held on the fifth day of the fifth month of the lunar year – for inscription on the UNESCO Representative List of the Intangible Cultural Heritage. This evoked nationwide anti-Korean sentiment in China because people believed that the festival originated in, and remained largely affiliated with, China's *Duanwu* (dragon boat) festival. Public accusations against South Korea proliferated in mass-media and internet forums. Many condemned South Korea for "stealing heritage from China." In fact, as the Chinese government and most heritage experts acknowledged, the festival proposed by South Korea was different from its Chinese equivalent. However, the general public did not appear willing to listen to the voices of experts.

This chapter aims to identify the mechanisms by which World Heritage as a new concept has been deeply integrated into China's political, cultural, and social fabric. Why is it so popular, and how is it understood and practiced? As the cases discussed here will reveal, World Heritage provides Chinese authorities with a discursive tool with which to claim and maintain political legitimacy and national solidarity. In short, World Heritage serves as a powerful concept for nation-building. Despite its universalistic claim, it is largely used in China as a signifier of the nation's image and self-esteem. The government even employs World Heritage to shape social discipline and to establish behavioral norms. In addition, however, the discursive tool is a double-edged sword, creating frustration and tension for the state, and, when applied in practice, challenging the government's political legitimacy.

World Heritage and Nation-Building

Heritage is highly involved in the process of nation-building. It is a political resource for nation-states (Tunbridge and Ashworth 1996). Thus, state authorities tend to create a totalizing and unitary narrative of the past, which is often manifested in material remains. Kate Moles, in her discussion of heritage issues relating to a Dublin park, finds that in spite of the multiplicity of narratives embedded in a particular heritage site, the state process of legitimation and authentication is always oriented toward creating a sole national narrative, which helps define and incorporate a concrete national history (Moles 2009: 130). As a political instrument, heritage is deliberately used to diffuse and disseminate state ideologies in order to secure the legitimacy of the state. Heritage, in this sense, resembles what Pierre Nora (1989) calls "the sites of memory," the control of which provides the authorities with a dominant narrative about heritage's innate meanings and values.

UNESCO's World Heritage List contains many sites of memory. Since coming into being in 1972, the World Heritage Convention has been a UNESCO flagship program. The rhetoric of Outstanding Universal Value develops a set of narratives that effectively makes the moral responsibility for and need for collaboration in cultural preservation a universal principle. Nevertheless, nation-states have been empowered, rather than disempowered, by the globalization of culture. As Tunbridge and Ashworth (1996) put it, a major challenge to the ideal of fostering a World Heritage preservation program lies in the power of states in the production and manipulation of national heritage. Barthel-Bouchier and Hui (2007) observe that World Heritage sites are still firmly embedded within national boundaries. The World Heritage program reflects a contradiction in that it superficially propagates universalism while stressing cultural identity with national sentiments at a more fundamental level.

To some extent, nation-states utilize rather than simply abide by UNESCO discourses. As William Logan observes:

> Some governments make use of the "external enemy" for domestic political reasons, such as the wish to forge national cohesion, rather than because of real differences over heritage issues. Other governments "collude" with UNESCO for similar domestic reasons, hoping to gain prestige and electoral support for being seen to operate "internationally" or obtain international recognition of the national culture. (Logan 2001: 53–54)

China's enthusiasm for World Heritage should be understood from the perspective of nation-building. First, the large quantity of the country's World Heritage sites offers a source of national pride. As stated in an official report, the quantity of World Heritage sites functions both as a representation of the nation's splendid history and its present level of civilization, public civility, and comprehensive national power (Tong, Gu, and Lu 2008). Second, World Heritage entails the nation's sense of independence in the world. As the same report continues, World Heritage "is the spiritual foundation and cultural skeleton for the Chinese nation to be independent among the nations of the world" (Tong, Gu and Lu 2008: 53). Given this, the state has employed World Heritage as an approach to the rhetorical constitution of patriotism. The implementation of World Heritage gives the state a new language to maintain and reinforce the connection between history and national pride. According to official documents, preserving World Heritage in China is imperative for the nation because it "educates the people for patriotism" (SACH 2009: 440), and in this way enhances "national spirits" (MoC *et al.* 2009: 509).

In particular, two dimensions of World Heritage in China are discursively deployed to support the official discourse of national pride: temporal continuity, and spatial unity – both of which help to articulate a unified China. A unified China is fundamental to the state's core ideology and striving for legitimacy.

Re-Defining China with World Heritage

Time: Historical Continuity

The rhetoric of historical continuity is one of the most important discursive devices through which the communist regime claims its legitimacy. Presenjit Duara argues that a linear grand historical narrative has been established in China, and it has silenced "different and non-narrative modes" (Duara 1997: 19). This linear grand history is widely employed by experts in heritage narratives. In 2007, State Administration of Cultural Heritage published an edited volume that summarized the accomplishments of China's cultural heritage preservation efforts. One chapter of the volume praised the

World Heritage efforts of China for its historical representation. It explicitly stated that, ranging from the Peking Man site dating back half a million years to the modern architecture of the historic town of Macao, World Heritage sites in China jointly "reflect the continuity and durability of the Chinese nation's cultural tradition" (Li 2007: 38).

One unparalleled example that shows the discursive construction of historical continuity is the Great Wall of China. Located beside the most famous scenic section of the Great Wall at Badaling, the Great Wall Museum presents China's foremost narrative of the Great Wall as a representation of China's long and continuous history. An introductory text at the exhibition states that, "the Great Wall started to be built in the Spring and Autumn Period over 2,500 years ago, and continued to be built in many dynasties afterwards. It was constructed by various peoples."[2] By placing this message within a firmly organized set of narratives, the museum provides a set of educational resources deployed for the dissemination of the state-sanctioned discourse of cultural identity.

Nevertheless, the narrative of historical continuity has been shown by historians to be factually incorrect. Julia Lovell finds that singularity is a myth of the Great Wall. People usually think of it as a series of structures with a coherently chronicled past. However, historical records show that the periods of construction were not contiguous: for over a thousand years of Chinese history, no sections of the Great Wall were built (Lovell 2006: 15). According to Arthur Waldron, "the Great Wall of China of the modern imagination is a historical newcomer" (Waldron 1983: 658). Discussing the 1994 International Symposium on the Great Wall, hosted by China, Waldron (1995) observes that many Chinese scholars blurred the difference between academic study and patriotic propaganda. These scholars, says Waldron, tend to pull together incompatible elements to articulate the Great Wall's mythical continuity and singularity.

Another example is the Grand Canal, which explicitly shows how World Heritage stimulates the Chinese government to maintain a narrative of historical linearity and continuity. As the official website of the Grand Canal's nomination for World Heritage status claims:

> The Grand Canal is the only water system in China that runs in a direction from south to north. It was first built in the Spring and Autumn Period (770 BC–476 BC) and was rebuilt during the Sui Dynasty (581–618) and the Yuan Dynasty (1271–1368), with its entire length now reaching 1,794 kilometers. (GCWHNO 2008)

To make it more recognizable and appealing to the public, the description continues to create an affinity between the Grand Canal and the Great Wall of China. "If the Great Wall is said to be the backbone of the Chinese people, then the Grand Canal is the flesh and blood of the Chinese" (GCWHNO 2008).

However, like the Great Wall, the construction and reconstruction of the Grand Canal was in fact not continuous in time. Hence, the Grand Canal should be more precisely defined as a series of canals that were constructed sporadically during different historical periods, and eventually connected together. The World Heritage nomination of the Grand Canal, however, promoted the idea of the canal's construction as being historically continuous. At a national symposium on World Heritage management, a presenter remarked: "the Grand Canal has been flowing for more than two thousand years. Its value is embedded in its historical antiquity" (Ye 2010: 207). Furthermore, representing the collective memory of the nation (Shu 2006: 56), the Grand Canal's historical continuity lies in the very fact that it is still "alive," a rhetorical stance that serves as the integral and constitutive element of its historical continuity. The Grand

Canal was added to the World Heritage List in June, 2014. It is believed that the inscription of the Grand Canal on the World Heritage List will help promote and maintain its continuity (Guo and Wang 2014).

Space: Ethnic Solidarity

In one respect, national unity in China relies fundamentally on the cooperative and harmonious relationship between China's ethnic groups. Long before the introduction of World Heritage, the preservation of cultural relics was employed to enhance ethnic harmony and political stability. In earlier official documents, cultural relics in the custody of ethnic minorities were treated specially and categorized separately (MoC and MFT 2009: 17). Ethnic solidarity and national unity were two concepts that often appeared hand in hand. The relationship between the cultural preservation of ethnic minorities and national solidarity was narrated as follows:

> China has endured as a multiethnic unified country since ancient times. The long history and splendid culture of the Chinese nation are created and owned by all its 56 ethnic groups. Each ethnic group uses its historical cultural relics to understand its own culture; it also uses the historical cultural relics of other groups to understand the others. Much historical cultural heritage … provides the people with a compelling sense of cohesion, and serves to maintain ethnic and national unification. (CPD *et al.* 2009: 243)

The Chinese state's approach to World Heritage echoes this assertion: "Properly protecting and preserving World Cultural Heritage is a symbol of a nation's … ethnic solidarity" (SACH 2009: 440). The sentiment expressed in this remark is also exemplified in China's World Heritage nominations. For instance, as James Hevia suggests, the designation of the Chengde Mountain Resort and Its Outlying Temples as a World Heritage site marked China's endeavor to claim ethnic integrity. Located in Hebei Province near Beijing, but distant from Tibet, some of Chengde's eighteenth-century temples were built in the architectural styles of ethnic minorities, especially those of Tibet and Mongolia. Indeed, one building was modeled on the Potala Palace of Tibet, a display of the asymmetrical power relationship between the Manchu Empire and the Tibetans. Hevia maintains that the original purpose of the Chengde site was "to awe the peoples of Inner and Central Asia into submission" (Hevia 2001: 233–34). However, Hevia points out that the World Heritage nomination claims it was built to "appease and unite the minority peoples living in China's border regions and to consolidate national unity" (Hevia 2001: 224), providing "historic evidence of the final formation of a unitary, multicultural China" (Hevia 2001: 224). The dominant Han ethnic group is hence characterized as sharing harmonious aspects of culture with the minorities of this particular site. Symbolizing "the unity of the Han, Manchu, Hui, Tibetan, and Uighur peoples" (Hevia 2001: 234), Chengde is thus an example of how national solidarity was forged and minority groups accepted their role in the nation.

The real Potala Palace represents a more compelling intertwining of ethnic essences and nationalist discourse. Between 2002 and 2008, the Potala Palace site underwent its most extensive renovation yet, which elicited sharp criticism from the Tibetan poet Woeser. She insisted that the ignorance of Chinese construction workers about Tibetan architecture made the renovation like a "children's game" that would destroy "the cohesiveness of the traditional Tibetan architecture of the Potala" (Woeser 2007: 50).

However, the state authorities were confident that the renovation respected Tibetan architectural and technological traditions. Li Zuixiong, an expert from Duanhuang Academy, claimed that the techniques used for the renovation of the wall paintings were authentically Tibetan (Yan 2007: 189). More explicitly, a number of Tibetan craftsmen were invited to demonstrate the authenticity of the work undertaken. One craftsman is reported as saying that "the renovation kept the authentic features of the structure." According to official media, the renovation was very successful, and the Communist Party and the government were strongly supported by most Tibetans, especially the religious people (Yan 2007: 189). Local praise for the preservation of authenticity was characterized as an embodiment of ethnic cooperation and solidarity. A state-run magazine, *Chinese Cultural Heritage*, commented on the highly positive role of the communist government in the restoration:

> The renovation is a vivid embodiment and splendid example of the [Communist] Party's and the government's cultural preservation of ethnic heritage. During the project, Tibetan and Han craftsmen worked cooperatively, composing a hymn of praise to ethnic solidarity … The designers, technicians and managers respected Tibetan tradition, ethnic style and science, combining Tibetan traditions with modern techniques for cultural conservation … which manifested the wisdom of ethnic solidarity. (Zhang 2009: 74)

"The Potala Palace is not only an outstanding representation of Tibetan architecture," wrote Nima Tsering, vice-chairman of the Standing Committee of the People's Congress of the Tibet Autonomous Region, "but also that of China and the world" (Nima 2009: 34). With this logic, it is not surprising that all cultural heritage in Tibet is articulated as material evidence of the Tibetan people's defense of Chinese national unity. Therefore, Tibetan heritage "undoubtedly functions in demonstrating the fact that 'Tibet is an inseparable part of the nation'" (TCRB 2009: 67).

Overall, by creating a set of temporal and spatial narratives of World Heritage, the party-state has endeavored to represent China as a vast nation imbued with national and ethnic cohesion, stability, and solidarity. In addition to the grand narratives discussed previously, nation-building also requires particular discursive frames by which the authorities can regulate and control people. To some extent, the Chinese heritage authorities employ World Heritage not only as a means of understanding, but also as a means of controlling to behavior. The next section will discuss how China's World Heritage is associated with the construction and control of social discipline.

World Heritage as Social Discipline

Preserving heritage entails behavioral discipline and the production of civility among the Chinese masses. The process of disseminating heritage knowledge has a patriotic and disciplinary function, what I call "heritage Enlightenment," which successfully combines the issue of heritage preservation with social discipline and moral education. World Heritage serves to create a discursive frame by which daily behavior is regulated. Preserving World Heritage is represented as having a civilizing effect, entangled with the issues of public health and communal relations. It is even believed to represent a moral quality: "Any behavior that damages and devastates cultural relics is ignorant and backward, and it must be condemned by future generations and all human beings"

(CPD *et al.* 2009: 244). Protecting cultural heritage is associated with the development of mental and moral, and scientific and cultural, qualities (SCPRC 2009: 544). World Heritage's social value lies primarily in its function in "constructing civilized society, [and] promoting a citizen's quality" (Li 2007: 41).

The discourse of behavioral regulation is manifested in World Heritage management and nomination. For example, in the documentation in support of the nomination of Fujian Tulou as a World Heritage site, preservation is explicitly represented as integral to the construction of a normative system of public hygiene and neighborhood safety (SACH 2008: 320–22). The nomination states that the residents should "foster a good habit of hygiene" and "should abide by social ethics"; even requiring them to "respect the aged and cherish the young" is mentioned as part of heritage conservation practices. Moral regulations are included "to help mediate disputes among the residents, resolve conflicts and bring about a harmonious neighborhood relationship" (SACH 2008: 321). At the end of the document, there is a section entitled "Residents' Pledges on Civilization," in which the residents agree to be "civilized and polite; to receive guests with warmth and keep good neighborly relations" and to "pay attention to public hygiene" (SACH 2008: 321).

From my work as a local assistant, I was present as a participant-observer during the nomination of the Grand Canal, and I saw that an important factor that the ICOMOS site mission checked was whether the canal communities agreed with the nomination and accepted the claim that they would maintain the canal environment's integrity. One initiative the state authorities have employed has been that of mobilizing key local communities to set up a public agreement. As a result, a number of community behavior regulations have been launched. The regulations involve not only heritage preservation, but also commitment to the maintenance of public security, neighborhood harmony, public hygiene, and other such factors. Again, the pledges are seen to constitute and represent a civilized community. World Heritage nominations thus encourage local communities to develop and reinforce a nexus of norms relating to heritage preservation and behavior. Failing to abide by these is taken as a symbol of personal failure, and would be shameful in the community concerned.

This process is analogous to Elias's contention that human behaviors are normalized and "civilized" by the social production of a sense of shame (Elias 2000). This civilizing mission, in the case of World Heritage in China, is particularly configured by the rhetorical proclamations of the state. Heritage Enlightenment is thus born of the intertwining of nationalist ethics and individual compliance and civility. By endowing cultural preservation with the significance of civility and discipline, the state lays down a model for social action. Consequently, the meaning of bodies and life is interwoven in the production of hegemonic power with the articulation and politics of discipline. This biopower is incorporated into the politics and constitution of heritage. Therefore, heritage preservation is firmly utilized as "a technology of power centered on life" (Foucault 1979: 44).

Mapping the Silk Road: Battles over Heritage in Kashgar

The state apparatus, being engaged in a series of discursive constructions of cultural preservation, is implicitly paradoxical. Often it finds itself constrained by an overriding framework that is simultaneously a discursive means of domestic hegemony and a challenge to that hegemony. For instance, the concept of cultural routes offers the state a discursive means of exercising historical and territorial control over of an array of scattered sites, such as the World Heritage nomination of the Silk Road. However, the Silk Road's nomination has turned out to be the most controversial and challenging case for the state-controlled heritage apparatus since China's ratification of the World Heritage Convention (1972).

The Silk Road was initially considered as a candidate for World Heritage status in August 2003, when UNESCO organized a visit of heritage experts to the Chinese sections of the Silk Road to investigate the concept of "cultural routes," which had then only just been adopted as a new category of cultural heritage. The mission was expanded to a transnational cooperative initiative in August 2006, when a UNESCO workshop on the Silk Road's World Heritage nomination was held in Turpan, Xinjiang Province, China, with participants including China's neighboring countries in Central Asia. At the workshop, China, along with Kazakhstan, Kyrgyzstan, Tajikistan, Turkmenistan, and Uzbekistan, developed and consolidated initiatives for World Heritage nomination cooperation, commencing with the Silk Road's formal World Heritage nomination. During the workshop, the Chinese experts outlined major Chinese sites for consideration, including the city of Kashgar in Xinjiang province (CCR 2006). The Old Town of Kashgar was described as having a recorded history stretching back 2100 years. Its streets and historic architecture marked its uniqueness as the most important trade hub along the Silk Road. Its historic and cultural significance endowed it with very high values, felt by both Chinese and international experts as a crucial heritage site that should be considered for high-level heritage preservation.

Although many official and media documents unequivocally recognized that Kashgar was one of the most important towns along the Silk Road, it was eventually excluded from the selected World Heritage nomination dossier,[3] which included eleven sites in five regions (Guo 2007).[4] The omission, according to a *Guardian* commentator, was deliberate (Jenkins 2009). More provocatively, not only was it omitted from the list, but it also faced demolition as part of a state-supported "reconstruction project." In February 2009, the local government of Kashgar, with the approval of and sponsored by the central government, launched a large-scale reconstruction in the central Old Town of Kashgar, taking in an area as wide as 5 million square meters and affecting as many as 49,000 households. The reconstruction initiative was officially justified as being intended to improve the town's infrastructure and reinforce old buildings to withstand earthquakes. However, it provoked vociferous protest among the domestic and international media. A survey showed that the whole project was generally disapproved of by local residents (Fan 2009), and it was charged with neither generating nor making known a detailed plan for the protection and preservation of the historic city.

An active NGO, the Beijing Cultural Heritage Protection Center, launched a campaign to call the public's attention to the reconstruction project. It was concerned that the it violated China's cultural heritage laws and policies, especially as Kashgar was a "historical and cultural famous city" at a national level (BCHPC 2009). In addition, the International Council on Monuments and Sites (ICOMOS) commented that "recent efforts by local Chinese authorities to modernize the settlement and address concerns for seismic vulnerability and risk preparedness access have resulted in large-scale loss" (ICOMOS 2010: 48). Accordingly, ICOMOS's International Scientific Committee on Earthen Architectural Heritage wrote an open letter to the Chinese government in June 2009, maintaining that the Old Town of Kashgar had been "[a]n important point of cultural, social, economic, and commercial exchange along the Silk Road for centuries" (ICOMOS 2010: 48), and one which should be respected and protected by the local and national authorities.

In the meantime, an array of international press articles appeared that openly questioned China's stated reasons for the reconstruction project. Some explicitly asserted that its purpose was politically motivated. The project was charged with aiming to break down potential ethnic tensions between Han and Uighur peoples by eradicating the cultural presence of the latter embedded in the old buildings and neighborhoods. The plans involved moving almost half of the town's residents, according to an article published on the web site of the US magazine *Time*, which indicated that the removal of the local population had been "executed with little to no consultation with those to be displaced" (Tharoor 2009). The article also claimed that "[t]he demolition of the city's historic core fits lockstep with what many consider a concerted effort on Beijing's part to bring Xinjiang firmly under its grasp and dilute Uighur identity" (Tharoor 2009).

To put this in a broader perspective, the concerns of the international press were raised against the backdrop of the violent riots that took place in Kashgar and many other places in Xinjiang Province in July 2009.[5] Thus, the state authorities were believed to have re-evaluated the Old Town's buildings as potential havens for terrorists and a potential threat to the region's stability (Jacobs 2009). This, however, produced a dilemma, given that the state had previously acknowledged that Kashgar was an important site along the Silk Road. Confronted with this, the central government was determined to place the issue of political stability before cultural heritage. Despite international criticisms, the reconstruction plan "had unusually strong backing high in the government" (Wines 2009).

Consequently, there emerged a series of appeals for the inclusion of the Old Town of Kashgar on the World Heritage List. Accompanying the aforementioned open letter, ICOMOS also sent a letter to the president of ICOMOS China, Tong Mingkang, who was also deputy director of the State Administration of Cultural Heritage. The letter, written by the president of ICOMOS, Gustavo Araoz, praised Kashgar's historic value as a strategic trade center along the Silk Road, stating that "Kashgar's inclusion in the proposed nomination would seem to merit serious consideration," and that "its destruction could be seen as a contradiction or even a major stain in the extraordinarily positive record of China in conserving and protecting the vastness of its cultural heritage" (ICOMOS 2010: 50–51). Besides the ICOMOS effort, a number of NGOs participated in the appeal. In 2009, the Save Kashgar web site was created, which hosted an online petition in 2009 in favor of Kashgar's World Heritage nomination, and received a great deal of attention around the world (Thompson 2009); and Radio Free Asia made multimedia resources available to protect Kashgar's vanishing memory in the same year.[6]

In response to the international petition for and outcry over Kashgar's World Heritage status, Tong Mingkang wrote to the president of ICOMOS, stating:

> Strict criteria and conditions are set for World Heritage nomination in accordance with the UNESCO World Heritage Convention and its Operational Guidelines. As numerous historic sites and monuments have been left over along the Silk Roads, the study, protection and nomination work pertaining to the Silk Roads will be a long and arduous task. According to the decision coordinated by UNESCO, nominated sites of the Silk Roads will be determined through consultations by countries involved. (ICOMOS 2010: 51)

The letter used a diplomatic tone, avoiding direct explanation for the exclusion of Kashgar from the World Heritage nomination. Although it stressed that China did not intend to desist from cooperating with international advisory bodies, it insisted that the involved States Parties be given the final decision over nomination, implying that international forces should not intrude on the rights of States Parties.

Ironically, although the Chinese government dismissed the international petition for Kashgar's World Heritage status, it attempted to use World Heritage as a pivotal concept in support of its widely criticized reconstruction project. As the Beijing Cultural Heritage Protection Center revealed, a government notice that appeared in Kashgar's streets alleged that the reconstruction plan was strongly supported by UNESCO. "UNESCO appraised that the reconstruction of the Old Town of Kashgar was human oriented" (BCHPC 2009). The Center claimed that the government had obviously made up the UNESCO endorsement to deliberately discourage protests by preservationists. Even more ironic was the fact that a local official claimed that the reconstruction project would be carried out in accordance with World Heritage standards (Ma 2009).

How can a project that contradicted the core principles of World Heritage be claimed to adhere to these principles? This notice on the streets of Kashgar revealed the state's ambivalent attitude regarding the issue of Kashgar, as well as other World Heritage sites. That is, although the state ostensibly controls and manipulates World Heritage with its nationalist rhetoric, the rhetoric itself draws on the very logic and power of World Heritage.

Heritage is inevitably a political project. As Cuneo (2011) has claimed, China's intention to nominate the Silk Road for World Heritage status is intended to champion its national ethnic multiplicity and identity. The ultimate political purpose of this, however, goes against the idea of multiculturalism, for its aim is to secure the state's totalizing rule over its border areas. As Li and Zhang, two scholars from Turpan's Cultural Relics Bureau, put it, the strengthening of World Heritage nomination and management in border areas has more than cultural implications. They maintain that World Heritage in national border areas is about the official proclamation of national unity, and, more critically, the state's attempt's to undermine separatist claims (Li and Zhang 2010: 183). In so far as both acts – preservation and reconstruction – are carried out to maintain the power of the state, the endeavor to champion ethnic multiplicity can be seen as not being at odds with the demolition of a heritage site.

The Powerful Nation

As Askew puts it, "despite the laudable universalist ideals of many dedicated intellectuals and practitioners involved in UNESCO's array of heritage conservation programs today, the globalized and institutionalized heritage system has not overcome nation-state-based power structures and nationalist agendas, but has rather enhanced them" (Askew 2010: 20). Characterizing World Heritage as a technical and normative system rather than an institutional one, Askew continues, "member states use the nomination process and promotion of world heritage sites for their own domestic agendas of cultural hegemony and state nationalism" (Askew 2010: 23). Askew is right, at least about the heritage system of China: while UNESCO consistently underlines the rhetorical universality of World Heritage, China primarily regards it as an embodiment of national solidarity.

This strategy is closely associated with the state's rhetorical approach to writing history, which, as Duara (1997) contends, aims to create a linear mode of narrative that integrates multiple voices into a cohesive and integrated frame. World Heritage is comprised of "sites of memory" (Nora 1989). The real environments of memory have been replaced by physical embodiments that are highly malleable and at odds with real memories. The state-sanctioned memory articulated in World Heritage has to be framed by the discourse of national solidarity. Moreover, World Heritage preservation has been characterized as an act that fulfills the development and advancement of behavioral and spiritual virtues. The concept provides a linguistic and rhetorical juxtaposition between the discourse of patriotism and nationalism, and that of behavioral civility and good citizenship. As a result, the state not only uses cultural heritage as a means for instituting national solidarity; it also articulates it with the politics of the body.

As a result, the term World Heritage itself instantiates a terminological ambivalence, as it is employed by the Chinese government precisely as "World-level National Heritage." Whereas the UNESCO definition of World Heritage emphasizes the uniqueness of each particular site, Chinese usage primarily emphasizes China's sense of its own collectivity. That is, only through being part of the World Heritage system can individual sites become meaningful. "World heritage is a national strategy" (SACH 2009: 439). It is not about particular heritage sites, but about World Heritage in China *sui generis.*

Finally, we may better understand the tears of the deputy mayor of Hangzhou in a deeper sense. Ostensibly, the tears seem to express a delicate personal emotion. However, behind the tender personal tears lies a hard and powerful state, which has established strong political authority in the realm of historic preservation and heritage management.

On January 30, 2012, the director-general of UNESCO, Irina Bokova, launched the fortieth-anniversary celebration of World Heritage. In her speech, Irina Bokova claimed that World Heritage embodies the heritage preservation efforts of all mankind as a "dream" and "beautiful adventure" (UNESCO 2012). It should be noted, however, that the dream and beauty are still nationally bounded. In spite of the ideal of creating a universally equal, peaceful, harmonious world, it is important to keep in mind that the nation-state remains the strongest agent, which regulates and shapes our heritage not only politically, but also socially and culturally.

Notes

1 In comparison, a search for "the Cultural Revolution" (in Chinese) received only 14.1 million.
2 This sentence, originally in English, is quoted from a display at the Great Wall Museum.
3 It must be noted that one site, Mehmud Qeshqeri Tomb of Kashgar, was included. But this inclusion had no link to the more famous and culturally influential site of the Old Town of Kashgar.
4 The nomination was later expanded to include 12 sites.
5 The events also had a deeper historical context. In the 1990s, Kashgar witnessed a series of bombings and terrorist attacks against Han people, culminating in the incident in which sixteen policemen were killed immediately before the Beijing Olympic Games (Jacobs 2009).

6 The Save Kashgar web site is available at: www.savekashgar.com/ (accessed November 11, 2011). Details of Radio Free Asia's campaign are available at: http://www.rfa.org/english/multimedia/kashgardemolition-03232010120925.html (accessed November 11, 2011).

References

Legislation

Convention Concerning the Protection of the World Cultural and Natural Heritage (World Heritage Convention) (UNESCO, 1972). Available at: http://whc.unesco.org/archive/convention-en.pdf (accessed March 19, 2015).

Other Works

Askew, M. (2010) The Magic List of Global Status: UNESCO, World Heritage and the Agendas of States. In S. Labadi and C. Long (eds), *Heritage and Globalization*. New York: Routledge, pp. 19–44.

Barthel-Bouchier, D., and Hui, M.M. (2007) Places of Cosmopolitan Memory. *Globality Studies Journal*. Available at: http://globality.cc.stonybrook.edu/wp-content/uploads/2011/03/no5.pdf (accessed July 1, 2014).

BCHPC (Beijing Cultural Heritage Protection Center) (2009) Kashi Laocheng Zhengfu Gongkai Xuancheng: Lianheguo Jiaokewen Zuzhi Zhichi Kashi Laocheng Gaizao Jihua [Local government publicly alleges: UNESCO supports the reconstruction project of the old town of Kashgar]. Available at: http://www.bjchp.org/?p=1849 (accessed November 18, 2011).

CCR (China Cultural Relics) (2006) Sichou Zhilu Kuaguo Lianhe Shenyi Tulufan Chubu Xingdong Jihua [The Silk Road Transnational World Heritage Nomination Turpan Initial Action Plan]. *China Cultural Relics*, September 1, p. 2.

CPD *et al.* (Central Propaganda Department of the Communist Party of China, Ministry of Culture, and State Administration of Cultural Heritage) (2009 [1989]) Guanyu Yinfa "Renren Aihu Zuguo Wenwu Xuanchuan Tigang" de Tongzhi. In State Administration of Cultural Heritage (ed.), *Zhongguo Wenhua Yichan Shiye Fagui Wenxian Huibian 1949–2009* [Collection of legal documents on china's cultural heritage enterprises]. Beijing: Cultural Relics Press, pp. 242–245.

Cuneo, A. (2011) The Silk Road Unraveled: The Politics of World Heritage. Presentation given at the international conference Why Does the Past Matter? University of Massachusetts–Amherst Center for Heritage and Society, Amherst, May 6.

Duara, P. (1997) *Rescuing History from the Nation: Questioning Narratives of Modern China*. Chicago: University of Chicago Press.

Elias, N. (2000) *The Civilizing Process: Sociogenetic and Psychogenetic Investigations*. Malden, MA: Blackwell.

Fan, M. (2009) An Ancient Culture, Bulldozed Away. *Washington Post*, March 24. Available at: http://www.washingtonpost.com/wp-dyn/content/article/2009/03/23/AR2009032302935.html (accessed November 13, 2011).

Foucault, M. (1979) *The History of Sexuality*. London: Allen Lane.

GCWHNO (Grand Canal World Heritage Nomination Office) (2008) The Grand Canals. Available at: http://chinagrandcanal.com/dyhen/lb.asp?lbid=356 (accessed November 6, 2011).

Guo, G., and Wang, Z. (2014) Shiwu Qianli de Wenhua Yichan Baohu Guojia Xingdong [Unprecedented national cultural heritage conservation]. *China Cultural Relics*, June 25, p. 1.

Guo, M. (2007) Guojia Wenwuju Kaocha Pinggu Silu Shenyi Xinjiangduan Gongzuo [State administration of cultural heritage inspects and evaluates progress on the Xinjiang section of the Silk Road World Heritage nomination]. *China Cultural Relics*, September 5, p. 2.

Hevia, J. (2001) World Heritage, National Culture and the Restoration of Chengde. *Positions: East Asia Cultures Critique*, 9, 219–243.

ICOMOS (2010) *Heritage at Risk: ICOMOS World Report 2008–2010*. Berlin: Hendrik Bäßler Verlag. Available at: http://www.international.icomos.org/risk/world_report/2008-2010/H@R_2008-2010_final.pdf (accessed November 13, 2011).

Jacobs, A. (2009) China Fears Ethnic Strife Could Agitate Uighur Oasis. *New York Times*, July 22, Available at: http://www.nytimes.com/2009/07/23/world/asia/23kashgar.html (access March 10, 2015).

Jenkins, S. (2009) As China Destroys its Culture, Hong Kong Proves that Its People Care. *Guardian*, May 28, p. 31.

Li, X., and Zhang, Y. (2010) Bianjiang Diqu Shenbao Shijie Wenhua Yichan Mianlin de Kunnan ji Duice [Challanges and solutions to World Heritage nomination of border areas]. In Z. Luo (ed.), *Zhongguo Shijie Yichan Baohu Wuyishan Gaofeng Luntan Wenji* [Papers from the Mount Wuyi summit on China's World Heritage preservation]. Beijing: Wuzho Communication Press, pp. 183–188.

Li, Y. (2007) Zhongguo de Shijie Yichan Baohu Shiye Gaishu [Overview of China's World Heritage conservation]. In *Zhongguo Wenhua Yichan Baohu Chengjiu Tonglan* [An overview of the achievements of China's cultural heritage conservation]. Beijing: Cultural Relics Press, pp. 38–44.

Logan, W. (2001) Globalizing Heritage: World Heritage as a Manifestation of Modernism and Challenges from the Periphery. In D. Jones (ed.), *Twentieth Century Heritage – Our Recent Cultural Legacy: 2001 Australian ICOMOS National Conference*. Adelaide: School of Architecture, University of Adelaide, pp. 51–57.

Lovell, J. (2006) *The Great Wall: China Against the World, 1000 BC to AD 2000*. New York: Grove Press.

Ma, S. (2009) Jiehe Kangzhen Anju Baohu Kashi Laocheng [Protecting the Old Town of Kashgar with quake-proof buildings]. Available at: http://www.xj.xinhua.org/2009-01/09/content_15408794.htm (accessed November 18, 2011).

MoC *et al.* (Ministry of Culture, Ministry of Construction, State Administration of Cultural Heritage, *et al.*) (2009 [2004]) Guanyu Jiaqiang Woguo Shijie Wenhua Yichan Baohu Guanli Gongzuo de Yijian [Suggestions on strengthening world cultural heritage preservation and management]. In State Administration of Cultural Heritage (ed.), *Zhongguo Wenhua Yichan Shiye Fagui Wenxian Huibian 1949–2009* [Collection of legal documents on china's cultural heritage enterprises]. Beijing: Cultural Relics Press, pp. 509–511.

MoC and MFT (Ministry of Culture and Ministry of Foreign Trade) (2009 [1960]) Guanyu Wenwu Chukou Jianding Biaozhun de Jidian Yijian [Suggestions on the evaluation standards for the exportation of cultural relics]. In State Administration of Cultural Heritage (ed.), *Zhongguo Wenhua Yichan Shiye Fagui Wenxian Huibian 1949–2009* [Collection of legal documents on china's cultural heritage enterprises]. Beijing: Cultural Relics Press, pp. 17–25.

Moles, K. (2009) A Landscape of Memories: Layers of Meaning in a Dublin Park. In M. Anico and E. Peralta (eds), *Heritage and Identity: Engagement and Demission in the Contemporary World*. London: Routledge, pp. 129–140.

Nima, T. (2009) Hongshan shang de Buda Lagong [The Potala Palace on Red Mountains]. *Chinese Cultural Heritage*, June, pp. 26–34.

Nora, P. (1989) Between Memory and History: Les Lieux de Memoire. *Representations*, 26, 7–24.

SACH (State Administration of Cultural Heritage) (2008) Fujian Tulou Nomination File. Available at: http://whc.unesco.org/uploads/nominations/1113.pdf (accessed December 19, 2011).

SACH (2009 [2002]) Guanyu Jiaqiang he Gaishan Shijie Yichan Baohu Guannli Gongzuo de Yijian [Suggestions on strengthening and promoting the protection and management of World Heritage]. In State Administration of Cultural Heritage (ed.), *Zhongguo Wenhua Yichan Shiye Fagui Wenxian Huibian 1949–2009* [Collection of legal documents on china's cultural heritage enterprises]. Beijing: Cultural Relics Press, pp. 439–441.

SCPRC (State Council of the People's Republic of China) (2009 [2005]) Guanyu Jiaqiang Wenhua Yichan Baohu de Tongzhi [Circular on strengthening the protection for cultural heritage) In State Administration of Cultural Heritage (ed.), *Zhongguo Wenhua Yichan Shiye Fagui Wenxian Huibian 1949–2009* [Collection of legal documents on china's cultural heritage enterprises]. Beijing: Cultural Relics Press, pp. 543–547.

Shu, Y. (2006) Yun He: Canque de Huihuang [The Grand Canal: fragmentary magnificence]. *Outlook Weekley,* September 18, p. 56.

TCRB (Tibet Cultural Relics Bureau) (2009) Xizang Wenwu Jianzhu Weixiu Buceng Jianduan de 50 Nian [Incessant 50 year renovation program of Tibetan architecutral heritage]. *Chinese Cultural Heritage*, June, pp. 64–68.

Tharoor, I. (2009) Tearing Down Old Kashgar: Another Blow to the Uighurs. *Time World.* Available at: http://www.time.com/time/world/article/0,8599,1913166,00.html (accessed November 18, 2011).

Thompson, R. (2009) Would UNESCO World Heritage Status Stop Uighur Kashgar Destruction? *Heritage Key.* Available at: http://heritage-key.com/blogs/rebecca-t/would-unesco-world-heritage-status-stop-uighur-kashgar-destruction (accessed November 13, 2011).

Tong, M., Gu, Y., and Lu, Q. (2008) Thirty Years of Reform and Open in World Cultural Heritage Enterprise. In State Administration of Cultural Heritage (ed.), *Thirty Years of Reform and Open in China's Cultural Relics Enterprise.* Beijing: Cultural Relics Press, pp. 53–63.

Tunbridge, J., and Ashworth, G. (1996) *Dissonant Heritage: The Management of the Past as a Resource in Conflict.* Chichester: John Wiley and Sons.

UNESCO (2011) Decision: 35 COM 8B.25. Decisions Adopted by the World Heritage Committee at Its 35th Session. WHC-11/35.COM/20. Available at: http://whc.unesco.org/document/107150 (accessed October 25, 2011).

UNESCO (2012) UNESCO and Goodwill Ambassador Herbie Hancock Launches 40th Anniversary of the World Heritage Convention. Available at: http://whc.unesco.org/en/news/834/ (accessed March 10, 2015).

Waldron, A. (1983) The Problem of the Great Wall of China. *Harvard Journal of Asiatic Studies* 43, 643–663.

Waldron, A. (1995) Scholarship and Patriotic Education: The Great Wall Conference, 1994. *China Quarterly*, 143, 844–850.

Wines, M. (2009) To Protect an Ancient City, China Moves to Raze It. *New York Times*, May 27. Available at: http://www.nytimes.com/2009/05/28/world/asia/28kashgar.html (accessed March 10, 2015).

Woeser, T. (2007) Decline of Potala Palace. Available at: http://hrichina.org/sites/default/files/oldsite/PDFs/CRF.4.2007/CRF-2007-4_Potala.pdf (accessed November 7, 2011).

Yan, D. (2007) *Zhongguo Jiyi: Wenhua Yichan Dangan* [Chinese memory: archives of Chinese cultural heritage]. Beijing: China Architecture and Industry Press.

Ye, P. (2010) Zhongguo Dayunhe: Zaireqing he Lixing Zhutuixia Zouxiang Shiyi [China's Grand Canal: toward World Heritage with passion and reason]. In Z. Luo (ed.), *Zhongguo Shijie Yichan Baohu Wuyishan Gaofeng Luntan Wenji* [Papers from the Mount Wuyi summit on China's World Heritage preservation]. Beijing: Wuzhou Communication Press, pp. 204–213.

Zhang, W. (2009) Shengshi Guibao Zouhuazhang: Xizang Sanda Zhongdian Wenwu Baohu Weixiu Goncheng Jishi [A beautiful poem composed in a flourishing age: records of the renovation project of Tibet's three major national heritage sites]. *Chinese Cultural Heritage*, June, pp. 69–76.

CHAPTER 17

War Museums and Memory Wars in Contemporary Poland

Julie Fedor

War heritage is always central to shaping and sustaining national identities and legitimizing political systems (Gegner and Ziino 2012), but in postsocialist Eastern Europe its importance has been especially great and the relevant issues especially fraught as the war heritage landscape entered a period of extreme flux and instability in the wake of the end of the Cold War. World War II heritage sites in what Timothy Snyder (2010) has called the "bloodlands" of Eastern Europe face a set of highly specific and difficult challenges. With the collapse of communism came the collapse of an entire symbolic universe, which has had to be remade anew. The experiences and legacy of World War II have been a central building block used in the creation of new national identities in this part of the world. This is especially true in the case of Poland, where the pre-existing traditions of a strong and highly distinctive memory culture focused on Polish martyrdom were further reinforced by the huge scale of the suffering and loss that the war brought.

Museums, and war museums in particular, are powerful tools for institutionalizing national memories and identities. Throughout Eastern Europe, war museums must negotiate and narrate a complex and heavily contested history. Previously, war museums in Soviet satellites had conformed to a monolithic, mythologized, and heavily policed narrative of the war dictated by Moscow, based on the central image of the Red Army's heroic liberation of Eastern Europe. In Eastern Central Europe (if not in Russia and other parts of post-Soviet space), this Soviet narrative has now been discarded, but devising new narratives to replace it for the next generation of war museums is no simple task. East European war experiences do not easily fit into the framework of the conventional, politically convenient, and reassuring West European narrative of the war as a two-sided struggle between good and evil that ended in unambiguous liberation.

A Companion to Heritage Studies, First Edition. Edited by William Logan, Máiréad Nic Craith, and Ullrich Kockel.
© 2016 John Wiley & Sons, Inc. Published 2016 by John Wiley & Sons, Inc.

The war proper cannot be neatly bracketed off from the waves of state-sponsored terror, repression, and destruction that preceded, followed, and accompanied the war, in some cases under multiple successive occupations, both Nazi and Soviet. Likewise, it can be difficult to disentangle cases of collaboration and complicity with Nazi war crimes from anti-Soviet national independence struggles. Furthermore, in the East European case, public debate on these questions, and public mourning for those categories of victims deemed "ungrievable" (Butler 2009) within the Soviet ideological framework, were banned for decades following the war. The situation is further complicated because the contested history of World War II is so closely entwined with the more recent history of the end of the Cold War and the transition from communism, and hence with the legitimacy of present-day governments across the region. The eastward expansion of the European Union (EU) has opened up an additional set of challenges linked to the struggle for recognition of East European experiences of the twentieth century and their integration into pan-European memory, including via memorialization of the dead, who have generally been absent or marginalized in the Western popular imagination. For all these reasons and more, issues surrounding war heritage carry a heightened charge in the East European context, and the past two decades have seen a series of memory wars, both domestic and transnational, fought throughout the region over the interpretation and representation of World War II. As important vehicles for the institutionalization and authorization of memory, museums have been key battlegrounds in these memory wars.

This chapter explores the case of recent Polish debates over how best to memorialize and narrate the Polish World War II experience in contemporary museums. Polish memory politics surrounding this question have tended to be strongly polarized, with the two main positions exemplified by two high-profile and high-budget war heritage institutions: the Museum of the Warsaw Uprising (opened 2004), on the one hand, and the planned Gdańsk Museum of World War II (scheduled to open in 2015), on the other. Both of these represent powerful bids to define and narrate the Polish war experience in a modern language accessible to both domestic and European audiences. To varying degrees, both museums reflect the worldwide shift towards remembering World War II in terms of violence and victimhood rather than heroism and glory (on which, see Confino 2005; Bessel 2010; Winter 2006), but their respective emphases and interpretations reflect very different visions of Polish identity. As Macdonald points out: "the museum is an institution of recognition and identity *par excellence*. It selects certain cultural products for official safe-keeping, for posterity and public display – a process which recognizes and affirms some identities, and omits to recognize and affirm others" (Macdonald 2011: 4). This chapter examines the selections made by the creators of these two museums and their connections to diverging views of Poland's past, present, and future, and on how best to resolve memory conflicts with Poland's neighbors.

Background: War Heritage in Postsocialist Europe

The Soviet Union drew its satellites into an "empire of memory" (Yekelchyk 2004), enforcing a monolithic and sacralized narrative of the war as the story of the Red Army's heroic liberation of Europe. This narrative was institutionalized in the form of museums and memorials that invariably conformed to a standardized model aimed at glorifying and mythologizing the sacrifices of the Red Army under the wise guidance of the Soviet state, and expressed via a standard symbolic repertoire: "grieving mothers, bronze warriors, stone columns [and] eternal flames" (Novikova 1999). Initiatives aimed at commemorating or narrating aspects of the war that were deemed to be ideologically suspect – such as the Warsaw Uprising (Davies 2003: 518, 592, 602) or the siege of Leningrad (Kirschenbaum 2006: 143–47), for example – were blocked by the party authorities.

The physical landscape of this East European memory empire was dotted with memorial tanks and statues of Soviet soldiers, including those erected at prominent strategic central urban sites immediately after the end of the war. These monuments stood guard over the core elements of the narrative of what was known as the Great Patriotic War, the Soviet label referring to the phase of the war that followed Hitler's invasion of the Soviet Union (1941 to 1945) and thus eliding the period of Nazi–Soviet cooperation (1939 to 1941).

This memorial landscape, together with the mythologized narrative that it embodied, entered a state of extreme flux and instability with the collapse of communism. Thousands of Soviet war monuments and memorials have been dismantled and relocated. Where they remain in place, they have sporadically attracted graffiti, protests, and unauthorized demolition, and have at times been flashpoints for violence, most notably in the 2007 "Bronze Soldier" riots in Estonia.

The regional war museum landscape has likewise undergone dramatic transformation over the past two decades. In some cases, new narratives of the war focused on the experience of dual occupations by Nazi and Soviet forces have been institutionalized, for example in the Estonian Museum of Occupations (opened 1998), the Museum of the Occupation of Latvia (1993), and the Lithuanian Museum of Genocide Victims (1992). The Hungarian House of Terror (2002) is perhaps the most prominent example of an attempt to build the foundations of a new national identity based on a narrative of victimhood at the hands of two totalitarian regimes. This model has been controversial for a number of reasons, and has been criticized variously for equating Nazism and Communism, for relativizing the Holocaust, and for eliding and whitewashing collaboration and complicity with Nazi war crimes.

The Polish War Heritage Landscape and Memory Wars

During the socialist period, a series of events central to the Polish war experience were erased from the official historical narrative, whose basic contours were put in place by Moscow and were heavily policed. The Soviet atrocities committed against Poles during the period of the Nazi–Soviet alliance (1939 to 1941) were among the unmentionable topics, as were the instances of Polish violence against Jews such as the 1941 Jedwabne massacre.[1] In some cases, the historical record was not simply excised or suppressed but actively distorted and falsified. Most notoriously, an extraordinarily elaborate cover story was devised by the Soviet authorities aimed at shifting blame for the NKVD's Katyn Forest massacres of Polish prisoners onto Nazi Germany.[2] The victims' relatives could not grieve their loved ones publicly unless they were prepared to sign up to what became known as "the Katyn Lie" (see Etkind *et al.* 2012). Strict taboos also governed representations of the failed Warsaw Uprising of 1944, such that the Red Army's role in standing by and allowing the Germans to destroy the city could not be mentioned (see Davies 2003; Imposti 2009; Bogumił and Wawrzyniak 2010: 10). These taboos generally had the opposite of the intended effect, only serving to keep alive within families and communities the memory of such events as powerful manifestations of national resistance and victimhood.

A constant aim throughout the post-1989 era has thus been to restore the fragmented and suppressed elements of Polish war memory. But this process has been accompanied by ongoing heated disputes over how to frame and narrate this history. Much like their late-twentieth-century counterparts elsewhere, such as the Australian indigenous history wars, or the *Enola Gay* controversy, these debates have centered on the issue of the admissibility of a critical approach to national history. In the Polish case, the key positions on this question reflect a basic cleavage over attitudes toward a dominant mode of Polish memory, in which Polish national identity is rooted in suffering, sacrifice, and martyrdom.

The Polish martyrological tradition can be traced back to the formative traumatic experience of the Partitions and Poland's erasure from the map, and the series of failed tragic insurrections of the nineteenth century.[3] As various scholars have pointed out (e.g. Davies 1984; Uffelmann 2013; Porter 1996; Walicki 2001), these events led to a strong emphasis on memory as a means of keeping Poland alive in the spiritual if not the physical realm. Narratives of national martyrdom, expressed in the idiom of Romantic idealism, offered a means of making sense of these events. The idea of Poland as the "Christ of Nations," participating in the Passion of Christ through suffering and carrying a mission to redeem humanity through suffering, became a key trope in the Polish national imagination (Chrostowski 1991).

This Catholic-inflected notion of Romantic martyrdom would also become the central prism through which the Polish experience of World War II was remembered. The (often well-justified) perception that Polish war suffering and Polish resistance had been insufficiently recognized or appreciated in the West served to foster this tendency (see e.g. Karski 2010: 258). The emphasis on Polish martyrdom was given institutional form in the key body tasked with creating, managing, and preserving Poland's war heritage sites: the Council for the Protection of Struggle and Martyrdom Sites, created in 1947.

The martyrological mode of memory subsided somewhat in the early postsocialist period. Prime Minister Tadeusz Mazowiecki (1989–1991) sought to draw a "thick line" between past and present, and President Aleksander Kwaśniewski (1995–2005) called upon Poles to look ahead, not back, with his electoral slogan "Let's Choose the Future." But the mythology of Polish martyrdom made a strong comeback to public life after the Kaczyński brothers' Law and Justice (PiS) party won parliamentary and presidential elections in 2005. The Kaczyński brothers spearheaded a campaign for active state intervention in defense of Polish collective memory (Brier 2009). They argued that it was the state's obligation to put in place an active "history policy" (see Traba 2010). They claimed that the governments of the 1990s had abdicated from their responsibilities when it came to preserving the memory of Poland's twentieth century and passing it on to younger generations of Poles, thereby undermining social coherence and continuity (see e.g. Ukielski, cited in Lasia 2012).

The Museum of the Warsaw Uprising

The embodiment and showpiece of the Kaczyński brothers' history policy was the Museum of the Warsaw Uprising, opened in 2004 to coincide with the uprising's sixtieth anniversary (see Etkind *et al.* 2012: 132–34; Bogumił and Wawrzyniak 2010: 10; Żychlińska 2009). The museum was the pet project of Lech Kaczyński, then mayor of Warsaw (2002–2005) and later national president (2005–2010), until he perished in the Smolensk air catastrophe while en route to a ceremony marking the seventieth anniversary of the Katyn massacres.

The museum's creators set out both to restore Polish memory and to educate the world about Polish history, in keeping with Lech Kaczyński's keen sense of a mission to fulfill these aims (Niżyńska 2010: 472–74). The creation of the museum was thus also linked to Poland's accession to the EU (in 2004). As the museum's director, Jan Ołdakowski, put it, the Polish community, like all communities, had a "basic obligation to define [it]self and to narrate [it]self to the outside" (Kosiewski 2012). One of the key messages of the Warsaw Uprising as defined by the museum's deputy director is that "the war was not a simple fight of good against evil (as it is often perceived in Western Europe), but that in fact three sides, each with different goals, were involved – two totalitarian systems and the world of Western democracies" (Ukielski 2011). In other words, this was intended as a challenge to the standard popular Western narrative of the war, and was part of a broader campaign aimed at gaining recognition for Polish suffering and resistance on the European stage.

Both the domestic and international aims of the museum were to be achieved through a strong focus on engaging the visitor, both emotionally and intellectually (Ukielski 2011), and by appealing to young people in particular through interactive multimedia and popular-culture based exhibitions. It is widely acknowledged that the museum's lavish hi-tech displays have set new standards for the Polish museum and heritage community.

The high-profile commemorations of the sixtieth anniversary of the Warsaw Uprising linked to the museum's opening were a major turning point in the evolution of Polish memory politics. As historian and publisher Zbigniew Gluza put it, the success of the sixtieth anniversary of the uprising and the wave of public interest in the past that it ushered in drove home the fact that political elites could derive advantage from turning to the past (cited in Lasia 2012). It was at this point, it has been claimed, that Polish politicians "fell in love with museums" (Kosiewski 2012).

The decision to focus on institutionalizing the memory of the Warsaw Uprising has attracted ongoing controversy. The Warsaw Uprising, and more broadly the martyrological mode of memory of which it is a cornerstone, have come under concerted attack over the past decade. For critics, the Warsaw Uprising epitomizes the flaws inherent in Polish identity and the source of Poland's historical misfortunes: a tendency towards irrationality, futile self-sacrifice, a lack of pragmatism (e.g. Sroczyński 2011; Kobiałka 2011; Pilawski 2009). Others have criticized the political instrumentalization and "privatization" of the memory of the uprising by PiS (e.g. Kowal 2009). Each year, heated media debates over the event's significance have accompanied the anniversary of the beginning of the uprising on August 1.

Attacks on the martyrological mode of memory intensified after Donald Tusk's Civic Platform party was elected to government in 2007.[4] Tusk is a trained historian who in 1987 ridiculed the Polish "Romantic-imperial-messianic" tradition as a "pathetic-grim-grotesque theatre of unfulfilled dreams and ungrounded longings" (Nowak 2011). Tusk's government has moved strongly to depart from the Romantic model of Polish memory and identity, viewing it as an anachronism and obstacle to Poland's modernization and European integration. This has been accompanied by a de-emphasis on the Warsaw Uprising. Tusk's foreign minister Radosław Sikorski caused a scandal in 2011 when he described the Warsaw Uprising as a "national catastrophe" and criticized the "cult" surrounding the event (cited in Dudek 2011).

The Gdańsk Museum of World War II Project

After its election in 2007, the Tusk government's position on museum politics was foreshadowed by Tusk's new minister for culture and national heritage, Bogdan Zdrojewski, who proclaimed that Poland should not become "a country of necropolises and museums" (cited in Smolar 2008: 61). The remark was a thinly veiled reference to Lech Kaczyński's politics of memory, a politics driven, in the view of Tusk and his allies, by a morbid fascination with victimhood and bloodshed (Romanowski 2010).

After Donald Tusk came to power, there was a major shake-up of several large-scale museum projects. Casualties included the planned Museum of Polish History in Warsaw, the Museum of the Western Lands in Wrocław, and the Museum of the Kresy (Eastern Borderlands) (Stańczyk 2013) – all projects associated to varying degrees with the patriotic memory politics of the previous government.

Instead, Tusk announced plans to build a new museum of World War II in his hometown of Gdańsk. Scheduled to open in 2015, this museum, which sets out to be the first international museum of the war in Europe, represents the most ambitious attempt to date to reintegrate Eastern and Western European memories of the war. It aims to be the first museum in Europe to cover the experiences of both Nazi and Soviet occupations, and to play a key role in incorporating the Eastern Central European experience of the war into broader European memory, as well as focusing on non-traditional aspects of the war such as the experiences of prisoners of war and civilians. The director of the Gdańsk project, Paweł Machcewicz, has announced that the museum will seek to present a multilayered narrative: individual, local, national, regional, European, and global (Machcewicz, cited in Daszczyński and Drzewicki 2011: 8). The project can also be read as representing a bid to recalibrate Polish memory, moving beyond previous divisions, both domestic and international, and putting in their place a synthesized and modernized narrative of the war.

The Gdańsk museum's creators have made clear that the project will narrate the history of World War II in a modern language. They have emphasized the fact that this will not be a martyrological museum (Machcewicz and Majewski 2008: 47). This is at times contrasted explicitly to the Museum of the Warsaw Uprising. Thus, for example, Paweł Machcewicz has said: "Obviously we'll show the Warsaw Uprising [in the Gdańsk museum], as one of many topics. We'll do this somewhat differently to the existing museum in the capital, but this is the natural right of each successive institution: to search for its own language of narration" (cited in Daszczyński and Drzewicki 2011: 8). Machcewicz has also linked this to the project's key aim of "introducing the Polish and Central European perspective to the world narrative and historical memory, within which sphere our [Polish] experiences are often only marginal and are not sufficiently well known and understood" (cited in Anon. 2013).

The Gdańsk museum project was originally conceived partly as an alternative to the proposed Berlin German Centre against Expulsions, aimed at narrating the experience of Germans deported from Poland at the end of the war. This subject has been the source of tensions between Poland and Germany since the emergence of the Federation of Expellees lobby group in Germany in the late 1990s, headed by Erika Steinbach. The Federation of Expellees seeks to gain recognition for a narrative of German victimhood which equates these deportations to other mass deportations in twentieth-century Europe, decoupling them from the history of Nazi German atrocities (Wieliński 2008).

According to Tusk's advisor on historical policy, Wojciech Duda, the Gdańsk museum is intended to offer a corrective to the narrative propagated by the Federation of Expellees (cited in Uhlig 2008). In December 2007, before announcing the plans, Tusk visited Berlin to discuss the Gdańsk museum proposal as a solution to the ongoing dispute over this issue (Smolar 2008: 53). The Gdańsk museum, which would be created in cooperation with German historians, was offered by Tusk as an alternative to the memorial to the deportations planned for Berlin. This represented a major shift in approach to German–Polish memory disputes, as the previous Polish government had not been willing to discuss the issue with its German counterparts (Wieliński 2007). The previous government had instead backed a project for a Wrocław Museum of Western Lands as a counterweight to Steinbach; this was planned as a museum similar to the Museum of the Warsaw Uprising in format and style (Anon. 2010), and was to emphasize the Polish contribution to post-war reconstruction in the western territories as a counterweight to the Federation of Expellees' claim to these territories (Ujazdowski 2011). Now, instead, the Gdańsk museum will narrate the stories of the German flight and deportations, but on its own terms, underlining the fact that, for example, mass forced migrations were carried out by the Third Reich and the Soviet Union (Machcewicz and Majewski 2008: 50). As Machcewicz put it, the best response to the Federation of Expellees is to:

> present one's own narrative focusing on World War II and its consequences. This would place the deportations in proper historical context, and first and foremost as a consequence of German crimes and occupation and not of Polish nationalism and striving to create a monolithic nation state as the Steinbach group has claimed. (Machcewicz 2012: 45)

Machcewicz had put forward this argument in a newspaper article in 2007, after which he was approached by Tusk's historical advisor Duda and invited to develop his idea; this eventually led to his appointment as director of the planned new museum. The museum's location at the site of the beginning of the German invasion will also serve to underline the connection drawn between the German flight and deportations, and the German attack on Poland.

In addition, the Gdańsk museum also engages with Russian–Polish memory disputes. The museum's stated aims include not only showing the decisive Soviet contribution to the victory over Nazi Germany, but also "restoring to the Russians themselves the memory of the wartime sufferings of Soviet citizens," such as the experiences of Soviet civilians living under Nazi occupation (Machcewicz and Majewski 2008: 48).

Jay Winter points out that battlefield sites are themselves "halfway between cemeteries and museums" (Winter 2012: 159). These are sites that make special claims on the visitor: "they enable (indeed they require) visitors to situate themselves geographically as well as temporally and thematically in a particular region or landscape marked by war" (Winter 2012: 159). As Julie Buckler writes, "Battlefield sites … have a special energy" (Buckler 2013: 204). Sites of battles and/or burials of the war dead are uniquely charged, and hence lend themselves as sites for forging new identity claims and for sacralization. The Gdańsk museum's creators point out that the museum's location at the site of the defense of Westerplatte will enhance the museum's attractiveness and "'persuasive' capacity," as well as lending it a "readable symbolic dimension, linking the narrative nature of the modern (multimedia) museum with authentic exhibits from the epoch (the Polish military fortifications at Westerplatte) and the site where World

War II began" (Machcewicz and Majewski 2008: 46). The site also serves to underline Poland's status as "the first victim" of Nazi Germany, as Tusk put it during the ceremonies held at the site in 2009; Poland was the "first victim," he said, while the Soviet Union was the "biggest victim" ("the main victim") (cited in Filatov 2009).

The symbolic load carried by the site has been further increased by a series of ritual ceremonies carried out at the museum's construction site. For example, delegations from a number of cities occupying a special place on the map of World War II, including Kharkiv in east Ukraine, were invited to bring soil which was placed within the foundations of the museum in an urn (Mirer 2009).

The museum's physical location will also be activated in support of another key linkage being drawn here: proximity to the Gdańsk shipyards also enables this history to be braided together with that of the Solidarity movement and Poland's role in ending communist power. In 2011, President Komorowski proclaimed that Gdańsk was a special place by virtue of its connections to Polish history, such that "here one breathes freedom" (cited in Anon. 2011). The Gdańsk museum is to be integrated and coordinated with a new European Centre of "Solidarity" in Gdańsk, devoted to the history of the Solidarity movement as well as other oppositional movements throughout Poland and Central and Eastern Europe (Machcewicz and Majewski 2008: 46). Thus the official commemorations held at Westerplatte in September 2009 featured the slogan "1939–1989–2009." As Tusk's historical advisor Duda put it: "In a sense it is precisely in 1989 that World War II ends for us" (cited in Uhlig 2008). Likewise, the connection is aimed at reminding Europe that the collapse of communism began in Poland (Duda, cited in Uhlig 2008). In this way, the museum project seeks to connect Polish resistance to Nazism and Polish opposition to Soviet communism, bringing both together within a single narrative of the Polish struggle for liberty.

As a symbol of resistance, Westerplatte is multifaceted and multilayered. In what was to become a famous address to young people during a visit to the site in 1987, Pope John Paul II emphasized the importance of Westerplatte as an "eloquent symbol"; everyone would face in life their own "Westerplatte moment" – a cause that could not be abandoned no matter what the odds. The ideal of resistance that the pope was describing here clearly also had contemporary political relevance in the context of the Solidarity movement.

Westerplatte was downplayed as a site of memory in the Stalinist period, presumably because of the awkward questions it raised regarding the events of the Nazi–Soviet pact between 1939 and 1941, but it became a central site of patriotic memory in the post-Stalinist period (see Garba and Westphal n.d.; Kostro 2013). The site was integrated into the Soviet Brezhnev-era war cult, and became used for staging international events performing Soviet–Polish brotherhood.

The site's history is also intertwined with the history of Solidarity in other ways. Periodically, the state authorities offered concessions regarding the site in an attempt to mollify patriotic feelings and damp down discontent. In 1971, for example, commander of the defense of Westerplatte Major Sucharski's ashes were brought back from Italy and interred at the site (Zajączkowski 2011: 367).

Finally, the museum might be read as a bid to forge a new consensus around a synthesized narrative. In the Polish memory wars of the early twenty-first century, Westerplatte as a site of memory sometimes featured as the antithesis of Jedwabne, the site of the notorious massacre of Jews by Poles which was the subject of prolonged debate in Poland from 2000: a site of pride rather than a site of shame and disgrace.[5]

The planned museum is an attempt to move beyond such binaries – as Machcewicz puts it, writing in response to an article by the historian Andrzej Nowak (2001), titled "Westerplatte or Jedwabne," the answer should be "both Westerplatte and Jedwabne" (Machcewicz 2012: 167–71).

Notes

1 Polish–Jewish relations are beyond the scope of this chapter; on this topic, see Webber's chapter (this volume).
2 The NKVD (the Soviet People's Commissariat for Internal Affairs) were a forerunner of the KGB, the Soviet state's secret police.
3 In the late eighteenth century Poland disappeared from the map after it was partitioned by its neighbors, Austria, Prussia, and Russia, in 1772, 1793, and 1795. A series of uprisings, most famously in 1830 and 1863, sought to restore Polish statehood but failed.
4 Between April 2010 and the present (February 2015), it has also held the presidency.
5 Machcewicz himself had previously led a major publication of documents and historical commentary on Jedwabne and other pogroms from the summer of 1941 (see Machcewicz and Persak 2002).

References

Anon. (2010) Muzeum Ziem Zachodnich: Nowa obietnica Kaczyńskiego. *Newsweek Polska*, June 29. Available at: http://polska.newsweek.pl/muzeum-ziem-zachodnich-nowa-obietnica-kaczynskiego,61217,1,1.html (accessed August 27, 2014).

Anon. (2011) Na gdańskim Westerplatte uczczono 72. rocznicę wybuchu II wojny światowej. *Gazeta.pl*, September 1. Available at: http://wiadomosci.gazeta.pl/wiadomosci/1,114873,10210431,Na_gdanskim_Westerplatte_uczczono_72__rocznice_wybuchu.html (accessed August 22, 2014).

Anon. (2013) Prof. Paweł Machcewicz: Muzeum II Wojny Światowej pokaże Polskę na szerszym tle. *Wiadomości*, June 30. Available at: http://wiadomosci.wp.pl/kat,1342,title,Prof-Pawel-Machcewicz-Muzeum-II-Wojny-Swiatowej-pokaze-Polske-na-szerszym-tle,wid,15775656,wiadomosc.html?ticaid=11222d (accessed August 22, 2014).

Bessel, R. (2010) Violence and Victimhood: Looking Back at the World Wars in Europe. In J. Echternkamp and S. Martens (eds), *Experience and Memory: The Second World War in Europe*. Oxford: Berghahn Books, pp. 229–269.

Bogumił, Z., and Wawrzyniak, J. (2010) Narracje zniszczenia: Trauma wojenna w muzejach miejskich Petersburga, Warszawy i Drezna. *Kultura i społeczeństwo*, 54 (4), 3–21.

Brier, R. (2009) The Roots of the "Fourth Republic": Solidarity's Cultural Legacy to Polish Politics. *East European Politics and Society*, 23 (1), 63–85.

Buckler, J. (2013) Taking and Retaking the Field: Borodino as a Site of Collective Memory. In J. Buckler and E.D. Johnson (eds), *Rites of Place: Public Commemoration in Russia and Eastern Europe*. Evanston, IL: Northwestern University Press, pp. 203–223.

Butler, J. (2009) *Frames of War: When Is Life Grievable?* London: Verso.

Chrostowski, W. (1991) The Suffering, Chosenness and Mission of the Polish Nation. *Occasional Papers on Religion in Eastern Europe*, 11 (4), 1–15.

Confino, A. (2005). Remembering the Second World War, 1945–1965: Narratives of Victimhood and Genocide. *Cultural Analysis*, 4, 46–75.

Daszczyński, R., and Drzewicki, M. (2011). Żyjemy w cieniu tamtej wojny. *Gazeta Wyborcza Trójmiasto*, 228, September 30, pp. 1, 8, 10.

Davies, N. (1984) *Heart of Europe: The Past in Poland's Present*. Oxford: Oxford University Press.

Davies, N. (2003) *Rising '44: "The Battle for Warsaw."* London: Macmillan.
Dudek, J. (2011) Sikorski: Powstanie to "narodowa katastrofa." *Rzeczpospolita*, July 31. Available at: http://www.rp.pl/artykul/695283.html (accessed August 27, 2014).
Etkind, A., *et al.* (2012) *Remembering Katyn*. Cambridge: Polity.
Filatov, Y. (2009) Bzhezinskii i Kachin'skii razoshlis' v otsenke Putina. *Km.ru*, September 1. Available at: http://www.km.ru/news/bzhezinskij_i_kachinskij_razoshl (accessed August 27, 2014).
Garba, B., and Westphal, M. (n.d.) Historia Półwyspu Westerplatte. Muzeum II Wojny Światowej. Available at: http://www.muzeum1939.pl/pl/ekspozycja/wystawa_plenerowa_na_westerplatte/symbol (accessed August 27, 2014).
Gegner, M., and Ziino, B. (2012) The Heritage of War: Agency, Contingency, Identity. In M. Gegner and B. Ziino (eds), *The Heritage of War*. Abingdon: Routledge, pp. 1–15.
Imposti, G.E. (2009) "God's Playground": Poland and the Second World War in Wajda's Cinema. In E. Lamberti and V. Fortunati (eds), *Memories and Representations of War: The Case of World War I and World War II*. Amsterdam: Rodopi, pp. 235–254.
Karski, J. (2010) *Story of a Secret State: My Report to the World*. London: Penguin.
Kirschenbaum, L.A. (2006) *The Legacy of the Siege of Leningrad, 1941–1995: Myth, Memories, and Monuments*. Cambridge: Cambridge University Press.
Kobiałka, M. (2011) Sąd nad Powstaniem Warszawskim. *Gazeta Wyborcza*, August 9. Available at: http://wyborcza.pl/1,76842,10085370,Sad_nad_Powstaniem_Warszawskim.html (accessed August 27, 2014).
Kosiewski, P. (2012) Muzeum na nowo pomyślane. *Tygodnik Powszechny*, April 26. Available at: http://tygodnik.onet.pl/historia/muzeum-na-nowo-pomyslane/j58fr (accessed August 22, 2014).
Kostro, R. (2013) Historia i mit. *Rzeczpospolita*, February 24. Available at: http://www.rp.pl/artykul/984046-Historia-i-mit.html (accessed August 27, 2014).
Kowal, P. (2009) Nie rzucać kamieniami w Muzeum Powstania. *Rzeczpospolita*, July 28. Available at: http://www.rp.pl/artykul/340952.html?print=tak&p=0 (accessed August 27, 2014).
Lasia, M. (2012) W naszej pamięci. *Dom Spotkań z Historią*. Available at: http://www.dsh.waw.pl/pl/3_1470 (accessed August 22, 2014).
Macdonald, S. (2011) Expanding Museum Studies: An Introduction. In S. Macdonald (ed.), *A Companion to Museum Studies*. Chichester: Wiley-Blackwell, pp. 1–12.
Machcewicz, P. (2012) *Spory o historię 2000–2011*. Kraków: Znak.
Machcewicz, P., and Majewski, P.M. (2008) Muzeum II Wojny Światowej: Zarys koncepcji programowej. *Przegląd Polityczny*, 91/92, 46–51.
Machcewicz, P., and Persak, K. (eds) (2002) *Wokół Jedwabnego*. Warsaw: IPN.
Mirer, P. (2009). Khar'kovskuiu zemliu polozhat v osnovu Muzeia Vtoroi mirovoi voiny v Gdan'ske. *Mediaport*, August 31. Available at: http://www.mediaport.ua/news/official/65709/ harkovskuyu_zemlyu_polojat_v_osnovu_muzeya_vtoroy_mirovoy_voynyi_v_gdanske (accessed August 22, 2014).
Niżyńska, J. (2010) The Politics of Mourning and the Crisis of Poland's Symbolic Language after April 10. *East European Politics and Societies*, 24 (4), 467–479.
Novikova, L. (1999) Stali prosto zemlei i travoi, a na bol'shee – deneg ne khvatilo. *Nezavisimaia gazeta*, December 25, p. x.
Nowak, A. (2011) Westerplatte czy Jedwabne. *Rzeczpospolita*, August 1. Available at: http://archiwum.rp.pl/artykul/347318-Westerplatte-czy-Jedwabne.html (accessed August 27, 2014).
Pilawski, K. (2009) Kult mitu powstania. *Przegląd*, August 16. Available at: http://www.przeglad-tygodnik.pl/pl/artykul/kult-mitu-powstania (accessed August 27, 2014).
Porter, B.A. (1996) The Social Nation and Its Futures: English Liberalism and Polish Nationalism in Late Nineteenth-Century Warsaw. *American Historical Review*, 101 (5), 1470–1492.
Romanowski, A. (2010) Z pamięcią katastrofa. *Gazeta Wyborcza*, July 26. Available at: http://wyborcza.pl/1,97737,8172183,Z_pamiecia_katastrofa.html (accessed August 27, 2014).
Smolar, A. (2008) Władza i geografia pamięci. In P. Kosiewski (ed.), *Pamięć jako przedmiot władzy*. Warsaw: Fundacja Batorego, pp. 49–74.

Snyder, T. (2010) *Bloodlands: Europe between Hitler and Stalin*. New York: Basic Books.

Sroczyński, G. (2011) Kłóćmy się o powstanie. *Gazeta Wyborcza*, August 2. Available at: http://wyborcza.pl/1,76842,10046325,Klocmy_sie_o_powstanie.html (accessed August 27, 2014).

Stańczyk, T. (2013) Kresy i ziemie zachodnie. *Uważam Rze*, January 23. Available at: http://www.historia.uwazamrze.pl/artykul/972321.html?print=tak&p=0 (accessed August 22, 2014).

Traba, R. (2010) Pol'skie spory ob istorii v XXI veke. *Polit.ru*, February 3. Available at: http://polit.ru/article/2010/02/03/traba/ (accessed August 27, 2014).

Uffelmann, D. (2013) Theory as Memory Practice: The Divided Discourse on Poland's Postcoloniality. In U. Blacker, A. Etkind and J. Fedor (eds), *Memory and Theory in Eastern Europe*. New York: Palgrave Macmillan, pp. 103–124.

Uhlig, D. (2008) 1939–1989–2009: Tusk planuje wielkie obchody. *Gazeta Wyborcza*, May 2. Available at: http://wyborcza.pl/dziennikarze/1,96017,5174218.html (accessed August 22, 2014).

Ujazdowski, K.M. (2011) To racje państwowe przemawiają za ustawą o Muzeum Ziem Zachodnich. *wPolityce.pl*, August 28. Available at: http://wpolityce.pl/dzienniki/dziennik-kazimierza-m-ujazdowskiego/13747-to-racje-panstwowe-przemawiaja-za-ustawa-o-muzeum-ziem-zachodnich-odpowiedz-na-niemiecka-polityke-historyczna (accessed August 22, 2014).

Ukielski, P. (2011) Warsaw Uprising in the Consciousness of Poles: Warsaw Rising Museum as a Place of Remembrance. *European Network Remembrance and Solidarity*, August 23. Available at: http://www.enrs.eu/en/articles/217-warsaw-uprising-in-the-poles-consciousness (accessed August 22, 2014).

Walicki, A. (2001) Traditions of Polish Nationalism in Comparative Perspective. *Dialogue and Universalism*, 11 (4), 5–50.

Wieliński, B.T. (2007) Steinbach nie jest ważna. *Gazeta Wyborcza*, December 11. Available at: http://wyborcza.pl/1,75968,4757527.html (last accessed February 2, 2013; URL now inactive).

Wieliński, B.T. (2008) Czy Niemcy przekonają Polaków do "widocznego znaku." *Gazeta.pl*, February 5. Available at: http://wiadomosci.gazeta.pl/wiadomosci/1,114881,4898233.html (accessed August 22, 2014).

Winter, J. (2006) *Remembering War: The Great War between Memory and History in the Twentieth Century*. New Haven: Yale University Press.

Winter, J. (2012) Museums and the Representation of War. *Museum and Society*, 10 (3), 150–163.

Yekelchyk, S. (2004) *Stalin's Empire of Memory: Russian–Ukrainian Relations in the Soviet Historical Imagination*. Toronto: University of Toronto Press.

Zajączkowski, K. (2011) Zakłócona rocznica: Wizyta niemieckickh weteranów w Gdansku w 1979 roku w świetle dokumentów Służby Bezpieczenstwa. *Pamięć i sprawedliwość*, 18, 365–381.

Żychlińska, M. (2009) Muzeum Powstania Warszawskiego jako wehikuł polskiej pamięci zbiorowej. *Kultura i społeczeństwo*, 53 (3), 89–114.

CHAPTER 18

Heritage in an Expanded Field: Reconstructing Bridge-ness in Mostar

Andrea Connor

> But, you know, I still feel that something has been murdered here. The Old Bridge had its recognizable patina. The builders do care, but this won't be that old bridge. I will dive, and I'll keep diving as long as my heart and body can endure that.
>
> —Emir Balic, "A Trip through Time"

An Expanded Field of Enquiry

What does heritage do? How does it work? What does it afford, enable, and enact? Questions about the "doing work" of heritage are not new, but they have taken on a somewhat renewed significance and different hue in the context of a much broader theoretical shift in the humanities and social sciences, a shift towards a more relational ontology concerned to probe the limits of a binary logic that serves to locate power and agency on either side of a subject/object divide. New conceptual metaphors, across a range of disciplines, mark this shift and a more expansive and distributed notion of agency. Bruno Latour's actor–network theory deploys the notion of assemblage to conceptualize the shifting associations and interactions between entities as they coalesce to form more or less stable social ties (Latour 2005). In archaeology, Ian Hodder writes of the entanglement of people and things and their mutual dependence (Hodder 2012) and Lynn Meskell of "permeability" in a "material lifeworld" where things can and do

A Companion to Heritage Studies, First Edition. Edited by William Logan, Máiréad Nic Craith, and Ullrich Kockel.
© 2016 John Wiley & Sons, Inc. Published 2016 by John Wiley & Sons, Inc.

work as "co-producers" (Meskell 2005: 3). In social anthropology, Tim Ingold, adapting the work of Deleuze and Guattari, develops a conceptual vocabulary around the notion of "fluxes and flows" and the social as a "meshwork" of "lines of force," fields of relations in which objects are not bounded entities but enlivened things (Ingold 2010). And in the field of human geography, Nigel Thrift considers the "lineage of inter-relations" in which human bodies co-evolve with all kinds of actors, forces, and entities, that in turn might be conceptualized as "thought in action" (Thrift 2008: 10).

All seek to address, in different ways, the limitations of a representational epistemology that privileges language and signification and restricts our understanding of how things matter to a reflection of their semiological value – that is, the meanings and cultural values we ascribe to the material world around us. All question "human centered" accounts of the social world that privilege the agency of human actors as fundamentally causal. Implicit in this theoretical shift is an epistemological imperative to understand the significance and work of entities, human and non-human, in an expanded field of enquiry encompassing a plurality of relations (Latour 2005), or even perhaps specific kinds of ecologies (Ingold 2013). Things take on social lives and "afterlives" as they are enmeshed and reassembled forming new associations, taking on new identities and use values in the process. They are enlivened. Ingold's work, in particular, points to the importance of understanding the liveliness of things and their material effects as "a process of formation" rather than the finality of matter:

> If we think of every participant as following a particular way of life, threading a line through the world, then perhaps we could define the thing, as I have suggested elsewhere as a "parliament of lines." Thus conceived, the thing has the character not of an externally bounded entity, set over and against the world, but of a knot whose constituent threads, far from being contained within it, trail beyond, only to become caught with other threads in other knots. Or in a word, things leak, forever discharging through the surfaces that form temporarily around them. (Ingold 2010: 3)

What might this theoretical shift offer heritage studies, a discursive field that has traditionally valorized the unique authenticity of the original and the belief that heritage value inheres in the materiality of the artifact (cf. Smith 2006). In this chapter I consider what might be at stake through a very concrete, historical example, the destruction and reconstruction of the Stari Most, or Old Bridge, in Mostar, Bosnia-Herzegovina.

A much-loved piece of heritage prior to the Bosnian War, the sixteenth-century footbridge spanned the Neretva River, and was widely recognized as a unique historical example of Bosnian Ottoman architecture, but was also a multivalent *thing*, a site of "living heritage" that occupied a privileged place in the urban fabric of the small city of Mostar and the everyday life of its citizens. Bombed and completely destroyed during the Bosnian War (1992 to 1995), it was reopened 11 years later as an intentional monument to reconciliation, a place through which to reanimate memory of a shared past and spatial history of cohabitation. In 2005 it gained official status as a World Heritage site, a designation that reinforced its symbolic reframing as a now idealized point of crossing. Implicit in UNESCO's rationale for World Heritage recognition was the assumption that the historical accuracy of the bridge's material reconstruction would work to restore its privileged status as a locus of identification, a symbolic agent in bridging not only a temporal divide between the past and the present, but also by extension a more contemporary political, spatial, and subjective divide, between the citizens of east and west Mostar, a city now divided along lines of ethnicity. But the 'new Old Bridge' is

Figure 18.1 The Stari Most (Old Bridge), Mostar. Source: photo by Andrea Connor.

now embedded in a post-war cultural landscape shaped by the identity politics of those seeking to both divide and unify the city. In such a context, the reconstruction of heritage becomes a highly politicized, contentious, and potentially divisive act.

This chapter considers the ambiguous and complex afterlife of the new bridge in a shifting political landscape, and the limits of a practice of heritage reconstruction that continues to derive its legitimating power from a materialist epistemology. I argue for a more expansive notion of heritage reconstruction encompassing not only the physical re-presencing of a material artifact, namely the bridge, but also the reconstruction of something wider and deeper but less immediately tangible: "bridge-ness." Taking my lead from Ingold and Latour, I want to highlight the importance of understanding the processual afterlife of the new bridge as a form of gathering or assemblage, a monumental thing whose affective intensities and mediating power is permeable rather than bounded. Analyzing the contested afterlife of this monument thus affords the opportunity to trace processes of transformation, and to understand the constellation of forces and interests that might work to sustain what Ingold calls the "leakiness" of things – their porosity and "immersion" in the circulations of emergence, not the finality or stasis of matter but their ongoing, processual realization (Ingold 2010: 6–7).

Implicitly then, this chapter addresses the practice of heritage reconstruction through the lens of this expanded field of enquiry, and considers the spatial, temporal, and material conditions of possibility that might work to reanimate a monumental bridge as an affecting, presencing thing, a site of gathering as much as crossing, with a form of mediating agency that is as much about the present as the past.

Permeability and the Agency of Destruction

On November 9, 1993, the world's longest span-arch bridge, the Stari Most, collapsed into the Neretva River, after weeks of intense bombardment by Croatian nationalist forces, during a vicious war that killed thousands, and eventually reshaped the political and cultural landscape of Bosnia. Despite the daily reportage of atrocities and mass killings, and the widespread destruction of heritage sites and cultural infrastructure, the destruction of the footbridge attracted international condemnation and an outpouring of grief and mourning throughout the former Yugoslavia. Whilst international organizations, such as UNESCO, condemned the bridge's destruction as a cultural crime against humanity, the citizens of Mostar and the former Yugoslavia expressed a sense of loss that spoke to the intertwined lives of a bridge and a people. The Croatian journalist Slavenka Drakulic wondered openly why reading about the death of the bridge was more devastating than hearing and reading about the deaths of real people during hostilities: "We expect people to die; we count on our own lives to end. The destruction of the monument of civilization is something else. The bridge in all its beauty and grace was meant to outlive us. It was an attempt to grasp eternity" (Drakulic 1993: 2). Others, like the architect Bogdan Bogdanovic, described the bridge's destruction as a potentially disorienting temporal loss, akin to losing part of oneself: "I ask myself how the people of Mostar will live without that bridge. They have now lost part of their being. With a loss like this people lose their place in time" (quoted in Sudetic 1993).

Both drew attention to the complex spatiotemporal work of the Stari Most, its mediating role in sustaining a collective sense of time and place, and its deep enmeshment in the material habitus or lifeworld of the city and its people. In 2004, on the eve of its symbolic reopening, the then director-general of UNESCO, Koïchiro Matsuura, expressed something of this enmeshment, describing the destruction of the Stari Most as a "serious spiritual and cultural blow" to the "ancient town" of Mostar – a loss felt as an "irreparable estrangement, as though the lost structure were a phantom limb" (Matsuura 2004). Matsuura's corporeal metaphor suggested not only a traumatic loss unable to be psychically integrated, individually and collectively, but a relationship of permeability between flesh and stone – an acknowledgement of the intertwined existence of entities usually understood as occupying separate, "impermeable worlds" (Meskell 2005: 3). Lynn Meskell has described this permeability, implicit in the notion of a "material lifeworld" as a "processual combining" of things, both material and immaterial, in ways that "cannot easily be disentangled or separated taxonomically" (Meskell 2005: 3). It was the affective content of this permeability that Matsuura, and others, traced in attempting to make sense of the absence, the material and symbolic void left in the wake of the bridge's destruction.

Built during the reign of the Ottoman ruler Suleiman the Magnificent in the sixteenth century, the Stari Most connected the east and west sides of the deep Neretva River that cuts through the city of Mostar, capital of the mountainous region of Herzegovina. The city itself grew up around the bridge, and a measure of its social significance is exemplified in the city's name: Mostar, an amalgamation of the words for bridge (Most) and bridge-keeper (Mostari) in Serbo-Croatian. Prior to its destruction, the social life of the Stari Most was realized iconographically as a cultural sign and emblem of the city; phenomenologically as a place of embodied encounter and social ritual; and metaphorically as an intense site of fantasy, imagining, and myth-making (Pasic 1995).

The multivalent quality of the Stari Most, its own specific form of "bridge-ness," reflected and reinforced a real and imagined urban landscape shaped by practices of coexistence, and strong affective ties to place.

Mostar was widely regarded as one of the most ethnically integrated cities in the former Yugoslavia prior to the outbreak of hostilities, with a high rate of intermarriage between people nominally identified as Croat, Bosniak, and Serb, but who also negotiated local and regional identities as Bosnians, and had a strong civic identification with their city as citizens of Mostar (Pasic 2005; Herscher 1998). The urban morphology of the city spoke to a history of ethno-religious diversity through the representational value of highly symbolic sites such as sacral heritage, but also through the everyday spatial practices of its inhabitants, to a history of spatial integration and cohabitation. The specific character and presencing power of the Stari Most can be understood in relation to its material embeddedness in the "spatial texture" (Lefebvre 1991: 10–45) of the city. To paraphrase Ingold (2010), the Stari Most was both a monumental thing that gathered *and* a gathering of things – spatial histories of use and engagement; a temporality that spoke to the durability of a material lifeworld and its continuous and permanent presence in a cultural landscape; collective and individual memories, meanings, associations, and attachments embedded over time. Its destruction was thus experienced as much more than the loss of an historical monument or representational object, but resonated subjectively at the level of identity reflecting what Edward Casey calls "emplacement" – a process in which the bridge had come to take up residence in the people, as much they had come to inhabit it (Casey 2001).

If the Stari Most's physical destruction produced a moment of traumatic rupture in which a form of permeability could be articulated, it was also paradoxically the transformation of a multivalent thing into a unified, representative object. When the Stari Most finally collapsed, Croatian HVO nationalist forces reportedly celebrated with gunfire the destruction of a "Muslim monument" that was now part of an alien culture, someone else's heritage, not theirs. Yet as Colin Kaiser, the UN's representative in Sarajevo, sagely remarked at the time, "Before the war, nobody in Mostar would have said that the Old Bridge was a 'Muslim monument.' Its destruction by Croat tanks turned it into one" (Kaiser 2000: 42). It was not, as the Croatian nationalists claimed, that the bridge was destroyed because it was a Muslim monument, a symbol of the "other"; rather, its metamorphosis occurred through the agency of destruction and the material and symbolic transformation of an urban landscape once held in common. Drained of its multivalent complexity, the Stari Most had been reduced to a "sign" of ethnicity.

Affective Landscapes: Materiality and Space

Whilst much attention has been paid to the so-called "cultural cleansing" that took place during the Bosnian War of the early 1990s,[1] there has been less focus on the transformation of the intangible but no less significant "spatial texture" (Lefebvre 1991) of cities like Sarajevo and Mostar. The destruction of the Stari Most was the most visibly symbolic moment in a campaign of destruction that was widespread, and included not only cultural sites and sacral heritage but also civic institutions, public spaces, libraries, archives, cultural institutions, museums, as well as public spaces such as cemeteries, parks, marketplaces, and whole streets.[2] These were places associated with forms of shared spatiality, civic identity, and collective gathering, exemplifying a history of coexistence (Grodach 2002). This destruction was a crucial strategy in materializing the territorial claims of ethno-nationalists, intent on carving out zones of ethnic purity, later manifested in the ethnic nationalism that has reshaped the political and cultural landscape of Mostar.

Two discourses emerged during and after the war to discursively frame and explain this destruction, and together exemplify the bifurcated logic that has informed the post-war reconstruction of Mostar and its most celebrated monument. On the one hand, a discourse of "cultural cleansing" situates this destruction as part of a wider strategy of "ethnic cleansing," targeting highly symbolic buildings and sacral heritage designed to erase the historical presence, collective memory, and material traces of identifiable ethnic groups. Implicit in this discourse is the assumption that specific material sites with heritage value are reflective of identity and contiguous with memory, and that their destruction is also by extension the erasure of both. Whilst the discourse of cultural cleansing spoke to the symbolic, representational status of material culture and its implication in the work of identity formation, it remained largely silent in relation to the spatial dimension and actualization of place through use and engagement.

This silence was made discursively visible in the 1990s through the discourse of "urbicide" that engaged with the destruction of the less tangible "spatial texture" of cities like Sarajevo and Mostar. An architect and former mayor of Belgrade, Bogdan Bogdanovic, articulated the rationale behind the targeting of an urban landscape:

> the deliberate targeting of cities, seeking to destroy the security, public order, civility and quality of life of all their citizens, and damage or destroy the viability and livability of the city itself... is a common element of acts of campaigns of terror of all kinds. (quoted in Safier 2001: 416)

The concept of urbicide explicitly recognized the destruction of cities in Bosnia as a strategy designed to reconfigure the social space of the city – and produce a realignment spatially and temporally, materially and symbolically, between place and identity, topography and ontology (Campbell 1998; Coward 2009) in relation to a fixed, bounded notion of ethnic identity.[3] Thus, whilst the notion of "cultural cleansing" focused on the representational status of discrete sites as identifiably "ethnic," the concept of urbicide drew attention to the spatial dimension of this destruction, and the processual, dynamic work of material culture as not simply reflective of culture or identity but mediative, implicated as coproducer in processes of being and becoming: animated and actualized through dynamic interaction and habitation.

The testimony of two experts, the UN's Colin Kaiser and the Harvard scholar Andras Riedlmayer, explicitly acknowledged both the spatial and material aspects of destruction. Whilst arguing that the targeting of heritage sites was consistent with a deliberate policy of cultural cleansing designed to kill off the collective memory of a "successfully shared past", and erase the historical presence, and attachment to place of a people" (Riedlmayer 1995, 2006), their testimony also went beyond the representational value of specific sites. Both noted the spatial syntax of the urban landscape – the juxtaposition of buildings and monuments, their proximity, and how this manifested a history of integration and a "common sense of ownership of sacral heritage" (Kaiser 2000: 41–42). Serbs, Croats, and Muslims, Kaiser argued, also took equal pride in their secular buildings such as the Stari Most (Kaiser 2000). When viewed in the context of a cultural landscape as an assemblage of buildings, public spaces, use values, memories, semantic associations, and spatial practices, a complex history of pluralistic habitation is revealed.

The transformation of Mostar, through the agency of destruction, was thus not only physical but was also a reconfiguration of the spatial materiality of an urban landscape – the assemblage of tangible and intangible entities that together work to animate place in specific ways, and through which space is socially imagined as particular kinds of place. Cultural landscapes are social, spatial, and imagined, invested with meaning, memory, and collective and individual significance, through processes of identification and place-making that also encompass people's affective ties to place (Hayden 1999: 142–45). The destruction of the urban landscape in Mostar has involved a reciprocal transformation in people's emotional sense of place, a psychic and affective remapping of social space. Processes of dis-identification and reorientation, in relation to a politically charged and contested post-war present, have been central to the shifting dialectic of collective and individual remembering and forgetting that has reconfigured the spatial and temporal landscape of Mostar (Herscher 1998). The rupturing of individual and collective memories, phantasmatic social meanings, and affective attachments that are integral to how material space is experienced subjectively as place are the less visible, but no less significant, effects of destruction. How can a practice of heritage reconstruction address this kind of transformation?

Representational Politics

The process of physically rebuilding an urban landscape as a means of redressing the erasure of the materiality of identity, and reinscribing the historical presence of a people or group and the durability of their social ties to place, would seem, on the face of it, to make enormous sense. The Dayton Agreement (1995), the document that finally ended hostilities and sealed an uneasy peace, recognized the potential significance of heritage reconstruction to support the rebuilding of civil society in Bosnia.[4] Fixed, tangible, sites of memory, intentional monuments, offer material loci around which to anchor political narratives about the past, and thus potentially mobilize an "imagined community" in the present. Heritage valuation and historical framing may also work as a potent form of "past-mastering" (Meskell 2012: 1–8), a means of renegotiating the memories, use values, and symbolic status of potentially dissonant, traumatic sites of memory. In disputed and contested contexts, heritage thus emerges as a significant form of "symbolic capital" (Scott 2002: 100), a potent resource around which to construct narratives of belonging and cultural legitimacy, particularly where ethnicity and notions of cultural difference are mobilized to assert possession over territory.

But in disputed and highly contested contexts such as Mostar, the physical reconstruction of heritage necessarily intersects with the identity politics and "competing nationalisms" (Makas 2006) of those working to solidify an ethnic division of the city, and with efforts to rebuild a civic culture based on something other than ethnic affiliation. Heritage has proved to be a tangible and highly visible means for ethno-nationalists to articulate historical differences and reinforce an essentialist nexus between territory and identity. The reconstruction of the Stari Most as an intentional monument to reconciliation and peace-building also negotiates a shifting cultural landscape in which the social processes of remembering and forgetting have been highly politicized in relation to their potential to reinforce and/or contest the spatial division of the city.

Over the last two decades, a "symbolic war" has been waged through the selective preservation and erasure of material sites now associated with the historical presence of what are conceived as "bounded ethnic identities" (Rowlands 2002: 117).[5] The contested rebuilding of sacral heritage, in particular, and its work in mapping this ethnicized territorial division, has garnered much scholarly attention (Makas 2006; Herscher 1998; Sells 1998, 2003). It is perhaps the most visible sign of the fractured internal politics that have reconfigured not only the physical but also the affective landscape of the city. Recently rebuilt mosques, financed by Saudi Arabia, mark the east side of the city, while on the now predominantly Croatian western side, a huge Franciscan clock tower has been rebuilt at three times its original height and now dominates the city skyline. This monumental reconstruction exemplifies the politicization of heritage and its significance as a symbolic agent in materializing and legitimizing ethno-religious claims of historical pre-eminence and originary occupation.[6]

This representational, ethnic mapping of material space is *amplified* by the dominant conceptualization of heritage as discrete and bounded, its valuation achieved through its material presence and tangible relationship to the past (Smith 2006: 29). What was once held in common through a shared history and collective memory of cohabitation and spatial proximity is now a highly politicized marker of ethnic identity. A representational politics has been invoked to both justify and defend monumental reconstruction as simply the restoration of a material artifact that merely reflects the multiethnic character of the city (Makas 2006). This causal, reflective rationale, materialized through heritage reconstruction, has worked to not only solidify an ethnicized division of social space in Mostar, but participates in an excision of particular sites from their spatial context in a move that reinforces their status as bounded, representational objects, but obscures their potential significance as things embedded in a wider social fabric or meshwork of relations including the intangible history of human–object interaction (Ingold 2010). In a city now socially imagined by many of its inhabitants as divided along lines of ethnicity and belonging to two unified ethnic groups, the reconstruction of what was once held in common is now viewed by many as "ethnic heritage": "theirs" not "ours." It is this bifurcated representational logic that has also informed the reconstruction of the "new Old Bridge" in Mostar.

Narrative Emplacement, Symbolic Forgetting

The official aim of the bridge's reconstruction, as expressed by UNESCO, was to reconnect the citizens of Mostar and Bosnia with a shared past, by restoring "part of the common heritage of Serbs, Croats and Muslims that had disappeared during the war" (Matsuura 2004). Implicit in this rationale is the assumption that the material reconstruction of the bridge will work to restore its privileged status as a site of "living heritage," a symbolic touchstone for a process of reconciliation in a post-war present. Its narrative reframing thus addressed the issue of memory and its animating force through the authorizing discourse of heritage, the dominant conceptualization of which, as argued, derives its own legitimating power from a materialist epistemology. Sites of heritage are ascribed cultural and in this case political value in relation to their capacity to "reference the past" (Lowenthal 1997: 28). The mediating power and narrative legitimacy of the heritage site thus revolves around its claims to authenticity, defined, within this dominant discourse, in historicist and materialist terms, as a quality of the object itself. The political claims attached to the "new Old Bridge" thus implicitly and problematically rested on establishing an authentic relationship to the past, through the historical accuracy of the bridge's material reconstruction. Its forensic reconstruction thus reflected this authorizing, causal logic.

In October 1998, UNESCO appointed an international committee of experts to oversee the reconstruction and ensure the "cultural integrity" and "architectural authenticity" of the process. Forensic attention to historical detail involved both significant historical reenactment and, paradoxically, the use of digital technology to reproduce sixteenth-century Ottoman building techniques. Pieces of stone remains dredged from the river were sent to a laboratory in Germany for scientific analysis of their exact compositional make-up, in the hope of gaining information about the traditional methods and construction techniques of the original (Armaly, Blasi, and Lawrence 2004: 11). Each stone was a composite of modern computer modeling and handcrafting – a hybrid process designed to ensure exact replication of the original. But when the structural engineers working on the bridge investigated its geometrical structure, they found imperfections that could not be explained with reference to what was known about the construction techniques of the original master architect Mimar Hajruddin and the Ottoman builders with whom he worked. The Stari Most's asymmetry, they concluded, could only have been produced by a seismic event – an earthquake at some point in its history (Armaly, Blasi, and Lawrence 2004: 15–17). It was precisely this trace of historicity, the singular, spatiotemporal trajectory of the bridge that could not be reproduced, no matter how accurate or scientific the process.

Lacking the imprint of temporal duration, and hence the authenticity of historicity, the new bridge's use value as a place of memory, a selective aide memoire, through which to anchor a narrative of reconciliation and national unity, is problematized by its own apparent newness and perfection. The "new Old Bridge" embodies the hybrid, paradoxical character of its reconstruction – a sixteenth-century design, recreated with modern research and digital technology, its discursive framing as "heritage" a form of "conceptual purification" that has worked to efface the composite character of its own specific, hybrid afterlife. As its popular name suggests, this "new Old Bridge" occupies an ambivalent relationship to the past, and is as much about intentional forgetting as it is about remembering. The contradictions implicit in its material reconstruction and discursive framing as "shared heritage" were manifested at its ceremonial reopening in 2004.

Hailed as a "new beginning" for the country, international dignitaries and political leaders enthusiastically took up the metaphor of "bridging," declaring it a bridge to peace, a bridge between cultures and peoples, a bridge between "Islam and the West," a bridge between a common multicultural past and a possible future. Its reframing as a technology of connection – a physical site through which to reconnect with a shared multiethnic past and thus re-imagine a unified future – foregrounded its representational, symbolic afterlife, but was largely silent in relation to its history as a place of spatial gathering. The specter of that history and its social significance was made manifest when, after all the speeches about unity, organizing officials allowed only a few select dignitaries to cross the bridge that day, much to the disappointment and protest of others present. Despite the political rhetoric of "new beginnings" and reconciliation, many citizens of Mostar were forced to watch the reopening of "their" bridge at home on television.

The symbolic reopening of the bridge exemplified the contradiction between the official, conceptual production of Mostar as a unified city, and what Lefebvre describes as the "perceived" space of the city, the routine, everyday spatial practices of citizens themselves, who "secrete" society's space (Lefebvre 1991: 38) through the individual and collective mapping of social space. Places, as Lefebvre and de Certeau remind us, are made of practice as well as discourse (Lefebvre 1991; de Certeau 1984). Sites are activated (or not) through their interaction with those who use and experience them, in a sensory and embodied way (Hayden 1997: 88). Thus specific sites also become mnemonic landscapes through various forms of "praxis," complex interactions between people and material space that reanimate landscapes as particular kinds of place. Officially, the "new Old Bridge" had been reframed as a material space through which to reconnect people with a shared past and reconfigure their affective ties to place. But if people would not, or could not, use "the bridge to peace," as UNESCO's director-general described the new bridge, then it risked becoming an indelible reminder of the international promise, and failure of reunification – a monumental site marking separation and division, in spite of official proclamations to the contrary.

Reassembling Authenticity, Reanimating Memory

In his essay on the "aura" of the artwork, Walter Benjamin argued that authenticity does not reside in the object itself but in the complex intermeshing of forces that produces a thing's unique spatiotemporal trajectory, a history that is imprinted on the artwork or artifact as a patina or trace (Benjamin 1969: 217–52). Benjamin's work foregrounds an essential dilemma associated with a practice of material reconstruction, no matter how historically accurate: its potential to undermine the authority of the original and thus, in this case, its capacity to work as an agent of authorization. But the notion of "trace" or "patina" as the imprint of a much wider spatiotemporal network of associations also implicitly locates authenticity in the realm of the social, and thus potentially as a form of "gathering" that might be reassembled in the present. The contradiction between the officially emplaced political narrative of reconciliation and the everyday mapping of social space by the citizens of Mostar themselves underlines not only the importance of the spatial actualization of place in reanimating sites of heritage, but also its potential significance in reassembling an authentic relationship to the past in a post-war present. We might then look beyond the physical destruction and reconstruction of the bridge as an authentic end point and consider the ongoing, processual realization of authenticity through the spatial, temporal, and material actualization of place.

One of the most socially significant spatial practices to occur in and around the Stari Most during its four-hundred-year life has been the tradition of diving from the bridge, and the annual Ikari, reputedly the world's oldest diving competition. Prior to the war, the Ikari had been held every year in the middle of summer at the end of July. A rite of passage for many young Bosnian men, and a tradition passed down from one generation to the next, diving from the bridge is part of the intangible spatial history of the city. It is the only day of the year that the bridge is closed to all but the divers and competition organizers. One week after the symbolic and spectacular reopening of the "new Old Bridge," divers gathered at dawn for the first competition to be held in Mostar in ten years. Whilst many citizens of Mostar had been unable to attend the official opening ceremony due to tight security, and had watched the event on television, some 30,000 gathered around the bridge to be part of the first diving competition since the end of the war. Zvezdan Grozdic, a high-diver from Belgrade who had dived from the Stari Most before its destruction, remarked that while the official opening ceremony resembled a "bodyguards' convention" with "too many politicians," the divers had given "some of the original spirit back to the bridge" (quoted in Mackenzie 2004). His comments implicitly acknowledged the auratic interaction between diver and bridge, and the possibility of reanimating the new bridge as an affecting, presencing thing. This collective annual ritual may be understood as what Lefebvre conceptualizes as representational or "lived space" – a mode of spatial production that crucially involves sensuous, embodied interaction:

> Representational space is alive: it speaks. It has an affective kernel or center: Ego, bed, bedroom, dwelling, house; or: square, church, graveyard. It embraces the loci of passion, of action and of lived situations, and thus immediately implies time. Consequently it may be qualified in various ways: it may be directional, situational or relational, because it is essentially qualitative, fluid and dynamic. (Lefebvre 1991: 42)

Bound up with the longitudinal relationship between bridge and city, the annual Ikari is a mode of spatial engagement and a performative event through which a network of relationships between bridge, divers, spectators, and landscape is reanimated in the present, and a historically and socially specific field of enactment is reiterated.

The lived, corporeal space of Mostar's annual diving competition thus foregrounds an embodied history of use and engagement that "speaks" to the long-standing, recursive relationship between a monumental thing and a history of shared habitation and heterogeneous coexistence. Now officially conceived and metaphorically reframed through the political discourse of reconciliation, the new bridge has been recast as an idealized point of connection and crossing between east and west Mostar. Its bridge-ness has been reconceived in relation to a post-war spatial division of the city and a re-territorialization of social space along ethnic lines. In contrast, the Ikari articulates a spatial history that is neither the conceived space of an officially unified city, nor the perceived space of a divided one, but a lived space that reconnects the new bridge temporally with a long history of human–object interaction, and reanimates it spatially as a site of gathering, an embodied space through which to reimagine the social space of the city.

The "new Old Bridge" does not unify the two sides of the city of Mostar, and today it is firmly located in what is socially imagined and spatially produced, through the everyday trajectory of its inhabitants, as the eastern, Bosniak side of the city. It remains an ambivalent and contested monument to reconciliation, a representative object whose post-war afterlife is enmeshed in the ethnicized identity politics of a divided city. The spatial practice of diving and the annual Ikari has also been somewhat politicized since the war, its associations realigned, a memory held in common slowly becoming part of a post-war history of separate traditions (Pasic 2005). However, the performative memory space opened up by the Ikari and the long-standing spatial practice of diving may also hold the potential to allow for a "memory ecology" to emerge, an ecology that gathers, in which things leak, and through which the body itself might emerge as a corporeal bridge between the past and the present.

Memory Ecologies

A central concern of this chapter has been the idea that a critical heritage studies needs to encompass a more expansive field of inquiry, and that the emphasis on a purely preservationist, materialist epistemology limits our understanding of *how* things work, the various forms of agency they acquire in specific spatiotemporal contexts, and how artifacts, objects, and places come to be enlivened as "living" sites of heritage through the present-oriented networks within which they are enmeshed and in turn work to shape. Memory work and the work of memory are crucial to animating heritage. But as the physical re-presencing of the Stari Most attests, the historical accuracy of a site's material reconstruction may be less important to its reanimation as an affecting presencing thing than how it is lived, interpreted, and actualized in the present. The bifurcated logic that has informed the reconstruction of this "new Old Bridge" has implicitly privileged a materialist aesthetic and representational politics that has worked to efface the spatial dimension and actualization of place through practices and histories of use and engagement. But the spatial and material aspects of heritage are neither mutually exclusive nor hierarchically dependent. They are rather *interwoven* in the constellation of forces and interests that sustains memory.

Perhaps a more useful concept with which to grasp and think through this complexity is that of an "ecology." Ecologies may be stable or unstable, durable or temporary, but they are not impermeable, bounded entities. A "memory ecology" may include the discursive valuation of material culture as heritage, but may also be sustained through the dialogical relationship between human and non-human actors, and histories of intangible associations that might be less immediately visible but are no less powerful for that. Ecologies are thus multifaceted, characterized by relations of interconnectedness and coexistence (Morton 2010: 4) that are never fixed but always potentially in flux, encompassing a relational ontology that defies any mono-causal logic or rationale. Memory does not reside in objects, but rather, as this chapter has argued, in the associative networks through which material objects might be reanimated as affecting, presencing things. The physical reconstruction of an artifact is thus only one element in reestablishing some kind of authentic relationship to the past, achieved not through material presence alone, but through the assemblage of forces and interests that coalesce to create and sustain an ecology that will allow for memory work to occur. As the very concrete, historical example of the Stari Most has shown, a memory ecology is not only or even primarily material or tangible; it is also spatial, conceptual, affective, and representational. The question for a critical heritage studies concerned with heritage reconstruction and conservation thus becomes: What are the conditions of possibility that might work to create a durable ecology of memory, an ecology that sustains the "leakiness" of things – human and non-human– and their capacity for ongoing processual gathering?

Notes

1 I use the term cultural cleansing to denote the widespread targeting and destruction of architecture, heritage sites, and artifacts associated with a particular cultural group as a means of erasing their historical presence and social ties to place. Robert Bevan (2006: 13), for example, has described this kind of destruction as "proto-genocidal" destructive acts which often occur before or alongside the ethnic cleansing of people, the two being inextricably intertwined.

2 The International Criminal Tribunal for the Former Yugoslavia heard evidence regarding the extent of the destruction from UNESCO representatives, NGOs, and unaffiliated experts like Riedlmayer.
3 The temporal dimension of this destruction and its implications for identity have been taken up by numerous scholars, including Robert Bevan (2006), who investigates the systematic destruction of architecture in a range of contexts, and its links with the destruction of identity and the logic of genocide.
4 A special provision within the Dayton Agreement set up the Commission to Preserve National Monuments. However, this has been largely ineffectual, not least because Bosnia remains an internally divided country with little cooperation between its constituencies, these being Republika Srpska and the different municipalities within the Federation of Bosnia and Herzegovina. Initially the responsibility of UNESCO, authority for the commission was handed over to the Bosnian government in 2000.
5 As Rowlands points out, the official recognition through the Dayton Agreement of three ethnic groups in Bosnia – Serbs, Croats, and Bosnian Muslims – as "the key cultural designators of identity" reinforced a conceptualization of identity in terms of an essential, homogeneous, ethnic, subject (Rowlands 2002).
6 The then director of the Institute for the Preservation of Cultural, Historic, and Natural Heritage in Mostar, Zijad Demirovic, described the tower's monumental presence in the urban landscape as out of all proportion to the other buildings of the skyline. In spite of his objections, the director had no jurisdiction on the Croat side of the city to stop its construction, another manifestation of the political and administrative division of the city.

References

Armaly, M., Blasi, C., and Lawrence, H. (2004) Stari Most: Rebuilding More than a Historic Bridge in Mostar. *Museums International*, 56 (4), 11–17.

Balic E. (2003) A Trip Through Time: Mostar, Bosnia and Herzegovina: 1993. *Time*, August 10. Available at: http://content.time.com/time/specials/packages/article/0,28804,2024035_2024499_2024962,00.html (accessed December 19, 2014).

Benjamin, W. (1969) *Illuminations: Essays and Reflections*, ed. H. Arendt, trans. H. Zohn. New York: Schocken Books.

Bevan, R. (2006) *The Destruction of Memory: Architecture at War*. London: Reaktion Books.

Campbell, D (1998) *National Deconstruction: Violence, Identity and Justice in Bosnia*. Minneapolis: University of Minnesota Press.

Casey, E. (2001) Body, Self, Landscape: A Geo-Philosophical Inquiry into the Place-World. In P. Adams *et al.* (eds), *Textures of Places: Exploring Humanist Geographies*. Minneapolis: University of Minnesota Press, pp. 403–425.

Coward, M. (2009) *Urbicide: The Politics of Urban Destruction*. London: Routledge.

De Certeau, M. (1984) *The Practice of Everyday Life*. Berkeley: University of California Press.

Drakulic, S. (1993) A Bridge too Dear. *Globe and Mail, December* 24, p. 2.

Grodach, C. (2002) Reconstituting Identity and History in Post-War Mostar, Bosnia-Herzegovina. *City*, 6 (1), 61–82.

Hayden, D. (1997) *The Power of Place: Urban Landscapes as Public History*. Cambridge, MA: MIT Press.

Hayden, D. (1999) Landscapes of Loss and Remembrance: The Case of Little Tokyo in Los Angeles. In E. Sivan and J. Winter (eds), *War and Remembrance in the Twentieth Century*. Cambridge: Cambridge University Press, pp. 142–160.

Herscher, A. (1998) Remembering and Rebuilding in Bosnia: An Architect Argues the Right Blend of Reconstruction Can Help Revive Multiculturalism. *Transitions*, 5 (3), 76–81.

Hodder, I. (2012) *Entangled: An Archaeology of the Relationships between Humans and Things*. Chichester: Wiley-Blackwell.

Ingold, T. (2010) Bringing Things to Life: Creative Entanglements in a World of Materials. Working Paper No. 15. Economic and Social Research Council National Centre for Research Methods, University of Manchester. Available at: http://www.socialsciences.manchester.ac.uk/medialibrary/morgancentre/research/wps/15-2010-07-realities-bringing-things-to-life.pdf (accessed December 12, 2012).

Ingold, T. (2013) *Making: Anthropology, Archaeology, Art and Architecture*. New York: Routledge.

Kaiser, C. (2000) Crimes Against Culture. *UNESCO Courier*, September, No. 4. Available at: http://web1.infotrac.galegroup.com/itw/infomark/109/511('Crimes against Culture') (accessed September 12, 2009).

Latour, B. (2005) *Reassembling the Social: An Introduction to Actor–Network Theory*, Oxford: Oxford University Press.

Lefebvre, H. (1991) *The Production of Space*, trans. D.N. Smith. Oxford: Blackwell.

Lowenthal, D. (1997) *The Heritage Crusade and the Spoils of History*. London: Viking Press.

Mackenzie, M. (2004) Extreme Sports: We Dive at Dawn. *Independent*, August 15. Available at: http://www.independent.co.uk/sport/general/extreme-sports-we-dive-at-dawn-6163835.html (accessed April 9, 2010).

Makas, G.E. (2006) Competing Visions of Post-War Mostar. Paper delivered at the European Association for Urban History conference Cultural Encounters in Urban Space, Stockholm, 2006. Available at: www.academia.edu/2211321/Competing_Visions_of_Postwar_Mostar_EAUH_Stockholm_2006_ (accessed December 10, 2012).

Matsuura, K. (2004) Why We Need the Mostar Bridge. *International Herald Tribune*, July 6. Available at: https://listserv.buffalo.edu/cgi-bin/wa?A2=JUSTWATCH-L;a5783e34.0407 (accessed February 28, 2015).

Meskell, L. (2005) Introduction: Object Orientations. In L. Meskell (ed.), *Archaeologies of Materiality*. Oxford: Blackwell, pp. 1–17.

Meskell, L. (2012) *The Nature of Heritage: The New South Africa*. Chichester: Wiley-Blackwell.

Morton, T. (2010) *The Ecological Thought*. Cambridge, MA: Harvard University Press

Pasic, A. (1995) *Islamic Architecture in Bosnia and Herzegovina*. Istanbul: Islamic Research Centre for Islamic History and Art.

Pasic, A. (2005) Mostar 2004 Program 1994–2004: Final Report. Studies on the History and Culture of Bosnia and Hercegovina No. 8. Istanbul: Islamic Research Centre for Islamic History and Art.

Riedlmayer, A. (1995) Genocide in Bosnia-Herzegovina: Hearing Before the Commission on Security and Cooperation in Europe, April 4, 1995. Available at: www.csce.gov/index.cfm?FuseAction=Files.Download&FileStore_id (accessed May 25, 2012).

Riedlmayer, A. (2006) Destruction of Cultural Heritage in Bosnia-Herzegovina, 1992–1996: A Post-War Survey of Selected Municipalities. Report prepared for the office of the prosecutor, International Criminal Tribunal of the Former Yugoslvia. Available at: http://archnet.org/system/publications/contents/3481/original/DPC1420.pdf?1384775281 (accessed March 11, 2015).

Rowlands, M. (2002) The Power of Origins: Questions of Cultural Rights. In V. Buchli (ed.), *The Material Culture Reader*. Oxford: Berg Books, pp. 115–133.

Safier, M. (2001) "Confronting Urbicide": Commentaries on September 11. *City*, 5 (3), 416–419.

Scott, J. (2002) World Heritage as a Model for Citizenship: The Case of Cyprus. *International Journal of Heritage Studies*, 8 (2), 99–115.

Sells, M. (1998) *The Bridge Betrayed: Religion and Genocide in Bosnia*. Berkeley: University of California Press.

Sells, M. (2003) Crosses of Blood: Sacred Space, Religion and Violence in Bosnia-Herzegovina. *Sociology of Religion*, 64 (3), 309–331.

Smith, L.J. (2006) *Uses of Heritage*. New York: Routledge.

Sudetic, C. (1993) Mostar's Old Bridge Battered to Death. *New York Times*, November 10. Available at: http://www.nytimes.com/1993/11/10/world/mostar-s-old-bridge-battered-to-death.html (accessed February 28, 2015).

Thrift, N. (2008) *Non-Representational Theory: Space, Politics, Affect*. New York: Routledge.

CHAPTER 19

Heritage Under Fire: Lessons from Iraq for Cultural Property Protection

Benjamin Isakhan

Heritage Under Fire

From as far back as military forces have been waging major campaigns in foreign lands, they have also been engaged in direct and indirect forms of damage to cultural property. This has included damage done to major structures such as castles, temples, and palaces, the destruction of local monuments and statues, and the looting of valuable treasures that are either returned to the country of the victors as a trophy of military conquest or sold off by soldiers looking to make a quick dollar. Military damage to cultural property has also ranged from collateral damage in which heritage sites are destroyed accidentally during a broader campaign to defeat the enemy, to the deliberate targeting of heritage sites precisely because they are thought to represent the ideology, religion, or culture of the enemy, even if the destruction does not specifically advance military goals (Miles 2011). While it is certainly true that such heritage destruction dates as far back as the military campaigns of the world's earliest civilizations, advances in modern military technology over the past two centuries have enabled armies to enact a level of devastation from land, sea, and air unthinkable in earlier times. This became increasingly obvious in the events of both World War I and World War II, which saw an enormous loss of life across the world, as well as the devastation of many significant heritage sites and the loss of invaluable cultural property (Kramer 2007; Simpson 1997).

A Companion to Heritage Studies, First Edition. Edited by William Logan, Máiréad Nic Craith, and Ullrich Kockel.
© 2016 John Wiley & Sons, Inc. Published 2016 by John Wiley & Sons, Inc.

Following this mass devastation, the international community ratified a series of international conventions, including the first such document to address the topic of heritage protection during times of war, the Convention for the Protection of Cultural Property in the Event of Armed Conflict (1954), commonly known as the Hague Convention. This document and its two subsequent protocols sought to establish an international framework for the legal obligations of militaries to avoid doing harm to cultural heritage, and to actively preserve it during times of armed conflict and occupation (Gerstenblith 2008, 2010; Kila 2012). Despite the significance of the Hague Convention, cultural property continued to suffer through many of the key conflicts – both between and within states – of the second half of the twentieth century. This has ranged from major international military endeavors such as Vietnam (Hardy, Cucarzi, and Zolese 2009), through to civil wars such as that in Lebanon (Sandes 2013), as well as domestic "cultural cleansing" campaigns such as that in Cambodia (Winter 2007) and during the Cultural Revolution in China (Liang 2002). It has also included relatively isolated incidents in which specific heritage sites have become a target of particular nationalist or fundamentalist groups – such as the destruction of the Babri Masjid Mosque by Hindu radicals in 1992, and the destruction of the Bamiyan Buddhas in Afghanistan by the Taliban in 2001 (Centlivres 2008; Layton and Thomas 2001).

However, academic investigations into such phenomena achieved perhaps their greatest urgency following the devastating events that tore apart the Balkans in the 1990s. The ethno-religious and asymmetric nature of the war clearly meant that the cultural property of opposing groups became a direct and deliberate target rather than a victim of collateral damage. The purpose of the "deliberate destruction of mosques, churches, museums, civil records, monuments and artifacts in the Balkans" was to suppress "evidence of a culturally diverse and hybrid past, in favor of a mythical 'golden age' of ethnic uniformity" (Layton and Thomas 2001: 12). Alongside their devastating human rights records, evidence of this deliberate targeting of cultural property was submitted to the International Court of Justice and the International Criminal Tribunal for the Former Yugoslavia at the Hague, and used as evidence in the trial of several key military figures, including Slobodan Milosevic (Herscher and Riedlmayer 2002; Riedlmayer 2002).

However, with the major military interventions of the new millennium in Afghanistan (2001 to 2014) and Iraq (2003 to 2011) led by the United States and the United Kingdom, the topic of the obligation to protect cultural property during military operations once again made global headlines. It is important to note that while at the onset of these two wars neither the United States nor the United Kingdom had ratified the Hague Convention (1954), their failure to protect cultural property during the war and subsequent occupation still contravened a vast body of international law (Gerstenblith 2008, 2010). Leaving aside the case of Afghanistan, this chapter traces the plight of Iraq's heritage since the intervention of 2003, which not only brought a devastating period of civilian loss of life and horrific violence, but also unprecedented damage to some of the world's most sensitive historical and heritage sites.

Given the unprecedented degree of cultural and historical devastation that Iraq has suffered since 2003, it is hardly surprising that a whole host of scholarly studies have attempted to document and analyze this destruction (Bogdanos 2005; Rothfield 2009). Foremost among these are a series of edited collections that bring together accounts by leading Iraqi and international archeologists, historians, cultural and heritage workers, diplomats, government officials, and military officers (Emberling and Hanson 2008; Rothfield

2008b; Stone and Bajjaly 2008b). What is curiously absent from the existing literature, however, is a sustained discussion of the various legacies that the Iraq War has had for Cultural Property Protection (CPP) during times of conflict.

This chapter therefore begins with a discussion of the impact of the war and subsequent occupation (2003–2011) on Iraq's heritage, documenting the most significant and devastating instances of heritage damage and destruction that occurred. Moving forward, this chapter continues with a discussion of the grave challenges facing Iraqi heritage beyond the withdrawal of US military forces in the forms of development, neglect, continued hostilities, and inexpert and haphazard excavation, preservation, protection, and restoration. Despite this troubling scenario, this chapter also examines the extent to which the Iraq conflict was a turning point for major Western military operations and the development of CPP programs which aim to better prepare military personnel for protecting cultural property in future conflicts.

Iraqi Heritage under Occupation, 2003–2011

When the bombing of Iraq began on March 19, 2003, it was clear that both the US administration and the British government had all but ignored several warnings concerning the plight of Iraqi heritage sites (Gibson 2008; P.G. Stone 2008). It was also clear that they had neglected to include cultural heritage in the list of things that would be taken into consideration in their relatively underdeveloped post-war plans. Such negligence by the coalition was to have devastating and irrevocable consequences for Iraq's cultural heritage. This began during the battle phase of the war (March 19 to April 9, 2003), the now infamous "shock and awe" campaign, which saw not only the death of many innocent Iraqi civilians and the destruction of sites of military significance, but also untold degrees of "collateral damage" done to sensitive historic and cultural sites across the nation. However, the damage done during the war pales when compared with that done during the subsequent nine-year military occupation of Iraq.

In the days immediately after the fall of Baghdad on April 9, 2003, from approximately April 10 to 15, Iraq witnessed an unprecedented and devastating degree of looting and arson in which key cultural and historical sites were the main target. No doubt the most widely publicized and internationally lamented event in these early days of chaos was the attack on the Iraq National Museum (INM). In the chilling firsthand accounts offered by Donny George, he recalls how, on the first day of looting (April 10), around "300–400 people gathered at the front of the Museum compound ... They were all armed with a variety of hammers, crow-bars, sticks, Kalashnikovs, daggers, and bayonets" (George 2008: 101). Once it began, the looting occurred in waves over the next three days, including both highly coordinated professional thieves who clearly knew where the most precious objects were stored, and opportunistic bandits who stole whatever they could and smashed almost everything else. Unbelievably, when museum staff pleaded with nearby US troops to intervene, they refused. When the looting subsided and it was safe for museum staff to re-enter the complex, they found that the looters had set fires, smashed cabinets, stolen documents and equipment, and destroyed anything that they could not remove (Rothfield 2009). As George writes:

> Fifteen thousand objects were stolen from the galleries and stores of the museum, including Abbasid wooden doors; Sumerian, Akkadian, and Hatraean statues; around five thousand

> cylinder seals from different periods; gold and silver material, along with necklaces and pendants; and other pottery material … [W]hat they could not take they smashed and destroyed. (George 2005: 1–2)

In the aftermath, George, along with US Colonel Matthew Bogdanos, set up an amnesty program in which objects could be returned without question or reprimand (Bogdanos 2005). This has seen some 4000 to 6000 objects returned to the INM, and a further 17,000 objects handed in that had been looted from archeological sites across Iraq (George 2008: 104).

Contemporaneous to the destruction of the INM, the Iraq National Library and Archive (INLA) suffered perhaps an even worse fate. Over the course of nearly one week, looters repeatedly targeted the building, carrying away material and equipment, and even going as far as lighting white phosphorous in the complex to ensure maximum damage. The results of their rampage was devastating, with one reliable estimate claiming that:

> Approximately 25% of the book collections were looted or burned … [A] full 60% of the archival collections were consumed by the fires, including much of the Ottoman-era documents, most of the Royal Hashemite-era documents, and all of those from the Republican period … The INLA also lost 98% of maps and photos and all of their storage cabinets. (Spurr 2008: 276)

To further indicate the scale of this destruction, Fernando Baez has calculated that "almost a million" books were destroyed and that about "ten million documents disappeared" from the INLA (Baez 2008: 270–72). It has also been speculated that much of this damage was deliberate and coordinated by Baathist loyalists who strategically burnt the classified documents of the former regime. Whatever the reason or intention of this destruction, the fact remains that much that was housed in the INLA was unknown to foreign or even Iraqi scholars, and a rich catalogue of Iraq's cultural heritage has now gone up in smoke and is lost forever.

However, while the well-known stories of the INM and the INLA are undeniably tragic, it should not be forgotten that at the same time a whole host of other cultural and historical institutions and sites were being targeted across Iraq. For example, on university campuses across the country – such as the University of Baghdad, Mustansiriya University, and the University of Mosul – looters destroyed degrees and registrars, burned libraries, looted offices, and stole everything from air conditioners to printers. Various other libraries were also attacked, such as the one housed at the College of Physicians, where classical Islamic and medieval texts on medicine were stolen; the library at the Al-Majma Al-Ilmi Al-Iraqi (Iraqi Academy of Sciences) lost manuscripts, periodicals, foreign books and scientific magazines; at the ninth-century Abbasid library, the Bayt Al-Hikma (House of Wisdom), looters took off with innumerable and priceless documents and totally destroyed an exhibition of materials relating to the Ottoman Empire (Baez 2008: 275–76); and at the Al-Awfaq Library in Baghdad, more than 5000 classical Islamic manuscripts were either stolen or turned to ash in another violent rampage. Museums and art galleries across the country also suffered, including those in Mosul, Basra, Kufa, Najaf, Nasiriyah, and Tikrit (Nisbett 2007). Perhaps most devastating among these was Iraq's Museum of Modern Art, where "[e]ight thousand works of art were removed," although around 3000 of these have since been recovered (Ghaidan 2008: 94). In terms of damage done to historic buildings, Usam Ghaidan has reported that in the earliest days of the occupation, the twelfth-century Abbasid palace had been damaged, as was the sixteenth-century Saray Mosque built by the famed Ottoman sultan Suleiman the Magnificent, as well as the Hashemite-era Parliament House. Famous Iraqi marketplaces, such as the Suq Al-Sari, the oldest book market in the Islamic world, and the historic Suq Al-Shorja in central Baghdad, have been destroyed by looting and arson. As Ghaidan goes on to note, between them these buildings not only catalogue every epoch of Iraq's long cultural history, they also "chronicle every architectural style of Iraq's heritage stock: courtyards, domes, vaults, iwans, and exposed brick walls, all of superior quality" (Ghaidan 2008: 93).

In addition to such wanton destruction, throughout the US-led occupation of Iraq, coalition forces set up a number of their key military bases at historically or culturally sensitive sites, such as in Saddam's palaces, government buildings, the Nasiriyah Museum, archeological sites, historic mosques, and the Martyr's Memorial. Perhaps the most devastating example is the military base that was set up by US troops at one of the world's most significant archeological sites, the ancient city of Babylon (Babel). Located around 90 kilometers south of Baghdad, Babylon was a US command post (known as Camp Alpha) from April 2003 until December 2004. The best accounts of the devastation incurred on this sensitive site are written by two Iraqi archeologists, Mariam Umran Moussa and Zainab Bahrani, who worked together to not only document the destruction but in their joint efforts to lobby the US to end their use of the site (Bahrani 2008; Moussa 2008). In her account of the destruction, Moussa painstakingly details the fact that the troops dug a series of approximately 8 trenches and 14 pits in and around the site, ranging up to 600 square meters in size. The soil – much of it riddled with artifacts – was then used to construct barriers, to fill sandbags, and to develop roads. They also scraped and leveled parts of the site in order to build a car park for military and other heavy equipment, build living quarters, and build two helipads. The damage also includes that done to the Ishtar Gate and the Procession Street of the ancient city. For example, nine of the animal bodies which adorned the Ishtar Gate and represent the mythical dragon emblem of the ancient god Marduk, the god of Babel, went missing (Moussa 2008: 145–49).

Sadly, as Bahrani has pointed out, Babylon is not the only archeological site to have been utilized by the US military as a base, and "at least seven or eight historical sites have been used in this way" since the start of the war (Bahrani 2008: 169). This tragedy is deepened by the fact that we know very little about the destruction that has gone on at these other sites. This was followed in 2005, when coalition forces used the ninth-century Malwiyya minaret at the Great Mosque of Samarra as the site for the construction of a barracks and training camp for 1500 members of the Iraqi National Police, leading to enemy fire on the site and permanent damage to the minaret (Stone and Bajjaly 2008a: 12). Together, the disregard for the key archeological sites of ancient Mesopotamia, as well as classical Islamic mosques, reveal the US-led coalition's disregard and disdain for the entire spectrum of Iraq's cultural heritage.

However, the military coalition also extended this disregard to Baathist sites, a whole collection of which were utilized by foreign occupying forces as military bases (Isakhan 2011). Two examples are worth mentioning here. The first occurred in January 2004, when the military coalition used the Baghdad Martyr's Memorial (Shaheed monument) as a military base. This site serves as a people's shrine dedicated to the 500,000 Iraqi soldiers who died defending their country in an unpopular, lengthy, and brutal war with Iran in the 1980s. Graffiti of US army mottos covered many of the names of the dead.

Damage has also been done to the mausoleum dedicated to the "father of pan-Arabism" and the co-founder of the Baath Party, Michel Aflaq. The site comprises a tomb and a statue built by Saddam Hussein upon Aflaq's death in 1989. As part of their program to symbolically eradicate the Baathist regime from Iraq, the mausoleum was initially slated for demolition by the Coalition Provisional Authority (CPA) before the decision sparked an outcry among Iraqi and international intellectuals. Instead, from 2003 to 2006, Aflaq's mausoleum, which falls inside Baghdad's Green Zone, was reportedly turned into something of a recreation center cum makeshift barracks for occupying forces. On the ground floor, and surrounding the tomb of Aflaq, soldiers would use various exercise equipment, as well as "foosball" tables. Directly underneath Aflaq's grave, soldiers slept in cramped plywood quarters. One cannot help but baulk at the insensitivity of turning such monuments into military bases for use by a foreign occupying power. Imagine the use of comparable historical sites in other nations: consider graffiti in a foreign language obscuring the names on the Vietnam memorial, or a foosball table in the Lincoln memorial, to begin to come to terms with how such actions might offend the Iraqi people.

Perhaps one of the most tragic and devastating elements of Iraq's cultural and historical destruction is that of the systematic looting of Iraq's sensitive archeological sites, particularly those in the south. Many of these sites have fallen prey to bands of treasure hunters and looters, who dig and smash their way through the underground catacombs in search of the highly prized artifacts of the ancient world. In fact this began the day the war started, and has intensified over the ensuing years, extending to sites such as those of Umma, Hatra, Nineveh, Ur, Nippur and Ashur (Hamdani 2008; E.C. Stone 2008). The people enacting this depredation range from destitute farmers who have no other source of income, through to the highly coordinated efforts of international black-market operatives. According to Melissa Nisbett, these more coordinated efforts involve "around 300 armed men who are using bulldozers and taking truckloads of artifacts, whilst guarded by another 40 men with Kalashnikovs" (Nisbett 2007). These very powerful gangs are then able to use their wealth and firearms to smuggle the antiquities out of Iraq and on to the international black market (Brodie 2008).

What is particularly devastating about this looting is that archeological relics lose a significant proportion of their scientific value once they are removed from their context and association (Hanson 2008). This means that even when some of these objects are recovered, the secret histories that they may once have revealed to the trained archeologist have been lost forever. To give an indication of just how widespread this devastation is, Lawrence Rothfield has estimated that "Iraq's ten thousand officially recognized sites [are] being destroyed at a rate of roughly 10 per cent per year" (Rothfield 2008a: xv). While the looting of archeological sites in remote rural areas is an extraordinarily difficult thing to prevent, the fact is that the coalition forces did not take early, decisive, or adequate action to prevent this devastating loss of Iraqi heritage.

Another important – but surprisingly understudied – aspect of cultural property destruction that has occurred since 2003 is that of the damage done to important religious sites such as mosques, shrines, and churches. The power vacuum that emerged following the toppling of the Baathist regime in 2003 was filled by a series of fundamentalists and ethno-religious power-mongers who viewed it as an opportunity to pedal their own relatively narrow and very divisive political rhetoric (Davis 2007; Isakhan 2012a). Such political divisions were a forerunner to the sharp upsurge in ethno-religious-motivated violence that was to follow. Indeed, through 2006 and 2007, Iraq descended into a particularly dark and unprecedented period with grim and complex battles being fought between the occupying forces, the Iraqi armed services, various insurgent groups, and terrorist organizations, as well as those between competing ethno-religious sectarian militias (Dawisha 2009: 258–71). Although things were generally more peaceful in the Kurdish north, the most horrific violence came with the dramatic division between the Sunni Arab minority (who had ruled the nation since 1921) and the Shia Arab majority (who had been actively oppressed and now held the bulk of power in the new Iraq). Such violence is said to have peaked after the bombing of the gold-domed tenth-century Al-Askari Mosque in Samarra on February 22, 2006 (it was bombed again on June 13, 2007). This site is highly revered by the Shia Arab population as the mausoleum of the tenth and eleventh *imams* of their faith. It is an incredibly important and significant heritage site, with deep historical and religious value for the Shia Arab population and for the world. It was deliberately targeted by Sunni insurgents (most likely Al-Qaeda in Iraq), and was clearly a "symbolic" attack – rather than a conventional terrorist or military attack – in the sense that while the attack almost destroyed the mosque it did not injure or kill a single person. This speaks volumes about the intention of the perpetrators to inflame passions rather than to target enemies or civilians.

While the bombing of the Al-Askari Mosque was certainly not the first incident in which religious sites were targeted after 2003, it not only proved to be a catalyst for ethno-religious violence but also for subsequent attacks on other heritage sites. For example, within 24 hours of the bombing of the Al-Askari Mosque in 2006, around 32 Sunni mosques were attacked across Iraq, up from zero the day before, and the death toll in Sunni majority areas spiked from approximately 5 people per day to 63 the day after (Isakhan 2012b, 2013a). Indeed, the ruins of the Al-Askari Mosque came to symbolize Iraq's alleged descent into civil war, and the bombing was thought of as a key turning point in relations between Sunni and Shia Arabs in Iraq (Fearon 2007).

The Legacy of Iraq for Cultural Property Protection during Times of War

Clearly, since the start of the US- and UK-led intervention in 2003, Iraq has suffered an extraordinary period of cultural and historical depredation. While this destruction is of particular concern because it represents the loss of some of humankind's greatest achievements and most spectacular wonders, it is also worth noting that it has had several distinct legacies that need to be considered here. The first such legacy concerns the impact that such destruction has had on Iraq. To begin with, the vast majority of heritage destruction in Iraq cannot be undone, and much has been lost forever: manuscripts that are turned to ash can never be studied by historians; looted archeological material – even if recovered – have lost the bulk of their scientific value; and important historical and religious sites that have been torn apart by deadly attacks will never regain their original architectural majesty. A second factor compounds these tragic losses, namely that both the United States and the United Kingdom failed to develop plans and policies that would protect Iraqi heritage beyond the final withdrawal of troops at the end of 2011. With the deadly onslaught of the Islamic State of Iraq and Syria (ISIS) in 2014, looting at archeological sites across Iraq continues unabated, as does ethno-religious sectarian attacks on places of religious significance (Isakhan 2015).

Beyond this, Iraq's cultural heritage also faces grave challenges in the face of an ever-widening knowledge and skills gap that has resulted from 35 years of Baathist dictatorship, 12 years of international sanctions and 9 years of military occupation. Iraqi heritage is also threatened by various additional factors: rapid and haphazard urban development and infrastructure projects (such as the recent plans for an oil pipeline to pass through the site of Babylon); neglect, with various sites left to decay as funds are understandably diverted to more urgent civil needs, such as potable water, sewerage, and electricity; and inexpert and piecemeal excavation, preservation, protection, and restoration.

Beyond this is the even more sensitive legacy of the destruction of Iraq's cultural heritage since 2003, and its intimate relationship to various competing, contested, and overlapping notions of identity. No matter what their religious or political persuasion, or their ethnic or cultural identity, for most Iraqis the past is not a distant and impenetrable discourse; it is a tangible force that informs the present. This is just as true for pious Shia Arabs who revere the holy sites found in Najaf and Karbala as it is for Assyrians who connect to Iraq's strong Christian heritage, or Sunni Arabs who admire the halcyon days of the Abbasid caliphate of Baghdad, or Kurds who may identify strongly with the achievements of Kurdish figures such as Salah Ad-Din. What is evident here is that Iraq is a complex ideological landscape in which the symbols, monuments, and artifacts of the past play a central role in the highly politicized efforts of a number of competing factions to assert notions of a historically legitimate identity (Isakhan 2011). As the case of the Al-Askari Mosque demonstrates, damage and destruction to heritage sites not only destroys the building itself, but can also be perceived as an attack on the identity of the community who derive significant cultural or religious meaning from that site. This can lead to a breakdown in social cohesion, as well as deadly waves of counter-attacks on the heritage sites and communities of the "other." Considering the scale of heritage destruction in Iraq since 2003, it is little wonder that inter-communal tension and violence is such a prominent sociopolitical force in the complex identity politics of contemporary Iraq (Isakhan 2013b, 2014).

If there is a silver lining to this very dark cloud, it is in the fact that the mass devastation of Iraqi heritage from 2003 onwards has also had an important legacy for the ways the United States, United Kingdom, and other militaries approach the issue of CPP during military operations (Kila and Zeidler 2013; Rush 2010). It is fair to say that the major failures of CPP in Iraq, such as the looting of the INM and the damage done during the military occupation of Babylon, were not only strategic mistakes, but also very bad public relations for the coalition. While this is certainly true for an international community and global media already skeptical about the merits and legality of the war, it was also bad public relations within Iraq, where various insurgents, terrorists, and militias used the failure to protect Iraq's cultural property as fodder in their deadly propaganda campaigns. The message was clear: coalition forces did not respect the proud history and culture of the Iraqi people.

To counter this overwhelmingly negative image, the United States and United Kingdom made several significant changes in their approach to CPP. First and foremost, although it did take several years, the destruction of heritage in Iraq provided the final impetus for the United States to finally ratify the Hague Convention (1954) in 2009, and has put additional pressure on the United Kingdom to do the same (Gerstenblith 2008, 2010).[1] Secondly, it saw the recruitment of many senior heritage professionals (archeologists, heritage conservation experts, and so on) who worked with the US and UK militaries in the field (Siebrandt 2010; Wegener 2010). These heritage experts also worked alongside local experts, authorities, and communities to protect and restore heritage sites, and develop initiatives such as local museums, tourism projects, and micro-finance initiatives associated with cultural heritage (Curtis 2008; Roberts and Roberts 2013). On a much larger scale, the United States and United Kingdom, along with the Iraqi government and various stakeholders, also funded several large-scale projects to restore significant heritage sites damaged since 2003, including the Future of Babylon Project and the restoration of the INM. Thirdly, various heritage professionals worked to develop a series of extensive and multistage programs for the training of military personnel in issues pertaining to CPP (Kila and Zeidler 2013; Rush 2010). This ranged from issuing soldiers with decks of playing cards that were adorned with images and information about Iraq's most important heritage sites, through to setting up a series of detailed training programs and strict protocols and procedures which enable soldiers to identify and manage any potential adverse effects to heritage sites during military operations.

Apart from its obvious good PR value, these types of initiatives had a series of positive outcomes. It is worth giving just one example to illustrate the point. At the ziggurat at Aqar Quf, west of Baghdad, US military personnel helped to protect and preserve the site and to stimulate the local economy via the development of tourism infrastructure. This had multiple positive outcomes, including "increase[d] security, further legitimizing local government … [and] … provid[ing] alternatives for unemployed workers (usually military age males) … away from conducting attacks against civilian or military targets" (Roberts and Roberts 2013: 171). Whatever ones views on the merits of the Iraq War or the many failings of the occupation, such efforts not only served to protect cultural property and give meaningful jobs to local constituents, but, most importantly, they saved lives.

Conclusion

With the invasion and occupation of Iraq since 2003, the nation has witnessed an unprecedented degree of cultural and historical destruction. The failures of the US- and UK-led occupation to protect key sites, and their use of others as military bases, have seen the supposed liberators deliver some of the more devastating blows to Iraq's past. In addition, Iraqi civilians have ransacked and vandalized important sites, including major institutions, libraries, and museums, as well as their systematic and highly coordinated efforts to inexpertly excavate places of enormous archeological significance, often aided and abetted by foreigners keen to capitalize on the highly sought after treasure. Finally, the ongoing hostility between varying factions within Iraq has had ruinous consequences for Iraq's cultural heritage, with artifacts, symbols, and monuments so often caught in the cross fire or deliberately targeted by opposing ethno-sectarian groups.

While the situation for cultural heritage in Iraq has continued to face a host of challenges beyond the withdrawal of foreign troops at the end of 2011, the Iraq War has left behind a complex legacy for the future of CPP in times of conflict. While the lessons learned from important projects such as the ziggurat at Aqar Quf came too late for many sites which had been damaged or destroyed since 2003, they do point to the important legacy of the Iraq War for CPP during military operations. This is most clearly demonstrated in the approach taken by major Western militaries since

Iraq, especially in the case of the NATO intervention in Libya in 2011, where the precision strikes of Operation Unified Protector have been widely praised for avoiding damage to heritage sites (Kila and Zeidler 2013). Although the brief NATO campaign in Libya cannot be compared to the major military intervention and subsequent occupation that occurred in Iraq, it does provide hope that future conflicts will take seriously the importance of CPP, and that the tragedy of Iraq's heritage losses will never again occur at the hands of a major military power. Only time will tell if this hope is realized.

Note

1 At the time of writing (February 2015) the United Kingdom has still not ratified the Hague Convention.

References

Legislation

Convention for the Protection of Cultural Property in the Event of Armed Conflict (Hague Convention) (UNESCO, 1954). Available at: http://unesdoc.unesco.org/images/0008/000824/082464mb.pdf (accessed March 19, 2015).

Other Works

Baez, F. (2008 [2004]) *A Universal History of the Destruction of Books: From Ancient Sumer to Modern Iraq*, trans. A. MacAdam. New York: Atlas.

Bahrani, Z. (2008) The Battle for Babylon. In P.G. Stone and J.F. Bajjaly (eds), *The Destruction of Cultural Heritage in Iraq*. Woodbridge: Boydell, pp. 165–171.

Bogdanos, M. (2005) *Thieves of Baghdad: One Marine's Passion for Ancient Civilizations and the Journey to Recover the World's Greatest Stolen Treasures*. New York: Bloomsbury.

Brodie, N. (2008) The Western Market in Iraqi Antiquities. In L. Rothfield (ed.), *Antiquities Under Siege: Cultural Heritage Protection after the Iraq War*. Lanham, MD: Alta Mira Press, pp. 63–73.

Centlivres, P. (2008) The Controversy over the Buddhas of Bamiyan. *South Asian Multidisciplinary Academic Journal*, 2. Available: http://samaj.revues.org/992 (accessed February 25, 2015).

Curtis, J. (2008) The Role of the British Museum in the Protection of the Iraqi Cultural Heritage. In P.G. Stone, and J.F. Bajjaly (eds), *The Destruction of Cultural Heritage in Iraq*. Woodbridge: Boydell, pp. 201–212.

Davis, E. (2007) The Formation of Political Identities in Ethnically Divided Societies: Implications for a Democratic Transition in Iraq. *American Academic Research Institute in Iraq Newsletter*, 2 (1), 3–4.

Dawisha, A. (2009) *Iraq: A Political History from Independence to Occupation*. Princeton: Princeton University Press.

Emberling, G., and Hanson, K. (eds) (2008) *Catastrophe! The Looting and Destruction of Iraq's Past*. Chicago: Oriental Institute of the University of Chicago.

Fearon, J.D. (2007) Iraq's Civil War. *Foreign Affairs*, 86 (2), 2–15.

George, D. (2005) Foreword. In M. Polk and A.M.H. Schuster (eds), *The Looting of the Iraq Museum, Baghdad: The Lost Legacy of Ancient Mesopotamia*. New York: Harry N. Abrams, pp. 1–3.

George, D. (2008) The Looting of the Iraq National Museum. In P.G. Stone, and J.F. Bajjaly (eds), *The Destruction of Cultural Heritage in Iraq*. Woodbridge: Boydell, pp. 97–107.

Gerstenblith, P. (2008) The 1954 Hague Convention on the Protection of Cultural Property in the Event of Armed Conflict: Its Background and Prospects for Ratification in the United States. In L. Rothfield (ed.), *Antiquities Under Siege: Cultural Heritage Protection after the Iraq War*. Lanham, MD: Alta Mira Press, pp. 79–88.

Gerstenblith, P. (2010) The Obligations Contained in International Traeties of Armed Forces to Protect Cultural Heritage in Times of Armed Conflict. In L. Rush (ed.), *Archaeology, Cultural Property and the Military*. Woodbridge: Boydell, pp. 1–14.

Ghaidan, U. (2008) Damage to Iraq's Wider Heritage. In P.G. Stone and J.F. Bajjaly (eds), *The Destruction of Cultural Heritage in Iraq*. Woodbridge: Boydell, pp. 85–96.

Gibson, M. (2008) The Looting of the Iraq Museum in Context. In G. Emberling and K. Hanson (eds), *Catastrophe! The Looting and Destruction of Iraq's Past*. Chicago: Oriental Institute of the University of Chicago, pp. 13–18.

Hamdani, A. (2008) The Damage Sustained to the Ancient City of Ur. In P.G. Stone, and J.F. Bajjaly (eds), *The Destruction of Cultural Heritage in Iraq*. Woodbridge: Boydell, pp. 151–156.

Hanson, K. (2008) Why Does Archaeological Context Matter? In G. Emberling and K. Hanson (eds), *Catastrophe! The Looting and Destruction of Iraq's Past*. Chicago: Oriental Institute of the University of Chicago, pp. 45–49.

Hardy, A., Cucarzi, M., and Zolese, P. (eds) (2009) *Champa and the Archaeology of My San*. Singapore: National University of Singapore Press.

Herscher, A., and Riedlmayer, A.J. (2002) The Destruction of Cultural Heritage in Kosovo, 1998–1999: A Post-War Survey. The Case of *Prosecutor v. Slobodan Milosevic (No. P486)*. The Hague: International Criminal Tribunal for the Former Yugoslavia.

Isakhan, B. (2011) Targeting the Symbolic Dimension of Baathist Iraq: Cultural Destruction, Historial Memory and National Identity. *Middle East Journal of Culture and Communication*, 4 (3), 257–281.

Isakhan, B. (2012a) *Democracy in Iraq: History, Politics, Discourse*. London: Ashgate.

Isakhan, B. (2012b) Measuring the Destruction of Heritage and Spikes of Violence in Iraq. Paper presented at the Centre for Middle East Studies, University of California at Berkeley, October 25.

Isakhan, B. (2013a) Bombing Mosques and Spikes in Violence in Iraq: Heritage Destruction and Ethno-Sectarian Violence, 2006/7. Paper presented at the Cambridge Heritage Research Group, Cambridge University, September 16.

Isakhan, B. (2013b) Heritage Destruction and Spikes in Violence: The Case of Iraq. In J.D. Kila and J. Zeidler (eds), *Cultural Heritage in the Crosshairs: Protecting Cultural Property During Conflict*. Lieden: Brill, pp. 219–248.

Isakhan, B. (2014) Creating the Iraqi Cultural Property Destruction Database: Calculating a Heritage Destruction Index. *International Journal of Heritage Studies*, 21 (1), 1–21.

Isakhan, B. (ed.) (2015) *The Legacy of Iraq: From the 2003 War to the "Islamic State"*. Edinburgh/New York: Edinburgh University Press/Oxford University Press.

Kila, J.D. (2012) *Heritage Under Siege: Military Implementation of Cultural Property Protection Following the 1954 Hague Convention*. Leiden: Brill.

Kila, J.D., and Zeidler, J. (eds) (2013) *Cultural Heritage in the Crosshairs: Protecting Cultural Property During Conflict*. Lieden: Brill.

Kramer, A. (2007) *Dynamic of Destruction: Culture and Mass Killing in the First World War*. Oxford: Oxford University Press.

Layton, R., and Thomas, J. (2001) Introduction: The Destruction and Conservation of Cultural Property. In R. Layton, P.G. Stone, and J. Thomas (eds), *Destruction and Conservation of Cultural Property*. London: Routledge, pp. 1–21.

Liang, W. (2002) The Confucius Temple Tragedy of the Cultural Revolution. In T.A. Wilson (ed.), *On Sacred Grounds: Culture, Society, Politics, and the Formation of the Cult of Confucius*. Cambridge, MA: Harvard University Press, pp. 376–400.

Miles, M.M. (2011) Still in the Aftermath of Waterloo: A Brief History of Decisions about Restitution. In P.G. Stone (ed.), *Cultural Heritage, Ethics, and the Military*. Woodbridge: Boydell, pp. 29–42.

Moussa, M.U. (2008) The Damages Sustained to the Ancient City of Babel as a Consequence of the Military Presence of Coalition Forces in 2003. In P.G. Stone, and J.F. Bajjaly (eds), *The Destruction of Cultural Heritage in Iraq*. Woodbridge: Boydell, pp. 143–150.

Nisbett, M. (2007) The End of History? The Impact of the Gulf Wars (1990–1991 and 2003–present) on Iraq's Cultural Heritage. *Cultural Policy, Criticism and Management Research*, 2. Available at: http://culturalpolicyjournal.wordpress.com/past-issues/issue-no-2/ (accessed February 25, 2015).

Riedlmayer, A.J. (2002) Destruction of Cultural Heritage in Bosnia-Herzegovina, 1992–1996: A Post-War Survey of Selected Municipalities. The Case of *Prosecutor v. Slobodan Milosevic (No. P486)*. The Hague: International Criminal Tribunal for the Former Yugoslavia.

Roberts, B.A., and Roberts, G.B. (2013) A Case Study in Cultural Heritage Protection in a Time of War. In J.D. Kila, and J. Zeidler (eds), *Cultural Heritage in the Crosshairs: Protecting Cultural Property During Conflict*. Lieden: Brill, pp. 169–193.

Rothfield, L. (2008a) Introduction. In L. Rothfield (ed.), *Antiquities Under Siege: Cultural Heritage Protection after the Iraq War*. Lanham, MD: Alta Mira Press, pp. xv–xx.

Rothfield, L. (ed.) (2008b) *Antiquities Under Siege: Cultural Heritage Protection after the Iraq War*. Lanham, MD: Alta Mira Press.

Rothfield, L. (2009) *The Rape of Mesopotamia: Behind the Looting of the Iraq Museum*. Chicago: University of Chicago Press.

Rush, L. (ed.) (2010) *Archaeology, Cultural Property and the Military*. Woodbridge: Boydell.

Sandes, C.A. (2013) Urban Cultural Heritage and Armed Conflict: The Case of Beriut Central District. In J.D. Kila, and J. Zeidler (eds), *Cultural Heritage in the Crosshairs: Protecting Cultural Property During Conflict*. Lieden: Brill, pp. 287–313.

Siebrandt, D.C. (2010) US Military Support of Cultural Heritage Awareness and Preservation in Post-Conflict Iraq. In L. Rush (ed.), *Archaeology, Cultural Property and the Military*. Woodbridge: Boydell, pp. 126–137.

Simpson, E. (ed.) (1997) *The Spoils of War: World War II and Its Aftermath: The Loss, Reappearance and Recovery of Cultural Property*. New York: Harry N. Abrams.

Spurr, J. (2008) Iraqi Libraries and Archives in Peril. In P.G. Stone, and J.F. Bajjaly (eds), *The Destruction of Cultural Heritage in Iraq*. Woodbridge: Boydell, pp. 273–281.

Stone, E.C. (2008) Archaeological Site Looting: The Destruction of Cultural Heritage in Southern Iraq. In G. Emberling and K. Hanson (eds), *Catastrophe! The Looting and Destruction of Iraq's Past*. Chicago: Oriental Institute of the University of Chicago, pp. 65–80.

Stone, P.G. (2008) The Identification and Protection of Cultural Heritage during the Iraq Conflict: A Peculiarly English Tale. In P.G. Stone, and J.F. Bajjaly (eds), *The Destruction of Cultural Heritage in Iraq*. Woodbridge: Boydell, pp. 73–84.

Stone, P.G., and Bajjaly, J.F. (2008a) Introduction. In P.G. Stone, and J.F. Bajjaly (eds), *The Destruction of Cultural Heritage in Iraq*. Woodbridge: Boydell, pp. 1–17.

Stone, P.G., and Bajjaly, J.F. (eds) (2008b) *The Destruction of Cultural Heritage in Iraq*. Woodbridge: Boydell.

Wegener, C. (2010) US Army Civil Affairs: Protecting Cultural Property, Past and Future. In L. Rush (ed.), *Archaeology, Cultural Property and the Military*. Woodbridge: Boydell, pp. 34–40.

Winter, T. (2007) *Post-Conflict Heritage, Postcolonial Tourism: Culture, Politics and Development at Angkor*. London: Routledge.

CHAPTER 20 The Intentional Destruction of Heritage: Bamiyan and Timbuktu

Christian Manhart

In recent years, cultural heritage has increasingly become the target of military and non-military destruction aimed at harming the opponent's cultural identity or attempting to sever the cross-cultural connections between different ethnic, religious, or social groups. In certain cases, we can even observe the deliberate destruction of a people's own cultural identity for the sake of ideology, as occurred in Afghanistan in 2001 and in Mali in 2012 and 2013. In this chapter, I intend to examine these two cases in more detail. I will also explain UNESCO's dual mandate to build peace and protect heritage, as stipulated in its Constitution and the activities to achieve these goals in Afghanistan and Mali.[1]

The Bamiyan Buddhas of Afghanistan

On February 26, 2001, the Islamic Emirate of Afghanistan issued the following edict from the city of Kandahar:

> On the basis of consultations between the religious leaders of the Islamic Emirate of Afghanistan, the religious judgments of the Ulema and the rulings of the Supreme Court of the Islamic Emirate of Afghanistan, all statues and non-Islamic shrines located in the different parts of the Islamic Emirate of Afghanistan must be destroyed. These statues have been and remain shrines of infidels and these infidels continue to worship and

A Companion to Heritage Studies, First Edition. Edited by William Logan, Máiréad Nic Craith, and Ullrich Kockel.
© 2016 John Wiley & Sons, Inc. Published 2016 by John Wiley & Sons, Inc.

> respect these shrines. Allah almighty is the only real shrine and all false shrines should be smashed. Therefore, the Supreme Leader of the Islamic Emirate of Afghanistan has ordered all the representatives of the Ministry of the Promotion of Virtue and Suppression of Vice and of the Ministry of Information and Culture to destroy all the statues. As ordered, by the Ulema and the Supreme Court of the Islamic Emirate of Afghanistan, all statues must be annihilated so that no one can worship or respect them in the future. (cited in Manhart 2009: 38)

As soon as this order was made public, UNESCO issued appeals to the Taliban leaders, exhorting them to preserve Afghan cultural heritage. These appeals were widely carried by the international press. The director-general of UNESCO addressed a personal letter to the Taliban leader, Mullah Omar, on February 28. The director-general also obtained the full support of the Islamic countries for UNESCO's activities to save Afghan cultural heritage. On March 1, Pierre Lafrance, special representative of the director-general, left for Islamabad, Kandahar, Kabul, the United Arab Emirates, Qatar, and Saudi Arabia. A number of Muslim religious leaders (*ulema*) from Egypt, Iraq, and Pakistan intervened at the request of UNESCO, issuing *fatwa*s against the Taliban's order. UNESCO launched an international petition for the safeguarding of Afghan cultural heritage on its web site, and a special funds-in-trust account has been created for this purpose. The crisis gained a great deal of international media attention, and UNESCO also received many letters of support for its actions in this matter from heads of state, ministers, other international organizations, and individuals. The director-general personally contacted the presidents of Egypt and Pakistan, as well as of the Organization of the Islamic Conference, all of whom tried to use their influence to persuade the Taliban to cancel the order. Following these interventions, a delegation of 11 international Muslim leaders went to Kandahar in order to try to convince Mullah Omar and his advisors that the Koran does not prescribe the destruction of statues. The emir of Qatar generously provided his private airplane to enable the group of *ulema* to travel directly to Kandahar. The meeting with Mullah Omar and his advisors lasted 4 hours and was, as we know, unfortunately not successful.

All these political, moral, and religious interventions proved to be in vain, and in March 2001, the Taliban destroyed not only the Buddhas of Bamiyan, but also a large number of statues in different Afghan museums.

Why did these efforts fail? Initially, in 1999 and 2000, the Taliban regime had rather efficiently forbidden the smuggling of antiquities and opium production, which were considered un-Islamic. Perhaps they hoped that they would rise in the estimation of the international community thanks to these measures. However, the opposite was the case. The country became even more isolated following Resolution 1333 of the UN Security Council (UNSC 2000), which urges all UN Member States to cease commerce with Afghanistan, to close all representation and offices of the Taliban, to freeze all their financial assets, to close all offices of Ariana (the national Afghan airline), and so on.

It also has to be noted that, at the time, Afghanistan faced a particularly harsh winter, with temperatures in the Bamiyan Valley temperatures falling as low as minus 40° Fahrenheit. This was preceded by a severe drought in summer 2000. The Afghan people were dying of cold and hunger in their thousands, and in spite of that, the international media had lost interest in Afghanistan. Almost no international aid was extended to the Afghans. It seemed as though the international community had turned its back on the country.

This situation strengthened the Taliban's links to Al-Qaeda even more – a fact the world realized only on September 11, 2001, with the destruction of the Twin Towers

Figure 20.1 Large Buddha niche, Bamiyan. Source: UNESCO/Graciela Gonzalez Brigas.

in New York City. However, in February and March of the same year, the Taliban wanted to attract the world's attention to Afghanistan and themselves, and the best means they found to do so was to destroy the Bamiyan statues. As far as attracting the world's attention was concerned, the operation was a total success, and the media was full of reports about this crime against cultural heritage. The consequence of this extreme radicalization of the Taliban was, however, also the war the United States fought in the fall of the same year, and which marked for the time being the end of the Taliban regime in Afghanistan.

It is worth mentioning that close contacts were kept just before and during the war between the US military and UNESCO for the protection of cultural sites in Afghanistan. UNESCO provided the US military with a list of important sites, including their geographical coordinates, which should be avoided by the military and protected from destruction and looting. This cooperation proved to very efficient, and no site was harmed during this war, with one exception: the fortress of Mazar-i-Sharif, in which the remaining Taliban fighters gathered at the end of the war, and which was slightly damaged by fighting. The US Army even employed an archeologist. It is therefore surprising that the same contacts between UNESCO and the US military were less fruitful in the case of the second Iraq War, where the Iraq National Museum and important archeological sites were left unprotected and exposed to looting and damage (see Isakhan, this volume).

Why were the international conventions in the field of culture insufficient to protect Afghan cultural heritage from the Taliban? The state of Afghanistan has not ratified the Convention for the Protection of Cultural Property in the Event of Armed Conflict (1954), commonly known as the Hague Convention. In 1979 it ratified the Convention Concerning the Protection of the World Cultural and Natural Heritage, or World Heritage Convention (1972), but no site was inscribed on the World Heritage List at the time. Only in July 2003 was the Bamiyan site inscribed on both the UNESCO World Heritage List and the List of World Heritage in Danger as part of the Cultural Landscape and Archaeological Remains of the Bamiyan Valley. However, as the Taliban regime was not recognized by the UN and the international community, except for Saudi Arabia, Pakistan, and the United Arab Emirates, it did not feel bound by any international convention. Also, at that moment the UN did not have any means to enforce conventions in Afghanistan.

In order to examine the position of the Muslim world toward the preservation of Islamic and non-Islamic heritage, UNESCO organized a joint international conference with the Organization of the Islamic Conference (OIC), the Islamic Educational, Scientific and Cultural Organization (ISESCO), and the Arab League Educational, Cultural and Scientific Organization (ALECSO). Those present included a number of *ulema*, and the conference met in December 2001 in Doha, Qatar (see UNESCO 2005). The conference resulted in a clear declaration of principles in favor of the protection of cultural heritage, including statues that can be appealed to in the future (UNESCO 2005).

It is worth mentioning one aspect of the destruction of the Bamiyan statues which could be considered positively: the end of disputes between art historians about their age, with competing proposals that they date from a period between the fourth and the eighth century AD. The exact dating of the statues was only possible through their destruction, liberating organic material that allowed scientific dating using carbon 14. Experts discovered in the rubble some wooden pegs and pieces of ropes, which the Buddhist monks had originally used to build the folds of cloth on the plastered surface. These pieces were examined in the scientific laboratory of the Bavarian Cultural Heritage Authority in Munich, Germany, and the results revealed that the Small Buddha originated from AD 550, and the Large Buddha from AD 600 (both dates plus or minus 20 years).

International Preservation Efforts

UNESCO, the UN's only specialized agency having responsibility for culture, had a duty to take action in order to try to avert future cultural disasters of this type. It responds firmly to the challenge of rehabilitating Afghanistan's endangered cultural heritage, which has suffered irreversible damage and loss during the past two decades of war and civil unrest. The safeguarding of all aspects of cultural heritage in the country, both tangible and intangible, including museums, monuments, archeological sites, music, art, and traditional crafts, is of particular significance in terms of strengthening cultural identity and a sense of national integrity. Cultural heritage can become a point of mutual interest for former adversaries, enabling them to rebuild ties, to engage in dialogue, and to work together in shaping a common future. UNESCO's strategy is to assist in the reestablishment of links between the populations concerned and their cultural history, helping them to develop a sense of common ownership of monuments that represent the cultural heritage of different segments of society. Heritage conservation also serves as a vector for sustainable development by offering training in different techniques, employment opportunities, and the building of the potential for future cultural tourism. This strategy is therefore directly linked to the nation-building process within the framework of the United Nation's mandate and concerted international efforts for rehabilitating Afghanistan.

With reference to the UN secretary-general's dictum during the January 2002 Afghanistan conference held in Tokyo, "Our challenge is to help the Afghans help themselves,"[2] policies and activities for the safeguarding of Afghanistan's cultural heritage focus on training and capacity-building activities related to preservation. In May 2002, UNESCO and the Afghan Ministry of Information and Culture organized the first International Seminar on the Rehabilitation of Afghanistan's Cultural Heritage, held in Kabul, which gathered 107 specialists in Afghan cultural heritage, as well as representatives of donor countries and institutions. The meeting was opened by President Hamid Karzai in the presence of his entire cabinet of ministers. Under the chairmanship of H.E. Makhdoum Raheen, the Afghan minister of information and culture, the participants gave presentations on the state of conservation of cultural sites across the country and discussed programs and coordination for the first conservation measures to be taken. The seminar resulted in more than US$7 million being collected for priority projects, allocated through bilateral agreements and UNESCO funds-in-trust projects. An eleven-page document containing concrete recommendations for future action was adopted, in which the need to ensure effective cooperation was emphasized. Bearing in mind the enormous need to conserve sites in immediate risk of collapse, it was clearly stated, and approved by the Afghan government, that the Bamiyan statues should not be reconstructed for the time being.

To this end, and following the Afghan authorities' request to UNESCO to play a coordinating role in all international activities aimed at the safeguarding of Afghanistan's cultural heritage, UNESCO established an International Coordination Committee. The International Coordination Committee's statutes were approved by UNESCO's Executive Board in October 2002. The committee consists of Afghan experts and leading international specialists belonging to the most important donor countries and organizations providing funds or scientific assistance for the safeguarding of Afghanistan's cultural heritage. It meets on a regular basis to review ongoing and future efforts to rehabilitate Afghanistan's cultural heritage.

In June 2003, the first plenary session of the International Coordination Committee was organized at UNESCO headquarters in Paris. The meeting was chaired by H.E. Makhdoum Raheen, in the presence of Prince Mirwais, son of the former king of Afghanistan, seven representatives of the Afghan Ministry of Information and Culture, and more than 60 international experts participating as members of the International Coordination Committee or as observers. The meeting resulted in concrete recommendations, which allowed the efficient coordination of actions to safeguard Afghanistan's cultural heritage to the highest international conservation standards. These recommendations concern key areas, such as: the development of a long-term strategy; capacity building; the implementation of the World Heritage Convention (1972) and the Convention on the Means of Prohibiting and Preventing the Illicit Import, Export and Transfer of Ownership of Cultural Property (1970); national inventories and documentation; the rehabilitation of the National Museum in Kabul; and the safeguarding of the sites of Jam, Herat, and Bamiyan. Several donors pledged additional funding for cultural projects in Afghanistan during and following the meeting.

In October 2002, a mission of Japanese experts noted that over 80 percent of the murals in Buddhist caves, dating from the sixth to the ninth century AD, had disappeared since their last evaluation in the 1970s. These losses occurred through neglect or looting. In one cave, experts even found the tools used by the thieves and the remains of freshly removed paintings. Since 2003 a large number of specialists from the Japanese National Research Institute for Cultural Properties have visited Bamiyan to safeguard the murals and prepare a master plan for the long-term preservation and management of the site. A Japanese company was contracted for the preparation of a topographic map of the valley and of a 3D model of the niches and cliffs.

Experts also noted with concern that large cracks have appeared in and around the niches where the Buddha statues had previously been situated, which could lead to the collapse of parts of the niches and inner staircases. After careful analysis, the UNESCO experts advised on appropriate measures to consolidate the cliffs and the niches, and the Japanese Foreign Ministry generously approved a UNESCO funds-in-trust for the safeguarding of the Bamiyan site, which is now in its fourth phase and has received nearly US$6.5 million in funding. The activities have been coordinated and implemented under the supervision of UNESCO in close collaboration with the Afghan Ministry of Culture and Information, the Ministry of Urban Development, and the provincial authorities of Bamiyan. Progress has been facilitated by regular meetings of members of these institutions forming the Expert Working Group on the Preservation of the Cultural Landscape and Archaeological Remains of the Bamiyan Valley, which met eleven times between 2002 and 2013. The most important outcomes are as follows: stabilization and consolidation of the cliffs and the two Buddha niches, that were threatened with collapse; conservation, monitoring, and documentation of the fragments of the two destroyed Buddha statues (implemented with additional funding of over €1 million from the government of Germany by ICOMOS Germany); safeguarding the remains of the murals in the Buddhist caves along the cliff, as well as in the adjacent valleys of Kakrak and Foladi; archeological research to define the exact boundaries of the various archeological zones, and register and document historical monuments, traditional settlements, irrigation systems and so forth; the elaboration of a cultural master plan consisting of protective zones with corresponding regulations to control urban development that could have a destructive effect on cultural heritage; the establishment of a management plan for the sustainable management of the World Heritage site; fighting against illicit excavations through site surveillance; and heritage management and conservation training of Afghan experts such as conservators, archaeologists, architects, and heritage professionals.

The main objectives of the current project Bamiyan Phase IV (costing just over US$ 1.5 million, with an implementation period of 2012 to 2015) are: to facilitate the feasibility study for the long-term preservation of the Buddha niches; promote institutional and community capacity-building in conservation, monitoring, planning, management, and community awareness for a cultural heritage-based sustainable development program, including the linkage of this Phase IV project to the creation of a Bamiyan Museum for Peace; and to ensure scientific documentation of site findings and operations. The current work at Bamiyan focuses on the eventual removal of the property from the List of World Heritage in Danger. While substantial progress has been made, a number of threats to the site remain. Development pressure is an imminent threat to the cultural landscape of the Bamiyan Valley and its archeological remains (Manhart and Lin 2014).

Figure 20.2 Results of the consolidation of the Small Buddha niche, Bamiyan, 2005. Source: UNESCO.

Proposals for the Future Preservation of the Buddha Niches

While there has been much debate about the possible reconstruction of the two Buddha statues, UNESCO is not pursuing this objective, nor is it involved in any initiative to achieve this aim. The cost of such a reconstruction would be extremely high, and in times where funding is lacking for the conservation of still intact monuments and sites, reconstructing something which has already been destroyed is hardly conceivable. Moreover, the technical feasibility has not been sufficiently researched. What also has to be taken into account is that the Buddhist monks who sculpted the statues with all their religious spirit in the sixth century are no longer there, and something new would therefore not express the Buddhist faith of that period. In addition, building new statues would destroy the relief and remains of the shoulders and arms that still subsist in the niches. Moreover, one has to consider the wisdom of rebuilding giant statues of the Buddha in an Islamic state in which with the Taliban remains a force to be reckoned with. However, the final decision will be entirely taken by the Afghan government and people. UNESCO's role is strictly advisory.

UNESCO's actions in Bamiyan focus on undertaking urgent conservation measures and protecting as much of Bamiyan's heritage as possible. Through UNESCO's

Figure 20.3 Conservation of fragments of the Large Buddha, Bamiyan, 2006.
Source: UNESCO.

projects, international experts and the Afghan authorities will elaborate possible technical options for the future use of the Buddha fragments, based on international conservation standards and in consultation with the World Heritage Committee. Such projects aim to support the Afghan government in taking their decision. The eleventh Expert Working Group meeting, which took place in Aachen, Germany, in December 2012, concluded again that, based on available scientific data and financial resources, a total reconstruction of either of the Buddha sculptures cannot be considered at present. In light of the policy of the Afghan Ministry of Information and Culture, the Large Buddha niche should be consolidated and left empty at present as testimony to the tragic act of its destruction. Nevertheless, the government of Afghanistan expressed its strong wish for the partial reassembly of the Small Buddha to be an option in the coming years, and a feasibility study should explore whether or not this is possible. Such a study should be in line with the World Heritage Committee's decision (see UNESCO 2012), which stated that feasibility studies on partial reassembly of the Small Buddha should consider an overall approach to conservation and presentation of the property, and an appropriate conservation philosophy based on the Outstanding Universal Value of the property, as well as the technical and financial possibilities for the implementation of the project proposals. Finally, safeguarding and preserving the entire cultural landscape of the Bamiyan Valley is paramount, with due regard to all of the archeological and architectural components necessary for the future development of Bamiyan.

The Destruction of Tangible and Intangible Heritage in Mali

In northern Mali, notably in Timbuktu and Gao, both tangible and intangible cultural heritage has been the subject of repeated attacks, and suffered heavy damage between May 2012 and September 2013 during raids by several more-or-less organized Islamist groups. Of the 16 mausoleums of the World Heritage site of Timbuktu, 14 were destroyed, including two of the Djingareyber Mosque, the largest mosque in the city, along with the holy door of the Sidi Yahia Mosque, and the El Farouk Independence Monument of the legendary white horseman who is believed to protect the city. Just before the liberation of the Timbuktu, 4203 manuscripts held in the new building of the Institute of Islamic Studies and Research Ahmed Baba were burned on January 27, 2013, by armed groups, as revenge for French military intervention. Fortunately, about 10,000 manuscripts are still safely conserved at the institute. However, serious concerns remain regarding the high risk of the physical deterioration of and illicit trafficking in some of the 300,000 estimated manuscripts held by government institutions and private families. In order to protect them from the Islamists, an estimated 90 percent of these manuscripts were removed from their original locations and taken to other places considered safer, such as Bamako or even neighboring countries. Many of these manuscripts are, however, in a bad state, and require conservation and restoration.

In Douentza, in the region of the Dogon people, the Grand Toguna in the village centre has been damaged and its sculpted pillars burnt. This is the meeting place for the decision-makers of the Dogon. In Gao, the World Heritage site of the Tomb of Askia was at risk of collapse for lack of maintenance during the occupation of the town by armed groups, as the caretakers and restorers had no access. The Mausoleum of El Kebir, belonging to the large family of Kounta, and situated about 330 kilometers from Gao, was destroyed by Islamist armed groups in October 2012. Most of the destruction of heritage by the Islamist groups was totally devoid of military or strategic necessity. Their only aim was to target the cultural and religious identity of the people, which is considered contrary to the Islamists' interpretation of the Koran.

In the north of Mali, community members have been repeatedly prevented by armed groups from using mausoleums or observing certain cultural and religious ceremonies. This means that not only monuments but also aspects of intangible cultural heritage have been heavily affected. Religious festivals, music, oral literature and traditions, and ceremonies linked to the mosques and mausoleums allow Mali's various peoples to express their values and knowledge. They also serve as precious tools for conflict resolution and inter-community cohesion. Many cultural practices have been interrupted since the start of the conflict, as people fear becoming targets of punishment meted out by Islamists. At present, six elements are inscribed on the Representative List of the Intangible Cultural Heritage of Humanity. One of them is the Manden Charter, one of the oldest constitutions in the world, albeit mainly in oral form. It contains a preamble of seven chapters advocating social peace in diversity, the inviolability of the human being, education, the integrity of the motherland, food security, the abolition of slavery, and freedom of expression and trade. The diverse populations of Mali possess an extremely rich intangible cultural heritage, which needs to be preserved to allow its transmission to future generations.

Resolutions 2056, 2071, and 2085, adopted by the UN Security Council in 2012, strongly condemn the destruction of cultural and religious sites and urge all parties to take appropriate measures to ensure the protection of the World Heritage sites in Mali (UNSC 2012a, 2012b, 2012c). In 2013, the UN Security Council adopted Resolution 2100, which established the United Nations Multidimensional Integrated Stabilization Mission in Mali (MINUSMA), and includes "support for cultural preservation" in its mandate, specifying that this is to be done in collaboration with UNESCO (UNSC 2013). This is the first time that a Security Council Resolution makes reference to culture, which shows the increasing importance of culture for peace-building. UNESCO is working with the UN Task Team on Mali and MINUSMA to prepare its action on the ground, and implement a training strategy of civil, military, and police personnel to be deployed as part of MINUSMA.

UNESCO Activities for Safeguarding Mali's Cultural Heritage

The UNESCO director-general, Irina Bokova, visited Mali together with the French president, François Hollande, on February 2, 2013, and confirmed UNESCO's commitment to do everything possible to safeguard and rebuild Mali's extraordinary cultural heritage, which the director-general described as a vital part of the country's identity and history, and fundamental for its future. Its restoration and reconstruction will give the people of Mali the strength and the confidence to rebuild national unity and look to the future.

UNESCO has developed and distributed maps and "heritage passports" with the geographical coordinates of important cultural sites, libraries, and museums in northern Mali, as well as relevant information on intangible cultural heritage, to facilitate their protection during military operations by the military as well as the general population, to which these small publications were widely distributed prior to the military operation, in particular to French troops. The "passport" contains a questionnaire which anyone can fill in to report on the state of conservation of or dangers to particular sites, and which can be transmitted by ordinary mail, text message, or e-mail to the Malian Ministry of Culture. This aims at encouraging the military and in particular the wider population to take increased responsibility for the protection of cultural heritage. These publications were reprinted in October 2013 for further distribution. UNESCO also initiated the inventorying and documentation of cultural objects. In addition, a series of posters of Mali's World Heritage were created for awareness-raising at meetings and events.

UNESCO organized a Day of Solidarity with Mali and an international experts meeting on the safeguarding of Mali's cultural heritage at UNESCO headquarters on February 18, 2013. Attended by over 200 participants, including managers of cultural sites in Mali, ministers, experts, and representatives from UNESCO Member States and international technical organizations, the meeting resulted in the adoption of an action plan estimated at US$11 million, with three main objectives: rehabilitating cultural heritage with the active participation of local communities; putting in place measures to protect ancient manuscripts; and providing training in conservation and site management.

UNESCO is now actively seeking funds for the implementation of this action plan. In this context, UNESCO participated in the international donors' conference convened by the European Commission President Barroso and the French President Hollande in Brussels on May 15, 2013. Funding has been provided under UNESCO's Emergency Fund and the World Heritage Fund. In addition, UNESCO established a special fund to support Mali in the safeguarding of its cultural heritage. So far, US$3 million have been received from the governments of Norway, the Netherlands, Croatia, Mauritius, and Switzerland, the Al Jaber Foundation and other private institutions, as well as the European Commission. These funds are presently being used for the restoration of mausoleums and mosques in Timbuktu, the rehabilitation of the municipal museum in Timbuktu, the conservation of manuscripts, and the safeguarding of intangible cultural heritage. Discussions are underway with other potential donors and partners.

A joint UNESCO-Mali expert mission went to Bamako and Timbuktu from May 28 to June 8, 2013, to evaluate the status of Mali's cultural heritage and ancient manuscripts. It resulted in a technical evaluation, and determined, in cooperation with the government of Mali, priority actions for the rehabilitation and conservation of World Heritage sites, museums, manuscripts, and intangible heritage. In August 2013, UNESCO started working on the ground on the first restoration activities initiated in Timbuktu at the Djingareyber Mosque. In October 2013 in Bamako, UNESCO launched the first of a series of training exercises aimed at the protection of cultural heritage for the military, police, and civilian personnel of MINUSMA from Benin, Côte d'Ivoire, Egypt, France, Romania, Rwanda, the United Kingdom and Togo (UNESCO 2013; Eloundou-Assomo 2014).

Figure 20.4 Ceremony for the start of the restoration of a mausoleum, Timbuktu, 2014. Source: UNESCO/MINUSMA/Marco Domino.

Mali and International Cultural Conventions

Mali ratified the World Heritage Convention (1972) in April 1977. On June 28, 2012, Timbuktu and the Tomb of Askia were inscribed on the List of World Heritage in Danger by the World Heritage Committee in order to mobilize the international community to help Mali in its efforts to safeguard these sites and prevent illicit trafficking in cultural property.

UNESCO, in partnership with MINUSMA, is offering support for cultural heritage preservation. It is also cooperating with the International Criminal Court in the Hague with respect to investigations into the situation in Mali, undertaken by the office of the prosecutor, in conformity with its statutes, in which "[i]ntentionally directing attacks against buildings dedicated to religion, education, art, science or charitable purposes, historic monuments" is classified as a war crime.[3] UNESCO is also cooperating under the framework of an article, which classifies persecution based on cultural grounds as a crime against humanity.[4]

In the framework of humanitarian international law, Mali has acceded to the Hague Convention (1954), and, on November 15, 2012, to its First Protocol (1961) and Second Protocol (1999). This accession allows Mali to benefit from international mechanisms for the protection of its cultural heritage.

Mali has also ratified the Convention on the Means of Prohibiting and Preventing the Illicit Import, Export and Transfer of Ownership of Cultural Property (1970), and cooperates with UNESCO mobilized partners (INTERPOL, World Customs Organization, neighboring countries) and regional organizations such as the African Union and the Economic Community of West African States (ECOWAS) in the fight against this illicit trafficking. UNESCO training programs were conducted in Dakar, Senegal, in September 2012, and in Bamako in April 2013, to reinforce the capacities of police and customs forces in Mali and bordering countries.

Mali is furthermore a State Party to the Convention for the Safeguarding of the Intangible Cultural Heritage (2003) and the Convention on the Protection and Promotion of the Diversity of Cultural Expressions (2005).

Conclusions

In contrast to Afghanistan, Mali has ratified almost all UNESCO conventions in the field of culture. However, as in Afghanistan in 2001, none of the conventions were applicable nor could they be enforced in this particular situation, with fighting groups which are not regular combatants or armies, and hence beyond the control of any recognized government.

In this context it is interesting to examine the effectiveness of the UNESCO Declaration Concerning the Intentional Destruction of Cultural Heritage (UNESCO 2003), or Intentional Destruction Declaration, which was adopted by the UNESCO General Conference on October 17, 2003, in the aftermath of the destruction of the Bamiyan Buddhas, with the aim of helping prevent such deliberate destruction of cultural heritage. Its preparation by UNESCO's Member States took two years of discussions in the Executive Board and the General Conference. The Intentional Destruction Declaration stipulates that Member States should take all appropriate measures to prevent acts of intentional destruction of cultural heritage, wherever such heritage is located, either in their own state or in another. It also encourages Member States to adopt appropriate legislative, administrative, educational, and technical measures to protect cultural heritage, and to become parties to the Hague Convention (1954) and other legal instruments in the field of culture. Member States should cooperate with each other and with UNESCO to protect cultural heritage from intentional destruction. The Intentional Destruction Declaration recommends that Member States take all appropriate measures to provide effective criminal sanctions against those persons who commit acts of intentional destruction of items of cultural heritage that are of great importance for humanity. However, a declaration does not need ratification by Member States, nor its implementation as national law – it is therefore not legally binding and of course does not apply to non-regular combatants and fighting groups.

In Bamiyan, Buddhist heritage was dynamited by Islamic extremists; in Mali, however, Islamic heritage is being destroyed by Muslims, which is far less understandable. In Malian tradition – and that of many other Muslim countries – shrines are erected over the tombs of great *ulemas* and *imams*. The population does not pray to these saints, but asks them for protection and help. However, the Malian Islamists hold the belief that God is unique in the extreme, and condemn any other form of veneration, such as that of saints. They destroyed shrines in order to prevent the population from venerating anything else than the one God, and to force them to pray to God only in the mosque. However, it has to be noted that these extremists comprise only a small minority of Malian society, but a minority which is heavily armed and has important financial means, coming from kidnapping, all kinds of illicit trafficking, and support from Al-Qaeda. Here again is a parallel with the Taliban, who were also under increasing influence of Al-Qaeda. In Mali, the Islamists' origins lie in the group Azawat, a liberation movement consisting mainly of Tuareg and Maurs who fought for the independence of the large north part of the country. They radicalized only recently when they joined hands with the Maghreb branch of Al-Qaeda and some other small extremist groups.

In conclusion, it can be said that the international community had almost no means of preventing the destruction of the Bamiyan statues or the cultural heritage of Mali. In spite of international conventions in the field of culture and cooperation between states, these extremist groups do not feel bound by international conventions, which are often ratified by the governments they seek to overthrow. We observe increasingly this constellation in conflicts, which considerably reduces the effectiveness of international conventions and national legal frameworks. The way to prevent these groups from harming heritage is in most cases only military intervention; in Afghanistan it was the United States and allied troops, and in Mali it was France. In both countries, military intervention by other countries came too late to prevent important damage – but it put a stop to more harm to cultural heritage.

Acknowledgements

Some of this chapter was previously published in Manhart and Lin (2014), and is included here with permission of Roland Lin, Claudio Margottini, and Springer-Verlag.

Notes

1 Disclaimer: the ideas and opinions expressed in this chapter are those of the author and do not necessarily represent the view of UNESCO.

2 The quotation is taken from an undated UN briefing, available at: http://www.un.org/News/dh/latest/afghan/un-afghan-history.shtml (accessed March 1, 2015).
3 Rome Statute (1998), art. 8.2.e.iv.
4 Rome Statute (1998), art. 7.1.h.iii.

References

Legislation

Convention Concerning the Protection of the World Cultural and Natural Heritage (World Heritage Convention) (UNESCO, 1972). Available at: http://whc.unesco.org/archive/convention-en.pdf (accessed March 19, 2015).

Convention for the Protection of Cultural Property in the Event of Armed Conflict (Hague Convention) (UNESCO, 1954). Available at: http://unesdoc.unesco.org/images/0008/000824/082464mb.pdf (accessed March 19, 2015).

Convention for the Safeguarding of the Intangible Cultural Heritage (Intangible Heritage Convention) (UNESCO, 2003). Available at: http://unesdoc.unesco.org/images/0013/001325/132540e.pdf (accessed March 19, 2015).

Convention on the Means of Prohibiting and Preventing the Illicit Import, Export and Transfer of Ownership of Cultural Property (UNESCO, 1970). Available at: http://unesdoc.unesco.org/images/0013/001333/133378mo.pdf (accessed March 19, 2015).

Convention on the Protection and Promotion of the Diversity of Cultural Expressions (UNECSO, 2005). Available at: http://unesdoc.unesco.org/images/0014/001429/142919e.pdf (accessed March 19, 2015).

Protocol to the Hague Convention of 1954 (UNESCO, 1954). Available at: http://unesdoc.unesco.org/images/0008/000824/082464mb.pdf#page=66 (accessed March 19, 2015).

Rome Statute of the International Criminal Court (ICC, 1998). Available at: http://www.icc-cpi.int/nr/rdonlyres/ea9aeff7-5752-4f84-be94-0a655eb30e16/0/rome_statute_english.pdf (accessed March 19, 2015).

Second Protocol to the Hague Convention of 1954 (UNESCO, 1999). Available at: http://unesdoc.unesco.org/images/0013/001306/130696eo.pdf (accessed March 19, 2015).

Other Works

Eloundou-Assomo, L.L. (2014) World Heritage Centre Briefing on Mali. Unpublished internal report. Paris: UNESCO.

Manhart, C. (2009) UNESCO's Activities for the Safeguarding of Bamiyan. In M. Petzet (ed.) *The Giant Buddhas of Bamiyan: Safeguarding the Remains.* Berlin: Hendrik Bassler Verlag, pp. 38–40.

Manhart, C., and Lin, R. (2014) UNESCO's Activities for the Safeguarding of Bamiyan. In C. Margottini (ed.), *After the Destruction of Giant Buddha Statues in Bamiyan (Afghanistan) in 2001.* Berlin: Springer Verlag, pp.61–67.

UNESCO (2003) UNESCO Declaration Concerning the Intentional Destruction of Cultural Heritage (Intentional Destruction Declaration). Available at: http://portal.unesco.org/en/ev.php-URL_ID=17718&URL_DO=DO_TOPIC&URL_SECTION=201.html (accessed June 3, 2014).

UNESCO (2005) *Proceedings of the Doha Conference of 'Ulamâ on Islam and Cultural Heritage.* Document CLT/CH/THS/2001/CD/H/1. Available at: http://unesdoc.unesco.org/images/0014/001408/140834m.pdf (accessed March 2 2015).

UNESCO (2012) Cultural Landscape and Archaeological Remains of the Bamiyan Valley (Afghanistan) (C 208 rev). Committee Decision 36 COM 7A.26. Available at: http://whc.unesco.org/en/decisions/4639/ (accessed June 3, 2014).

UNESCO (2013) Emergency Actions in Mali. Available at: http://www.unesco.org/new/en/unesco/themes/pcpd/special-pages/emergency-actions-in-mali/ (accessed June 3, 2014).
UNSC (2000) Resolution 1333. Document S/RES/1333. Available at: http://daccess-dds-ny.un.org/doc/UNDOC/GEN/N00/806/62/PDF/N0080662.pdf?OpenElement (accessed April 10, 2015).
UNSC (2012a) Resolution 2056. Document S/RES/2056. Available at: http://www.un.org/en/ga/search/view_doc.asp?symbol=S/RES/2056(2012) (accessed March 2, 2015).
UNSC (2012b) Resolution 2071. Document S/RES/2071. Available at: http://www.un.org/en/ga/search/view_doc.asp?symbol=S/RES/2071(2012) (accessed March 2, 2015).
UNSC (2012c) Resolution 2085. Document S/RES/2085. Available at: http://www.un.org/en/ga/search/view_doc.asp?symbol=S/RES/2085(2012) (accessed March 2, 2015).
UNSC (2013) Resolution 2100. Document S/RES/2100. Available at: http://www.un.org/en/ga/search/view_doc.asp?symbol=S/RES/2100(2013) (accessed March 2, 2015).

CHAPTER 21

Heritage and the Politics of Cultural Obliteration: The Case of the Andes

O. Hugo Benavides

The Andes run the length of the South American continent from the northern Colombian landscapes to the southern sections of Argentina's and Chile's Tierra del Fuego. As expected in such a large cultural region, the varied historical legacies are quite diverse. However, central to these differing sociohistorical legacies is the traumatic genocidal and ethnocidal practices imposed upon the region's Native American population as a result of Europe's colonial expansion into the continent. The last five centuries have been marked with the violent manner in which different native communities have been victimized, but also with the ways they have creatively resisted different forms of cultural obliteration.

Since the 1990s, the field of heritage studies has constituted itself as a burgeoning area of intellectual and political focus. In the Andes this has expressed contradictory elements that have both implicated this field in the colonial discourses of official historical memory, but also helped reformulate new means for understanding the postcolonial production of identity and memory. Traditional approaches to heritage studies (that is, claiming UNESCO World Heritage status for sites, revitalizing tourism at pre-Hispanic monuments, and so on) unfortunately work to reassert white and *mestizo* notions of cultural property, and the commoditization of history, that are ever present in the production of political and economic power over indigenous communities.

This problematic development of heritage studies is an important part of the focus of this Andean case study. The present chapter aims to assess some of the ways in which cultural heritage has been developed in the region, giving way to distinctive identity

A Companion to Heritage Studies, First Edition. Edited by William Logan, Máiréad Nic Craith, and Ullrich Kockel.
© 2016 John Wiley & Sons, Inc. Published 2016 by John Wiley & Sons, Inc.

formations and political agency. Central to this discussion is the work of the anthropologist and writer José María Arguedas (1911–1969), who, during his lifetime, developed a significant intellectual oeuvre that critically looked at assessing the politics of heritage in the region. In his work, Arguedas examined from varying vantage points the complex processes by which cultural heritage has both contributed to and helped to resist the differing official forms of hegemonic control and ethnic decimation in the Andes. Not surprisingly, the cultural analysis proposed by Arguedas proved heavy to bear (and would directly contribute to his suicide), yet would still propel him to becoming one of the central figures in the rethinking of heritage, culture, and identity in the region.

Both Arguedas's Peruvian ancestry and his theoretical contributions provide a more nuanced manner of understanding the initial colonial decimation experienced by Native American populations as a result of the European conquest of the New World initiated in the early 1500s. The particular form of European expansion into the region would provide the violent legacies that acted as the default model upon which myriad of generations would reconstruct their livelihood (and culture) for the next five centuries. These particular cultural reformulations would be central in Arguedas's literary and ethnographic explorations, providing an incisive look into the historical legacies that continue to fuel the present problematic of heritage for the nation-states of the Andes.

The first section of this chapter provides a succinct overview and discussion of Arguedas, particularly how his unique racial location allowed him to rethink Andean cultural heritage from a singularly hybrid viewpoint. I argue that it is this particular hybrid process of miscegenation (*mestizaje* in the local context) which allowed Arguedas to take in both indigenous and Western contributions as equally central to the production of cultural heritage in the Andes. It is this same process of *mestizaje*, as I discuss in the following section, that one sees enacted in one of the main Andean ports, the city of Guayaquil, Ecuador. With its population of almost 4 million people and one of the central historical centers linking the colonial Caribbean slave trade to the Andean highlands, Guayaquil continues to effusively contend with the pervasive legacies that both produce and contest the differing ways in which cultural heritage is represented in the region.

The third section and conclusion uses Arguedas's insights to assess the contemporary manner in which both archeological sites (in this case, Cochasquí) and the Confederation of National indigenous Communities of Ecuador (CONAIE) continue to offer new and varied practices of cultural heritage production. The site of Cochasquí, currently directed by the Cosejo Provincial de Pichincha (Pichincha's provincial council), provides evidence of continued occupation in the area for several millennia. Not surprisingly, the site's cultural heritage provides powerful ideological resources to the state's national imaginary, and to the sustaining of a viable national cultural identity in the region. CONAIE's political and cultural agenda is "similarly different" (see Hall 1997a, 1997b) in its form of heritage production. As one of the largest indigenous movements not only in the Americas but in the world, CONAIE continues to reproduce powerful representations of cultural heritage, reminding us of Faulkner's popular yet profound admonition: "The past is not dead. It's not even past" (Faulkner 1951: 126).

Ultimately, based on Arguedas's analyses and anthropological research, this chapter assesses the manner in which Andean Native American communities and their descendants continue to reinvent and reassess their heritage, providing counter-hegemonic ways to understand their histories and the production of the West in the Americas. In many ways this also posits an inherent contradiction in the field of heritage studies, since as an integral part of the academic establishment it belies the interest of those in power, in contrast to the indigenous communities of the Andes who have been decimated by these same European and Anglo practitioners for at least the last two centuries. The question is whether or not an academic and political discourse like heritage studies can realign itself, at least in some manner, with its humane objective of recuperating the past, and in the process acknowledge the fact that the West has benefited from the erasure of native history, and from the removal and export of native historical objects to museums all over the world. After all, as many indigenous activists claim, museums are the dirty closets of colonial power.

José María Arguedas: The Politics of *Mestizaje*

More so than any other Andean intellectual, José María Arguedas developed a consistent cultural oeuvre that interrogated the underlying racial symptoms that fueled the national imaginings of the region (see Arguedas 1941, 1958, 1961, 1964, 1971). The initial colonial conquest of the indigenous communities of the Andes by a mixed (European, Jewish, Arab, and African) Spanish population reified as racially superior and white, is still being played out in multiple settings within the region. The violent origins of the contemporary Andean nation-states speaks to a long-standing tradition of racism and exclusion, which is central to the forms of governance carried out by these states, but also embedded within the different protest movements, including *indigenismo* and *indianismo*, that have looked to address this social malady over the last century. It is this particular painful "coloniality of power" (Quijano 1993: 33) that Arguedas addresses in his work, and that would be responsible for his untimely death.

Arguedas was born into an upper-class, white Peruvian family, but was brought up by the Indian servants that his family practically owned. His mother died at an early age, and Arguedas was sent to live in the servant quarters by his stepmother. He would learn Quechua along with Spanish as his native tongues, and be able to feel intimately an Indian world that did not correspond to his racial designation as white. This initial split between an Indian and a white cosmology would be heightened throughout his life. It was this alienation from two conflicting worlds, making him a hybrid subject, that was an essential part of Arguedas as Andean, and it would motivate his vocation as an anthropologist. However, it would not just be his anthropological research or academic positions that he would be remembered for (he was a dean at the Universidad Nacional Agraria La Molina when he finally succeeded in killing himself at the age of 58). Rather, it would be his fiction along with his ethnographic explorations that would contribute to his intellectual legacy as the most important contributor to work on the politics of race, sexuality, and class in the Andes.

This initial split between a subsumed (and more real) Indian cosmology that related to his own early life, and the later (and more superficial) *mestizo* or white world that corresponded to his class affiliation, would be heightened throughout his life. In many ways one can easily see that it was this initial alienation from two insurmountable worlds that although conflicted were an essential part of his Andean world. This hybrid existence was what also motivated him to become an anthropologist and dedicate his career to rescuing an Indian past, and present, that he thought had been wrongfully vilified; an Indian culture that ultimately represented for him what Peru, the Andes, and Latin America in general was all about.

It is this complex vision that comes across most strongly in his landmark novel *Los ríos profundos* (1958) where he uses a young *mestizo* boy to express the "deep rivers" of Indian history that flood the bodies and geography of the Andes. This particular contribution was, of course, not only not recognized in his own lifetime, but many times used to question his own patriotic allegiance and to present physical exile from Peru as the only viable option for his survival. However, it was his reluctance to physically abandon the Andes that both enriched his work and complicated his life, since it was this geographic proximity and his unwillingness to ignore the violent origins of Peruvian society that contributed to his continuous bouts of depression and eventual suicide. Arguedas would provide several key texts in terms of assessing the conflicting social nature of Andean society, including the novels *Los ríos profundos*, *Yawar Fiesta* (1941), *El Sexto* (1961), *Todas las sangres* (1964), and the posthumous *El zorro de arriba y el zorro de abajo* (1971).[1]

Race plays an essential role in the Andes, and as such is primal in Arguedas's understanding of the cultural politics of the region. However, far from embracing a xenophobic discourse of racial purity, Arguedas argues for a complex understanding of race that distanced itself from both the utopian visions of pure whiteness and Indianness that were popular during his time. On the one hand, you have a series of global and local elements that re-emphasize a particular white Western version of the world, where whiteness, first Spaniard, now North American, is claimed to have a superior cultural standing based on skin color; while on the other hand you have a millenarian understanding of Indian identity that looks to reclaim a native culture untouched by centuries of unequal and violent forms of social relations and exchange.

It is this unwillingness to appease either side that made Arguedas a viable target for many of his compatriots, who did not want, and to some degree were unable, to accept the horrors that their historical incongruencies would bring in the decades to come. For Arguedas, the racial conundrum of the Andes is a unique one that cannot be shied away from. It is also one marked by the centuries of miscegenation that are an essential part of assessing the manner in which identities have been dynamically articulated. It is in this sense that *mestizaje*, a complex process of mixing at multiple levels, is highlighted in Arguedas's work, and is particularly reified in the figure of the *cholo* – a racial category used throughout the Andean region to depict a hybrid person, although more indigenous than white or mestizo. Ronald Stutzman (1981), in a key article on miscegenation in Ecuador written over 30 years ago, defined *mestizaje* as an all-inclusive ideology of exclusion. For him, and for generations of progressive scholars, *mestizaje* was nothing else than, or at least most successful as, a state ideology that looked to celebrate the mixing of races, Spanish/white, Indian, and African, without really being interested in understanding the uneven and hierarchical manner in which these identities were produced. For Stutzman and others, the ideology of *mestizaje* was more than anything else a hierarchical tool that oppressed non-white identities and yet was still able to rhetorically claim to be democratic. *Mestizaje* in this sense is really about whiteness and being white, and, through this ideological artifice, hide all other difference under the rug.

It is this particular racial ideology that would allow the Ecuadorian dictator, General Guillermo Rodríguez Lara, to claim in the 1970s that there was no longer a racial problem in his country since, like most Ecuadorians, he also thought that we are simply all mestizos now. In one sentence he was able to deny centuries of Indian exploitation while still having Indians as indentured servants on his own hacienda (plantation). The vision of *mestizaje* expounded by Rodríguez Lara and shared by others underlay the subtle manner in which Andean states used a democratic rhetoric of racial equality while still calmly benefiting from long-term mechanisms of labor exploitation. It was only through these ideological mechanisms of *mestizaje* that Brazil could talk about a racial democracy which never existed, or Mexico was able to claim itself an Indian nation while the majority of Indians suffered horribly under the ruling political party, the PRI.

However, this particular vision of *mestizaje* as a form of Marxist false consciousness failed to account for the actual violent miscegenation that had profoundly marked the continent. It would be the singular contribution of the late Gloria Anzaldúa (1987) that would sustain a more nuanced idea of *mestizaje*. For Anzaldúa, *mestizaje* was not simply a reactionary form of state ideology, but also a more intimate form of cultural expression in the Americas. It was this *mestizaje*, which she referred to as the "borderlands," that signaled a way out of the violent historical legacy that constantly condemned (rather than celebrated) difference.

It is at this point, and with Anzaldúa's contribution in mind, that Arguedas's own work can be made to make even more sense. As his own bilingual upbringing signaled, it is only in these hybrid "borderlands" that the Andean subject can make any sense of their life. Even though one's external life is related to particular socioeconomic conditions, the internal construction of identity is not simply defined in class terms but rather in terms of the intertwining of racial, class, and sexual elements that continuously defy categorization.

Arguedas offers ethnographic glimpses of Indian markets, aged ritual dancers, exploited Indian laborers, and castrated condors as a symbolic metaphor of the greater emasculation suffered by Andean subjects in general over the last five centuries, marking if anything the particular vulnerability of men towards this particular repressive political process. And yet it is this ambivalent sexual place where any kind of particular redemption might occur. It is only through these different kinds of sexual ambivalences that one can escape the binary of victim/oppressor, of either being the condor or its repressive guard. And this binary form of sexual and gender violence is precisely afforded by a reified, yet invisible, white heteronormative ideology that intimately restructures everything from the inside out, including what one desires, when we desire it, and who one ultimately turns out to be.

It is not so much Indianness, or blackness, or even homosexuality that could be held responsible for some type of abnormal or perverse behavior, but rather how these particular ideologies have been demonized into their provocative existence in the Andes. It is the normative tropes of whiteness and heteronormativity, now expressed in neocolonial and postcolonial terms, which frame the violent structure in which Peruvians, and all Andean subjects, construct their own daily livelihood. And it is this particular struggle – at once local and global – of striving to makes sense within a local reality of racial and sexual desires that have been globally reinforced that constitutes the ultimate challenge for people in the Andes today.

There is a wealth of cultural heritage in terms of Indian identity but also in terms of black and Spanish ancestry in the Andes that must be accounted for before any kind of political resolution can be obtained. It is this particularly problematic issue of cultural heritage that Arguedas worked over in his writing, assessing the ways in which the varied racial, sexual, and cultural elements that had been continuously oppressed, repressed, and reused needed to be allowed to resurface as consciously as possible.

However, it was this same disturbing idea, of letting the cultural past claim its contemporary hold, that most Andean people, particularly those in positions of power, were (and are) most terrified of.

Guayaquil and its Modern Heritage

The *mestizo* population of the Andes has historically distanced itself from the Indian population, and even from its original assimilated term of *cholo*. This distancing trend inherited from the Spanish racial system has been invigorated by a new global Western order in which whiteness still constitutes itself as a marker of civilization. However, now English and the United States, not Spanish and Europe, are the markers of civilizing culture. It is this particular racial construction for *mestizos* as a group and *mestizaje* for the nation (Stutzman 1981) that has been the prevalent reality of the ethnic formation of the new white/*mestizo* elite of Guayaquil's economy; an ethnic formation that inspired a progressive liberal revolution (1895 to 1905) at the turn of the century that linked the nation to an international capitalist economy, and introduced the nation's lower classes to a proletarian existence (Ayala Mora 1986).

This particular form of ethnic competition, which over five centuries has allowed a significant number of *mestizos* to if not belong at least to closely identify with the elite white population, has not gone without its particular difficulties and provocative social experimentation. One of these provocations is its historically ambiguous relationship to Indian heritage. This ambiguous relationship is ontologically implied in multiple ways with contemporary Indian communities, but perhaps much more subtly in the representation of an indigenous heritage that is shared by the contemporary Indian and white/*mestizo* population of Guayaquil. This indigenous heritage is not exclusively about a racial legacy, but also about a class-based and sexual one, mainly because this racial legacy is not only dependent upon the sexual reproduction of their common ancestors but also of the mechanisms of social reproduction and contemporary representation that each group has put into place for their own historical continuity and legitimization.

This form of historical ambiguity for the political ruling *mestizo* population and their corresponding ideological and identity framework is particularly inescapable because it refers back to the haunting question of cultural authenticity (Silva 1991). One of the essential contradictions constantly replayed in reclaiming an Indian heritage is that while it supports the legitimization of a much needed historical authenticity, it also reiterates the problem of ethnic differentiation between *mestizos* and European colonizers. However, this same European legacy of racial division demands that *mestizos* separate themselves from their Indian ancestors, and so to some degree separate themselves from themselves, and/or the image that they may produce of themselves. In this manner, there is an internal incongruence of striving and conducting oneself as white, of Spanish descent, and yet also claiming, or struggling to claim, Indian ancestry; combined with this is the fact that in your day-to-day existence you are also in desperate need of distinguishing yourself as superior to the contemporary Indian population.

In Guayaquil this particular historical representation has had interesting results. One of these is the widespread form of *regionalismo*, whereby people from the coast distinguish themselves from the highland population (Maiguashca 1994). For the people of the coast, the *serranos* (as highland people are pejoratively referred to) represent the backwardness, hypocrisy, and "Indianness" of the country. Highlanders also holds the coastal population in low esteem, referring to them as *monos* (monkeys) because they are popularly held to be cunning, good imitators, always eager to "con" one for their own benefit, economic or otherwise. In a specific manner this regional representation mimics the geographical legacy of colonial government: while the coastal Indian groups were quickly assimilated into the colonial structure, one could say by "imitating" or "mimicking" the colonizers, highland Indian groups have not only maintained an Indian identity for the last five centuries of colonial and neocolonial domination, but along with Amazonian groups they have also been able to form the strongest social movements in the last decade through the aforementioned CONAIE and Pachakutik Nuevo País.

The *regionalismo* held by the coast, and most fiercely by Guayaquileños, in many ways could be interpreted as another distancing mechanism – one that helps them deny the existence of an Indian component of their existence, but not necessarily of their heritage. This connection is even afforded in a clearer way by the fact that most of the visible Indian migrants in the city, many of whom are vendors in the food markets and plazas (*mercados*), are of highland extraction and are phenotypically, linguistically, and in their clothing distinct from the *mestizo* Guayaquileños. For Guayaquileños, *serranos* represent more clearly the Indian past toward which they have such ambivalent feelings of longing for ancestral recognition, and, fear and hatred of racial rejection. The pervasiveness of the city's *regionalismo* is also a marker of its own administrative separation and distinctiveness from the nation's capital, Quito, a centralized political control that has been a cause of resentment throughout the country's colonial and republican existence.

However, this *regionalismo* not only points to political resentment but perhaps even more to a deeper sense of internal colonialism and self-loathing (see Freire 1992). The hatred towards highlanders seems to reflect the city's own ambivalent feelings toward itself and its Indian heritage, especially since many Guayaquileños as national migrants have highland ancestry themselves. *Regionalismo* is a sign of the difficulty of effectively valuing those elements of a historically constructed sense of regional identity that have been deemed of less value in the progressive Western self-image that Guayaquil set out for itself almost five centuries ago. This was a Western (that is, anti-indigenous) construct that is an essential component of what Guayaquil and Guayaquileños are today. We can also see in the discourse of *regionalismo* the reason why the legacy of the *enchaquirados* (a homosexual harem of young male religious and sexual servants) has so often been ignored and misconstrued. In the modern construction of Guayaquil's historic identity there is very little representational room for an Indian element, specially a "problematic" sexual one (a point to which I will return).

Most educational institutions, historical texts, and Guayaquileños assume that the original Indian inhabitants of the area on which the city now stands were the now long-gone Huancavilcas (Navas Jimenez 1994). The Huancavilcas are represented as a community of fierce warriors that resisted initial attempts at conquest by the Inca state, and that fought to the bitter end against the Spanish conquistadors. This image of fierce resistance and proud heritage is enshrined in the most popular explanation given for the origin of the city's name: Guayaquil is supposed to have come from the name of the leader of the Huancavilca, Guayas, and his wife, Quil, who resisted the Spanish up to their death; that is, while Guayas was killed by the Spanish, his wife preferred to take her own life by jumping into the river (named Guayas after her husband) rather than "belong" to any of the (male) Spanish conquerors.

This particular origin myth is quite similar to the racial and gender problematics of other American settings, such as those of Malinche in Mexico and *mestizas* in Peru (Mallon 1996; De la Cadena 2000). As in these other regions, contemporary politicians quite quickly understand the lucrative possibilities that can come from drawing on ancient myth and historical heritage. In this fashion, Andean politicians, educators, and other public spokespersons call upon a heritage of great resistance, on which has precisely gendered and sexual specifications (see Radcliffe and Westwood 1996). In terms of these discourses, to be from Guayaquil means, as well as demands, having courage, physical strength, and moral superiority. It is this particular brand of *machismo*, with its precepts of engendered behavior and an implicit heterosexuality, which is reinforced in Guayaquil's normative behavior. Ethnohistorical accounts about the Manteño-Huancavilcas and other pre-Hispanic communities in the area provide an opportunity to contextualize Guayaquil's contemporary regional construction in terms of its sexual past. The pervasive presence of a transgendered community in the non-urban setting of Ecuador's Santa Elena Peninsula, particularly the town of La Libertad, has much to offer us not only in assessing the nature of sexual identities in general, but also in terms of resistance, accommodation, and daily existence in the face of capitalist cultural dynamics.

This somewhat triumphant tone of recognition of a possibly local gay identity at La Libertad, however, is only half of the picture. The other half is afforded by five centuries of religious and moral ideology that has shaped and constituted transgendered identities in the Andes. In this manner, it is likely that Catholicism has paradoxically both enabled and oppressed Andean transgendered communities. The question to entertain is how has the sexually repressive ideology of Catholicism contributed to rather than simply repressed the present expression of queer identities. This is particularly complex in light of the Church's explicit condemnation of homosexual activity, and through its political power by helping to create a homophobic secular ideology that has significantly ostracized transgendered communities. To complicate matters further, this homophobic ideology has been further reinforced by racial ideology, through white/*mestizo* control of public policies, national images, political representation, and a particular discourse of *regionalismo*. In the Andes, this racialized control has meant the almost complete erasure and outright denial of a different or alternative pre-Hispanic sexual practice, one that is at odds with that advocated by the Catholic Church.

This binary opposition, however, does not fully explain the complex involvement and centrality of religion and sex in the construction of contemporary cultural identities. There is no doubt that the Church's homophobic desire to enforce heteronormativity remains unfulfilled – the large transgendered communities along the Andean coast is testament to this. But one must wonder if the annihilation of "sodomites" was ever the Church's ultimate or unique objective. After all, as Foucault's (1998) work so explicitly shows, deviants are essential if we are interested in normalizing any form of social or sexual behavior. Following this lead, I would suggest that more subtle forms of domination were being instituted during this repressive period, forms which combined both pre-Hispanic and Spanish religious beliefs. Both the Church and Indian communities could be seen as points of struggle within greater Andean webs of hegemonic constraint.

Contemporary formulations of Guayaquil's Indian heritage, with its specific sexual representation, are highly indebted not only to the actual descriptions contained in ethnohistorical accounts, but also to their religious tone, morality, and sentiments. The city's dismissal of any public reference to homosexuality speaks to the systematic production by Spain and the Church of a sexual discourse devoid of non-heterosexual elements. In this light, the officialization of homophobic historical interpretations has been part of the production of a way of racially being (*regionalismo*) and a set of class dynamics that has repeatedly drawn on an idea of Europe as the civilizing cultural center.

The *enchaquirados* have been a historical resource close at hand for both Guayaquil's historians and the population at large (Benavides 2002). The *enchaquirados* are described in the same ethnohistorical accounts that have been used to reconstruct Guayaquil's colonial heritage. These accounts, however, have not only been consistently scrutinized to reconstruct Ecuador's history (see Pareja Diezcanseco 1990; Efrén Reyes 1967), and have been used to produce and legitimize a particular heteronormative national discourse. Not surprisingly, the proponents of this heteronormative discourse have relied precisely on the supposed objectivity of official history to support its veracity, denying the inherent circularity in the hermeneutic process of representation which always "obscur[es] the conditions of its own creation, [and] cover[s] its own tracks" (Hale 1996: 2; see also Alonso 1988).

In this sense it is not surprising that the *enchaquirados* have escaped historical notice, because in terms of official historiography they really did not exist. As part of this official discourse, one could take Julio Estrada's discussion of Cieza de León's chronicle of his time in the Andes (Estrada 1987).[2] Estrada systematically avoids any mention of homosexuality or sodomy in Cieza de León's texts, even though they quite significantly appear in direct quotes in the notes to the main text (Estrada 1987: 243). Estrada even argues against these "unmentioned" (*nefando*) sins by blaming Cieza de León and other ethnohistorical chroniclers for attributing unspeakable acts to Indian communities whose actions ran contrary to the writer's explicit agenda. In this way, Estrada blames others for what he himself does, using historical sources biased by his own unconscious desires, which constitutes an inescapable dilemma for any conscientious and committed historian (Alonso 1988). In this regard, even when other national historians have mentioned evidence of homosexuality in their texts, the evidence has not been sufficient to cause them to question the reigning heteronormative discourse.

The discussion of Guayaquil's cultural heritage, including the legacy of the *enchaquirados*, illustrates how claims concerning the pre-Hispanic past construct particular forms of sexual and racial practices and understandings, and in doing so contribute to the region's national normalizing cultural discourse. Ultimately, the contradiction between alternative constructions of heritage within a hegemonic heritage discourse is an essential factor in the constitution of all national heritage projects in the Andes. It is this larger, dynamic hegemonic discourse, constantly in the making, that ultimately benefits from and redefines the varied attempts at constructing heritage and negotiating identity.

Conclusion: Cultural Heritage in the Andes

Arguedas's insights readily allow us to understand cultural heritage production in other areas in the Andes as well, such as in the archeological recovery of the past at Cochasquí (see Programa Cochasquí 1991; Benavides 2004) and the powerful reproduction of the indigenous movement by CONAIE (1989, 1997, 1998). These two different cultural phenomena exemplify the wide variation in historical debate and the hegemonic implications of any discussion of Andean archeological and cultural heritage. Other case studies, such as that of the archeological sites of Culebrilla and Agua Blanca, present scenarios in which the local population fought against the state's willingness to destroy archeological sites for development purposes. In both instances the communities reinterpreted the archeological heritage embedded at the sites to legitimize their own claims of being defenders of archeological ruins, and thereby provide a dynamic reinterpretation of their own past and identities.

These cases, either of state control at sites such as Cochasquí and Inga Pirca (the largest Inca ruin in Ecuador today), or where local contestation is immediately effected and mobilized through the population's reinterpretation of the official past, as with CONAIE, are dynamic examples, I would argue, of the complex overarching hegemonic structure in which heritage constructions operate. Rather than seeing these cases as contrasting examples, they all express similar processes of interpretation, appropriation, and a dynamic and constantly changing hegemonic ambiguity. In other words, they all express similar constraints of national historical hermeneutics, embedded within the very nature of the claims made regarding archeological and cultural heritage.

What has become clearer in the last couple of decades is what we have always known: that no individual, group, or institution can survive without a heritage claim to the past. The greatest difference, perhaps, is that it is now possible to theorize about the appropriation of the past, mainly because through the burgeoning field of heritage studies the discipline of archaeology has been forced to adapt its own hegemonic claims regarding science and Western legitimacy in a less stringent fashion. This adaptation of the discipline's hegemonic stronghold over the past is, I believe, afforded by a postcolonial critique that has given a voice, albeit in an extremely complicated manner, to precisely those natives and locals who used to be only "objects" of study (Spivak 1999; Mignolo 2000).

However, it is important in this regard to recognize how native discourses are always reinserted within neocolonial reformulations of power. Local forms of historical production are never visible in the global scene, unless of course they are asserted within the global reproduction of power. It is this basic contradiction in which native or local forms of historical identification can only be recognized within the greater hegemonic structure of elite academic institutions that makes it essential to reassess the manner in which the past (and heritage studies) restructure contemporary political alliances.

It is in this manner that all heritage claims, particularly ones with nationalizing implications, present at Cochasquí and inherent in CONAIE's reformulation of the past, will always imply a political struggle to redefine and legitimize one's identity, and therefore one's right to exist. Baldwin, perhaps better than any other scholar, has captured this ambiguous relationship, between the past and our identities:

> The disputed passage [of our identities] will remain disputed so long as you do not have the authority of the right-of-way – so long, that is, as your passage can be disputed: the document promising safe passage can always be revoked. Power clears the passage, swiftly: but the paradox, here, is that power, rooted in history, is also, the mockery and repudiation of history. The power to define the other seals one's definition of oneself – who, then, in such a fearful mathematics, is trapped? (Baldwin 1990: 481)

The case studies from the Andes discussed here, I would argue, cogently express the fact that the process of domination inherent in all heritage claims invites a different form of analysis, one that will, at least not blindly, offer itself to hegemonic control, even though it cannot totally escape it. And yet the ambiguous elements of domination and resistance are always present in the recovery of heritage. So the trap is most precisely set when we look at either resistance or domination, instead of seeing how both are inherent in all heritage enterprises, reconstructions of the past, and reformulations of our historical identities. But precisely because of the dynamic nature of these social processes, something always eludes signification and thrusts us into new and old reformulations (Hall 1997b). It is also in escaping from of precise signification that our hopes are most secure and least betrayed, since supposedly "true" and "authentic" heritage reconstructions will only lead us into greater webs of domination (Malkki 1995), and historical misrepresentations.

Notes

1 Some of Arguedas's novels are available in English. *Los ríos profundos* was published as *Deep Rivers* (trans. F.H. Barraclough, University of Texas Press, 1978), *Yawar Fiesta* ("Blood festival") has appeared under its Spanish title (trans. F.H. Barraclough, University of Texas Press, 1985), and *El zorro de arriba y el zorro de abajo* was published as *The Fox from Up Above and the Fox from Down Below* (trans. F.H. Barraclough, University of Pittsburgh Press, 2000). At the time of writing, both *El Sexto* (the name of an infamous federal prison in Lima) and *Todas las sangres* ("All the blood") remain unavailable in English.

2 Cieza de León traveled in the Andean region in the 1530s and 1540s, and is best known for his four-part work *Crónicas del Perú*.

References

Alonso, A.M. (1988) The Effects of Truth: Re-Presentation of the Past and the Imagining of a Community. *Journal of Historical Sociology*, 1 (1), 58–89.

Anzaldúa, G. (1987) *Borderlands/La Frontera: The New Mestiza*. San Francisco: Aunt Lute Books.

Arguedas, J.M. (1941) *Yawar fiesta*. Lima: Librería Mejía Baca.

Arguedas, J.M. (1958) *Los ríos profundos*. Buenos Aires: Editorial Losada.

Arguedas, J.M. (1961) *El Sexto*. Lima: Librería Mejía Baca.

Arguedas, J.M. (1964) *Todas las sangres*. Buenos Aires: Editorial Losada.

Arguedas, J.M. (1971) *El zorro de arriba y el zorro de abajo*. Buenos Aires: Editorial Losada.

Ayala Mora, E. (1986) *Los Partidos Políticos en el Ecuador: Síntesis Histórica*. Quito: La Tierra.

Baldwin, J. (1990) *Just Above My Head*. New York: Laurel.

Benavides, O.H. (2002) The Representation of Guayaquil's Sexual Past: Historicizing the Enchaquirados. *Journal of Latin American Anthropology*, 7 (1), 68–103.

Benavides, O.H. (2004) *Making Ecuadorian Histories: Four Centuries of Defining Power*. Austin: University of Texas Press.

CONAIE (Confederación de Nacionalidades Indígenas del Ecuador) (1989) *Las nacionalidades indígenas en el Ecuador: Nuestro proceso organizativo*. Quito: Editorial TINCUI-CONAIE and Abya-Yala.

CONAIE (1997) *Proyecto político de la CONAIE*. Quito: CONAIE.

CONAIE (1998) *Las nacionalidades indígenas y el estado plurinacional*. Quito: CONAIE.

De la Cadena, M. (2000) *Indigenous Mestizos: The Politics of Race and Culture in Cuzco, Peru, 1919–1991*. Durham, NC: Duke University Press.

Estrada, J. (1987) *Andanzas de Cieza por tierras americanas*. Guayaquil: Banco Central del Ecuador and Archivo Histórico del Guayas.

Efrén Reyes, O. (1967) *Breve Historia General del Ecuador*, 3 vols. Quito: Chávez.

Faulkner, W. (1951) *Requiem for a Nun*. New York: Vintage.

Foucault, M. (1998) Nietzsche, Genealogy, History. In *Aesthetics, Method and Epistemology: Essential Works of Michel Foucault*, vol. 2, ed. J. Faubion. New York: New Press, pp. 369–418.

Freire, P. (1992 [1970]) *Pedagogy of the Oppressed*. New York: Continuum.

Hale, C. (1996) Introduction. *Journal of Latin American Anthropology*, 2(1), 2–3.

Hall, S. (1997a) The Local and the Global: Globalization and Ethnicity. In A. King (ed.), *Culture, Globalization and the World-System: Contemporary Conditions for the Representation of Identity*. Minneapolis: University of Minnesota Press, pp. 19–39.

Hall, S. (1997b) Old and New Identities, Old and New Ethnicities. In A. King (ed.), *Culture, Globalization and the World-System: Contemporary Conditions for the Representation of Identity*. Minneapolis: University of Minnesota Press, pp. 41–68.

Maiguashca, B. (1992) The Role of Ideas in a Changing World Order: The Case of the International indigenous Movement, 1975–91. Paper delivered at the conference "The Changing World Order and the United Nations System," Yokohama, Japan, March.

Malkki, L. (1995) *Purity and Exile: Violence, Memory, and National Cosmology among Hutu Refugees in Tanzania*. Chicago: University of Chicago Press.

Mallon, F. (1996) Constructing Mestizaje in Latin America: Authenticity, Marginality, and Gender in the Claiming of Ethnic Identities. *Journal of Latin American Anthropology*, 2 (1), 170–181.

Mignolo, W. (2000) *Local Histories/Global Designs: Coloniality, Subaltern Knowledges, and Border Thinking*. Princeton: Princeton University Press.

Navas Jimenez, M. (1994) *Historia, Geografía y Civica*. Quito: Grafica Mediavilla Hermanos.

Pareja Diezcanseco, A. (1990) *Breve Historia del Ecuador*. Quito: Libreas.

Programa Cochasquí (1991) *Replanteamiento Programático*. Quito: Honorable Consejo Provincial de Pichincha.

Quijano, A. (1993) América Latina en la economía mundial. *Problemas del Desarrollo*, 24, 5–18.

Radcliffe, S., and Westwood, S. (1996) *Remaking the Nation: Identity and Place in Latin America*. New York: Taylor and Francis.

Silva, E. (1995) *Los Mitos de la Ecuatorianidad: Ensayo Sobre la Identidad Nacional*. Quito: Abya-Yala.

Spivak, G. (1999) *A Critique of Postcolonial Reason: A History of the Vanishing Present*. London: Routledge.

Stutzman, R. (1981) El Mestizaje: An All-Inclusive Ideology of Exclusion. In N. Whitten (ed.), *Cultural Transformations and Ethnicity in Modern Ecuador*. Urbana: Illinois University Press, pp. 45–94.

PART III Recasting Heritage

CHAPTER 22

The Economic Feasibility of Heritage Preservation

Ron van Oers

Every Crisis Harbors an Opportunity

Against the backdrop of building collapses and deterioration at World Heritage sites in Italy (Donadio and Povoledo 2013; Le Roux 2013), the progressive sale of iconic monuments in France, as well as the "great sell-off" in Italy (Dinmore and Segreti 2013), and the splitting up of English Heritage (Clark 2013), statutory advisor for cultural heritage in England and Wales, many are questioning what will remain of Europe's once considered superior system of cultural heritage preservation. Now that support and funding for cultural heritage preservation by national governments is drying up, it seems that the bedrock of preservation in these countries is less stable than most realized. Much to the dismay of old-time preservationists, issues concerning cultural heritage management are now becoming part of ordinary struggles for survival played out in the public realm.

To be fair, this has always been the case with cultural heritage preservation in practically all other parts of the world, regardless of economic booms or busts. Arguably, what we are witnessing can be traced back to an uncomfortable truth: in spite of the many successes (Casini 2011: 374),[1] the European system of cultural heritage preservation and its management is apparently not robust enough. This chapter puts forward the argument that, on the one hand, this can be related to the fact that its base of support is still too narrow, primarily being the educated elite; and on the other, the absence of a sustainable mechanism of financing, with an over-reliance on government funding.

A Companion to Heritage Studies, First Edition. Edited by William Logan, Máiréad Nic Craith, and Ullrich Kockel.
© 2016 John Wiley & Sons, Inc. Published 2016 by John Wiley & Sons, Inc.

Both the narrow support base and a state-controlled financial mechanism are related. Essentially they stem from the nineteenth century, when concern for historical and artistic heritage was an affair foremost related to nation-building (Muñoz Viñas 2005: 30), and not to the livelihoods and well-being of local communities. Both are also at the core of the Recommendation on the Historic Urban Landscape (UNESCO 2011), which was adopted by UNESCO's General Conference on 10 November 2011 after a long and at times arduous process that de facto started in 2003. That year, during a heated debate at the annual session of the World Heritage Committee, this intergovernmental decision-making body called for the development and elaboration of updated guidelines for urban conservation to better address the multitude of development pressures exerted on World Heritage sites (Van Oers 2010: 8). Over the course of eight years and several dozen expert meetings, workshops, and symposia, all relevant international charters, recommendations, and other supporting guidelines were reviewed and critically examined. The heart of the matter, in technical terms, concerned the viewpoint that urban conservation had become "a moving target, to which a static, monumental approach as inherited from the previous century is wholly inadequate, or perhaps downright destructive" (Bandarin and Van Oers 2012: 111). But this technicality, of course, has political implications as well.

The Recommendation on the Historic Urban Landscape (UNESCO 2011), in building upon more than half a century of established international conservation doctrine, advocates the recognition of the changing nature and conditions of living urban heritage. This necessitates an approach for greater social inclusion, a broadening of stakeholder groups, and for stronger engagement between policy-makers, decentralized governments, the corporate sector, and local communities, among others. It calls for the building of bridges to improve mutual understanding that is often lacking in "preservation versus development" debates. The aim would be to streamline heritage preservation into the urban development process in order to reduce tensions and conflicts, and redirect some of these often massive funds to strengthen heritage preservation programs. To gather supporting evidence for this position, currently a series of pilot projects in China and other countries in the Asian region are being set up under the umbrella of the Historic Urban Landscape approach (Van Oers and Taylor 2015).

This will add to the growing body of research and literature that is being published on projects initiated by major actors, such as the World Bank, UNESCO, the Inter-American Development Bank and the Aga Khan Trust for Culture. These projects all demonstrate the broad range of benefits to be had when heritage preservation is integrated into the planning and design of a sustainable development process.

However, when working directly with local and decentralized governments, it often turns out that this range of benefits, and how it can be generated, is still poorly understood. Consequently, departments or units dealing with cultural heritage preservation are mostly operating in a silo, instead of being integrated into broader territorial and socioeconomic development planning. This obviously reduces the efficiency and effectiveness of preservation efforts, and hampers a full realization of the potential of cultural heritage to contribute to broader socioeconomic development. Hence, the publicly held opinion that heritage preservation is a luxury that contributes little to, or perhaps even arrests, economic progress, and is therefore only feasible for rich countries that have money to spare. Naturally, the issues playing out in Europe at the moment just reinforce this idea.

Rather than throwing the baby out with the bathwater, the current crisis should be taken as an opportunity "to take a fresh look at the discipline and the ways and means in which it operates, in particular the modalities of management and financing," as argued elsewhere (Van Oers 2009: 55). In search of the economic feasibility of heritage preservation, therefore, this chapter will address several key issues, including:

1 the need to consider the overall state of infrastructure, legal-institutional as well as technical, when trying to determine the costs and benefits of cultural heritage preservation;
2 the complexity of relationships when looking for direct and indirect spin-offs;
3 the imperative of including environmental, social, and cultural parameters when aiming for a sustainable economic performance in the urban development process;
4 the need to search for innovative ways in which a broadened engagement in cultural heritage preservation can be achieved, the support base can be enlarged, and the budget constraints can be overcome.

What, if Anything, Does World Heritage Status Bring?

When examining the economic feasibility of heritage preservation, it would seem that the first and best place to look for clear directions is the UNESCO Convention Concerning the Protection of the World Cultural and Natural Heritage, or World Heritage Convention (1972), or more precisely, the rationale behind nominating properties (natural, cultural, or mixed) to the World Heritage List. The enormous popularity and visibility of this internationally acclaimed instrument over the last 40 years induces one to readily accept that the benefits, including economic ones, must be considerable (see UNESCO 2012). Why otherwise would governments spent several years, on average, in developing a nomination dossier? As this exercise was estimated in 2008 to be costing up to £400,000 in the UK, or US$234,250 (RC and TBR 2009), plus the effort to lobby the international community for the site's inscription on the World Heritage List, why would governments make such an effort, if it wasn't for a handsome return?

An International Monetary Fund Working Paper, based on the World Heritage List and a large cross-section of countries for the period 1980 to 2002, investigated whether tourism specialization is a viable strategy for development. The authors concluded "that the gain from tourism specialization *can* be significant" (Arezki, Cherif, and Piotrowski 2009: 16. emphasis added). But this is by no means a given.

On close inspection, it appears a clear causality between costs incurred and benefits gained in the World Heritage nomination process is difficult to demonstrate. When examining a range of research reports and commissioned studies (Buckley 2004; PwC 2007; Gravari-Barba and Jacquot 2008; Nicot and Ozdirlik 2008; Talandier 2008), the overall outcome dispelled the myth that World Heritage listing per se generates significant positive impacts. Apparently, the evidence for this was difficult to extract from the often scarce or incomplete data available. Additionally, a 2008 report to the Australian Department of the Environment, Water, Heritage and the Arts on the economic activity of 15 of Australia's World Heritage sites examined economic activity that arose from expenditures associated with management of the sites, as well as expenditure of visitors to the sites. It concluded that of the more than AUS$16 billion (US$17.1 billion) in annual direct and indirect national output or business turnover, generating more than AUS$4 billion (US$4.29 billion) in direct and indirect national household income and over 83,000 direct and indirect national jobs, 95 percent of these impacts were from visitor expenditure, with the remainder from management expenditure. The conclusion continued, however, that the methodology used analyzed all expenditure associated with visitors to World Heritage areas (WHAs), in accordance with standard practice, but "there is no way to tell from the secondary data utilized, how much of that visitor expenditure is attributable to the WHAs alone" (GE and BDA 2008: 7). From the multitude of forces at work at any given moment and the complexity of inter-relationships, it is hard to distinguish precisely the impacts they generate when looking for direct and indirect spin-offs. However, what does seem to emerge very clearly from these studies is that much will hinge on the existence or establishment of an enabling environment in which the benefits from World Heritage designation can be nurtured and optimized. Contrary to most people's perception – including those of decision-makers – in the absence of such an enabling environment little will take root and flourish. The World Heritage List is replete with sites that, in spite of their coveted international status, have not benefited at all in terms of generating significant returns on investment (Van Oers 2009: 60).

Hence, World Heritage status, at best, functions as a catalyst. It *can* be a powerful tool, a means to an end, which has the potential to bring about significant socioeconomic benefits *if* coupled with investments in infrastructure and targeted programs and actions that are part and parcel of an enabling environment.

What Constitutes an Enabling Environment for Heritage Preservation?

An enabling environment for heritage preservation practically involves two aspects. Firstly, it concerns the existing legal-institutional framework under which cultural heritage is protected, financially supported, and, aligned with other related public policies, is implemented. Secondly, it involves the available technical-managerial capacities through which sites are managed, presented, branded, and promoted, made accessible and subsequently can be experienced. To derive any benefits at all, let alone an optimum, the two must work in tandem.

On purpose, financial resources have not been singled out as a separate aspect, but should be embedded as an element under both legal-institutional frameworks (as incentives included in tax codes and land-use regulations, for example) and management capacity (as part of business administration and destination marketing, for instance). Similar to assuming that World Heritage status per se brings economic gains, all too easily the assumption is made that given enough money any preservation project will be successful. Again, the reality is more fuzzy.

Drawing on several Latin American experiences involving adaptive rehabilitation of cultural heritage properties, Eduardo Rojas (Rojas and Lanzafame 2011: 5; Rojas 2013: 179) posits that the institutional framework for managing the process is as critical as the financial means to effectively implement urban heritage preservation programs. The effective use, he argues, of financial resources to achieve objectives and expected results is part of a multi-sector strategy, and largely depends on an efficient structure and working of institutional mechanisms to mobilize and streamline various contributions, in cash as well as in kind. This includes the capacity of stakeholders to carry the risks and capture the returns of the preservation process, in which the effective coordination of key actors must be ensured.

Since the 1970s, due to diminishing state-controlled finance for the management and financing of heritage preservation, the field of economics as applied to heritage preservation has developed rapidly. While the need for more objective reasoning and scientific measuring is legitimate (see Vernieres *et al.* 2012), however, it remains important to remember that a significant part of the values and meaning of heritage preservation cannot be captured in monetary terms alone (see Wilson 2009). The World Bank's latest publication in this field (Licciardi and Amirtahmasebi 2012), to which ten economists made contributions, paints a complex picture in which effective heritage management is determined by values and aspirations, constrained by political realities and markets, characterized by shortcomings and externalities, and supported by tailor-made schemes involving incentives, regulation, and investments, through multiple-source financing, complex cost-recovery mechanisms, and subsidies. In the space available here it is not possible to outline each aspect, but for the purpose of this chapter, Donovan Rypkema handsomely sums up the economic rationale, when he states that:

> growing body of research findings, based on studies of international examples, consistently demonstrates that heritage conservation pays. And the most straightforward evidence that heritage pays is the willingness of buyers not just to pay for heritage properties, but to pay extra for them. This commonly found economic premium has a multitude of public policy implications. Rising property values will often mean increased revenues for local governments, a greater willingness of financial institutions to make loans, a greater likelihood of private-sector investment, and fewer heritage buildings lost to demolition by inaction or neglect. (Rypkema 2013: 139)

Eduardo Rojas and Francesco Lanzafame (2011) arrive at a similar conclusion by correlating the experiences of preservation of ten World Heritage sites in Latin America, Europe, and the Arab states. They conclude that the sustainability of the process of urban heritage preservation will be enhanced when heritage areas have been made attractive for a variety of users interested in a variety of heritage values. "Preservation efforts must promote the economic values of the heritage as a complement and support for the preservation of the socioeconomic values that have motivated actions in the past" (Rojas and Lanzafame 2011: 9–10; see also Bigio and Licciardi 2010).

Instead of continuing to argue whether or not the preservation of cultural heritage is worthy of our efforts and resources, given international experiences it seems more meaningful to work on creating an enabling environment and to make this system robust.

How Can We Enhance the Robustness of the Cultural Heritage Preservation System?

Enhancing the robustness of the system of cultural heritage preservation would involve three key aspects.

Firstly, reaching the understanding that economic performance can only be sustained when it is closely linked to sound environmental management, social inclusion, and cultural diversity.[2] These are prerequisites to ensuring the wise use of finite resources, to fully tap into the potential of human population groups with each performing a task best suited to it, and to optimize conditions for creativity and innovation, as convincingly argued by Edward Glaeser (2011). While we should be aware of a world where the only yardstick to measure progress by is "economic growth," and where "value" is expressed in monetary terms alone,[3] nevertheless, coupling heritage preservation with economic performance generates mutual benefits and increases sustainability. Indeed, as part and parcel of sustainability, a community's and city's identity based on heritage values and local culture generates opportunities for development, which in turn will set in motion a process that, if properly managed, will further strengthen it. For this to occur, however, it will be necessary to align all related public policies in order to connect and integrate heritage preservation with strategic planning and socioeconomic development. Making the city or region more sustainable – in which both preservation and economic performance play a critical role – means realigning the relevant policies towards this goal, including those on housing, labor, education, and everything you do in terms of business and how you invest your money in the city and region. If this process remains incomplete, then the result will be incomplete – both in terms of the effectiveness of preservation programs and the achievements in sustainability.

Secondly, enhancing robustness would involve enlarging constituencies in support of cultural heritage preservation, as the base of support is still too narrow. In part this is related to certain conservative, rather elitist attitudes residing in the cultural heritage preservation discipline, as recalled by David Throsby (2013: 46),[4] which prefers to keep the ranks specialized and closed. It also relates to the late-capitalist phase of our societies, in which unbridled materialism and consumerism have gained the upper hand, leaving the majority of the population passive and indifferent to the plight of cultural heritage. Then, aside from individual attitudes, within the cultural heritage preservation discipline itself not all is well organized. Much of the field remains fragmented and divided on key issues, such as the meaning and extent of authenticity, as shown through continuing debates on the significance of the Nara Document on Authenticity (ICOMOS 1994), or on contemporary architecture in historic context, which has been a hotly debated topic for over 40 years now (Frampton 2003). One might also point to the calls for a "New Heritage" (Holtorf and Fairclough 2013), which would deny over half a century of carefully built-up international conservation awareness – albeit including some mistakes and flaws. But rather than helping to create stronger support for heritage preservation, it would only lead to further confusion, and therefore be a waste of human endeavor, present and past. These are just some examples of the discipline's internal disarray.

In this regard, the cultural heritage sector has a lot to learn from its colleagues in natural heritage preservation. Generally and publicly they speak with one voice; they have managed to convey to society at large the urgency regarding the plight of rainforests, whales, tigers, and now polar bears; they have established scientific global databases on the state of natural heritage to support their arguments;[5] and, on top of this, they have successfully lobbied governments and global institutions to include their concerns in planning and funding mechanisms.[6] Clearly, the cultural heritage sector has a long way to go.

The third key aspect involving robustness is equally pressing. It entails the search for innovative ways to finance cultural heritage preservation and its management. As argued at the beginning of this chapter, over-reliance on government support is a remnant of a previous age, when the centralized state was solely responsible for the protection and management of cultural heritage. Since the progressive push for decentralization that started in the 1980s, local governments have increasingly taken over this role, though seldom with corresponding levels of capacity or financing (Van Oers 2009: 56). With today's cash-strapped local and national governments and large population groups experiencing severe austerity measures, this system has become politically untenable. Moreover, there is also an economic rationale for avoiding full public financing of preservation efforts. As Rojas argues:

> The overwhelming presence of the public actors in the financing and implementation of the rehabilitation projects in historic city cores may crowd out other stakeholders. The seemingly intractable scale of the problem of restoring and revitalizing historic city cores, coupled with the stream of private benefits that this can generate, makes full public funding impractical, inefficient, and unequal. It is impractical for the simple reason that it is not possible to raise the amount of funds required from all levels of public administration to bear the costs of the conservation effort; it is inefficient because public investment may crowd out private investments when applied to assets that have use value through demand in the real estate market; it is unequal when public funds benefiting private-sector owners and users are not returned to the public treasury. (Rojas 2013: 168)

As such, it seems more important and necessary, given the urgency of the situation, to look for new partnerships, rather than new heritage, to sustain the efforts and build upon the achievements of the existing system of heritage preservation.

What Types of Partnership and Financing Are There for Cultural Heritage Preservation?

It is not just the preservation of cultural heritage that has come under pressure as regards the sustainability of its financing. Many charities and nonprofit organizations are experiencing a roll-back of government support and a tightening of purses, prompting a wave of exploratory and innovative ideas to try to fill the ensuing gap, with some remarkable results. Fueled in part by the economic crisis, but also by the search for greater social responsibility, innovative schemes such as micro-donations,[7] crowdsourcing,[8] philanthro-capitalism,[9] impact investing,[10] and a profit-driven stock market for nonprofit organizations[11] all have one aspect in common: the creation of linkages between different sectors and the application of concepts from one sector, that of business administration, to those of the social and cultural domains – or, in a broader perspective, an evolution of concepts and practices through a process of cultural selection.

When looking into the potential role of the corporate sector in supporting heritage preservation, through public–private partnerships (PPPs) and corporate social responsibility (CSR) initiatives, Fiona Starr found that "cultural heritage is not generally perceived by the private sector as a priority for support since it is not considered to be of interest to company stakeholders, nor considered relevant to core business" (Starr 2013: 149), adding that the "private sector considers involvement with heritage to be bureaucratic and challenging" (Starr 2013: 151). However, this doesn't mean that the preservation of cultural heritage cannot be aligned with the business strategy of corporations and the goals of CSR. Quite the contrary. By way of an extensive discussion of the involvement of American Express, through its partnership with the World Monuments Fund, in the restoration and consolidation of the temple complex of Preah Khan at Angkor in Cambodia, she demonstrates the sustainable benefits of the preservation project to local communities and the development-oriented local government, as well as the American Express company. Respectively, these involved specialized skills training in crafts and project management, employment, financial stability, and improved livelihoods for the local communities; the safeguarding of an important resource for sustainable development, with increased visitation and revenues from tourism, which created a diversification of economic activities, and improved infrastructure and communication for the local government; and improved visibility, reputation enhancement, and competitive positioning for the corporation.

When considering this range of benefits, and those to whom it applies, it is all the more remarkable that CSR and cultural heritage partnerships are most commonly initiated by companies instead of recipient partners. Thus, "the potential of private sector financing for cultural heritage has been limited because the cultural heritage sector has not yet engaged with the corporate social responsibility movement" (Starr 2013: 147).

It is imperative for the cultural heritage sector to actively engage and position itself within the CSR process, or other innovative strategies, if it does not want to miss the boat when it sets sail to new horizons of increased social engagement and sophisticated business partnerships. Because if it does, the consequences might be dire as fewer people today automatically accept that cultural heritage is important. If it is, or so the thinking goes, then this needs to be demonstrated through its relevance to society, in one way or another, instead of taking the moral high ground and practicing a sit-and-wait strategy.

Fortunately, some careful steps are being undertaken to seek new ways and means of financing urban heritage preservation. In a recent study commissioned by the Asia-Europe Foundation, PPP as a construction in the management of heritage cities was examined through a total of 36 case studies in Asia and Europe.[12] Many cases (37 percent) dealt with revitalization efforts through the use of tourism, while the issue of good governance (26 percent) also appeared high on the agenda. In general, it turns out that the PPP approach is used in a wide variety of contexts, from setting up a strategy for fund raising to developing a new business model for operating a museum, or for the development of conservation management plans to rehabilitate housing complexes or whole historic precincts. What became clear from this study is that PPPs are growing in importance as part of the management of heritage cities, and they have proved to be a creative and powerful tool for the safeguarding of urban heritage, be it tangible or intangible. More particularly, several of the PPP cases demonstrate a key role for local communities, either in taking the initiative or in driving the process.

While most of them merit recognition for their efforts, I will briefly highlight three of the more noteworthy cases.

In Edinburgh (Scotland), a PPP between the Edinburgh World Heritage Trust and individual building owners aimed at implementing the concept of "conservation-led regeneration." More than a 1000 repairs have been executed, according to the highest conservation standards, through national and local government funding since 1971, and which ultimately led to World Heritage status for the city in 1995.

In Manila (Philippines), the Far Eastern University Campus Conservation Program was started in 1989 in one of Manila's most depressed urban areas. It aimed at rehabilitating the university's oldest campus buildings in their original landscape, thereby re-establishing the former identity of the university. However, the program gradually developed into a wholesale grassroots movement, engaging surrounding communities, which initiated a private–public initiative for neighborhood revitalization, with the backing of the mayor of Manila.

Leipzig (Germany), meanwhile, has attempted to halt and reverse the dramatic decline in the population of the city (once part of the former East Germany), which has lost 50 percent of its inhabitants (100,000 people) in just two decades. A PPP was established to manage the city's 45,000 empty apartments, and to preserve and rehabilitate its architectural heritage. Through the establishment of the Leipzig City Forum, 15 associations and many local community groups, as well as individuals, committed to the implementation of a sustainable urban development strategy, working closely with the City Forum's volunteers on innovative initiatives which facilitated the adaptive reuse of heritage buildings and the regeneration of neighborhoods.

A case of PPP that merits special attention is the conservation and rehabilitation of the inner city of Amsterdam in the Netherlands. Since its foundation in 1956, a for-profit company, Stadsherstel Amsterdam, has invested capital in buying historic properties in a (very) poor state of conservation, which are subsequently restored, rehabilitated, and put back on the property market. These activities are undertaken with financing from the company's own capital, supplemented by subsidies from various government departments, local as well as national. After the building is rented out, the revenues are put back into the company, which results in a steadily growing capital base that covers the maintenance as well as the acquisition of new properties, or any further restoration and upgrading interventions. It also generates a return for the company's shareholders of 5 percent per annum, which is exempt from tax (Tung 2001: 242). Next to the municipality of Amsterdam, large Dutch banks and insurance companies are among its shareholders, who in the spirit of CSR accept lower than usual profits in view of a mutually beneficial sociocultural program for the city, which provides visibility and improves their image with the general public. Since its foundation 58 years ago, Stadsherstel Amsterdam has rehabilitated 500 houses and 30 larger monuments, such as churches and industrial monuments like pumping stations and a shipyard (Stadsherstel 2011: 5). It has invested on average €10 million (US$13.26 million) annually in restoration and rehabilitation activities, 30 percent of which comes from state or municipal subsidies (€3 million, or US$4 million). By 2006, the total value of the company's assets had already reached a surplus of €178 million, and it owned 921 residential buildings in the inner city of Amsterdam, all rented out on the market, with a possibility of incremental sale (Bandarin and Van Oers 2012: 174).

After a process of almost ten years in which the concept and dossier for nomination was arduously developed and refined, the seventeenth-century canal rings of Amsterdam, which contain a significant portion of Stadsherstel's properties, were inscribed on UNESCO's World Heritage List in 2010.

Conclusion: The Costs Precede the Benefits

The World Heritage designation of the historic centre of Amsterdam was significant as it constituted the crowning achievement of efforts that effectively started in 1956, and which have subsequently led to arguably one of the most successful cases of urban heritage preservation and inner-city revitalization in Europe. With a critical mix of social concerns, cultural continuity, broad-based community and private-sector support, and innovative financing, the historic centre of Amsterdam is both a protected area as well as a locus for investment and development largely based on a social pact between the local government, its citizens, and several city-based companies. This constitutes an enabling environment for multiple sectors, for both heritage preservation and entrepreneurial businesses, for social experiments as well as cultural highlights, which is advanced by political determination and fostered by stability and continued commitment.

Painted on the cornice of one of the historic buildings at the entrance to the old harbor of Amsterdam is the text "the costs precede the benefits" (*de cost gaet voor de baet uyt*), which was an important motto during the Dutch Golden Age of the seventeenth century. It still reminds the population of Amsterdam of the need for sustained investment, innovation, thorough planning and coordination, and hard work, in order to generate a good return; that is, a profit.

Instead of the perceived deterioration of the preservation apparatus in Europe, as posited at the start of this chapter, perhaps we could view the unfolding events also as a positive sign, as indicators of systemic changes that are currently underway. Only time will tell. But changes are sorely needed to advance from a largely twentieth-century modernist approach to heritage preservation as being the sole responsibility of central governments and based on a strict and fragmented division of largely mechanistic tasks among specialized agencies, to the next postmodern phase, where responsibility is shared among all stakeholders and executed through an integration of vision, political will, community leadership, and corporate social responsibility. Only this will safeguard our finite heritage resources, ensure the economic feasibility of their preservation, and keep them available for enjoyment, inspiration, and sustainable development for present and future generations.

Notes

1 Since its inception, the largest number of inscribed sites on the World Heritage List have been located in the European region, currently standing at 458 out of a total of 981 sites, with Italy topping the list with 49 World Heritage sites (as of January 2014).
2 India and China are currently learning this the hard way, with disturbing records in air and water pollution, soil degradation, and looming civic unrest, which threatens to hamper their economic growth and social progress (see Mandhana 2012; Anon. 2013a; Anon. 2013b; Wu, Jiang, and Tang 2013; Kynge 2013).
3 See the Framework Convention on the Value of Cultural Heritage for Society (2005), which recognizes "the need to put people and human values at the centre of an enlarged and cross-disciplinary concept of cultural heritage" (preamble).
4 Throsby recalls: "In a paper first published in 1995, Sir Alan Peacock pointed to the simple economic principle of opportunity cost as a constraint on resource allocation to heritage projects. At that time, given the budgetary constraints, more often than not, heritage projects received lesser funds from administrators in comparison to other projects on the scale of priorities. Since in most cases it was public funds that were being deployed, Peacock argued that public preferences should be taken into account in the decision making process. These suggestions drew a spirited response from the heritage profession, whose members feared that their expert judgements on the cultural significance of heritage items would soon be displaced by crude financial criteria and lowest-common-denominator popular opinion in decisions concerning the allocation of heritage resources" (Throsby 2013: 46).
5 See UNEP and IUCN's Protected Planet (www.protectedplanet.net), or the Equator Initiative Case Study Database (http://www.equatorinitiative.org/index.php?option=com_winners&view=casestudysearch&Itemid=685, accessed September 11, 2012), which has developed detailed case studies of 127 Equator Prize winners, all outstanding efforts to reduce poverty through the conservation and sustainable use of biodiversity and ecosystems.

6 Examples include the Environmental Impact Assessment, Global Environment Facility (www.thegef.org/gef/), or the Equator Principles (www.equator-principles.com/).

7 Micro-donations are gifts so tiny that donors do not even notice they are giving them, obtained through a small tax on products such as airplane tickets, which revolutionized the world of medical aid to poor countries (see Kuper 2012).

8 Crowdsourcing is a form of citizen sponsorship usually for the arts and organized through social media (see Greffe 2012).

9 Philanthro-capitalism is the term used to refer to high-profile big public giving by the business world. It started with Ted Turner's US$1 billion gift to the United Nations in the late 1990s, which led to other billionaires like Bill Gates and Warren Buffett following suit, and that is reshaping philanthropy by bringing business sensibility with greater rigor and evaluation into this domain (see Kristof 2012).

10 Impact investing is an emerging concept aiming to provide a clear social benefit as well as a financial return that originated in the United Kingdom and is being pioneered by the Rockefeller Foundation (see Johnson 2013).

11 A stock market for nonprofit organizations is a concept that seeks the trading of bonds of nonprofit organizations on the stock market, in which investors replace donors (see Sorkin 2013).

12 This study was based on the outcomes of "Managing Heritage Cities in Asia and Europe: The Role of Public–Private Partnerships," Experts' Meeting in Preparation for the Fifth ASEM Culture Ministers' Meeting, Yogyakarta, Indonesia, July 12–14, 2012 (see Van Oers 2012). PPPs refer to "innovative methods used by the public sector to contract with the private sector, which brings in their capital and their ability to deliver projects on time and to budget, while the public sector retains the responsibility to provide these services to the public, in a way that benefits the public and delivers economic development and an improvement in the quality of life" (UNECE 2007: 1).

References

Legislation

Convention Concerning the Protection of the World Cultural and Natural Heritage (World Heritage Convention) (UNESCO, 1972). Available at: http://whc.unesco.org/archive/convention-en.pdf (accessed March 19, 2015).

Framework Convention on the Value of Cultural Heritage for Society (Faro Convention) (Council of Europe, 2005). Available at: http://conventions.coe.int/Treaty/en/Treaties/Html/199.htm (accessed March 19, 2015).

Other Works

Anon. (2013a) "Study: Air Pollution Fifth Biggest Killer in India," *Times of India*, February 13, p. 13.

Anon. (2013b) "The East is Grey," *Economist*, August 10, pp. 17–20.

Arezki, R., Cherif, R., and Piotrowski, J. (2009) Tourism Specialization and Economic Development: Evidence from the UNESCO World Heritage List. Working Paper WP/09/176. Washington: International Monetary Fund.

Bandarin, F., and Van Oers, R. (2012) *The Historic Urban Landscape: Managing Heritage in an Urban Century*. Oxford: Wiley-Blackwell.

Bigio, A., and Licciardi, G. (2010) *The Urban Rehabilitation of Medinas: The World Bank Experience in the Middle East and North Africa*. Urban Development Series No. 9. Washington: World Bank.

Buckley, R. (2004) The Effects of World Heritage Listing on Tourism to Australian National Parks. *Journal of Sustainable Tourism*, 12 (1), 70–85.

Casini, L. (2011) "Italian Hours": The Globalization of Cultural Property Law. *International Journal of Constitutional Law*, 9 (2), 369–393.

Clark, N. (2013) "Plans to Divide English Heritage Put Historic Sites' Future 'In Peril'," *Independent*, December 1. Available at: http://www.independent.co.uk/news/uk/home-news/radical-plan-to-break-up-english-heritage-rushed-and-not-viable-9195984.html (accessed on July 17, 2014).

Dinmore, G., and Segreti, G. (2013) Property Investors Buy Into Italy's "Dolce Vita." *Financial Times*, November 16–17, p. 8.

Donadio, R., and Povoledo, E. (2013) Pompeii's Peril: The Italian State. *International Herald Tribune*, April 22, p. 3.

Equator Initiative (n.d.). Equator Initiative Case Study Database. Available at: http://www.equatorinitiative.org/index.php?option=com_winners&view=casestudysearch&Itemid=685 (accessed September 11, 2012).

Frampton, K. (2003) Foreword. In P. Collins, *Changing Ideals in Modern Architecture 1750–1950*. Montreal: McGill-Queen's University Press, p. xiii.

GE and BDA (Gillespie Economics and BDA Group) (2008) Economic Activity of Australia's World Heritage Areas: Final Report. Report to the Department of the Environment, Water, Heritage and the Arts, New South Wales.

Glaeser, E. (2011) *Triumph of the City*, London: Macmillan.

Gravari-Barba, M., and Jacquot, S. (2008) Impacts socio-économiques de l'inscription d'un site sur la liste du Patrimoine Mondial: une revue de la littérature. Research report for the World Heritage Centre. Paris UNESCO.

Greffe, X. (2012) *L'artiste-entreprise*. Paris: Dalloz.

Holtorf, C., and Fairclough, G. (2013) The New Heritage and Re-Shapings of the Past. In A. González-Ruibal (ed.), *Reclaiming Archaeology: Beyond the Tropes of Modernity*. London: Routledge, pp. 197–201.

ICOMOS (1994) Nara Document on Authenticity. Available at: http://whc.unesco.org/archive/nara94.htm (accessed July 17, 2014).

Johnson, S. (2013) Impact Investing Is Doing Well by Doing Good. *Financial Times*, April 29, p. 2.

Kristof, N. (2012). How Giving Became Cool. *International Herald Tribune*, December 28, p. 4.

Kuper, S. (2012) How to Change the World on the Quiet. *Financial Times*, October 6–7, p. 2.

Kynge, J. (2013) The Migrant Millions Crucial to China's Rebalancing. *Financial Times*, April 23, p. 7.

Le Roux, G. (2013) Concerns over State of Italy's Historic Locations. *China Daily*, July 3, p. 2.

Licciardi, G., and Amirtahmasebi, R. (eds) (2012) *The Economics of Uniqueness: Investing in Historic City Cores and Cultural Heritage Assets for Sustainable Development*. Urban Development Series. Washington: World Bank.

Mandhana, N. (2012) Indian Capital Struggles to Control Heavy Smog. *International Herald Tribune*, December 28, p. 3.

Muñoz Viñas, S. (2005) *Contemporary Theory of Conservation*. Oxford: Elsevier Butterworth-Heinemann.

Nicot, B.-H., and Ozdirlik, B. (2008) Les impacts socio-économiques de l'inscription sur la liste du Patrimoine Mondial: Deux comparaisons en Turquie. Research report for the World Heritage Centre. Paris: UNESCO.

PwC (PricewaterhouseCoopers) (2007) The Costs and Benefits of UK World Heritage Site Status. Literature review for the UK Department for Culture, Media and Sport, London. Available at: https://www.gov.uk/government/uploads/system/uploads/attachment_data/file/78450/PwC_literaturereview.pdf (accessed March 16, 2015).

RC and TBR (Rebanks Consulting and Trends Business Research) (2009) World Heritage Status: Is There Opportunity for Economic Gain? Report for the Lake District World Heritage Project.

Available at: http://rebanksconsultingltd.com/resources/WHSTheEconomicGainFinalReport.pdf (accessed January 12, 2014).

Rojas, E. (2013) Governance in Historic City Core Regeneration Projects. In G. Licciardi and R. Amirtahmasebi (eds), *The Economics of Uniqueness: Investing in Historic City Cores and Cultural Heritage Assets for Sustainable Development.* Urban Development Series. Washington: World Bank, pp. 160–174.

Rojas, E., and Lanzafame, F. (eds) (2011) *City Development: Experiences in the Preservation of Ten World Heritage Sites.* Washington: Inter-American Development Bank.

Rypkema, D. (2013) Heritage Conservation and Property Values. In G. Licciardi and R. Amirtahmasebi (eds), *The Economics of Uniqueness: Investing in Historic City Cores and Cultural Heritage Assets for Sustainable Development.* Urban Development Series. Washington: World Bank, pp. 175–185.

Sorkin, A.R. (2013) Vision of For-Profit Tactics to Help Charities. *China Daily,* November 24, p. 6.

Stadsherstel (2011) *Stadsherstel Amsterdam 2006–2011: The Company for City Restoration.* Amsterdam: Stadsherstel Amsterdam.

Starr, F. (2013) *Corporate Responsibility for Cultural Heritage: Conservation, Sustainable Development, and Corporate Reputation.* London: Routledge.

Talandier, M. (2008) Le classement UNESCO favorise-t-il l'activité touristique et le développement économique local? Une étude économétrique du cas de la France. Research report for the World Heritage Centre. Paris: UNESCO.

Throsby, D. (2013) Heritage Economics: A Conceptual Framework. In G. Licciardi and R. Amirtahmasebi (eds), *The Economics of Uniqueness: Investing in Historic City Cores and Cultural Heritage Assets for Sustainable Development.* Urban Development Series. Washington: World Bank, pp. 45–74.

Tung, A. (2001) *Preserving the World's Great Cities.* New York: Random House.

UNECE (United Nations Economic Commission for Europe) (2007) *Guidebook on Promoting Good Governance in Public–Private Partnerships.* Geneva: UNECE.

UNESCO (2011) Recommendation on the Historic Urban Landscape. Available at: http://portal.unesco.org/en/ev.php-URL_ID=48857&URL_DO=DO_TOPIC&URL_SECTION=201.html (accessed March 16, 2015).

UNESCO (2012) *World Heritage: Benefits beyond Borders.* Paris/Cambridge: UNESCO/Cambridge University Press.

Van Oers, R. (2009) Sleeping with the Enemy? Private Sector Involvement in World Heritage Preservation. In F. Descamps (ed.), *Proceedings Xth World Congress of the Organization of World Heritage Cities, 8–11 September 2009, Quito.* Los Angeles: Getty Conservation Institute, pp. 55–64.

Van Oers, R. (2010) Managing Cities and the Historic Urban Landscape Initiative: An Introduction. In R. van Oers and S. Haraguchi (eds), *Managing Historic Cities.* World Heritage Papers No. 27. Paris: UNESCO, pp. 7–17.

Van Oers, R. (2012) Public–Private Partnerships in Asia and Europe in the Management of Heritage Cities and the Role of UNESCO. Report. Singapore: Asia-Europe Foundation.

Van Oers, R., and Taylor, K. (2015) Asian Theoretical and Best-Practice Framework for the Historic Urban Landscape: Heritage for the Future. In K. Taylor, A. St Clair, and N. Mitchell (eds), *Cultural Landscape Conservation: Issues and Challenges.* London: Routledge, pp. 198–215.

Vernieres, M., Patin, V., Mengin, C., Geronimi, V., Dalmas, L., Noel, J-F., Tsang King Sang, J. (2012) *Methods for the Economic Valuation of Urban Heritage: A Sustainability-Based Approach.* Paris: Agence française de développement.

Wilson, M. (2009) Nominating Chief Roi Mata's Domain (Vanuatu) for World Heritage Listing: An Assessment of Costs and Benefits. Report for World Heritage Centre. Paris: UNESCO.

Wu W., Jiang X., and Tang Y. (2013) A Growing Thirst for Water Safety. *China Daily,* June 28, pp. 1, 6.

CHAPTER 23

UNESCO and Cultural Heritage: Unexpected Consequences

Christina Cameron

The roots of international cultural heritage discourse go back to the 1920s and 1930s, when concepts of common heritage and international cooperation as well as a distinctive style of international diplomacy developed through the League of Nations (Titchen 1995: 12–24). Following the creation of UNESCO in 1945 on the heels of World War II, ideas abounded for global standards to protect and use cultural heritage, to build technical capacity, and to intervene directly to protect threatened heritage. These ideas were fueled by outrage at the destructive consequences of global conflict, and by optimism that a new era was at hand that could reach across national borders and build a robust international society.

In response to specific circumstances, UNESCO has fostered the creation of standard-setting instruments and international organizations like the International Centre for the Study of the Preservation and Restoration of Cultural Property (ICCROM) and the International Council on Monuments and Sites (ICOMOS). Standard-setting instruments include sets of recommendations on archaeological excavations (UNESCO 1956), landscapes (UNESCO 1962), cultural property endangered by public or private works (UNESCO 1968), and historic urban areas (UNESCO 1976, 2011b). In addition, there are the fully fledged UNESCO conventions, such as the Convention for the Protection of Cultural Property in the Event of Armed Conflict (1954), the Convention on the Means of Prohibiting and Preventing the Illicit Import, Export and Transfer of Ownership of Cultural Property (1970), the Convention Concerning the Protection of the World Cultural and Natural Heritage, or World Heritage Convention

A Companion to Heritage Studies, First Edition. Edited by William Logan, Máiréad Nic Craith, and Ullrich Kockel.
© 2016 John Wiley & Sons, Inc. Published 2016 by John Wiley & Sons, Inc.

(1972), the Convention on the Protection of the Underwater Cultural Heritage (2001), the Convention for the Safeguarding of the Intangible Cultural Heritage (2003), and the Convention on the Protection and Promotion of the Diversity of Cultural Expressions (2005).

From a philosophical perspective, the conceptual frameworks underpinning these international instruments are being re-evaluated in light of present-day values and perceptions of fairness. Today's holistic approach to heritage conservation makes UNESCO's achievements appear fragmented and only partially effective – witness the ongoing erosion of historic urban centers, the encroachment of new infrastructure, and the deliberate destruction of monuments in conflict zones. This chapter on UNESCO's activities in cultural heritage focuses mainly on the World Heritage Convention (1972). It examines aspects that were not foreseen at the outset, in particular changes to the understanding of key concepts like Outstanding Universal Value, authenticity, and cultural landscapes, as well as changes to the role of experts and the involvement of civil society. The chapter then turns to unintended consequences, both positive and negative, with regard to public awareness, heritage discourse, conservation and "in danger" listing, tourism, politicization, and emerging international legal status.

Evolving World Heritage Concepts

Outstanding Universal Value

The World Heritage Convention (1972) establishes Outstanding Universal Value as the threshold for inscription on the World Heritage List. During the drafting process in April 1972, the proposed term "universal interest" was replaced in the definitions of cultural and natural heritage with Outstanding Universal Value (Cameron 2009: 127). Although used thirteen times in the World Heritage Convention text, the term is not defined and takes form through the World Heritage Committee's application of inscription criteria. The interpretation of the concept is not static. It has evolved through changes to the criteria, as well as through precedent-setting committee decisions on nominations. Early interpretations of cultural heritage focused on high-style architectural monuments, archeological sites of ancient civilizations, and historic cities, now viewed as evidence of bias in favor of properties from the Western world (Cameron and Rössler 2013a: 83; Labadi 2013: 59–63).

While the meaning of "outstanding" is defined through the application of comparative studies related to a nominated property, the notion of "universal" was challenged from the outset by the nomination of sites from diverse cultural contexts. The World Heritage Committee rapidly acknowledged that some properties "may not be recognized by all people, everywhere, to be of great importance and significance," and interpreted "universal" as "referring to a property which is highly representative of the culture of which it forms part" (UNESCO 1977a: 7). A later interpretation suggests that the term "can be understood as defining the quality of a site of being able to exercise a universal attraction for all humanity and exhibit importance for the present and future generations" (Francioni 2008: 19).

In response to increasing diversity and pluralism, the World Heritage Committee made various attempts to enlarge the interpretation of Outstanding Universal Value, including the adoption of the Global Study in 1983 and the Global Strategy in 1994 (Cameron and Rössler 2013a: 75–76, 82–83). The Global Strategy in particular demonstrates a shift towards a more anthropological perspective, one focused on cultural exchange and human experiences on the land and in society (Cameron and Rössler 2013a: 75–85). By the turn of the century, however, these efforts were still deemed insufficient. In her analysis of the World Heritage Convention (1972) at that time, Blake notes that there is a need "to employ a broader anthropological notion of cultural heritage that encompasses intangibles (such as language, oral traditions and local know-how) associated with monuments and sites and as the social and cultural context within which they have been created" (Blake 2001: v). During the twenty-first century, participation by almost all States Parties to the World Heritage Convention as well as the growing influence of the discourse of intangible heritage further sharpened a culturally relativist interpretation of Outstanding Universal Value. During the drafting of the 2003 UNESCO Convention for the Safeguarding of the Intangible Cultural Heritage (UNESCO 2002a: 11.2), the replacement of the phrase "outstanding specific value" by "representative list" also had an impact on World Heritage, since many delegates participated in both conventions. Subsequent decisions by the World Heritage Committee show its determination to list under-represented types of cultural heritage with strong intangible dimensions. While interpretation of the concept has evolved, criticism of the World Heritage Convention's high threshold continues. Nonetheless, the pride with which States Parties join the exclusive World Heritage List is palpable.

Authenticity

Another concept that has undergone significant reinterpretation is the condition of "authenticity," a requirement for World Heritage inscription. Until the final draft of the text of the World Heritage Convention (1972), the term was "integrity," proposed by American expert E.A. Connally, who drew on his experience with criteria for the United States National Register of Historic Places. Stovel claims it was changed to "authenticity" because European experts believed that "use of the integrity concept might limit analysis to concern for original form or design" (Stovel 1995: 394–96). After some initial minor adjustments to the definition, the attributes of authenticity remained unchanged for more than a decade (Cameron 2008: 19–21). With four attributes of design, materials, workmanship, and setting, the initial understanding of authenticity leaned towards tangible characteristics of properties, a reflection of European conservation philosophy at the time.

The first modification to the definition came in 1992, when the phrase "in the case of cultural landscapes their distinctive character and components" was added to reflect the presence of people living within such landscapes (UNESCO 1994: 24.b.i). But the most significant change to the understanding of authenticity as it applies to World Heritage sites emerged from the 1994 Nara Conference on Authenticity. Under the leadership of Japan, ICOMOS, and UNESCO, the Nara process brought together international experts with diverse cultural perspectives. The Nara Document on Authenticity (ICOMOS 1994) represents a paradigm shift in conservation theory because it interprets authenticity as a relative concept that must be understood within its own cultural context. It marked, in the view of one of the rapporteurs, Herb Stovel, "the final stage of the move from belief in universal international absolutes, first introduced by the Venice Charter, towards acceptance of conservation judgments as necessarily relative and contextual" (Stovel 2008: 9). For administrative reasons, the new list of attributes crafted at the Nara conference only received official approval a decade later by the World Heritage Committee.

These were: form and design; materials and substance; use and function; traditions, techniques and management systems; location and setting; language, and other forms of intangible heritage; and spirit and feeling (UNESCO 2005: 82). These attributes enlarge the concept to include intangible and associative aspects. This broader definition of authenticity has paved the way for listing properties like Aapravasi Ghat (Mauritius), where value is associated with memories of indentured workers from India, and the Old Bridge area of Mostar (Bosnia and Herzegovina), a reconstruction which ICOMOS judged to have overall authenticity with strong intangible dimensions (Cameron 2008: 23). It is interesting to note that the Intangible Heritage Convention (2003) does not include authenticity as a consideration for listing intangible cultural heritage, preferring to leave such judgments to associated communities (Labadi 2013: 132).

Cultural Landscapes

The development of the definition and categories of cultural landscapes in 1992 expanded the interpretation of cultural heritage, and helped bridge the gap between culture and nature. In the World Heritage Convention (1972), the definition of cultural heritage includes sites that demonstrate the "combined works of man and nature."[1] Although both natural and cultural heritage are included, early implementation of the World Heritage Convention focused on each end of the spectrum, avoiding the interface of culture and nature until the French delegation introduced a debate on rural landscapes in 1984. The ensuing discussions mark the first time that experts in cultural and natural heritage worked together to tease out the meaning and implications of this continuum between culture and nature. Important results include an understanding that such humanized landscapes will evolve and change over time, and that this holistic idea of heritage means that values are derived largely from the interaction between human beings and the land, and not from outstanding characteristics of the landscape itself (Cameron and Rössler 2013a: 60–71).

A philosophical breakthrough that deeply affected the interpretation of cultural landscapes came during a 1992 meeting of UNESCO experts at La Petite Pierre, France. The meeting developed a definition and framework for World Heritage cultural landscapes that included three categories: designed, organically evolved, and associative landscapes. The most important change was the new intangible dimension "justified by virtue of powerful religious, artistic or cultural associations of the natural element rather than material cultural evidence, which may be insignificant or even absent" (UNESCO 1992, Annex I: 5). Credit for this paradigm shift is attributed to an Australian participant, Isabel McBryde, who promoted the recognition of the spiritual aspects of indigenous landscapes (Gfeller 2013: 497). This expansive approach to associative cultural landscapes has facilitated the inscription of sites like Tongariro National Park (New Zealand) as cultural landscapes. The linkages with the Intangible Heritage Convention (2003) are evident.

Changes in the Role of Experts

Implementation of the World Heritage Convention (1972) depends on three players identified in the text: the States Parties who nominate and conserve eligible sites; UNESCO as registrar, secretariat, and coordinator of activities; and the Advisory Bodies, ICOMOS, ICCROM, and the International Union for the Conservation of

Nature (IUCN). Like a three-legged stool, each pillar is necessary to maintain equilibrium. With regard to technical expertise, ICOMOS, IUCN, and ICCROM use their professional networks to prepare criteria amendments, studies, and monitoring frameworks, as well as nomination evaluations and reports on the state of conservation. Their work has been supplemented by countless UNESCO expert meetings to more deeply study specific concepts and conservation issues, bringing together States Party practitioners and scholars from different regions and cultures of the world. Taken collectively, these activities constitute an extraordinary and continuous learning cycle as the World Heritage Convention adapts to new manifestations and perceptions of cultural heritage.

The role of expertise has evolved over time. For the evaluation of nomination documents, arguably one of the most sensitive activities in World Heritage, ICOMOS and IUCN have adjusted their methods to respond to new scientific studies and the diversity of cultures and sites. From an initial period when literature reviews and informal consultation were deemed adequate, both Advisory Bodies established new processes and introduced obligatory site visits to better understand local contexts. Significantly, both organizations have shifted from a single evaluator model to an institutional process which develops a corporate position with participation from their global memberships (Cameron and Rössler 2013a: 174–97).

In spite of the high quality of Advisory Body work, there has been a gradual and escalating rejection of expert advice in the twenty-first century, especially for nominations, due to unremitting pressure from States Parties who seek to inscribe sites immediately on the World Heritage List. This rejection flies in the face of consistent World Heritage Committee instructions to ICOMOS and the IUCN to be "as strict as possible in their evaluations" (UNESCO 1983: 38.a), now rephrased as "objective, rigorous and scientific in their evaluations" (UNESCO 2013b: 148.b). An argument can be made that technical evaluations are more and more thorough, taking into account new types of heritage and evolving concepts. But as a recent UNESCO audit confirms, "the decisions of the [World Heritage] Committee diverge more and more frequently from the scientific advice of the Advisory Bodies" (UNESCO 2011a: 172). Just how much the situation has changed is demonstrated by the growing gap between advice on nominations from ICOMOS and IUCN, and World Heritage Committee decisions. From 85 percent agreement in 2005, the numbers decline to 56 percent agreement in 2010 and 29 percent in 2011 and 2012 (UNESCO 2011a, Annex 5; Meskell 2013: 486–87).

This weakening of one leg of the three-legged stool has not gone unnoticed. On several occasions, Irina Bokova, director-general of UNESCO, has urged the World Heritage Committee and States Parties to return to scientific principles. At the 2012 World Heritage Committee session in St Petersburg, she observed that "some developments within the inscription process have weakened the principles of scientific excellence and impartiality that are at the heart of the [World Heritage] Convention … The credibility of the inscription process must be absolute at all stages of the proceedings" (UNESCO 2012: 2). At the 2013 General Assembly of States Parties, she reiterated her ongoing concern: "Let me be clear – in recent years, a number of developments within the inscription process have weakened the principles of objectivity and impartiality at the heart of the [World Heritage] Convention. It undermines everything the Convention stands for, everything we have sought for over 40 years" (UNESCO 2013a: 2).

The Growing Involvement of Civil Society

The World Heritage Convention (1972) does not mention the need for broad participation by civil society in its work. As an international treaty among national governments, observers and scholars have correctly criticized it for its concentration of power at the national level. Some argue that it enables governments to reinforce mainstream narratives while excluding those of minority groups and indigenous peoples. In this case, nationalism has not disappeared as a result of globalization, but instead it "continues to shape the way countries interact with global processes and with global institutions" (Labadi and Long 2010: 5). While recognizing the "laudable universalist ideals" that underpin UNESCO's work, Askew asserts that "the globalised and institutionalised heritage system has not overcome nation-state-based power structures and nationalist agendas, but has rather enhanced them, and this severely compromises the ideal of forging a countervailing meta-national zeitgeist evoked by the term 'World Heritage'" (quoted in Labadi and Long 2010: 20).

Aware of the absence of civil society in the World Heritage Convention (1972), drafters of the Intangible Heritage Convention (2003) explicitly added the requirement for countries to involve local communities in the identification and safeguarding of their intangible cultural heritage. Matsuura, former director-general of UNESCO, supports this approach: "I do think the 2003 convention is a better frame, giving more weight to the role of local communities. This is something the 1972 convention should have more carefully looked into."[2]

In the early years, the World Heritage Committee made deliberate choices to minimize the participation of interested stakeholders. This practice is explicitly spelled out in the 1988 operational guidelines which give directions for preparing nominations:

> In all cases, so as to maintain the objectivity of the evaluation process and to avoid possible embarrassment to those concerned, States Parties should refrain from giving undue publicity to the fact that a property has been nominated for inscription pending the final decision of the [World Heritage] Committee on the nomination in question. (UNESCO 1988: 14)

Milne, an American with long involvement in World Heritage matters, sums it up well: "I felt that the early decisions with regard to basically closed meetings and denying access to a variety of institutions and bodies has been in a way a weakness, and has, I believe, contributed to the general lack of public understanding or appreciation of what goes on."[3]

In the 1994 guidelines, the World Heritage Committee gave a somewhat reluctant nod to the role of communities: "Participation of local people in the nomination process is essential to make them feel a shared responsibility with the State Party in the maintenance of the site, but should not prejudice future decision-making by the [World Heritage] Committee" (UNESCO 1994: 14). It was only in the 2005 operational guidelines that the phrase about prejudicing the work of the World Heritage Committee was replaced with the positive encouragement of civil society: "States Parties are encouraged to prepare nominations with the participation of a wide variety of stakeholders, including site managers, local and regional governments, local communities, NGOs and other interested parties" (UNESCO 2005: 123).

With regard to organizations and professional associations, only those already associated with UNESCO were officially included in the World Heritage Convention. Attempts by various groups to achieve official status within the World Heritage system have been systematically rebuffed. For example, the Organization for World Heritage Cities, established after a 1991 international symposium in Quebec, applied without success for formal recognition as a Category B UNESCO organization (Cameron and Rössler 2013a: 217–18). The most serious case occurred in 2001, when a proposal to foster the development of a World Heritage Indigenous Peoples Council of Experts (WHIPCOE) was summarily rejected. The initiative came from a small group of countries, including Australia, Canada, and New Zealand, with large natural World Heritage sites inhabited by indigenous populations. The group believed that it was essential to provide an opportunity for indigenous voices to be heard in protecting the world's natural and cultural heritage. While some World Heritage Committee members, observers, and Advisory Bodies representatives were in favor, stating that "indigenous peoples have a special role with respect to certain World Heritage properties and that a network could provide a positive forum for an exchange of information and experience concerning their protection," others presented carefully crafted statements that raised legal concerns about WHIPCOE's status and the definition of indigenous peoples. In a clear demonstration of the fragility of nation-states, "the [World Heritage] Committee did not approve the establishment of WHIPCOE as a consultative body of the Committee or as a network to report to the Committee" (UNESCO 2002b: 57; see also Logan 2013: 164–65).

It is not by accident that a WHIPCOE participant, Tumu Te Heu Heu, paramount chief of the Ngati Tuwharetoa people of New Zealand and chair of the 2007 World Heritage session in Christchurch, proposed an amendment to the World Heritage Committee's strategic objectives to include a fifth "C" for "Community," a small step towards formalizing community involvement in World Heritage matters. In this second decade of the twenty-first century, civil society and communities are deeply involved in World Heritage matters, although still not formally within the statutory bodies of the World Heritage Committee. The powers of the World Heritage Committee remain unchanged. Nonetheless, evidence of public participation includes a thriving World Heritage partnerships program that involves many corporations and NGOs, as well as attendance at World Heritage Committee meetings by over one thousand people physically, and untold numbers virtually through streaming the event live on the internet.

Unexpected Consequences

Public Awareness

Public awareness of the World Heritage Convention (1972) has exceeded the expectations of its creators. Often referred to as a flagship program, it is UNESCO's best-known ambassador with a tangible presence at sites around the world. Evidence of the World Heritage Convention's popularity can be measured in several ways: the almost complete roster of countries that have ratified it, currently 191 States Parties; the number of participants at World Heritage Committee sessions, now well over a thousand in attendance; the number of sites on the World Heritage List (1007) and the waiting list (1611) as of June 2014; daily media coverage of World Heritage issues; an impressive array of private, public and not-for-profit partners; and eight UNESCO

Category 2 capacity-building centers related to World Heritage sponsored by States Parties in all regions of the world. Such a high level of global public awareness was not envisaged at the outset. According to Pressouyre:

> In the 1980s, the [World Heritage] Convention did not seem destined to this future, yet is now known around the world and is, I would say, an extremely powerful instrument for awareness-raising in all countries … It is necessary to pay attention now when a property is put on the World Heritage List because everyone is watching and de facto … it belongs to everyone more than in the past.[4]

Not only is awareness of this UNESCO program widespread, it is also positive. Admittedly, the primary focus is on the World Heritage List and less on conservation and protection goals. Nonetheless, international interest in World Heritage suggests that many people share the sentiment that "parts of the cultural or natural heritage are of outstanding interest and therefore need to be preserved as part of the world heritage of mankind as a whole."[5]

Heritage Discourse

One of the unexpected impacts of the World Heritage Convention (1972) is the emergence of a significant cultural heritage discourse with a strong interdisciplinary flavor. It was predictable that those directly involved in World Heritage implementation would develop concepts, methodologies, and research studies as part of their work (Cameron and Rössler 2013a: 187–201). As an off-shoot of the work of international ICOMOS, several national ICOMOS committees developed independent conservation charters to provide guidance for heritage sites in their own countries. Through the platform of World Heritage, some have influenced global practice, including the groundbreaking Australia ICOMOS Burra Charter (1979), which introduced innovative concepts like cultural (not heritage) significance and values-based decision-making (Australia ICOMOS 1979: arts. 1, 5, 6).

What was unpredictable is the impetus that World Heritage has given to the rapid development of academic courses and research in the field. Graduate heritage conservation programs located in different disciplinary contexts now exist in many countries and regions. Added to the university roster are over twenty UNESCO university chairs in as many countries focused on heritage conservation from diverse disciplinary perspectives including resource management, architecture, sustainable tourism, urban studies, World Heritage, museology, science, economics, and preventive maintenance. As a result of this academic activity, there is a growing body of published research including works on Outstanding Universal Value, authenticity, cultural landscapes, sustainable tourism, heritage theory, and many other subjects connected to World Heritage.

The flowering of these academic pursuits is an achievement that echoes the unfulfilled ambitions of the first director of the World Heritage Centre, Bernd von Droste. In 1992, he envisaged the creation of a centralized World Heritage Academy based in Paris with a "hundred leading people of more scientific standing" and "the world's largest collection of books" so as to have a "very strong scientific basis for World Heritage" (Cameron and Rössler 2013a: 205). As it has unfolded, the development of a global heritage discourse has occurred through an independent and geographically distributed academic sector, a more appropriate response to the diverse cultures and contexts of the world.

Conservation and the List of World Heritage in Danger

At the heart of the World Heritage Convention (1972) is protection of the planet's most precious cultural and natural heritage. Concerns about how to conserve listed sites emerged early, beginning in 1982 with an unsuccessful American proposal for a monitoring regime. In the early years, the World Heritage Committee developed an ad hoc reporting system on the state of conservation, and later added a formal system-wide monitoring regime known as periodic reporting (Cameron and Rössler 2013b). The spirit of international solidarity materialized in cooperative initiatives to share technical know-how, and to provide financial support for capacity building and safeguarding measures at specific sites. In these respects the World Heritage Convention met the expectations of its creators.

But a crucial unintended consequence is the marked resistance from States Parties to inscribing their sites on the List of World Heritage in Danger. The original intention was to identify those sites that were "threatened by serious and specific dangers" that needed major operations. The idea was to prepare estimates for the cost of these operations and to publicize them to attract donor funding, a process reminiscent of the earlier UNESCO international safeguarding campaigns.[6] Regrettably, few countries interpret this mechanism in a positive light. Almost all States Parties now view endangered listing as a black mark, an implicit criticism that their countries are not deemed capable of protecting World Heritage sites situated in their territories. Evidence of this attitude can be found by comparing the relatively low and stable number of properties on the List of World Heritage in Danger, which did not exceed 38 sites until 2013, when 6 in war-torn Syria were added, while the steadily increasing number of inscribed sites is just over the one-thousand mark. Drafters of the Intangible Heritage Convention (2003) learned from this, choosing to call a similar mechanism the List of Intangible Cultural Heritage in Need of Urgent Safeguarding.[7] The black-mark syndrome has deprived many World Heritage sites of timely aid for their conservation. Perhaps an informal change of nomenclature to something like the List of World Heritage sites for Priority Funding could reverse the trend and facilitate conservation at the most needy sites.

Tourism

When the World Heritage Convention (1972) was created, tourism was not at the top of the list. Drafters focused on conservation issues due to widespread destruction of cultural heritage during World War II, and escalating environmental degradation due to the development surge of the post-war years. In the first ten years, tourism was rarely part of World Heritage discourse. The word "tourism" appears only six times in World Heritage Committee minutes, consistently expressing concern about potential adverse impacts on the values of the sites, and cautioning that "socio-economic benefits from tourism should not jeopardize the state of preservation of the property" (UNESCO 1977b: 45). Over the years, the World Heritage Committee has treated tourism with caution. Its operational guidelines still refer to tourism as a pressure and potential threat, asking States Parties to explain whether sites can absorb visitors without adverse effects and urging countries to prepare tourism development plans that outline the steps taken to manage visitors and tourists (UNESCO 2013b, Annex 5: 4.b.iv).

On the other hand, the tourism industry has enthusiastically embraced World Heritage as an extraordinary business opportunity, developing hotel networks and travel itineraries based solely on World Heritage sites. Such attractions are essential to service the astounding growth in mass tourism. In the 1950s there were 25 million international arrivals; today there are over one billion.[8] The World Heritage system has been slow to understand the increase in what one study calls "World Heritage literacy," a global consumer awareness that comes from a critical mass of designated sites. The study concludes that the network effect of World Heritage sites automatically generates increased local, national, and international media attention. Specifically for tourism, it influences the travel choices of individuals as well as the itineraries of guidebook publishers and tour operators who have confidence in the World Heritage label as an indicator of quality (RC and TBR 2009: 24, 30). But statistics from the World Heritage Centre's state of conservation database indicate that almost 50 percent of World Heritage sites are experiencing negative impacts from tourism. The unexpected surge in mass tourism presents challenges for responsible stewards to develop new strategies to protect the Outstanding Universal Value of these properties.

Politicization

As an agreement among national governments, the World Heritage Convention (1972) is inherently political. Nonetheless, the creators of the treaty set out specific measures to downplay politics and to emphasize the importance of science by formally establishing the three Advisory Bodies and by indicating that "States Parties shall choose as their representatives persons qualified in the field of the cultural or natural heritage."[9] The World Heritage Committee translated this directive into its operational guidelines, beginning in 1980 and continuing to the present day in slightly modified form, by stating that "decisions must be based on considerations which are as objective and scientific as possible" and that they depend upon "evaluation by qualified experts and the use of expert referees" (UNESCO 1980: 5). In the early years, discussions at World Heritage Committee sessions were by and large technical, with a focus on criteria, conservation processes, and so forth. The gradual shift towards a more political discourse arose primarily through debates on a series of high-profile sites, including Auschwitz and Jerusalem (Cameron and Rössler 2013a: 165–74). By the year 2000, scientific principles were overshadowed by escalating politicization, and the ensuing years have only reinforced the trend. The 2013 amendment to the Rules of Procedure institutionalizes a system of lobbying and advocacy by invited States Parties to present their views after Advisory Body evaluations and reports (UNESCO 2013c: 22.7). This unexpected politicization is a reflection of the global situation, where national interests and regional alliances vie for a greater say and a fair distribution of power and resources.

Emerging International Legal Status

UNESCO plays a leadership role in setting international standards in the field of cultural heritage. Signatories to any UNESCO instrument undertake obligations and duties that are meaningful. In a 1983 landmark case concerning the Franklin Dam, Tasmania, one of the Australian High Court judges opined that signing the World Heritage Convention (1972) was not merely a statement of aspiration or political accord:

> Unless one is to take the view that over 70 nations have engaged in the solemn and cynical farce of using words such as "obligation" and "duty" when neither was intended or

> undertaken, the provisions of the Convention impose real and identifiable obligations and provide for the availability of real benefits for properties on the World Heritage List. (quoted in Peek and Reye 2006: 206–7)

Few countries have translated World Heritage obligations into national legislation. The United States was the first, followed shortly thereafter by Australia. In 1980, the Americans amended an existing law, the National Historic Preservation Act (1966), to assign responsibility for directing and coordinating World Heritage activities to the secretary of the interior in coordination with the secretary of state, the Smithsonian Institute and the Advisory Council on Historic Preservation (Reap 2006: 234). The Australian government faced a different situation because of the particular division of powers between the Commonwealth and state governments. The federal government used its constitutional responsibility for international treaties to pass World Heritage legislation, thereby acquiring additional powers in the federal–state tug-of-war over natural resources. The World Heritage Properties Conservation Act (1983) was subsequently replaced by provisions in the Environment Protection and Biodiversity Conservation Act (1999) (Peek and Reye 2006: 206).

The World Heritage Convention (1972) sets the parameters for a delicate balance between sovereignty rights of nations and international obligations.[10] An unexpected development is the emerging status of cultural heritage in international law. Evidence is being gathered through research led by Francesco Francioni, an international environmental lawyer and chair of the 1997 session of the World Heritage Committee. This team of legal researchers is documenting adjudications in international courts that concern cultural heritage. While acknowledging that no international court or tribunal currently exists with a specific cultural heritage focus, the team claims that international law shows a "remarkable intensification of interest in cultural property and a significant expansion of the legal tools for its protection" (Francioni and Gordley 2013: 1). While many national jurisdictions give weight to heritage concerns in planning decisions, an example from an investment arbitration context shows the influence of cultural heritage on treaty implementation. In 2007, the International Centre for Settlement of Investment Disputes (ICSID) gave "considerable weight" to cultural heritage impacts, although cultural heritage is not technically part of the treaty, in a judgment concerning an infrastructure project in Vilnius, Lithuania, a World Heritage site: "This award breaks new ground in introducing cultural heritage concerns as legitimate aims that the host state may pursue in adopting regulations or taking measures that have an impact on the economic interests of an investor" (Francioni and Gordley 2013: 18–19). The importance of cultural heritage in international law is a welcome but unexpected consequence of the UNESCO convention.

Conclusion

Expectations for a brave new world order for cultural heritage, fostered by UNESCO in the euphoric era of the 1960s and 1970s, could not be met. Even the approach of treating different aspects of cultural heritage separately, as demonstrated by the various UNESCO conventions and sets of recommendations, seems from a present-day perspective to be piecemeal and no longer aligned with current ideas about treating cultural heritage in a holistic way. The World Heritage Convention (1972) has proven its ability to adapt to different cultural perspectives, as shown by the evolution of concepts like Outstanding Universal Value, authenticity and cultural landscapes. Over time, an unfortunate politicization has undermined scientific principles and threatened the credibility of the World Heritage system. While there is a marked increase in the engagement of civil society and communities in the work of World Heritage, there is no real power-sharing as States Parties remain firmly in control. Implementation measures to date have not yet succeeded in systematically bringing the most threatened World Heritage sites to international attention, or achieving an acceptable balance between tourism and conservation. On the other hand, the World Heritage Convention has exceeded expectations in attracting public attention, in fostering a culturally diverse heritage discourse, and in developing international legal status for cultural heritage. Like all human activity, it is a work in progress.

Notes

1 World Heritage Convention (1972), art.1.
2 Interview with Koïchiro Matsuura, Paris, 2009.
3 Interview with Rob Milne, Paris, 2009.
4 Interview with Léon Pressouyre, Paris, 2008.
5 World Heritage Convention (1972), preamble.
6 See World Heritage Convention (1972), art. 11.4.
7 Intangible Heritage Convention (2003), art. 17.
8 Figures from "International Tourism Exceeds Expectations with Arrivals up by 52 Million in 2013." Press release 14004, UN World Tourism Organization, Madrid, January 20, 2014. Available at: http://media.unwto.org/press-release/2014-01-20/international-tourism-exceeds-expectations-arrivals-52-million-2013 (accessed January 20, 2014).
9 World Heritage Convention (1972), art. 9.3.
10 World Heritage Convention (1972) art. 6.1.

References

Legislation

Convention Concerning the Protection of the World Cultural and Natural Heritage (World Heritage Convention) (UNESCO, 1972). Available at: http://whc.unesco.org/archive/convention-en.pdf (accessed March 19, 2015).

Convention for the Protection of Cultural Property in the Event of Armed Conflict (Hague Convention) (UNESCO, 1954). Available at: http://unesdoc.unesco.org/images/0008/000824/082464mb.pdf (accessed March 19, 2015).

Convention for the Safeguarding of the Intangible Cultural Heritage (Intangible Heritage Convention)(UNESCO,2003).Availableat:http://unesdoc.unesco.org/images/0013/001325/132540e.pdf (accessed March 19, 2015).

Convention on the Means of Prohibiting and Preventing the Illicit Import, Export and Transfer of Ownership of Cultural Property (UNESCO, 1970). Available at: http://unesdoc.unesco.org/images/0013/001333/133378mo.pdf (accessed March 19, 2015).

Convention on the Protection and Promotion of the Diversity of Cultural Expressions (UNESCO, 2005). Available at: http://unesdoc.unesco.org/images/0014/001429/142919e.pdf (accessed March 19, 2015).

Convention on the Protection of the Underwater Cultural Heritage (UNESCO, 2001). Available at: http://unesdoc.unesco.org/images/0012/001246/124687e.pdf#page=56 (accessed March 19, 2015).

Environment Protection and Biodiversity Conservation Act (Government of Australia, 1999). Available at: http://www.comlaw.gov.au/Details/C2015C00063 (accessed March 19, 2015).

National Historic Preservation Act (United States Government, 1966, with amendments). Available at: http://www.ncshpo.org/nhpa2008-final.pdf (accessed March 19, 2015).

World Heritage Properties Conservation Act (Government of Australia, 1983). Available at: http://www.austlii.edu.au/cgi-bin/download.cgi/cgi-bin/download.cgi/download/au/legis/cth/num_act/whpca1983427.txt (accessed March 19, 2015).

Other Works

Australia ICOMOS (1979) Charter for Places of Cultural Significance (Burra Charter). Available at: http://australia.icomos.org/wp-content/uploads/Burra-Charter_1979.pdf (accessed January 22, 2014).

Blake, J. (2001) *Developing a New Standard-Setting Instrument for the Safeguarding of Intangible Cultural Heritage: Elements for Consideration*. Paris: UNESCO.

Cameron, C. (2008) From Warsaw to Mostar: The World Heritage Committee and Authenticity. *APT Bulletin*, 39 (2/3), 19–24.

Cameron, C. (2009) The Evolution of the Concept of Outstanding Universal Value. In N. Stanley-Price and J. King (eds), *Conserving the Authentic*. Rome: ICCROM Conservation Studies, pp. 127–136.

Cameron, C., and Rössler, M. (2013a) *Many Voices, One Vision: The Early Years of the World Heritage Convention*. Farnham: Ashgate.

Cameron, C., and Rössler, M. (2013b) The Shift towards Conservation: Early History of the 1972 World Heritage Convention and Global Heritage Conservation. In M.-T. Albert, R. Bernecker, and B. Rudolff (eds), *Understanding Heritage: Perspectives in Heritage Studies*. Berlin: De Gruyter, pp. 69–76.

Francioni, F. (2008) *The 1972 World Heritage Convention: A Commentary*. Oxford: Oxford University Press.

Francioni, F., and Gordley, J. (eds) (2013) *Enforcing International Cultural Heritage Law*. Oxford: Oxford University Press.

Gfeller, A. (2013) Negotiating the Meaning of Global Heritage: "Cultural Landscapes" in the UNESCO World Heritage Convention, 1972–92. *Journal of Global History*, 8 (3), 483–503.

ICOMOS (1994) Nara Document on Authenticity. Available at: http://www.icomos.org/charters/nara-e.pdf (accessed January 16, 2014).

Labadi, S. (2013) *UNESCO, Cultural Heritage and Outstanding Universal Value: Value-Based Analyses of the World Heritage and Intangible Cultural Heritage Conventions*. Plymouth, UK: AltaMira Press.

Labadi, S., and Long, C. (eds) (2010) *Heritage and Globalisation*. London: Routledge.

Logan, W. (2013) Australia, Indigenous Peoples and World Heritage from Kakadu to Cape York: State Party Behaviour under the World Heritage Convention. *Journal of Social Archaeology*, 13 (2), 153–176.

Meskell, L. (2013) UNESCO's World Heritage Convention at 40: Challenging the Economic and Political Order of International Heritage Conservation. *Current Anthropology*, 54 (4), 483–494.

Peek, M., and Reye, S. (2006) Judicial Interpretation of the World Heritage Convention in the Australian Courts. In B.T. Hoffmann (ed.), *Art and Cultural Heritage: Law, Policy and Practice*. New York: Cambridge University Press, pp. 206–209.

Reap, J.K. (2006) The United States and the World Heritage Convention. In B.T. Hoffmann (ed.), *Art and Cultural Heritage: Law, Policy and Practice*. New York: Cambridge University Press, pp. 234–238.

RC and TBR (Rebanks Consulting and Trends Business Research) (2009) World Heritage Status: Is There Opportunity for Economic Gain? Report prepared for the Lake District World Heritage Project. Available at: http://rebanksconsultingltd.com/resources/WHSTheEconomicGainFinalReport.pdf (accessed January 12, 2014).

Stovel, H. (1995) Considerations in Framing the Authenticity Question for Conservation. In K.E. Larsen (ed.), *Nara Conference on Authenticity in Relation to the World Heritage Convention, Nara, Japan, 1–6 November 1994: Proceedings*. Trondheim: Tapir Publishers, pp. 393–398.

Stovel, H. (2008) Origins and Influence of the Nara Document on Authenticity. *APT Bulletin*, 39 (2/3), 9–17.

Titchen, S. (1995) On the Construction of Outstanding Universal Value: UNESCO's World Heritage Convention (Convention Concerning the Protection of the World Cultural and Natural Heritage, 1972) and the Identification and Assessment of Cultural Places for Inclusion in the World Heritage List. Ph.D. dissertation. Canberra: Australian National University.

UNESCO (1956) Recommendation on International Principles Applicable to Archaeological Excavations. Available at: http://portal.unesco.org/en/ev.php-URL_ID=13062&URL_DO=DO_TOPIC&URL_SECTION=201.html (accessed February 24, 2015).

UNESCO (1962) Recommendation Concerning the Safeguarding of Beauty and Character of Landscapes and Sites. Available at: http://portal.unesco.org/en/ev.php-URL_ID=13067&URL_DO=DO_TOPIC&URL_SECTION=201.html (accessed February 24, 2015).

UNESCO (1968) Recommendation Concerning the Preservation of Cultural Property Endangered by Public or Private Works. Available at: http://portal.unesco.org/en/ev.php-URL_ID=13085&URL_DO=DO_TOPIC&URL_SECTION=201.html (accessed February 24, 2015).

UNESCO (1976) Recommendation Concerning the Safeguarding and Contemporary Role of Historic Areas. Available at: http://portal.unesco.org/en/ev.php-URL_ID=13133&URL_DO=DO_TOPIC&URL_SECTION=201.html (accessed February 24, 2015).

UNESCO (1977a) Operational Guidelines for the Implementation of the World Heritage Convention. Document CC-77/conf.001/8. Available at: http://whc.unesco.org/archive/opguide77a.pdf (accessed January 16, 2014).

UNESCO (1977b) Report of the Rapporteur on the First Session of the World Heritage Committee in Paris, 27 June to 1 July 1977. Document CC-77/CONF.001/9. Available at: http://whc.unesco.org/archive/1977/cc-77-conf.001-9en.pdf (accessed January 14, 2014).

UNESCO (1980) Operational Guidelines for the Implementation of the World Heritage Convention, WHC/2/revised. Available at: http://whc.unesco.org/archive/opguide80.pdf (accessed January 6, 2014).

UNESCO (1983) Operational Guidelines for the Implementation of the World Heritage Convention, WHC/2/revised. Available at: http://whc.unesco.org/archive/opguide83.pdf (accessed January 10, 2014).

UNESCO (1988) Operational Guidelines for the Implementation of the World Heritage Convention, WHC/2/revised. Available at: http://whc.unesco.org/archive/opguide88.pdf (accessed January 10, 2014).

UNESCO (1992) Report of the Expert Group on Cultural Landscapes, La Petite Pierre (France) 24–26 October 1992, Revision of the Operational Guidelines for the Implementation of the World Heritage Convention. Document WHC-92/conf.002/10/add., Annex I. Available at: http://whc.unesco.org/archive/pierre92.htm (accessed January 16, 2014).

UNESCO (1994) Operational Guidelines for the Implementation of the World Heritage Convention, WHC/2/revised. Available at: http://whc.unesco.org/archive/opguide94.pdf (accessed January 10, 2014).

UNESCO (2002a) Preliminary Draft of the International Convention on Intangible Cultural Heritage, Paris, 10 June 2002. Document GRR2/CH/2002/WD/5. Available at: http://www.unesco.org/culture/ich/doc/src/04844-en.doc (accessed January 14, 2014).

UNESCO (2002b) Report of the Twenty-Fifth Session of the World Heritage Committee in Helsinki, 11–16 December 2001. Document WHC-01/conf.208/24. Available at: http://whc.unesco.org/archive/2001/whc-01-conf208-24e.pdf (accessed January 12, 2014).

UNESCO (2005) Operational Guidelines for the Implementation of the World Heritage Convention, WHC.05/2. Available at: http://whc.unesco.org/archive/opguide05-en.pdf (accessed January 10, 2014).

UNESCO (2011a) Final Report of the Audit of the Global Strategy and the PACT Initiative, Paris, 27 May 2011. Document WHC-11/35.com/inf. 9. Available at: http://whc.unesco.org/archive/2011/whc11-35com-INF9Ae.pdf (accessed January 14, 2014).

UNESCO (2011b) Recommendation on the Historic Urban Landscape, Including a Glossary of Definitions. Available at: http://portal.unesco.org/en/ev.php-URL_ID=48857&URL_DO=DO_TOPIC&URL_SECTION=201.html (accessed February 24, 2015).

UNESCO (2012) Address by Ms Irina Bokova, UNESCO Director-General, on the Occasion of the Opening of the 36th session of the World Heritage Committee: Let Us Rejuvenate the World Heritage Convention, St Petersburg, 24 June 2012. Document DG/2012/096. Available at: http://unesdoc.unesco.org/images/0021/002167/216700e.pdf (accessed January 14, 2014).

UNESCO (2013a) Address by Irina Bokova, Director-General of UNESCO, on the Occasion of the Open Debate on Item 11 Follow-up of the Director-General's Meeting on "The World Heritage Convention: Thinking Ahead" during the 19th General Assembly of States Parties to the World Heritage Convention, Paris, 21 November 2013. Document DG/2013/213. Available at: http://unesdoc.unesco.org/images/0022/002250/225052m.pdf (accessed January 6, 2014).

UNESCO (2013b) Operational Guidelines for the Implementation of the World Heritage Convention, WHC.13/01. Available at: http://whc.unesco.org/archive/opguide13-en.pdf (accessed February 24, 2015).

UNESCO (2013c) Rules of Procedure: Intergovernmental Committee for the Protection of the World Cultural and Natural Heritage, WHC-2013/5. Available at: http://whc.unesco.org/en/committee (accessed January 17, 2014).

CHAPTER 24

The Limits of Heritage: Corporate Interests and Cultural Rights on Resource Frontiers

Rosemary J. Coombe and Melissa F. Baird

Introduction

"Critical heritage studies" (Baird 2009, 2012) positions heritage within a wider field of global institutions, discourses, and power relations. For example, the new emphasis upon cultural heritage as a development resource by international institutions, states, NGOs, and local governing bodies is criticized by scholars who call attention to the new governmentalities that neoliberal heritage regimes engender (Coombe 2012), and their impacts on local "communities" reduced to mere "stakeholders" in reconfigured fields of power. In this vein, we draw upon ethnographic studies in Australia, Romania, and Madagascar to show how heritage claims emerge in new terrains of contestation involving local residents, resources, and extractive industries. International heritage institutions face new challenges as heritage becomes imbricated in industry strategies on "resource frontiers" (Tsing 2003, 2005), limiting social expectations for its governance. Rights-oriented institutions and movements, however, also afford communities and indigenous peoples the means to insist upon new forms of participation and accountability, and assert territorialities that expose the limits of universalizing heritage discourses.

A Companion to Heritage Studies, First Edition. Edited by William Logan, Máiréad Nic Craith, and Ullrich Kockel.
© 2016 John Wiley & Sons, Inc. Published 2016 by John Wiley & Sons, Inc.

Contentious Terrain: Heritage, Resources, and Rights

Heritage is everywhere: Viking heritage is rebranded as a "Disney-style amusement park," urban trail systems promote a city's "brewing heritage," and national parks protect indigenous cultural heritage from industrial development. The exponential growth of heritage is part of a proliferation of culturalized claims to property and rights in an era of neoliberalism, informational capital, and indigenous politicization (Coombe 2009). Cultural heritage is positioned as a resource to alleviate poverty, provide sources of human dignity, sustain livelihoods, prevent rural to urban migration, reinforce social cohesion, and provide new forms of enterprise for "communities," culturally conceived.

UNESCO and its advisory bodies, moreover, are increasingly preoccupied with negotiations around resources and the proliferation and impact of extractive industries. These institutions are now called upon to respond to global conflicts and to mediate issues of development and human rights, while negotiating boundaries between zones of permissible actors and permitted activities. They find themselves engaged with industry actors and private sector institutions to broker issues of natural resource extraction, environmental impact, and social benefit. Such involvements are especially intense on resource frontiers, a concept that delineates places of emergent agency at the intersection of industrial enterprise, transnational governmentalities, international norms, and local interests (Tsing 2003, 2005). Resource frontiers concentrate action: investment, extraction, negotiation, development, and resistance. These are zones in which natural heritage and sustainable development initiatives uneasily coexist with extractive industry and peoples who have cultural attachments to lands. In such contexts, the definition, rhetorical framing, and rights to lay claims to heritage are all matters of contention.

Corporate discourses of responsibility may become reconfigured around expressions of heritage (Weiss 2014) in what we might cynically deem a new heritage industrial complex. Development priorities provoke international heritage bodies to legitimate new dispensations. The World Heritage Committee's decision in 2012 to allow Tanzania to excise village lands in a wildlife corridor in the Selous Game Reserve for the Mkuju River Uranium Project, overturning their earlier decision that mining was incompatible with heritage status, illustrates these new pressures from state and industry interests. The uranium project was majority owned by a Russian corporation, and the decision was made when Russia was chairing the World Heritage Committee session, in clear violation of rules regarding conflicts of interest. International mining activists charge that Tanzania has not complied with the conditions set by the World Heritage Committee, and has no intention of so doing (Uranium Network 2013). The project has provoked unprecedented international opposition on health, environmental, economic, and human rights grounds that has spurred interfaith cooperation and support from civil society organizations and aboriginal peoples with extensive experience with the industry (Kuhne 2013).

The UN Special Rapporteur on the Rights of Indigenous Peoples, James Anaya, made critical evaluation of extractive industries in and near indigenous territories an international priority in 2013. His earlier report to the UN Human Rights Council asserted that dominant models for advancing natural resource extraction were contrary to the international principle of indigenous self-determination, and that most states and industry actors failed to understand the basic minimum standards of their responsibilities (UNHRC 2011). Most global governance bodies, however, understand the negative consequences of resource extraction within or near indigenous territories, and a wide variety of NGOs seek to assist indigenous peoples and other local communities to control and limit extractive practices or to develop partnerships that assure community benefits.

Global heritage institutions must at least nominally show adherence to a new body of international indigenous rights in which cultural heritage grounds new political claims (Wiessner 2011). As we explain below, the International Union for the Conservation of Nature (IUCN) has become obligated to demonstrate its commitment to respect international indigenous rights. Indigenous rights, however, are only one category of rights in which the heritage significance of lands and resources grounds collective cultural rights that may be used to discipline states and the industrial developments they condone (FPP 2013). In its reporting procedures and a newly established complaints process, the UN Committee on Economic, Social and Cultural Rights (CESCR) affirms that the right to participate in cultural life may be exercised by communities in the ways that they occupy lands and use resources, and the rights of minorities to conserve and develop their own culture includes protection of the cultural heritage of communities in economic development and environmental policies. This requires that States Parties obtain free, prior, and informed consent (FPIC) when the preservation of a group's cultural resources, especially those associated with their way of life, are at risk. Indigenous peoples, moreover, seek to embed compliance with customary law principles into the very definition of FPIC. Clearly rights-based struggles on resource frontiers will increasingly engage issues of indigenous territoriality.

The International Convention on the Elimination of all Forms of Racial Discrimination (1969) that binds 175 nation-states affirms the cultural rights of ethnic groups, and the UN Committee on the Elimination of Racial Discrimination (UNCERD) recently called for the government of Laos to "review its land regime with a view to recognizing the cultural aspect of land as an integral part of the identity of some ethnic groups" in mountainous areas (UNCERD 2012: 4). UNCERD has extended the principle of FPIC as a requirement in *all* resource-based projects that affect the way of living, livelihood, and culture of ethnic groups. In early warning and urgent action procedures as well as its general recommendations, it affirms the collective property rights of ethnically and racially identified peoples "in cases where their ways of life and culture are linked to the utilization of lands and resources" (UNCERD 2011: 2). New regional rights bodies have also extended recognition of culturally based land and resource rights. The tenure rights of non-indigenous "forest peoples" governed by customary law, for instance, are increasingly articulated as human rights in the face of accelerated land grabs in Africa (De Schutter 2011). For communities whose ancestral lands and traditional livelihoods are significant aspects of their cultural identity, logging, industrial agriculture, aquaculture, and even large-scale tourism may be considered extractive enterprises. Cultural heritage, in short, grounds an increasing number of human rights laws, principles, and norms. Nonetheless, representatives of States Parties to UNESCO's international heritage conventions and heritage professionals often seem to be either ignorant of these rights and/or actively hostile to their exercise as the recent treatment of the World Heritage Indigenous Peoples Council of Experts illustrates (Logan 2013; Meskell 2013).

Industry Engagement with Heritage

If social scientists now trace the discursive logic and material apparatus through which private actors deploy international heritage languages in new forms of heritage governance (Golub and Rhee 2013; Patterson and Telesetsky 2012, Starr 2013), heritage scholars must now attend to the ways in which cultural heritage responsibilities are taken up in highly publicized statements by corporate bodies (e.g. Baird 2013; Weiss 2014). What work does such discourse accomplish, and how does it align with or legitimate industry practices? We need to study global flows of discourse, imagery, capital, normative principles, and the frictions between these (Tsing 2005, 2009). Such investigations need to follow specific discourses, political agendas, and forms of expertise (ethnographically, archivally, and through zones of publicity and personal experience) as these are framed by heritage concepts. Does corporate publication of finely crafted heritage policy statements serve as a way to develop community capacities, or does it make an extractivist agenda more acceptable to a wider group of interlocutors?

With these questions in mind, Baird visited two sites in Western Australia and Northern Territory presented in an oft-cited publication by the mining company Rio Tinto (Bradshaw and Rio Tinto 2011), and found that the company was working closely with Aboriginal communities and developing best practices of some benefit to them (Baird 2013). At the same time, it is clear that publications such as *Why Cultural Heritage Matters* (Bradshaw and Rio Tinto 2011) reframe contentious debates in a celebratory language of partnership that ignores power relations and obscures environmental impacts. Corporate discourse contains, manages, and packages heritage in nostalgic, ahistorical, and apolitical ways, and presents a view of good governance that ignores issues of coercion, levels of political recognition, and struggles to control lands and identities. Ongoing contested claims are presented as resolved and indigenous communities are unilaterally represented as partners in development projects in which they have had little if any choice.

Corporate heritage discourse produces corporate literary forms that deploy a standardized array of rhetorical techniques to frame local heritage so that it serves as evidentiary legitimation of corporate social responsibility (CSR) principles and company respect for international legal norms for community protection (Kirsch 2010). Rio Tinto's communities and social performance indices, for example, clearly draw upon earlier iterations of social impact assessment and redefine these around business priorities (Rio Tinto 2011). Key documents delineate corporate attention to communities, gender relations, and rights principles in a way that fulfills the company's ultimate responsibilities to shareholders and investors. Who assesses their veracity? While the protection of heritage may be offered up by corporate interests as a bargaining chip to negotiate enhanced access to land and resources, our critical inquiries need to go further. In any given context we need to ask whether heritage is a shared point of reference in overall negotiations, a consideration required by national or regional legislation, an attempt to align development with human rights norms, an effort to appease NGOs, a way to ensure eligibility for "ethical" investment, or an endeavor to limit and sequester the agency of indigenous and local communities. In addition to corporate intent, we need to consider global pressures, national contexts, and local effects and consequences.

Indigenous peoples, moreover, are now linked with powerful international networks as a consequence of the global recognition of indigenous rights and the support of transnational environmental organizations. Regional associations of indigenous peoples have become increasingly proactive in naming, blaming, and shaming states, development banks, and industry actors whose activities fail to accord with recognized indigenous and collective rights. They have circulated their own statements of best practices in attempts to educate communities about the kinds of pressure they can assert on funding bodies, industry groups, and particular companies. For example, the Asia Indigenous Peoples Pact recently published a community guide for indigenous peoples designed to educate communities about their rights pursuant to the Asian Development Bank's safeguard policy statement (AIPP 2013). This financial institution funds projects in regions where 70 percent of the world's indigenous peoples live; it is the third largest donor to developing countries in Asia and the Pacific.

Over 20 years, indigenous peoples have pressured the Asian Development Bank (ADB) to develop safeguard policies and procedures to hold member states accountable. These remain poorly known, making widespread violations of these safeguards inevitable unless and until indigenous peoples and their supporters find effective ways of using grievance, redress, and accountability mechanisms to pressure member states. Heritage scholars could play an important role in this education process. Significantly, safeguards are to be initiated if a project directly or indirectly affects the human rights, livelihood, and culture of indigenous peoples or their natural and cultural resources.[1] In the absence of regional human rights instruments, this is an important lever for indigenous peoples seeking recognition, participation, and the sharing of benefits. The ADB will neither finance projects that have not complied with safeguards, nor support those in which a member state has failed to comply with international legal obligations. As we have seen, such obligations include many rights that are premised upon collectively held cultural heritage. What role might critical heritage scholars play in identifying potential violations of rights in the face of development proposals and publicizing impending harms?

The Australian context might be used as an example of how the specificities of national legislation limit and shape the political expectations we might have for heritage governance. The value of Australian mineral exports exceeded AUS$107 billion in 2012, and the development of extractive industries in Western Australia is unprecedented (Scambary 2013). Yet, despite 60 percent of mineral operations occurring in or near indigenous communities (Taylor 2012), most Australian Aboriginal peoples have seen little benefit (Langton and Longbottom 2012). Unlike most settler colonies, there is no treaty in Australia that formally recognizes indigenous peoples' prior occupancy of lands and waters. Heritage legislation in Northern Territory and South Australia provided the baseline for securing Australian Aboriginal peoples' rights and restricting activities on areas or sites of significance. Indeed, the limits of heritage governance regimes focused on sites, places, and objects (Teehan and Godden 2012) spurred movements to recognize Aboriginal legal title, culminating in the High Court's recognition of native title in the case of *Mabo v. Queensland (No. 2)* (1992) and the Native Title Act (1993), which ensured legal and political recognition, and rights to negotiate and claim benefits, transforming the way that mining companies and industrial actors more generally conducted their operations. Disparities in power and benefit have fundamentally shifted. In 2001, Rio Tinto announced an agreement with Aboriginal owners in the Pilbara region of Western Australia to provide AUS$2 billion over 40 years (Anon. 2011). The Argyle Diamond Mine Indigenous Land Use Agreement incorporated a rights-based policy framework, which recognized the Daa'man and Dawange peoples as "bosses for the country," and shared benefits through payments to community controlled trusts, guaranteed employment, and provided for developing Aboriginal enterprise (Doohan, Langton, and Mazal 2012). Although contractual partnership models have political limits (O'Faircheallaigh 2008), they are now the dominant means to address issues of indigenous cultural sustainability (Ritter 2009). Still, Aboriginal peoples complain that native title as recognized in Australia falls far short of their rights under international law and gives resource corporations the upper hand in negotiations (NCAFP 2012).

On most resource frontiers, environmental resources, biodiversity, and sustainable development principles coexist uneasily with both extractive industry and peoples dependent upon land. The latter may "culturalize" claims and grievances to appeal to a broad range of potential partners and allies so as to gain greater leverage to shape local economic development efforts. In such contexts, the definition and management of heritage may serve diverse, contradictory, and conflicting political and economic needs. Rather than criticize these new corporate engagements and community articulations as instrumental agencies, we need critical inquiries that more precisely explore the configurations of this new terrain. In what specific ways do industries call upon heritage as a way to gain access to lands and resources and provide legitimacy for business practices? When are they successful, and when does the evocation of heritage act as a limit on corporate practices? Under what conditions can communities use these rhetorical frameworks to bargain for new forms of economic opportunity and/or political recognition? What leverage does the corporate use of heritage discourse provide to indigenous peoples seeking enhanced recognition of their rights from states or local government? When does it limit or undermine them?

New Expectations and Demands on Heritage Bodies

The jurisdictions of global advisory heritage bodies are shifting. The World Heritage advisory body the International Council on Monuments and Sites (ICOMOS) was originally mandated to evaluate cultural and cultural properties proposed for the World Heritage List, while the IUCN came into being to evaluate natural and environmental heritage. Historically, the latter had little interest in recognizing or protecting cultural heritage. Although the cultural landscape designation brought together natural and cultural values, in indigenous contexts, cultural heritage values were often subordinated to the natural values of heritage sites (see Baird 2009, 2012). Since the ratifications of the Convention on Biological Diversity (1992) and the Declaration on the Rights of Indigenous Peoples (United Nations 2007), however, the IUCN has had to move into a rights terrain characterized by culturally based collective and community rights.

The IUCN's Commission for Environmental, Economic and Social Policy embraced the promotion of biocultural diversity as a policy principle, and thereby indexed sympathy to organized indigenous peoples' political work. Including "Biocultural Diversity and Indigenous Peoples" as one of the "journeys" at the 2008 World Conservation Congress, indigenous peoples were involved in more than 60 events, culminating in the adoption of resolutions integrating culture and cultural diversity into IUCN policy (McIvor, Fincke, and Oviedo 2008). Significantly, the IUCN endorsed the Declaration on the Rights of Indigenous Peoples (United Nations 2007) and resolved to incorporate indigenous rights requirements in all of its programs (Oviedo and Puscharsky 2012). The recognition of community conservation in accordance with customary law was taken up as topic of research, and biocultural indigenous territories governed by traditionally constituted authorities were affirmed, along with recognition that many of the world's so-called community conserved areas were formed without indigenous peoples' FPIC. This legitimates the Permanent Forum on Indigenous Peoples' complaints about these sites' constitution. The number of indigenous community members in the IUCN has also increased; a revisiting and restructuring of World Heritage Sites in accordance with rights-based principles may result as a consequence of these changes.

International recognition of the role of indigenous peoples and local communities in the management of protected areas is evidenced by new practices, such as collaborative management of protected areas and new categories of territory, such as indigenous and community conserved areas, in what has been described as "a new paradigm linking conservation, culture and rights" (Stevens 2014). These are accompanied by a new willingness in international environmental circles to acknowledge conservation landscapes as having cultural dimensions that may be crucially linked to the biological resources they harbor (Pretty *et al.* 2009). Thousands of protected areas are home to large numbers of people dispossessed of livelihood resources under former conservation paradigms that are now seen as both counterproductive and violations of human rights (Kothari 2008). Co-managed and community-conserved areas have been established as relatively autonomous zones in which indigenous cultural norms and customary law have normative stature, following upon global recognition that indigenous peoples' traditional environmental knowledge and practices are inherently linked to their cultural heritage.

The IUCN has recognized these new forms of governance in its global systems of protected area categories, and acknowledged indigenous peoples and local communities as legitimate guardians of landscapes. The formal introduction of a rights-based approach to conservation inevitably means that the IUCN must support local and indigenous community involvement in UNESCO nomination processes and site management plans and activities (IUCN 2011). Recognizing that many inscribed sites overlap with traditional indigenous lands, the IUCN is obliged to consider if and to what extent traditional tenure and access rights were addressed in nomination processes and site management. Noting that indigenous intangible cultural heritage is constitutive of many World Heritage Sites, the IUCN acknowledges that rights monitoring and traditional governance will require more attention in all of them, and that in future nominations indigenous peoples' and local communities' rights will need to be secured in the official dossiers from the outset.

During the same period that it was acknowledging culturally based rights, the IUCN implemented a Business and Biodiversity Programme and operational guidelines for private sector engagement to promote discussions of indigenous peoples' rights and extractive industries (IUCN 2011), no doubt prompted by the UN Special Rapporteur's professed concerns. In response to growing controversies over the environmental impacts of mining operations in the global South, the IUCN had already identified mining as a priority, establishing a relationship with the International Council on Mining and Metals (ICMM) – an industry group focused on issues of sustainable resource development – while positioning mining companies as legitimate "stakeholders" in territories of global heritage significance (ICCM 2013). The IUCN also developed a working relationship in "dialogue" with indigenous communities, making the institution an increasingly important mediator in development disputes involving cultural heritage.

At the fourth session of the World Conservation Congress in 2008, the IUCN passed the "responsible mining" resolution and established the Extractive Industry Responsibility Initiative. Rio Tinto responded proactively, seeking to clarify relationships between industry and sustainability via a three-year collaboration with the IUCN beginning in 2010, devoted to developing best practices. In predictable neoliberal fashion, objectives include increasing "capacities for market-based approaches to environmental management and conservation" that bring awareness to conservation and business challenges (IUCN 2010). The parties agreed to collaborate on issues of land management and biodiversity, to integrate "natural capital" into business decisions, and to indicate how land can deliver ecosystem services. To what extent the IUCN's combined emphases on rights-based approaches to conservation and the development of neoliberal vehicles to build value from ecosystem protection may be reconciled is unclear. This is a paradox that indigenous peoples negotiate on many fronts, including climate change and carbon markets, in which they continually articulate FPIC principles in furtherance of self-determination.

Despite this recent and more progressive approach to indigenous and community rights by the IUCN, and perhaps, indeed, because of it, there appears to be a clear erosion of the power of the advisory bodies to the World Heritage Committee and a new, assertive ascendancy of state signatories to the Convention Concerning the Protection of the World Cultural and Natural Heritage (1972), who increasingly overturn recommendations with respect to nominations (Meskell 2013) and leverage heritage for political purposes. Select countries have formed key alliances in the process of garnering voting support. Heritage scholars thus face new challenges unraveling the processes through which development banks, industry interests, indigenous peoples, NGOs, and new social movements pressure Member State governments so as to shape this new landscape and the ways in which state signatories comply with or evade such pressures. Similarly, the new focus on "communities" as subjects of neoliberal cultural governmentality (Coombe 2012) is giving rise to a host of new discourses and technologies for cultural management, as well as new forms of local political agency (Coombe 2011; Coombe and Weiss 2015).

Heritage and Development Scenarios: Limits and Opportunities

We now provide ethnographic glimpses of three historical landscapes in which heritage looms large in political contexts where communities, governments, NGOs, and international heritage advisory bodies encounter corporate actors and negotiate issues of development, sustainability, environmental resources, indigenous rights, and modes of governance. Not surprisingly, the combination of variables differs in each instance, and available data is limited, especially with respect to some of the newer tendencies we have outlined. Each case distinctly illustrates the "limits" of heritage, but the new political contexts we have delineated also suggest that relevant actors have potential new opportunities to assert claims on heritage grounds. Each poses new research and ethical questions for heritage scholars.

The Australian Mining Boom

Resource frontiers are clearly situated in areas of significant indigenous heritage values. The Pilbara, located in the northwestern region of Western Australia, is Aboriginal "country," a term that Aboriginal people use to describe ancestral and inherited places, and the practices and law that guide behavior there. This once remote and environmentally vulnerable coastal region is in the midst of a breathtaking economic transition – with physical, political, and social infrastructure being built to support expanding iron ore, liquefied natural gas (LNG), and salt operations. These comprised 81 percent of the value of Western Australia's mineral and petroleum production in 2012 (McKenzie 2013). Such development is occurring on or near heritage lands, as exemplified by the Burrup Peninsula, which features hundreds of thousands of unique pictographs. The archipelago is country to its traditional custodians – the Ngarluma/Yindjibarndi, Yaburara Madudhunera, and Wong-goo-tt-oo peoples – and has been at the center of heated debates involving conservation and heritage groups, local residents, and traditional owners who have protested the Burrup Peninsula's physical degradation and the cultural loss wrought by the destruction of pictographs and sacred sites. Developers have divided the land into industrial tracts that ignore how this archipelago functions as a holistic cultural landscape for Aboriginal peoples.

In 2013, the minister for environment announced the creation of Murujuga, Western Australia's one hundredth national park, a community co-managed protected area on the footprint of land designated as non-industrial under a 2003 management plan between industry, the government, and native title holders. One consequence is that the majority of the peninsula is thereby opened up for industrial development. The park is jointly managed by the Department of Environment and Conservation (DEC) and the Murujuga Aboriginal Corporation under a management plan developed "in consultation" with the community and prepared by a council comprised of traditional owners, DEC representatives, and the minister of indigenous affairs. It is geographically bound by the Indian Ocean and the LNG plant operated by Woodside Petroleum Limited. Protected as a cultural and environmental heritage site, the park is a very small portion of a peninsula where 64 percent of the land is available for industrial development. Represented as creating "a lasting partnership between Aboriginal people … [that] balances the protection of its ancient and living heritage with the sustainable use of the region's natural resources," it is doubtful that rights to FPIC were respected in its establishment.[2]

Clearly, there are great challenges in mediating and managing heritage adjacent to an industrial estate of this size. The sheer physicality of an LNG exporting plant next to a park sized for a small community and its traditional modes of usage is incongruent; adverse effects include the displacement of livelihood activities, noise, air pollution, and unknown chemical releases. How will the divergent interests of park residents, visitors, and the nearby industry be reconciled? What role do traditional authorities have, and to what extent will customary legal protocols be respected? Heritage managers are faced with mediating starkly different uses and meshing these with conservation and cultural values.

There are reasons to suspect that attention to heritage values in this instance may serve to deflect attention from issues of environmental protection. While traditional owners have achieved new positions of relative power with respect to a small area in which they can exercise some autonomy, the majority of the Burrup Peninsula is primed for industrial development about which they may be deprived of capacities to grieve. How do acknowledgements of limited heritage protection in areas set aside for indigenous stewardship shape the ways in which the larger concept of sustainability is understood within contiguous mining development projects? In Murujuga, a focus on heritage values displaces discussions about larger environmental impacts in coastal areas affected by extractive industry. What is gained and what is lost by communities who accept the constitution of small portions of their territories as parks by way of state recognition of their cultural and environmental values? We do not need to judge the work of traditional custodians to recognize the wider fields of power and possibility potentially at play. The emergence of new divisions of labor in heritage management on resource frontiers challenges us to consider a more complicated terrain of environmental and political consequence.

Industrial Heritage in Roşia Montană, Romania

Roşia Montană is a community of villages in the South Apuseni Mountains in west-central Romania, whose heritage includes archeological sites, funerary monuments, and an industrial landscape of early-twentieth-century gold mining. It is also promoted as one of the best-preserved natural environments in Europe. The local cultural foundation asserts that the Roşia Montană is not simply part of local but of European patrimony of great natural and cultural significance. Nonetheless, the region is in dire need of new economic growth opportunities, and municipal authorities have sought sources of sustainable development in which natural resources can be preserved and invested in by way of public–private partnerships. With rich mineral resources, an industrial history, and a desire to combine environmental sustainability with economic growth, Roşia Montană attracted the interest of global mining industries willing and able to play heritage politics for financial gain (Egresi 2011).

The proposal by a Canadian corporate investor to develop an open-pit gold mining operation – the Roşia Montană Gold Corporation (RMGC) – divided local stakeholders and attracted international attention when local heritage institutions, failing to find government ears receptive to their opposition, appealed to ICOMOS and the World Heritage Committee (considering the area's nomination as a heritage site) to help prevent this proposed industrial growth. Shrewdly, RMGC pitched its plan to forge "lasting cultural heritage together with an environmental legacy" by using best practices of environmental management. They drew upon local heritage discourses that romanticized the regional practice of mining as organically rooted in the landscape and, following common industry practice, divorced the culture of mining from the social, economic, and environmental dispossession it historically effected. In contexts such as this, even the available scholarship needs to be approached with caution. Gligor and Tămaş (2009) cite the historical basis for considering mining as an essential aspect of people's heritage in the area, one which they *should* sustainably develop and from which they could derive future environmental, cultural, and economic benefits (a proposition that at first glance seems to echo the position of local officials). Foreign investment in the project, they argued, would "create major assets for the community and at the same time … certify that modern mining and cultural heritage can well coexist" (Gligor and Tămaş 2009: 53). But because the lead author is an employee of the open-pit mining operation, the heritage concept appears to be deployed in an effort of "green washing" – "efforts to project more socially and environmentally friendly images to consumers, investors or regulators" (Bebbington 2010: 1).

This brief example gives us a glimpse of the rhetorical politics at play in new landscapes of heritage where foreign interests, global institutions, state parties, and local elites broker discourses of naturalized patrimony, cultural significance, environmental preservation, and economic development. Local communities may well struggle to find voice in the municipal, national, and international regimes of governance in which they find themselves located. In this instance, it appears that the landscape of heritage policy was fractured into discrete understandings of natural, cultural, and industrial heritage, whose very compartmentalization enabled commercial interests to use the concept strategically. RMGC pointed to historic mining activities as corroboration of the region's industrial heritage, which they sought only to sustainably develop. Heritage, however, did not feature in the RMGC's consideration of its operation's concrete economic and environmental impacts.

Organized local interests, on the other hand, saw the proposed World Heritage status as a means of leverage with which to navigate international bureaucracies and find powerful allies to protect the area from unwanted industrialization. A report sent to ICOMOS by the local heritage organization's Romanian president recorded alarm about how intensified mining would negatively impact the heritage considered outstanding for global heritage protection purposes. Ultimately, the government was swayed by the outpouring of protest and the feared environmental damage, refusing to issue the necessary permits. RMGC insisted that failure to implement the proposed development merely ensured that the region would soon suffer from 80 percent unemployment, and had lost the opportunity for sustainable development that their remediation of the environmental damage done by the historic mining activities would afford. We neither have the data nor the expertise to weigh up the merits of the respective arguments, nor do a full range of community interests appear to be represented in the available documentation. How did unemployed residents, for example, respond to this initiative by local cultural experts? What environmental impact studies were done?

Malagasy Custom and Universalist Heritage

Despite recent efforts to embrace and "safeguard" the heritage of "communities" as a source of local cultural meaning and identity (Coombe and Weiss 2015; Forsyth 2012), heritage has always been amenable to capture by universalist discourses. UNESCO's definitions of cultural heritage, even in the more expansive field of intangible cultural heritage, embrace both local meanings and global values. If intangible cultural heritage is transmitted from generation to generation, constantly recreated in response to environment and interactions with nature and history, while providing a sense of identity and continuity to groups and communities, its safeguarding must also promote global values of cultural diversity and sustainable development, and be compatible with human rights.

Those local "communities" who claim land as part of their cultural heritage, however, usually do so in highly specific ways that express their cosmologies grounded in human knowledge and practices which reproduce social worlds and local livelihoods. For example, Malagasy peoples use the concept of *fomba gasy* to refer to their own customs regarding land as the basis of "a social, existential, and ontological web, which ties past, present and future generations" (Evers and Seagle 2012: 97). Many now do so, however, in the context of a multi-billion dollar ilmenite mine, run by Rio Tinto and its subsidiary, QIT Madagascar Minerals (QMM) near Fort Dauphin, that encompasses a rare 6000 hectare littoral forest prized for its biodiversity, as well as the ancestral lands of the Antanosy and Antesaka people who have tombs in the area.

In the context of controversial African "land grabs," protected conservation areas have grown in size, scope, and popularity in Madagascar, attracting international conservation NGOs and provoking multinational corporate interests to find new vocabularies to legitimate extractivist industries. Since 1999, Rio Tinto has adopted sustainability discourses in new partnerships with international conservation NGOs, adding a new discourse of universalized needs and interests to the rhetorical means through which the company justifies its practices. Conservationists often refer to biodiversity itself as "world heritage" and a universal entitlement. In exchange for their rights to strip-mine the forests in which these Malagasy people live, Rio Tinto/QMM have leased 30,000 hectares of forest land elsewhere by way of "biodiversity offsets," a form of offsite compensation for their activities. They also entered into an agreement with Kew Gardens in London to send seeds of plants endemic to the forest for safekeeping in its international seed banks. Both activities represent "commitments" to preserving biodiversity as a global, human heritage.

In terms of local heritage values, however, sustainable development should only take place in harmony with the processes through which the deceased become ancestors. For Malagasy, ancestors are the true owners of the land; their heirs merely derive its fruits until they too become ancestors through the portals that permanent, inalienable tombs provide. Evers and Seagle (2012) suggest that the dynamic and processual nature of *fomba gasy* is at odds with an international concept of heritage focused upon static, defined, bounded pieces of land and heritage "sacred sites" "located" upon such lands, which, according to corporate interpretations of global policy, should not be "disturbed." Malagasy concepts of heritage are not limited to objects or places, however, but encompass the embodied human uses of land as both a material and spiritual medium of social reproduction. Moreover, the institutions put into place to engage communities are wholly inadequate to address local social complexities.

Rio Tinto/QMM assert that their activities have no social impact on the use of territory because no complaints have been registered, while acknowledging that there is no functioning complaint mechanism for communities to use (Kraemer 2012; QMM 2010). New contractual institutions created by the state in the 1990s and dominated by local lineage elites are used to register compliance with *dina* as an authentic cultural expression of local customary law and community consent that has little legitimacy with local farmers (Bérard 2009). The poorest, most marginalized people are those most dependent upon the forest in the mining zone for daily livelihood resources such as energy, construction, handicrafts, medicine, and the performance of ancestral services. They are also those least likely to qualify as participants in the local "community" recognized in corporate socioenvironmental mitigation programs (Kraemer 2012).

How is it that carbon offsets are sold on ancestral lands without community permission in circumstances where there are no mechanisms enabling communities living in or near mining "protected areas" to be heard or compensated? Under what circumstances is the work of some cultivators recognized as a contribution to crop genetic resources and successfully asserted as biocultural heritage (Coombe and Griebel 2014), while the livelihoods of others are accepted as so "degrading" to forests that foreign corporations are entitled to destroy them in the name of protecting biodiversity? This is only possible, critics suggest, in a still relatively isolated island environment characterized by entrenched social hierarchies, where movements for indigenous and forest peoples' rights have made few inroads, legal tenure is insecure, the state recognizes no resource rights, and Malagasy peoples find few opportunities for transnational partnerships or international representation (Ferguson 2010). Certainly, these Malagasy are amongst the non-indigenous communities whose heritage-based rights the Forest Peoples Programme seeks to articulate, and for whose claims they seek wider support.

This is also a site of biocultural diversity in which the IUCN might seek to reconcile dedication to community-based conservation and customary law, protecting traditional environmental knowledge and insisting upon responsible industry practice. It might serve as a good test case of the compatibility of its commitments to responsible mining practices, sustainable development, and human rights norms.

Closing Comments

Heritage is obviously being taken up as a political resource in new and surprising ways. As international heritage bodies are called upon to involve and engage local communities in the project of protecting heritage and safeguarding intangible cultural heritage, their work is increasingly imbricated in encounters with corporate, indigenous, and transnational actors who have incorporated heritage norms into their own agendas. If such intersections pose limits to the emancipatory expectations we should have for heritage governance in some instances, they also suggest that heritage governance on resource frontiers is a site of intensified struggles whose outcomes are unpredictable.

Industry actors are using international heritage vocabularies in new exercises of corporate social responsibility that might be considered novel forms of public–private policy in which industrial and community agents voluntarily take up and reframe global legal principles of sustainability, community, and heritage for their own ends (e.g. Luning 2012; Welker 2009). Mining companies have attempted to usurp or co-opt global norms that position heritage as a development resource by funding tenure-track faculty positions, endowing research chairs, and offering their own staff as experts to serve in global heritage institutions. Rio Tinto is at the forefront of efforts to articulate corporate "best practices" in heritage management, including "cultural heritage offsets." To what extent should heritage scholars participate in these corporate efforts, providing documentation of intangible cultural heritage (for oral histories, museums, and publications), or contribute to the corporate conservation of culturally significant landscape features which provide rationales for indigenous dispossession elsewhere, or function to "compensate" peoples displaced from cultural landscapes and alienated from practices of intangible cultural heritage embedded in ancestral territories?

Indigenous peoples may increasingly culturalize their claims to local resources and livelihoods in order to appeal to an ever broadening range of international legal norms that respect their rights to control their cultural heritage. In so doing, they may seek or find alliances with other rights-based movements. Some communities, faced with extractivist encroachments upon livelihood resources, may find an indigenous subject position attractive precisely because of the enhanced legitimacy their cultural norms assume in the international arena of indigenous rights. We see this logic at work throughout the world, where communities constitute themselves as indigenous peoples through their opposition to industries destructive to what they come to understand as ancestral territories to which they have historical claims. Alex Golub (2014), for example, writes about how the Ipili in Manus Province, Papua New Guinea, came to more fully constitute themselves as a group holding cultural heritage precisely as they forged their opposition to one of the world's largest gold mines (see also Logan 2013). Indeed, even where local peoples do not identify themselves as indigenous, attention to international indigenous rights regimes and the affordances they offer to local communities dealing with extractivist industry on resource frontiers is strategically advised (Langton and Longbottom 2012). Heritage scholars will be compelled to situate themselves in such politics.

We need to move beyond critiques which focus primarily upon the ways in which heritage does or does not faithfully represent actual histories and culture as it is experienced, or communities as they see themselves, to understand the political and economic work that heritage is doing for diverse agents seeking multiple audiences in performative utterances in various venues and multiple scales in conditions of neoliberal governmentality (Coombe and Weiss 2015). We must pay more attention to the "publics" heritage rallies, the accounting norms through which it may become an offset, and the NGOs for whom its citation and site location provides places for new investment. For example, we find extractive industries and ecotourism enterprises working side by side (Buscher and Davidov 2013) in areas in which "community" cultural difference has been targeted for entrepreneurial investment.

Heritage struggles for rights and resources are clearly politicized on resource frontiers. The exploitation of heritage resources in unfamiliar places will engage social scientists, heritage managers, conservation activists, indigenous peoples' movements, traditional communities, NGOs, and state actors in unforeseen ways. Scholars have new responsibilities to critically explore assemblages of actors and institutions as well as the legitimating logics of these new heritage landscapes, attending to the international discourses and institutional norms that provide political resources for these new projects, while exploring how these are put to use by various parties to serve particular interests. Such projects are inherently transnational ones in which corporate policy, public relations, market measures, environmental norms, indigenous rights, and nationally and internationally recognized forms of territoriality are at least as important as international heritage organizations in France and Switzerland.

Acknowledgements

The authors wish to thank the editors of the volume for the opportunity for this collaboration. Coombe would like to acknowledge the support of the Canada Research Chairs Program and the research assistance of Marc Griebel. Baird acknowledges the support of the Stanford Archaeology Center, the Woods Institute for the Environment, and the Department of Anthropology at Stanford University.

Notes

1 The indigenous peoples safeguards are triggered if a project directly or indirectly affects the dignity, human rights, livelihood systems, or culture of indigenous peoples or affects the territories or natural or cultural resources that they own, use, occupy, or claim as an ancestral domain or asset. The term "indigenous peoples" is used in a generic sense to refer to a distinct, vulnerable, social, and cultural group possessing the following characteristics in varying degrees: (i) self-identification as members of a distinct indigenous cultural group and recognition of this identity by others; (ii) collective attachment to geographically distinct habitats or ancestral territories in the project area and to the natural resources in these habitats and territories; (iii) customary cultural, economic, social, or political institutions that are separate from those of the dominant society and culture; and (iv) a

distinct language, often different from the official language of the country or region. In considering these characteristics, national legislation, customary law, and any international conventions to which the country is a party will be taken into account. A group that has lost collective attachment to geographically distinct habitats or ancestral territories in the project area because of forced severance remains eligible for coverage under this policy.

2 The quoted passage comes from "State's 100th National Park Announced." Press release, GovernmentofAustralia,2013.Availableat:http://www.mediastatements.wa.gov.au/_layouts/mobile/dispform.aspx?List=b389bce3-6767-405e-8870-a68d6925cac7&View=623ecd10-6172-412f-9eaa-e4ad246dd06a&ID=7107 (accessed March 2, 2015).

References

Legislation

Convention Concerning the Protection of the World Cultural and Natural Heritage (World Heritage Convention) (UNESCO, 1972). Available at: http://whc.unesco.org/archive/convention-en.pdf (accessed March 19, 2015).

Convention on Biological Diversity (United Nations, 1992). Available at: http://www.cbd.int/doc/legal/cbd-en.pdf (accessed March 19, 2015).

International Convention on the Elimination of All Forms of Racial Discrimination (United Nations, 1969). Available at: http://www.ohchr.org/Documents/ProfessionalInterest/cerd.pdf (accessed March 19, 2015).

Native Title Act (Government of Australia, 1993). Available at: http://www.comlaw.gov.au/Details/C2014C00631 (accessed March 19, 2015).

Case Law

Mabo v. Queensland (No. 2) (1992), High Court of Australia. HCA 23; 175 CLR 1. Available at: www.austlii.edu.au/au/cases/cth/high_ct/175clr1.html (accessed January 22, 2015).

Other Works

AIPP (Asia Indigenous Peoples' Pact) (2013) *We Have Rights: A Community Guide for Indigenous Peoples on the 2009 ADB Safeguard Policy Statement and Accountability Mechanism.* Chiang Mai: AIPP Printing Press.

Anon. (2011) Landmark Rio Deal to Deliver Billions to Aborigines. *The Age*, June 3, 2011. Available at: http://www.theage.com.au/national/landmark-rio-deal-to-deliver-billions-to-aborigines-20110602-1fiwq.html (accessed November 1, 2012).

Baird, M.F. (2009) The Politics of Place: Heritage, Identity, and the Epistemologies of Cultural Landscapes. Ph.D. dissertation. Eugene: University of Oregon.

Baird, M.F. (2012) "The Breath of the Mountain Is My Heart": Indigenous Cultural Landscapes and the Politics of Heritage. *International Journal of Heritage Studies*, 19 (4), 327–340.

Baird, M.F. (2013) Mining and the New Heritage Landscapes. Paper presented at the American Anthropological Association, Chicago, November 2013.

Bebbington, A. (2010) Extractive Industries and Stunted States: Conflict, Responsibility and Institutional Change in the Andes. In R. Raman (ed.), *Corporate Social Responsibility: Discourses, Practices and Perspectives.* London: Palgrave MacMillan, pp. 97–116.

Bérard, M.H. (2009) Légitimité des normes environnementales et complexité du droit: L'exemple de l'utilisation des DINA dans la gestion locale de la forêt à Madagascar (1996–2006). Ph.D. dissertation. Quebec: Université Laval.

Bradshaw, E., and Rio Tinto (2011) *Why Cultural Heritage Matters: A Resource Guide for Integrating Cultural Heritage Management Into Communities Work at Rio Tinto.* London: Rio Tinto.

Buscher, B., and Davidov, V. (eds) (2013) *The Ecotourism-Extraction Nexus: Political Economies and Rural Realities of (Un)Comfortable Bedfellows.* London: Routledge.

Coombe, R.J. (2009) The Expanding Purview of Cultural Properties and their Politics. *Annual Review of Law and Social Sciences*, 5, 393–412.

Coombe, R.J. (2011) Cultural Agencies: The Legal Construction of Community Subjects and Their Properties. In M. Woodmanse, M. Biagioli, and P. Jaszi (eds), *Making and Unmaking Intellectual Property.* Chicago: University of Chicago Press, pp. 79–88.

Coombe, R.J. (2012) Managing Cultural Heritage as Neoliberal Governmentality. In R. Bendix, A. Egert, and A. Peselmann (eds), *Heritage Regimes and the State.* Gottingen: Universitatsverlag Gottingen, pp. 375–387.

Coombe, R.J., and Griebel, M. (2014) An Amodern Territory: Working Potatoes and Properties in an Era of Informational Capital. Paper presented at the Alternative Property Practices Symposium, International Institute for the Sociology of Law, Onati, Spain, April 4.

Coombe, R.J., and Weiss, L. (2015) Neoliberalism, Heritage Governmentality, and Rights-Based Politics. In L. Meskell (ed.), *Global Heritage: A Reader.* London: Wiley Blackwell, pp. 43–69

De Schutter, O. (2011) The Green Rush: The Global Race for Farmland and the Rights of Land Users. *Harvard International Law Journal*, 52, 504–559.

Doohan, K., Langton, M., and Mazel, O. (2012) From Paternalism to Partnership: The Good Neighbour Agreement and the Argyle Diamond Mine Indigenous Land Use Agreement in Western Australia. In M. Langton and J. Longbottom (eds), *Community Futures, Legal Architecture: Foundations for Indigenous Peoples in the Global Mining Boom.* London: Routledge, pp. 231–250.

Egresi, I. (2011) The Curse of the Gold: Discourses Surrounding the Project of the Largest Pit-Mine in Europe. *Human Geographies*, 5 (2), 57–68.

Evers, S.J.T., and Seagle, C. (2012) Stealing the Sacred: Why "Global Heritage" Discourse Is Perceived as a Frontal Attack on Local Heritage-Making in Madagascar. *Madagascar Conservation and Development*, 7 (2S), 97–106.

Ferguson, H.B. (ed.) (2010) Voices from Madagascar's Forests: Representation and Rights of Malagasy Forest People. Report on a conference held at the University of East Anglia, Norwich, UK, June 5–6. Norwich: University of East Anglia. Available at: http://www.redd-monitor.org/wp-content/uploads/2010/09/VoicesfromMadagascarFinalReport2010.pdf (accessed February 22, 2015).

Forsyth, M. (2012) Lifting the Lid on the Community: Who Has the Right to Control Access to Traditional Knowledge and Expressions of Culture? *International Journal of Cultural Property*, 19, 1–31.

FPP (Forest Peoples Programme) (2013) The Rights of Non-Indigenous "Forest Peoples" with a Focus on Land and Related Rights: Existing International Legal Mechanisms and Strategic Options. Available at: http://www.forestpeoples.org/topics/rights-land-natural-resources/publication/2013/rights-non-indigenous-forest-peoples-focus-land (accessed March 2, 2015).

Gligor, A. and Tămaş, C. (2009) Roşia Montană: Cultural Heritage in the Context of a New Mining Development. *Studia UBB, Geologia*, 54 (1), 49–54.

Golub, A. (2014) *Leviathans at the Gold Mine: Creating Indigenous and Corporate Actors in Papua New Guinea.* Durham, NC: Duke University Press.

Golub, A., and Rhee, M. (2013) Traction: The Role of Executives in Localizing Global Mining and Petroleum Industries in Papua New Guinea. *Paideuma*, 59, 215–236.

ICCM (International Council on Mining and Metals) (2013) Identifying Potential Overlap between Extractive Industries (Mining, Oil and Gas) and Natural World Heritage Sites. Final report. Available at: http://www.icmm.com/document/6950 (accessed March 25, 2014).

IUCN (2010) IUCN's Collaboration Agreement with Rio Tinto. Available at: http://cms.iucn.org/?uNewsID=5674 (accessed June 16, 2014).

IUCN (2011) Report Submitted by IUCN to the Tenth Session of the United Nations Permanent Forum on Indigenous Issues. Document E/C.19/2011/CRP.8. 2 May 2011. Gland: IUCN.

Kirsch, S. (2010) Sustainable Mining. *Dialectical Anthropology*, 34 (1), 87–93.

Kothari, A. (2008) Protected Areas and People: The Future of the Past. *Parks*, 17 (2), 23–35.

Kraemer, A. (2012) Whose Forests, Whose Voices? Mining and Community Based Nature Conservation in Southeastern Madagascar. *Madagascar Conservation and Development*, 7 (2S), 5–16.

Kuhne, E. (ed.) (2013) *Uranium Mining: Impact on Health and Environment*. Dar es Salaam: Legal and Human Rights Centre/Rosa Luxemburg Stiftung. Available at: http://www.uranium-network.org/images/pdfs_tanzania/Uranium_Mining_Impact.pdf (accessed June 18, 2014).

Langton, M., and Longbottom, J. (eds) (2012) *Community Futures, Legal Architecture and Indigenous Peoples in the Global Mining Boom*. New York: Routledge.

Logan, W. (2013) Australia, Indigenous Peoples and World Heritage from Kakadu to Cape York. *Journal of Social Archaeology*, 13 (2), 153–176.

Luning, S. (2012) Corporate Social Responsibility (CSR) for Exploration: Consultants, Companies and Communities in Processes of Engagements. *Resources Policy*, 37 (2), 205–211.

McIvor, A., Fincke, A., and Oviedo, G. (2008) Bio-Cultural Diversity and Indigenous Peoples' Journey. Report from the 4th IUCN World Conservation Congress Forum, Barcelona, Spain, October 6–9. Gland: IUCN. Available at: http://cmsdata.iucn.org/downloads/bcd_ip_report_low_res.pdf (accessed March 2, 2015).

Mckenzie, F.H. (2013) Delivering Enduring Benefits from Gas Development: Governance and Planning Challenges in Remote Western Australia. *Australian Geographer*, 44 (3), 341–358.

Meskell, L. (2013) UNESCO and the Fate of the World Heritage Indigenous Peoples Council of Experts (WHIPCOE). *International Journal of Cultural Property*, 20 (2), 155–174.

NCAFP (National Congress of Australia First Peoples) (2012) First Peoples and Extractive Industries: Good Practices. UN Special Rapporteur, Professor James Anaya. Report of roundtable meeting, Melbourne, August 20–21. Available at: http://nationalcongress.com.au/wp-content/uploads/2012/09/ExtractiveIndustriesRoundTableReport.pdf (accessed March 2, 2015).

O'Faircheallaigh, C. (2008) Negotiating Cultural Heritage? Aboriginal–Mining Company Agreements in Australia. *Development and Change*, 39 (1), 25–51.

Oviedo, G., and Puschkarsky, T. (2012) World Heritage and Rights-Based Approaches to Nature Conservation. *International Journal of Heritage Studies*, 18 (3), 285–296.

Patterson, R., and Telesetsky, H. (2012) Heritage Inc.: A Mini Symposium on Heritage Protection and Private Actors. *International Journal of Cultural Property*, 19 (4), 549–571.

Pretty, W. *et al.* (2009) The Intersections of Biological Diversity and Cultural Diversity: Towards Integration. *Conservation and Society*, 7 (2), 100–112.

QMM (QIT Madagascar Minerals) (2010) Exploitation des sables minéralisés de Fort-Dauphin: Bilan des suivis sociaux et environnementaux 2005–2009, phase construction, parties 7 à 12. Report submitted to the Office National pour l'Environnement de Madagascar, Antananarivo.

Rio Tinto (2011) Communities and Social Performance Fact Sheet. Available at: http://www.riotinto.com/sustainabledevelopment2011/pdf/communities_factsheet.pdf (accessed March 31, 2014).

Ritter, J. (2009) *The Native Title Market*. Crawley: University of Western Australia Press.

Scambary, B. (2013) *My Country, Mine Country: Indigenous People, Mining and Development Contestation in Remote Australia*. Canberra: Australia National University E-Press. Available at: http://press.anu.edu.au/titles/centre-for-aboriginal-economic-policy-research-caepr/my-country-mine-country/(accessed, February 27, 2015).

Starr, F. (2013) *Corporate Responsibility for Cultural Heritage: Conservation, Sustainable Development and Corporate Reputation*. New York: Routledge.

Stevens, S. (ed.) (2014) *Indigenous Peoples, National Parks and Protected Area: A New Paradigm Linking Conservation, Culture, and Rights*. Phoenix: University of Arizona Press.

Taylor, J. (2012) Measuring Indigenous Outcomes from Mining Agreements in Australia. In M. Langton and J. Longbottom (eds), *Community Futures, Legal Architecture: Foundations for Indigenous Peoples in the Global Mining Boom.* Oxford: Routledge, pp. 59–75.

Teehan, M., and Godden, L. (2012) Legal Forms and their Implications for Long-Term Relationships and Economic, Cultural and Social Empowerment: Structuring Agreements in Australia. In M. Langton and J. Longbottom (eds), *Community Futures, Legal Architecture: Foundations for Indigenous Peoples in the Global Mining Boom.* Oxford: Routledge, pp. 111–132.

Tsing, A.L. (2003) Natural Resources and Capitalist Frontiers. *Economic and Political Weekly.* 38 (48), 5100–5106.

Tsing, A.L. (2005) *Friction: An Ethnography of Global Connection.* Princeton: Princeton University Press.

Tsing, A.L. (2009) Worlds in Motion. In A.L. Tsing and C. Gluck (eds), *Words in Motion: Toward a Global Lexicon.* Durham, NC: Duke University Press, pp. 11–20.

UNCERD (2011) General Recommendation No. 34 Adopted by the Committee, Racial Discrimination against People of African Descent. Document CERD/C/GC/34. Available at: http://www2.ohchr.org/english/bodies/cerd/docs/GR34_English.pdf (accessed March 2, 2015).

UNCERD (2012) Consideration of Reports Submitted by States Parties Under Article 9 of the Convention, Concluding Observations of the Committee on the Elimination of Racial Discrimination, Lao People's Democratic Republic. Document CERD/C/LAO/CO/16–18. Available at: http://www2.ohchr.org/english/bodies/cerd/docs/CERD.C.LAO.CO.16-18.pdf (accessed March 2, 2015).

UNHRC (2011) Report of the Special Rapporteur for Indigenous Peoples, James Anaya: Extractive Industries Operating within or Near Indigenous Territories. Document A/HRC/18/35. Available at: http://unsr.jamesanaya.org/annual-reports/report-to-the-human-rights-council-a-hrc-18-35-11-july-2011 (accessed June 16, 2014).

United Nations (2007) Declaration on the Rights of Indigenous Peoples (UNDRIP). Document A/RES/61/295. Available at: http://www.un-documents.net/a61r295.htm (accessed March 19, 2015).

Uranium Network (2013) Statement re. Mkuju River Uranium Project and Selous Game Reserve World Heritage Site. Available at: http://www.uranium-network.org/images/pdfs_tanzania/u-n_Statement-Selous-2013.pdf (last accessed June 18, 2014).

Weiss, L.M. (2014) Informal Settlements and Urban Heritage Landscapes in South Africa. *Journal of Social Archaeology*, 14 (1), 3–25.

Welker, M. (2009) Corporate Security Begins in the Community: Mining, the Corporate Social Responsibility Industry, and Environmental Advocacy in Indonesia. *Cultural Anthropology*, 24 (1), 142–179.

Wiessner, S. (2011) The Cultural Rights of Indigenous Peoples: Achievements and Continuing Challenges. *European Journal of International Law*, 22 (1), 121–140.

CHAPTER 25 Indigenous Peoples' Rights and the World Heritage Convention

Stefan Disko

Introduction

Adopted before the entry into force of both the International Covenant on Civil and Political Rights (1966) and the International Covenant on Economic, Social and Cultural Rights (1966), as well as almost all other core international human rights instruments, UNESCO's Convention Concerning the Protection of the World Cultural and Natural Heritage, or World Heritage Convention (1972), finds itself increasingly at odds with internationally agreed human rights standards as well as interrelated principles and values such as cultural diversity, sustainable development, and good governance.[1] This is particularly evident when one considers the experiences of indigenous peoples with the implementation of the World Heritage Convention against the backdrop of their status and rights under international human rights law. While indigenous peoples and human rights organizations have repeatedly called on UNESCO and the World Heritage Committee to bring the implementation of the World Heritage Convention into line with international standards concerning the rights of indigenous peoples by adopting appropriate changes to procedures and operational guidelines, these efforts have so far been unsuccessful. Instead, there have been several cases in recent years where the rights of indigenous peoples were violated in the processes of the convention, not only at the national level in the management of specific World Heritage sites, but also at the international level in the practice of the World Heritage Committee, its Advisory Bodies and its Secretariat (the UNESCO World Heritage Centre). They have

A Companion to Heritage Studies, First Edition. Edited by William Logan, Máiréad Nic Craith, and Ullrich Kockel.
© 2016 John Wiley & Sons, Inc. Published 2016 by John Wiley & Sons, Inc.

attracted the attention of international human rights bodies and mechanisms, and undermine the credibility of UNESCO as an organization committed to human rights, intercultural understanding and democratic principles.

This chapter begins with a brief overview of indigenous peoples' rights relevant to the context of the World Heritage Convention, and related obligations and commitments of UNESCO and the United Nations system. It then discusses some of the key shortcomings in the implementation of the World Heritage Convention (1972) from an indigenous rights perspective. In doing so, the chapter draws on recent efforts and proposals of indigenous organizations and human rights bodies aimed at resolving these shortcomings, and making the implementation of the World Heritage Convention consistent with international human rights standards. These efforts began in 2000 with an unsuccessful proposal to establish a World Heritage Indigenous Peoples Council of Experts (WHIPCOE) as a consultative body to the World Heritage Committee, and were reinvigorated with the adoption of the UN Declaration on the Rights of Indigenous Peoples (United Nations 2007). More recently, the fortieth anniversary of the World Heritage Convention in 2012, celebrated by UNESCO under the theme World Heritage and Sustainable Development: The Role of Local Communities, provided a framework for increased attention on this issue.

Heritage Sites and Indigenous Peoples: Relevant Human Rights Standards

The primary reference point for identifying human rights standards relevant to indigenous peoples is the UN Declaration on the Rights of Indigenous Peoples (United Nations 2007), commonly known as the UNDRIP. Adopted by the UN General Assembly with the approval of an overwhelming majority of Member States,[2] it is the most comprehensive universal international human rights instrument explicitly addressing the rights of indigenous peoples. According to the UNDRIP, the rights recognized therein "constitute the minimum standards for the survival, dignity and well-being of the indigenous peoples of the world" (United Nations 2007: art. 43). As the UN Special Rapporteur on the rights of indigenous peoples, James Anaya, has noted, the UNDRIP does not attempt to bestow indigenous peoples with a set of special or new human rights, but rather elaborates upon existing human rights standards and principles of general applicability in the specific cultural, historic, social, and economic context of indigenous peoples. While itself not a binding legal instrument, the UNDRIP "represents an authoritative common understanding, at the global level, of the minimum content of the rights of indigenous peoples, upon a foundation of various sources of international human rights law" (Anaya 2008: 24).[3] Anaya emphasizes that the standards affirmed in the UNDRIP "share an essentially remedial character, seeking to redress the systemic obstacles and discrimination that indigenous peoples have faced in their enjoyment of basic human rights" (Anaya 2008: 24).

The UNDRIP affirms a wide range of political, economic, social, cultural, spiritual, and environmental rights of indigenous peoples and provides states, international organizations, and others with a clear-cut frame of reference for the formulation, implementation, and evaluation of programs and projects targeted at or impacting indigenous peoples. Special emphasis is placed on the collective rights of indigenous peoples, which are "indispensable for their existence, well-being and integral development as peoples"

(United Nations 2007: preamble). While a comprehensive discussion of the various human rights standards affirmed in the UNDRIP is beyond the scope of this paper, the following rights are some of the most relevant in the context of the protection and conservation of cultural and natural heritage sites, and will therefore be briefly outlined below: rights to lands, territories, and resources; the right to self-determined development; and participatory rights. Other, interrelated rights that may be of special relevance in the context of specific heritage sites include, among other things, indigenous peoples' right to enjoy their own culture and to continue their traditional way of life; their right to maintain, control and develop their cultural heritage and traditional knowledge; their right to health and a healthy environment; their right not be forcibly removed from their lands or territories; and their right to reparation and redress for wrongs suffered.

Rights to Lands, Territories, and Resources

As the UN Permanent Forum on Indigenous Issues (UNPFII) has observed, lands, territories, and natural resources "are of fundamental importance to indigenous peoples since they constitute the basis of their life, existence and economic livelihood, and are the sources of their spiritual, cultural and social identity" (UNPFII 2007: 2). Therefore:

> Land rights, access to land and control over it and its resources are central to indigenous peoples throughout the world, and they depend on such rights and access for their material and cultural survival. In order to survive as distinct peoples, indigenous peoples and their communities need to be able to own, conserve and manage their territories, lands and resources. (UNPFII 2007: 2)

The land and resource rights of indigenous peoples have been recognized and affirmed by several of the international human rights courts and treaty monitoring bodies, and in various international instruments including the UNDRIP and the International Labour Organization's Indigenous and Tribal Peoples Convention (1989). The UNDRIP states: "Indigenous peoples have the right to own, use, develop and control the lands, territories and resources that they possess by reason of traditional ownership or other traditional occupation or use, as well as those which they have otherwise acquired" (United Nations 2007: art. 26.2).

The UNDRIP also recognizes indigenous peoples' right to determine and develop priorities and strategies for the development or use of their lands, territories and resources, and requires states to obtain their free, prior, and informed consent (FPIC) before approving any project affecting their lands or resources (United Nations 2007: art. 32). A number of other articles recognize related rights, including the right of indigenous peoples not to be forcibly removed from their lands or territories (United Nations 2007: art. 10); their right to the conservation and protection of the environment and the productive capacity of their lands and resources (United Nations 2007: art. 29); their right to be secure in the enjoyment of their own means of subsistence and to engage freely in all their traditional and other economic activities (United Nations 2007: art. 20); their right to the protection of their traditional medicinal plants and animals (United Nations 2007: art. 24); their right to maintain and develop their traditional knowledge and cultural heritage associated with their lands and territories (United Nations 2007: art. 31); and their right to redress for lands, territories, and resources which they have traditionally owned, occupied, or used, and which have been confiscated, taken, occupied, used, or damaged without their consent (United Nations 2007: art. 28).

From this list of rights it is obvious that respect for indigenous peoples' land and resource rights is, as the former UN Special Rapporteur Rodolfo Stavenhagen, has remarked, "a precondition for the enjoyment of other rights such as the rights to food, health, adequate housing, culture and free exercise of religion" (Stavenhagen 2007: 15).

The Right to Self-Determined Development

Article 3 of the UNDRIP, which mirrors Article 1.1 of both the International Covenant on Civil and Political Rights (1966) and the International Covenant on Economic, Social and Cultural Rights (1966), affirms that indigenous peoples, like all peoples, have the right to self-determination. This means, among other things, that they have the right to determine their own economic, social, and cultural development, and to manage, for their own benefit, their own natural resources (see EMRIP 2011: 26). The UNDRIP also affirms indigenous peoples' "right to development in accordance with their own needs and interests" (United Nations 2007: preamble), and their "right to determine and develop priorities and strategies for exercising their right to development" (United Nations 2007: art. 23). This includes, in particular, "the right to be actively involved in developing and determining ... programmes affecting them and, as far as possible, to administer such programmes through their own institutions" (United Nations 2007: art. 23). It is also stressed that "control by indigenous peoples over developments affecting them and their lands, territories and resources will enable them to maintain and strengthen their institutions, cultures and traditions, and to promote their development in accordance with their aspirations and needs" (United Nations 2007: preamble).

As established in the UN Declaration on the Right to Development (United Nations 1986), the right to development is an inalienable human right that entitles every human person and all peoples "to participate in, contribute to, and enjoy economic, social, cultural and political development, in which all human rights and fundamental freedoms can be fully realized" (United Nations 1986: art. 1.1). The declaration also highlights that the right to development "implies the full realization of the right of peoples to self-determination, which includes ... the exercise of their inalienable right to full sovereignty over all their natural wealth and resources" (United Nations 1986: art. 1.2). This correlation is also clear from the UNDRIP, which notes in its Preamble that indigenous peoples, as a result of colonization and dispossession of their lands, territories, and resources, have been prevented from exercising their right to development in accordance with their own needs and interests.

Participatory Rights

All over the world, indigenous peoples have been systematically excluded and marginalized from decision-making on matters affecting them (Stavenhagen 2007: 11). The UNDRIP therefore emphasizes their "right to participate in decision-making in matters which would affect their rights, through representatives chosen by themselves in accordance with their own procedures" (United Nations 2007: art. 18). States have a duty to consult and cooperate in good faith with indigenous peoples through their own representative institutions, in order to obtain their FPIC before approving or implementing any measures or projects that may affect them (United Nations 2007: arts. 19, 32).

These rights of indigenous peoples, and corresponding duties of states, are essential elements of the right of indigenous peoples to self-determination, and have been repeatedly affirmed by international human rights courts and treaty bodies (see EMRIP 2011: 24–27).

Human rights bodies, as well as intergovernmental organizations and conservation organizations, have on many occasions acknowledged the special importance of respecting indigenous peoples' participatory rights in the context of conservation activities affecting their lands. For instance, the World Conservation Congress of the International Union for the Conservation of Nature (IUCN) has adopted a series of resolutions underlining the need to ensure respect for indigenous peoples' participatory rights in the establishment of new and the management of existing protected areas (see e.g. IUCN 2008). Similarly, the Conference of Parties to the Convention on Biological Diversity (1992) has recognized that "the establishment, management and monitoring of protected areas should take place with the full and effective participation of, and full respect for the rights of, indigenous and local communities" (CBD 2004: para. 22). Also notable is the Programme of Action for the Second International Decade of the World's Indigenous People, adopted by the UN General Assembly in 2005, which underscores that: "programmes and initiatives relating to indigenous cultures should follow the principle of free, prior and informed consent of indigenous peoples. Particular caution should be exercised when elaborating tourism and national park projects in indigenous territories" (United Nations 2006: para. 19).

On a practical level, respect for indigenous peoples' participatory rights requires the creation of mechanisms that enable their full and effective participation in all stages of an initiative or project, from design, implementation, monitoring, and evaluation to benefit-sharing (UNDESA 2008: 17). While mechanisms for participation can vary depending on the specific circumstances, participation must be through representatives chosen by the indigenous peoples themselves, in accordance with their own procedures. Indigenous representatives should be involved in all regular participatory mechanisms, such as multi-stakeholder meetings, civil society consultations, or meetings with government officials. Additionally, specific and culturally appropriate consultation mechanisms may need to be established. It is important to emphasize, as the United Nations Development Group has done, that "[p]articipation implies going further than mere consultation and should lead to concrete ownership of projects by indigenous peoples" (UNDG 2009: 27).

The principle of FPIC implies among other things that there is an absence of coercion, intimidation, or manipulation. Consent must be sought sufficiently in advance of any authorization or commencement of activities, with due respect for the time requirements of indigenous decision-making processes in all phases of a project. Full and understandable information on likely impacts must be provided, including information on potential risks and benefit-sharing mechanisms (see UNDG 2009: 30; FAO 2014).

Obligations and Commitments of UNESCO and the UN System

The promotion of respect for human rights is one of the fundamental objectives of the United Nations system as a whole. According to Article 1(3) of the United Nations Charter (1945), a main purpose of the United Nations is "promoting and encouraging respect for human rights and for fundamental freedoms for all without distinction as to race, sex, language, or religion". This commitment has been reaffirmed by the UN General Assembly, other UN organs, and individual Member States in countless declarations, conventions, and other instruments. It is also reflected in Article 1 of the UNESCO Constitution (United Nations 1945), the treaty which created UNESCO as a specialized agency of the United Nations. UNESCO's Constitution establishes the furthering of universal respect for human rights as one of the fundamental purposes of the organization.

As a declaration solemnly proclaimed by the UN General Assembly with the approval of an overwhelming majority of Member States, the UNDRIP represents a commitment on the part of the United Nations and Member States to its provisions, within the framework of the obligations established by the UN Charter to promote and protect human rights on a non-discriminatory basis (Anaya 2008: 13). Additionally, Articles 41 and 42 of the UNDRIP explicitly require the organs and specialized agencies of the UN system, other intergovernmental organizations, and states to act in accordance with the standards expressed in the UNDRIP, and to promote respect for and full realization of the provisions of the UNDRIP.

When the UNDRIP was adopted, UNESCO's director-general publicly welcomed this development as "a milestone for indigenous peoples and all those who are committed to the protection and promotion of cultural diversity and intercultural dialogue," promising that the declaration would "undoubtedly provide the foremost reference point [for UNESCO] in designing and implementing programmes with and for indigenous peoples" (Matsuura 2007). UNESCO's commitment to the UNDRIP was renewed by its General Conference in the organization's Medium-Term Strategy 2014–2021, where it is declared that:

> The needs of indigenous peoples will also be addressed by UNESCO's action. They continue to be disproportionately represented among the most marginalized and impoverished segments of society, while being recognized as the stewards of the major part of the world's biological, cultural and linguistic diversity ... [UNESCO] will implement the UNDRIP across all relevant programme areas. (UNESCO 2013c: para. 20)

An obligation and responsibility of UNESCO to protect and promote the rights of indigenous peoples can also be deduced from the organization's expressed commitment to principles and values such as cultural diversity, sustainable development, and good governance. All of these objectives imply a commitment to human rights, and in particular the rights of indigenous peoples, as UN Member States have consistently affirmed.[4]

Moreover, the UNESCO General Conference has repeatedly emphasized that UNESCO will integrate a human rights-based approach into all its programs and activities (UNESCO 2003, 2008). This means in practice that "all activities should contribute to the realization of human rights," and that "human rights principles and standards should guide the programming process in all fields and all stages, including design, implementation, monitoring and evaluation" as the UNESCO Strategy on Human Rights notes (UNESCO 2003: 2, 5).

Lack of Implementation of the UNDRIP in the Context of the World Heritage Convention

Of the roughly one thousand sites inscribed on UNESCO's World Heritage List as of 2014, a large number are fully or partially located within the ancestral lands or territories of indigenous peoples, and are of great significance to the respective peoples who depend upon them for their livelihoods and their spiritual, social, and cultural well-being. The vast majority of these sites are inscribed as "natural" World Heritage sites, often with no recognition whatsoever of their cultural, economic, and spiritual significance to indigenous peoples in the justification for inscription (Statement of Outstanding Universal Value).[5] Therefore, more often than not, the heritage values of these places to local indigenous peoples were completely disregarded when they were classified as World Heritage by UNESCO's World Heritage Committee. Obviously, this can have significant implications for conservation strategies, management frameworks, and priorities, and has in many cases facilitated or caused the imposition of various kinds of prohibitions and restrictions on indigenous peoples' land-use practices and access (see Disko and Tugendhat 2013, 2014).

Ever since the first World Heritage sites were inscribed in the late 1970s and early 1980s, there have been frequent protests by indigenous peoples about their lack of involvement in particular World Heritage nomination processes and rights violations in the management of particular sites. While it is important to note that there are also some positive cases, where indigenous peoples have been fully involved in the designation of World Heritage sites and where their rights are generally respected in ongoing site management, this is to a large extent due to the domestic policies of respective States Parties and not a result of the guidelines and requirements of the World Heritage Committee.

To this day, the operational guidelines used for the implementation of the World Heritage Convention (1972) contain no safeguards for the rights of indigenous peoples and merely "encourage" States Parties to "ensure the participation of a wide variety of stakeholders … in the identification, nomination and protection of World Heritage properties" (UNESCO 2013d: para. 12). Until the mid 1990s, these guidelines even promoted non-transparent and non-participatory nomination processes, urging States Parties to "refrain from giving undue publicity to the fact that a property has been nominated for inscription" (see e.g. UNESCO 1992: para. 14).[6] While this sentence was deleted in 1996 and a phrase was added noting that the participation of local people in the nomination process is essential to make them feel a shared responsibility in the maintenance of the site, the World Heritage Committee to this day does not firmly insist on the full and effective involvement of indigenous peoples in World Heritage nominations and other decision-making processes that affect them, as many instances testify. Moreover, no mechanisms are in place that would ensure that indigenous peoples can effectively participate in the World Heritage Committee's own decision-making affecting them.

In 2000, a forum of indigenous peoples held during the World Heritage Committee meeting in Cairns, Australia, called for the establishment of a World Heritage Indigenous Peoples Council of Experts (WHIPCOE) as a consultative body to the committee, out of concern about the "lack of involvement of indigenous peoples in the development and implementation of laws, policies and plans … which apply to their ancestral lands within or comprising sites now designated as World Heritage areas" (UNESCO 2001a: 2). The forum considered that such a council was needed to advise on "the appropriate identification, evaluation and management of 'mixed' properties and 'cultural' properties with indigenous associations," as well as "the identification, management and possible renomination of properties listed for their 'natural' World Heritage values that may also hold indigenous values" (UNESCO 2001a: 5). While the proposal was discussed by the World Heritage Committee in 2001, it did not approve the establishment of WHIPCOE as a consultative body or network to report to it (see Logan 2013; Meskell 2013). One of the stated reasons for this decision was that "[s]ome members of the [World Heritage] Committee questioned the definition of indigenous peoples and the relevance of such a distinction in different regions of the world" (UNESCO 2002: 57). The former chairperson of the World Commission on Protected Areas, Adrian Phillips, attributed the decision to a "dismissive attitude towards indigenous peoples' issues" among some of the World Heritage Committee's members (quoted in IUCN 2002: 15).

Since the adoption of the UNDRIP in 2007, there has been renewed attention to the inadequacy of the existing mechanisms for ensuring respect for the rights of indigenous peoples in the implementation of the World Heritage Convention (1972). In 2010, the UNPFII, which has a mandate to promote the UNDRIP within the UN system, for the first time sent a representative to a session of the World Heritage Committee. The purpose of this was to inform the committee about the numerous concerns related to World Heritage sites that indigenous organizations had brought to the UNPFII's attention since its first session in 2002. In a written submission to UNESCO, the UNPFII highlighted that it had received complaints about a "list of indigenous sites inscribed in the World Heritage List without the adequate participation and involvement of indigenous peoples," and underlined the need for states and intergovernmental bodies to do proper consultations with indigenous peoples and obtain their FPIC before bringing any development or conservation projects into their territories (UNPFII 2010). It recommended that "efforts to set up an appropriate mechanism whereby indigenous experts can provide advice to the World Heritage Committee and the World Heritage Center be revived," and that the UNDRIP and the guidelines on indigenous peoples' issues developed by the United Nations Development Group (UNDG) be used as frameworks for the nomination and management of World Heritage sites in indigenous peoples' territories and missions done in these areas (UNPFII 2010).

In May 2011, a coalition of over 70 indigenous organizations and NGOs submitted a joint statement to both the World Heritage Committee and the UNPFII expressing serious concern about the disrespect of the principle of FPIC by the committee when it designates sites in indigenous territories as World Heritage sites. The statement denounced three World Heritage nominations under consideration (Western Ghats, Sangha Trinational, and Kenya Lake System in the Great Rift Valley), which had been prepared without meaningful involvement and consultation of affected indigenous peoples, and stated that insufficient consideration had been given to indigenous peoples' cultural values and their role as stewards of the respective places. It urged the World Heritage Committee not to approve these nominations until the indigenous peoples affected had been adequately involved and their FPIC had been obtained (EWC *et al.* 2011).

However, the objections expressed in the joint statement of EWC *et al.* did not receive substantive consideration by the World Heritage Committee. Kenya Lake System was inscribed on the World Heritage List in June 2011, and the Western Ghats and Sangha Trinational in June 2012, although the concerns had not been resolved in any of these three cases. In the latter two instances, the indigenous peoples concerned had not even seen the final versions of the nomination documents, which had not been made publicly available (IWGIA *et al.* 2012).

The case of Kenya Lake System is especially noteworthy in the context of this chapter as it prompted significant responses from human rights bodies and international institutions. Kenya Lake System includes the Lake Bogoria National Reserve, which was the subject of a landmark ruling of the African Commission on Human and Peoples' Rights (ACHPR), the so-called Endorois Decision (ACHPR 2009). In this ruling, the ACHPR condemned the forcible eviction of the indigenous Endorois people from their ancestral lands surrounding Lake Bogoria during the creation of the reserve in the 1970s. The ACHPR found that the evictions and the failure to subsequently involve the Endorois in the management and benefit-sharing of the reserve had violated their human rights to property, natural resources, development, culture, and religion. It ordered Kenya, among other things, to "Recognise rights of ownership to the Endorois and Restitute [*sic*] Endorois ancestral land," and to "Pay adequate compensation to the community for all the loss suffered" (ACHPR 2009). The ruling also underlined that in the case of any development projects that would have a major impact within Endorois territory, "the State has a duty not only to consult with the community, but also to obtain their free, prior, and informed consent, according to their customs and traditions" (ACHPR 2009: para. 291).

The World Heritage listing of Lake Bogoria happened less than two years after the Endorois Decision, although the Endorois community had sent several communications to UNESCO informing them both about the ruling and the fact that they had not been consulted or included in the nomination process (IWGIA *et al.* 2012). This provoked the ACHPR to adopt a specific resolution on World Heritage in which it expressed deep concern about the listing, denouncing it as a contravention of the Endorois Decision and a violation of the Endorois' right to development (ACHPR 2011). The resolution also noted with concern that numerous World Heritage sites in Africa had been inscribed without the FPIC of the indigenous peoples in whose territories they are located, and were managed in ways not consistent with the principles of the UNDRIP. The ACHPR urged the World Heritage Committee and UNESCO to review and revise the operational guidelines of the World Heritage Convention in order to ensure that the implementation of the latter is consistent with the UNDRIP and that indigenous peoples' rights are respected, protected, and fulfilled in World Heritage areas. It further called on the World Heritage Committee to consider establishing an appropriate mechanism through which indigenous peoples can provide advice to it and effectively participate in its decision-making processes (ACHPR 2011).

A related resolution, also responding to the World Heritage listing of Lake Bogoria, was adopted by the 2012 World Conservation Congress of the IUCN in Jeju, South Korea. In addition to endorsing the ACHPR's recommendations to the World Heritage Committee, the resolution calls on the IUCN, the World Heritage Committee's technical advisory body on natural heritage, to develop clear policy and practical guidelines to ensure that the principles of the UNDRIP are respected in the IUCN's work as an advisory body. It underlines that the IUCN should "fully inform and consult with indigenous peoples when sites are evaluated or missions are undertaken on their territories" (IUCN 2012). Further, drawing attention to the fact that indigenous peoples have "suffered dispossession and alienation from their traditional lands and resources as a result of the establishment and management of protected areas, including many areas inscribed on the World Heritage List," the resolution urges the World Heritage Committee to "work with States Parties to establish mechanisms to assess and redress the effects of historic and current injustices against indigenous peoples in existing World Heritage sites" (IUCN 2012). The resolution notes that the World Heritage Convention "can and has played a leadership role in setting standards for protected areas as a whole," and that "World Heritage sites with their high visibility and public scrutiny have the potential to act as 'flagships' for good governance in protected areas" (IUCN 2012).

A process for bringing the implementation of the World Heritage Convention (1972) in line with the UNDRIP has been proposed by the UN Expert Mechanism on the Rights of Indigenous Peoples (EMRIP), a subsidiary body of the UN Human Rights Council. Emphasizing that "robust procedures and mechanisms" should be established to ensure that indigenous peoples are adequately consulted and involved in the management of World Heritage sites, and that their FPIC is obtained when parts of their territories are inscribed on the World Heritage List, EMRIP has:

> Encourage[d] the World Heritage Committee to establish a process to elaborate, with the full and effective participation of indigenous peoples, changes to the current procedures and operational guidelines and other appropriate measures to ensure that the implementation of the World Heritage Convention is consistent with the UNDRIP and that indigenous peoples can effectively participate in the World Heritage Convention's decision-making processes. (EMRIP 2012: 7)

This recommendation has been endorsed by the UN Special Rapporteur on the rights of indigenous peoples, James Anaya,[7] as well as at the International Expert Workshop on the World Heritage Convention and Indigenous Peoples that took place in September 2012 in Copenhagen, Denmark, in the context of the fortieth anniversary of the convention. The expert workshop was organized by the Danish Agency for Culture, the government of Greenland and the International Work Group for Indigenous Affairs (IWGIA), and brought together indigenous experts and representatives, human rights experts, and actors in the World Heritage system. It resulted in a "call to action" containing recommendations on how to align the implementation of the World Heritage Convention (1972) with the UNDRIP, as well as a set of proposed amendments to the World Heritage Convention's operational guidelines aimed at ensuring respect for indigenous peoples' right to FPIC in the context of World Heritage designations (Disko and Tugendhat 2013).[8]

Conclusions and Assessment

Throughout the history of the World Heritage Convention (1972), there have been repeated objections by indigenous peoples and human rights organizations about violations of indigenous rights in the implementation of the convention, not only at the domestic level in the management of specific World Heritage sites, but also at the international level in the practice of the World Heritage Committee, its Advisory Bodies and its Secretariat. Human rights concerns include, among other things, frequent disrespect for indigenous peoples' right to FPIC in the nomination and inscription of sites, the marginalization of indigenous peoples in the on-site decision-making and management of many World Heritage sites, violations of their right to participate equitably in tourism benefits, a common lack of involvement of indigenous peoples in monitoring missions and site evaluations, and a serious lack of transparency in some of the World Heritage Convention's processes.[9]

Moreover, in some World Heritage areas, indigenous peoples are essentially treated as threats to their own territories, and tight restrictions and prohibitions are placed on traditional land-use practices such as hunting, gathering, farming, or animal husbandry in violation of their cultural and subsistence rights. These restrictions and prohibitions have had severe consequences for some indigenous peoples' food security, health, and well-being, which in some cases can be directly linked to the World Heritage status of a site.[10] The World Heritage List also contains several protected areas from which indigenous peoples have been forcibly removed, in some instances, a former staff member of UNESCO's World Heritage Centre has acknowledged, with the intention of "justifying inscription of an area on the World Heritage List as a place of natural importance devoid of what is perceived as the negative impact of local inhabitants" (Titchen 2002).

The numerous rights violations, which are in many ways the result of the inadequacy of the World Heritage Convention's procedures and operational guidelines, have drawn the attention of international human rights bodies and mechanisms, and stand in sharp contrast to UNESCO's mission, the principles upon which it was founded, and the overarching values which it promotes. The violations are damaging the reputation and credibility of UNESCO as an institution committed to furthering respect for human rights, cultural diversity, sustainable development, and intercultural understanding, and threaten to overshadow the positive role that the World Heritage Convention can play and, in many cases, undoubtedly has played for indigenous peoples by helping them protect their lands, cultures, and heritage. They are also incompatible with UNESCO's vision of World Heritage sites as places that "serve as an example, and become conservation models for all sites, including those of more local interest" (UNESCO 2004).

There are various reasons for the lack of concern and respect for indigenous rights in the processes of the World Heritage Convention (1972), two of which will be highlighted here. First, for many if not most States Parties, including many of those serving as members of the World Heritage Committee, the main interest in the World Heritage Convention today lies in the prestige, tourism profits, and economic development that World Heritage sites can bring to a country or region. This is not least due to the fact that UNESCO has actively and successfully promoted World Heritage as a "brand," which has become a premium marketing tool for the tourism industry with considerable commercial value. The inscription of new sites on the World Heritage List has become a highly politicized affair that is marked by aggressive lobbying, political maneuvering, and bargaining (see e.g. Meskell 2012). This has resulted in a climate and culture within the World Heritage Committee where economic and political interests all too often override all other concerns, including human rights principles and even conservation considerations. The director of the World Heritage Centre, Kishore Rao, recently remarked:

> [The question is] whether safeguarding our common heritage for present and future generations is the real motivation for identifying and adding sites to the World Heritage List, or has it been eclipsed by other considerations, such as economics and national prestige … [T]he general impression is often of intense pressure to have sites designated as World Heritage because of the expected economic benefits or the prestige involved. Perhaps we are failing in our narrative to effectively communicate a coherent message about the true objectives of the Convention. (UNESCO 2013a: 83)

Secondly, due to the fact that the World Heritage Convention was drawn up as far back as 1972, it contains no references to human rights or indigenous peoples, unlike more recently adopted UNESCO instruments in the field of culture, such as the Convention for the Safeguarding of the Intangible Cultural Heritage (2003) or the Convention on the Protection and Promotion of the Diversity of Cultural

Expressions (2005). At the same time, the World Heritage Committee acts in many ways as if the World Heritage Convention existed in a vacuum, and it pays little to no regard to international legal standards developed in other intergovernmental forums, or legal obligations of states under other international instruments. In particular, the World Heritage Committee has been oblivious to developments in human rights law since 1972.[11] This also seems to be true for many of the government representatives participating in its sessions. For instance, during discussions at an official working group at the June 2013 meeting of the World Heritage Committee in Phnom Penh, Cambodia, several government representatives expressed opposition to including provisions on indigenous peoples in a revised set of operational guidelines for the World Heritage Convention due to reservations about the concept and questions about the definition of "indigenous peoples."[12] Astonishingly, these included representatives of governments that voted for the adoption of UNDRIP and who have repeatedly expressed their commitment to advancing recognition and respect for the rights of indigenous peoples as enshrined in it. This ignorance among government representatives participating in World Heritage Committee sessions is shocking considering the unquestionable significance of indigenous rights for protecting the common heritage of humankind and for preserving the world's cultural and biological diversity, a significance that has been recognized by states and UNESCO on numerous occasions.

While the overall conduct and attitudes of the World Heritage Committee and its general lack of accountability pose significant obstacles to making the implementation of the World Heritage Convention (1972) consistent with the principles and requirements of the UNDRIP, it needs to be acknowledged that there is some awareness within UNESCO of the problems and the need for corrective action. UNESCO's ability to influence the decision-making of the World Heritage Committee is limited by the fact that the latter, though "established within UNESCO" according to the World Heritage Convention, is an independent and largely autonomous intergovernmental body.[13] However, there have been increasing efforts in recent years by UNESCO to enhance respect for indigenous rights in the processes of the World Heritage Convention.[14] In November 2011, UNESCO launched a process to develop a policy for engaging with indigenous peoples "to ensure that [the] Organization performs in accordance with the minimum internationally agreed standards," and to "build awareness and provide guidance to staff and committees in order to effectively implement the UNDRIP in all components of UNESCO's work" (UNESCO 2011b). In launching this process, Irina Bokova, the UNESCO director-general, stressed that UNESCO, as the Secretariat for the World Heritage Convention, was "consciously working to improve and promote the FPIC and the full and effective participation of indigenous peoples in the establishment and management of heritage sites" (UNESCO 2011b). The issue was also highlighted by UNESCO representatives at the closing event of the World Heritage Convention's fortieth anniversary in November 2012, held in Kyoto, Japan. UNESCO's assistant director-general for culture, Francesco Bandarin, encouraged the World Heritage Committee to reconsider the 2000/2001 proposal to create a World Heritage Indigenous Peoples Council of Experts in light of the UN General Assembly's adoption of the UNDRIP in 2007 (UNESCO 2013a: 43). The director of the World Heritage Centre remarked, on the same occasion, that the World Heritage Committee should seriously consider the appeal of the UNPFII "for the principle of FPIC to be introduced within the *Operational Guidelines*" (UNESCO 2013a: 84).

Significantly, the World Heritage Centre proposed in May 2013 that the World Heritage Committee consider, at its thirty-seventh session in Phnom Penh, the reflections and proposals of the International Expert Workshop on the World Heritage Convention and Indigenous Peoples that took place in Copenhagen in September 2012 under the agenda item Revision of the Operational Guidelines (UNESCO 2013b). The World Heritage Committee held some preliminary discussions on the matter, in the above-mentioned working group, but decided to "re-examine the recommendations of this meeting [the Copenhagen expert workshop] following the results of the discussions to be held by the Executive Board on the UNESCO Policy on indigenous peoples" (UNESCO 2013e).

One can only hope that the UNESCO policy, once adopted, will provide the necessary impetus for the World Heritage Committee to finally adopt a human rights-based approach to those of its activities that impact upon indigenous peoples, and take the necessary steps to ensure that the management and protection of World Heritage sites occurs in accordance with the principles contained in the UNDRIP. At stake is not only the credibility of the World Heritage Convention (1972), but the credibility of UNESCO as a whole.

Notes

1 Although both the International Covenant on Civil and Political Rights and the International Covenant on Economic, Social and Cultural Rights were drawn up in 1966, the two did not come into force until 1976, some four years after the adoption of the World Heritage Convention.

2 The UNDRIP was adopted by a vote of 143 in favor to 4 against, with 11 abstentions. However, all 4 opposing UN Member States (Australia, Canada, New Zealand, United States) and some abstaining States have since endorsed it.

3 Anaya notes that the UNDRIP not only reflects existing human rights obligations of states under international treaties, but that some aspects of the provisions of the UNDRIP can also be considered a reflection of norms of customary international law, insofar as they connect with a pattern of consistent international and state practice (Anaya 2008: 13). For details on which provisions of the UNDRIP correspond to existing state obligations under customary international law, see ILA (2012).

4 See e.g. UNESCO (2001b: art. 4), United Nations (2002: para. 5), United Nations (2000: sec. V), United Nations (2012: paras. 43, 49), and UNHRC (2008).

5 Between a third and half of the 228 natural World Heritage sites (as of July 2014) are inhabited by indigenous peoples.

6 "In all cases, so as to maintain the objectivity of the evaluation process and to avoid possible embarrassment to those concerned, States Parties should refrain from giving undue publicity to the fact that a property has been nominated for inscription pending the final decision of the [World Heritage] Committee on the nomination in question" (UNESCO 1992: para. 14). Similar thinking continues to be contained in Annex 6 of the operational guidelines (which concerns the ICOMOS procedures for the evaluation of cultural sites), where States Parties "are requested to ensure that ICOMOS evaluation missions are given a low profile so far as the media are concerned" (UNESCO 2013d: 116).

7 See Anaya's video message *World Heritage Convention and Indigenous Peoples* (2012). Available at: http://unsr.jamesanaya.org/videos/video-mensaje-world-heritage-convention-and-indigenous-peoples (accessed January 31, 2014).

8 The expert workshop was organized in response to World Heritage Committee Decision 35 COM 12D (2011), which encouraged State Parties to carry out activities to celebrate the anniversary. Acknowledging the statements made by the UNPFII at the 2010 and 2011

sessions of the World Heritage Committee, the Decision explicitly noted that considerations relating to indigenous peoples "should be included in the theme of the 40th anniversary" (UNESCO 2011a). For the outcome documents and report of the expert workshop, see UNESCO (2012).

9 For instance, there is no requirement for World Heritage nominations and monitoring mission reports to be made publicly available before the World Heritage Committee takes a decision. This has in many cases prevented indigenous peoples from reviewing such documents and providing their perspectives to the World Heritage Committee, although such documents can have far-reaching implications for indigenous peoples' rights and interests.

10 A case in point is the Ngorongoro Conservation Area in Tanzania, where an array of restrictions on land use, including a ban on subsistence cultivation, has been imposed on the conservation area's Maasai residents. The imposition in 2009 of the cultivation ban has led to serious hunger and malnutrition that has affected most of the area's 70,000 residents, and resulted in the deaths of several people. According to local indigenous organizations, the cultivation ban, and therefore the hunger situation, can be directly traced to the area's World Heritage status and the interventions of UNESCO and IUCN (PINGOs Forum *et al.* 2012).

11 This is plainly evident from the World Heritage Convention's operational guidelines, which contain a list of the conventions the World Heritage Committee considers relevant to the protection of cultural and natural heritage (UNESCO 2013d: para. 44). None of the international human rights instruments are included in this list.

12 This is a personal observation. Specifically, these were the representatives of France, Algeria, India, and Côte d'Ivoire.

13 On the World Heritage Committee being "established within UNESCO," see World Heritage Convention (1972), art. 8.1. The independence and autonomy of the World Heritage Committee was also highlighted as a challenge in a recent report by UNESCO on the organization's progress in implementing the UNDRIP and the objectives of the Second International Decade of the World's Indigenous People (UNESCO 2014: 2). For details on the relationship between the World Heritage Committee and UNESCO, see Vrdoljak (2008: 224–25).

14 Additionally, there have been efforts by the Advisory Bodies to promote the use of human rights-based approaches in the World Heritage context (see Ekern *et al.* 2012; Larsen, Oviedo, and Badman 2014).

References

Legislation

Charter of the United Nations (United Nations, 1945). Available at: http://www.un.org/en/documents/charter/ (accessed March 19, 2015).

Constitution of the United Nations Educational, Scientific and Cultural Organization (1945). Available at: http://unesdoc.unesco.org/images/0022/002269/226924e.pdf#page=6 (accessed March 19, 2015).

Convention Concerning the Protection of the World Cultural and Natural Heritage (World Heritage Convention) (UNESCO, 1972). Available at: http://whc.unesco.org/archive/convention-en.pdf (accessed March 19, 2015).

Convention for the Safeguarding of the Intangible Cultural Heritage (UNESCO, 2003). Available at: http://unesdoc.unesco.org/images/0013/001325/132540e.pdf (accessed March 19, 2015).

Convention No. 169: Indigenous and Tribal Peoples Convention (International Labour Organization, 1989). Available at: http://www.ilo.org/dyn/normlex/en/f?p=NORMLEXPUB:12100:0::NO::P12100_ILO_CODE:C169 (accessed March 19, 2015).

Convention on Biological Diversity (United Nations, 1992). Available at: http://www.cbd.int/doc/legal/cbd-en.pdf (accessed March 19, 2015).

Convention on the Protection and Promotion of the Diversity of Cultural Expressions (UNESCO, 2005). Available at: http://unesdoc.unesco.org/images/0014/001429/142919e.pdf (accessed March 19, 2015).

International Covenant on Civil and Political Rights (United Nations, 1966). Available at: http://www.ohchr.org/Documents/ProfessionalInterest/ccpr.pdf (accessed March 19, 2015).

International Covenant on Economic, Social and Cultural Rights (United Nations, 1966). Available at: http://www.ohchr.org/Documents/ProfessionalInterest/cescr.pdf (accessed March 19, 2015).

Other Works

ACHPR (African Commission on Human and Peoples' Rights) (2009) Centre for Minority Rights Development (Kenya) and Minority Rights Group International on behalf of Endorois Welfare Council v. Kenya. Decision of the ACHPR, November 2009. Communication 276/2003. Available at: http://www.achpr.org/communications/decision/276.03 (accessed March 5, 2015).

ACHPR (2011) Resolution on the Protection of Indigenous Peoples' Rights in the Context of the World Heritage Convention and the Designation of Lake Bogoria as a World Heritage Site. Res.197(L)2011. Available at: http://www.achpr.org/sessions/50th/resolutions/197/ (accessed March 5, 2015).

Anaya, J. (2008) Report of the Special Rapporteur on the Situation of Human Rights and Fundamental Freedoms of Indigenous People. Report to the UN Human Rights Council. UN document A/HRC/9/9. Available at: http://unsr.jamesanaya.org/docs/annual/2008_hrc_annual_report_en.pdf (accessed March 5, 2015).

CBD (2004) Decision VII/28 of the Conference of Parties to the Convention on Biological Diversity. Programme of Work on Protected Areas. Available at: http://www.cbd.int/decision/cop/?id=7765 (accessed March 5, 2015).

Disko, S., and Tugendhat, H. (2013) Report on the International Expert Workshop on the World Heritage Convention and Indigenous Peoples, 20–21 September 2012. Available at: http://whc.unesco.org/document/122252 (accessed March 5, 2015).

Disko, S., and Tugendhat, H. (eds) (2014) *World Heritage Sites and Indigenous Peoples' Rights*. Copenhagen: IWGIA, Forest Peoples Programme, and Gundjeihmi Aboriginal Corporation.

Ekern, S., Logan, W., Sauge, B., and Sinding-Larsen, A. (2012) Human Rights and World Heritage: Preserving Our Common Dignity through Rights-Based Approaches to Site Management. *International Journal of Heritage Studies* 18 (3), 213–225.

EMRIP (UN Expert Mechanism on the Rights of Indigenous Peoples) (2011) Expert Mechanism Advice No. 2 (2011): Indigenous Peoples and the Right to Participate in Decision-Making. UN document A/HRC/18/42, Annex. Available at: http://www.ohchr.org/Documents/Issues/IPeoples/EMRIP/Advice2_Oct2011.pdf (accessed March 5, 2015).

EMRIP (2012) Report of the Expert Mechanism on the Rights of Indigenous Peoples on Its Fifth Session. Report to the Human Rights Council. UN document A/HRC/21/52. Available at: http://www.ohchr.org/Documents/HRBodies/HRCouncil/RegularSession/Session21/A-HRC-21-52_en.pdf (accessed March 5, 2015).

EWC (Endorois Welfare Council) *et al.* (2011) Joint Statement on Continuous Violations of the Principle of Free, Prior and Informed Consent in the Context of UNESCO's World Heritage Convention. Available at: http://www.iwgia.org/iwgia_files_news_files/0314_UNPFII_2011_Joint_Statement_on_FPIC_and_World_Heritage.pdf (accessed January 31, 2014).

FAO (UN Food and Agriculture Organization) (2014) *Respecting Free, Prior and Informed Consent: Practical Guidance for Governments, Companies, NGOs, Indigenous Peoples and Local Communities in Relation to Land Acquisition*. Governance of Tenure Technical Guide No. 3. Rome: FAO.

ILA (International Law Association) (2012) Rights of Indigenous Peoples. Resolution No. 5/2012. Available at: http://www.ila-hq.org/en/committees/index.cfm/cid/1024 (accessed May 14, 2014).

IUCN (2002) Local Communities and Protected Areas. *Parks Magazine*, special issue, 12 (2).

IUCN (2008) Indigenous Peoples, Protected Areas and Implementation of the Durban Accord. World Conservation Congress Resolution 4.048. Available at: www.iucn.org/congress_08/assembly/policy/ (accessed March 5, 2015).

IUCN (2012) Implementation of the UNDRIP in the Context of the UNESCO World Heritage Convention. World Conservation Congress Resolution WCC-2012-Res-047-EN. Available at: http://www.iucnworldconservationcongress.org/member_s_assembly/resolutions/ (accessed March 5, 2015).

IWGIA *et al.* (2012) Joint Submission on the Lack of Implementation of the UNDRIP in the Context of UNESCO's World Heritage Convention. Available at: http://www.forestpeoples.org/sites/fpp/files/publication/2012/05/joint-submission-unpfii.pdf (accessed January 31, 2014).

Larsen, P., Oviedo, G., and Badman, T. (2014) World Heritage, Indigenous Peoples, Communities and Rights: An IUCN Perspective. In S. Disko and H. Tugendhat (eds), *World Heritage Sites and Indigenous Peoples' Rights*. Copenhagen: IWGIA, Forest Peoples Programme, and Gundjeihmi Aboriginal Corporation, pp. 65–82.

Logan, W. (2013) Australia, Indigenous Peoples and World Heritage from Kakadu to Cape York: State Party Behaviour under the World Heritage Convention. *Journal of Social Archaeology* 13 (2), 153–176.

Matsuura, K. (2007) Message from the Director-General of UNESCO on the Occasion of the Approval of the UNDRIP by the UN General Assembly. Available at: http://portal.unesco.org/en/ev.php-URL_ID=39604&URL_DO=DO_TOPIC&URL_SECTION=201.html (accessed January 31, 2014).

Meskell, L. (2012) The Rush to Inscribe: Reflections on the 35th Session of the World Heritage Committee, UNESCO Paris, 2011. *Journal of Field Archaeology* 37 (2), 145–151.

Meskell, L. (2013) UNESCO and the Fate of the World Heritage Indigenous Peoples Council of Experts (WHIPCOE). *International Journal of Cultural Property*, 20, 155–174.

PINGOs Forum (Pastoralists' Indigenous Non-Govermental Organisations Forum) *et al.* (2012) Hunger in a World Heritage Site? Where Is the World? Available at: http://www.pingosforum.or.tz/index.php/home/3-newsflash/129-hunger-in-a-world-heritage-site (accessed January 31, 2014).

Stavenhagen, R. (2007) Report of the Special Rapporteur on the Situation of Human Rights and Fundamental Freedoms of Indigenous People. Report to the Human Rights Council. UN document A/HRC/6/15. Available at: http://daccess-dds-ny.un.org/doc/UNDOC/GEN/G07/149/23/PDF/G0714923.pdf?OpenElement (accessed March 5, 2015).

Titchen, S. (2002) Indigenous Peoples and Cultural and Natural World Heritage Sites. Presentation at panel discussion on Cultural Heritage and Sacred Sites: World Heritage from an Indigenous Perspective, New York University, May 15. Available at: http://www.dialoguebetweennations.com/n2n/pfii/english/SarahTitchen.htm (accessed January 31, 2014).

UNDESA (2008) Resource Kit on Indigenous Peoples' Issues. Available at: http://www.un.org/esa/socdev/unpfii/documents/resource_kit_indigenous_2008.pdf (accessed March 5, 2015).

UNDG (2009) Guidelines on Indigenous Peoples' Issues. Document HR/P/PT/16. Available at: http://www.un.org/esa/socdev/unpfii/documents/UNDG_guidelines_EN.pdf (accessed March 5, 2015).

UNESCO (1992) Operational Guidelines for the Implementation of the World Heritage Convention. Document WHC/2/Revised, 27 March 1992. Available at: http://whc.unesco.org/en/guidelines/ (accessed March 6, 2015).

UNESCO (2001a) Report on the Proposed World Heritage Indigenous Peoples' Council of Experts (WHIPCOE). Document WHC-2001/CONF.205/WEB.3. Paris: UNESCO.

Available at: http://whc.unesco.org/archive/2001/whc-01-conf205-web3e.pdf (accessed March 6, 2015).
UNESCO (2001b) Universal Declaration on Cultural Diversity. Document A/RES/66/154. Available at: http://unesdoc.unesco.org/images/0012/001246/124687e.pdf#page=67 (accessed March 19, 2015).
UNESCO (2002) Report of the Twenty-Fifth Session of the World Heritage Committee (Helsinki, Finland). Document WHC-01/CONF.208/24. Available at: http://whc.unesco.org/archive/2001/whc-01-conf208-24e.pdf (accessed March 6, 2015).
UNESCO (2003) UNESCO Strategy on Human Rights. Document SHS-2007/WS/15. Available at: http://unesdoc.unesco.org/images/0014/001457/145734e.pdf (accessed March 6, 2015).
UNESCO (2004) Report by the Director-General of UNESCO on the United Nations Year for Cultural Heritage 2002 and on its Follow-up. Available at: http://unesdoc.unesco.org/images/0013/001332/133255e.pdf (accessed March 6, 2015).
UNESCO (2008) Medium-Term Strategy 2008–2013. Document 34 C/4. Available at: http://unesdoc.unesco.org/images/0014/001499/149999e.pdf (accessed March 6, 2015).
UNESCO (2011a) Celebration of the 40th Anniversary. Decision 35 COM 12D of the World Heritage Committee. Available at: http://whc.unesco.org/en/decisions/4405 (accessed March 6, 2015).
UNESCO (2011b) Towards a UNESCO Policy on Engaging with Indigenous Peoples. Speech by Gretchen Kalonji on behalf of UNESCO Director-General Irina Bokova, November 10, 2011. Available at: http://www.unesco.org/new/en/indigenous-peoples/related-info/unesco-policy-on-indigenous-peoples/launch-event-policy-on-indigenous-people (accessed January 31, 2014).
UNESCO (2012) International Expert Workshop on the World Heritage Convention and Indigenous Peoples. UNESCO World Heritage Centre. Available at: http://whc.unesco.org/en/events/906 (accessed March 6, 2015).
UNESCO (2013a) *Celebrating 40 years of the World Heritage Convention*, November 2012, Kyoto, Japan: Proceedings. Paris: UNESCO. Available at: http://whc.unesco.org/document/125846 (accessed March 6, 2015).
UNESCO (2013b) Item 12 of the Provisional Agenda: Revision of the Operational Guidelines. World Heritage Committee, Thirty-Seventh Session. Document WHC-13/37.COM/12. Paris: UNESCO. Available at: http://whc.unesco.org/document/122839 (accessed March 6, 2015).
UNESCO (2013c) Medium-Term Strategy 2014–2021. Document 37/C4. Available at: http://unesdoc.unesco.org/images/0022/002278/227860e.pdf (accessed March 6, 2015).
UNESCO (2013d) Operational Guidelines for the Implementation of the World Heritage Convention. Document WHC.13/01, July 2013. Available at: http://whc.unesco.org/archive/opguide13-en.pdf (accessed March 6, 2015).
UNESCO (2013e) Revision of the Operational Guidelines. Decision 37 COM 12.II of the World Heritage Committee. Available at: http://whc.unesco.org/en/decisions/5186 (accessed March 6, 2015).
UNESCO (2014) Report on the Achievement of the Goal and Objectives of the Second International Decade of the World's Indigenous Peoples (2005–2014): Questionnaire Response. Available at: http://www.un.org/esa/socdev/unpfii/documents/2014/unesco.pdf (accessed July 12, 2014).
UNHRC (2008) The Role of Good Governance in the Promotion and Protection of Human Rights. UN Human Rights Council Resolution 7/11. Available at: http://ap.ohchr.org/documents/E/HRC/resolutions/A_HRC_RES_7_11.pdf (accessed March 6, 2015).
United Nations (1986) Declaration on the Right to Development. Document A/RES/41/128. Available at: http://www.ohchr.org/Documents/Issues/Development/DeclarationRightDevelopment_en.pdf (accessed March 19, 2015).
United Nations (2000) United Nations Millennium Declaration. UN General Assembly Resolution A/RES/55/2. Available at: http://www.un.org/millennium/declaration/ares552e.htm (accessed March 16, 2015).

United Nations (2002) Plan of Implementation of the World Summit on Sustainable Development. Available at: http://www.un.org/esa/sustdev/documents/WSSD_POI_PD/English/WSSD_PlanImpl.pdf (accessed March 16, 2015).

United Nations (2006) Programme of Action for the Second International Decade of the World's Indigenous People. Document A/60/270, adopted by UN General Assembly Resolution A/RES/60/142. Available at: http://daccess-dds-ny.un.org/doc/UNDOC/GEN/N05/464/96/PDF/N0546496.pdf?OpenElement (accessed March 6, 2015).

United Nations (2007) United Nations Declaration on the Rights of Indigenous Peoples (UNDRIP). Document A/RES/61/295. Available at: http://www.un-documents.net/a61r295.htm (accessed March 19, 2015).

United Nations (2012) The Future We Want. Outcome document of the UN Rio+20 Conference on Sustainable Development. Available at: http://www.uncsd2012.org/content/documents/727The%20Future%20We%20Want%2019%20June%201230pm.pdf (accessed March 16, 2015).

UNPFII (2007) Permanent Forum on Indigenous Issues: Report on the Sixth Session. Document E/2007/43. Available at: http://daccess-dds-ny.un.org/doc/UNDOC/GEN/N07/376/75/PDF/N0737675.pdf?OpenElement (accessed March 6, 2015).

UNPFII (2010) Statement at the Thirty-Fourth Session of the World Heritage Committee. Available at: http://xa.yimg.com/kq/groups/20674633/27593986/name/UNPFII+Statement+WHC+Final.docx (accessed January 31, 2014).

Vrdoljak, A. (2008) Article 13: World Heritage Committee and International Assistance. In F. Francioni (ed.), *The 1972 World Heritage Convention: A Commentary*. Oxford: Oxford University Press, pp. 219–241.

CHAPTER 26

UNESCO, the World Heritage Convention, and Africa: The Practice and the Practitioners

George Okello Abungu

Introduction

The Convention Concerning the Protection of the World Cultural and Natural Heritage (1972), popularly known as the World Heritage Convention, is the only international accord that protects the world's cultural and natural heritage under one umbrella. This prestigious convention celebrated its fortieth anniversary in 2012, and currently has 1,007 sites in 161 countries from across the world on its list (as of 2014). It recognizes heritage of Outstanding Universal Value, which presupposes that all forms of heritage are important, but that some are so significant that their value transcends national borders and their conservation should be the responsibility of all humanity (UNESCO 2012).

This chapter looks at the World Heritage Convention (1972), its use and evolution through time, and the constantly dynamic and at times conflicting relations among practitioners. It also interrogates UNESCO's role through the World Heritage Convention in the protection of Africa's heritage, the challenges faced, and the results realized so far. It further reflects on what direction heritage practice in Africa should take in the future in light of the various challenges, opportunities, and changing dynamics in the continent, and in particular Africa's perceived position as the continent of the future. "Practice" here is considered as the implementation of the World Heritage Convention, with its attendant challenges and opportunities, and "practitioners" are those responsible and/or involved in one way or another in that practice. While Africa

A Companion to Heritage Studies, First Edition. Edited by William Logan, Máiréad Nic Craith, and Ullrich Kockel.
© 2016 John Wiley & Sons, Inc. Published 2016 by John Wiley & Sons, Inc.

refers to the entire continent, for the purposes of this chapter I omit discussion of the Arabic-speaking north.

Practitioners, broadly defined, include diverse stakeholders with multiple voices, and not always similar expectations, values, and approaches. These range from people on the ground where sites are located, NGOs both national and international, government agencies and UNESCO States Parties, UNESCO Advisory Bodies, and funding organizations and pressure groups interested in world heritage affairs whose roles and responsibilities also often differ. At present, States Parties to the World Heritage Committee (a group of 21 states elected from States Parties divided into regions) and Advisory Bodies – the International Council on Monuments and Sites (ICOMOS), the International Union for Conservation of Nature (IUCN), and International Centre for the Study of Preservation and Restoration of Cultural Property (ICCROM) – play central and dominant roles in the implementation of the World Heritage Convention (1972). These roles have, at times, created situations of conflict, especially when communities' pasts and their heritage spaces are appropriated, even as their voices are left out of decisions. As Meskell (2013: 485) has pointed out, the States Parties that are today mostly represented in the World Heritage Committee by state-appointed ambassadors and politicians have become even more domineering, often overturning the recommendations of Advisory Bodies. While I draw on my experience from dynamics in Africa, the tensions that I see as inherent in managing heritage resources in the context of the World Heritage Convention are broadly relevant across the heritage sector.

Although the World Heritage Convention (1972) is managed by the UNESCO World Heritage Centre in Paris, its effects are felt on the ground worldwide as heritage is increasingly recognized as a major player in world affairs. Differing practitioners, values, working dynamics, and methods of practice create a complex web of interests, actions, and interactions. Recent happenings at UNESCO, including budget cuts to the World Heritage Centre, and attendant restructuring resulting from withdrawal of funding by the United States as a result of UNESCO's recognition and admission of Palestine to the World Heritage Convention, an "increasing and overt politicization of the [World Heritage] Committee" (Meskell 2013: 484), has made matters even worse. Integral to this web is the construction and use of power, and the alignment of groups, interests, and hierarchies. Meskell states that "these external challenges in the global political arena are also matched by escalating internal tensions from within among the three pillars of the organization: the World Heritage Centre, the Advisory Bodies, and the World Heritage Committee" (Meskell 2013: 484). She identifies a major challenge within the committee in the form of emerging interest groups or "pacting," observing "pacting between certain blocs, the maintenance of colonial connections, the escalating attacks on the Advisory Bodies, and the overturning of many conservation recommendations" (Meskell 2013: 484).

The question is: Where does Africa find itself in relation to all these? Does it need to carve out its own space and create a voice for itself that would address its unique challenges and opportunities within the spectrum of the World Heritage Convention (1972) and the international heritage community? With the lowest representation of sites on the World Heritage List and the highest on the List of World Heritage in Danger, Africa has immense resources already attracting a scramble from without. Many of the resources are located either in or adjacent to some of the World Heritage sites, making exploitation inadmissible according to the World Heritage Convention despite high expectations by surrounding communities and States Parties' stated commitments to uplifting the living standards of their poor majority. Currently any attempt to exploit mineral and other natural resources meets with stiff opposition from the World Heritage Committee's Advisory Bodies and the so-called "neutral" countries on the committee, a group that claims to stand for the credibility of the convention. To be able to understand both practice and practitioners, and the workings of the World Heritage Committee and the World Heritage Convention, one has to understand UNESCO's historical context, the convention as an instrument of ranking and appropriation of values, the politics surrounding its implementation, and the operational procedures and players involved.

Setting the Stage: UNESCO's Historical Background

UNESCO, a top player in the heritage arena, claims an agenda that foregrounds human understanding, cooperation, development, and empowerment on the premise that better communication, dialogue, and intercultural understanding is the way to preserve peace in the world. Its view of heritage includes ranking, with all heritage being seen as important but some seen as more important than others.

UNESCO's founders aspired to an organization that embodied "a genuine culture of peace" that would "establish the 'intellectual and moral solidarity of mankind,'" and as such prevent outbreak of another world war (UNESCO n.d.). It set itself as the moral authority on human relations – setting the bar pretty high considering that it represented the same states that had engaged in World War II. However, as Meskell (2013) notes, given its history of recognition and reconciliation, the long-standing ethos of cultural diversity, and the protection of minority life-ways, UNESCO has emerged as the only structural avenue to global governance and the promotion of cultural heritage.

Founded in the aftermath of this devastating war, its primary objective was to use education and culture to "build peace in the minds of men" (UNESCO n.d.). Culture and heritage held privileged status, and here begin the challenges. A Western European construct with American input, it became the international intergovernmental body speaking on behalf of many states. Since the major stakeholders are States Parties, from the start UNESCO had no alternative but to promote the notion of heritage as a national responsibility. It perceived heritage in terms of global, national, and local significance, and claimed interest in what it deemed to be "world heritage," letting states classify national or local levels according to their own legal instruments. Nevertheless, states had the power to advance national heritage as the heritage of humanity on the UNESCO World Heritage List. This of course is problematic since it opens the door to value judgments, spiced with political manipulation and competition at all levels. Having sites inscribed on the World Heritage List garners international and national prestige, enables access to the World Heritage Fund, and heightens public awareness, tourism, and economic development, all trappings that endears the World Heritage Convention (1972) to the States Parties and create a sense of want and control.

Since its inception and through its history, UNESCO has done commendable work in a remarkable range of areas linked with cultural resilience. It has excelled in areas dealing with mutual understanding and respect for all cultures, education for all, and the reduction of illiteracy. It has spearheaded the fight against discrimination on the basis of gender, race, or color, the protection of human rights, the promotion of the diversity of cultural expression, the protection of humanity's heritage, the protection of linguistic diversity, oral traditions, rituals, and festivals, the freedom of the media and press, and the reduction of poverty. The reflexive interrogation of focus, language, representation, and content can also be seen in numerous meetings and outcomes: the Mexico Declaration (UNESCO 1982); the World Decade for Cultural Development, running from 1988 to 1997; the UN's Agenda 21 action plan (United Nations 1992); the World Conference on Human Rights, held in June 1993; the Millennium Development Goals Achievement Fund, from 2006 onward; and the UN Resolution on Culture and Sustainable Development (UNGA 2013). Coupled with this are the numerous multilateral agreements, such as the Convention on the Protection and Promotion of the Diversity of Cultural Expressions (2005) and the Declaration on the Rights of Indigenous Peoples (United Nations 2007).

The important debates, discussions, decisions, and programs on cultural heritage provide the context in which the World Heritage Convention (1972) has evolved since its adoption in 1972, reflected to a large extent in the way its implementation has evolved through the flexibility of the convention's updated sets of operational guidelines, which has allowed for the inclusion of other forms (categories) originally not included, such as cultural landscapes, mixed sites, and archeological heritage.

As the "property" of Member States, UNESCO has its limitations, since it must often abide by those states' needs and expectations, some of which are purely political. Conventions including the World Heritage Convention (1972) by extension belong to the States Parties, and cannot be independent of their influence, despite stated scientific independence. Some scholars (e.g. Askew 2010; Logan 2012) have questioned the perception that UNESCO's power is wielded from its headquarters in Paris, stating that as an intergovernmental body and part of the UN family, States Parties that are signatories to the convention are the most powerful decision-makers in World Heritage, especially those that have representation on the World Heritage Committee. World Heritage Convention practice and practitioners are therefore caught up in a discourse that often lapses into polarized political theatrics that, in turn, inform relations between peoples, regions and issues.

It's about Heritage: A Theoretical Framework

The World Heritage Convention (1972) is a victim of its creation: it was the West that wanted to rediscover its past, glorifying and protecting it in the name of humanity. This past is tangible and monumental, conceived as a physical legacy; its focus is culture (for archeologists and architects) and nature (for conservationists and park managers). Naturally, the management system that developed under the World Heritage Convention favored that part of the world which had invested in monument building, an activity that was reified through the production of a dominant narrative of what constituted heritage. This narrative was grounded in the Venice Charter, the precursor to the World Heritage Convention, with its "principles for the preservation and restoration of ancient monuments, respect for original material and the concepts of authenticity and integrity" (ICASHB 1964: arts. 9, 14; see also Petzet 2004). Although the principles have largely been maintained, there has been flexibility in relation to understanding and incorporating local cultures and practices (ICOMOS 1994; Stovel 2008),[1] as well as an expansion of the idea of the heritage of humanity that extends it beyond the monuments and gardens of Europe.

Archaeology and architecture provided the dominant view of what and whose heritage constituted Outstanding Universal Value. However, as the discussion of broader definitions of heritage began to interest many, the World Heritage Convention's supposed neutrality, inclusivity, and representativeness came into question, especially in relation to parts of the world outside Europe and North America. This challenge was met by one of the World Heritage Committee's positive actions, a corrective measure in 1994 known as the Global Strategy for a Representative, Balanced and Credible World Heritage List (UNESCO 2005: 47). This "noble" effort introduced new categories of heritage for listing, such as cultural landscapes, industrial sites, and archeological heritage, thought to address the needs of other parts of the world. However, new categories did not achieve the desired effect: Europe was quick to embrace them, and prepare faster and better nominations. The disparity in designations went from bad to worse.

The Global Strategy has, however, had some success in the area of capacity-building among others in the developing world. Projects such as Africa 2009 made possible the establishment of regional training and capacity-building centers, and subsequently the founding of such heritage-funding institutions as the African World Heritage Fund (AWHF), all tremendous achievements. A course on nomination processes, for example, has resulted in strong nomination dossiers from the African continent and an increase in sites being listed. This is also attributable to a new "up-streaming process" of the World Heritage Committee designed to assist underrepresented countries in preparing robust conservation dossiers, and in identifying the criteria for Outstanding Universal Value, optimally leading to site inscription. The last two decades have also seen improvements in networking, professionalism, and the capacity of heritage practitioners to deal with issues around livelihood. Today in Africa, the heritage sector is a strong network of professionals who call upon each other for assistance. They are not only well-trained, but have a strong sense of commitment to effective practice, and utilize tools that have been made available through the AWHF, various states, as well as training institutions such as the Ecole Patrimoine Africaine (EPA) in Porto Novo, Benin, and the Centre for Heritage Development in Africa (CHDA) in Mombasa, Kenya, both partners of the AWHF in program implementation. Another indirect benefit of the Global Strategy is increasing recognition of the value of traditional management systems in the management of World Heritage sites.

The aim of the Global Strategy to achieve regional balance in site representation has, however, not succeeded. Deeply embedded challenges cause much of the world to lag behind Western Europe in listings (Labadi 2005). With its origins in Europe under the influence of the Venice Charter (ICASHB 1964), the World Heritage Convention (1972) has favored Europe. Meskell states that, "UNESCO largely began as an organization to preserve European architectural achievements after the devastation of World War II and subsequently has had to embrace other heritage forms and practices worldwide" (Meskell 2013: 488). Despite the flexibility of the Operational Guidelines as expounded by Labadi (2013: 31), a working document that has been revised repeatedly by the World Heritage Committee, the challenge of global inclusivity still exists.

Scholars and communities, including indigenous populations, now demand a voice within the corridors of the World Heritage system. Groups are questioning the dominant views that defined heritage in the past, thereby privileging some aspects while excluding others, with certain oppressive practices now coming under scrutiny (Mapunda and Lane 2004; Pikirayi 2011; Abungu and Abungu 2006; Abungu 2013).

Laurajane Smith has stated that there is no such thing as heritage, and that heritage is a performance or a construct with sites, monuments, and other so-called heritage being the theatre in which these performances are done.[2] Processes of value attachment and accompanying decisions come into question, and the possibility of dominant voices manipulating the World Heritage Convention (1972) declines when the values attached to many heritage places cease to be obvious.

Webber Ndoro (2001) contends that communities around the Great Zimbabwe National Monument, a World Heritage site, do not share the World Heritage Committee's view that it is an archaeological and architectural marvel requiring protection against use. To these communities, Great Zimbabwe is a site of great spiritual value. Classification and listing has brought no benefit to these communities – just restrictions on access to and use of their holy shrines. The values and narratives that supported its listing were developed by archeologists and architects without consultation with the communities to which they belong. Thus, despite meeting World Heritage inscription criteria, the fact that rationales for listing were constructed outside community domains has come to haunt the implementation of the World Heritage Convention (1972).

Historically, too, what are seen as architectural achievements are often attributed to people from outside the African continent. Great Zimbabwe is not an exception (Ndoro 2001), and the same approach is observed along the coast of East Africa, where the building of Swahili towns was ascribed to Arabs based on the Western assumption that there was a lack of creativity in Africa until colonial times (Chittick 1965, 1967, 1984). This discourse constructed by colonial scholars found favor with European powers seeking a reason to colonize and "civilize the African," a discourse that dominated the heritage scene in Africa until the 1980s.

The legacy of the colonial agenda of control remained after independence (Abungu 1996; Mumma 2008b), with the control and management of heritage and its study and interpretation remaining intact, with heritage managers hardly consulting communities and archeologists and other heritage researchers considering local communities uninformed and ignorant (Chirukure *et al.* 2010; Pikirayi 2011; Schmidt 2006; Abungu 2011). Archaeology, with its elitist tendency to exclude non-archaeologists from the interpretation of its findings, has contributed especially in Africa to the marginalization of communities, making them bystanders toward their own past (Ndoro and Pwiti 2001; Chirukure *et al.* 2010; Pikirayi 2011; Mumma 2008a; Schmidt 2006; Abungu 2011). Pikirayi (2011) has correctly pointed out that archeologists have failed to recognize the ways in which knowledge of local communities would benefit their own research. Instead, they tend to side with those who appropriate others' pasts and decline to listen to the voices of the wise, the sages of the communities concerned (Abungu 2011). Many World Heritage properties in Africa are hardly known as such by local communities.

The lack of community participation has led to an agitation for community rights, evidenced by the now famous phrase "Not for Us without Us" heard in Southern Africa, a sentiment that cuts across the continent and has created division among practitioners. With increasing demands in the developing world to use World Heritage in a manner perceived to be contradictory to the norms of the World Heritage Convention (1972) – especially for economic activities associated with extractive industries – the World Heritage List is becoming increasingly politicized, creating a division between North and South in the meetings of the World Heritage Committee.

Narrating her experience of the thirty-fifth World Heritage Committee session, Meskell states:

> I have witnessed the geopolitical machinations within the Committee and the excessive lobbying by nominating nations. The pacting between certain blocs, the maintenance of colonial connections, the escalating attacks on the Advisory Bodies, and the overturning of many conservation recommendations have been insightful for an archaeologist such as myself. (Meskell 2013: 484)

Strasser (2002) has attributed sustained critiques of the World Heritage system to postcolonial interventions against what is seen to be a traditionally European-dominated body, while Meskell (2013) observes that recent critiques may also be read as overt attempts to displace the hegemony of the North that has historically characterized the World Heritage List in historic terms.

Meskell notes that in the past few years European representatives on the World Heritage Committee have come from smaller, less powerful nations like Estonia, Switzerland, and Sweden, while challenges were mounted by large, powerful, emerging nations, including Brazil, Mexico, India, and South Africa. Meskell suggests that:

> for those State Parties leading the challenge, this could be seen as a revolution against the so-called expert adjudicators and their role in the contest that site nomination has become. Since ICOMOS has attracted criticism for appearing too white and European, this could be positioned as a strategic defiance of long-held hegemonic positions on the places where World Heritage is located, how it is understood, and the ways in which it can be legitimately practiced and lived. (Meskell 2013: 489)

This rift within the World Heritage family calls for reflexivity on the part of practitioners, and the need to decolonize the discourse of heritage listing.

Politics, International Relations, and Heritage

Despite many excellent decisions in areas of education, science, communication, and culture, because most representatives of states at UNESCO meetings tend to be technocrats, decisions are often spiced with political considerations. The "I have to consult my capital" mentality is alive and often heard during crucial discussions. Capitals mean political centers or entities where States Parties' interests are imagined, discussed, approved, and activated. The States Parties give advice based on how this serves their interest. It is therefore a fallacy to imagine that the World Heritage Convention (1972) can remain neutral and non-political, with all decisions based on the interests of science. And even in situations of democracies, the interests of States Parties are paramount with a give-and-take approach.

UNESCO Member States decide what to implement (or not) depending in their interests. As an example, an African minister from a State Party to the World Heritage Convention (1972), and who was also sitting on the World Heritage Committee, declined to approve the nomination of an extension to a site in their country, declaring listing would only happen "over my dead body." This was because the World Heritage Committee declined to approve mineral extraction next to a World Heritage site as the proposed development was considered to threaten the site's Outstanding Universal Value. The committee was in this case perceived to be anti-development and inconsiderate, especially to a case from the developing world. The case concerned non-extension of the Cape Floral Kingdom after the committee failed to approve open-pit coal mining in the Mapungubwe area.

UNESCO conventions are supposed to be made relevant to local stakeholders through the enactment of relevant national legislation. This rarely takes place, especially in the developing world (see Munjeri 2008). However, even when conventions are domesticated, they are often not fully implemented. National legislation dealing with mining, transportation, and the economy often overrides heritage laws.

The tensions inherent in listing are also illustrated in an example from an African country where the president, after hearing that the nomination dossier for a fine natural heritage site had been submitted, decreed that it should be withdrawn because "UNESCO will not allow us to even plough our farms once this place is listed." This was a reaction to the World Heritage Committee's non-approval of uranium mining in Selous Game Reserve, a World Heritage site. The property cited is the Eastern Arc in Tanzania and parts of Kenya.

Other difficulties emanate from World Heritage Committee's reluctance to approve projects when it is feared that local management will undermine the Outstanding Universal Value of the heritage property. Kenya planned a seven-berth port 20 kilometers from Lamu Old Town, a World Heritage property, with a potential negative impact on the property (Ndoro, Mumma, and Abungu 2008; Bakker, Odiaua, and Abungu 2013). In Zanzibar, the government gave permission for the development of a hotel in one of the historical landmark buildings on the island with hardly any consultation with the locals and in disregard to the World Heritage Convention (1972). Despite advice from a UNESCO mission (Bakker and Abungu 2012) on what would have been a win-win situation, the construction commenced in violation of expert advice. The exercise was stopped when a threat was made to place the property on the List of World Heritage in Danger. Cases such as these abound. Today a number of States Parties see listing as a flagrant denial of their right to tap resources for the well-being of their people. Uncertainty, a sense of victimization, and resistance to World Heritage Committee decisions or non-cooperation in their implementation seem to be a normal cycle of UNESCO challenges.

UNESCO is a political entity by design, with international tensions that characterize its membership, its priorities, and power relations among the membership. It would be folly therefore to imagine that it is faultless in its application, apolitical and neutral, and only driven by scientific considerations. The call for credibility that rings within the halls of every World Heritage Committee meeting, especially from so-called "neutral" members of the committee, can only be said to be a call for caution, and not for the elimination of politics in implementation. It is through these controversies that new practices as well as new heritage are imagined, figured, configured, and reconfigured.

The World Heritage Convention: Origins, Practice, and Inherent Contradictions

The World Heritage Convention (1972) is UNESCO's central instrument for recognizing and protecting that part of the heritage of humanity considered to be of Outstanding Universal Value. Grounded in the belief that heritage transcends national boundaries, this flagship convention remains the most ratified international treaty for cultural and natural heritage conservation in the world four decades after its inception. Nevertheless, it has a range of challenges based on history and the way it is organized. The World Heritage Convention is cast in stone and no changes can be made except additional improvements. However, as Labadi (2013) notes, its implementation is subject to constantly changing operational guidelines that address the omissions or inadequacies of the convention.

The World Heritage Convention (1972), implemented by the World Heritage Committee, and assisted by the World Heritage Centre, the Secretariat, ICOMOS, ICCROM, and the IUCN as advisory bodies (UNESCO 2012), all have their ways of operation, interests, and set-ups. Often what they see and recommend is not necessarily in line with what the broader heritage community thinks.

Although participation in the World Heritage Committee is through direct election, and each region is supposed to be more or less equally represented, there is so much solicitation that without resources and patronage, countries find it difficult to get elected. The desire to achieve membership of the committee is attributed to the fact that it ensures countries of nomination of their property to the World Heritage List. Meskell states that there is a correlation between the countries represented on the World Heritage Committee and the location of properties nominated: from 1977 to 2005, in 314 nominations, 42 percent benefited those countries with committee members at the time (Meskell 2013: 489). Small countries with unlimited resources have of late found their way on to the committee, while big countries with no resources, especially from the African continent, have been less successful, leading to them having less influence and a smaller numbers of listed sites. This conflict of interest has never been "corrected."

UNESCO's overall focus on cultural heritage evolved slowly. The notion that there is some heritage that is so important that its loss would be significant to the global community was born in 1959 when the presidents of Egypt and Sudan called on UNESCO to assist in salvaging monuments that were to be flooded due to the construction of the Aswan High Dam (Munjeri 2008). Given their worldwide significance, the concept of international action to address a threat to heritage emerged. The operation was not only massive in scale but also inclusive in nature, emphasizing a collective commitment to heritage of Outstanding Universal Value to which all humanity could subscribe.

The efforts of the IUCN several years later led to the World Heritage Trust that mobilized "international cooperation to protect the world's superb natural and scenic areas and historical sites" (UNESCO n.d.). This growing attention to formal strategies for designation and support was formalized in a recommendation at the UN meeting on the human environment, held in Stockholm in 1972, where it was decided that UNESCO should have a "World Heritage Convention" (UNEP 1972). It was adopted at the General Conference of UNESCO in November 1972.

Inevitably there were political undertones. Early influences came from the presidents of Egypt and Sudan through the Aswan Dam project, while President Nixon wanted the convention to be in place for the centennial celebrations of Yellowstone National Park. These hidden but significant factors demonstrate that heritage is at times a construct that depends on negotiations between competing interest groups, with persuasion and even coercion used as means for arriving at a consensus.

Today there are questions to be asked about the performance of the World Heritage Convention (1972). While the convention sought to link and balance, for the first time, concepts of natural and cultural heritage conservation, it is an open question whether or not this has been achieved. This is a critical issue, particularly in relation to natural sites, mixed sites, and cultural landscapes, where ICOMOS and the IUCN often read from different scripts. While ICOMOS celebrates the human imprint on sites, the IUCN often see this as a problem, and may insist on the removal of populations from sites considered to be of natural or even of mixed significance. Different perspectives among practitioners lead to inherent contradictions within practice.

The reaction to the practice of World Heritage listing is so region-specific that one wonders whether the concept of Outstanding Universal Value is applicable across the board. When looked at closely, differences are possibly due to ways in which World Heritage listing is valued. In Europe and parts of Asia, communities and regional governments line up to include their heritage. In Africa, however, many see World Heritage listing as limiting rather than enabling due to the exclusion of local communities from decision-making and management.

The issue outlined and discussed above lead to a number of important questions relating to the World Heritage Convention (1972) and its implementation:

- Can it or its implementation evolve beyond the inherent European bias that originally gave too much weight and favored gardens and cathedrals over the cultural and religious landscapes of Africa or South America? Of course recognition must be given to the various attempts that UNESCO has made in the past in addressing such issues, including through the aforementioned Global Strategy for a Representative, Balanced and Credible World Heritage List; the Nara Document on Authenticity (ICOMOS 1994); the Convention for the Safeguarding of the Intangible Cultural Heritage (2003); and the introduction of categories of heritage such as cultural landscapes.
- How does it deal with the appropriation of heritage from the periphery to the center, from communities to national institutions that then treat communities as a problem rather than a solution?
- How does it integrate traditional and community-based management systems within externally prescribed and top-down systems?
- How does it deal with imbalances created when prestige and investment opportunities linked with listing attract the wealthy, leading them to buy properties and invest in tourism while at the same time restricting what the local poor can do within the "core" and "buffer" zones of the heritage site?
- How does it deal with biases that exclude communities from using the past and shaping its interpretation, relying instead on scholarly work that in itself is exclusive and elitist, devoid of community input and local knowledge?
- How does it deal with multiple voices on the ground that offer a diversity of opinion and action regarding the management of World Heritage?
- How does it deal with genuine community needs regarding the exploitation of natural resources to alleviate poverty in the face of negative opinion from well-funded environmental propagandists working in the name of conservation concerns?
- And how can conservation practice become inclusive regarding different kinds of heritage in their varied contexts without practitioners working against the World Heritage Convention's restrictive approach and rigid definitions?

These issues are at the core of contemporary practice and of practitioners' engagement, especially in the African context.

Hidden beneath the Convention: Challenges and Opportunities for Practice and Practitioners

The World Heritage Convention (1972), although a project of political entities, is implemented by professionals in heritage management and conservation. Based on the Venice Charter (ICASHB 1964), the World Heritage Convention was conceived as based on a set of apolitical scientific principles and processes that were informed by conservation science in the spirit of preserving the world's most outstanding heritage. However, given its origins, its international context, and the values it serves, this well-intentioned accord can hardly be apolitical and neutral, a dilemma that lies at the core of practice.

The Venice Charter (ICASHB 1964) is a work of architects, and a document of conservation policy and practice heavily influenced by European thinking. These biases clearly shape the World Heritage Convention (1972). The cultural part of the convention focus on the built environment rather than on the associated spiritual and intangible heritage that imbues it with meaning. Instead, these aspects are now covered by the later Convention for the Safeguarding of the Intangible Cultural Heritage (2003), a convention that some major Western states initially declined to sign.

Interpretation of the World Heritage Convention (1972) has also been dominated by particular subjects. Architecture has promoted views of heritage that are not universal and inclusive in approach. The same can be said of archaeology, a subject that claims to be rigorous and scientific, and has no room for speculation. These disciplines each have their own language and ways of imagining the world, often rooted in Western philosophical studies that reverberate with articulations of "other" and expert knowledge, where the definition of that "other" is a preserve of the West and not always flattering. Even scholars of heritage studies are not exempt from complaining about their perceived absence at UNESCO. Meskell, for example, notes:

> I was once told UNESCO is a fascinating topic for an archaeologist to research. On the one hand, the organization signifies everything, a powerful and universal symbol, providing the only global standard for recognizing and protecting archaeological heritage. And on the other hand, it means so little to archaeologists: they scarcely understand its processes and are often outside its capillary networks of power. It is this uneasy polarity I find compelling. In theory, UNESCO constitutes the arena where archaeology reaches worldwide attention and yet archaeologists themselves are largely invisible in the political processes, governance, and public profile of the organization. (Meskell 2013: 492)

Regarding nature, the World Heritage Convention's approach is shaped by subjects like biology and geology, particularly in the work of the IUCN. The disciplines that claim to be strictly scientific leave no room for consultation with communities since these are deemed not to be "experts." Exclusion from the first stage of defining the values and significance of heritage, and from participating in the process of nominating one's heritage, automatically has implications for practice and practitioners.

Tension inevitably emerges in engaging with communities in heritage management. However, change is being embraced through provisions for "participatory culture" embedded in additions to the World Heritage Convention's Operational Guidelines, including emerging recognition of traditional management systems. Although accepted grudgingly, it has been demonstrated that traditional practices can be effective. While there has been quite a change in mindset and practice in recent years, especially with efforts by ICOMOS and the IUCN to work with communities, there is still a long way to go for communities to be counted among true practitioners, with direct implications in Africa where heritage is still lived and used. The reluctance on the part of ICOMOS to engage States Parties during the development of nomination dossiers as part of the upstream process, claiming conflicts of interest, has not been well received.

While ICOMOS sees its representatives as evaluators rather than collaborators, it is itself perceived as opposing new nominations and recommending properties be placed on the List of World Heritage in Danger, all of which has led to suspicions among many States Parties that they have become victims of international heritage politics.

The relations between the colonized and the colonizers, of the rich "enlightened" and patronizing North and the poor "illiterate" and patronized South, of the master and servant, have been dilemmas that confront both practice and practitioners. There are undercurrents in World Heritage Committee discussions that show that unequal relationships between the two worlds are still present, and what Meskell refers to as "the pacting between certain blocs, the maintenance of colonial connections" (Meskell 2013: 484).

There is, however, a start being made to reframing values within heritage discourses worldwide as the issue of community roles increasingly takes center stage at international forums. This can be traced to the evolution of the World Heritage Convention (1972), and today this reframing influences World Heritage Committee decisions and those of major practitioners. The World Heritage Convention mentions the word "community" in passing, calling for their involvement. While the World Heritage Committee recognized a number of key actions in its 2002 list of Cs for conservation practice (UNESCO 2005) – credibility, conservation, capacity-building, and communications – it did not add a C for community until 2007.

There is no doubt that UNESCO and the World Heritage Convention (1972) has led to many positive benefits the world over, and for Africa in particular. The Global Strategy for a Representative, Balanced and Credible World Heritage List; the identification and inclusion of heritage more specific to the African continent, such as cultural landscapes and archeological and paleontological sites; capacity-building in the heritage sector; the founding of the dedicated African World Heritage Fund; the introduction and support for "upstreaming processes," designed to assist underrepresented countries in preparing robust conservation dossiers and identifying the criteria for Outstanding Universal Value, optimally leading to site inscriptions that have yielded positive results; the introduction of the fifth C, leading to the recognition of the role of community in World Heritage matters, and recognition of traditional management systems at World Heritage sites – these have all, albeit conditionally, contributed immensely to the course of the World Heritage Convention in Africa. However, the convention has also encountered many challenges. Meant to be an instrument of high moral standards, of scientific excellence, and of rigor and integrity, it is also a tool open to political manipulation, used by States Parties to negotiate strategies and exercise power, including at times rights of intervention in others' culture and heritage.

Changing Dynamics, Paradigm Shift, or Temporary Truce?

Current debates have shown that heritage has political, social, and economic dimensions, and that it is not apolitical, innocent, or neutral. It can be misused, contested, appropriated, and even used to divide or unify entities. While misunderstandings can create conflict, heritage can also build identity, a sense of belonging, and an appreciation of diversity.

Heritage is becoming popular both for its intrinsic value and as a commodity. The making and use of heritage is central to contemporary debates on the roles of World

Heritage, as more people discuss production, consumption, and the challenges associated with ownership, use, and misuse. This puts heritage discourse squarely on the platform of contestation as various practitioners jostle for advantageous position.

Heritage and heritage places are no longer perceived as static in this discourse, but constantly evolving and changing. While the concept of Outstanding Universal Value may imply permanency, there is a developing awareness that rigidity in interpretation may lead to the loss of some of the most outstanding heritage places from the list. This phenomenon has been highlighted in debates over conservation and development currently raging in Africa. Communities are demanding a say in the definition of their "past" as they continue to create "heritage," define and redefine their spaces, meanings, and uses, and influence power relations. They are also demanding that their views on the use of heritage and heritage places be respected. Others are demanding their "past" back, including what they see as having been appropriated by scholars and institution of learning. The return of human remains to the World Heritage site in Mapungubwe, South Africa, from the University of Pretoria many decades after their excavation and appropriation is a good example (Pikirayi 2011; Meskell 2011). In most cases, due to the need for economic advancement, poverty alleviation, and job creation, communities do not perceive conflict in the use of heritage places in a way that the World Heritage Committee or its Advisory Bodies do. In this argument, even UNESCO and its agencies become agents of imperialism. For example, the communities of Mapungubwe do not see how coal mining seven kilometers away will affect their site. For them, opposition to the venture means a lack of concern for their well-being and support for the interests of owners of nearby eco-lodges who are benefiting from Mapungubwe's World Heritage listing at their expense (Pikirayi 2011).

In Tanzania, the Maasai of the Ngorongoro Conservation Area do not see why the IUCN opposes grazing animals within the park when, according to them, they have always done this. They take pride in protecting the wild animals that they have coexisted with for centuries, and oppose measures to separate or control their activities just because the place has been inscribed on the World Heritage List. Further south, the government of Tanzania does not see why it cannot mine a small section (about 0.09 percent of the total acreage of a park the size of Belgium) of the massive Selous Game Reserve for uranium that will not only create jobs but will also strengthen the national economy and alleviate poverty in the region. After the government decided to proceed with the project, the Selous Game Reserve was placed on the infamous List of World Heritage in Danger – a list that many African States Parties see as an instrument of punishment.

In Kenya, the government is proceeding with building a seven-berth port near Lamu. They do not accept that this facility will compromise the Outstanding Universal Value of Lamu Old Town, located 20 kilometers away. Concerns about destroying views and vistas, or compromising the spirit of place, do not seem sufficient to overturn their quest to create wealth and jobs (Abungu *et al.* 2009; Bakker, Odiaua, and Abungu 2013).

Many examples from Africa can be used to illustrate arguments that the North exercises domination by stopping development in the South. African developers observe that some World Heritage sites in Europe are old mines, the very same thing that the World Heritage Committee condemns. In this narrative, they have the support of local populations and communities who have "suffered" at the hands of conservation, and who want to escape cycles of poverty and want. The politicians, often the beneficiaries of developmental projects and wanting support from communities, have no hesitation contradicting the very convention that their states have acceded to. It is not uncommon to see the mighty and powerful preside over heritage days, festivals, and exhibition openings as an investment in votes of confidence.

These challenges have led to conflicts in practice, particularly in relation to the World Heritage Convention's emphasis on permanency over flexible change. Today among the key practitioners on the World Heritage Committee and advisory bodies on the one hand, and States Parties on the other, there is a constant question of change or no change. This has grouped those claiming that change is not necessarily destructive on one side, and those championing the preservation of the status quo on the other.

The notion of "them" and "us" is evident in World Heritage Committee meetings, even if it is not uttered due to sensitivities. At times it is caused by the North/South divide, but at other times former colonial powers support their former colonies, especially when the interests of the powerful are at stake. The high moral standards espoused as a cornerstone of the World Heritage Convention (1972) can temporarily be put aside if there is need for deal-making. This observation has also been made by Strasser (2002) and Meskell, the latter stating that "sustained critiques of the World Heritage system may seem like critical organizational and postcolonial interventions against what is seen to be a traditionally European-dominated body" (Meskell 2013: 488).

Is the World Heritage Convention capable of adapting to address present societal needs without compromising its stated aims and goals? What kind of practices and practitioners will ensure that the gains made are kept and mistakes are corrected to ensure the survival of a convention that is truly inclusive of all in the face of constant antagonism and criticism between politically powerful States Parties, the partners to the World Heritage Convention.

The Power of Heritage

Giving communities voice requires a paradigm shift with practitioners engaging in serious reflexivity regarding their own roles and practices in the past and today (Pikirayi 2011; Abungu 2013). Such a transition involves acknowledging as partners those who were custodians of heritage long before any conventions came into place (Mumma 2008a). As community members demand their rightful place in heritage management, they also must shape interpretation, including the production of knowledge. This calls for a change of mindset among researchers who have monopolized this process. Knowledge is power, and when one's voice is not captured, one's interests are not represented. This has produced complications with regard to sacred sites in Africa, where the very owners of these sites find access restricted as narratives are developed without their participation (Chirukure *et al.* 2010; Abungu 1996, 1997, 2011; Ndoro 2001, 2004). Ownership comes with expected benefits and responsibility. Most communities within and around World Heritage sites in Africa have for years remained spectators as States Parties and the business community often have benefited. It is not uncommon to come across World Heritage sites where the communities have no idea of a site's heritage status. And even if they do hear, they are not informed of what it means to be a World Heritage site.

When nations assumed responsibility for preserving and interpreting the past, they also assumed exclusive power over owning the past, creating the present and determining the future through such things as museums, departments of antiquities, tourism, culture, wildlife management, and forestry among others. This top-down heritage management approach characterized practice for over a hundred years in many places in the African continent, where colonization and its attendant discriminatory actions such as land alienation and heritage appropriation led in some instances to total alienation of populations from their heritage (Rodney 1973). Independence and democracy never brought an answer as systems established in the past persisted, ensuring that communities are hardly players in heritage discourse. In the process, institutions of heritage have had troubled relationships with communities who are often perceived as the problem when it comes to protecting "innocent nature and the wild and exotic."

However, the past is not just the past, nor does it belong to the state. The past and the making of the present have become an arena of contestation and debate. The notion of the silent majority willing to listen no longer applies in a heritage discourse of production and consumption. As people continue to reappropriate and reinterpret their heritage through such instruments as stakeholder forums, community empowerment programs, voter education programs, self-help groups, NGOs, and other community-based activities, heritage management discourse is changing, with a paradigm shift occurring with regard to practice and the attitude of practitioners, empowering communities as equals in heritage protection and interpretation.

UNESCO and its States Parties have been accused of a top-down approach to heritage management that has failed to recognize the central role of communities, so important in a continent like Africa. UNESCO has also been accused of creating a flat cultural map of the world, rather than viewing culture as a phenomenon entangled in process, negotiation, and contestation (Wright 1998), as well as romanticizing culture and diversity (Ericksen 2009). Heritage conservation practices, especially World Heritage and the World Heritage Convention (1972), provides a platform for political, cultural, and socioeconomic dialogue among practitioners despite these persistent challenges.

Conclusion: Africa, the World Heritage Convention, and the Future

Africa as a continent has had a checkered history, and even today complaints about discrimination and exploitation still abound. The question is whether this is reality or it is about a continent caught in a time warp. From the discussion, it appears there are reasons to complain. Heritage management both at local and at international level still excludes many, and it remains caught up in conflicts, contradictions, and levels of political expediency that require serious reflection. Heritage theory is still dominated by Western thought and practices, and heritage practice has to change, with sensitive and informed practitioners ready to open doors for communities. Numerous issues remain in need of address, and many questions remain unanswered. There is need to positively challenge the scope and meaning of heritage practices and, most importantly, heritage practitioners; we must also align custodians and owners alongside professional practitioners; align the interests of communities with those of the World Heritage Convention (1972); and develop genuine conservation strategies that also serve the interests of the local majority without necessarily compromising the spirit and principles of the convention.

Ways must be found in which the formal and informal, and the community and the state, operate in unity; the voices of communities must be included in the management of their own heritage. The question of the economic benefit of heritage (Throsby 1999, 2001; O'Brien 2010) must be part of the heritage agenda. The traditional systems that for centuries have sustained sites, especially in Africa, need to be integrated into their management, and so must the roles of women and youths as practitioners.

The latter issue begs an answer as these groups are major stakeholders, and Africa has had substantial support from Scandinavian countries for training, a region that insists on gender parity. Through this assistance, Africa has shifted and corrected imbalances in heritage practice, especially in connection with female representation, and this must be maintained.

The challenge emerging out of neglect and the failure to address the many issues discussed here is that social and ecological concerns are increasingly overshadowed by economics. People require food, good healthcare, better roads, and more jobs; such needs can prompt dominant parts of society to manipulate a community's collective consciousness. Heritage practitioners have, however, failed to demonstrate the stability that cultural and ecological values can bring to society. How do we align heritage management with local needs and expectations? Engagement and ownership, and the increased use of traditional indigenous knowledge are sure ways of achieving this. Practitioners who care about the future of heritage have an obligation to change the fundamentals of heritage practice to fit into the current world of high expectations and compelling rights. Africa, with its numerous challenges but immense untapped resources, and a developing rebellious attitude, stands a good chance of helping redraw a heritage discourse that is diverse yet inclusive, respectful of the local and yet global and cosmopolitan, supportive of the World Heritage Convention and yet cares about people. It must be a true discourse representative of all humanity, a principle of the World Heritage Convention.

Notes

1 Also relevant here is the Burra Charter (Australia ICOMOS 2013).
2 Laurajane Smith, personal communication, March 27, 2014. See also Smith (2006).

References

Legislation

Convention Concerning the Protection of the World Cultural and Natural Heritage (World Heritage Convention) (UNESCO, 1972). Available at: http://whc.unesco.org/archive/convention-en.pdf (accessed March 19, 2015).

Convention for the Safeguarding of the Intangible Cultural Heritage (Intangible Cultural Heritage Convention) (UNESCO, 2003). Available at: http://unesdoc.unesco.org/images/0013/001325/132540e.pdf (accessed March 19, 2015).

Convention on the Protection and Promotion of the Diversity of Cultural Expressions (UNESCO, 2005). Available at: http://unesdoc.unesco.org/images/0014/001429/142919e.pdf (accessed March 19, 2015).

Other Works

Abungu, G. (1996) Heritage, Community and the State in the Nineties: Experiences from Africa. Paper presented at the conference The Production of History in a Changing South Africa, University of the Western Cape, South Africa, July 10–12.

Abungu, G. (1997) Museums, Archaeology and the Public. In C. Ardouin (ed.), *Museums and Archaeology in West Africa*. Washington: Smithsonian Institution Press, pp. 142–154.

Abungu, G. (2011) Africa's Rich Intangible Heritage: Managing a Continent's Diverse Heritage. In M.I. Stefano, P. Davis, and G. Corsane (eds), *Safeguarding Intangible Heritage*. Woodbridge: Boydell Press, pp. 57–70.

Abungu, G. (2013) Walking the Long Path to Partnership: Archaeology and Communities in Eastern Africa – Relevance, Access and Ownership. Paper presented at the International Conference on Community Archaeology, University of Florida, Gainesville, March 24–28.

Abungu, G., and Abungu, L. (eds) (2006) Africa: A Continent of Achievements. *Museum International*, 229/230, special issue.

Abungu, G., Abungu, L., Coulson, D., Pavitt, N., Fisher A., and Beck, C. (2009) *Lamu: Kenya's Enchanted Island*. New York: Rizzoli.

Askew, M. (2010) The Magic List of Global Status: UNESCO, World Heritage and the Agendas of States. In S. Labadi and C. Long (eds), *Heritage and Globalization*. London: Routledge, pp. 19–44.

Australia ICOMOS (2013) Charter for Places of Cultural Significance (Burra Charter), revised version. Available at: http://australia.icomos.org/wp-content/uploads/The-Burra-Charter-2013-Adopted-31.10.2013.pdf (accessed June 29, 2014).

Bakker, K.A., and Abungu, G. (2012) Heritage Impact Assessment for the Proposed Hotel Complex at Mambo Msiige, Zanzibar Stone Town. Report for the Government of Zanzibar.

Bakker, K.A., Odiaua, I., and Abungu, G. (2013) Heritage Impact Assessment for Lamu Port–South Sudan–Ethiopia Transport (LAPSSET) Corridor and the New Lamu Port and Metropolis Development Project, as well as Related Development in the Lamu Archipelago, Kenya. Report for National Museums of Kenya, the Government of Kenya, and UNESCO.

Chirukure, S., *et al.* (2010) Unfulfilled Promises? Heritage Management and Community Participation at Some of Africa's Heritage Sites. *International Journal of Heritage Studies*, 16 (1/2), 29–42.

Chittick, H.N. (1965) The Shirazi Colonization of East Africa. *Journal of African History*, 6 (3), 275–294.

Chittick, H.N. (1967) Discoveries in the Lamu Archipelago. *Azania*, 2, 37–67.

Chittick, H.N. (1984) *Manda: Excavations at an Island Port on the Kenyan Coast*. Nairobi: British Institute in Eastern Africa.

Ericksen, T.H. (2009) Between Universalism and Relativism: A Critique of the UNESCO Concept of Culture. In M. Goodale (ed.), *Human Rights: An Anthropological Reader*. Malden, MA: Wiley-Blackwell, pp. 356–371.

ICASHB (International Congress of Architects and Specialists of Historic Buildings) (1964) International Charter for the Conservation and Restoration of Monuments and Sites (Venice Charter). Available at: http://www.icomos.org/charters/venice_e.pdf (accessed March 9, 2015).

ICOMOS (1994) Nara Document on Authenticity. Available at: http://www.icomos.org/charters/nara-e.pdf (accessed April 1, 2015).

Labadi, S. (2005) A Review of the Global Strategy for a Balanced, Representative and Credible World Heritage List, 1994–2004. *Conservation and Management of Archaeological Sites*, 7, 89–102.

Labadi, S. (2013) *UNESCO, Cultural Heritage and Outstanding Universal Value*. Walnut Creek, CA: AltaMira Press.

Logan, W. (2012) States, Governance and the Politics of Culture: World Heritage Places in Asia. In P. Daly and T. Winter (eds), *The Routledge Handbook of Heritage in Asia*. London: Routledge, pp. 113–128.

Mapunda, B., and Lane, P. (2004) Archaeology for Whose Interest, Archaeologists or Locals? In N. Merriman (ed.), *Public Archaeology*. London: Routledge, pp. 211–223.

Meskell, L.M. (2011) From Paris to Pontdrift: UNESCO Meetings, Mapungubwe and Mining. *South African Archaeological Bulletin*, 66, 149–156.

Meskell, L.M. (2013) UNESCO's World Heritage Convention at Forty: Challenging the Economic and Political Order of International Heritage Conservation. *Current Anthropology*, 54 (4), 483–494.

Mumma, A. (2008a) Framework for Legislation on Immovable Cultural Heritage in Africa. In W. Ndoro, A. Mumma, and G. Abungu (eds), *Cultural Heritage and the Law: Protecting Immovable Heritage in English-Speaking Countries of Sub-Saharan Africa*. Rome: ICCROM, pp. 97–107.

Mumma, A. (2008b) Heritage Policy and Law-Making Processes. In W. Ndoro, A. Mumma, and G. Abungu (eds), *Cultural Heritage and the Law: Protecting Immovable Heritage in English-Speaking Countries of Sub-Saharan Africa*. Rome: ICCROM, pp. 109–112.

Munjeri, D. (2008) Introduction to International Conventions and Charters on Immovable Cultural Heritage. In W. Ndoro, A. Mumma, and G. Abungu (eds), *Cultural Heritage and the Law: Protecting Immovable Heritage in English-Speaking Countries of Sub-Saharan Africa*. Rome: ICCROM, pp. 13–23.

Ndoro, W. (2001) *Your Monument, Our Shrine: The Preservation of Great Zimbabwe*. Uppsala: Societas Archaeologica Upsaliensis.

Ndoro, W. (2004) Traditional and Customary Heritage Systems, Nostalgia or Reality? The Implications of Managing Heritage Sites in Africa. In E. Merode, R. Smeets, and C. Westrik (eds), *Linking Universal and Local Values: Managing a Sustainable Future for the World Heritage*. Paris: UNESCO, pp. 81–84.

Ndoro, W., Mumma, A., and Abungu, G. (eds) (2008) *Cultural Heritage and Law: Protecting Immovable Cultural Heritage in English-Speaking Countries of Sub-Saharan Africa*. Rome: ICCROM.

Ndoro, W., and Pwiti, G. (2001) Heritage Management in Southern Africa: Local, National and International Discourse. *Public Archaeology*, 2, 21–34.

O'Brien, D. (2010) Measuring the Value of Culture: A Report to the Department for Culture, Media and Sports. London: Department of Arts and Culture/Arts and Humanities Research Council. Available at: https://www.gov.uk/government/uploads/system/uploads/attachment_data/file/77933/measuring-the-value-culture-report.pdf (accessed April 1, 2015).

Petzet, M. (2004) Principles of Preservation: An Introduction to the International Charters for Conservation and Restoration, Forty Years after the Venice Charter. *Monuments and Sites*, 1, 7–29. Available at: http://openarchive.icomos.org/432 (accessed January 26, 2015).

Pikirayi, I. (2011) *Tradition, Archaeological Heritage Protection and Communities in the Limpopo Province of South Africa*. Addis Ababa: Organization for Social Science in Eastern and Southern Africa.

Rodney, W. (1973) *How Europe Underdeveloped Africa*. Dar es Salaam/London: Tanzania Publishing House/Bogle-L'Ouverture Publications.

Schmidt, P. (2006) *Historical Archaeology in Africa: Representation, Social Memory, and Oral Traditions*. Lanham, MD: AltaMira Press.

Smith, L. (2006) *Uses of Heritage*. London: Routledge.

Stovel, H. (2008) Origins and Influence of the Nara Document on Authenticity. *APT Bulletin*, 39 (2/3), 9–10.

Strasser, P. (2002) "Putting Reform into Action": Thirty Years of the World Heritage Convention: How to Reform a Convention without Changing Its Regulations. *International Journal of Cultural Property*, 11, 215–266.

Throsby, D. (1999) Cultural Capital. *Journal of Cultural Economics*, 23, 3–12.

Throsby, D. (2001) *Economics and Culture*. Cambridge: Cambridge University Press.

UNEP (1972) Declaration of the United Nations Conference on the Human Environment, Stockholm, June 5–16. Available at: http://www.unep.org/Documents.Multilingual/Default.asp?documentid=97&articleid=1503 (accessed April 1, 2015).

UNESCO (1982) Mexico City Declaration on Cultural Policies. Declaration adopted by the UNESCO World Conference on Cultural Policies, Mexico City, July 26 to August 6. Available at: http://portal.unesco.org/culture/en/files/12762/11295421661mexico_en.pdf/mexico_en.pdf (accessed April 1, 2015).

UNESCO (2005) Basic Texts of the 1972 World Heritage Convention. Available at: http://whc.unesco.org/en/activities/562/ (accessed April 10, 2015).
UNESCO (2012) Operational Guidelines for the Implementation of the World Heritage Convention. Available at: http://whc.unesco.org/archive/opguide12-en.pdf (accessed April 1, 2015).
UNESCO (n.d.) Introducing UNESCO. Available at: https://en.unesco.org/about-us/introducing-unesco (accessed September 30, 2014).
UNGA (2013) Resolution on Culture and Sustainable Development. Document A/RES/68/223. Available at: http://www.unesco.lacult.org/lacult_en/docc/Res_ONU_68_263_Eng.pdf (accessed April 1, 2015).
United Nations (1992) Agenda 21. Report from the United Nations Conference on Environment and Development Rio de Janeiro, Brazil. Available at: https://sustainabledevelopment.un.org/content/documents/Agenda21.pdf (accessed April 1, 2015).
United Nations (2007) Declaration on the Rights of Indigenous Peoples (UNDRIP). Document A/RES/61/295. Available at: http://www.un-documents.net/a61r295.htm (accessed March 19, 2015).
Wright, S. (1998) The Politicization of "Culture." *Anthropology Today* 14 (1), 7–15.

CHAPTER 27

World Heritage Sites in Africa: What Are the Benefits of Nomination and Inscription?

Webber Ndoro

It has been argued that the major reason why little domestic attention is given to World Heritage places in Africa is the inability of heritage to contribute to the development agenda espoused by most African governments. As a developing continent, Africa is faced with challenges in achieving sustainable development whilst maintaining its social and cultural fabric, as well as ensuring that heritage places such as World Heritage sites are preserved (Keitumetse 2007; Kigongo and Reid 2007; Jopela 2010; Sinamai 2014). At times the issues of heritage conservation and the improvement of livelihoods are perceived as opposite sides of the same coin. Issues relating to the incompatibility of resource utilization and conservation have dominated heritage discourse on the continent (Meskell 2011). The issue is how heritage managers develop international conservation practice when surrounded by a sea of poverty. Does excellence in conservation and the management of a specific site have to concern itself with the issue of livelihoods? Rarely does UNESCO and the World Heritage Committee concern itself with people's lives, particularly local communities, although it has been argued that tourism and World Heritage places can lead to sustainable development and the stimulation of local industries (see Galla 2012).

Sustainable development is a model of resource utilization that aims to meet human needs while preserving the environment, and ensuring that these human needs can be met without compromising environmental needs. Sustainable development therefore respects the limited capacity of ecosystems to absorb the impact of human activity, and aims at ensuring that today's development needs do not compromise the ability of

A Companion to Heritage Studies, First Edition. Edited by William Logan, Máiréad Nic Craith, and Ullrich Kockel.
© 2016 John Wiley & Sons, Inc. Published 2016 by John Wiley & Sons, Inc.

future generations to develop. On the whole, sustainable development ensures environmental protection, social growth, and economic development. Do World Heritage sites and tourism promote environmental protection initiatives that incorporate social and economic growth? The International Cultural Tourism Charter recognizes that heritage belongs to all people, and that it "records and expresses the long processes of historic development, forming the essence of diverse national, regional, indigenous and local identities and is an integral part of modern life. It is a dynamic reference point and positive instrument for growth and change" (ICOMOS 1999: 2). It can be argued that World Heritage nomination and inscription acts as a catalyst in making a place an important destination, and it can be a strong driver of economic development (see Shackley 1998; Leask and Fyall 2006; Salazar 2010).

Heritage and Development

Problems of poverty, unemployment, and inequality have persistently stifled economic development in the Third World. This is particularly true in Africa, where the majority of people who reside in rural areas live below the poverty line. Often, capital and employment opportunities are scarce, effectively leaving communities with few options to meet their development needs. Heritage, which is a strong aspect of the indigenous knowledge systems, has emerged as one of the most powerful engines for economic development (Galla 2012). As a resource, heritage can provides an opportunity for job creation, infrastructure development, and educational opportunities in both rural and urban areas. Perhaps one of the most common ways of exploiting heritage resources is through the promotion of heritage-based tourism, as many tourists visit iconic heritage places every year. The value chain associated with such visits is assumed to have many positive impacts. For example, the development of heritage places for tourism requires infrastructure development, which in turn feeds into sectors such as the construction industry. When fully functional, developed heritage places will employ people who will provide services in areas such as hotels and catering, which is another strong sector of the economy. Therefore, what normally starts as a visit to a heritage place is interlinked with the local economy in many positive ways, a fact that is not always easily recognized.

The role of development has always been seen as a double-edged. Whilst tourism has been given as one of the ways heritage can contribute to development, it has also been regarded as a threat to the very places that the heritage sector is trying to preserve (Keitumetse and Nthoi 2009; Mowforth and Munt 2009; Comer 2011).

In 2000, following on from the United Nations Millennium Declaration (UNGA 2000), the United Nations proposed eight Millennium Development Goals (MDGs) to promote concrete actions for the world to address extreme poverty in its many dimensions: income poverty, hunger, disease, lack of adequate shelter, and exclusion. With a target date of 2015, the MDGs are a first attempt to subject the development process to the discipline of showing that it can improve lives on a large scale within an agreed time frame. When they were made public, however, many within the heritage profession must have wondered why there was no reference to cultural heritage and the role that it could play in development.

In the last few years, the role of cultural heritage in sustainable development has been highlighted. For example, it is very much reflected in the report from the Rio Plus 20

Conference (United Nations 2012). Here the importance of cultural heritage in creating jobs and entrepreneurial opportunities is stressed. The debate of the role of culture and heritage in sustainable development has also featured prominently in the post-2015 MDGs program discussion (Barthel-Bouchier 2013). One of the most important aspects of the MDGs is the focus not only on lack of income but also on accompanying problems such as lack of education, gender inequality, infectious diseases, and a feeling of hopelessness, loss of identity, and lack of self-esteem. The effects of poverty go beyond the individual, impacting on whole communities and nations, affecting their ability to sustain themselves and their way of life, including their cultural heritage and historic environment (Ndoro and Jaquinta 2006). Yet it can be argued that cultural heritage and the historic environment help reinforce meaning and identity in individuals and cohesion in communities. It follows therefore that the conservation and protection of historic buildings, towns, landscapes, and heritage places in general have an important role to play in any meaningful poverty reduction program leading to sustainable economic development (Ndoro and Jaquinta 2006).

This sort of development is only possible through the empowerment and involvement of local communities in the decision-making process. For example, the government of Mongolia galvanized support for national development though the rebuilding of one of the country's most important cultural assets: a bronze statue which had been destroyed in the early part of the twentieth century. Rebuilding the statue after the collapse of the communist regime united Mongolians and made them proud of their own culture. By focusing first on this important symbol of their heritage, the government paved the way for a more healthy development process (see Palmer 2003).

Conservation projects can also have a more direct effort on development goals. Heritage professionals should try where possible to link development objectives to conservation work. An example of this type of link can be found in a site project which took place in Kokologho, Burkina Faso, and was carried out as a partnership between the national Directorate of Cultural Heritage and the local chief and residents of the eight villages which make up Kokologho. The project called for the promotion and reinforcement of traditional conservation practices to ensure the ongoing protection of the chief's palace. To aid in the conservation work at the site, a solar lighting system was installed and a borehole drilled. This infrastructure, necessary for the conservation work, now supplies lighting and water to the surrounding communities. In addition, the project brought the community together and encouraged involvement in a way that reinforced the values of their heritage. Thus both conservation and development objectives were achieved within the same project.

Heritage and Tourism

There is recognition that tourism, which depends on peoples' culture as the main source of attraction and entertainment, is the world's largest industry, and has great potential to contribute to sustainable development in Africa. At the Rio Earth Summit in 1992, Agenda 21 underlined the possibilities for using sustainable tourism as a tool for poverty eradication (United Nations 1992). However, for tourism to be sustainable, it must take into account environmental and sociocultural considerations. The extent of environmental and sociocultural changes must be determined by those who have to live with those changes – that is, local communities as the recipients of tourist flows, governmental organizations as the policy planners and managers of the activity, and the private sector as the providers of the service.

Heritage has always been regarded as one of the most significant and fastest-growing parts of the tourism sector (Timothy 1997). Heritage tourism refers to the utilization of both cultural and natural heritage assets and resources to attract tourists (Chang 1999). Apart from the economic role which heritage tourism might bring, it is also seen as a driver of social cohesion and cultural education around the globe. At times it provides local pride and allows local communities to connect with the world (Edson 2004).

There are also negative aspects of heritage tourism, such as the introduction of global products and norms that might lead to the suppression of local cultural values and memories. In other contexts, tourism at heritage places has been regarded as destructive and leading to the commoditization of heritage experiences (Lowenthal 1998; Teutonico and Matero 2003). In Africa, as indicated elsewhere, it has led to the displacement of people as heritage places are reorganized to satisfy the interest of foreign visitors (Ndoro 2005). The construction of infrastructure to facilitate tourist movement and accommodation does not always necessarily bring the required or desired effects to the local population.

The relation between tourism and heritage resources is strong and is evident in Africa. Tourism-generating markets are aware of the pressure and threats on the environment in Africa. Protected status is often considered a prerequisite for an attraction: if it is not protected, it is not worth visiting. This is why tourism development in many African countries starts around protected sites and parks. A protected status indicates scarcity: if the resource is available everywhere, it would not be worth the effort to travel to see it. This principle is behind official government-controlled parks and reserves, World Heritage sites, and national monuments, as well as the entry of community and privately controlled areas into the ecotourism market.

In Africa, tourism marketing is largely geared to attract Western tourists, and very little effort has been made to attract domestic tourists. Despite the policies of such countries as Zimbabwe, the number of tourists from Asia and more specifically China still remains small in comparison (Karambakuwa *et al.* 2011). Even for Zimbabwe, the policy of attracting Asian visitors has been forced on them due to the sanctions imposed on the government by Western countries (Chigora and Chisi 2009).

UNESCO has proposed looking at culture as "ways of living together" (UNESCO 1996: 22) and has defined culture as: "the whole complex of distinctive spiritual, material, intellectual and emotional features that characterize a society or social group. It includes not only arts and letters, but also modes of life, the fundamental rights of the human being, value systems, traditions, and beliefs" (UNESCO 1982: 1)). Other global bodies, such as the World Bank, now accept this definition (see e.g. Serageldin and Taboroff 1992: 2). This reflects the separation of culture and cultural heritage into both movable and immovable forms. It also recognizes that the "cultural landscape" includes expressions of traditions and lifestyles that must be taken into consideration when looking at effective ways of safeguarding a community's cultural heritage.

Heritage is crucial to people's identity, self-respect, and dignity. This applies to both affluent and poor societies (Lowenthal 1998). Tangible heritage may be an avenue through which the tourist starts to grasp a basic understanding of the past and/or living culture, which has adapted to and influenced the environment that they are trying to make intelligible. Provided these basic facts are understood, and serve as guidelines for presentation and communication between tourists and the local population, cultural tourism has great potential to improve understanding and respect among different cultures, and in a long-term perspective may be regarded as a tool for creating and preserving peace (Galla 2012). Cultural tourism has long existed, but recent demographic, social, and cultural changes in the main countries from which tourists come have led to an increasing number of new niche markets in destination countries, including culture-oriented holidays. Though sun, sand, and surf holidays are not expected to disappear, they have declined in relative importance as more and more visitors seek challenging, educational, and/or relatively unique experiences. These changes have led to increased popularity for tourism involving culture and nature as attractions. Various sites and countries are responding to the opportunity provided by this growth in demand. For example, South Africa has historically relied on its climate, beaches, and nature to attract tourists, but between 1997 and 1999 it implemented a marketing campaign titled "Explore South Africa – Culture" to attract culture-oriented tourists. Though most of the attention in this area has been on tourism involving Western/Northern visitors to destinations in the global South, there has also been a general increase in intra-regional (South–South) tourism.

In their search for new sources of growth and job creation, developed countries have begun to pay more attention to the role of culture in today's economies. In the European Union, for example, the cultural sector was growing three times faster than the overall economy before the global financial crisis that began in 2008. Its cultural industries contribute about 7 percent of jobs, and 2.1 percent of EU's collective GDP, more than automobile and construction activities combined (Nypan 2007). Heritage promotes development in three ways: by supporting social capital, creating an environment that is attractive for residents as well as tourists, and providing leverage for the creation of products that draw from a local cultural dimension.

The Contribution of Heritage to Development

There are many benefits to be gained from a well-planned, sustainable form of tourism based on realistic market analyses. Such a form of tourism represents an attractive diversification opportunity for jobs and investment. It has the potential to bring high foreign exchange returns for relative low capital investment, whilst also being an appealing private-sector enterprise accessible to the poor in Africa. Tourism has the ability to foster development, empowerment, and social cohesion.

Tourism has proven to be a driver of growth and a source of new private-sector investment in Southern Africa; in 2007 it amounted to 11 percent of total investment. It has since grown to over 15 percent of total regional exports, and international tourism arrivals and receipts grew at consistently more than 8 percent between 2000 and 2005. Tourism employs about 4 million people in Sub-Saharan Africa, and an estimated 10.6 million if indirect linkages and the informal sector are considered (Rivett-Carnac 2011).

Africa's natural and cultural heritage assets are lasting comparative advantages that cannot be "grown" or "manufactured" elsewhere. There are proven environmentally sustainable benefits to developing tourism, such as national parks maintained through tourism, as well as contributing positively to good governance (parks which are sustainable turn out to have good governance structures) (see Arezki, Cherif, and Piotrowski 2009). For example, well-governed and well-managed sites turn out to be frequented more by tourists. Equally evident is the fact that where political crises occur, there is

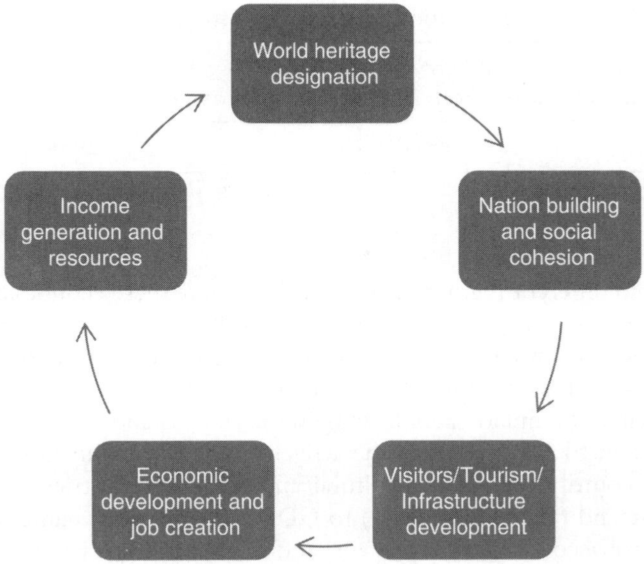

Figure 27.1 World Heritage sites contributing to economic growth.

usually an accompanying decline in tourism, as demonstrated by the political crises in Zimbabwe beginning in 2000, when a drastic fall occurred in the number of visits to heritage attractions. The political crisis and conflicts in the Democratic Republic of Congo in the past decade have also led to a lack of care in safeguarding heritage places, resulting in five of the country's World Heritage sites being inscribed on UNESCO's List of World Heritage in Danger.

Southern Africa continues to be a preferred long-haul destination for Europe and the United States, while large increases in arrivals from mainland China and the Middle East have been recorded in recent years. With the exception of Zimbabwe (due to the political crisis mentioned above), the region is perceived as a good tourism destination.

Evidence from various countries in the world, including South Africa, demonstrates that World Heritage status of places serves as a catalyst, not only for conservation, partnerships, social cohesion, skills development, and education, but also for job creation, infrastructure development, foreign direct investment, all leading to an increase in GDP (see Galla 2012). A study commissioned by the International Monetary Fund argues that the presence of cultural or natural UNESCO World Heritage sites is likely to affect long-term GDP growth (Arezki, Cherif, and Piotrowski 2009). The study indicates that international tourism at World Heritage sites can affect growth in several ways other than the direct revenue gained from receipts. The foreign direct investment associated with tourism can bring managerial skills and technology with potential spillover benefits to other sectors. Policies designed to foster tourism, by improving security, stability, and openness, can also enhance growth in other sectors.

Cultural and natural heritage also supplies raw material for the creative entertainment industries, such as film, fashion, advertising, television, and video games. It constitutes a stage for a whole array of motion pictures for these industries. For one French castle alone, the income from one single film production was €11 million in 2004 (Nypan 2007). These issues are summarized in Figure 27.1.

Table 27.1 The contribution of various industries to European GDP.

Cultural and creative industries (including cultural heritage)	*Food, beverages, and tobacco*	*Textile industry*
2.6%	1.9%	0.5%

Source: Greffe (2002: 7).

Examples from different regions of the world illustrate these economic gains in more detail. In Europe, the European Commission states that the region's tourism industry is driven by two non-renewable resources: nature and culture/cultural heritage. Cultural heritage is an essential asset in the European cultural and creative industries sector of the economy. A total 5.885 million people work in the cultural and cultural tourism sectors, which is equivalent to 3.1 percent of the actively employed population (Nypan 2007). The economic contribution of the cultural and creative industries sector (including cultural heritage and related businesses) to GDP is 2.6 percent, higher than the food, beverages, and tobacco sector (1.9 percent) and the textile industry (0.5 percent).

A prominent example comes from Spain, where Bilbao repositioned itself on the international cultural tourism landscape by building a new museum, the Museo Guggenheim, designed by renowned American architect, Frank Gehry. In this, Bilbao was following the example of the Sydney Opera House, which is now inscribed on the World Heritage List as a great architectural work of the twentieth century that brings together creativity and innovation. In 1998, when the museum was finished, Bilbao was mentioned in 8,500 press articles, 60 percent of which were in the international media. The museum has attracted 1.3 million visitors since it opened, and these visitors have spent US$450 million in Bilbao (Ayoub and Zouain 2009).

The diversity of European cultures, combined with a multitude of attractive landscapes and cuisines, is an important factor in the region's competition with other tourist destinations around the world. It is important to remember that research shows that only 6 to 10 percent of visitors' daily spending is left at the sites visited. The remaining 90 percent of spending falls to other businesses the visitor uses.

Infrastructural Development at the Tsodilo Hills

On the African continent, World Heritage sites are a potential catalyst for improving livelihoods. However, the experience so far has been mixed. The management of the Tsodilo Hills cultural landscape in Botswana clearly demonstrates some of the benefits of inscription on the World Heritage List. "The mountains of the gods" or Tsodilo Hills were the first World Heritage site nomination in Botswana in 2001. Before designation as a place of Outstanding Universal Value, Tsodilo was the ancestral home of the San and the Hambakushe groups of Botswana, who used the place as a hunting and grazing area. However, the Tsodilo Hills were considered to be a culturally rich place, with some of the most spectacular rock art paintings in Southern Africa. Made a protected area for its archeological heritage, it was thought that locals could contaminate the region's scientific evidence, and above all compromise its conservation by hunting and grazing in the hills. This was despite the fact that these groups had lived

Figure 27.2 A Tsodilo homestead in 1998. Source: photo by Phenyo Thebe.

Figure 27.3 The results of World Heritage tourism: a homestead near Tsodilo in 2011. Source: photo by Phenyo Thebe.

in the area from time immemorial. Thus, in order to nominate the place, the Botswana government and ICOMOS experts thought that the resident groups had to be moved at least 3 kilometers away, and the area had to be fenced off to ensure that no encroachment took place.

Before World Heritage listing, the Tsodilo Hills were visited by less than 3000 people annually, and these were largely foreign visitors as the site could only be accessed by 4x4. After listing, the visitor numbers increased from less than 3000 to 10,000 per year between 2001 and 2005, representing approximately a 40 percent growth (ECOSURV 2005). Between 2005 and 2014, visitor numbers fluctuated between 10,000 and 12,000 visitors per year. An even larger percentage of visitors to the Tsodilo Hills are foreigners (43.1 percent) who come to the site through tour operators, while domestic Botswana visitors make up 34.6 percent. An important category contributing to the visitor record is school groups (21.2 percent), who come from virtually all parts of the country, while church groups account for the remaining 1.1 percent. Being the only World Heritage site in Botswana, Tsodilo Hills, like other heritage sites in the country, is incorporated into the school curriculum, and as such most schools visit the site. It should be mentioned that with the increase in visitors to the Tsodilo, the site has certainly contributed to Botswana's GDP.

The granting of World Heritage status to the Tsodilo Hills encouraged the Botswana government to commit to providing infrastructural development at the site. This includes an access road from the Maun–Nxamasere highway to the site, which improved the journey from a 6-hour to a 45-minute drive, thereby not only improving local and international tourism but also improving access to the Tsodilo Hills catchment area. Accommodation businesses in the area, as well as local tour guides, restaurants, and retail outlets have grown and benefited from the increase in visitor numbers. As local tourism was boosted, the Botswana government created the Botswana Tourism Board in 2004 in order to ensure sustainable and diversified tourism development for the country.

Apart from infrastructural development, community life changed. Clay and grass huts were replaced by cement and asbestos houses, a change seen as a marker of modernization and progress. This was due to local communities providing crafts and other tourist-related products like tour guiding to visitors to the World Heritage site. Although the tourism venture has led to some changes in the way traditional materials for rituals are made, this has led to craft specialization, the acquisition of new skills, and new business ventures for the community and Botswana in general (Keitumetse and Nthoi 2009). Thus, it can be argued that the nomination of the Tsodilo Hills seems to have had an impact not just on local community livelihoods, but also on regional infrastructural development objectives.

The Great Zimbabwe World Heritage Site

Close to Masvingo in the south of Zimbabwe, Great Zimbabwe comprises the remains of an African kingdom, and it has significant national importance as a symbol of the country's heritage; indeed, the site gave its name to the country at independence. The Great Zimbabwe area has an estimated population of 30,000 people under the traditional authority of three chiefs. Managing local stakeholder dynamics for the management authority of the site is a balancing act between community groups. The demands and expectations of the communities have been limited by their own fragmentation. The result is that stakeholder groups often have conflicting interests and agendas (Salazar and Porter 2005). There are no people living on the site, residents having been removed earlier to create a protected area under Rhodesian law.[1]

Great Zimbabwe was inscribed on the World Heritage List in 1986, and with its listing a number of developments were undertaken within and outside the property. These developments included the upgrading of the access road from the provincial capital Masvingo, and the establishment of several tourist lodges and a craft market. Through listing it became part of a family of sites that are managed as part of the UNESCO World Heritage system. This has attracted private-sector engagement, particularly from those companies which saw an opportunity in the tourism industry.

Becoming a World Heritage site usually brings benefits to both the site and local communities. A World Heritage site has advantages of international marketing, and Great Zimbabwe is no exception. Between 1989 and 2000, visitor numbers at Great Zimbabwe increased from around 30,000 to over 100,000 per year, with a peak of 121,000 in 1997.

Great Zimbabwe has two fully owned private-sector hotels within the demarcated core area and in the buffer zone of the site. The Great Zimbabwe Hotel, owned and run by the African Sun hotel group, is the largest. It was established in the early 1900s, and as a result the hotel has full title to the land and pays no rental or other fees to the National Monuments and Museums of Zimbabwe as its construction predates the inscription of the site. This is despite the fact that the hotel benefits directly from the World Heritage site due to its privileged location.

While the hotel has maintained the 49 rooms that it had before the inscription of the World Heritage site, a massive investment in upgrading the rooms was undertaken to meet international tourism standards. By 2010 a spacious conference center had also been constructed, accommodating 250 people, so that including the old building's carrying capacity of 100 people, the hotel can now accommodate 350. The construction of the conference center was undertaken during the period of political crisis in the country (discussed earlier). Another up-market hotel has also built, in addition to more than ten other hotels and lodges around the World Heritage site. This has meant employment and investment opportunities for local communities. The inscription of Great Zimbabwe has also led to several infrastructural developments, adding to employment and providing a stronger basis for future economic development.

There have, however, been several negative impacts brought about by the promotion of the heritage site as a tourist destination. Chief among them is a decline in agricultural output and the area under crop production in the villages around Great Zimbabwe (Ndoro 2005). With more foreign tourists coming, the local population has moved more into the craft sector and neglected the cultivation of crops. It can be argued perhaps that this is a choice the local communities have made. However, the sale of craft items turns out to be seasonal, and with a decline in the number of tourists visiting the site, income has declined for the community. Besides, there has also been a marked increase in the population living around the site. The number of tourists and the infrastructural developments at the site have attracted people to settle in its environs in the hope of benefiting from the jobs and economic opportunities that the site offers. The rising population has also puts pressure on the conservation needs of the site as there has been an increased demand on resources like firewood and grazing land.

Job Creation at the Cradle of Humankind and Other Sites

The Cradle of Humankind is managed by an authority under the provincial government of Gauteng in South Africa. It is a peri-urban area covering several local authorities. It borders industry and residential developments, housing both affluent and impoverished communities. The population is heterogeneous and includes many South African farm-workers and their descendants, as well as migrants from other provinces of South Africa and neighboring countries. At the Cradle of Humankind site, many tourism businesses are in operation, some pre-dating its inscription. Furthermore, there are no homogeneous community groups, or fully representative structures. Stakeholder coordination is thus difficult, with a myriad of government, private, and community players in the area, and various conflicting agendas and expectations.

The Cradle of Humankind Authority was explicitly set up as a special-purpose trading entity for managing the site, but also as a high-impact priority project for the province with a focus on tourism promotion. It has a formal public–private partnership agreement in place with a private sector operator of the visitor facilities. Awarded by competitive process, the operator has taken responsibility for the day-to-day running of the visitor facilities, marketing, and the displays and other interpretative materials. As the UNESCO significance of the site relates to fossils, much of the expenditure on the Sterkfontein Caves experience and Maropeng visitor center has been on providing an interpretative experience that is both educational and fun.

By 2010 the Gauteng provincial government had invested ZAR 163 million (US$16.3 million),[2] primarily on construction at Sterkfontein, Maropeng, and roads in the area. Management plans recommend strong direct investment in infrastructure after inscription on the World Heritage List in order to generate sustainable growth in visitor numbers.

The listing of the Cradle of Humankind as a World Heritage site has had the desired effect on growth in the tourism sector. Site tourism products such as accommodation, tours, guiding, and so on have more than quadrupled – from 68 in 1999 to 405 in 2010. The construction of the Sterkfontein and Maropeng tourism attractions has created 600 permanent and 1200 temporary jobs, while the construction of roads in the area has created a further 600 posts. An extensive study conducted in 2008 (GPG 2010) reported that tourist spending from visits to the Cradle of Humankind generated a total of about ZAR 695 million (US$69.5 million), about 0.1 percent of Gauteng's GDP. It is estimated that about ZAR 334 million (US$33.4 million) of the ZAR 695 million (US$69.5 million) was spent at the site, with the remaining ZAR 361 million (US$36.1 million) spent outside of it. The same study reported that, in 2008, tourists visiting the Cradle of Humankind generated about 6175 employment opportunities; that is, a 0.2 percent of Gauteng's employment total. About 4100 employment opportunities were created at the Cradle of Humankind site itself, and the remaining 2075 job opportunities were created outside the site (GPG (2010).

In 2010, a socioeconomic impact assessment was completed for the Cradle of Humankind site (GPG 2010), and it found that the numbers generated by the 2008 study for job creation and GDP contribution were extremely conservative (see Table 27.2). It is estimated that the annual wage bill from tourism-related establishments totals ZAR 228.1 million (US$22.81 million), and that ZAR 148.3 million (US$14.83 million) of this is spent in a 10 kilometer radius of the tourism establishments.

Table 27.2 Tourism-related employment at the Cradle of Humankind.

Establishment category	*Average number of permanent employess*	*Average number of part-time employess*	*Average number of total employess*	*Total number of activities*	*Total number of permanent employess*	*Total number of part-time employess*	*Total number of employees*	*Total number of dependents*
Hotel	43	2	45	21	911	38	949	4926
Country Lodge	27	2	29	63	1688	139	1827	9482
Restaurant	16	3	19	125	2000	375	2375	12326
Camping and Caravanning	12	0	12	9	108	0	108	561
Conference	10	4	14	100	1040	400	1440	7474
Game Lodge	10	1	10	10	95	8	103	535
Guest House	6	1	7	34	201	27	228	1182
Wedding Venue	5	0	5	65	325	0	325	1687
Mixed	4	8	12	10	40	80	120	623
Bed and Breakfast	3	0	3	12	32	4	36	187
Self-Catering	2	0	2	26	44	0	44	229
Totals	**15**	**2**	**16**	**475**	**6485**	**1070**	**7555**	**39211**

Source: GPG (2010).

Gauteng's GDP for 2009 was estimated at ZAR 579.3 billion (US$57.93 billion), while tourism-related expenditure at the Cradle of Humankind was ZAR 2.658 billion (US$265.8 million). The total estimated GDP contribution of the site is ZAR 2.362 billion (US$236.2 million), or 0.59 percent of Gauteng's GDP. The site's consumption activity is estimated at ZAR 1.58 billion (US$158 million), with direct employment amounting to 10,484 jobs and indirect employment to 11,226 jobs.[3]

Similar information and impacts can be seen at other South African World Heritage sites, such as iSimangaliso Wetland Park, Robben Island, and the uKahlamba Drakensburg Park. Along with the Cradle of Humankind, these examples clearly demonstrate that the designation of World Heritage status provides an opportunity for economic and social development.

Twyfelfontein

The potential for heritage to produce local benefits is clearly demonstrated by Twyfelfontein, also known as /Ui-//aes, a World Heritage site located in a sparsely populated rural area of northwest Namibia. It is famous for its rock engravings and was inscribed in 2007. The remoteness of Twyfelfontein has meant that the number of stakeholders and potential beneficiaries from the site are limited and easier to coordinate. The site is managed as a "conservancy" and this provides the local community with management control over the land. Conservancies are very common in Namibia as a vehicle to ensure stakeholder participation in land-use practices. They provide local communities with the use of land from which they can draw income though their own activities, or through concession-style arrangements with private-sector operators.

At Twyfelfontein, the community thus benefits directly not only from the site and its entrance fees but also from concession fees. The conservancy arrangement has afforded the local community a mechanism to obtain formally structured benefits from the activities of accommodation lodges, for example by charging a levy based on bed occupancy (Rivett-Carnac 2011). In addition, the lodges provide a number of services to the site and the local communities, which includes banking, water, and telephone services. The World Heritage site has also provided a forum for local craft specialists to exhibit and sell their produce through the site shop and visitor center.

Although there has been minimal infrastructural development at Twyfelfontein, the small population of the area has meant that the benefits are shared by the whole community. There is also a high level of participation in stakeholder meetings, with every member involved.

Kilwa Kisiwani

The designation of World Heritage status does not always bring increased socio-economic benefits or development, as demonstrated by the site of Kilwa Kisiwani in Tanzania. The site is an island that, together with the neighboring island of Songo Mnara, was inscribed as a World Heritage site in 1981. Located on the southern coast of Tanzania, some 333 kilometers south of Dar es Salaam, Kilwa Kisiwani has been inhabited since at least the ninth century AD. The ruins that exist on the island today – a great number of structures – remain from what was once a great Swahili city-state, and

Figure 27.4 Lodges at Twyfelfontein. Source: photo by Webber Ndoro.

Figure 27.5 The World Heritage site of Kilwa Kisiwani. Source: photo by Webber Ndoro.

are the reason for the site's inscription. Residents of Kilwa Kisiwani live among the ruins, but have seen little direct economic benefit of inscription.

Kilwa Kisiwani has a population of around 15,000 people, mainly subsistence farmers. Despite the great number of interested stakeholders, the benefits of designation have been minimal. The district government does not have a dedicated person to deal with promoting the site or developing a tourism strategy. Yet Kilwa Kisiwani has received considerable funds for the conservation of the fabric of the site from World Monuments Watch, the Aga Khan Foundation, and the French, Japanese, and Norwegian governments. None of these funds have been targeted at community development or projects that could be beneficial to both the site and local communities.

There is no private-sector investment on the island of Kilwa Kisiwani. There are, however, a number of lodges on the mainland, opposite the island, that have been developed largely on leasehold land. These lodges are relatively small and have no formal community benefit structures in place. They are also not active in cooperative marketing, or broader destination development plans. Thus the private sector at Kilwa does not play a particularly large role in local development, and consequently the benefits in terms of either jobs or infrastructure are limited. Kilwa Kisiwani has nothing in place to benefit local people through tourism in the area. The visitor fee is very low, and not currently apportioned to the islanders. Nor are there formal providers of transport to or services on the island. Of the five tour guides, three are from Kilwa Kisiwani, while two are from the mainland. A number of community groups have, however, organized themselves for tourism, such as the Kilwa Cultural Centre on the island, and Chagamoto and Mkudje amongst others on the mainland. The trickle of visitors to the area does not yet support regular activities or generate income for these community groups.

Kilwa Kisiwani has had a number of factors working against it, most notably institutional fragmentation and weak public and private players in the area. Access to the site has also been severely compromised, although this is changing with the development of a paved road connecting Kilwa to Dar es Salaam. Competition from other nearby World Heritage sites, like Selous Game Reserve and Ngorongoro Conservation Area, has also affected its positioning and marketing. Kilwa Kisiwani has not yet made a marked contribution to the socioeconomic development of the Kilwa district. It remains to be seen if the access road from Dar es Salaam will change the situation and make it easier for tourists to visit the site.

Conclusion

World Heritage sites can be seen as important resources that have the potential to drive socioeconomic development, provided the right mix is attained. A variety of public-sector and private-sector facilities are necessary to attract and satisfy visitors, and tour operators are needed to package the area, and its accommodation, restaurants, transportation services, and information offices.

From the case studies discussed here it is clear that World Heritage sites can play a part in job creation, the development of infrastructure, small-scale business, and they can generally yield economic benefits. However, the pattern in Africa is that most of the investors at World Heritage sites are foreign, more specifically international tour operators, hotel chains, and airlines. For example, levels of unemployment in the area of the Victoria Falls World Heritage site on the Zambia–Zimbabwe border are high. Here, there are more than twenty hotels and lodges, but they obtain supplies of their products externally, even having vegetables flown in from Johannesburg and Cape Town. They also rely on outside workers. Thus the local population is forced to rely on the making and selling of handicrafts as a means of ensuring their survival. This means putting pressure on the local rainforest, the source of wood for the craft industry.

Although World Heritage inscription is generally considered to act as a catalyst for economic development, there are many issues in Africa which create obstacles to sustainable development and heritage conservation. These include the actions of local communities and local government, ownership of and access rights to the resources that form the site, and the forced displacement of local populations from sites as governments seek to comply with UNESCO-imposed management systems (Ndoro 2005; Hampton 2005).

The money visitors spend at World Heritage sites on admission fees, souvenirs, transport, food, and accommodation represents a substantial contribution to the global economy, and the sites employ millions of people directly and indirectly (Timothy and Boyd 2003). However, although some heritage sites have generated forms of economic development, as some of the case studies discussed here show, it is generally perceived in Africa that most of the benefits do not trickle down to local communities. In this regard, it is telling that many of Africa's famous heritage sites, such as Ngorongoro, Kruger National Park, Great Zimbabwe, Zanzibar, Timbuktu, and the Serengeti National Park, are surrounded by a sea of poverty. Here, the benefit of inscription as a World Heritage site and the knock-on effects generated by global tourism seem to be limited, and local communities are yet to see significant improvements in their lives and livelihoods.

Notes

1 Initially colonized by the British in the 1890s, Zimbabwe was known as Rhodesia during the period of the minority white government that ruled the country from 1964 until 1980. White rule ended when the country gained independence in 1980, at which point it adopted the name Zimbabwe.
2 The national currency of South Africa is the rand, known by the abbreviation ZAR.
3 Due to sometimes wild fluctuations in exchange rates, the amounts in this paragraph are given using 2004 prices.

References

Arezki, R., Cherif, R., and Piotrowski, J. (2009) Tourism Specialisation and Economic Development: Evidence from the UNESCO World Heritage List. IMF Working Paper WP/09/176. Washington: International Monetary Fund.

Ayoub, L., and Zouain, G. (2009) Art and Heritage: Instruments of Urban Regeneration. In V. Chesnot *et al.* (eds), *Culture as a Tool for Development: Challenges of Analysis and Action*. Brussels: ARCADE, pp.94–109. Available at: http://www.creativeideasbank.eu/wp-content/uploads/2012/10/Culture-as-a-tool-for-development.-Challenges-of-analysis-and-action.pdf (accessed March 13, 2015).

Barthel-Bouchier, D. (2013) *Cultural Heritage and the Challenge of Sustainability*. Walnut Creek, CA: Left Coast Press.

Chang, T. (1999) Local Uniqueness in the Global Village: Heritage Tourism in Singapore. *Professional Geographer*, 51, 91–103.

Chigora, P., and Chisi, T.H. (2009) The Eight Years of Interaction: Lessons from Zimbabwe's Look East Policy and the Future of African Countries and the Asia-Pacific Region. *Journal of Sustainable Development in Africa* 10, (4). 147–161.

Comer, D. (2011) *Tourism and Archaeological Heritage Management at Petra*. New York: Springer.

ECOSURV (2005) Planning Work on the World Heritage Site at Tsodilo Hills. Report. Gaborone: ECOSURV.

Edson, G. (2004) Heritage: Pride or Passion, Product or Service? *International Journal of Heritage Studies*, 10 (4), 333–348.

Galla, A. (ed.) (2012) *World Heritage: Benefits beyond Borders*. Cambridge: Cambridge University Press.

GPG (Gauteng Provincial Government) (2010) Socio Economic Impact Assessment of Cradle of Humankind World Heritage Site. Report. Johannesburg: GPG.

Greffe, X. (2002) *La valorisation économique du patrimoine*. Rapport au Dep et à la Dapa. Paris: Ministère de la culture et de la communication.

Hampton, M. (2005) Heritage, Local Communities and Economic Development. *Annals of Tourism Research*, 32 (3), 735–759.

ICOMOS (1999) International Cultural Tourism Charter: Managing Tourism at Places of Heritage Significance. Available at: http://international.icomos.org/charters/tourism_e.pdf (accessed October 1, 2014).

Jopela, A. (2010) Traditional Custodianship of Rock Art Sites in Southern Africa: A Case Study from Central Mozambique. M.A. dissertation. Johannesburg: University of the Witwatersrand.

Karambakuwa, R.T., Shonhiwa, T., Murombo, L., Mauchi, F.N., Gopo, N.R., Denhere, W., Chingarande F.T.A., and Mudavanhu, V. (2011) The Impact of Zimbabwe Tourism Authority Initiatives on Tourist Arrivals in Zimbabwe (2008–2009). *Journal of Sustainable Development in Africa*, 13 (6), 68–77.

Keitumetse, S. (2007) Celebrating or Marketing the Indigenous? International Rights Organisations, National Governments and Tourism Creation. In P.M. Burns and M. Novelli (eds), *Tourism and Politics: Global Frameworks and Local Realities*. Oxford: Elsevier, pp. 109–122.

Keitumetse, S.O., and Nthoi, O. (2009) Investigating the Impact of World Heritage Site Tourism on the Intangible Heritage of a Community: Tsodilo Hills World Heritage Site, Botswana. *International Journal of Intangible Heritage* 4, 144–149.

Kigongo, R., and Reid, A. (2007) Local Communities, Politics and the Management of the Kasubi Tombs, Uganda. *World Archaeology*, 39 (3), 371–384.

Leask, A., and Fyall, A. (eds) (2006) *Managing World Heritage Sites*. Oxford: Butterworth-Heinemann.

Lowenthal, D. (1998) *The Heritage Crusade and the Spoils of History*. Cambridge: Cambridge University Press.

Meskell, L. (2011) *The Nature of Heritage: The New South Africa*. Oxford: Wiley-Blackwell.

Mowforth, M., and Munt, I. (2009) *Tourism and Sustainability*. New York: Routledge.

Ndoro, W. (2005) *The Preservation of Great Zimbabwe: Your Monument, Our Shrine*. Rome: ICCROM.

Ndoro, W., and Jaquinta, M. (2006) Millennium Development Goals and Cultural Heritage. *ICCROM Newsletter*, 32, 12–13.

Nypan, T. (2007) *Cultural Heritage Monuments and Historic Buildings as Value Generators in a Post-Industrial Economy with Emphasis on Exploring the Role of the Sector as an Economic Driver. Paper presented at the conference Economics and Built Heritage*, Hämeenlinna, Norway.

Palmer, M. (2003) *Faith in Conservation: New Approaches to Religions and the Environment*. Washington: World Bank.

Rivett-Carnac, K. (2011) Cultural World Heritage Site Scan: Lessons from Four Sites. Development Planning Division Working Paper Series No. 19. Midrand: Development Bank of Southern Africa.

Salazar, N.B. (2010) The Globalization of Heritage through Tourism: Balancing Standardization and Differentiation. In S. Labadi and C. Long (eds), *Heritage and Globalisation*. London: Routledge, pp. 130–147.

Salazar, N.B., and Porter, B. (2005) Heritage Tourism, Conflict and the Public Interest. *International Journal of Heritage Studies*, 11 (5), 361–370.

Serageldin, I., and Taboroff, J. (eds) (1992) *Culture and Development in Africa*. Proceedings of the International Conference Held at the Headquarters of the World Bank, Washington, April 2–3. Washington: World Bank.

Shackley, M.L. (ed.) (1998) *Visitor Management: Case Studies from World Heritage Sites*. Oxford: Butterworth Heinemann.

Sinamai, A. (2014) An Un-Inherited Past: Preserving the Khami World Heritage Site, Zimbabwe. Ph.D. dissertation. Melbourne: Deakin University.

Teutonico, J.M., and Matero, F. (ed.) (2003) *Managing Change: Sustainable Approaches to Conservation of the Built Environment*. Los Angeles: Getty Conservation Institute.

Timothy, D. (1997) Tourism and Personal Heritage Experience. *Annals of Tourism Research*, 24 (3), 751–754.

Timothy, D., and Boyd, S. (2003) *Heritage Tourism*. Harlow: Pearson.

UNESCO (1996) Our Creative Diversity. Document CLT-96/WS-6. Available at http://unesdoc.unesco.org/images/0010/001055/105586e.pdf (accessed November 19, 2014).

UNGA (2000) United Nations Millennium Declaration. Resolution 55/2. Document A/RES/55/2. Available at: http://www.refworld.org/docid/3b00f4ea3.html (accessed July 10, 2014).

United Nations (1992) Agenda 21. United Nations Conference on Environment and Development Rio de Janeiro, Brazil. Available at: https://sustainabledevelopment.un.org/content/documents/Agenda21.pdf (accessed October 11, 2014).

United Nations (2012) The Future We Want. Rio Plus 20 Conference Report. Available at: https://sustainabledevelopment.un.org/rio20 (accessed October 19, 2014).

CHAPTER 28

Heritage in the "Asian Century": Responding to Geopolitical Change

Zeynep Aygen and William Logan

Many would argue that the Western world – essentially Europe and North America – has dominated the cultural heritage field for too long. Indeed, references to this dominance are commonly seen in the global heritage discourse, as, for instance, in the manifesto of the Association of Critical Heritage Studies (ACHS 2013) or in Silva and Chapagain's recent compilation on Asian heritage management, where the heritage field is described as "primarily Euro-centric in its origin, premise, and praxis" (Silva and Chapagain 2013: i). This Eurocentric dominance is certainly seen in the World Heritage system, UNESCO's flagship program created under the auspices of the Convention Concerning the Protection of the World Cultural and Natural Heritage (1972), or as it is commonly known, the World Heritage Convention (Meskell 2013: 488–89). The system's headquarters are located in Paris (at the UNESCO World Heritage Centre) and the advisory bodies named in the World Heritage Convention – the International Council on Monuments and Sites (ICOMOS), the International Centre for the Study of the Preservation and Restoration of Cultural Property (ICCROM), and the International Union for the Conservation of Nature (IUCN) – are situated respectively in Paris, Rome, and Gland, Switzerland. Moreover when the system's centerpiece, the World Heritage List, was created in the late 1970s, it soon began to lean towards Europe. A quarter century later, nearly two-thirds of the 216 cultural places inscribed in the period 1996 to 2000 were European. The credibility of the World Heritage List as a representation of the world's cultural heritage was clearly at risk. Even though important steps have been taken to correct the balance, in January 2014 Europe and

A Companion to Heritage Studies, First Edition. Edited by William Logan, Máiréad Nic Craith, and Ullrich Kockel.
© 2016 John Wiley & Sons, Inc. Published 2016 by John Wiley & Sons, Inc.

North America still had 48 percent of all World Heritage properties and 53 percent of Cultural properties.

Over the same period, the world has been witnessing a fundamental geopolitical shift, such that the twenty-first century has already been tagged the "Asian century." Building on the rapid modernization of Japan and South Korea, the growing economies of China and India are seen by many to be challenging the economic dominance that the United States has enjoyed for the last hundred years. If this global shift is sustained, it is possible that it will eventually be reflected in the field of cultural heritage conservation as in other forms of cultural production. It follows that the heritage profession, especially practitioners in the West, need to know more about Asia's heritage places, site management projects, and conservation approaches. In accepting the need to learn more about Asian ways of understanding and managing heritage, however, we should not underestimate the significance of the impact that Asia has already had on heritage practice across the world. Indeed, we should recognize that insofar as heritage is concerned, the Asian century began in the 1980s. Nor should we underestimate the sheer size and complexity of the Asian continent and its diverse range of communities in terms of their histories, cultural characteristics, and standards of living. We need to tread carefully in our representation of "Asian" heritage in this challenging continent of diversity and often of dissonance, and generalizations about Asian heritage, thought, and practice need to be carefully couched.

This chapter summarizes Asia's impact on heritage theory and practice thus far, with a particular emphasis on Japan and China. It then proceeds to identify other ways in which Asia may influence our understandings of heritage and how to protect it in the coming years. In doing so, the chapter questions the use of the simplistic East/West binary in heritage scholarship and practice, and it calls for greater attention to be paid to understanding the meta-values that apply to humans everywhere. The chapter concludes by commenting on some of the heritage challenges currently confronting Asia, including the rapid redevelopment of major historic cities, the treatment of ethnic minority heritage, and the use of heritage as a way of strengthening dialogue between neighboring states and communities.

Questioning the East/West Binary

It is bound to be risky to characterize a century based on the experience of its first fifteen years, especially when the economic fortunes of world regions and their constituent states have recently been showing considerable volatility. Asia's demographic size alone suggests that its voice (or voices) will be increasingly heard. By 2050, Asia's population is predicted to reach 5 billion – half of humanity – and its share of global economic wealth is expected to grow to 52 percent (Kohli, Sharma, and Sood 2011: 205, 299). This demographic and economic growth is expected to lead to a realignment of geopolitical power (Mahbuhani 2008). We can anticipate that the "Western" (European and North American) approach to many things will be challenged, including the field of cultural heritage conservation. Although the emergence of an "Asian century" is not entirely assured at this early stage, the overall trend makes it prudent to consider what such a possibility would mean to the world if it materialized. This may mean insisting on greater weight being given by the international heritage bodies – UNESCO and its Advisory Bodies in particular – to Asian heritage philosophical stances, identification and management approaches, and technical practices. Non-Western members of the World Heritage Committee are already flexing their muscle (Logan 2012; Meskell 2013). It may even mean finding a new geographical balance in its organizational structure.

Cultural heritage discourse, as represented by books and journal articles, most of which were published by Western companies and associations, has been dominated by European, North American, and Australasian scholars and practitioners. Aygen (2013: 30–33) describes the "clashes and reactions" when global (read Western) practices sideline local practices (for example, Asian) in conferences and publications. Many of the more progressive Western scholars, such as Smith (2006: 99–100), have railed against the imposition of "Western" concepts of heritage and conservation practices onto the "East." The sub-text here is that the East is powerless to resist the dominating West. It is important to avoid lapsing into another form of Orientalism in relation to cultural heritage. Indeed, it is both misleading and potentially dangerous for heritage discourse to base itself on a simplistic West versus East view of the world. The West/East binary is misleading to the extent that there is great local variation within both the West and the East, and that the overlapping and sharing of histories between the two makes distinguishing Western from non-Western ideas and theories problematic. A critique is emerging that seeks to move away from this binary, with scholars such as Nguitragool (2012), for instance, maintaining that the boundaries between Western and non-Western political thinking are less well pronounced than previously claimed. Winter goes further to claim that "the attempt to define conservation according to certain cultural or geographical criteria has, paradoxically, led to its abstraction and decontextualisation" (Winter 2014: 135).

A growing number of Asian scholars and heritage practitioners are now taking a more nuanced view of the colonial period, and the protection of colonial heritage is increasingly accepted by government authorities across Asia. Mishra argues that this is because European colonization in Asia was not merely economic, political, and military, but also intellectual, moral, and spiritual, and it "left its victims resentful but also envious of their conquerors and, ultimately, eager to be initiated into the mysteries of their seemingly near-magical power" (Mishra 2012: 45). Thus Japan and Thailand went out and deliberately borrowed modernizing ideas from the West. The city of Qingdao in eastern China experienced the imposition of Western architectural and urban planning ideas, although the colonizers here were German followed by Japanese. Western influences coming by way of imperial Japan in the first half of the nineteenth century also impacted on cities in Korea and Taiwan. In Malaysia, George Town and Malacca (Melaka) have been working since the late 1980s to protect their shop-houses, villas, and other colonial-period buildings (Jenkins 2010), and Yangon (Rangoon) is now promoting its British colonial heritage strongly as Myanmar emerges from a long period of political and economic isolation (Logan 2015). In Vietnam, the layering of built forms from successive periods and regimes, including the French colonial era, has been internationally recognized as a key heritage feature of the capital city, Hanoi, and was one of the reasons for the World Heritage listing of Hanoi's Thang Long citadel in 2010.

It is important, as Hägerdal (2009) advises, not to underestimate Asian agency – the agency that enabled Asians to work with, adjust to, make use of, and ultimately defeat colonialism. Take Vietnam as an example. There, as in all societies, can be found a range of attitudes to and interest in heritage. In Hanoi and the north, the French colonial period lasted only 70 years, but it had a transforming and indelible impact on the city's physical and social fabric. It created "home" for Hanoians, and the impact of French architectural and town planning has come to be seen as part of Hanoi's essential heritage; it is now well outlined by local historians, exploited by international and regional tourism operators, and conserved with Vietnamese funds and help from foreign embassies based in the city. The Vietnamese have a reputation for "bending with the wind" (Logan 2000: 9). Throughout history they have appeared to acquiesce to the will of foreign overlords but stubbornly followed their own agenda, as, for instance, in their dealings with the Chinese, with the Russians over the design of Ho Chi Minh's mausoleum, and with the Australians over the large Hanoi Planning and Development Control Project (Logan 2000: 1; 2015). This infuriates foreign investors, aid workers, and other foreigners working in the country, but, given their history of repeated invasions and wars, the Vietnamese are determined to stay in control, use what they like, and reject what they don't.

Hägerdal and other scholars reject the certainty that globalization is leading to Western economic and cultural dominance and further Asian "victimhood." Far from being totally put upon, postcolonial regimes have used and continue to use the legacy of colonialism when advantageous for them to do so. Nor was the colonial era a one-way street: studies are now showing that the colonizer was frequently influenced by the colonized, and what has been thought of as "imposed colonial" in character has in fact considerable local content (Hägerdal 2009: 11, 15). Logan (2002) has questioned the East/West dichotomy and argued that the drive behind economic and cultural globalization comes from both directions. Investment in urban development both within and beyond Asia, as well as architectural design influences, have come from Japan, Korea, China, Malaysia, and Indonesia. Meanwhile, Asian cultural influences – Indian haute couture, Japanese manga, movies from Iran, Hong Kong and Bollywood, and Taiwanese and Korean pop music – have not just been felt within Asia but have flowed out to the rest of the world, where they have been internalized as part of living culture, especially among young people. People learn to live with the multiplicity of cultural forms around them. Sometimes they opt for the dominant, so-called "mainstream" culture at work and in other public spheres, while also keeping alive their ethnic minority, tribe, clan, or family culture within the home. What is developing in many parts of the world is a vibrant hybrid culture – a "creolized" culture that overcomes the East/West binary. Recognition of agency and the complexity of cultural arrangements that result is essential if our theory and practice is to reflect today's world.

Asia's Global Impact on the Heritage Field

The title of this chapter implies that Asian influences on heritage conservation will be felt in the twenty-first century, the "Asian century." It is important, however, to acknowledge that Asia has already had a great influence on the heritage field across the world, with Japan and China in particular at the forefront of this counter-movement.

Japan has long had a strong national system for protecting tangible and intangible heritage, and many of its conservation experts have not been comfortable with some of the principles being promoted by UNESCO and ICOMOS. Their concerns have revolved around the definition of authenticity, which in the Venice Charter (ICASHB 1964) was judged primarily in terms of the building fabric, and with the principle of minimum intervention. These were seen as inappropriate for countries where the main building material is timber, a material that suffers from humid climatic conditions, insect infestation, and destruction by fire. Restoration, even rebuilding, can also be appropriate in many cultures for religious and commemorative buildings, since keeping structures in good repair has been an important way of showing respect to the ancestors, gods, and heroes to which the buildings are dedicated. In such societies, the emphasis is on "living cultures," and maintaining the uses to which buildings are put is more important than the fabric itself.

One of these concerned Japanese experts is Nobuo Ito, who was awarded ICOMOS's prestigious Piero Gazzola Prize in 2011 for his support of cultural heritage in Japan and internationally. He was involved in drawing up the Principles for the Preservation of Historic Timber Structures that was approved at the ICOMOS General Assembly in Mexico City in 1999 (ICOMOS 1999). These principles recognized that, in certain circumstances, minimum intervention can mean that preservation or conservation may require complete or partial dismantling and subsequent reassembling, preferably using traditional methods. "What a beautiful modification of the Venice Charter it is!" Ito wrote, "We hope similar flexible and practical principles would be adopted for the structures made of other materials" (Ito 2000: 18). Furthermore, East Asia insisted, as Ito put it, that "the primary responsibility belongs to the countries concerned" and that "respect to the sovereignty of member states" must be embodied in World Heritage processes (Ito 2000: 18).

In fact, although Japan was relatively late in signing up to the World Heritage Convention (only doing so in June 1992), its interventions over the next few years had enormous impact on the World Heritage system globally. A major activity was hosting the 1994 Nara Conference on Authenticity in relation to the World Heritage Convention (1972), at which a new charter, the Nara Document on Authenticity (ICOMOS 1994), was adopted. This set forward the principle that each nation is entitled to develop conservation approaches that are appropriate to its own cultural context. This principle has had enormous effects not only on conservation practice related to heritage places, but also on professional practice in museums and galleries (Kreps 2003).

Akagawa (2014) ties Japan's active global and regional engagement in heritage conservation to its post-war constitution. Still anxious to have influence internationally, but now unable to do so by military means, it moved to soft diplomacy, including interventions in the heritage field. Japan's post-war economic growth helped, of course, enabling it to become the largest financial contributor to UNESCO when the United States, United Kingdom, and Singapore left the organization in the mid 1980s. It was no accident that the Japanese diplomat, Koïchiro Matsuura, became UNESCO director-general in 1999, a position he held for ten years. Under his leadership, UNESCO moved its heritage system to embrace intangible heritage, first with the Masterpieces of the Oral and Intangible Heritage of Humanity scheme in 2000, and then with the Convention for the Safeguarding of the Intangible Cultural Heritage (Intangible Heritage Convention) in 2003, with its new system of committees, and inscription and monitoring processes. This shift towards intangible forms of heritage reinforced efforts to protect the "associative" values of cultural landscapes and spiritual places within the World Heritage system. As well as having a major impact at the global level, Japan has also sought to assist countries within the Asian region, such as Vietnam, as part of its soft diplomacy.

Reflecting East Asia's focus on intangible heritage, Japan and China were among the first, in 2004, to become States Parties to the Intangible Heritage Convention, with South Korea following a year later. Table 28.1 shows the rapid growth of the system developed under this convention, and the prominence of Asian states in terms of the numbers of elements inscribed on the Representative List of the Intangible Cultural Heritage of Humanity. Western states as a whole have smaller inscription numbers, but it should be noted that Germany joined only in 2013 and has yet to have an element inscribed on the Representative List, and Australia, Canada, Ireland, the United Kingdom and the United States have not signed the convention. Non-Western states that have not signed include South Africa and, in Asia, Thailand.

In contrast to Japan, which has led with new ideas, China has tended to pick up existing global statements of heritage practice and adapt them to their own purposes, and to use existing global heritage protection systems, quickly overtaking other states in terms of conservation interventions and heritage inscriptions. Lee and du Cros (2013) show how China's recently developed heritage management system has been strongly influenced by Western thinking and practice. An example is the way in which China's State Administration of Cultural Heritage (SACH) took the Australian ICOMOS Burra Charter (2013) and, working with the Getty Conservation Institute and Australian Heritage Commission, developed some of its key notions into the Principles for the Conservation of Heritage Sites in China, commonly referred to as the China Principles (SACH 2000). Other Asian countries, such as Indonesia and India, have also developed national charters to guide professional practice (ICOMOS Indonesia 2003; INTACH 2004), but China's determination to protect its cultural heritage and to make use of it for nation-building and tourism purposes is unparalleled. The China Principles give a clear indication that China's heritage serves the national interest, and it may take second place to major construction projects deemed of national importance (SACH 2000: art. 18).

According to Qian (2003), far from being locked into traditional ways of protecting its traditional heritage, China has seen the adoption of Western heritage approaches as

Table 28.1 States Parties to the Intangible Heritage Convention (2003) having the most elements inscribed on the Representative List of the Intangible Cultural Heritage of Humanity, February 2014.

	Elements	
State party	*No.*	*%*
China	30	10.6
Japan	22	7.8
Republic of Korea	16	5.7
Spain	11	3.9
France	11	3.9
Turkey	11	3.9
India	10	3.5
Iran	8	3.4
Mexico	7	2.8
Italy	5	1.8
World Total	**282**	**100.0**

Source: compiled by W. Logan from UNESCO (n.d.).

Table 28.2 States Parties to the World Heritage Convention (1972) having the most inscriptions on the World Heritage List, July 2014.

	Inscriptions		*Tentative list*	
State party	*No.*	*%*	*No.*	*%*
Italy	50	5.0	40	2.5
China	47	4.7	46	2.8
Spain	44	4.5	27	1.7
France	39	3.9	38	2.3
Germany	39	3.9	9	0.6
Mexico	32	3.3	25	1.5
India	32	3.3	40	2.5
United Kingdom	28	2.9	13	0.8
Russian Federation	26	2.6	25	1.5
USA	22	2.2	12	0.7
Australia	19	1.9	2	0.1
Brazil	19	1.9	18	1.1
Japan	18	1.8	11	0.7
Canada	17	1.7	7	0.4
Greece	17	1.7	15	0.9
Iran	17	1.7	51	3.1
World Total	**1007**	**100**	**1627**	**100**

Source: compiled by W. Logan from UNESCO (2015a, 2015b).

part of the country's modernization, and it aims to show that it can do better in the field than the West. China's success can be seen in many conservation projects carried out across the country, some of which are innovative and effective by world standards, such as the reuse of an industrial complex in Beijing as the District 798 art zone.[1] China's success can be seen, too, in its engagement in the World Heritage system. It entered the system relatively late, being the eighty-seventh of the current 190 Member States when it ratified the World Heritage Convention in 1985. But it has made up for lost time and now has the second largest number of inscriptions on World Heritage List. As Table 28.2 shows, following the 2014 World Heritage Committee meeting in Qatar, China has 47 places on the World Heritage List, and has overtaken Western strongholds such as Spain, France, and Germany, although not yet Italy. As an indication of its future nomination intentions and potential dominance of the World Heritage system, China now has 46 sites on its Tentative List.

Distinctive Asian Heritage Thought and Practice

The argument we are making in this chapter is that whether or not we have entered an "Asian century," clearly Asia is enormous demographically, rich culturally, and expanding economically, and that suggests that more needs to be known about Asian heritage places, site management projects, and conservation approaches. There are many challenges facing heritage and heritage studies in coming decades. One of these is to more carefully identify what is meant by the "Asian approach" or "Asian approaches" to understanding and protecting heritage. Fong *et al.* note that, despite numerous publications, declarations and conferences dedicated to the "Asian approach" theme, the argument remains "nebulous and elusive" (Fong *et al.* 2012: 41). Of course it is not equitable that Europe, North America, and Australia should dominate the field, and realignment is needed. The rationale for making this shift, however, should not be solely or even primarily based on ideological positions and polemical debates. We need to analyze sensitively the claims made for an Asian approach, and to clarify what is truly and essentially distinctive. We need also to ensure that such claims are not based on inaccurate characterizations of the "West" and so-called "Western approaches." It may be that so much intermingling of ideas and practices has occurred that neat differentiation is no longer possible.

It is sometimes argued, for example, that there is a marked difference between the West and Asia with regard to nature and the place of people in it. For the West, it is said, nature has been seen as something to be manipulated and tamed, even though the notion of wilderness and the push for national and global protection of wilderness areas came out of North America. The Asian approach, it is said, is to see people as being an integral, if not organic, part of cultural landscapes, but this overlooks the fact that indigenous populations in Western countries such as Canada, Australia, and New Zealand have never conceived of the land and the people on it as separate entities. Holding such an "Asian" view does not exclude the Asian practice of shaping the environment to enhance landscapes and create beautiful gardens, often now on the World Heritage List, as in Suzhou and Shalimar. Certainly a spiritual meaning is attributed to many places found in most parts of Asia based on a variety of religious and spiritual worldviews, including animism, cosmology, and *feng shui*. Peleggi (2012) and Chapagain (2013) show how this occurs in Buddhism, while Ariffin (2013) considers the same issue in the Islamic context, and Tom (2013) and Singh (2013) look at Hinduism and its sacred geography. But such spiritual ways of understanding the world are not exclusively Asian. Indigenous peoples in many parts of the world have deeply valued spiritual landscapes, as at Tongariro in New Zealand, Uluru in Australia, and Chief Roi Mata's Domain in Vanuatu. Nor should the persistence and impact of old forms of worship in the West, such as Roman Catholicism or Greek and Russian Orthodoxy, be overlooked, or the emergent fundamentalist branches of Christianity. Perhaps Shinde is right in asserting that, "Religious heritage is common to most societies and includes both tangible and intangible cultural properties" (Shinde 2012: 328).

We know that Asian countries like China, India, and Iran are descended from great civilizations, and it is claimed that Asians venerate longevity. On the other hand, there is no word for "heritage" in some Asian languages (Daly and Winter 2012: 8), and major Asian religions – Buddhism and Hinduism – focus on cycles of birth, decay, and rebirth. Pride in a long history clearly does not preclude an enormous tolerance for rapid change of the kind experienced in Asia over the last half century, particularly in pursuit of improved standards of living. And, as we have seen, ancient buildings may be venerated, but not when they are in a state of dilapidation. The intangible values of these places count most, whereas the physical materials can be renewed. Some Asian societies, however, such as the Vietnamese, display a religious syncretism in which successive incoming religions are added to, rather than replace, the existing ones. Does this frame of mind open the way for a greater tolerance of physical change on the part of Asian heritage professionals, for an easier acceptance of the accretions of time, and for the development of hybrid forms?

Perhaps as a consequence there may also be a softer attitude towards reconstruction and re-creation in Asia than is seen in Western heritage charters. In the eighteenth century, the Qing dynasty of Chinese emperors created replicas of palaces from all parts of the kingdom at the Chengde Imperial Summer Palace mountain resort, which is now inscribed on the World Heritage List. The new Chinese city of Shenzhen has created a Window of the World Park with replicas of heritage wonders from around the world. In Western heritage practice, "Disneyland" is usually a derogatory term, but perhaps Asians – some Asians? all Asians? – see such reconstructions as more geographically and intellectually accessible to most people. In any case, it is a distortion to see European heritage practice as rigorously following the Venice Charter (ICASHB 1964). There is a long history of reconstruction in Europe too, as in Viollet-le-Duc's post-Revolution reconstruction of Vézelay, Carcassonne, and Notre Dame, all now on the World Heritage List. After World War II, whole city centers were rebuilt, and currently Berlin is reconstructing Frederick the Great's baroque palace, although not without considerable political wrangling and public debate. Foddle (2010) bemoans the disappearance of vernacular architecture in the post-Soviet Central Asian republics as well as the spate of monument restoration projects and fantasy reconstructions that are used by national governments for the celebration of city anniversaries and other important events. Such Central Asian showcasing of recently "saved" buildings is no different from that carried out elsewhere in Asia or, indeed, the West.

Critical Issues for Asian Heritage in Twenty-First Century

To a large extent, the challenges currently confronting Asia vary according to the state of each country's economy and standard of living. Kohli, Sharma, and Sood (2011) divide Asia's 49 countries into three groups: those that grew rapidly in the 1950s to become high-income, developed economies, some 7 in all, and including Japan, South Korea, and Singapore; those that have grown since 1990 to reach middle-income status, totaling 11, including China and India; and the majority, 31 in all, that remain behind. The more affluent countries can of course pay more attention to environmental quality and heritage issues, and have more human resources, technical facilities, and funds to implement heritage programs. But most countries around the world, even the poorest, have adopted cultural policies and allocate some funding to heritage protection programs. Nonetheless, people everywhere want improved standards of living, and often heritage and other environmental quality issues are not high on the popular or business agenda. A difficult challenge for governments – in Asia as elsewhere, and particularly in cities – is to manage a wide set of objectives, especially where they appear to be in conflict, and to adopt cultural and urban planning measures that enable effective cultural heritage protection while also supporting economic development and improvements in living conditions.

A survey of selected Asian heritage specialists conducted for this chapter showed that in some countries, recent increases in national wealth as measured by GDP have been accompanied by increased government funding for heritage protection, mostly for built heritage. Eric Babar Zerrudo indicates that funding in the Philippines more than tripled between 2001 and 2012, during which time growth in the country's GDP catapulted from 1.1 to 7 percent per annum. Zerrudo notes, however, that a causal relationship has yet to be demonstrated.[2] Neel Kamal Chapagain suggests that the increased funding seen in Nepal may simply be due to heritage professionals and organizations becoming more persuasive. He notes, however, that, despite the increase, the absolute level of funding remains low.[3] Other countries have seen no funding increases at all, and the situation for site protection is dire. Sri Lanka, for instance, had a brief burst of heritage funding in the late 1980s and early 1990s, when several sites were inscribed on the World Heritage List, but funds have since declined.[4] This is partly due to the realignment of national finances to provide for infrastructure development and revitalization in the northern and eastern provinces following the end of the civil war in 2009. Heritage funding continues to be focused on monuments, despite Sri Lanka having many unique forms of performing arts and craft practices, as well as traditional construction techniques and agricultural practices, all with associated belief systems.

Population growth presents many serious challenges. While this applies worldwide, it is the enormous scale of growth in Asia that is different and new. It is one of the reasons for the rapid redevelopment of major historic cities. The rise of a middle class with disposable income enabling increased leisure time and tourism is leading to huge visitor numbers at heritage sites, intense wear and tear on their physical fabric, and the deterioration of sensory experiences. The old ways of managing visitors at heritage sites are frequently inadequate at Asian sites (Hitchcock, King, and Parnwell 2010: 266), particularly at tourism magnets like Angkor. Winter (2007: 41) sees the problem being partly that visitor management still follows European models. Often UNESCO is criticized for imposing a Western agenda of "museumification" on World Heritage sites (Logan 2012: 113–19). But what is happening at many Asian sites is neither Western nor required by UNESCO. Clearing out the long-term inhabitants of sites is the local understanding of how to deal with a heritage site. The commoditization and distortion of intangible heritage is also occurring, and is likely to escalate. Emphasizing the livability of cities should allow the creation of more energy-efficient, greener, and safer urban environments, and allow a stronger focus on protecting cultural heritage assets. Urbanization and the growth of an educated population can provide "unparalleled opportunities to increase productivity and improve the quality of life of citizens" (Kohli, Sharma, and Sood 2011: 287), but there is a need to build better conservation of significant heritage elements into planning and development.

Chapagain believes that, "The beauty of Asian heritage lies in its cultural pluralism" (Chapagain 2013: 3). The treatment of the heritage of ethnic minorities in many Asian states, however, undercuts this belief to a large extent. Twenty years ago, the Nara Document on Authenticity recognized that "the search for cultural identity is sometimes pursued through aggressive nationalism and the suppression of the cultures of minorities" (ICOMOS 1994: para. 4). Nothing much has changed. China is sometimes singled out for criticism in this respect. Ethnic harmony and efforts to protect the heritage of the Naxi ethnic minority seem to exist in Lijiang (Logan 2012: 122), but numerous authors have questioned the situation in Tibet (e.g. Shepherd and Yu 2013; Sinding-Larsen 2013) and Xinjiang Province (e.g. Bennett 2012; Aygen 2013: 78). Such criticism is not confined to China, of course, and insensitivity towards ethnic minority heritage can be found in many Asian states. Sometimes ethnic minority groups are also exploited for tourism purposes, as with the long-necked Kayan Lawhi women who fled the Myanmar army and now live in villages near Mae Hong Son in northern Thailand. And sometimes minorities are discriminated against for reasons other than ethnicity, as for example the Dalit in caste-ridden India (Ram 2012).

Occasionally heritage claims have been the basis of legal and even military conflicts between states. The dispute between Cambodia and Thailand over the World Heritage site of Preah Vihear has been well covered in the heritage literature (Croissant and Chambers 2011; Silverman 2011). Less has been said about the construction of a replica of Angkor Wat on the banks of the Ganges River in Bihar, India, which caused a diplomatic confrontation between Cambodia and India in 2012, the former describing the building of the replica as means of creating the world's largest Hindu shrine as a "shameful act" that could affect future relations between the two countries (Murdoch 2012). Contestation over ownership escalates as states become more engaged in safeguarding intangible cultural heritage under the Intangible Heritage Convention (2003), both to acquire international status and to expand tourism. The use of dances and songs in tourism campaigns has sparked diplomatic rows between Cambodia and Thailand, and between Indonesia and Malaysia (Anon. 2009). While such conflicts usually have a longer history of animosity and develop for a variety of reasons, cultural heritage can nevertheless become a powerful symbol for national, regional, and local claims.

A challenge facing Asia, and other parts of the world, will be to find new ways to promote inter-ethnic and international understanding and reconciliation, and enhanced cooperation in heritage protection. Governance arrangements offer part of the solution. Within the global heritage organizations, improved procedures for dealing with contentious World Heritage nominations, and a higher prioritization of transnational nominations, may be instituted. It will be important that the move towards establishing a rights-based approach to World Heritage management (Ekern *et al.* 2012) flows through into the workings of nation-states and their constituent provinces. Cooperation between adjacent states will also improve the survival chances of the intangible heritage of ethnic minorities that straddle today's political boundaries.

Conclusion: Communicating Asian Heritage Ideas

Based on the economic and political trends of the last quarter century, we appear to have entered an "Asian century," unless, of course, political changes occur to upset current trends – and nothing surprises like politics. Kohli, Sharma, and Sood sum up the situation by saying the Asian century is "plausible, but by no means, preordained" (Kohli, Sharma, and Sood 2011: 28). In the heritage field, however, we are certainly into an Asian century as measured by the impact that Asia has already had in terms of global leadership and innovation. Heritage theory and practice have already made major adjustments to incorporate Asian viewpoints, and this is likely to continue, although the extent to which Asian approaches are different from Western, African, indigenous and other approaches has yet to be fully explored and clarified. If current trends continue, the next decades will see a two-way flow of heritage ideas and influences, leading to hybridization rather than a simple East versus West division. The role of heritage theorists and practitioners in this is to move beyond East/West tribalism, and to identify and prioritize the meta-values that apply to all people.

Asian states will use what they want from international heritage discourse, but they are likely to be less interested in ageing Western models. A major change is that Asian heritage professionals are no longer so dependent on the West for sources of information and inspiration. Up until the recent past there were no major Asian presses dealing with heritage, and few Asian university centers and scholars, certainly not of the "critical" kind. Today, however, there are many new means of communicating Asian ideas, including university teaching and research programs, networks of Asian academics, and practitioners such as the Academy of Asian Heritage Management, Modern Asian Architecture Network (known as MAAN), and the Asian Cultural Landscape Association. There are also new vocational training schools, such as Manila's Escuela Taller Intramuros. As for publishing, Silkworm, the National University of Singapore (NUS), and other presses are now active in the field, and the authorship of books and journal articles is shifting from non-Asians talking about Asian heritage, albeit often focusing on colonial influences (e.g. Logan 2000; Spodek 2011), to Asian scholars writing monographs (e.g. Akagawa 2014) and editing collections (e.g. Ismail, Shaw, and Ooi 2009; Silva and Chapagain 2013). In addition, there is now a fine crop of recent Asian doctoral graduates coming out of universities both in Asia and beyond.

Asian states have also learnt how to work within the global heritage system. China's hosting of the major Hangzhou conference in 2013, which resulted in the Hangzhou Declaration (UNESCO 2013), being a recent case in point. China has also established two of the nine current UNESCO Category 2 Centres in the heritage field: the World Heritage Institute for Training and Research in Asia and the Pacific (WHITR-AP) in 2007, and the International Centre on Space Technologies for Natural and Cultural Heritage (HIST) in 2011. Meanwhile, Japan continues to fund its Asia/Pacific Cultural Center for UNESCO, and South Korea seems to be focusing its efforts on intangible heritage. These centers feature strongly in these countries' cultural diplomacy in the region. In terms of leadership positions, Koïchiro Matsuura was replaced at UNESCO by Irina Bukova from the East European bloc, and while the Arab world is lining up to follow, China and India must also be regarded as future providers of UNESCO director-generals. Such developments reinforce the key point made in this chapter regarding the importance of Asian agency in the heritage field.

Asian states will no doubt want more say in decision-making in the global heritage system, pushing further the recent politicization in the workings of the World Heritage Committee. Nationalistic considerations are likely to increase at the expense of the Advisory Bodies, especially ICOMOS. This is fed by the view that States Parties to the World Heritage Convention (1972) should run the show. International rivalries and tensions may, however, continue to flow over into the heritage field, and the need will increase to find ways to use heritage for strengthening dialogue between neighboring states and communities rather than highlighting differences. While conservation management techniques may remain much as we have seen them emerge over the last 25 years, geopolitical shifts will undoubtedly lead to changes in governance arrangements, both within the global heritage system and within Asia's states. Over coming decades this will provide a challenging work context for field policy-makers and practitioners, and a fertile agenda for heritage researchers.

Acknowledgements

The authors are grateful for the kind cooperation in the preparation of this chapter of Dr Neel Kamal Chapagain (Center for Heritage Management, Ahmedabad University, India, and a member of ICOMOS Nepal), Prof. Anila Naeem (NED University, Karachi, Pakistan), Dr Kapila D. Silva (School of Architecture, Design and Planning,

University of Kansas), Prof. Nalini Thakur (Faculty of Architecture, University of New Delhi, India), and Prof. Eric Babar Zerrudo (Center for Conservation of Cultural Property in the Tropics, University of Santo Tomas, Manila, and vice chair of the UNESCO Philippine Commission and Philippines representative on the World Heritage Committee).

Notes

1 See Figure 13.1 in Winter (this volume).
2 Eric Babar Zerrudo, personal communication, October 4, 2013.
3 Neel Kamal Chapagain, personal communication, October 8, 2013.
4 Kapila Silva, personal communication, November 7, 2013.

References

Legislation

Convention Concerning the Protection of the World Cultural and Natural Heritage (World Heritage Convention) (UNESCO, 1972). Available at: http://whc.unesco.org/archive/convention-en.pdf (accessed March 19, 2015).

Convention for the Safeguarding of the Intangible Cultural Heritage (Intangible Heritage Convention) (UNESCO, 2003). Available at: http://unesdoc.unesco.org/images/0013/001325/132540e.pdf (accessed March 19, 2015).

Other Works

ACHS (Association of Critical Heritage Studies) (2013) Manifesto. Available at: http://archanth.anu.edu.au/heritage-museum-studies/association-critical-heritage-studies (accessed January 7, 2014).

Akagawa, N. (2014) *Heritage Conservation and Japan's Cultural Diplomacy: Heritage, National Identity and National Interest.* London: Routledge.

Anon. (2009) Indonesian Outrage over a Dance, *Asia Sentinel*, August 25. Available at: http://www.asiasentinel.com/society/indonesian-outrage-over-a-dance/ (accessed February 18, 2014).

Ariffin, S.I. (2013) Islamic Perspectives and Malay Notions of Heritage. In K.D. Silva and N.K. Chapagain (eds), *Asian Heritage Management: Contexts, Concerns, and Prospects.* London: Routledge, pp. 65–84.

Australia ICOMOS (2013) Charter for Places of Cultural Significance (Burra Charter), revised version. Available at: http://australia.icomos.org/wp-content/uploads/The-Burra-Charter-2013-Adopted-31.10.2013.pdf (accessed June 29, 2014).

Aygen, Z. (2013) *International Heritage and Historic Building Conservation.* London: Routledge.

Bennett, G.P. (2012) National History and Identity Narratives in the People's Republic of China: Cultural Heritage in Xinjiang. In C.W. Hartley, G.B. Yazicioglu, and A.T. Smith (eds), *The Archaeology of Power and Politics in Eurasia: Regimes and Revolutions.* Cambridge: Cambridge University Press, pp. 37–56.

Chapagain, N.K. (2013) Heritage Conservation in the Buddhist Context. In K.D. Silva and N.K. Chapagain (eds), *Asian Heritage Management: Contexts, Concerns, and Prospects.* London, Routledge, pp. 49–64.

Croissant, A., and Chambers, P. (2011) A Contested Site of Memory: The Preah Vihear Temple. In H.K. Anheier and Y.R. Isar (eds), *Cultures and Globalization: Heritage, Memory and Identity.* London: Sage, pp. 148–156.

Daly, P., and Winter, T. (2012) *Routledge Handbook of Heritage in Asia*. London: Routledge.

Ekern, S., Logan, W., Sauge, B., and Sinding-Larsen, A. (2012) Human Rights and World Heritage: Preserving Our Common Dignity through Rights-Based Approaches to Site Management. *International Journal of Heritage Studies*, 18 (3), 213–225.

Foddle, E. (2010) Conservation and Conflict in the Central Asian Silk Roads. *Journal of Architectural Conservation*. 16 (1), 75–94.

Fong, K.L., Winter, T., Rii, H.U., Khanjanusthiti, P., and Tandon, A. (2012) "Same but Different?" A Roundtable Discussion on the Philosophies, Methodologies, and Practicalities of Conserving Cultural Heritage in Asia. In P. Daly and T. Winter (eds), *Routledge Handbook of Heritage in Asia*. London: Routledge, pp. 39–54.

Hägerdal, H. (ed.) (2009) *Responding to the West: Essays on Colonial Domination and Asian Agency*. Amsterdam: Amsterdam University Press.

Hitchcock, M., King, V.T., and Parnwell, M. (2010) Heritage Futures. In M. Hitchcock, V.T. King, and M. Parnwell (eds), *Heritage Tourism in Southeast Asia*. Honolulu: University of Hawaii Press, pp. 264–273.

ICOMOS (1994) Nara Document on Authenticity. Available at: http://www.icomos.org/charters/nara-e.pdf (accessed March 12, 2014).

ICASHB (International Congress of Architects and Specialists of Historic Buildings) (1964) International Charter for the Conservation and Restoration of Monuments and Sites (Venice Charter). Available at: http://www.icomos.org/charters/venice_e.pdf (accessed March 9, 2015).

ICOMOS (1999) Principles for the Preservation of Historic Timber Structures. Available at: http://www.international.icomos.org/charters/wood_e.pdf (accessed March 11, 2015).

ICOMOS Indonesia (2003) Piagam Pelestarian Pusaka/Indonesia Charter for Heritage Conservation. Jogjakarta: ICOMOS Indonesia. Available at: http://www.international.icomos.org/charters/indonesia-charter.pdf (accessed March 11, 2015).

INTACH (Indian Trust for Art and Cultural Heritage) (2004) Charter for the Conservation of Unprotected Architectural Heritage and Sites in India. Delhi: INTACH. Avalable at: http://www.intach.org/about-charter.php (accessed March 11, 2015).

Ismail, R., Shaw, B.J., and Ooi, G.L. (eds) (2009) *Southeast Asian Culture and Heritage in a Globalizing World: Diverging Identities in a Dynamic Region*. Farnham: Ashgate.

Ito, N. (2000) World Cultural Heritage and Self-Enlightenment of Conservation Experts. In *Report of the Consultative Meeting on Regional Cooperation in Cultural Heritage Protection in Asia and the Pacific*. Nara: Asia Pacific Cultural Center for UNESCO, pp. 15–18.

Jenkins, G. (2010) Interpreters of Space, Place and Cultural Practice: Processes of Change through Tourism, Conservation and Development in George Town, Penang, Malaysia. In M. Hitchcock, V.T. King, and M. Parnwell (eds), *Heritage Tourism in Southeast Asia*. Honolulu: University of Hawaii Press, pp. 147–172.

Kohli, H.S., Sharma, A., and Sood, A. (2011) *Asia 2050: Realizing the Asian Century*. London: Sage.

Kreps, C. (2003) *Liberating Culture: Cross-Cultural Perspectives on Museums, Curation, and Heritage Preservation*. London: Routledge.

Lee, F., and du Cros, H. (2013) A Comparative Analysis of Three Heritage Management Approaches in Southern China: Guangzhou, Hong Kong and Macau. In K.D. Silva and N.K. Chapagain (eds), *Asian Heritage Management: Contexts, Concerns, and Prospects*. London: Routledge, pp. 105–121.

Logan, W. (2000) *Hanoi: Biography of a City*. Seattle: University of Washington Press.

Logan, W. (ed.) (2002) *The Disappearing "Asian" City: Protecting Asia's Urban Heritage in a Globalizing World*. Hong Kong: Oxford University Press.

Logan, W. (2012) States, Governance and the Politics of Culture: World Heritage in Asia. In P. Daly and T. Winter (eds), *Routledge Handbook of Heritage in Asia*. London: Routledge, pp. 111–128.

Logan, W. (2015) Heritage in Times of Rapid Transformation: A Tale of Two Cities – Yangon and Hanoi. In G. Bracken (ed.), *Asian Cities: Colonial to Global*. Amsterdam: University of Amsterdam Press, pp. 279–300.

Mahbuhani, K. (2008) *The New Asian Hemisphere: The Irresistible Shift of Global Power to the East*. New York: Public Affairs.

Meskell, L. (2013) UNESCO's World Heritage Convention at 40: Challenging the Economic and Political Order of International Heritage Conservation. *Current Anthropology*, 54 (4), 483–494.

Mishra, P. (2012) *From the Ruins of Empire: The Revolt against the West and the Remaking of Asia*. London: Penguin.

Murdoch, L. (2012) Fury at Plan for Indian Replica of Angkor Wat. *Canberra Times*, March 20. Available at: http://www.canberratimes.com.au/travel/travel-news/fury-at-plan-for-indian-replica-of-angkor-wat-20120319-1vfr7.html (accessed March 11, 2014).

Nguitragool, P. (2012) God-King and Indonesia: Renegotiating the Boundaries between Western and Non-Western Perspectives on Foreign Policy. *Pacific Affairs*, 85 (4), 723–743.

Peleggi, M. (2012) The Unbearable Impermanence of Things: Reflections on Buddhism, Cultural Memory and Heritage Conservation. In P. Daly and T. Winter (eds), *Routledge Handbook of Heritage in Asia*. London: Routledge, pp. 55–68.

Qian, F. (2003) Shanghai's Western Townscape and Changing Perceptions of Cultural Heritage in China. Ph.D. dissertation. Melbourne: Deakin University.

Ram, R. (2012) Beyond Conversion and Sanskritization: Articulating an Alternative Dalit Agenda in East Punjab. *Modern Asian Studies*, 46 (3), 703–729.

SACH (State Administration of Cultural Heritage, People's Republic of China) (2000) Principles for the Conservation of Heritage Sites in China. Beijing: SACH. Available at: http://www.getty.edu/conservation/publications_resources/pdf_publications/pdf/china_prin_heritage_sites.pdf (accessed February 28, 2015).

Shepherd, R., and Yu, L. (2013) *Heritage Management, Tourism and Governance in China*. New York: Springer.

Shinde, K.A. (2012) Shifting Pilgrim-Trails and Temple-Towns in India. In P. Daly and T. Winter (eds), *Routledge Handbook of Heritage in Asia*. London: Routledge, pp. 328–338.

Silva, K.D., and Chapagain, N.K. (eds) (2013) *Asian Heritage Management: Contexts, Concerns, and Prospects*. London: Routledge.

Silverman, H. (2011) Border Wars: The Ongoing Temple Dispute between Thailand and Cambodia and UNESCO's World Heritage List. *International Journal of Heritage Studies*, 17 (1), 1–21.

Sinding-Larsen, A. (2013) Lhasa Community, World Heritage and Human Rights. *International Journal of Heritage Studies*, 18 (3), 297–306.

Singh, R.P.B. (2013) *Hindu Tradition of Pilgrimage: Sacred Space and System*. New Delhi: Dev Publishing.

Smith, L. (2006) *Uses of Heritage*. London: Routledge.

Spodek, H. (2011) *Ahmedabad: Shock City of Twentieth Century India*. Bloomington: Indianan University Press.

Tom, B. (2013) *Jiirnnoddharana*, the Hindu Philosophy of Conservation. In K.D. Silva and N.K. Chapagain (eds), *Asian Heritage Management: Contexts, Concerns, and Prospects*. London: Routledge, pp. 35–48.

UNESCO (2013) The Hangzhou Declaration: Placing Culture at the Heart of Sustainable Development Policies. Available at: http://www.unesco.org/new/fileadmin/MULTIMEDIA/HQ/CLT/images/FinalHangzhouDeclaration20130517.pdf (accessed March 12, 2014).

UNESCO (2015a) World Heritage List. Available at: http://whc.unesco.org/en/list/ (accessed February 28, 2015).

UNESCO (2015b) Tentative Lists. Available at: http://whc.unesco.org/en/tentativelists/ (accessed February 28, 2015).

UNESCO (n.d.) Lists of Intangible Cultural Heritage and Register of Best Safeguarding Practices. Available at: http://www.unesco.org/culture/ich/index.php?lg=en&pg=00559 (accessed February 28, 2015).

Winter, T. (2007) Rethinking Tourism in Asia. *Annals of Tourism Research*, 34 (1), 27–44.

Winter, T. (2014) Beyond Eurocentrism? Heritage Conservation and the Politics of Difference. *International Journal of Heritage Studies*, 20 (2), 123–137.

CHAPTER 29

(Re-)Building Heritage: Integrating Tangible and Intangible

Máiréad Nic Craith and Ullrich Kockel

Although it looks emphatically to the past, "heritage" as a process is deeply present-centered. From our contemporary perspective, we interpret resources (both tangible and intangible) that are drawn from a perceived past in order to generate meanings in the present and for the future. These meanings may be revised and even discarded as our present context and needs change. The identification of significant tangible and intangible heritage involves a selection discourse that reflects power relations and differentials. Although a dynamic process, this discourse has reproduced certain dominant ideologies and authorities over the centuries. The state has frequently played a major role in this "power game" because cultural heritage has the potential to be used as a political tool in the "national" interest, however defined. Particular aspects of the past may be emphasized or removed, in line with political ambitions and the will to shape public opinion.

This chapter explores changing discourses of heritage with reference to the built environment. In previous generations, many of our historic sites were regarded as "tabernacles, sacred groves tended by a professional priesthood equipped with esoteric rituals" (McCrone 2005: 25). Important buildings generated a sense of monolithic power and dominance over the public at large. Castles, palaces, and cathedrals, for example, were also monuments commissioned by rulers, and designed to impress as well as control the common people. However, more recent iconic buildings have "broken the mold," signaling a layered approach to power – one that communicates *with* people, rather than merely communicating dominance *to* them.

A Companion to Heritage Studies, First Edition. Edited by William Logan, Máiréad Nic Craith, and Ullrich Kockel.
© 2016 John Wiley & Sons, Inc. Published 2016 by John Wiley & Sons, Inc.

Our focus will be on changing discourses of power within the context of an expanding concept of heritage that emphasizes the confluence and interdependence of tangible and intangible elements in creating meaning. As anthropologists, we take a comparative perspective on an international context that has seen an expansion in the interpretation of heritage. This, in turn, has signaled a change in the way people think about architecture. An assessment of the impact of various ICOMOS and UNESCO charters and documents will provide the framework for this chapter, in which we will explore an approach to what Frank Lloyd Wright termed "organic architecture" (Wright 1992).

Authorized Heritage Discourse

The Convention Concerning the Protection of the World Cultural and Natural Heritage, commonly known as the World Heritage Convention (1972), defines cultural heritage in largely tangible terms as monuments, groups of buildings, and sites, with natural heritage being defined separately. Central to the World Heritage Convention is the concept of Outstanding Universal Value. This may apply to individual or groups of buildings "which, because of their architecture, their homogeneity or their place in the landscape, are of outstanding universal value from the point of view of history, art or science."[1] The concept has also been located in the European cultural tradition that derives from classical philosophy (Cleere 2001), and has been criticized as rooted in processes of colonization, and military and imperial expansion (Smith and Akagawa 2009).

Established after the World Heritage Convention (1972), UNESCO's World Heritage List incorporates many majestic castles, historic cathedrals, and other iconic buildings. Some well-known examples include the Acropolis (Athens), the Taj Mahal (Agra), the Kremlin and Red Square (Moscow), and the Tower of London. Architectural masterpieces such as these are often imposing buildings symbolizing victory and power. Many symbolized nobility, wealth, or a sense of monolithic authority over the public at large, and reflected the grand narratives of the era in which they were built. These were historic statements of power representing military might or force, and could be regarded as "power from above," expressed architecturally.

The World Heritage List has been "dominated by monumentally grand and aesthetic sites and places" (Smith and Akagawa 2009: 1). Laurajane Smith (2006) suggests that much of the list has been determined by what she terms a Western Authorized Heritage Discourse – European in origin, but historically dominant and of continuing global influence. This discourse defines heritage as tangible, powerful, and monumental in scale. Thus it determines not simply the meaning of heritage, but also how that heritage is conserved and managed. With her emphasis on discourse, Smith draws on Foucault's (1991) argument that discourses reflect relationships between power and knowledge.

Reframing Heritage

Over the past two decades or so, there has been a shift in the way we think about buildings. This is reflected, for example, in the celebration of the *genius loci* by the film *Cathedrals of Culture*, initially showcased in Berlin in February 2014.[2] Wim Wenders, the driving force behind the project, invited other directors to explore the souls of their favorite buildings. The six filmmakers selected the Berliner Philharmonie, the National Library of Russia in St Petersburg, Halden Prison in Norway, the Salk Institute in La Jolla, California, the Oslo Opera House, and the Centre Georges Pompidou in Paris. The resulting six documentaries have been regarded as an amazing experience of buildings by both audiences and the filmmakers themselves.

"Who would have thought that Halden maximum security prison … known as the 'humane prison,' would provoke a fascinating architectural discussion?" asked one reviewer (Young 2014). One of the film's co-directors, Michael Madsen, opted to begin with a quote from Foucault reflecting on the similarity of discourses of power with regard to factories, schools and prisons. The building is heard describing itself (in the voice of the prison psychologist) as tall, huge, and long, and "relieving" the prisoners of their individuality. The notion of power and control is reinforced by the building's "1000 eyes," which maintain a constant watch over the prisoners. However, all is not dismal, and the building observes that "people who have done terrible things also have a bit of good in them" (Young 2014).

The entire venture was described as an exploration of what buildings would say to us if they could speak, and in these documentaries the buildings themselves are given voices. "I am a house," says the Oslo Opera House, in director Margreth Olin's lyrical ode, co-written by Bjørn Olaf Johannessen, and continues: "I am an immigrant, an intruder on the edge of your fjord" (Birchenough 2014). The Berliner Philharmonie tells its own story in a female voice. Reflecting on its great German architect, Hans Scharoun, who was dismissed by the Nazis as degenerate, the building says: "I am his crowning achievement … I am a huge musical instrument myself, with an exceptional spatial structure." The voice of the narrator of the National Library in St Petersburg reads from Gogol, Dostoevsky, and Brodsky "as if the building spoke the literature in which it is seeped" (Birchenough 2014). Few human beings are visible in the documentary on the library, and those that do feature are primarily women. While the older women look after the card catalogues, the younger ones are "plunged into the labyrinth of words" (Birchenough 2014). While visitors may have their laptops, the library itself is devoid of computers, and there is barely a light to switch on. One reviewer describes it as "a place out of time, like the Kafkaesque reading room" (Birchenough 2014).

In his documentary, Robert Redford seeks to explore "the issue of just what an inspired architect can create" (Birchenough 2014). Selecting the Salk Institute for this, Redford accompanies his images with the voices of selected scientists for whom it has served as a creative base. Redford says: "every now and then there is a building that I think has soul and therefore it speaks to you, it speaks to you in a different way. Rather than just being objective, it suddenly makes things subjective" (quoted in Macnab 2014).

The *Cathedrals of Culture* project illustrates a significant shift in the way we think about buildings and places for which, in the heritage context, the 1999 version of Australia ICOMOS's Burra Charter was a primary catalyst. This version of the Burra Charter moved the emphasis away from Outstanding Universal Value to the notion of cultural significance. Coming from an Australian context, the Burra Charter stated that "[p]laces of cultural significance enrich people's lives, often providing a deep and inspirational sense of connection to community and landscape, to the past and to lived experiences," and noted that: "[p]laces of cultural significance reflect the diversity of our communities, telling us about who we are and the past that has formed us and the Australian landscape. They are irreplaceable and precious" (Australia ICOMOS 1999: pmbl.).

Figure 29.1 The "dual trajectories" of heritage.

Central to the 1999 version of the charter and its subsequent revisions is the recognition of the dynamic nature of cultural heritage, the significance of which may change over time and with use: "Understanding of cultural significance may change as a result of new information" (Australia ICOMOS 1999: 2). The Burra Charter also notes the range of values a particular place can have for different individuals and groups. This reflects a shift not just in the way we look at heritage, but also in how its value is determined. The discourse of power has been fractured and there is greater inclusivity. While previously the value of heritage was determined by those in authority, it is now determined rather more collaboratively. This constitutes a shift, however gradual, in the balance of power, and the necessary renegotiation of power relations.

Symbiotic Heritage

Following on from the Burra Charter and a number of UNESCO initiatives, such as the Convention for the Safeguarding of the Intangible Cultural Heritage (2003), there has been growing recognition of the significance of the living dimension of material heritage. However, it seems as if material and non-material heritage are still treated as following separate and distinct trajectories (Figure 29.1), with primacy given to the former.

Postulating separate trajectories for material and non-material heritage is, of course, deeply problematic, and a number of charters and documents have sought to overcome this separation and promote an integrated concept of heritage – one that merges the tangible with the intangible, and thus reinforces the indivisible nature of heritage, transcending the conventional dualism. The Charter on the Built Vernacular Heritage, ratified by the ICOMOS 12th General Assembly in Mexico, stated that "[t]he vernacular embraces not only the physical form and fabric of buildings, structures and spaces, but the ways in which they are used and understood, and the traditions and the intangible associations which attach to them" (ICOMOS 1999: 2).

Mounir Bouchenaki has captured this interdependence between tangible and intangible. He describes cultural heritage as "a synchronized relationship involving society (that is, systems of interactions connecting people), norms and values (that is, ideas, for instance, belief systems that attribute relative importance)," arguing that the "symbols, technologies and objects are tangible evidence of underlying norms and values" (Bouchenaki 2003: 2). Interestingly, he suggested a symbiotic concept of

Figure 29.2 A symbiotic concept of heritage.

heritage (Figure 29.2) where the intangible provides the context and "should be regarded as the larger framework within which tangible heritage takes on shape and significance" (Bouchenaki 2003: 2). A similar argument can be made with regard to natural heritage, since all heritage is a mental construct, including valued elements of the natural environment – and the values, perceptions, and cultural practices associated with natural heritage are inherently intangible. This is in keeping with the "holistic heritage" argument promoted by Smith (2006).

The holistic approach to heritage was reinforced by the Declaration of the Kimberley Workshop on the Intangible Heritage of Monuments and Sites (ICOMOS 2004). The document began with recognition of "the indivisible nature of tangible and intangible heritage" and went on to argue that "intangible heritage gives meanings, values and context to objects and places. The individual elements cannot be separated, they are inextricably linked" (ICOMOS 2004: pmbl.).

More recently, Robin Turner, a member of Historic Environment Scotland, compared the heritage spectrum to the electro-magnetic spectrum.[3] Just as the electro-magnetic spectrum has a visible part that is sandwiched between significant dimensions at either end of the spectrum, the physical environment also lies in the middle of a spectrum with natural heritage at one end and intangible cultural heritage at the other (Figure 29.3). His main concern was to illustrate the "whole picture" of visible and invisible – a combination of the things we can see (the physical environment) and the things we cannot (stories, rituals, and a sense of place). He also emphasized that the "cultural" environment is part of the same heritage spectrum as the "natural," just as radio waves and visible light are part of the same electro-magnetic spectrum.

Heritage and a Sense of Place

This reframing of heritage can be demonstrated by different architectural case studies. Consider, for example, the National Museum of the American Indian (NMAI) in Washington (see Figure 29.4). Its sweeping and curvilinear architecture was designed by Douglas Cardinal, a Canadian architect of Blackfoot and Métis ancestry, who worked in collaboration with tribes and communities from across the Western hemisphere.

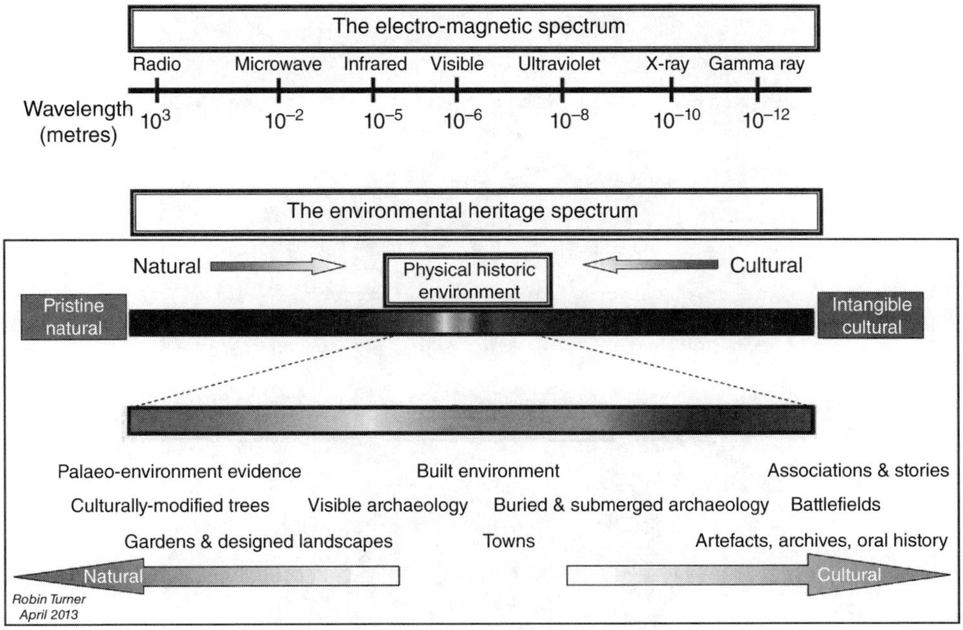

Figure 29.3 The environmental heritage spectrum. Source: image courtesy of Robin Turner © Royal Commission on the Ancient and Historical Monuments of Scotland. Used by permission.

The museum's architecture differs significantly from the other buildings on Washington's National Mall: "In sharp contrast to the Capitol and its setting, the museum presents crisp, contemporary forms and organic curves redolent of natural shapes, announcing its own message and character" (Blue Spruce 2008: 18). Indeed, as Phillips has suggested, "Cardinal's undulating, organic strata and the warmth of his preferred gold-hued stone contrast sharply with the grey historicism of official architecture" that surrounds it (Phillips 2006: 76).

The challenge to conventionality is also visible in the Sydney Opera House, placed on the World Heritage List in 2007. This iconic building was designed by Danish architect Jørn Utzon and brought to fruition by engineer Ove Arup. The shell-shaped structure is instantly recognizable and is designed to emphasize its setting in Sydney harbor. At the time of its construction, the building marked a radically new approach in architecture. As the World Heritage nomination dossier noted, "Sydney Opera House breaks new ground in terms of complex sources of architectural representation, innovation in structure and technology and an empathetic relationship between a large public building and its dramatic natural setting" (GoA 2006: 92).

The building was compared with other iconic architectural masterpieces, such as the city of Brasilia, the Getty Center in Los Angeles, the Guggenheim Museum in Bilbao, and the Pompidou Center in Paris (UNESCO 2007: 92). It breaks new ground in terms of its complex sources of architectural representation, innovation in structure and technology, and an empathetic relationship between a large public building and its dramatic physical setting.

Equally radical is the new Scottish Parliament in Edinburgh, opened in 2004. The building tells Scotland's national story in a design "vocabulary" that reflects multiple

Figure 29.4 National Museum of the American Indian, Washington. Source: Raul654 via Wikimedia Commons. Attribution-ShareAlike 3.0 Unported (CC BY-SA 3.0).

aspects of Scotland's living landscape and cultural heritage, using indigenous materials in as far as possible, with different Scottish rocks embedded in its walls facing the Canongate end of Edinburgh's Royal Mile. The complex is designed to be viewed from below and above. Since the fishing industry is a significant part of Scotland's heritage, the view from above features distinctive boat motifs (Figure 29.5). Buildings such as this represent "the bricolage of the twenty-first century" rather than the "grand narrative of modernity" (McCrone 2005: 25). In the case of the Scottish Parliament, the Catalan architect Enric Miralles was determined that the building should reflect the land. He saw the building as sitting "in the land because it belongs to the Scottish land. The Parliament should be able to reflect the land which it represents" (quoted in Bowditch 2009: 13). Such was his desire to connect the building to the landscape around it that he designed long (and what are euphemistically called) "concrete branches" at the ends of the buildings. It was his ambition to construct a building that is located in, but also emerges from the land. Thus the landscape shaped around the actual Scottish Parliament takes up 60 percent of his designed site. Miralles described the land as "a physical building material" (Jencks 2005: 18). The building is heavily embellished with the iconography of both land and sea.

Figure 29.5 Scottish Parliament, Edinburgh. Source: © Royal Commission on the Ancient and Historical Monuments of Scotland (Aerial Photography Collection). Licensor: www.rcahms.gov.uk.

There is a similar focus on connections with the land in the design of the NMAI. "The design team conceived of the museum building as a rock formation carved by wind and water, a formation emerging from the earth rather than being set down upon it" (Blue Spruce 2008: 17). To reinforce the connection, the base of the building and its immediate exterior hardscape were built of American Mist granite. The surrounding landscaping was designed by Navajo botanist Donna House, who opted for four habitats: forest to the north, cropland to the south, wetland to the east, and meadow to the southwest (Nelson 2006: 57). The landscape aims to reinforce the connection between indigenous people and the land. It has elements such as 40 large un-carved rocks called Grandfather Rocks that represent enduring relations between Native American peoples and their land (Smith 2005: 427). With almost 30,000 trees, shrubs, and plants, the site "was designed to reflect a return to the natural world, offering a respite from the otherwise groomed and sculpted National Mall" (Lea 2008: 124). This is in sharp contrast to the "monumental, monolithic, and monochromatic landscape" designed by the French-born American architect Pierre Charles L'Enfant and others to accompany "the most important federal buildings of the United States" (Lea 2008: 124).

Escobar's observation that being connected with the land remains "an integral part of the contemporary modern life of … communities, even in cases in which such connectedness might be a vehicle for the exercise of power over them" (Escobar 2001: 146), puts that focus on the land into a critical perspective. For all its emphasis on representing an American Indian perspective, the NMAI has faced several ideological contradictions, most significantly that of "how to build a museum to display cultures which have a deep ambivalence about the notion of being displayed," since museums "are simply part of the cultural apparatus of expansion and colonization" (Conn 2006: 69). Arguably, the NMAI "exemplifies decolonisation in practice" (Smith 2005: 437) as "a significant new site of postIndian identity making and place making" (Nelson 2006: 43). That significance arises partly from "the desire of Native American communities to tell the stories of contemporary survival and Native cultural continuance, rather than have this museum serve as a shrine to pain and suffering" (Nelson 2006: 43).

To facilitate this, the US Congress delegated the development of the NMAI largely to Native Americans, thereby ostensibly inverting established power relationships (Phillips 2006: 76). Thus "the NMAI had the potential to transform the organisation of knowledge" (Smith 2005: 426) and tell a different story – or tell the story differently. Smith argues that the absence of power differentials from the meta-vocabulary of the NMAI "derives from its role as forum rather than temple" (Smith 2005: 434).

The principles underpinning the installations are related to storytelling (West 2002): community ("our tribes are sovereign nations"), locality ("this is Indian land"), vitality ("we are here now"), viewpoint ("we know the world differently"), and voice ("these are our stories"). Smith (2005: 431–32) cites various press articles about the opening of the NMAI that reveal the incomprehension of observers whose conventional expectations were challenged when they were faced with the very different way in which the museum, in the stories it tells, orders – and thus makes sense of – the world. This may indeed be reflective of decolonization. However, critics have remarked that the NMAI has been curated by a new kind of Native American elite, and Phillips, following Althusser, points out that "the sponsoring of a new representation by a nation state can only happen if the representation is seen to serve the state's ideological needs" (Phillips 2006: 79). Rather than power relationships being inverted, we may in fact see them being reconfigured by dominant interests continuing to control the discourse.

A similar reconfiguration of power relationships is evident in the case of the Scottish Parliament. While the building seeks to represent the people's relationship with the land, and "embedded in Scottish identity is the sense of belonging not to a tribe and ethnic group, but a place, a territory" (McCrone 2005: 31), the siting of the building can be seen as putting Scottish national aspirations firmly in their place within the context of the United Kingdom. Unlike the NMAI, which is given pride of place with its location on the National Mall, the Scottish Parliament was not located in an elevated position, such as the initially proposed Calton Hill, "studded with British architectural gems" (Riddoch 2013: 285) and overlooking the city center from the end of its main boulevard. Instead, after a devolved administration for Scotland was finally introduced in 1997, its parliament was almost tucked away on the low-level site of a disused brewery, connected with the city's otherwise dense public transport network by a single bus route. Albeit located next to the Royal Palace of Holyrood House, and thus symbolically close to the local residence of the monarch of the United Kingdom to which Scotland remains subordinate, its siting suggests an aggrandized county or provincial council rather than a national parliament, thus reflecting the esteem in which it is held by the United Kingdom's main political parties (Riddoch 2013).

The architects of both the Scottish Parliament and the NMAI had great empathy with the intangible heritage of the people represented by their respective buildings. The importance of such a sense of empathy was noted by ICOMOS (2004), when it committed itself to giving attention to the intangible values of place, a position it subsequently reinforced in the Xi'an Declaration (ICOMOS 2005). The declaration attributed immense significance to the conservation of context, which it defined in terms of physical and visual aspects along with people's interactions with the natural environment, past and present. Interactions may include rituals, customs, and practices, and any other forms of intangible heritage that cultivate a sense of and relationship with place. Such relationships, gradually accumulated over time, make an integral contribution to the spirit of place.

The Québec Declaration on the Preservation of the Spirit of Place (ICOMOS 2008) reinforced previous initiatives by ICOMOS to promote both tangible and intangible dimensions of place. The declaration asserts that "intangible cultural heritage gives a richer and more complete meaning to heritage as a whole" (ICOMOS 2008: art. 1). Sites, buildings, and other tangible elements such as routes and objects all contribute to a strong sense of place. However, intangible elements such as memories, narratives, festivals, colors, and odors also contribute significantly to giving spirit to a place. The design and management of the NMAI have made extensive use of such elements.

Both the NMAI and the Scottish Parliament are urban buildings created emphatically to express both tangible and intangible heritage. Other examples of urban structures with strong dimensions of intangible heritage include the Royal Exhibition Building and the Shrine of Remembrance, both in Melbourne. The Royal Exhibition Building was inscribed on the World Heritage List under criterion (ii): to exhibit an important interchange of human values, over a span of time or within a cultural area of the world, on developments in architecture or technology, monumental arts, town-planning or landscape design. The building was originally designed for the 1880 International Exhibition, and used again for the 1887 International Exhibition. In fact, it is the only remaining principal building from the nineteenth-century International Exhibition movement. Although the building is a copy of classical architecture (Brunelleschi's Dome in Florence), it reflects the people who built it and its subsequent history. It was used for the opening of the first Australian national parliament in 1901, when the colonies federated. It still functions today as an exhibition hall, and is much loved by the inhabitants of Melbourne. When referring to its nomination for World Heritage listing in 2003, the then federal minister for the environment and heritage noted that "World Heritage listing of this extraordinary place would for the first time recognize post-European settlement and built heritage as part of Australia's rich and internationally important heritage" (Willis 2004: 55).

The Shrine of Remembrance in Melbourne is also strong architecturally, but it is its intangible heritage that makes it a great, indeed moving, building. It was built between 1928 and 1934 to mark the extensive loss of life during World War I. Some 114,000 volunteers had enlisted; of these, 89,000 had served abroad, and 19,000 of these were killed in battle. Since they were buried abroad at a time when overseas transport was limited and the repatriation of Australia's war dead was not countenanced, the Shrine of Remembrance served as a place at home in Australia where their relatives and friends could grieve individually or collectively (SoR 2011). The site also pays tribute to soldiers who fought in subsequent wars, thereby adding to its wealth of intangible heritage.

Not all urban structures with a political function were originally built with a view to representing heritage. The Reichstag in Berlin, for example, both in its original and in its reconstructed form, was clearly built with heritage in mind, whereas the Berlin Wall most certainly was not. However, in the course of the Cold War, it acquired an intangible heritage dimension that remains vivid even after the tangible built structure has almost entirely disappeared, raising peculiar issues of heritage conservation (Merbach 2011). This highlights a differential in the embedding of tangible in intangible heritage (Figure 29.2), between a deliberate political act and incidental historical accrual. Of course, these are not binary opposites; any politically driven design may, and most likely will, become associated over time with aspects of intangible heritage, just as incidental historical accrual of such associations can be, and frequently has been, instrumentalized politically.

Cities are often rich in symbolically significant buildings, but as sites of structures built to represent a conjunction of tangible and intangible heritage at a broader scale, such as that of an entire nation, any signification remains necessarily abstract because it is inevitably decontextualized, despite the best efforts of curators and other stakeholders. Where imperial, military, or industrial heritage is expressed in the built environment, the abstraction may seem less obvious, since the symbols tend to have urban resonances. But where the emphasis is on "the land," as in the NMAI and the Scottish Parliament, the dichotomy between an urban and a rural symbolic repertoire becomes evident, and can make the built structure appear somewhat incongruous – an out-of-place place. Whether such symbolic misplacement reflects a tacit acknowledgement of the actual displacement of the subjects purportedly represented by the building is a question for another occasion. Nelson laments that the NMAI failed to engage openly with displacement, and thus "missed an opportunity to educate the public about the 'disease of displacement' and the intergenerational trauma created by the 'erasure of place'" (Nelson 2006: 43).

The (re-)creation of rural habitats in any urban setting tends to have either recreational or Romantic connotations, which raises questions of who it is targeted at, in terms of both the actual visitors and any specific wider range of stakeholders. Without wishing to overstate the urban/rural dichotomy, it may be worth noting that societies where power is concentrated in urban centers seem to create at these centers representations of their cultural hinterland that inscribe the dichotomy. By bringing the rural into the urban in a post-Romantic manner, they may thus reaffirm rather than diminish the power distance, and consolidate rather than change existing power relationships.

However, the (re-)building of heritage in a post-Romantic manner can also have change-inducing effects, thereby contributing to a gradual altering of power relationships. Examples of this can be found in cities, but more usually in peripheral areas. A case in point may be the Museum of Local Cultures in Zagora, Morocco. An Italian team of architects, in collaboration with local authorities, tourism organizations, and other stakeholders, proposed developing the museum in the shape of a traditional caravanserai (Biondi, Cirinna, and Mecca 2006). The symbolic significance of caravanserais as places of encounter and exchange between different cultures and traditions is an important aspect of this project (Biondi, Cirinna, and Mecca 2006: 5), and has been acknowledged in the redevelopment of historical caravanserais elsewhere for tourism purposes (Bryce, O'Gorman, and Baxter 2013). Moreover, "the physical form of caravanserais traditionally embodied dimensions of expectation and behaviour" (O'Gorman and Prentice 2008), and this is another element the project seeks to capture. It is envisaged as what may be termed a "living and working museum," combining exhibits with the making on site of traditional artifacts, using traditional skills, adapted to contemporary needs.

In the construction of the building itself, the emphasis was placed on local building traditions and materials, and on integration with the surrounding landscape. The team therefore chose "a specific building technique and a defined building typology … [using] … raw earth" (Biondi, Cirinna, and Mecca 2006: 4–5), which – much like the NMAI – would make the architectural structure itself an integral part of the museum display. The aim was to create a "modern" caravanserai, "with rooms and spaces arranged around the central courtyard, represent[ing] an experimental way to retrieve and communicate important knowledge" of the diverse cultures that share this region (Biondi, Cirinna, and Mecca 2006: 5).

Similar in its intention and aspirations to the NMAI, the Museum of Local Cultures, however, is not located at a high profile, high exposure site, but rather in a remote area. Conceived as a local center for the recovery, maintenance, and development of traditional skills and other forms of intangible heritage, not merely for purposes of conservation but for their use in everyday life, it appears less as a representational stage for the display of heritage to an audience of mostly outsiders than the NMAI does in the eyes of many of its critics. This is partly to do with the difference of scale: the NMAI, like the Scottish Parliament, is a national institution with representational ambitions to match, while the Museum of Local Cultures appears very much as a local institution. However, as critical nodes along long-distance routes, places of cultural encounter, and places of exchanges in goods, knowledge, and skills, caravanserais represent very much the global connectedness of place as part of their intangible heritage. Whether the Museum of Local Cultures project will succeed in capturing this, or produce just another local craft center attracting the occasional tourist, remains to be seen.

In both examples, the location of the exhibits is of great significance. The NMAI was built on the National Mall in an elevated position in Washington. This contrasts sharply with the Museum of Local Cultures, which is located on the edge of the Sahara Desert. Both museums are designed to represent indigenous heritage, but the NMAI has much bigger aspirations. It is located in a major urban center that is also the national capital, and thus designed to host mass tourism, but it is also located far away from the homes of the peoples it represents. In contrast, the Museum of Local Cultures is set within an environment affording close proximity to its historically multi-ethnic population (Biondi, Cirinna, and Mecca 2006: 3). It is a local exhibition representing local people. Is it meaningful to ask which of these representations is the more authentic and why.

The NMAI and the Museum of Local Cultures are both examples of planned heritage, and built for the purpose of exhibiting heritage. This contrasts with many of the stately homes and castles on the World Heritage List, which were originally built as homes of the rich and powerful, and acquired official heritage status when the rich were no longer able (or willing) to maintain them. In some instances the narrative is even more complex. Consider the example of the Royal Exhibition Building. "At a world level, it remains as the World's oldest surviving exhibition hall and a legacy of the great nineteenth century exhibitions of arts and manufactures" (Riddett 2000: 76). Originally built to provide a stage for the exhibition of heritage, including designated heritage of the future, the building itself has now achieved iconic status. This contrasts with the Shrine of Remembrance, intentionally built as an object of tangible heritage to represent the memory of sacrifice as intangible heritage.

The New Heritage Paradigm: Implications and Challenges

With the expansion of the concept of heritage, there has also been a change in the way the built environment is perceived and understood. When looking at a historic building, one no longer simply sees a tangible structure of greater or lesser aesthetic value, encapsulating a significant achievement in the linear progression towards the height of civilization. The perspective on the built environment has broadened and deepened, and become more complex. When we seek to understand Chartres Cathedral, we do not simply look at the stone and glass, or even at what it has in common with other cathedrals. Rather, we are urged also to comprehend "the specific concepts of the relations among God, man, and architecture that, since they have governed its creation, it consequently embodies" (Geertz 1973: 50–51). This is very much an anthropological approach to heritage – one that "leads us to consider [any building] as a social ensemble of many different, complex and interdependent manifestations" (Bouchenaki 2003: 1).

The expansion of the concept of heritage has also resulted in the redefinition of conservation, with a new emphasis on the cultural significance of place (as found in the Burra Charter). The purpose of values-driven conservation and management is "not to preserve material for its own sake but, rather, to maintain (and shape) the values embodied by the heritage" (Avrami, Mason, and de la Torre 2000: 7). However, this expansion in the concept of heritage, and the subsequent redefinition of conservation, raises many challenges. For example, many of the majestic cathedrals on the World Heritage List were built at a time when society was predominantly religious in orientation. Ordinary people were infused with religious values. Contemporary society is much more secular. We have moved into a different universe of meaning. This has implications for a values-based approach towards the conservation of a religious building. While contemporary society can still appreciate the great architectural achievements of magnificent cathedrals, or value these for the skills and techniques involved in their construction, the spiritual dimensions of such buildings may no longer be relevant. In such contexts, does one aim to conserve as intangible heritage the spiritual values of the building as they were at a time when religion was clearly part of the social fabric of society, or does one seek to translate that religious dimension for present-day society in ways that transcend our distancing from the past? Approaches to making historical contexts accessible in the present all too often suffer from such distancing, which alienates the present from the past rather than aiding closer understanding. Even where concerted attempts have been made to overcome – or at least mediate – this distance, the challenges have been considerable, as the case of the NMAI highlights.

The anthropological approach to material culture, including the built environment and the cultural landscape, has long conceptualized these objects as "cultural expressions," along similar lines to cultural practices and beliefs. This highlights the value of material objects as dependent on a culture that frames and creates them. The new heritage paradigm also draws attention to the reverse dependency. One can thus no longer regard intangible heritage as an independent entity without material foundations, not just in a Marxian sense of the formative influence of material (that is, economic) conditions, but in an even more metaphysical, intimate sense – people make places and objects, but are also made by them. Stories and colors are linked to rivers and landscapes. Dances are danced by people, often in special costumes and usually accompanied by musicians playing instruments of sorts. Traditions and rituals are associated with particular places that are frequently marked by some physical signifier. The material artifacts that go with festivals constitute an entire industry in themselves.

Whether tangible or intangible, the designation of any cultural expression as heritage will have involved a process of selection, which implies recognition and evaluation. Dealing with material objects requires a particular expertise in such objects. The concern is primarily with the physical properties of the building and how these interact with the physical environment. Evaluating intangible heritage is a challenging task, since recognition as "heritage" is a selection process that must take account of the dynamic nature of stories and rituals. How does the conservation of stories as official "heritage" affect the nature of the stories themselves? Traditionally, stories are dynamic – constantly evolving as they are handed down from one generation to the next – and that dynamic is part of their cultural value. For example, how does fixating a particular version of a story impact on all the other versions? Whose version is authorized? And who does the authorizing (and who authorizes them)? What happens when these authorities disagree on the meaning of a story or building? Who owns the building or the story, once the disagreement has been settled? How do they "own" it, and what for?

Even more challenging are those instances where the tangible dimension has been lost – when all that is left may be the absence where a structure once stood. Take the case of the Berlin Wall as an example. Multiple meanings of the Wall have accumulated over time – the history of what happened along and in relation to it, as well as the way it happened, have contributed to the layers of cultural significance. And although the Wall has now effectively disappeared, its "web of significance" (Geertz 1973: 5) continues to hold. It has even given rise to a commonplace metaphor: *die Mauer in den Köpfen* (the Wall in the heads) refers to a tendency of mental and emotional retreat into a nostalgized Cold War frame of reference in the face of the socioeconomic changes following German unification – another instance of the intangible outliving the tangible.

Ultimately, the new, more inclusive definition of heritage is a broader interpretation of the concept and recognizes human beings' creative coexistence with buildings and the landscape. People are no longer merely a disturbance and a danger to the conservation of heritage. The new heritage paradigm entails a different appreciation of history. Rather than being about historic buildings or landscapes only, this deeper understanding of the history is about both the culture and the architecture, and about the spirit of place. This new paradigm requires an integrated management process that is more than just a "twin-track" approach dealing with intangible heritage alongside, in parallel with, tangible heritage. Either form of heritage, whether seen as process, product, or both, is a construct, and when we are dealing with constructs, regardless of any value judgments, we need to ask not only what is being constructed, how and why, but also who for. As key agencies in providing infrastructure, governments in particular need to think about their overarching strategies for heritage, taking a holistic approach towards historic built environments and national treasures that engages equitably with different stakeholders, one that does not reinforce a divide between material and non-material heritage. In this context, it could be argued, UNESCO ought to review whether separate lists and definitions for tangible and intangible heritage should be continued.

Notes

1 World Heritage Convention (1972), para. 1.
2 W. Wenders, M. Glawogger, M. Madsen, R. Redford, M. Olin, and K. Aïnouz (dirs.) *Cathedrals of Culture*, 165 mins. (London: Metrodome, 2014). See the *Cathedrals of Culture* web site, available at: http://kathedralenderkultur-derfilm.de (accessed May 14, 2014).
3 Robin Turner, personal communication, 2013.

References

Legislation

Convention Concerning the Protection of the World Cultural and Natural Heritage (World Heritage Convention) (UNESCO, 1972). Available at: http://whc.unesco.org/archive/convention-en.pdf (accessed March 19, 2015).

Convention for the Safeguarding of the Intangible Cultural Heritage (Intangible Heritage Convention) (UNESCO, 2003). Available at: http://unesdoc.unesco.org/images/0013/001325/132540e.pdf (accessed March 19, 2015).

Other Works

Australia ICOMOS (1999) Charter for Places of Cultural Significance (Burra Charter), revised version. Available at: http://australia.icomos.org/publications/burra-charter-practice-notes/burra-charter-archival-documents/ (accessed February 26, 2015).

Avrami, E., Mason, R., and de la Torre, M. (2000) Values and Heritage Conservation. Research Report. Los Angeles: Getty Conservation Institute. Available at: http://hdl.handle.net/10020/gci_pubs/values_heritage_research_report (accessed December 31, 2014).

Biondi, B., Cirinna, C., and Mecca, S. (2006) Natural Landscape, Local Culture and Traditional Architecture Meet Each Other in a Building: The Museum of Local Cultures in Zagora, Morocco. Revised version of a paper presented at the Forum UNESCO University and Heritage 10th International Seminar, Cultural Landscapes in the 21st Century, Newcastle-upon-Tyne, April, 11–16, 2005.

Birchenough, T. (2014) Berlinale 2014: Cathedrals of Culture. *TheArtsDesk.com*, February 14. Available at: http://www.theartsdesk.com/film/berlinale-2014-cathedrals-culture (accessed May 14, 2014).

Blue Spruce, D. (2008) Honoring our Hosts. In D. Blue Spruce and T. Thrasher (eds), *The Land Has Memory: Indigenous Knowledge, Native Landscapes, and the National Museum of the American Indian*. Chapel Hill, NC: University of North Carolina Press/Museum of the American Indian/Smithsonian Institution, pp. 11–31.

Bouchenaki, M. (2003) The Interdependency of the Tangible and Intangible Cultural Heritage. Paper presented at the ICOMOS 14th General Assembly and Scientific Symposium. Available at: http://openarchive.icomos.org/468/1/2_%2D_Allocution_Bouchenaki.pdf (accessed May 14, 2014).

Bowditch, L. (2009) *The Scottish Parliament Official Guidebook*. Edinburgh: Scottish Parliamentary Corporate Body.

Bryce, D., O'Gorman, K., and Baxter, I. (2013) Commerce, Empire and Faith in Safavid Iran: The Caravanserai of Isfahan. *International Journal of Contemporary Hospitality Management*, 25 (2), 204–226.

Cleere, H. (2001) The Uneasy Bedfellows: Universality and Cultural Heritage. In R. Layton, P.G. Stone, and J. Thomas (eds), *Destruction and Conservation of Cultural Property*. London: Routledge, pp. 3–29.

Conn, S. (2006) Heritage vs. History at the National Museum of the American Indian. *Public Historian*, 28 (2), 69–74.

Escobar, A. (2001) Culture Sits in Places: Reflections on Globalism and Subaltern Strategies of Localization. *Political Geography* 20, 139–174.

Foucault, M. (1991) Governmentality. In G. Burchell, C. Gordon, and P. Miller (eds), *The Foucault Effect*. London: Wheatsheaf Harvester, pp. 87–104.

Geertz, C. (1973) *The Interpretation of Cultures*. New York: Basic Books.

GoA (Government of Australia) (2006) Sydney Opera House Nomination for the World Heritage List. Available at: http://whc.unesco.org/uploads/nominations/166rev.pdf (accessed May 14, 2014).

ICOMOS (1999) Charter on the Built Vernacular Heritage. Available at: http://www.international.icomos.org/charters/vernacular_e.pdf (accessed May 14, 2014).

ICOMOS (2004) Declaration of the Kimberley Workshop on the Intangible Heritage of Monuments and Sites. Available at: http://www.international.icomos.org/victoriafalls2003/kimberley.pdf (accessed May 14, 2014).

ICOMOS (2005) Xi'an Declaration on the Conservation of the Setting of Heritage Structures, Sites and Areas. Available at: http://www.international.icomos.org/charters/xian-declaration.pdf (accessed May 14, 2014).

ICOMOS (2008) Québec Declaration on the Preservation of the Spirit of Place. Available at: http://whc.unesco.org/document/116778 (accessed May 14, 2014).

Jencks, C. (2005) *The Scottish Parliament*. Edinburgh: Scala.

Lea, M (2008), Facing Challenges and Maintaining Balance. In D. Blue Spruce and T. Thrasher (eds), *The Land Has Memory: Indigenous Knowledge, Native Landscapes, and the National Museum of the American Indian*. Chapel Hill, NC: University of North Carolina Press/Museum of the American Indian/Smithsonian Institution, pp. 124–135.

McCrone, D. (2005) Devolving Scotland. In A. Balfour (ed.), *Creating a Scottish Parliament*. Edinburgh: Finlay Brown, pp. 5–33.

Macnab, G. (2014) Robert Redford and Wim Wenders on New Architecture Film "Cathedrals of Culture." *Independent*, February 12. Available at: http://www.independent.co.uk/arts-entertainment/films/features/robert-redford-and-wim-wenders-on-new-architecture-film-cathedrals-of-culture-9122224.html (accessed May 12, 2014).

Merbach, A. (2011) The Berlin Wall: Managing a Difficult Heritage. In L. Schmidt, S. Pant, and H. Türk (eds), *Forschen, Bauen, Erhalten. Jahrbuch 2010/2011*. Berlin/Bonn: Westkreuz, pp. 83–86.

Nelson, M. (2006) Ravens, Storms, and the Ecological Indian at the National Museum of the American Indian. *Wicazo Sa Review*, 21 (2), 41–60.

O'Gorman, K., and Prentice, R. (2008) Iranian Hospitality: From Caravanserai to Bazaar to Reporting Symbolic Experience. Paper presented at the EuroCHRIE 2008 Congress, Dubai, October 11–14.

Phillips, R. (2006) Disrupting Past Paradigms: The National Museum of the American Indian and the First Peoples Hall at the Canadian Museum of Civilization. *Public Historian*, 28 (2), 75–80.

Riddett, R. (2000) Melbourne's Royal Exhibition Building: A Case for World Heritage Significance. *Historic Environment, World Heritage*, 14 (5), 75–78.

Riddoch, L. (2013) *Blossom: What Scotland Needs to Flourish*. Edinburgh: Luath.

Smith, C. (2005) Decolonising the Museum: The National Museum of the American Indian in Washington, DC. *Antiquity*, 79, 424–439.

Smith, L. (2006) *Uses of Heritage*. London: Routledge.

Smith, L., and Akagawa, N. (2009) Introduction. In L. Smith and N. Akawaga (eds), *Intangible Heritage*. London: Routledge, pp. 1–9.

SoR (Shrine of Remembrance) (2011) History. Available at: http://www.shrine.org.au/The-Shrine-Story/History (accessed May 14, 2014).

UNESCO (2007) Sydney Opera House. Advisory Body Evaluation No. 166 rev. Available at: http://whc.unesco.org/en/list/166/documents/ (accessed June 15, 2014).

West, R. (2002) Museums in the Twenty-First Century: By Whose Authority? Paper presented at the South Australian Museum, Adelaide, March.

Willis, E. (2004) *The Royal Exhibition Building, Melbourne: A Guide*. Melbourne: Museum Victoria.

Wright, F.L. (1992) *Truth Against the World: Frank Lloyd Wright Speaks for an Organic Architecture*, ed. P.J. Meehan. Boston: John Wiley & Sons.

Young, D. (2014) Cathedrals of Culture: Berlin Review. *Hollywood Reporter* February 9. Available at: http://www.hollywoodreporter.com/review/cathedrals-culture-berlin-review-678678 (accessed May 12, 2014).

CHAPTER 30

The Elephant in the Room: Heritage, Affect, and Emotion

Laurajane Smith and Gary Campbell

In *Uses of Heritage*, Smith (2006) argued that heritage is an embodied cultural performance of meaning-making, which has important consequences for social recognition, and relies heavily on claims to "emotional authenticity" (see Bagnall 2003). Smith also introduced the idea of the Authorized Heritage Discourse, a discursive and rhetorical justification for understanding heritage as old, aesthetic, material, Western, and expert-interpreted, which is not just found in heritage texts but also operates as a dominant sentiment and professional mindset of heritage professionals (see also Waterton, Smith, and Campbell 2006).

Subsequently, Smith applied these insights in a project examining the commemoration of the 1807 abolition of the slave trade in Great Britain (Smith *et al.* 2011). One of the key insights of this research was the extent to which people were managing a range of complex emotions about the subject, ranging from active attempts to work through difficult issues, negotiating cognitive dissonance to mitigate their nation's involvement in the slave trade, to "passive" refusals to extend empathy and recognition. People with such 'passive' frames of mind were in themselves active in their unwillingness to engage either their thoughts or their emotions with the historical experience of slavery or its contemporary legacy. On the other hand, most African-Caribbean British visitors were emotionally engaged with the exhibitions and the issues, actively seeking recognition and empathy, not just for past wrongs, but to sustain a lively sense of engagement with contemporary racial politics (Smith 2011).

A Companion to Heritage Studies, First Edition. Edited by William Logan, Máiréad Nic Craith, and Ullrich Kockel.
© 2016 John Wiley & Sons, Inc. Published 2016 by John Wiley & Sons, Inc.

Smith's current research, based on further interviews, using the same instrument as in the above projects (although slightly adapted for different sites), pursues these ideas in the United States and Australia. By 2013, after conducting close to 4500 interviews at 45 museums, exhibitions, and heritage sites in England, Australia, and the United States, it has become clear that rather than being simply or solely a learning experience, heritage and museum visitors' experiences can only be explained if the emotional aspects of their visits are taken in to account (Smith 2013, 2015a). As we show, this can work on two levels: the more emotionally charged, indeed often febrile, engagements with traumatic or nationalist issues, and something which has been to date ignored in the literature, the emotionally flat, "common sense" performance of dutiful visiting that reinforces consensus narratives of class, race, gender and nation.

Smith has previously suggested that there is an elephant in the room of heritage and museum studies (see Smith and Waterton 2009: 49). This pachyderm is the recognition, or rather lack of recognition, of affect and emotion as essential constitutive elements of heritage making. Despite nascent signs of an interest in emotion in recent literature, our contention in this chapter is twofold: first, this lacuna dramatically detracts from the ability of a range of disciplines interested in studying the past in the present to ask meaningful questions about how people use the past as a contemporary cultural resource; and second, it requires theoretically robust work, drawing on the recent growth in research on affect and emotion, as well as recent critical writing on museum and heritage studies, to inform a pragmatic agenda of empirical research that will speak to researchers, policy-makers, and practitioners in the areas of heritage and museum studies, memory studies, and public history.

In this chapter we outline why we see it is important, indeed essential, to understand how emotions work to frame the staging and experience of heritage and museums. In doing so we suggest some reasons why emotion has been avoided in discussions of heritage and museums until relatively recently, and discuss the work of some authors who have redressed that lacuna. We will also make some preliminary suggestions about directions for future research, and intellectual sources for guiding that research, and raise some caveats about theoretical wrong turns and dead ends that might limit useful research on emotions in heritage and museums research.

Emotional Heritage: Registers of Engagement

Before exploring the literature in and outside of heritage and museum studies, it is useful to outline some of the insights emerging from interviews Smith has been undertaking in the United States and Australia to illustrate not simply the importance of understanding emotion, but the range of emotional engagements with heritage that interviews with visitors have revealed. It is not possible to report in detail on this work, but rather to sketch a very brief overview and identify key issues.[1] One of the key issues emerging from this work is that there are a range of emotional responses to heritage, and a range of intensities in those responses. We develop the idea of "registers of engagement" to describe this observation.

It is, of course, a prosaic observation that individuals will engage differently with a particular aspect of history, and that different heritage sites may engender varying levels of engagement. However, measuring different levels or registers of engagement reveals the limitations of much of the heritage and museum-interpretation literature that draws on educational studies that argue deep engagement is more significant than shallow engagement. Some visitor engagement can be quite shallow, banal even, but nonetheless this form of engagement does important cultural and political work, while some deep engagement can generate a lot of emotional feeling, but does not necessarily go far in developing critical insight for the visitor. Deep and shallow visitor engagement can also produce either conservative/reactionary or liberal/progressive outcomes. However, understanding registers of engagement is important for assessing both the emotional and intellectual investments that visitors may make in their visits, the ways emotions and critical insight interact, and the meanings that are subsequently rehearsed or constructed during visits.

Indeed, the notion of "registers of engagement," in incorporating an understanding that individuals can react and engage differently to the same site or exhibition, acknowledges the agency of individuals in creating their own meanings and understandings of exhibitions and heritage sites. In doing so, a wide range of ways in which heritage sites and museums are used by visitors has been identified. Overall, it is quite clear that museums and heritage sites are places where people go to feel (Smith 2015a), and indeed they are arenas where people go to "manage" their emotions. That is, museums and heritage sites may be defined as perhaps "safe" or simply "appropriate" or permissible places for people to not only feel particular emotions, but to work out or explore how those emotions may reinforce, provide insight, or otherwise engage with aspects of the past and its meaning for the present.

In interviews, visitors have expressed a range of emotions from rage to happiness and delight, from fear to confidence and affirmation, from mild and banal nationalism to deep patriotism, from sadness for others to deep and tearful empathy, from a commonplace sense of having a nice day out to cognitive and emotional epiphanies. Each affective response occurs through a complex interaction of place or exhibition, personal agency, and social and cultural context. Affective responses do not just happen spontaneously and uncontrollably, a point we will return to, but occur through the ability of the visitor to both desire, seek out, and mediate that response. It is, therefore, a contextual response, depending not only on the site or exhibition, but the visitors' relationship to it, their own political and social contexts, and their own skills at recognizing and working with their emotional responses – a skill that can be defined as emotional intelligence (see Mayer, Salovey, and Caruso 2008).

People use sites in many ways, from places where people go to experience, express, or experiment with emotions, as places where families pass on familial memories and social and/or political values, places were individuals go to remember and find affirmation of personal or collective social and political values, as places where some visitors seek reinforcement of what they already know, believe, and feel about the past and its relationship with the present, or to offer recognition and respect for groups other than themselves; occasionally, they are also places where people go to learn about the past or other cultures or social groups (Smith 2015a). Above all, they are places where people feel.

Take, for example, the following statements made by visitors to the Tenement Museum in New York.[2] Their comments focus on their own or others' feelings in revealing ways:

> grabbing the banister going up the first two flights of stairs – allows me to feel more connected, that's a meaning for me, to my roots.
>
> (TM41: male, 45–54, insurance broker, Jewish American)[3]

> To me it [being here] means feeling connected.
> (TM30: female, 55–64, teacher, Jewish American)

> A little bit excited, but also sad and in some ways stronger.
> *LS: Would you mind elaborating on that a little?*
> Absolutely not. When I said stronger I mean in the sense that being able to relate one's present experiences with the past experiences of individuals or groups of individuals, be those families or larger communities, allows me anyway to draw more of a direct line between who I am and how I'm living my life today, and how that may relate back to people in communities that inform again who I am and what I'm doing.[4]
> (TM41: male, 45–54, insurance broker, Jewish American)

> It does in the – as what was said again about the heritage – there's something about actually physically going into the space, physically sort of feeling that kind of tightness that you have to experience to really understand, to get an idea, anyway.
> (TM70: female, 45–54, writer, American)

Empathy was a frequent and important emotion for many visitors, and was triggered not only in response to the content of the tours, exhibitions, or interpretive material, but from a sense of physically being in place. For example, being at the Tenement Museum, "grabbing the banister" of the tenement building, as one visitor put it, was significant in facilitating an empathetic response. A sense of place helped facilitate an emotional authenticity – the emotions that were expressed in interviews were very real to most visitors and, consequently, facilitated either visitors' reflections about the meaning of the history they were viewing and/or their sense of connection to it. These emotions then underpinned and validated the way visitors engaged or disengaged with the information contained in exhibitions and heritage sites, and were used to affirm, rethink, negotiate, or ignore the histories that were on display.

Emotion in Heritage and Museum Studies

Mapping the terrain of emotion in the heritage and museum studies literature is quite complex, because when issues of emotion have been approached, it has been done so in a piecemeal and not entirely systematic way. We can trace the history of heritage studies back to the 1980s (museum studies, of course, has a much longer pedigree) with the publication of two works that set the tone for the intellectual development of the Anglophone field, particularly with regard to issues of emotion: Lowenthal's *The Past is a Foreign Country* (1985) and the collection by Chase and Shaw, *The Imagined Past: History and Nostalgia* (1989). Much of the early literature following up on the issues explored by these works eschewed emotion as entirely problematic, focusing in particular on the apparent problematic of nostalgia as a reactionary backward glance at the past, while also being critical of the triumphant nationalism rightly seen to be espoused by most heritage sites and museums at the time (e.g. Wright 1985; Hewison 1987; Lowenthal 1989; Walsh 1992; Goulding 2001). Criticism of nostalgia in particular was and continues to be rampant, and linked to reactionary and conservative views, commercialization, sentimentalism, and outright ignorance (e.g. Lowenthal 1985, 1989; Wright 1985; Hewison 1987; Jenkins 2011). Although there has been a sustained critique of this characterization of nostalgia, both within and outside of heritage studies (e.g. Samuel 1994; Cashman 2006; Smith 2006; Bonnett and Alexander 2012; Keightley and Pickering 2012), the idea of the "duped" public, consuming a sanitized and consensual national narrative via heritage and museum visiting, underwrote and continues to frame approaches to emotion in heritage and museum studies. Indeed, emotion was seen as somehow "dangerous" to achieving a balanced understanding of the importance of the past in the present.

This position is often reasserted in response to two ongoing developments in heritage and museum practices. The first is in response to an increasing emphasis on experiences which include tactile, visual, aural, and even olfactory aids to interpretation, and to "hands on" approaches, often electronically mediated – together often seen as being populist and puerile by traditionalists. The second is in response to an increasing tendency toward more risk taking in the sector, with emotionally charged issues like slavery, immigration, "forgotten" histories, and class and ethnic conflicts becoming an emerging feature of modern heritage and museum practice (see Bonnell and Simon 2007; Witcomb 2013). Lowenthal encapsulates this ongoing distrust in heritage and museum studies regarding issues of emotion:

> Museums' new found sensitivity to empathy leaves them at the mercy of those who would bend them to national or tribalist aims or, still worse, enlist them in the generalized politics of memory, which sacralizes the emotional salience of remembrance to the detriment of historical understanding. Empathetic concerns have their place. But they should not be allowed to overshadow the detached distancing that enables museums uniquely to serve, and to be widely seen, as reliable vehicles of public illumination. (Lowenthal 2009: 29–30)

Empathy is questioned as something that substitutes shallow identification for appropriately rigorous historical understanding. Jenkins, in writing about the increasing numbers of memorial museums, argues that rather than "celebrating human achievement" (which she seems to see as the proper role of a museum, and yet fails to recognize that celebration is also an emotive performance), such museums are more concerned with a "focus on experience, and on the victims," and that this subsequently "does not allow for complicated reflection" (Jenkins 2011), though she cites no evidence to support this. Whether it is David Lowenthal railing against "too much empathy," museums focusing on "education" as their primary purpose (Trofanenko 2014), or all too many historians still insisting that imposing the moral sentiments of the present on the study of the past compromises the study of history (see e.g. Reddy 2001; Southgate 2007; Kalela 2012), emotion is, when it comes to those fields that study the meaning of the past in the present, all too often actively excluded as an area of valid research.

The tendency to wariness toward issues of emotion, or to see emotional issues as potentially reactionary, is not confined to heritage studies, and it is in many ways symptomatic of the reluctance to engage with emotion in many disciplines in the twentieth century, and perhaps an artifact of modernity itself. Emotion and affect were not taken seriously as an area of research in the twentieth century, at least until what Clough (2007) and Damasio (2006) respectively identify as a recent turn to affect in the social sciences and neurosciences. Reddy (2001) notes that the same applies to the discipline of history, which is still rather resistant to recent findings in the social and cognitive sciences about emotion and affect, and despite a number of notable exceptions (e.g. Agnew 2007; de Groot 2011) it remains suspicious of popular and "emotive" manifestations of interest in history (see also Kalela 2012).

Emotions have also commonly been dismissed as subjective and unreliable, especially in relation to individual and social memory (Ahmed 2004; Campbell 2003, 2006; Wetherell 2012). However, as Andrew Sayer (2007: 90–91) argues, emotion is a form of evaluative judgment of matters that are understood as affecting our well-being. Indeed, there is now a substantive literature that argues that reasoning, cognition, and memory depend on emotion. The point has been made that too much emotion can at times undermine rationality; conversely, too much abstract rationality can likewise undermine sound reasoning (e.g. Ahmed 2004; Damasio 2006; Protevi 2009; Hoggett 2009; Mercer 2010; Frevert 2011; Wetherell 2012).

The Authorized Heritage Discourse, which privileges a certain mentality in the management of heritage and museums, has also played an important role in maintaining negative attitudes to emotion in heritage. This mentality is overly concerned with expert judgments on the significance of the past, and is based on technical and aesthetic forms of expert knowledge and the mobilization of their practitioners, such as archeologists, art historians, architects, and historians, whose "value free" knowledge can be used to arbitrate over and govern how the past should be understood. Ironically, these experts have a massive emotional investment in professing not to have an emotional, but rather a technical, "rational" and disinterested approach to heritage, museums, and history. Some of the foundational studies in the sociology of emotions and work demonstrate that the emotional commitment and emotional intelligence of workers can be effectively utilized by employers in the workplace, especially in the "knowledge economy" and the service sector (Hochschild 1983; see also Mercer 2010; Pedwell 2013). The stress on not being emotional, on maintaining professional objectivity, may be viewed as being both performative and itself an emotional state. Thus, strangely enough, workplace studies of emotion work quite well to explain why so many people in heritage, museums, and history are averse to dealing with emotions. In the first instance, these insights rather compromise experts' emotional commitment to denying that their avocations are in themselves emotional as well as reasoned career choices, and in the second it all too clearly shows how imbricated their work is in the governance of a field whose politics is intensely and unavoidably emotional – the contemporary significance of the past.

What has also problematized engaging with emotion has been the tendency for market-led research in museums and heritage studies, often fostered by tourism studies, to undertake quantitative visitor surveys and analyses of how affective responses could be used to increase visitor revenue (see e.g. Forrest 2013). This work only cultivated suspicion by some that promoting affective responses through heritage and museum interpretations was part of the co-called "Disneyfication" or commoditization of the past, and played on perceived nostalgic tendencies in the population. The negativity with which much of the heritage field has regarded tourists and tourism has been well documented (Graburn and Barthel-Bouchier 2001; Ashworth 2009); it is, however, this negativity that has facilitated the dismissal both of engaging with non-expert users of heritage sites and ultimately the issue of the emotional content and consequence of heritage.

Ray Cashman's pointed observation that the tendency in the social sciences to overstate the reactionary and subjective nature of emotions such as nostalgia "may be due in part to the fact that many of these critics are not the sort who engage in ethnographic fieldwork" (Cashman 2006: 155) is well made. One may wonder whether an uneasiness with emotion may go hand in hand with being unwilling to do empirical research that actually involves talking to people. It is perhaps no accident that the first key pieces of research to start to address issues of emotion arose from qualitative research undertaken with visitors to heritage sites and museums. Yaniv Poria and colleagues in a study of visitors to religious sites in Jerusalem identify the emotional significance of the visit, noting the more emotionally engaged visitor tended to define the site as part of their personal or cultural heritage (Poria, Butler, and Airey 2003; Poria 2007). Their observation, that heritage sites are places where people go to feel, drew attention to the legitimacy of visitor experiences at sites that went beyond a linear understanding of visitors as recipients of curatorial or interpretive educational messages.

Their findings were backed by work from within tourism studies, that had started to argue that visitors to heritage sites and museums were not necessarily the mindless dupes identified in the literature of the 1980s and early 1990s, but rather altogether more mindful and discerning (Moscardo 1996; Mcintosh and Prentice 1999; Prentice and Andersen 2007). The sociologist Gaynor Bagnall (2003), in an analysis of in-depth visitor interviews at Wigan Pier and the Museum of Science and Industry, Manchester, identified what may be termed "emotional authenticity" as a key element in visitor engagement with heritage sites and museums. She argued that authenticity of emotions engendered by people's interaction with place, which was itself framed by individual social contexts and biographies, was significant in the degree to which visitors engaged with the site or exhibition.

Smith (2006), meanwhile, utilized Bagnall's concept in analyzing visitor responses to heritage sites and museums in England. She argued that the emotional authenticity of the site was something visitors mediated in relation to a sense of place, and emotional responses to sites, artifacts, and exhibitions underpinned the ways in which visitors engaged in memory work and the negotiation and renegotiation of historical narratives about nation, class, and community. Smith argued that visitors and other users of heritage were engaged in an embodied, emotional, performance of negotiating and creating the meaning of the past for the present. Work by Bagnall and Smith echoes more recent work from within geography that argues the sense of place embodied by people engaging with heritage sites and landscapes tends to be dismissed by heritage agencies and experts in formal assessments of historical and cultural significance of sites and places (Cresswell and Hoskins 2008).

Much of the work within heritage and museum studies that has engaged with ethnographic and other forms of qualitative research has tended, much like memory studies, to draw attention to the highly energized emotional content of traumatic histories (e.g. Smith 2010a; Sather-Wagstaff 2011; Witcomb 2012; Kidron 2013) or with expressions of nationalism (Palmer 2005; Smith 2006). We are not critical of this focus, as it has illustrated the overall importance and complexity of emotional responses and interactions with heritage. However, a significant absence is the understanding of the emotional consequences of the everyday, common-sense, or more banal aspects of the past and visitor responses to it. A charting of the emotional terrain of heritage must include the unremarkable as much as the dissonant and contested. As Billig (1995) has so powerfully argued, the banal and everyday can have deeper and ongoing consequences to issues of nationalism, identity, and belonging than the extraordinary. Smith's work has demonstrated that emotional responses that are not heightened play a significant role in the performance of many heritage and museum visits, and have a central role in the emotional embedding of consensus nationalist and racial narratives, and deferential social attitudes (Smith 2015a).

Other work has focused on the ways in which emotion has contributed to pedagogy within the work of museums and heritage sites (e.g. Soren 2009; Gregory and Witcomb 2007; Witcomb 2013; Trofanenko 2014; Smith 2015b). This body of research has documented how emotions can be used to destabilize received narratives and understandings of history, so that greater engagement with hidden or marginalized histories and contemporary group sympathy may occur. Central in this process has been the identification of deep empathy, or empathy that moves beyond the "I feel sad" for this other, as key to triggering a response that engages the imagination in such a way that visitors start to question what they know and understand (Witcomb 2013; Smith 2015a, 2015b). Still other work, drawing on extensive ethnographic interviews with visitors, has illustrated the ways in which visitors may use emotion to close down engagement with attempts to subvert received or consensus histories, and thus maintain more comfortable or treasured historical narratives and the sense of identity and self that they underpin (Smith 2010a, 2011).

Ethnographic work with communities or other groups has also illustrated that the emotional attachment of groups to their heritage and the narratives they represent play important work in affirming community or group identity (e.g. Linkon and Russo 2002; Byrne *et al.* 2006; Smith 2006; Smith and Campbell 2011; Cashman 2006; Bonnett 2010a, 2010b; Bonnett and Alexander 2012). This attachment is not simply mawkish sentimentalism, but rather is illustrative of the emotional investment people make in their heritage as a cultural and emotional resource. Heritage as a resource in the interplay of the politics of representation and recognition should not be understated; heritage has become, during the latter part of the twentieth century, an explicitly identifiable political resource. This is because heritage, through its ability to represent and give material "legitimacy" to claims about cultural and social identity, is mobilized within the demands and negotiations groups make with the state and policy-makers for social justice and equity in negotiations over the distribution of welfare resources.[5]

It is this literature that has questioned the classification of nostalgia as simply reactionary backward glances. Smith (2006: 237–75) and Smith and Campbell (2011), in their study of the self-identified working-class community of Castleford, in northern England, have argued that nostalgic reflections by this community about their past is about explicitly recognizing both the negative and positive aspects of the past, and identifying valued aspects of the past that they want to see reinstated in the present and future. Similar ethnographic work by Cashman (2006) in Ireland and Bonnett and Alexander (2012) in Newcastle, England, with community groups argues that nostalgia is a negotiation between past and present, and a form of activism that seeks to use the past to reflect on and take action in the present for a better future (see also Pickering and Keightley 2006; Keightley and Pickering 2012). The political work of nostalgia may be either progressive or reactionary, but it is not a languid lament that can or should be dismissed. Indeed, Bonnett (2009, 2010a) identifies what he calls radical nostalgia, and asserts that nostalgia is integral and constitutive of modern life, and an "inevitable emotion in an era of rapid and enforced change" (Bonnett 2010b: 2365), and as such it is worthy of attention.

A further recent strand of work on emotion in heritage and museums draws on non-representational theory (NRT). NRT derives from geography, and, as Creswell argues, has its antecedents in the School of Geographical Sciences at the University of Bristol. It is, as he characterizes it, "very British and very male" (Creswell 2012: 96).[6] It emerges from the work of Gilles Deleuze and Félix Guattari, as well as Nigel Thrift (Crouch 2010). The work in this area within heritage studies is led by Waterton and Watson (2013: 554–55), who, drawing on Thrift, privilege the non-cognitive and precognitive – that is, the intuitive, habitual, and the biological – to focus on the affective moment as caught up in a continuous process of composition.

This emphasis on the idea that "affect" is something that is prior to cognition, apprehension, or emotion, and is a biologically based process not mediated by representation, culture, or discourse, has received significant criticism. These ideas are borrowed from what Wetherell (2012, 2013a) and Leys (2011) argue are dubious foundations in the biological sciences and deeply problematic psychology (see also Wolff 2012). Non-representational theorists are concerned by an overemphasis on language and discourse, and certainly the point that there is more than representation (Lorimer 2005) is important. However, in NRT, affect becomes an "unspecific force, unmediated by consciousness, discourse, representation and interpretation" (Wetherell 2012: 123), and analysis is focused on the moment, on "atmosphere," and the event, to the extent that context, and issues of class, race, and gender in particular, become obscured or disregarded.[7] This disregard has been criticized by a number of feminist scholars, who also note that as emotion is analyzed outside consciousness, NRT makes a number of androcentric and Eurocentric assumptions about how such emotion is expressed and understood (see e.g. Thien 2005; Tolia-Kelly 2006; Wetherell 2012; Cresswell 2012). Although the issue of power and context is noted by Waterton and Watson (2013), the underlying assumptions of NRT, which separates affect from consciousness and representation, forces analysis away from dealing with issues of politics, human labor, and agency (Creswell 2012: 104; Wetherell 2013b). This failure is also exacerbated by a tendency toward poetical treatments of the event or moment of affect that NRT aims to analyze, and a tendency to stress the complexity of theory by excessive wordiness and obscurantism. NRT is a theoretical dead end, particularly for research that aims to understand the interrelationship between heritage and the social, and political contexts within which heritage, and the emotions it generates and facilitates, work (Wetherell 2012).

Moving Away from Suspicion: Affect, Emotion and Heritage

We called earlier in this chapter for a pragmatic and considered program of research on emotion and the contemporary relevance of the past and its uses, which would be able to speak to practitioners, researchers, and other communities of interest. There are two starting points for any understanding of affect and emotion. Firstly, that our understanding must commence from an acknowledgement that the social, cultural, and political structures or contexts in which we live matter. Secondly, that affect and emotion have a range of material, individual, and systemic consequences on the contexts in which we live. As Stuart Hall notes, those things connected "with the psychic – with emotions and identifications and feelings" are part of the institutional and personal structures that we live and experience (Hall 1996: 488). Emotions are socially, culturally, discursively, and politically mediated, and indeed how we talk about emotions and the language we use to do so also impacts on our emotional experiences and all that flows from these (Reddy 2001: 103–5).

While we are stressing the point that emotions are social, it is important, as Wetherell (2012: 62) notes, to acknowledge that affect and emotion are part of a highly complex interplay of autonomic bodily responses (such as sweating, trembling, blushing), other body actions (such as approaching or avoiding), as well as subjective feelings and cognitive processing. While it is important to note the biological aspects of emotion, it is also important to remember that psychology and neuroscience, when it comes to the social aspects of emotion, are often unsubtle in dealing with such a complex relationship, especially in terms of its cultural and historical dimensions (Reddy 2001; Frevert 2011; Wetherell 2012). Certainly, biological responses are themselves understood and mediated within a sociocultural context (Mesquita and Albert 2007: 487), and thus, above all, emotions may be understood as relational and social events that are discursively mediated, and work to underpin and influence meaning-making (Wetherall 2012: 74; 2013a). There is a dizzying wealth of research on emotions that identifies the various ways in which affect and emotion have a range of consequences. Our aim now is to identify aspects of this literature that facilitate research and understanding of the interplay of emotion in heritage, drawing particular attention to issues of: memory; emotion and cognition and meaning-making; and emotional management and regulation.

Memory and Emotion

Like emotion, individual and social memory is not something we simply "have"; it is also mediated and reconstructive (Wertsch 2002). Emotion is significant in the way memory is interpreted, given meaning, and judged as "accurate." The work of Sue Campbell is instructive here, as she notes: "emotions are themselves rich in representational quality. The emotion through which we represent the past is a significant component of recollective accuracy" (Campbell 2006: 373; see also Campbell 2003). We would like to suggest that recognizing reason/cognition, affect/emotion, and memory as being mutually constitutive and reinforcing of each other is a positive step for anyone interested in understanding and researching the contemporary significance of the past, both in terms of how individuals utilize the past and the sets of institutions and practices that Sharon Macdonald calls "memory complexes" (Macdonald 2013) and Landsberg calls "prosthetic memory" (Landsberg 2004), which implicate heritage, museums, memory, and history. Sutton (2006) and Campbell (2006) suggest some interesting ways in which both memory and cognition can be seen as both embodied and distributed, so cognition is not individual but enabled by cognitive practices and context. In this fashion, memory, as well as cognition, can be seen as "potentially spreading across the world and body as well as brain" (Sutton 2006: 282), so that the "remembering and feeling embodied subject is thoroughly embedded in natural, technological, social, and internal environments" (Sutton 2006: 287). Consequently, memory complexes, the suite of institutions such as museums, heritage sites, history education, and memory practices, can be seen as elements of both individual and social cognition and memory, which have affective/emotional dimensions that are not arbitrary or marginal, but essential constitutive and linking elements.

Campbell's (2003, 2006) work makes some very evocative links between personal and social memory, and emotion and performance, drawing on Ricoeur's (2004) injunction that being faithful to the past requires both judging aspects of the past by the concerns of the present, and sharing remembering via narrative, representations in public space, and interactions with others. She argues for the importance of significance in remembering, in that significance is important for both accuracy and integrity, and points to the power of emotion in energizing this: "an important way we are guided by the past is through the emotion in memory that both represents the significance of the past, and, in its evocation, continues to give the past power" (Campbell 2006: 364).

Drawing on the work of the philosopher Alan Morton (2002), Campbell develops the idea of "emotional truth," in which ideas of accuracy or truth do not require minute details, but rather captures the salience of context, which addresses both the situation as it is and the potential for a range of possible outcomes. Campbell draws two important conclusions about emotion and memory from this. Firstly, she stresses how this formulation builds on the emerging tendency not to dismiss emotion as a-rational or irrational, but rather to stress "the complex notion of *appropriateness* or fit, an evaluation sensitive to how we represent the world through responses that have a central role in guiding action via framing attention" (Campbell 2006: 370, original emphasis). Secondly, she stresses the importance of assessing context, which is, she argues: "important to the accuracy of psychological states that have a key role in directing ongoing response. Recollective memory as well as emotion can be assessed along this dimension of accuracy" (Campbell 2006: 370). This process is emotionally charged, and she notes that an "important way in which memory evolves is through the emotion with which recollection is imbued" (Campbell 2006: 372). Indeed, recollection here is defined as an embodied performative act, a performance that both Campbell (2006) and Sutton (2006) stress is not embodied or directed by place or artifact, but rather performative acts bring together people with divergent positions, to negotiate a sense of what the past might mean in the present. This is an argument similar to Smith's (2006) approach to heritage. The point we are trying to tease out here is not just that heritage and museums have a performative element, but that these performances are embodied acts involving complex relationships between emotion, memory (both personal and social), and cognition. These are issues, perhaps not fully formed, that researchers such as Bagnall (2003), Smith (2006, 2010a, 2011), Witcomb (2012), and Byrne (2013) have attempted to explore in heritage studies, explorations, we argue, that can be given further depth by the work of Sue Campbell.

Emotion and Meaning

Underlying Wetherell's (2012) position on emotion is the idea that affect and emotion have consequences for the way people understand and experience the world in which they live. Indeed, it is now well established in the literature that reason and cognition can no longer be separated from emotion (e.g. Reddy 2001; Ahmed 2004; Protevi 2009; Frevert 2011). Research has shown that judgments and evaluations are based on assessments of what Campbell (2006) calls "emotional truth." As Illouz (2007: 2) notes, emotions are not themselves actions, but they provide an inner energy that propel us toward an act; they provide the energy for cognition and evaluation. This energy, Illouz argues, is drawn from the observation that emotion concerns both "the self and the relationship of the self to culturally situated others" (Illouz 2007: 3). Further, as Mercer (2010) argues, emotions are used as evidence in making judgments and in underpinning beliefs, and feelings not only thus influencing what a person believes, but also their actions. Indeed, emotions are central to our moral lives (Morton 2013).

This is illustrated in the chapters in Thompson and Hoggett (2012) that outline the ways in which emotions underpin the work of political campaigning and public policy. Work by Eran Halperin and others has also demonstrated the ways in which emotions are used in altering people's political views and in mediating conflicts (Halperin 2013; Halperin *et al.* 2013; Gross, Halperin, and Porat 2013; Kappas 2013). The point of this is not only to stress the importance of emotions to cognition, but to point out that if an aim of heritage and museum interpretation is to educate or otherwise influence how people understand and use the past to understand themselves and others, then an understanding of emotion needs to become a central concern of exhibition and interpretive strategies.

In developing such strategies, however, it is useful to consider the interplay between memory, remembering, emotion, and imagination. Emily Keightley and Michael Pickering (2012) offer the idea of mnemonic imagination, which provides a conceptual framework to understand how remembering and imagination work together. They argue that remembering is a process of reassessing past experience, while imagination is what animates the material on which remembering draws. Thus, the interplay between remembering and imagination are vital in comprehending the significance or value of the past for the present and future (Keightley and Pickering 2012: 8). This work finds sympathy with Landsberg's (2004) idea of prosthetic memory, which also emphasizes the interplay of individual and collective memory with imagination and emotion. For Landsberg (2004), the idea of prosthetic memory describes the encounters people have with historical narratives in places such as museums, and the process whereby that narrative takes on a more personal and deeply felt memory, even though it may not be a past through which that person has lived. In this theorization, Landsberg identifies the "realness" of the material culture contained in museum as what she calls a "transferential space" to facilitate the uptake of prosthetic memories – new memories that are based on an understanding of difference, a difference bridged by empathy (Landsberg 2004: 135). These conceptualizations help to highlight the interplay between not only imagination and memory, but also emotion. As Morton argues "all emotion involves imagination" (Morton 2013: 3), where imagination allows us to grasp and comprehend possibilities. Imagination heightens not only the social or personal significance of feeling a particular emotion; it also underpins the energy it provides to action and cognition. For our purposes, understanding the emotion of empathy in relation to imagination, memory and remembering is vital.

Empathy has been identified as a key emotion for facilitating and swaying public debate on social justice issues (see Johnson 2005; Clohesy 2013). However, the idea of empathetic imagination, and the way it is often uncritically embedded in liberal discourse as a "feel good" concession, has been strongly criticized as a way of reasserting existing power relations when socially privileged subjects choose to confer or withhold empathy (Pedwell 2013). Certainly, there is a sense that "feeling sad" for another can stand in for acknowledging and acting on the observations of the existence of social injustices. Nonetheless, empathy coupled with imagination remains "a necessary condition for justice, democracy and ethics … [and] for us to live well in the world" (Clohesy 2013: 1). Empathy does not mean, as Sontag (2004) points out, that one can or should ever believe we can understand or imagine the experiences of others, but is important for sincerity. Further, as she argues, how one engages with issues of social justice depends on the context in which they are encountered; and it is important to understand these contexts, particularly those which can insulate and foster denial in the individual or collective being asked to empathize. As Clohesy (2013: 59) notes, Sontag's observations mean that it has become vital for researchers to understand the political, social, and cultural contexts that inform different emotional responses to issues of social justice. This has immediate implications for research into both how museums and heritage institutions construct such issues, and the ways in which their audiences respond to them.

Managing Emotion

The final point we wish to stress about both emotion and affect is that an appreciation that emotion is socially and culturally mediated requires us to consider the ways in which emotion can be consciously managed and regulated. This has important implications for developing interpretive strategies at heritage sites and museums, but also in allowing us to rethink the ways such places may be used by their audiences. The moment of affect may come upon us unexpectedly, as various commentators assert (Ahmed 2004; Thrift 2008), but this does not mean that affective moments are always unexpected and that they cannot be sought and regulated, or even if emotions do surprise us, that they are not then managed. Individuals do regulate and manage their emotional state. Indeed, as Mesquita and Albert (2007: 491) observe, people can choose situations and engage with or avoid certain people, places, or objects to regulate or otherwise manage their emotions. Certainly choosing to go to a particular museum exhibition or heritage site may be about regulating your emotional response to particular historical or cultural narratives. The point here is that individuals have emotional agency and make choices about how and where they express themselves emotionally, and what they then "do" with that emotional response. In short, people manage their emotions, and that management will be influenced by their personal, social, cultural, and political contexts, and by their skill in perceiving and utilizing their emotions, a skill some refer to as emotional intelligence (Mayer, Salovey, and Caruso 2008). The implication of this is that research in heritage and museum studies cannot simply confine itself to the event or instance of affect, but rather must engage with the agency, context, and above all consequences of the affective moment.

Conclusion

Traditional studies of heritage, museums, and history tend to privilege a modernist view of the rational subject, and as a consequence have either neglected or viewed issues associated with affect and emotion with suspicion. A recent focus in the social sciences on emotion presents us with an array of studies and arguments about the nature, significance, and consequences of emotions. What we draw from this is that not only is a focused analysis on emotional issues important, but also that they need integration into the discursive practices we use to understand and engage with heritage and museums. Moreover, this engagement needs to be based on a pragmatic approach to affect and emotion that starts from an understanding that not only are emotions cultural and socially mediated, but that they also have moral and political consequences and impacts. If we accept that heritage is political, that it is a political resource used in conflicts over the understanding of the past and its relevance for the present, then understanding how the interplay of emotions, imagination, and processes of remembering and commemoration are informed by people's culturally and socially diverse affective responses must become a growing area of study for the field.

Notes

1 These issues are the subject of current research by Smith.
2 Eighty interviews with visitors to the Tenement Museum were conducted between June 30 and July 3, 2012, as part of an Australian Research Council research grant (ARC FT0992071). The interviews consisted of a number of demographic questions to determine, among other things, age, gender, occupation, and distance traveled. These were followed by a core set of 12 open-ended questions. Responses to the open-ended questions were recorded with the permission of the interviewee. Interviewees were convenience sampled, and interviews were generally administered just before people exited the museum. Of the 80 interviewed, 30 (38.5 percent) were male and 50 (62.5 percent) were female; there was a roughly even spread of age groups, although those between 18 and 24 represented only 5 percent of those interviewed; 83 percent held a university or higher degree; 63 percent defined themselves as Caucasian American; and 76 percent had traveled from a vacation address.
3 The descriptions of occupation and ethnic/national identity are as self-described by the interviewees.
4 After the interview, the interviewee wrote in the visitor book: "It [the tour] reminded me of the stories my grandmother told me when I was a child! She came from the Czech Republic around 1919 through Ellis Island. She came alone when she was 16 years old with a single cloth suitcase. She was very brave and determined."
5 For fuller discussion, see Smith (2010b) and Smith and Campbell (2011).
6 For a discussion of NRT, see Anderson and Harrison (2010).
7 The over idealization of affect found in NRT is also a criticism leveled at the work of Ahmed (2004) by Wetherell, while more specifically Wetherell finds issue with the way embodiment becomes lost in Ahmed's theorizations (Wetherell 2012: 158–60).

References

Agnew, V. (2007) History's Affective Turn: Historical Reenactment and its Work in the Present. *Rethinking History*, 11 (3), 299–312.

Ahmed, S. (2004) *The Cultural Politics of Emotion*. London: Routledge.

Anderson, B., and Harrison, P. (eds) (2010) *Taking-Place: Non-Representational Theories and Geography*. Farnham: Ashgate.

Ashworth, G.J. (2009) Do Tourists Destroy the Heritage They Have Come to Experience? *Tourism Recreation Research*, 34 (1), 79–83.

Bagnall, G. (2003) Performance and Performativity at Heritage Sites. *Museum and Society*, 1 (2), 87–103.

Billig, M. (1995) *Banal Nationalism*. London: Sage.

Bonnell, J., and Simon, R.I. (2007) "Difficult" Exhibitions and Intimate Encounters. *Museum and Society*, 5 (2), 65–85.

Bonnett, A. (2009) The Dilemmas of Radical Nostalgia in British Psychogeography. *Theory, Culture and Society*, 26 (1), 45–70.

Bonnett, A. (2010a) *Left in the Past: Radicalism and the Politics of Nostalgia*. New York: Continuum.

Bonnett, A. (2010b) Radicalism, Antiracism, and Nostalgia: The Burden of Loss in the Search for Convivial Culture. *Environment and Planning A*, 42, 2351–2369.

Bonnett, A., and Alexander, C. (2012) Mobile Nostalgias: Connecting Visions of the Urban Past, Present and Future amongst Ex-Residents. *Transactions of the Institute of British Geographers*, 38, 391–402.

Byrne, D. (2013) Love and Loss in the 1960s. *International Journal of Heritage Studies*, 19 (6), 596–609.

Byrne, D., Goodall, H., Wearing, S., and Cadzow, A. (2006) Enchanted Parklands. *Australian Geographer*, 37 (1), 103–115.

Campbell, S. (2003) *Relational Remembering: Rethinking the Memory Wars*. Lanham, MD: Rowman and Littlefield.

Campbell, S. (2006) Our Faithfulness to the Past: Reconstructing Memory Value. *Philosophical Psychology*, 19 (3), 361–380.

Cashman, R. (2006) Critical Nostalgia and Material Culture in Northern Ireland. *Journal of American Folklore*, 119 (427), 137–160.

Chase, M., and Shaw, C. (eds) (1989) *The Imagined Past: History and Nostalgia*. Manchester: Manchester University Press.

Clohesy, A.M. (2013) *Politics of Empathy: Ethics, Solidarity, Recognition*. London: Routledge.

Clough, P.T. (2007) Introduction. In P.T. Clough and J. Halley (eds), *The Affective Turn: Theorizing the Social*. Durham, NC: Duke University Press, pp. 1–33.

Cresswell, T. (2012) Nonrepresentational Theory and Me: Notes of an Interested Sceptic. *Environment and Planning D: Society and Space*, 30, 96–102.

Cresswell, T., and Hoskins, G. (2008) Place, Persistence, and Practice: Evaluating Historical Significance at Angel Island, San Francisco, and Maxwell Street, Chicago. *Annals of the Association of American Geographers*, 98 (2), 392–413.

Crouch, D. (2010) The Perpetual Performance and Emergence of Heritage. In E. Waterton and S. Watson (eds), *Culture, Heritage and Representation: Perspectives on Visuality and the Past*. Farnham: Ashgate, pp. 57–71.

Damasio, A. (2006) *Descartes' Error*. London: Vintage.

de Groot, J. (2011) Affect and Empathy: Re-enactment and Performance as/in History. *Rethinking History*, 15 (4), 587–599.

Forrest, R. (2013) Museum Atmospherics: The Role of the Exhibition Environment in the Visitor Experience. *Visitor Studies*, 16 (2), 201–216.

Frevert, U. (2011) *Emotions in History – Lost and Found*. Budapest: Central European University Press.

Goulding, C. (2001) Romancing the Past: Heritage Visiting and the Nostalgic Consumer. *Psychology and Marketing*, 18 (6), 565–592.

Graburn, N.H.H., and Barthel-Bouchier, D. (2001) Relocating the Tourist. *International Sociology*, 16, 147–158.

Gregory, K., and Witcomb, A. (2007) Beyond Nostalgia: The Role of Affect in Generating Historical Understanding at Heritage Sites. In S.J. Knell, S. Macleod, and S. Watson (eds), *Museum Revolutions: How Museums Change and Are Changed*. Abingdon: Routledge, pp. 263–275.

Gross, J.J., Halperin, E., and Porat, R. (2013) Emotion Regulation in Intractable Conflicts. *Current Directions in Psychological Science*, 22 (6), 423–429.

Hall, S. (1996) The Formation of a Diasporic Intellectual. In D. Morley and K.H. Chen (eds), *Stuart Hall: Critical Dialogues in Cultural Studies*. London: Routledge, pp. 484–503.

Halperin, E. (2013) Emotion, Emotion Regulation, and Conflict Resolution. *Emotion Review*, 6 (1), 68–76.

Halperin, E., Pliskin, R., Saguy, T., Liberman, V., and Gross, J.J. (2013) Emotion Regulation and the Cultivation of Political Tolerance: Searching for a New Track for Intervention, *Journal of Conflict Resolution*, 58 (6), 1110–1138.

Hewison, R. (1987) *The Heritage Industry: Britain in a Climate of Decline*. London: Methuen.

Hochschild, A.R. (1983) *The Managed Heart: Commercialization of Human Feeling*. Berkeley: University of California University Press.

Hoggett, P. (2009) *Politics, Identity, and Emotion*. Boulder, CO: Paradigm.

Illouz, E. (2007) *Cold Intimacies: The Making of Emotional Capitalism*. Cambridge: Polity.

Jenkins, T. (2011) Lest We Should Ever Be Allowed to Forget. *Independent*, September 13. Available at: http://www.independent.co.uk/arts-entertainment/art/features/lest-we-should-ever-be-allowed-to-forget-2353599.html (accessed September 14, 2011).

Johnson, C. (2005) Narratives of Identity: Denying Empathy in Conservative Discourses on Race, Class, and Sexuality. *Theory and Society*, 34, 37–61.

Kalela, J. (2012) *Making History: The Historian and Uses of the Past*. Basingstoke: Palgrave Macmillan.

Kappas, A. (2013) Social Regulation of Emotion: Messy Layers. *Frontiers in Psychology*, 4 (51).

Keightley, E., and Pickering, M. (2012) *The Mnemonic Imagination: Remembering as Creative Practice*. Basingstoke: Palgrave Macmillan.

Kidron, C.A. (2013) Being There Together: Dark Family Tourism and the Emotive Experience of Co-Presence in the Holocaust Past. *Annals of Tourism Research*, 41, 175–194.

Landsberg, A. (2004) *Prosthetic Memory: The Transformation of American Remembrance in the Age of Mass Culture*. New York: Columbia University Press.

Leys, R. (2011) The Turn to Affect: A Critique. *Critical Inquiry*, 37 (3), 434–472.

Linkon, S.L., and Russo, J. (2002) *Steeltown U.S.A.: Work and Memory in Youngstown*. Lawrence: University of Press of Kansas.

Lorimer, H. (2005) Cultural Geography: The Busyness of Being "More-than-Representational." *Progress in Human Geography*, 29 (1), 83–94.

Lowenthal, D. (1985) *The Past Is a Foreign Country*. Cambridge: Cambridge University Press.

Lowenthal, D. (1989) Nostalgia Tells It Like It Wasn't. In M. Chase and C. Shaw (eds), *The Imagined Past: History and Nostalgia*. Manchester: Manchester University Press, pp. 18–32.

Lowenthal, D. (2009) Patrons, Populists, Apologists: Crises in Museum Stewardship. In L. Gibson and J. Pendleburry (eds), *Valuing Historic Environments*. Farnham: Ashgate, pp. 19–31.

Macdonald, S. (2013) *Memorylands: Heritage and Identity in Europe Today*. London: Routledge.

Mayer, J.D., Salovey, P., and Caruso, D.R. (2008) Emotional Intelligence: New Ability or Eclectic Traits? *American Psychologist*, 63 (6), 503–517.

McIntosh, A., and Prentice, R. (1999) Affirming Authenticity: Consuming Cultural Heritage. *Annals of Tourism Research*, 26 (3), 589–612.

Mercer, J. (2010) Emotional Beliefs. *International Organization*, 64, 1–31.

Mesquita, B., and Albert, D. (2007) The Cultural Regulation of Emotions. In J.J. Gross (ed.), *Handbook of Emotion Regulation*. New York: Guilford Press, pp. 486–503.

Morton, A. (2002) Emotional Accuracy. *Proceedings of the Aristotelian Society*, supplementary volume, 76, 265–275.

Morton, A. (2013) *Emotion and Imagination*. Cambridge: Polity.

Moscardo, G. (1996) Mindful Visitors: Heritage and Tourism. *Annals of Tourism Research*, 23 (2), 376–397.

Palmer, C. (2005) An Ethnography of Englishness: Experiencing Identity through Tourism. *Annals of Tourism Research*, 32 (1), 7–27.

Pedwell, C. (2013) Affect at the Margins: Alternative Empathies in *A Small Place*. *Emotion, Space and Society*, 8, 18–26.

Pickering, M., and Keightley, E. (2006) The Modalities of Nostalgia. *Current Sociology*, 54 (6), 919–941.

Poria, Y. (2007) Establishing Cooperation between Israel and Poland to Save Auschwitz Concentration Camp: Globalising the Responsibility for the Massacre. *International Journal of Tourism Policy*, 1(1), 45–57.

Poria, Y., Butler, R., and Airey, D. (2003) The Core of Heritage Tourism. *Annals of Tourism Research*, 30 (1), 238–254.

Prentice, R., and Andersen, V. (2007) Interpreting Heritage Essentialisms: Familiarity and Felt History. *Tourism Management*, 28, 661–676.

Protevi, J. (2009) *Political Affect: Connecting the Social and the Somatic*. Minneapolis: University of Minnesota Press.

Reddy, W.M. (2001) *The Navigation of Feeling: A Framework for the History of Emotions*. Cambridge: Cambridge University Press.

Ricoeur, P. (2004) *Memory, History, and Forgetting*, trans. K. Blamey and D. Pellauer. Chicago: University of Chicago Press.

Samuel, R. (1994) *Theatres of Memory*, Vol. 1: *Past and Present in Contemporary Culture*. London: Verso.

Sather-Wagstaff, J. (2011) *Heritage that Hurts: Tourists in the Memoryscapes of September 11*. Walnut Creek, CA: Left Coast Press

Sayer, A. (2007) Class, Moral Worth and Recognition. In T. Lovell (ed.), *(Mis)recognition, Social Inequality and Social Justice: Nancy Fraser and Pierre Bourdieu*. London: Routledge, pp. 88–102.

Smith, L. (2006) *Uses of Heritage*. London: Routledge.

Smith, L. (2010) "Man's Inhumanity to Man" and Other Platitudes of Avoidance and Misrecognition: An Analysis of Visitor Responses to Exhibitions Marking the 1807 Bicentenary. *Museum and Society*, 8 (3), 193–214.

Smith, L. (2010b) Ethics or Social Justice? Heritage and the Politics of Recognition. *Australian Aboriginal Studies*, 2 (2010), 60–68.

Smith, L. (2011) Affect and Registers of Engagement: Navigating Emotional Responses to Dissonant Heritage. In L. Smith, G. Cubitt, R. Wilson, and K. Fouseki (eds), *Representing Enslavement and Abolition in Museums: Ambiguous Engagements*. New York: Routledge, pp. 260–303.

Smith, L. (2013) Visitor Emotion, Affect and Registers of Engagement at Museums and Heritage Sites. Unpublished paper presented at the annual meeting of the American Anthropological Association, Chicago, November.

Smith, L. (2015a) Theorising Museum and Heritage Visiting. In A. Witcomb and K. Message (eds), *Museum Theory*. Chichester: Wiley-Blackwell, in press.

Smith, L. (2015b) Changing Views? Emotional Intelligence, Registers of Engagement and the Museum Visit. In V. Gosselin and P. Livingstone (eds), *Museums as Sites of Historical Consciousness: Perspectives on Museum Theory and Practice in Canada*. Vancouver: University of British Columbia Press, forthcoming.

Smith, L., and Campbell, G. (2011) Don't Mourn, Organize: Heritage, Recognition and Memory in Castleford, West Yorkshire. In L. Smith, P. Shackel, and G. Campbell (eds), *Heritage, Labour and the Working Class*. London: Routledge, pp. 85–105.

Smith, L., Cubitt, G., Wilson, R., and Fouseki, K. (eds) (2011) *Representing Enslavement and Abolition in Museums: Ambiguous Engagements*. New York: Routledge.

Smith, L., and Waterton, E. (2009) *Heritage, Communities and Archaeology*. London: Duckworth.

Sontag, S. (2004) *Regarding the Pain of Others*. London: Penguin.

Soren, B.J. (2009) Museum Experiences that Change Visitors. *Museum Management and Curatorship*, 24 (3), 233–251.

Southgate, B. (2007) Memories into Something New: Histories for the Future. *Rethinking History*, 11 (2), 187–199.

Sutton, J. (2006) Memory, Embodied Cognition, and the Extended Mind. *Philosophical Psychology*, 19 (3), 281–289.

Thien, D. (2005) After or Beyond Feeling? A Consideration of Affect and Emotion in Geography. *Area*, 37 (3), 450–456.

Thompson, S., and Hoggett, P. (eds) (2012) *Politics and the Emotions: The Affective Turn in Contemporary Political Studies*. New York: Continuum.

Thrift, N. (2008) *Non-Representational Theory: Space, Politics and Affect*. London: Routledge.

Tolia-Kelly, D. (2006) Affect – An Ethnocentric Encounter? Exploring the "Universalist" Imperative or Emotional/Affectual Geographies. *Area*, 38, 213–217.

Trofanenko, B.M. (2014) Affective Emotions: The Pedagogical Challenges of Knowing War. *Review of Education, Pedagogy and Cultural Studies*, 36 (1), 22–39.

Walsh, K. (1992) *The Representation of the Past: Museums and Heritage in the Post-Modern World*. London: Routledge.

Waterton, E., Smith, L., and Campbell, G. (2006) The Utility of Discourse Analysis to Heritage Studies: The Burra Charter and Social Inclusion. *International Journal of Heritage Studies*, 12 (4), 339–355.

Waterton, E., and Watson, S. (2013) Framing Theory: Towards a Critical Imagination in Heritage Studies. *International Journal of Heritage Studies*, 19 (6), 546–561.

Wertsch, J.V. (2002) *Voices of Collective Remembering*. Cambridge: Cambridge University Press.

Wetherell, M. (2012) *Affect and Emotion: A New Social Science Understanding*. London: Sage.

Wetherell, M. (2013a) Affect and Discourse – What's the Problem? From Affect as Excess to Affective/Discursive Practice. *Subjectivity*, 6 (4), 349–368.

Wetherell, M. (2013b) Feeling Rules, Atmospheres and Affective Practice: Some Reflections on the Analysis of Emotional Episodes. In C. Maxwell and P. Aggleton (eds), *Privilege, Agency and Affect*. Basingstoke: Palgrave Macmillian, pp. 221–239.

Witcomb, A. (2012) On Memory, Affect and Atonement: The Long Tan Memorial Cross(es). *Historic Environment*, 24 (3), 35–42.

Witcomb, A. (2013) Understanding the Role of Affect in Producing a Critical Pedagogy for History Museums. *Museum Management and Curatorship*, 28 (3), 255–271.

Wolff, J. (2012) After Cultural Theory: The Power of Images, the Lure of Immediacy. *Journal of Visual Culture*, 11 (3), 3–19.

Wright, P. (1985) *On Living in an Old Country*. London: Verso.

CHAPTER 31

Cross-Cultural Encounters and "Difficult Heritage" on the Thai–Burma Railway: An Ethics of Cosmopolitanism rather than Practices of Exclusion

Andrea Witcomb

The town of Kanchanaburi, in Thailand, attracts over 5 million tourists a year. They do not come for Thailand's beach resorts, to visit remote ethnic villages, or famous World Heritage sites. Kanchanaburi does not offer any of these things. Young Thai come to Kanchanaburi mainly for the river cruise boats, which, on Saturday nights, become floating discos. Family groups come for the region's national parks, to the north of the town. But a growing number of Thai, alongside a significant number of international tourists, come to see what has become known as the Death Railway, made famous by David Lean's 1957 film *Bridge on the River Kwai*.[1] Known officially as the Thai–Burma railway, this railway was built during World War II under the command of the Japanese by Allied prisoners of war and Asian forced laborers under terrible conditions. The Japanese wanted to create a link between the Gulf of Thailand and Burma in order to support their war efforts into India, which were under threat from Allied naval attack. The railway now looms large in both popular culture and in the memories of those countries that lost thousands of people to its construction.

A Companion to Heritage Studies, First Edition. Edited by William Logan, Máiréad Nic Craith, and Ullrich Kockel.
© 2016 John Wiley & Sons, Inc. Published 2016 by John Wiley & Sons, Inc.

Amongst the growing number of places associated with the railway and its history that tourists can visit is a small, now increasingly decrepit, museum in one of the local Buddhist temples. It is known as the JEATH Museum, an acronym drawing on the names of the countries with the closest ties to the railway's beginnings: Japan, England, Australia, Thailand, and Holland. The museum was established in 1977 by the then head abbot of the temple in response to the growing number of tourists and former POWs that were coming to Kanchanaburi to see the bridge on the River Kwai and pay their respects at the main Commonwealth War Graves Cemetery in Kanchanaburi and at Chung Kai over the river to all those who had died on the railway. While the town already had a memorial built during the war by the Japanese to those who died in the construction of the Thai–Burma railway, there was no information available as to what had actually occurred. In a U-shaped replica of the attap huts the POWs had lived in, the chief abbot of the temple put together a display to tell the story, largely using photographs from the Australian War Memorial and copies of various articles in magazines and newspapers detailing events. The abbot understood this museum as fitting in with the mission of the temple, which is to promote peace.[2] In their understanding, it was necessary to forgive but not forget. As the little pamphlet that accompanies an entry ticket puts it, "Dear visitors, JEATH museum has been constructed not for the maintenance of the hatred among human beings, especially among the Japanese and allied countries, but to warn and teach us the lesson of HOW TERRIBLE WAR IS. MAY PEACE ALWAYS CONQUER VIOLENCE" (JEATH Museum 2012, original capitals).

Figure 31.1 The JEATH Museum, with its transnational image clearly represented in the range of flags on display. Source: photo by Mike Knopp.

In a relatively short period of time, this museum became the center of POW attention, particularly from Australia, but also from other Allied countries whose men had died and suffered on the railway – Dutch and British in particular. Former POWs began to send the abbot photographs of themselves, either at home or at the museum itself. Sometimes, these photos are of entire groups of former POWs coming on a pilgrimage to Kanchanaburi. The abbot displayed these photographs in a small room near the entrance to the temple, implicitly making the statement that reconciliation was possible and that friendship between nations was the way to peace. Local Thai also participated during this early period by donating objects held by their families. These had been received in payment for essential items such as food and medicine on the part of POWs. In the museum, these objects came to represent an interpretation in which local Thai were depicted as helping the POWs and taking pity on them, thus establishing a history of cooperation and friendship rather than allowing a narrative of enmity or, alternatively, of being a bystander to atrocity from dominating. At the same time, former POWs themselves donated objects still in their possession, such as cooking items, to help the temple tell their story.

This history of exchange is now embodied in an annual pilgrimage by the current abbot of the temple to Benalla, a small country town in rural Victoria, Australia, to conduct a memorial service at the Weary Dunlop Memorial. Edward "Weary" Dunlop was a former Australian POW who was a trained doctor. He used his medical knowledge and his rank as an officer to establish makeshift hospitals to deal with outbreaks of infectious deceases and care for the ill and dying. He has become a symbol of sanity and the possibility of reconciliation and peace in both Kanchanaburi and in Australia, embodying the potential of friendship between nations.

I am interested in how this message of peace, embodied in the photographs and material culture of the POWs on display, produced by former POWs and local Thai people during an intense period of cross-cultural encounters in the late 1970s and early 1980s, can be understood as a manifestation of something other than either the production of "enclave" heritage (Ashworth and Van der Aa 2002) on the part of POWs, or narrow nationalist interests on the part of the Thai. "Enclave heritage" is a term coined by Ashworth and Van der Aa to describe what happens when the heritage of one group is not spatially located within that group's home territory, with the result that their minority status within a cross-cultural situation results in a strident affirmation of that heritage despite the cross-cultural circumstances. The problem is particularly evident around war heritage, when sites of significance to one group are not necessarily located within the boundaries of their nation-state, leading to the production of isolated enclaves that defy their cross-cultural location and which are thus inherently unsustainable in the long term because they cannot accommodate the existence of multiple interpretations of the same event. The more general association between the memorialization of war and national interests is of course widespread (an issue I will return to).

In this chapter, my aim is not to add yet more examples in support of either of these arguments – examples of which also exist in the Kanchanaburi region such as Hellfire Pass Museum, which was funded by the Australian government (Beaumont 2012). Instead, I wish to work with examples that cannot be entirely comprehended within these nationalist frameworks. More specifically, my aim is to use the traces of cross-cultural encounters at places like the JEATH Museum as an entry point into a discussion about the ways in which, sometimes, the construction of war heritage is used not for jingoistic, patriotic causes but their opposite: attempts to argue for peace, demonstrate remorse, and engage in acts of reconciliation and atonement (see also Logan and Witcomb 2013; Witcomb 2012) in ways that seem to be motivated by an ethics of cosmopolitanism (Meskell 2009, this volume). As the examples I want to engage with show, however, these moments tend to be produced by private individuals and organizations rather than the state, are of the moment, and respond to particular conjunctures. They are, as a consequence, essentially ephemeral in nature. This ephemerality, however, should not be seen as undermining the significance of the cultural work involved in such practices.

In giving attention to these phenomena, I am aiming to produce a space for the analysis of heritage that does more than produce either an ideological reading of the site or exhibition in question in terms of a politics of identity, or a political and economic analysis of the processes involved in the production of heritage. This is not because I discount the value of such analyses, but because I do not think they encompass all that there is to be noticed and understood within the landscape of heritage. We need to find ways of training our gaze towards the ephemeral, to that which appears to be of little consequence, perhaps quaint and antiquarian in sensibility or the work of amateurs rather than professionals, and add our understanding of these phenomena to our understanding of the work that heritage does in society. What I am after is a space for the analysis of heritage which sets in motion a conversation between the more conventional discussion of heritage as a site of ideological productions which reflect hegemonic interests by supporting particular economic and political investments, and the growing recognition that heritage also embodies far more localized, personal, emotional, and affective relationships. While some of these may concur with large-scale interests that are often exclusionary in nature, this is not always the case. My arguments however, are not simply located in a call for "heritage from below" in a repeat of the heritage debates of the late 1980s and early 1990s (see e.g. Samuels 1984). They are in fact located in using what many are calling the "material turn," with its links to theories of affect, the recognition of the role played by emotion in expressions of heritage, and the ways in which all these things impact on people's understanding of their sense of self in relation to others.[3]

In what follows, then, my method of analysis is not dominated by the more traditional textual or discursive mode of analysis. Instead, I focus on moments of encounter, played out through various performative practices, which, I argue, produce a form of heritage practice in their own right. In doing so I will also be making use of a particular suite of theoretical ideas that help me to identify these moments, and to analyze them in ways that are sensitive to the ideals they embody. In the cases I wish to engage with, these ideals are not the reinforcement of fixed identities but the production of spaces for cross-cultural encounters that encourage a more cosmopolitan approach to the politics of identity.

Conventional Approaches to Heritage and Identity

To say that heritage is strongly associated with identity and that, for many, its purpose is to differentiate one group from another is a truism. We talk of heritage in a way that implies that heritage is something that can be first of all owned, and that there is a clear owner – it belongs to somebody (Davison 2000). Heritage has thus been understood as a differentiating machine, constructing, reproducing, and representing a variety of heritage resources (places, artifacts, landscapes, and intangible forms of cultural practices) to valorize some forms of identity over others, and to associate a territory with a particular group (Graham, Ashworth, and Tunbridge 2000; Graham and Howard 2008).

This is perhaps no more evident than in the production of war heritage. War is an experience that is universally taken as a nation-defining moment, and attains a quasi-religious status in which the death of young men is taken as the ultimate sacrifice for the nation, and thus it is given a redemptive meaning (Ashplant, Dawson, and Roper 2000). It is thus not surprising, as Martin Gegner and Bart Ziino put it, that "The political heritage of war has been the building of nations and empires" (Gegner and Ziino 2012: 1). In Australia, where the attainment of nationhood is universally associated with the failed Gallipoli campaign during World War I, in which 8700 young Australians died, this is particularly true. Despite many critical voices (see Lake *et al.* 2010), the experience of war still defines what many understand it is to be Australian, through the values of what has come to be known as the ANZAC legend in which mateship, courage, and fierce determination define national identity. As in other examples around the world, this is a classic case of the production of an "imagined community" (Anderson 1983), in which heritage resources are put to work, recycling and reinforcing national narratives (Graham, Ashworth, and Tunbridge 2000) in ways that support celebratory narratives through the reinforcement of well-established historiographies that have a deep anchor within national collective memory. The memorialization and commemoration of war is thus interpreted as reflecting national narratives of identity in which national interests and perspectives are foremost (see e.g. Linantud 2008; Daugbjerg 2009).

The Development of More Pluralist Understandings of Heritage

Both critical heritage practice and critical heritage studies have sought ways in which this exclusivist mode of practicing and thinking about heritage can be challenged. In the main, I would argue that this has been done through a politics of pluralism, a politics that attempts to give equal weight to the representation of diverse forms of heritage, and through that to multiple communities and their identities. That has involved, as Ashworth and Tunbridge (1996) put it, a recognition that heritage can be "dissonant" as it may not mean the same thing to all people. Its interpretation thus needs to be polysemic, addressing multiple viewpoints (see also Ashworth, Graham, and Tunbridge 2007; Graham and Howard 2008).

While such strategies recognize dissonance and the cultures of minority groups, they also reinforce the strong association between heritage and identity and, by extension, fixed understandings of culture. There is not a lot of space, within this perspective, for paying much attention either to transnational cultural formations or even to the possibility that the production of heritage might not always be about the production of a fixed notion of identity. A collateral problem, as many critics of multiculturalism point out, is that these strategies actually work to reinforce differences in ways that produce enclave communities that are exclusive in nature (Hage 1998; Lydon 2009). As Ghassan Hage put it, in the context of museums these strategies have promoted a "zoological multiculturalism" (Hage 1998: 160–63) in which each group remains not only within its pigeon hole but is marked as different from a dominant mainstream. The problem then is that these strategies leave the other as "other," and they do not promote what might be described as a cosmopolitan ethic – an ethic where the willingness to open up oneself to the "other" results in some form of transformative experience which shakes the roots of established identities and ways of thinking (see Meskell 2009; Appiah 2007; Beck 2006). In situations where a particular place might be important to multiple stakeholders, who may not have the same memories of the past, or in contexts where heritage is not only dissonant but also difficult (Logan and Reeves 2009; Macdonald 2009a), in that it brings into the present a past than many would prefer to forget and even erase, this seems to be a particularly important question to address.

It is in this context that I have become interested in exploring more fleeting and momentary encounters between self and other at heritage sites and museums, using a different theoretical tool kit from that normally associated with the production of identity narratives – one that borrows from recent work on the ways in which our sense of self owes as much to our embodied experiences of the world, realized through our affective response to both material and non-material encounters in the form of objects, places, and people.[4] This work forms part of what has been more widely described as a material or "sensorial turn" (Dudley 2010), or even a "performative turn" (Latour and Weibel 2007), which places importance on experience rather than representation, and is thus often referred as a movement for looking at the "more than representational" (see Lorimer 2005; Waterton and Watson 2013).

Much of this work is increasingly applied to understanding how we engage with heritage practices by focusing on the personal, the ordinary, and the everyday as they are manifested through "sensorial, haptic, corporeal and kinaesthetic experiences" (Cromby 2007: 96) that occur as we engage with heritage sites through such practices as ritual performances, dialogues with interlocutors, and interactions with objects, landscapes, and people (Crouch 2012; Dudley 2010; Macdonald 2009a; Byrne 2013). Within a wider theoretical landscape, this focus could also be understood as part of actor-network theory, in which relations between material and non-material worlds, between people and objects, is understood as forming a network of agents called an "assemblage" (Law 2004; Latour 2005). As Sharon Macdonald has observed in her work on the difficult Nazi heritage of Nuremberg, "Taking an assemblage perspective on heritage directs our attention less to finished 'heritage products' than to processes and entanglements involved in their coming into being and continuation" (Macdonald 2009b: 118). It also points our attention to the point of contact and to processes of enactment, in which both moments of established forms of identity and moments of instability are performed. Recognizing these moments involves letting go of the idea that museums and heritage sites offer prepackaged representations for the visual consumption of audiences in a way that presupposes a distance between viewer and viewed. The idea that this distance is integral to the ways in which exhibitions work is well established. As Tony Bennett (2004) reminds us, the nineteenth-century museum produced "ways of seeing" which supported this distance by presuming it was possible to represent the world in an ordered way, such that those undertaking the viewing were outside of the frame, looking down on it. However, it is also the case that if we understand exhibitions and heritage sites from the perspectives of encounter and assemblage, there is no distinction between viewer and viewed as they are both involved in a performative relationship, where meanings are produced through the relationships that are established at the moment of encounter rather than given a priori. While collective memories and identities will inevitably inform these encounters, there is also a space in which the experience of the encounter itself can play a role in the production of meaning. The point is that this space can dislodge received understandings as much as reinforce them. From this perspective, both distance and closeness are an effect of the entanglements that occur during processes of heritage-making.

Encounters at the JEATH Museum

If we apply these ideas to the JEATH Museum and its traces of past cross-cultural encounters between former POWs and the local community in Kanchanaburi, a number of themes emerge. The poor state of the displays, with their fading photographs, layers of dust, and amateur presentation, does not make it easy to recapture the ways in which the process of meaning-making in the early years of the museum revolved around interactions between people from different backgrounds in real time. And yet, while all we can do now is look at the displays, what is significant about them is not that they are a representation of past atrocities, but that they are a trace of real cross-cultural encounters between groups who were enacting in the process of that encounter something other than a fixed understanding of their identity. In its early years, the museum was as much about the social present as about the past it documented. In this sense it was not a deeply nationalistic but a transnational social space, valuing a notion of community which Nancy Fraser (2000: 119) describes as one that values a politics of recognition over separatism and group enclaves. As visitors to this museum now, we are witnesses to a time in which the temple, the local community that supported it, and the POWs that came to it, were intent on developing a cosmopolitan practice. By this I mean that, in producing a space in which their encounters with one another resulted in an exchange of objects and conversations that led to a sense of a shared though differently experienced past, they were also building a shared future. They were linked. In a very real sense, former POWs were constructing their own personal geographies (Anderson and Gale 1999) in ways that linked their personal biographies to Thailand as much as to their country of birth. They were announcing that their experiences during the war had made them part of Thailand as well as their countries of birth, and that despite the hardships they endured there, the place had become important to them in ways that went beyond those experiences. The displays are thus significant for the ways in which they register the traces of these performances, embodying real attempts at cross-cultural encounters and acts of reconciliation. This, I would suggest, is what visitors can sense and are respectful of when they walk, mostly in silence, past these displays.

On the other side, local people were also engaging in a process of laying claim to their local history and place in world history in a context where World War II is hardly dealt with in the national historiography of the country, let alone the atrocities that occurred during the building of the Thai–Burma railway. The history of World War II in Thailand is deeply problematic for the Thai, who have always claimed that what happened around the railway was the responsibility of the Japanese and not them. Officially, they do not regard the railway as part of their history, and the tendency is to fudge the degree to which they were allies of the Japanese or involved in its construction (Reynolds 1994: 236). In Thai historiography, the alliance with the Japanese is depicted as a pragmatic accommodation to the realities of power balances in the Asia-Pacific, a devil's choice that was the only option available if the Thai wished to preserve their sovereignty and some semblance of independence (Syamananda 1971: 184–85).

While Thailand was forced to buy the railway from the British, as part of war reparations, they actually destroyed much of it, particularly its northern part, as they did not want a link with Burma, their traditional enemy. Much of it disappeared under a large dam, while other sections were simply reused for local purposes. In the 1950s, the line was reopened as far as Nam Tok, north of Kanchanaburi. The railway's historical value, however, was never recognized by the authorities – that is, until David Lean's film *Bridge on the River Kwai* made its appearance, and tourists started pouring in to Kanchanaburi wanting to see the film's setting. Despite the fact that the bridge in Kanchanaburi is not a wooden but a metal bridge, and thus different from that depicted in the film, and that its river was not the Kwai but the Mae Klong, the town responded. In an act of local agency, both the bridge and the river were renamed by the local authorities in order to capture the growing tourist interest in the railway after the release of the film. So popular is the bridge and the image of what has become locally known as the Death Railway, that the bridge now serves as the visual icon for the city, making it, as Joan Beaumont argues, the visual equivalent of the Eiffel Tower for Paris (Beaumont 2013).

Neither the bridge nor the railway itself are on any Thai heritage list, however, since this type of heritage resource does not conform to Thai notions of heritage, which are focused on royal sites and sites associated with Buddhism, such as the royal city of Sukhothai (Peleggi 2002). It would be easy, therefore, to assume that the visual

Figure 31.2 The "Bridge on the River Kwai," Kanchanaburi. Source: photo by Andrea Witcomb.

prominence of imagery concerning the bridge and the Death Railway – on banners, signs, tourist pamphlets, a local sound and light festival – is merely designed to grasp the tourist dollar which is now supported by around 5 million people a year, of which 7 percent come specifically for the railway (TAT 2011).

The actions of individual citizens and institutions such as the Buddhist temple that put together the JEATH Museum could be understood, however, as running counter to this narrative, and making a claim not only to recognize the railway as part of local history, but also to use that history to claim a significance for the Kanchanaburi region that goes beyond the nation-state. While public agencies have, in the main, not interpreted this history,[5] private carriers of memory have,[6] indicating perhaps something deeper than merely the desire to engage in the economic opportunity provided by dark tourism. The recognition that there is heritage of a transnational kind in Kanchanaburi that involves the local Thai could be seen to support a more cosmopolitan desire, as well as willingness to engage with global tourism. Inevitably, the two are in tension as, over time, this cosmopolitan desire also became an economic proposition as much as a utopian desire to effect reconciliation between former enemies, and even, perhaps, to help to atone for any role in the disaster. This should not, however, undermine the recognition that at the time of these activities there was a real desire to prevent future wars by facilitating cross-cultural encounters that worked through what had occurred during the war.

Weary Dunlop Peace Park: Contemporary Cross-Cultural Encounters

The Weary Dunlop Peace Park (WDPP), located about an hour's drive upriver from Kanchanaburi, is another attempt to express friendship and reconciliation on the part of Thai people. The WDPP is a testimony to an extraordinary friendship between two men: Kanit Wanachote, and Weary Dunlop. The men first met in 1984 when Dunlop was following the River Kwai by boat with some other former POWs, on a mission to find the Hintock River camp where he had once been a prisoner of war and had set up a field hospital. The group saw Kanit and his family in their residence – a significant home set amongst landscaped gardens above the river – which they took to be a restaurant. He called out in a friendly way, asking him if he had a beer. They were invited in and became steadfast friends.[7] Dunlop educated Kanit about the history of the area during World War II as, not surprisingly, the latter had not known about the railway given its place in Thai historiography, and explained why he was there and what he was looking for.

Dunlop became a role model for Kanit, and the two established a series of links between their two countries to strengthen the bonds between them. When Dunlop died in 1993, one third of his ashes were buried at Hellfire Pass,[8] which had, by that time, become a sacred site of memory for Australians. A further third of his ashes were set afloat on the River Kwai from Kanit's home in a lavish Buddhist ceremony, while the remaining third are in Benalla, his birthplace in Australia. Kanit built the WDPP on his property, going to great lengths to explain the ingenuity of Dunlop and other doctors in treating the sick, the kinds of conditions they lived in, and the illnesses they treated. One large covered space is devoted to an exhibition of images, objects, and media representations of the friendship between the two men. The park is dominated by a large wooden sculpture of Dunlop at its entrance.

Figure 31.3 View of the text explaining the Weary Dunlop Peace Park. Source: photo by Andrea Witcomb.

Most of the year, the WDPP is empty. It is not on the main tourist route, and it was only seen by the young people Kanit hosted on a regular basis at special youth camps that aimed to build cross-cultural understanding. However, every year, around ANZAC Day, April 25, when Australians commemorate their war dead in ceremonies in Australia as well as at major war heritage sites overseas, such as at Hellfire Pass, Kanit's place comes alive. An Australian organization called the Quiet Lions takes a tour to Thailand with former POWs and their families, as well as a large number of high-school children and army cadets from Western Australia. For almost a week they are based in Home Phu Toey, Kanit's resort. From here they explore the heritage landscape of the railway and attend the ANZAC Day dawn ceremony at Hellfire Pass, as well as the 10 o'clock service in the Commonwealth War Graves Cemetery in Kanchanaburi. They also attend a number of events organized by Kanit to celebrate the bond between the two countries and to remember the dead.

Thus the day before ANZAC Day, every guest at Home Phu Toey is invited to attend three ceremonies. Here I want to focus on two of them. The first is a memorial event for Kanit's wife, who, attendees are told, was a great friend of Weary Dunlop's.[9] In attending this ceremony, Australians are made honorary members of Kanit's family, paying homage to the friendship between the two families as a symbol of post-war reconciliation. The site is set amongst a landscaped rose garden in honor of Kanit's wife's love of gardening, with beautiful views to the distant hills. Respect for the occasion amongst the Australians dominates, even if most are a bit confused as to why they are there. There is a sense in which everyone understands, without having to be told, that their job is to embody and enact the continuation of this friendship into the future. The Kanits become part of ANZAC Day, and the Australians, a part of Kanit's family.

This is followed by a memorial ceremony for the spirits of the dead POWs in the WDPP itself, a ceremony that is, in a sense, a reciprocal gift. Sitting below the large sign with the ever-present phrase "The Death Railway," monks from the nearby temple conduct a prayer for the dead in which everyone participates. Within Thai culture, as in many other parts of Southeast Asia, there is always a concern for the spirits of those who die in difficult circumstances and who are not given proper burials (see Cornwel-Smith 2005: 178–183; Gesick 1995: 69). Their spirits are said to hang about and endanger the lives of those who remain. Special prayers are said to help the spirits release themselves. Those who died on the railway belong in this category. The ceremony is thus not only a memorial service but an attempt to assuage the spirits of the dead, to calm them. Those who attend often have a personal connection to those who either died or who endured the conditions of being a POW. In engaging with it, placing their hands together and bowing their heads in the prayer position, they become participants rather than simply an audience, and are thus brought into a Thai approach to commemorating the dead. At this moment, the possibility of a memorializing practice that is transnational and not steeped within a narrow patriotism is made possible, however fleetingly. Members of the audience become active participants in the ritual, participating in the giving of food and money to the monks in exchange for their services in releasing the spirits and preventing them from harming those present.

Figure 31.4 Australian school choir singing as part of the memorial service for Kanit's wife. Source: photo by Andrea Witcomb.

The net effect of the ceremony is, I would argue, to demonstrate that the responsibility to care for the dead and to remember them is now a joint one. Once again, connections between people are produced, enacted, and made to stand for peace. But central to this particular experience is the knowledge of the deep friendship between Kanit Wanachote and Weary Dunlop. If Kanit were not there, embodying that friendship, the ceremony would not have the same impact. This is because the audience would not be witnessing, in the presence of the testifier, what Kanit and Weary Dunlop stood for. The presence of both testifier and witness is needed since, as Auerhahn and Laub (1990) argue, a testimony only comes into full force if there is a listener that can carry that testimony forward into the future. That the audience engages with their role using their feelings as well as their bodies adds, I would argue, to the affective power of this witnessing experience as well, adding to the sense of responsibility that is incumbent on those who listen to testimonies (see also Simon 2007).

Kanit Wanachote, however, died in 2014, posing a question as to whether the Quiet Lions can continue to use this place as their base on an indefinite basis. Of perhaps even greater concern, however, is the ability to continue to embody what has come to make it so distinctive – the enactment of friendship. For without this park and the ceremonies that accompany it, without Kanit, the tour will lose the affective power that lies at the base of the performance of its cross-cultural values. When I attended the Anzac Day ceremonies the following day on April 25, 2012, the contrast could not have been starker.

Figure 31.5 The interactive nature of the ceremony to assuage the spirits of the dead: three of surviving POWs thank Buddhist monks for their prayers with offerings of rice. Source: photo by Andrea Witcomb.

At the dawn service in Hellfire Pass, I overheard one group of Australians saying, in reference to Thai dignitaries who had come to pay their respects as part of the service, "Why are they here? This is an Australian Ceremony!" Their remark was spoken loudly, and they were completely unaware and unconcerned about their location or their uncritical and exclusivist patriotism.

What is it, then, that makes these performances so powerful? There is, first of all, the lack of strong historical master narratives based on identity and national collective memory. Instead, we see an attempt at two important practices: the use of personal biographies to establish a bulwark against war, and an attempt to value direct social contact between different national groups in the present. Unlike enclave forms of heritage, which tend to value a single group's memories and understandings of events, these sites use what happened in World War II to establish a "heritage of peace" for Kanchanaburi which marks it as different from the rest of Thailand, effecting some kind of reconciliation and attempting to work with both local and international memories of what happened there. Crucial to this is the space they provide for a complex series of cross-cultural encounters. It is these encounters, rather than instances of "enclave heritage," I would argue, that might provide a base from which to build what Joan Beaumont described as a "memory of the past that is shared between the peoples of the host country and those outsiders who claim an intense interest in a land not their own" (Beaumont 2012: 21).

In pointing to the significance of these encounters for the issue of how to deal with heritage sites that invoke multiple collective memories, I am also guided by Michael Carolan's suggestion that "our understandings of the world are lived, embodied and tangled up with how we do things: our doings and our enactments in the moment" (Carolan 2008: 410). If this is so, our own bodily experiences and performances in the spaces offered by these museums and sites are integral to the way they work in ways that go beyond the telling of "what happened" toward the creation of a contemporary heritage landscape for the Thai–Burma railway not as sites of representation but as sites that enable the enactment of what we might call the contemporary intangible heritage of the war. In an important sense, the heritage significance of these sites lies not so much in archival knowledge, though they certainly refer to that, but to a repertoire of embodied performances (Taylor 2003: xvi) that speak to the ways in which these sites enable the production of heritage as a participative process, in a perpetual process of becoming. In this sense, they do not use archival knowledge to construct a narrative that recycles pre-established understandings of the significance of the railway. The uses of the past at both the JEATH Museum and the Dunlop Peace Park have contributed to the production of an intangible heritage in the present based on cross-cultural encounters post-World War II, raising a question as to what this might mean for our understanding of heritage, and whether this kind of heritage is sustainable or, by definition, of the moment only.

The focus on the future rather than on the past is also worth pondering upon. In an important sense there is something very different about the role memory plays in Thailand from the way Western nations have come to represent difficult histories. In the West, we tend to focus on the victims, driven mainly by the legacy of the Holocaust and the significance accorded to testimony. The focus is on the past. In Thailand the focus is on getting away from the past rather than dwelling on it. As Winichakul (2002) has argued, there are problems with this tendency, which makes it all to easy to avoid difficult discussions about the role of the state in overpowering opposition to its policies.

What it does do, however, at least in the case of the Thai–Burma railway, is facilitate a space in which cross-cultural encounters can be practiced and supported. In these ways, what is enabled here is something that goes beyond "enclave heritage."

Despite the lack of a direct confrontation with their own role during World War II at the national level, these Thai sites all embody a process through which the history of the Thai–Burma railway has become incorporated into local identity. They are therefore, a form of heritage in their own right. As I have shown, however, these sites are also extremely fragile, and at risk of disappearing all together as their founders disappear from view. We should not be surprised at this, however. After all, if heritage is the result of a process that uses the past for present-day purposes, then it stands to reason that it will come and go depending on whether or not there is an assemblage of agents that can support it. What I have shown though, is that its value lies not only in narratives about the past, in representation, but in public performances that embody relationships between people and place. These relationships are often deeply personal, but can also reach out towards others and produce new collective memories. However, if the carriers of memory are no longer there to animate it, it can become almost impossible to maintain those performances, and those particular forms of heritage may well become lost to both our view and our experience.

Finally, we could think of these examples as early instances of what others are calling a turn towards the pacification of war heritage (Becker 2014; Daugbjerg 2009). These discussions argue that the current pacifist discourse within the commemoration of war is made possible by a turn towards a more cosmopolitan ethic in which the recognition that these sites are of significance to multiple nations is part of what enables a less jingoistic interpretation to emerge. Annette Becker (2014), for example, has argued that current memorialization of World War I in France is doing precisely that: recognizing that its battlefields are important to other nations as well, and that, in the moment of death, all people are equal. Rather than a celebration of war, current memorialization efforts have turned instead to a pacifist narrative.

Others, however, such as Mads Daugbjerg (2009), argue that this turn to pacifism is attuned to what they call cosmopolitan nationalism rather than outright cosmopolitanism. In other words, it suits contemporary multicultural societies to develop more inclusive strategies of interpretation when it comes to articulating the national significance of their war heritage sites. For Daugbjerg, the turn towards a more cosmopolitan interpretation of Dybbøl, the battlefield site through which Danes commemorate their loss to the Prussians in 1864 through narratives of sacrifice and valor, is symbolized by a turn away from an ethnic understanding of nationalism. This involves a shift away from an interpretation of the battle seen entirely from an exclusively Danish perspective to one that makes space for the Prussian viewpoint, and which does not carry an anti-German narrative. This is in turn interpreted as a response to the need to develop a more international and humanitarian response to war, and the inclusion of international peace-keeping forces around the world in which Danes and Germans fight side by side rather than against each other. It is in Denmark's national interest, Daugbjerg argues, to develop a more cosmopolitan outlook on its own war heritage, and to make Denmark the birthplace of peace-keeping efforts.

While I would see the developments I have described in this chapter as an early instance of the emergence of this pacifist discourse, there are some important differences. Daugbjerg is concerned with softening the claims that cosmopolitanism is a social fact that is increasingly doing away with the nation. While not wanting to disagree with the need to take a less utopian approach to the emergence of cosmopolitanism, both as a term that describes a new social reality (Beck 2006) or an ethical disposition (Meskell 2009), the cases I have described are interesting because they do not spring from a nationalist but a local motivation. These sites are anathema within Thailand's own historiography and collective memory. They are not part of official discourse. And yet it is this cosmopolitan, pacifist rhetoric that enables Kanchanaburi to bypass the lack of interest on the part of Thai national heritage agencies in the heritage of the Thai–Burma railway and catapult itself onto the international stage.

These two sites are now on their way out as the life forces that brought them into being peter out. What has replaced them undertakes different work. At the ANZAC Day ceremony at the Kanchanaburi Commonwealth War Graves Cemetery, it is not only the Australian dead that are commemorated. The event has become a diplomatic ceremony with representatives not only from those countries directly involved in the building of the Thai–Burma railway. Also present are a range of countries with whom Thailand has a diplomatic relation and who were also involved in World War II, though not this particular site of atrocity – such as Russia for example. In some ways, while an Australian event, it has become a day of commemoration for Thailand, which does not have a day set apart to commemorate World War II, enabling it to participate in a transnational narrative. The ceremony shows just how hard it is not to frame the commemoration of war within national frames, and how easily local specificities can be taken over by larger narratives.

Figure 31.6 Wreaths from the ANZAC Day ceremony 2012 at the Kanchanaburi Commonwealth War Graves Cemetery. Source: photo by Andrea Witcomb.

Acknowledgements

This chapter is one of the outcomes of "Australian Heritage Abroad: Managing Australia's Extraterritorial War Heritage," funded by an Australia Research Council Discovery Grant. It was undertaken by the author together with Professor William Logan (Deakin University), Professor Joan Beaumont (Australian National University), and Dr Bart Ziino (Deakin University).

Notes

1 D. Lean (dir.), *Bridge on the River Kwai*, 161 mins. (London: Horizon Pictures, 1957).
2 Interview with the abbot of Wat Chaichumpol, undertaken by Joan Beaumont and myself, 2010.
3 For a summary of these, see Waterton and Watson (2013).
4 For examples of work in this vein, see Witcomb (2010, 2013).
5 The one exception to this is a memorial wall near the "Bridge on the River Kwai," which has some interpretative text.
6 As well as the sites discussed here, there are two more private sites built by local Thai families. One tells the story of Boon Pong, a local merchant who smuggled radio parts and information to the POWs and was part of the resistance movement. The other is the War and Peace Museum, built by a man in memory of his father who died from wounds suffered during an Allied bombing attack on the bridge.
7 Interview with Kanit Wanachote, undertaken by Joan Beaumont and myself, 2010.
8 This was an area of the railway that the POWs created by blasting a cutting through the rock during what became known as the "speedo" period, in which POWs and indentured Asian laborers worked both day and night. They did so under the light of dozens of fires and at a cracking pace imposed under brutal conditions by the Japanese, and which resulted in thousands of deaths. The name Hellfire Pass reflects the appalling conditions under which they labored.
9 Since Mr Wanachote's death on 1 April 2014, this ceremony is now conducted in both of their memories. The description here is based on the 2012 ceremony.

References

Anderson, B. (1983) *Imagined Communities*. London: Verso.

Anderson, K., and Gale, F. (eds) (1999) *Cultural Geographies*, 2nd edn. Melbourne: Pearson Education.

Appiah, K.A. (2007) *Cosmopolitanism: Ethics in a World of Strangers*. London: Penguin Books.

Ashplant, T.G., Dawson, G., and Roper, M. (2000) *The Politics of War Memory and Commemoration*. London: Routledge.

Ashworth, G.J., Graham, B., and Tunbridge, J.E. (2007) *Pluralising Pasts: Heritage, Identity and Place in Multicultural Societies*. London: Pluto Press.

Ashworth, G.J., Tunbridge, J.E. (1996) *Dissonant Heritage: Managing the Past as a Resource in Conflict*. Chichester: John Wiley & Son.

Ashworth, G.J., and Van der Aa, B.J.M. (2002) Bamyam: Whose Heritage Was It and What Should We Do About It? *Current Issues In Tourism*, 5 (5), 447–457.

Auerhan, N.C., and Laub, D. (1990) Holocaust Testimony. *Holocaust and Genocide Studies*, 5 (4), 447–462.

Beaumont, J. (2012) Hellfire Pass Memorial Museum, Thai–Burma Railway. In M. Gegner and B. Ziino (eds), *The Heritage of War*. London: Routledge, pp.19–40.

Beaumont, J. (2013) The Thai–Burma Railway: A Cultural Route? *Historic Environment*, 25 (3), 100–113.

Beck, U. (2006) *The Cosmopolitan Vision*. Cambridge: Polity Press.

Becker, A. (2014) French First World War Centenary Commemorations and the Politics of War Memory Today. Paper delivered at a seminar at the Alfred Deakin Research Institute, Deakin University, Melbourne, July 17.

Bennett, T. (2004) *Pasts Beyond Memory: Evolution, Museums, Colonialism*. London: Routledge.

Bennett, T. (2006) Civic Seeing: Museums and the Organisation of Vision. In S. Macdonald (ed.), *A Companion to Museum Studies*. Chicester: Wiley-Blackwell, pp. 263–281.

Byrne, D. (2013) Gateway and Garden: A Kind of Tourism in Bali. In R. Staiff, R. Bushell, and S. Watson (eds), *Heritage and Tourism: Place, Encounter, Engagement*. London: Routledge, pp. 26–44.

Carolan, M.S. (2008) More-than-Representational Knowledge/s of the Countryside: How We Think as Bodies. *Sociologia Ruralis*, 48, 408–422.

Cornwel-Smith, P. (2005) *Very Thai: Everyday Popular Culture*. Bangkok: River Books.

Cromby, J. (2007) Towards a Psychology of Feeling. *International Journal of Psychology*, 21, 94–118.

Crouch, D. (2012) Meaning, Encounter and Performativity: Threads and Moments of Space-Times in Doing Tourism. In L. Smith, E. Waterton, and S. Watson (eds), *The Cultural Moment in Tourism*. London: Routledge, pp. 19–37.

Daugbjerg, M. (2009) Pacifying War Heritage: Patterns of Cosmopolitan Nationalism at a Danish Battlefield Site. *International Journal of Heritage Studies*, 15 (5), 431–446.

Davison, G. (2000) *The Use and Abuse of Australian History*. St Leonards, NSW: Allen and Unwin.

Dudley, S. (ed.) (2010) *Museum Materialities: Objects, Engagements, Interpretations*. London: Routledge.

Fraser, N. (2000) Rethinking Recognition. *New Left Review*, 3, 107–120.

Gegner, M., and Ziino, B. (2012) The Heritage of War: Agency, Contigency, Identity. In M. Gegner and B. Ziino (eds), *The Heritage of War*. London: Routledge, pp. 1–15.

Gesick, L.M. (1995) *In the Land of Lady White Blood*. Ithaca, NY: Cornell University Press.

Graham, B., Ashworth, G.J., and Tunbridge, J.E. (2000) *A Geography of Heritage: Power, Culture and Economy*. London: Arnold.

Graham, B., and Howard, P. (eds) (2008) *The Ashgate Research Companion to Heritage and Identity*. Aldershot: Ashgate.

Hage, G. (1998) *White Nation: Fantasies of White Supremacy in a Multicultural Society*. Sydney: Pluto Press.

JEATH Museum (2012) Museum Pamphlet. Kanchanaburi: JEATH Museum, Wat Chaichumpol.

Lake, M., Reynolds, H., Damousi, J., and McKenna, M. (2010) *What's Wrong with ANZAC? The Militarization of Australian History*. Sydney: University of New South Wales Press.

Latour, B. (2005) *Reassembling the Social: An Introduction to Actor–Network Theory*. Oxford: Oxford University Press.

Latour, B., and Weibel, P. (2007) Experimenting with Representation: *Iconoclash* and *Making Things Public*. In P. Basu and S. Macdonald (eds), *Exhibition Experiments*. Oxford: Blackwell, pp. 94–108.

Law, J. (2004) *After Method: Mess in Social Science Research*. London: Routledge.

Linantud, J.L. (2008) War Memorials and Memories: Comparing the Philippines and South Korea. *International Journal of Heritage Studies*, 14 (4), 347–361.

Logan, W., and Reeves, K. (eds) (2009) *Places of Pain and Shame*. London: Routledge.

Logan, W., and Witcomb, A. (2013) Messages from Long Tan, Vietnam: Memorialisation, Reconciliation and Historical Justice. *Critical Asian Studies*, 45 (2), 255–278.

Lorimer, H. (2005) Cultural Geography: The Busyness of Being "More-than-Representational." *Progress in Human Geography* 29 (1), 83–94.

Lydon, J. (2009) Young and Free: The Australian Past in a Global Future. In L. Meskell (ed.), *Cosmopolitan Archaeologies*. Durham, NC: Duke University Press, pp. 28–47.

Macdonald, S. (2009a) *Difficult Heritage: Negotiating the Nazi Past in Nuremberg and Beyond.* Abingdon: Routledge.

Macdonald, S. (2009b) Reassembling Nuremberg, Reassembling Heritage. *Journal of Cultural Economy*, 2 (1), 117–134.

Meskell, L. 2009. Cosmopolitan Heritage Ethics. In L. Meskell (ed.), *Cosmopolitan Archaeologies.* Durham, NC: Duke University Press, pp. 1–27.

Pellegi, M. (2002) *The Politics of Ruins and the Business of Nostalgia.* Bangkok: White Lotus Press.

Reynolds, E.B. (1994) *Thailand and Japan's Southern Advance, 1940–1945.* New York: St Martin's Press.

Samuels, R. (1984) *Theatres of Memory.* London: Verso.

Simon, R. (2007) The Terrible gift: Museums and the Possibility of Hope without Consolation. *Museum Management and Curatorship*, 21, 187–204.

Syamananda, R. (1971) *A History of Thailand.* Bangkok: Chulalongkorn University Press.

Taylor, D. (2003) *The Archive and the Repertoire: Performing Cultural Memory in the Americas.* Durham, NC: Duke University Press.

TAT (Tourism Authority of Thailand) (2011) Tourism Authority of Thailand: Tourism Statistics. Available at: http://www2.tat.or.th/stat/web/static_tst.php (accessed April 10, 2011).

Waterton, E., and Watson, S. (2013) Framing Theory: Towards a Critical Imagination in Heritage Studies. *International Journal of Heritage Studies*, 19 (6), 546–561.

Winichakul, T. (2002) Remembering/Silencing the Traumatic Past: The Ambivalent Memories of October 1976 Massacre in Bangkok. In S. Tanabe and C.F. Keyes (eds), *Cultural Crisis and Social Memory: Modernity and Identity in Thailand and Laos.* Honolulu: University of Hawaii Press, pp. 243–283.

Witcomb A. (2010) Remembering the Dead by Affecting the Living: The Case of a Miniature Model of Treblinka. In S. Dudley (ed.), *Museum Materialities: Objects, Engagements, Interpretations.* London: Routledge, pp. 39–52.

Witcomb, A. (2012) On Memory, Affect and Atonement: The Long Tan Memorial Cross(es). *Historic Environment*, 24 (3), 35–42.

CHAPTER 32

Heritage and Cosmopolitanism

Lynn Meskell

Cosmopolitanism describes a wide variety of important positions in moral and socio-political philosophy brought together by the belief that we are all citizens of the world and have responsibilities to others. This ethical commitment is the thread that connects cosmopolitan thought from the Classical tradition to contemporary philosophy. Similarly, it is this ethical concern that has been debated in anthropology and the social sciences (Appiah 2006; Breckenridge *et al.* 2002; Brown and Held 2010b; Cheah and Robbins 1998; Hannerz 2006; Latour 2004; Werbner 2008). As archaeologists and heritage practitioners, our obligations may entail addressing the political and economic ravages of past regimes, enhancing local livelihoods, publicizing the impacts of war or extractive economies, and tackling head-on the incursions of transnational companies and institutions. Increasingly we find ourselves embedded within these processes in our fieldwork and scholarship.

In recent decades, archaeologists have been called upon to straddle these multiple scales, in large part because of the nature of our fieldwork, but also, more importantly, because heritage now occupies a new position in the global movements of development, conservation, post-conflict restoration, and indigenous rights (Meskell 2009a). Access to one's own cultural heritage as a fundamental human right represents a new challenge that is fast appearing on our disciplinary horizon (Disko 2010; Hodder 2010; Lilley 2009; Logan 2008; Meskell 2009c, 2010; O'Keefe 2000; Schmidt 1996; Silverman and Fairchild Ruggles 2008; Sinding-Larsen 2012). Rights to heritage and heritage rights have gradually emerged within archaeological discourse, and whereas once researchers were ill-prepared to enter debates that traversed international, national, and indigenous

A Companion to Heritage Studies, First Edition. Edited by William Logan, Máiréad Nic Craith, and Ullrich Kockel.
© 2016 John Wiley & Sons, Inc. Published 2016 by John Wiley & Sons, Inc.

platforms, that can no longer be the case. This chapter asks how might cosmopolitan heritage discourse and practice prepare us for these emergent struggles, in which archaeological pasts are drawn into contemporary struggles for recognition and self-determination.

A Cosmopolitan Perspective

The principles of cosmopolitanism can be found in the writings of the Cynics, Stoics, of Kant and J.S. Mill, then forward to Habermas, Held, Gilroy, Appiah, Kymlicka, and Nussbaum. We can say that, on the one hand, the world is becoming a smaller and more interconnected place, while on the other, our networked relations and responsibilities are now more expansive, multi-scalar, and multifarious. Recently, the global financial crisis and the impacts of climate change underscore the fact that events in one part of the world have a significant widespread impact globally (Brown and Held 2010a). There are longer historic trends, too, including numerous international crises in humanitarian intervention, the upsurge in genocide, ongoing military mobilization in the Middle East, as well as the long-standing global concerns of indigenous groups. Disciplines like geography, anthropology, political and social theory, law, and international relations have all re-engaged with cosmopolitan theory (Beck and Sznaider 2006: 1), suggesting that cosmopolitanism is not isomorphic with the global, the world system, world polity, and so on, as each rests on the basic dualisms of national/international, domestic/foreign which have become increasingly polymorphous and ambiguous. Nor is it simply another version of international relations, concerned with the workings of states and global power imbalances: cosmopolitanism is primarily concerned with people, and respect for individuals as citizens of the world regardless of their race, gender, ethnicity, religion, culture, and so on.

The tenets of cosmopolitanism challenge older notions of globalization or homogenization. The shorthand of local and global, caricatured by imputed cultural designations of traditional versus capitalist, falls short of the current complexities we all necessarily face on the ground. The utility of the term globalization, once descriptive of the macroeconomic turn, is further restricted by the fact that it now stands for everything and nothing simultaneously. What is appealing about cosmopolitanism is that while the processes of globalization lay claim to an overarching homogeneity of the planet in economic, political, and cultural spheres, the term cosmopolitanism might be employed as a counter to globalization from below. It also effectively overturns any notion that the local, situated contexts in which we work are isolated, traditional, disengaged, or disconnected from larger processes, institutions, organizations, consumer networks, and knowledges (Meskell 2009b).

Cosmopolitan theory and its application is being redefined by scholars across a wide swathe of disciplines. Cosmopolitans evince a willingness to engage with cultural difference coupled with an intellectual and aesthetic openness (Hannerz 1996: 103) that has become the hallmark of much recent postcolonial, collaborative, and indigenous archaeology. They may be against slavery and torture, but they do not seek to impose a universal set of normative practices: toleration is a fundamental principle, as is the recognition of our obligations to others. Anthony Appiah argues that cosmopolitans

> take seriously the value not just of human life but of particular human lives, which means taking an interest in the practices and beliefs that lend them significance. People are

> different, the cosmopolitan knows, and there is much to learn from our differences. Because there are so many human possibilities worth exploring, we neither expect nor desire that every person or every society should converge on a single model of life. Whatever our obligations are to others (or theirs to us) they often have the right to go their own way. As we'll see, there will be times when these two ideals – universal concern and respect for legitimate difference – clash. There's a sense in which cosmopolitanism is the name not of the solution but of the challenge. (Appiah 2006: xv)

Cosmopolitanism describes the situation we find ourselves in today; it is not a description of causal relationships, nor does it offer predictable outcomes.

It is easy to see how the archaeological past and present are situated firmly within a suite of cosmopolitan dispositions and practices (Szerszynski and Urry 2006: 114–15): extensive mobility and travel; consuming places and environments; curiosity about people, places, and cultures; experiencing risks in encountering others; mapping various cultures and societies; semiotic skills in interpreting others, openness to different languages and cultures. On the ground we also need to endorse cosmopolitan principles in our archaeological and heritage practices. Here it is instructive to consider the eight principles put forward recently by David Held (2010: 230). He urges us to adhere to principles of (1) equal worth and dignity; (2) active agency; (3) responsibility and accountability; (4) consent; (5) collective decision-making; (6) inclusiveness; (7) avoidance of serious harm; and (8) sustainability.

Cosmopolitan heritage work would support tolerance and diversity, and acknowledge that we share responsibility and obligations. In Habermasian terms, a rooted cosmopolitanism must address the tension between the principle of equal treatment and the aim of protecting cultural identity. Cosmopolitans advocate the survival of cultural diversity, value the inherent differences between societies, and support the maintenance of those differences whether among locals, minorities, or indigenous communities. In this sense, cosmopolitans want to challenge simple notions of globalization or homogenization. They are committed to the equal worth and dignity of different cultures and their implications for social justice. That commitment operates not simply on a state-to-state basis but to all those individuals and groups within and beyond borderlines. And they are open to different local and human ways of being (Ivison 2006).

Cosmopolitanism may not provide a stock set of solutions, but I would argue that it offers a useful lens through which heritage practitioners might consider this new set of multi-scalar engagements. On the one hand it encompasses the overarching framework of global politics and, on the other, it directs our attention to the concerns of the individual and the community.

Cosmopolitan Heritage Rights

Global justice is perhaps the primary and oldest theme within cosmopolitan writing, specifically concerned with how we create the conditions of global justice and the exploration of what moral, political, and economic responsibilities are owed to each individual. Responding to this concern for global justice has taken many forms in contemporary cosmopolitan thought (Brown and Held 2010a: 10). This *institutional* cosmopolitanism has inherent implications at the local level, so that *cultural* cosmopolitanism can be understood as forging a sense of global justice in a culturally pluralistic world. Given these different scales, how might cosmopolitan heritage practice prepare us for emergent struggles in which archaeological pasts are drawn into contemporary claims for recognition and self-determination?

Cosmopolitans tend to be strong proponents of the survival of cultural diversity. They value the inherent differences between societies and support the maintenance of those differences. But as a cautionary note, we cannot assume that striving for cultural diversity is a necessary good for everyone in the arena of heritage and identity politics. Surely it is problematic to privilege diversity for its own sake, and rather more important to recognize the situations in which individuals and groups actually choose to retain their distinctive traditions and relationships to the material past. There is a danger that we might force indigenous and minority groups to succumb to oppressive legal frameworks in order to gain recognition, or to even claim their heritage through the language of international rights. We should not presume that the maintenance of cultural diversity is an a priori desire for all people in all places.

It is notable that cultural heritage does not feature in the primary human rights document, the Universal Declaration of Human Rights (United Nations 1948), but rather the more polymorphous categories of "culture" and "tradition." Some authors (Hodder 2010; Meskell 2010) suggest that one way to think about heritage and human rights would be to demonstrate that destruction or appropriation patently deforms human capabilities and well-being (Nussbaum 1997, 2006; Sen 1999) and does damage for multiple generations. With the first clear mention of archaeological heritage in the Declaration on the Rights of Indigenous Peoples (United Nations 2007), there may now be some leverage to consider extreme cases where the willful decimation or controlling of heritage may do significant harm to the capacities or flourishing of a people or community. However, as a rule the discourse of human rights is so often caught up in exclusions and boundaries (Stacy 2009) that they may not always mesh well with contested heritage sites, where archaeologists strive to include more constituencies, to forge inclusivity rather than exclusivity given our long temporal perspectives. Human rights may, in some places, be the wrong medium for the complex ethnic and community connections archaeologists have become used to negotiating. Experts might potentially abrogate responsibility to higher legal orders and tribunals. Yet what really makes a difference in many communities is what happens on the ground, in more informal and integrative settings on the local, regional, and national scale, hence the appeal of a cosmopolitan sensibility.

Indigenous rights and the possibilities of transnational or cosmopolitan justice bring to the fore twofold tensions, namely between states and their minorities (or majorities), and states and the international community as defined by particular ruling bodies. The fraught relationship between national sovereignty and international intervention for the purpose of social justice thus resurfaces. The present aporia recognizes that nationalism, even in its most oppressive times, cannot be easily transcended by cosmopolitan solidarity (Cheah 1998: 312). The international public sphere is typically represented by nation-states – the United Nations is the obvious case in point, and exemplifies the uneven nature of member representation. At present a decentralized political system is operative where global allegiance is thin and populated largely by intellectuals and activists. Ultimately, for transnational agencies to be modified, progress must occur in cooperation with and through nation-states, and in those negotiations reside the same potentials for emancipation as there are for domination.

An example of the potentials of this approach is demonstrated in the writing of Chip Colwell-Chanthaphonh (2010; Colwell-Chanthaphonh and Ferguson 2004) and his development of an indigenous conceptual framework that embraces cultural difference.

In recent work (Colwell-Chanthaphonh 2009) he employs ethnographic archaeologies from contemporary Zuni, Hopi, and Navajo communities to underscore our obligations to embrace indigenous practices and worldviews, rather than retreating into a narrow view of protectionism. He concludes that there is no "universal" preservation ethic, since preservation itself is a cultural construct, yet international bodies like UNESCO insist that we universalize just such an ethic. Instead, our only recourse as practitioners is to a cosmopolitan heritage ethic. He calls for a "complex stewardship" modeled on rooted cosmopolitanism that acknowledges that preservation is both locally enacted and universally sought. For Colwell-Chanthaphonh, this translates into maximizing "the integrity of heritage objects for the good of the greatest number of people, but not absolutely" (Colwell-Chanthaphonh 2009: 155).

His views have strong resonance with the tenets of postcolonial liberalism, which assert that "cultural difference is real, especially in the case of clashes between liberal institutions and indigenous societies, but it does not follow from this that the differences are therefore radically incommensurable" (Ivison 2002: 36). Negotiation and discussion is key, as Colwell-Chanthaphonh himself has demonstrated. Heritage practitioners are increasingly learning that process is everything, and that their commitment to inclusion, participation, and ongoing discussions with affected groups is paramount. Importantly, cosmopolitanism entails openness to divergent cultural experiences (Hannerz 2006), which has inevitably become the hallmark of recent writing in interpretive, contextual, collaborative, and indigenous archaeologies (see also Colwell-Chanthaphonh 2003b, 2010; Colwell-Chanthaphonh and Ferguson 2007).

Those working within the heritage sphere could benefit from the insights of liberal and cosmopolitan philosophies that take seriously cultural difference, that identify both past and present identities as constitutive, and trace the concomitant ramifications for social justice. Taking culture seriously entails paying attention to its internal complexity. More generally, multinational societies still attempt to craft nationalism and continue to fall back on the flawed taxonomies of language, common culture, history, religion, or "homeland" in an attempt to forge common identity. A more cosmopolitan engagement would see the construct of shared identity as emanating from the various forms of practical accommodations and negotiations that emerge over time between the different peoples who share that territory (Ivison 2002: 166), and often these may in fact cross state lines. Jürgen Habermas places this engagement with changing cultural meanings that reside at the heart of individuals' and groups' understandings of themselves and the world. The historicity of cultural identities and their inherent fluidity are underlined, yet this is no ground for their dismissal under the law or international mandates. In that spirit, cosmopolitan theorists are committed to pluralism.

But cosmopolitanism is at variance with theories of multiculturalism, even if there appear to be superficial resemblances. Multiculturalism, I would argue, seeks to extend equitable status or treatment to different cultural or religious groups within the bounds of a unified society (see Benhabib 2002, 2004). While the ideals of multiculturalism are admirable, many cosmopolitans find this position problematic in practice since it can de-privilege certain forms of cultural difference, and subsequently disempower indigenous and minority communities who already have less visibility and representation under the state (Ivison 2006). Such tensions have arisen in multicultural states, such as Australia and the United States, with diverse populations and manifold tensions over the claims of culture, economic opportunity, and indigenous rights. Charles Taylor (1994: 61–64) argues that multiculturalism results in the imposition of some cultures upon others with a tacit assumption of superiority. Western liberal societies are visibly guilty in this regard. Claims upon the past are increasingly employed in land claims and other forms of reparation for indigenous groups (Coombe 2005; Goodale and Merry 2007; Lilley 2000; Robins 2002). A multiculturalist position might challenge indigenous privilege in the management and control of sacred places or objects for the democratic ideals of free and equal access for all. Alternatively, a cosmopolitan stance might go beyond this recognition of equal value and access by considering whether cultural survival and indigenous practice should be considered legitimate legal goals within a specific society. Many archaeologists would consider the claims of connected communities primary and, in many contexts, give them greater weight than other stakeholders. But we must also be prepared that while some groups may opt for cultural "preservation" and distinctiveness, other groups may prefer cultural integration and sometimes even "destruction" of the material past (see Colwell-Chanthaphonh 2003a; Meskell 2002).

Compelling work by Denis Byrne has underlined the strong cultural differences that resonate around heritage objects and sites across Southeast Asia, as opposed to the traditional philosophies espoused by Western heritage agencies. Whether looking at local modes of restoration and conservation in Thai stupas (Byrne 1995), or the excavation and ownership issues surrounding ancient objects and amulets (Byrne 2009), his work challenges familiar and entrenched dichotomies. Byrne positions Thai cosmopolitanism as sharply contrastive with the strict taxonomies that heritage practitioners and archaeologists regularly enforce. Through adopting the local point of view he details how ancient sites become the receptacles of empowerment, despite the fact that foreign scholars have failed to integrate indigenous religion into their own field practice. In a sense they elide the very magic in the present that they desperately seek to uncover in the past (Byrne 2007). Such an elision has grounded consequences, since local people and popular religion have been decoupled from heritage management, leaving both parties somewhat bereft. Acknowledging those embodied and affective perspectives toward materiality, however, might lead to more tolerant and less polarized decision-making processes regarding heritage, preservation, conservation, and use. As Byrne reminds us, popular religious practice does not require our consent, but rather it is the students of heritage who stand to gain by taking a cosmopolitan approach.

Margaret Swain (2013: 33) takes us in another direction altogether by asking how understandings of cosmopolitanism are inherently shaped by national cultures rather than existing solely as global concepts. It then follows that we question what is at stake when we simply and uncritically map Western concepts onto non-Western, albeit globalized contexts like China. From the perspective of Chinese philosophy, Swain argues that we could incorporate Confucian-inspired notions of a heritage-based worldview (*tianxia guan*) or a "worldism" that recognizes an engagement with a changing world (*shijie zhuyi*). For example, the idea of *tianxia* embodies the physical (the earth), the philosophical (the heart), and the political (global governance). *Shijie* can be defined as the dynamic and relational understanding of the world. Taken together, there is a focus on harmony for all humanity, rather than the Western idea of global citizenship founded on the nation-state (Swain 2013: 37). Both of these concepts, Swain suggests, are reflective of cosmopolitan ideals. In the context of China's heritage landscape today, two forms of cosmopolitan thinking are mobilized simultaneously. There is a Western cosmopolitan ethos that is strategically employed in the realm of academic research, tourism development, and through the efforts of international agencies like UNESCO. Running parallel to this are the Chinese concepts of *tianxia* and *shijie* that mobilize minority national unity as well as global tourism marketing. A Chinese cosmopolitanism or Confucian worldview could also be seen as a "kind of soft power, [which] shapes official nationalism, state sovereignty, and territorial integrity" (Swain 2013: 36). Perhaps the next step for those considering the relevance of cosmopolitan philosophy globally is to take seriously the ontological differences that particular cultural inflections bring, and the ways in which engaging with local knowledges is not only more relevant and culturally appropriate but in keeping with the fundamental notions of cosmopolitan responsibility. To some degree we have seen the same process in the field of ethics, where scholars have taken seriously the long histories and epistemic specificities of Buddhist ethics or Muslim ethics.

Multi-Scalar Approaches

Heritage studies have lately evinced the local dimension, placing local communities and understandings at the forefront of our research agendas (Atalay 2007; Chirikure and Pwiti 2008; De Cesari 2010; Hodder 2009; Kersel, Luke, and Roosevelt 2008; Salazar 2010). Simultaneously, many want to demonstrate global relevance, the impact of global networks and forces, and the implications of international efforts, whether aid, development, protectionism, conservation, humanitarianism, and so on. Both ends of the spectrum, local and global, have their limitations if considered in isolation, and do not fully consider the "processes of self-transformation in which new cultural forms take place and where new spaces of discourse open up leading to a transformation in the social world" (Delanty 2006: 44). The situations heritage researchers now routinely face warrants a closer look at the potentials of cosmopolitan theories for getting beyond the narrow binaries of local and global, to see how nations and territories themselves position international efforts and discourses, and how those are shot through with the specific contextual sensibilities of time and place. How the world is imagined in particular places is greatly at variance.

These developments do not only pertain to individual practitioners but to our collaborative projects, many of which are international and strive to make a difference in our host countries. Archaeological and heritage projects are increasingly self-styled as NGOs and charities, and, in turn, they are supported by other NGOs. World Heritage sites across the globe have a longer history of entanglement with World Bank schemes, USAID funding, and other transnational adventures (Brand 2001; Lafrenz Samuels 2010; Lilley 2009; Mitchell 2000, 2002). Governments, donor agencies, and corporations have all come to see heritage and tradition as reified public *goods* that could be mobilized for the greater public *good*. But more than simply its economic instrumentality, heritage is increasingly called upon to serve as a novel vehicle for national pride, spiritual recovery, and reconciliation. I suggest that cultural heritage today is always "future perfect," and is increasingly imagined as a vehicle for development and modernizing, as well as reconciliation and uplift. Capitalizing culture in these ways increasingly means that archaeologists and heritage professionals have to work with and between international agencies like UNESCO, transnational projects, national governments, and indigenous groups, while tackling questions as to whether cultural heritage contributes to the emergent human rights, diversity and sustainability, development and capacity-building, as well as human and global well-being.

Cosmopolitan perspectives typically find wide resonance with the concerns of political and postcolonial liberalism (Ivison 2002; Rawls 1993), as I have argued previously in my work on post-apartheid South Africa (Meskell 2012). Indeed, it is typically indigenous and impoverished communities in postcolonial nations like South Africa that have the most to lose, or win, in the recognition and restitution that might logically follow from the acknowledgement of history. Without an admission of the human past, I would argue, recognition premised upon historical and genealogical grounds cannot move forward in the present. In cosmopolitan terms, we need to counter South Africa's continued residual racism that imputes that certain people do not matter (Appiah 2006: 153).

Much of my recent work has been conducted in and around Kruger National Park, the jewel in the crown of South Africa's conservation, biodiversity, and wilderness heritage program (Meskell 2012). That research has examined the ongoing tensions surrounding the privileging of nature over culture, and the continuing sacrifice of historic recognition and restitution for neighboring black communities for the "greater good" of conservation. An archaeological ethnography (Meskell 2005, 2007) based around heritage sites and projects across the park further exemplifies the displacement of the historic past, and this has serious implications for the claims and rights of black descendant communities today. Such rights to culture and to the past, Weiss (2014) reminds us, are construed subjectively, individually, and collectively, thus questioning what we can do about safeguarding the freedom to meaningfully participate in such a cultural heritage. Her work comes with the warning that researchers must be clear about those instances where cultural heritage enhances human rights freedoms and claim-making, and those where heritage projects are largely rhetorical exercises that further risk injury or misrecognition.

At another level, the case of Kruger National Park also reveals the cosmopolitan frictions among transnational organizations, funding agencies, state projects, heritage bodies, and indigenous communities in and around the place of culture in a nature reserve. Both natural and cultural heritage are imagined in particular local and national ways, and each is influenced and impacted upon by global organizations and mandates. Funding for the running of and research at Kruger National Park is supplied by North American government agencies, private foundations, international organizations, universities, research grants, NGOs, and state and private revenues (McKinsey Report 2002). In this way, rights and responsibilities extend well beyond state borders. Notions of local, state, global, and indigenous are all pieced together from this complex mosaic of sources, resources, inspirations, and agendas. Thus researchers must increasingly examine new cosmopolitan configurations characterized by changing networks and alliances. Moreover, the burgeoning promotion and commoditization of nature and culture alike, with all the attendant promises, cannot be overlooked, nor can the widening gap between rhetoric and reality (Büscher and Dressler 2007: 588).

Conservation and biodiversity mandates, I would argue, have become cosmopolitan concerns in South Africa, while cultural heritage remains a troubled and very local affair. Yet on the wider, world stage, discourses of nature and culture conservation share a legacy and are now mobilized through cosmopolitan networks (Meskell 2009c). Resource use and sustainability largely inform cultural heritage priorities about site usage, occupation, and lived traditions, often undervaluing them when it comes to indigenous owners and stakeholders. Conservation is seen very much as a global good for a common humanity, whether natural or cultural. The language of sustainability

(Norton 2005), so prevalent in nature conservation, is fast becoming the rallying cry for heritage development as an economic growth industry worldwide. It is thus useful to ask how is the preservation and deployment of an archaeological past, or natural heritage, to be construed as a global good, yet simultaneously mobilized in practices of sanctioning, or worse, victimizing national or local constituencies in a new landscape of "culture wars"? Bruno Latour has critiqued this singular view of the globe, arguing that cosmopolitics cannot rely on the "first modernity" dream of an already existing common sphere. He underlines the tragic mistake of pursuing peace by dragging in the defunct globe as a locus for the common world (Latour 2004: 462). Here too we are forced to confront the tensions of privileging the global over the local, and ask who wins and loses when researchers superimpose international heritage and conservation agendas on communities who have been previously excluded from decision-making.

Final Thoughts

In crafting a cosmopolitan heritage, practice must continue to traverse the global and the local, whether we are uncovering global historical processes, international organizations and mandates, or shared responsibilities as well as attending to local communities, concerns, and ethics on the ground. We live in an "age of overlapping communities of fate," Brown and Held reminds us, "where the fate and fortunes of countries are increasingly entwined with one another" (Brown and Held 2010a: 13). It is for these reasons that cosmopolitanism has sustained a "growing interest and relevance because it is a philosophy and ethical orientation that takes account of the dense enmeshment of human beings – the connections between them, the bonds that link them, the interests that divide them, and the clashes of ethical and political outlook" (Brown and Held 2010a: 13). As they rightly propose, in this age of human interconnectedness, cosmopolitanism is a philosophy that generates a politics for our small world.

While there are various kinds of cosmopolitanism, attesting to the encompassing and plural nature of the philosophy, there are also important elements that are shared by all positions. Following Pogge (2010: 114), there is a commitment to human beings or persons, rather than to larger structural units, be they tribes, religions, or states. That is not to say that cosmopolitan theorists do not consider the position of nations or ethnic groups, but it is rather their members or citizens who are the primary concern within theorists' frameworks. There is also a universal element to that concern which attaches to individuals, and considers them to be equal, rather than to a subset based on religion, class, or ethnicity. Lastly, there is a generalizing commitment of concern for everyone. Individuals are the primary unit of concern, and must be not only for their fellow nationals or members of their particular group, but for all the citizens of the world.

References

Appiah, K.A. (2006) *Cosmopolitanism*. New York: Norton.

Atalay, S. (2007) Global Application of Indigenous Archaeology: Community Based Participatory Research in Turkey. *Archaeologies*, 3, 249–270.

Beck, U., and Sznaider, N. (2006) Unpacking Cosmopolitanism for the Social Sciences: A Research Agenda. *British Journal of Sociology*, 57, 1–23.

Benhabib, S. (2002) *The Claims of Culture: Equality and Diversity in a Global Era*. Princeton: Princeton University Press.

Benhabib, S. (2004) *The Rights of Others*. Cambridge: Cambridge University Press.

Brand, L.A. (2001) Development in Wadi Rum? State Bureaucracy, External Funders, and Civil Society International Journal of Middle East Studies, 33, 571–590.

Breckenridge, C., Bhabha, H., Pollock, S., and Chakrabarty, D. (eds) (2002) *Cosmopolitanism*. Durham, NC: Duke University Press.

Brown, G.W., and Held, D. (2010a) Editor's Introduction. In G.W. Brown and D. Held (eds), *The Cosmopolitanism Reader*. Cambridge: Polity, pp. 1–15.

Brown, G.W., and Held, D. (eds) (2010b) *The Cosmopolitanism Reader*. Cambridge: Polity.

Büscher, B., and Dressler, W. (2007) Linking Neoprotectionism and Environmental Governance: On the Rapidly Increasing Tensions between Actors in the Environment-Development Nexus. *Conservation and Society*, 5, 586–611.

Byrne, D. (1995) Buddhist Stupa and Thai Social Practice. *World Archaeology*, 27, 266–281.

Byrne, D. (2007) *Surface Collection: Archaeological Travels in Southeast Asia*. Walnut Creek, CA: AltaMira Press.

Byrne, D. (2009) Archaeology and the Fortress of Rationality. In L.M. Meskell (ed.), *Cosmopolitan Archaeologies*. Durham, NC: Duke University Press, pp. 68–88.

Cheah, P. (1998) Given Culture: Rethinking Cosmopolitical Freedom in Transnationalism. In P. Cheah and B. Robbins (eds), *Cosmopolitics: Thinking and Feeling Beyond Nation*. Minneapolis: University of Minnesota Press, pp. 290–328.

Cheah, P., and Robbins, B. (eds) (1998) *Cosmopolitics: Thinking and Feeling Beyond Nation*. Minneapolis: Minnesota University Press.

Chirikure, S., and Pwiti, G. (2008) Community Involvement in Archaeology and Cultural Heritage Management: An Assessment from Case Studies in Southern Africa and Elsewhere. *Current Anthropology*, 49, 467–485.

Colwell-Chanthaphonh, C. (2003a) Dismembering/Disremembering the Buddhas: Renderings on the Internet during the Afghan Purge of the Past. *Journal of Social Archaeology*, 3, 75–98.

Colwell-Chanthaphonh, C. (2003b) Signs in Place: Native American Perspectives of the Past in the San Pedro Valley of Southeastern Arizona. *Kiva*, 69, 5–29.

Colwell-Chanthaphonh, C. (2009) The Archaeologist as a World Citizen: On the Morals of Heritage Preservation and Destruction. In L. Meskell (ed.), *Cosmopolitan Archaeologies*. Durham, NC: Duke University Press, pp. 140–165.

Colwell-Chanthaphonh, C. (2010) *Living Histories: Native Americans and Southwestern Archaeology*. Lanham, MD: AltaMira Press.

Colwell-Chanthaphonh, C., and Ferguson, T.J. (2004) Virtue Ethics and the Practice of History: Native Americans and Archaeologists along the San Pedro Valley of Arizona. *Journal of Social Archaeology*, 4, 5–27.

Colwell-Chanthaphonh, C., and Ferguson, T.J. (eds) (2007) *The Collaborative Continuum: Archaeological Engagements with Descendent Communities*. Thousand Oaks, CA: AltaMira Press.

Coombe, R. (2005) Legal Claims to Culture In and Against the Market: Neoliberalism and the Global Proliferation of Meaningful Difference. *Law, Culture and the Humanities*, 1, 35–52.

De Cesari, C. (2010) World Heritage and Mosaic Universalism. *Journal of Social Archaeology*, 10, 299–324.

Delanty, G. (2006) The Cosmopolitan Imagination: Critical Cosmopolitanism and Social Theory. *British Journal of Sociology*, 57, 25–47.

Disko, S. (2010) World Heritage Sites in Indigenous Peoples' Territories: Ways of Ensuring Respect for Indigenous Cultures, Values and Human Rights. In D. Offenhäußer, W. Zimmerli, and M.-T. Alberts (eds), *World Heritage and Cultural Diversity*. Cottbus: German Commission for UNESCO, pp. 167–177.

Goodale, M., and Merry, S.E. (2007) *The Practice of Human Rights : Tracking Law between the Global and the Local*. Cambridge: Cambridge University Press.

Hannerz, U. (1996) *Transnational Connections.* London: Routledge.
Hannerz, U. (2006) Cosmopolitanism. In J. Vincent and D. Nugent (eds), *A Companion to the Anthropology of Politics.* Oxford: Blackwell, pp. 69–85.
Held, D. (2010) Principles of Cosmopolitan Order. In G.W. Brown and D. Held (eds), *The Cosmopolitanism Reader.* Cambridge: Polity, pp. 229–247.
Hodder, I. (2009) Mavili's Voice. In L.M. Meskell (ed.), *Cosmopolitan Archaeologies.* Durham, NC: Duke University Press, pp. 184–204.
Hodder, I. (2010) Cultural Heritage Rights: From Ownership and Descent to Justice and Well-Being. *Anthropological Quarterly*, 83, 861–882.
Ivison, D. (2002) *Postcolonial Liberalism.* Cambridge: Cambridge University Press.
Ivison, D. (2006) Emergent Cosmopolitanism: Indigenous Peoples and International Law. In R. Tinnevelt and G. Verschraegen (eds), *Between Cosmopolitan Ideals and State Sovereignty.* New York: Palgrave, pp. 120–134.
Kersel, M.M., Luke, C., and Roosevelt, C.H. (2008) Valuing the Past: Perceptions of Archaeological Practice in Lydia and the Levant. *Journal of Social Archaeology*, 8, 298–319.
Lafrenz Samuels, K. (2010) Mobilizing Heritage in the Maghrib: Rights, Development, and Transnational Archaeologies. Ph.D. dissertation. Stanford, CA: Department of Anthropology, Stanford University.
Latour, B. (2004) Whose Cosmos, which Cosmopolitics? *Common Knowledge*, 10, 450–462.
Lilley, I. (ed.) (2000) *Native Title and the Transformation of Archaeology in the Postcolonial World.* Oceania Monographs No. 50. Sydney: University of Sydney.
Lilley, I. (2009) Strangers and Brothers? Heritage, Human Rights, and Cosmopolitan Archaeology in Oceania. In L.M. Meskell (ed.), *Cosmopolitan Archaeologies.* Durham, NC: Duke University Press, pp. 48–67.
Logan, W. (2008) Cultural Diversity, Heritage and Human Rights. In B. Graham and P. Howard (eds), *The Ashgate Companion to Heritage and Identity.* Farnham: Ashgate, pp. 439–454.
McKinsey Report (2002) SANParks and McKinsey Final Meeting. Pretoria: South Africa National Parks.
Meskell, L.M. (2002) Negative Heritage and Past Mastering in Archaeology. *Anthropological Quarterly*, 75, 557–574.
Meskell, L.M. (2005) Archaeological Ethnography: Conversations around Kruger National Park. *Archaeologies: Journal of the World Archaeology Congress*, 1, 83–102.
Meskell, L.M. (2007) Falling Walls and Mending Fences: Archaeological Ethnography in the Limpopo. *Journal of Southern African Studies*, 33, 383–400.
Meskell, L.M. (ed.) (2009a) *Cosmopolitan Archaeologies.* Durham, NC: Duke University Press.
Meskell, L.M. (2009b) Cosmopolitan Heritage Ethics. In L.M. Meskell (ed.), *Cosmopolitan Archaeologies.* Durham, NC: Duke University Press, pp. 1–27.
Meskell, L.M. (2009c) The Nature of Culture in Kruger National Park. In L.M. Meskell (ed.), *Cosmopolitan Archaeologies.* Durham, NC: Duke University Press, pp. 89–112.
Meskell, L.M. (2010) Human Rights and Heritage Ethics. *Anthropological Quarterly*, 83, 839–860.
Meskell, L.M. (2012) *The Nature of Heritage: The New South Africa.* Oxford: Blackwell.
Mitchell, T. (2000) Making the Nation: The Politics of Heritage in Egypt. In N.A. Sayyad (ed.), *Global Forms/Urban Norms: On the Manufacture and Consumption of Traditions in the Built Environment.* London: E & F Spon/Routledge, pp. 212–239.
Mitchell, T. (2002) *Rule of Experts.* Berkeley: University of California Press.
Norton, B.G. (2005) *Sustainability: A Philosophy of Adaptive Ecosystem Management.* Chicago: University of Chicago Press.
Nussbaum, M.C. (1997) Capabilities and Human Rights. *Fordham Law Review*, 66, 273–300.
Nussbaum, M.C. (2006) *Frontiers of Justice: Disability, Nationality, Species Membership.* Cambridge, MA: Belknap Press.
O'Keefe, P. (2000) Archaeology and Human Rights. *Public Archaeology*, 1, 181–194.

Pogge, T. (2010) Cosmopolitanism and Sovereignty. In G.W. Brown and D. Held (eds), *The Cosmopolitanism Reader*. Cambridge: Polity, pp. 114–133.

Rawls, J. (1993) *Political Liberalism*. New York: Columbia University Press.

Robins, S. (2002) Land Struggles and the Politics and Ethics of Representing "Bushman" History and Identity. *Kronos: Journal of Cape History*, 26, 56–75.

Salazar, N.B. (2010) The Glocalisation of Heritage through Tourism. In S. Labadi and C. Long (eds), *Heritage and Globalisation*. London: Routledge, pp. 131–145.

Schmidt, P. (1996) The Human Right to a Cultural Heritage: African Applications. In P.R. Schmidt and R. McIntosh (eds), *Plundering Africa's Past*. Bloomington: Indiana University Press, pp. 18–28.

Sen, A. (1999) *Development as Freedom*. New York: Random House.

Silverman, H., and Fairchild Ruggles, D. (eds) (2008) *Cultural Heritage and Human Rights*. New York: Springer.

Sinding-Larsen, A. (2012) Lhasa Community, World Heritage and Human Rights. *International Journal of Heritage Studies*, 18 (3), 297–306.

Stacy, H.M. (2009) *Human Rights for the Twenty-First Century: Sovereignty, Civil Society, Culture*. Stanford, CA: Stanford University Press.

Swain, M.B. (2013) Chinese Cosmopolitanism (Tianxia He Shijie Zhuyi) in China's Heritage Tourism. In T. Blumenfield and H. Silverman (eds), *Cultural Heritage Politics in China*. New York: Springer, pp. 33–50.

Szerszynski, B., and Urry, J. (2006) Visuality, Mobility and the Cosmopolitan: Inhabiting the World from Afar. *British Journal of Sociology*, 57, 113–131.

Taylor, C. (1994) The Politics of Recognition. In A. Gutmann (ed.), *Multiculturalism: Examining the Politics of Recognition*. Princeton: Princeton University Press, pp. 25–73.

United Nations (1948) Universal Declaration of Human Rights. Resolution 217 A (III). Available at: http://www.un.org/en/documents/udhr/ (accessed March 19, 2015).

United Nations (2007) Declaration on the Rights of Indigenous Peoples (UNDRIP). Document A/RES/61/295. Available at: http://www.un-documents.net/a61r295.htm (accessed March 19, 2015).

Weiss, L.M. (2014) Informal Settlements and Urban Heritage Landscapes in South Africa. *Journal of Social Archaeology*, 14 (1), 3–25.

Werbner, P. (ed.) (2008) *Anthropology and the New Cosmopolitanism*. Oxford: Berg.

CHAPTER 33

"Putting Broken Pieces Back Together": Reconciliation, Justice, and Heritage in Post-Conflict Situations

Patrick Daly and Benjamin Chan

Phsas phsa, the Khmer expression for reconciliation, means "putting broken pieces back together" (Ciorciari 2011: 438). In a discussion about reconciliation in Cambodia, Ciorciari (2011) argues that the approaches used to secure peace have come at the expense of justice and accountability. In this chapter, we will argue that heritage has been an integral part of this – possibly facilitating stability and peace, but also denying satisfaction and healing to victims of genocide. This exposes a major fault within heritage when it comes to war and genocide remembrance, and questions whether it is possible to balance supporting open and inclusive dialogue that might be valuable for healing, while eliminating violence and tension in post-conflict environments.

The positioning of heritage within conflict situations has received extensive attention from scholars, largely documenting the impacts – intentional and otherwise – of violence upon cultural patrimony (Meskell 1998; Tunbridge and Ashworth 1996). This maturing body of work by the heritage community examines the consequences of cultural loss on affected communities and ways to increase the protection of heritage. This dovetails with literature about the memorialization of suffering, tragedy, and atrocity (e.g. Logan and Reeves 2009; MacDonald 2009; Kugelmass 1995; Williams 2008; Viejo-Rose 2011), which we discuss in more detail below. Heritage has increasingly

A Companion to Heritage Studies, First Edition. Edited by William Logan, Máiréad Nic Craith, and Ullrich Kockel.
© 2016 John Wiley & Sons, Inc. Published 2016 by John Wiley & Sons, Inc.

become situated within a nexus of post-conflict reconstruction, economic development, and nation-building, which has received scrutiny by a number of scholars (Winter 2006, 2014). Recently, there has been discussion about the roles that heritage can play to repair fractured societies, offer solace, and facilitate reconciliation in post-conflict environments (Meskell and Scheermeyer 2008; Giblin 2013; Lehrer 2010; Rowlands 2008). A number of major NGOs, such as the World Bank and UNESCO, have advocated the practical application of heritage in post-conflict areas. The use of heritage by such organizations to contribute towards social cohesion and recovery emphasizes tolerance, respect for diversity, pluralism, and an implicit connection between healing, reconciliation, and remembrance. Heritage is seen as a potential platform for airing grievances, searching for truth and accountability, and providing a lasting testimony to injustices committed.

However, post-conflict situations are complicated, messy, and unique, with conflicting narratives, agendas, and various levels of empowered stakeholders. It is difficult to build a consensus about the needs of post-conflict environments and compose narratives of guilt, responsibility, and accountability that all stakeholders agree with and support – making it incredibly difficult to utilize a standard tool kit, including heritage, to remedy such situations. As we outline below, stakeholders in post-conflict situations often have disparate views when it comes to narrative construction, remembrance, and heritage representation that reflects contemporary agendas. There are also uncomfortable questions about whether it is helpful to engage with the past openly (which many heritage practitioners seem to support), or to forget and let the tensions of the past fade away, allowing people to focus on the future. Additionally, it is important to understand whose narratives are promoted, what voices are at the table, and whom expression, or silence, benefits or harms. All of this needs to be considered against the realities of post-conflict environments, which are commonly plagued by overwhelming social and economic problems, traumatized populations, and often internecine internal politics and power struggles.

In this chapter we discuss how heritage is used by different stakeholders to construct and rework narratives of conflict, and lay the foundation for longer-term recovery. We briefly outline some of the needs in a post-conflict environment, and how they intersect with heritage.[1] We then address current debates about post-conflict heritage, remembrance, and representation. We argue that the post-conflict construction of narratives is almost entirely problematic and selectively exclusionary, and rarely satisfies all concerned stakeholders. We find that heritage can contribute towards some combination of stability, justice, and reconciliation, but usually never all three at the same time, and often with significant compromises. We draw upon a range of cases and provide more in-depth discussions about post-Khmer Rouge Cambodia and post-World War II Japan.

Justice, Accountability, and Reconciliation

The cessation of armed hostilities is only the first step on the difficult path to sustainable peace in conflict-ridden societies. Issues and grievances are unlikely to have been fully addressed, even after the formal end of armed conflict, and it is common for animosities to endure, especially in cases of heightened brutality and civilian hardships (Berdal 2009). This is amplified in conflicts in which identity is one of the motivations behind violence. In some cases, such as civil war, combatants find themselves living side by side with their "enemies" post-conflict – further complicating reconciliation. Each post-conflict setting has a unique combination of needs, conditions, stakeholders, and objectives.

Of particular relevance to heritage is the tension between preventing continued violence and fostering stability, accountability, and justice. A pragmatic approach to conflict resolution focuses on providing humanitarian support for affected persons, demobilization and disarmament, the reintegration of combatants within productive society, and an overall reconstitution of "normal" social and economic functioning. This approach can overshadow "moral" needs, such as punishment for crimes committed, justice for victims, and accountability. It is widely recognized in theory that truth, accountability, and justice are important, both in terms of recovery and reconciliation, laying the longer-term foundation for an enduring peace, and setting precedent for conduct in future conflicts. Most scholars agree that reconciliation is an important part of the peace building process, and that it can bring about the "personal healing of survivors, the reparation of past injustices, the building or rebuilding of non-violent relationships between individuals and communities and the acceptance by the former parties to a conflict of a common vision and *understanding of the past*" (Bloomfield, Barnes, and Huyse 2003: 19, emphasis added). Successful reconciliation consists of multiple stages: fostering non-violent coexistence and initial dialogue; rebuilding trust and differentiating levels of guilt; and finally empathy, where both sides can begin to understand the positions and emotional responses of the other (Bloomfield, Barnes, and Huyse 2003: 19). In an ideal world, as the result of a transparent process, all parties would acknowledge responsibility for acts carried out, justice would be served, and all parties could be free to reconcile (which is the theoretical foundation of truth and reconciliation commissions). In such a case, heritage would best serve peace by bearing testimony to the facts of the situation, and reinforcing truth, accountability, and an inclusive set of narratives in which victims are allowed an open platform for their grievances, and have an opportunity to confront the perpetrators of crimes against them.

The moral demands of justice for victims, and the political requirements of peace, which often take the form of a compromise by key actors in the conflict, can be mutually exclusive. History suggests that pragmatic solutions usually prevail, as can be seen in the often token and symbolic "punishment" of those involved in war crimes. It is widely acknowledged that punishing all "guilty" participants is not practical or conducive to post-conflict stability and rebuilding (Bass 2002; Ball 1999). Post-World War II Japan and Germany are both examples of situations where strong interests wanted to retain existing power structures and administrative infrastructure, allowing guilty parties to slip through because of their functional role in managing society. People are needed to police, govern, and make sure that the trains run on time. In many post-conflict situations, perpetrators such as military elites often remain in positions of influence. Any attempt to hold them accountable for atrocities might be perceived as a continuation of conflict by judicial means. Prosecuting or even implicating key actors as part of enacting justice could threaten the fragile accommodation that led to the termination of the conflict, an argument that has been made by the Cambodian government to limit the scope of the post-Khmer Rouge investigation (Ciorciari 2011). In that case, amnesty and a lack of inquiry into wrong-doings were used to end the conflict, and played keys roles in an internal power struggle for control of the country. As we discuss in more detail below, all of the parties jockeying for power in post-Khmer Rouge Cambodia strategically manipulated narratives of conflict and genocide. The Vietnamese publicly held up evidence of Khmer Rouge atrocities, and established the foundations of what are now some of the killing field memorial sites and the genocide museum to justify in part their invasion and decade-long occupation of Cambodia (Williams 2004). Given Cold War politics, many in the West, led by the United States, opposed Vietnamese narratives, and went as far as to support the Khmer Rouge at the United Nations as the official representatives of Cambodia. Subsequent leaders in Cambodia, including the late King Sihanouk, current Prime Minister Hun Sen (Cambodian People's Party), Prince Ranariddh (FUNCINPEC), and Sam Rainsy (Sam Rainsy Party), have added their own spin to the events leading up to and following the period between 1975 and 1979. It is questionable to what extent any of this has brought about justice to victims, or fostered reconciliation at a vernacular level, but it has certainly influenced heritage in Cambodia.

Post-Conflict Heritage and Narrative Construction

The interconnected issues surrounding heritage in post-conflict situations have been neatly summarized by Viejo-Rose:

> In a post-war reconstruction context, the past is called on to serve various functions … Central to this process is the fact that [heritage] is selective; choices are made about what to explicitly "remember" or deliberately silence. As old symbols are reinterpreted, familiar landscapes change and new ideological connotations are added. Memorials can be used to construct a mythology for the emerging power structure, one that supports its claims of legitimacy and power. (Viejo-Rose 2011: 469).

Much of how we memorialize atrocity has been profoundly influenced by the Holocaust, and the heritage sites dedicated to the suffering and extermination of European Jews during World War II (Williams 2008). Part of the influence of post-Holocaust memorials is their perceived success at sustaining remembrance of suffering and laying out a clear case of blame. The construction of post-Holocaust heritage was facilitated by a near universal condemnation of the Nazis, and the manner in which post-war Germany accepted responsibility for atrocities carried out by the Nazi regime. There was a clear admission of guilt and a strong will and effort to atone. Given their total defeat, the Germans had no choice but to accept the resultant heritage narratives as their place in post-war Europe was dependent upon reconciling and paying reparations. However, the Germans were able to skillfully frame narratives in ways that gave Germans a unique historical reprieve by allowing them to accept full and complete responsibility, while deflecting the blame away from the German people and toward the Nazi party, a defunct political entity, and its fanatical leaders.

Since World War II it has become increasingly rare for war to result in absolute defeat, and common for it to be mired in internal tensions. Decolonization and the Cold War spawned countless civil wars, separatist movements, and low-intensity conflicts. In such environments, blame and responsibility are murky, and even when they are clear, it has proven difficult to enforce accountability, raising questions about the applicability of Holocaust heritage as a suitable model. The singular-blame approach has proven problematic when applied in other situations. In a detailed analysis of perspectives on reconciliation in Rwanda, Thomson (2011) outlines the powerful negative impacts of the authoritarian scripting of post-genocide blame narratives, which have led to the demonization of all Hutu, irrespective of their involvement in atrocities. The author makes a powerful case about how powerful elites can construct and enforce an official historical narrative of blame that can potentially limit healing and reconciliation. Framed around peace and reconciliation – and ostensibly influenced by Holocaust heritage – the Rwandan government has overseen a massive project that combines forgetting, forced abdication of ethnicity and identity, and a focus on the colonial roots of the divisions that led to the genocide, which has been systematically implemented top-down (Giblin 2013; Meierhenrich 2011; Hilker 2011; Buckley-Zistel 2009). It is accompanied by severe limitations on free-expression, diverging opinion, and critical assessment.

The results of several field surveys suggest that citizens in Rwanda, from both sides, might prefer different strategies to manage trauma and reconciliation, such as avoiding public acknowledgement of atrocities (Buckley-Zistel 2006). This echoes the findings of Rowlands (2008) in Liberia, where many citizens are eager to forget and move on from the trauma of the recent past. He details how contemporary heritage has been structured in a way to encourage "forgetting in order to remember in a suitable way" (Rowlands 2008: 138). As part of this strategy, people look to reconnect with their pre-conflict past through re-establishing familiar landscapes, sites, and places, which can also be seen in post-disaster situations (Daly and Rahmayati 2012). Post-conflict scholars suggest that deliberate or forced amnesia can prolong trauma, and potentially allow unresolved issues to fester to the point of renewed conflict. However, from the perspective of heritage, there is a conflict between respecting the wishes of local stakeholders when it comes to remembrance, and encouraging them down pathways that external parties feel are conducive to healing.

Respecting the views of all stakeholders within post-conflict situations can challenge peace and stability in a number of ways. Examples such as Northern Ireland clearly demonstrate how open platforms and multivocality can perpetuate sectarian divides (McDowell 2008). Through the use of murals, memorials, flags, and marches, both Republicans and Unionists craft heritage and promote tourist engagement in ways that promote their own narratives of the conflict (McEvoy 2011). As Long and Reeves (2009) point out, allowing former Khmer Rouge to extol the virtues of the Pol Pot regime at heritage sites in northern Cambodia might be inappropriate given the nature of the atrocities carried out by the regime. In situations like Uganda and Sierra Leone, the number of stakeholders, based upon ethnic groups, makes it incredibly difficult to map out responsibility and demand accountability (Giblin 2013). Finally, Basu (2008) raises the important question about how open to be about blame and guilt, as in many cases too much truth can undermine reconciliation and exacerbate difference, bringing us to the question posed by Long and Reeves (2009) as to whether there can be both justice and reconciliation, and which side heritage should support.

Representing the Khmer Rouge in Post-Conflict Cambodia

On April 17, 1975, the city of Phnom Penh in Cambodia was emptied by rumors of an imminent bombing raid by American aircraft. This led to the installation of one of the more improbable and certainly infamous regimes of the twentieth century: the Communist Party of Kampuchea. Commonly known as the Khmer Rouge, they brought about a four-year period of chaos, in which cities and towns were depopulated, most of the country's population displaced, and up to 3 million people were killed (Chandler 1991; Kiernan 2008). This was carried out by Cambodians as part of a tragic plan of political and social reform, which still has a powerful influence in Cambodia over thirty years later.

Since the early 2000s there has been tremendous growth in tourism in Cambodia, with landmines, the Khmer Rouge, and genocide playing a major role alongside the famous temples of Angkor in framing the visitor experience (Winter 2006). This has helped raise a new level of awareness of the civil war and genocide in international circles, and raised some fundamental challenges in terms of how such things should be remembered and presented to both Cambodians and visitors (Long and Reeves 2009; Wood 2006). This has coincided with the start of the first major trials of top Khmer Rouge leaders through a special tribunal, the Extraordinary Chambers in the Courts of Cambodia (ECCC). The construction of heritage narratives reveal tensions between different stakeholders, which include former Khmer Rouge, victims of Khmer Rouge activities, the government, civil society, the international community, tourists, and Cambodians born after the conflict. In this section we unpack several of the key issues that have defined post-conflict engagement with the Khmer Rouge since 1979, and look at how the country is still struggling with how to position the Khmer Rouge within a broader national narrative that seeks to move on from the atrocities of the past toward a stable path of economic development. A central part of this is how ideas of justice and reconciliation, which have become core parts of post-conflict vocabulary, play out (or not) in the Cambodian context.

Our analysis draws on examples from the main vehicle for officially representing the Cambodian national version of events, the Tuol Sleng Genocide Museum in Phnom Penh. Following its use as a prison and torture center, it has found new life as both a heritage and documentation center. Situated within a former school compound, the site was initially preserved and displayed soon after the Vietnamese captured Phnom Penh in 1979, and it has changed little since then. The museum utilizes a mixture of primary material culture, such as torture equipment, an extensive selection of photographs of persons incarcerated in the prison (and ultimately killed), and an assortment of paintings depicting atrocities to convey to visitors the horrors that occurred within the prison.[2] There is a paucity of explicit accompanying text, and only a limited wider context is provided. Most visitors view the museum in groups accompanied by museum guides, who usually mine their personal experiences living under the Khmer Rouge to impart additional gravity. Our analysis of the museum suggests that there have been long-standing efforts to obscure the nature of Khmer Rouge activities, and only limited efforts to seek truth, accountability, and justice among the Cambodian ruling elite. This is embodied in Prime Minister Hun Sen's widely quoted desire to "dig a hole and bury the past and look to the future." While he has not been able to do that fully, the evolution of the genocide museum provides an interesting window into post-conflict heritage construction in Cambodia.

On display are thousands of photos taken by the prison authorities of persons "processed" by the detention center – almost all of whom were eventually killed in the surrounding countryside. These photos form the center of the exhibit, and have been selected to elicit emotional reaction – representing both the scale of the crimes, and the callous ways that people were dealt with. However, while there are very detailed depictions of the victims, there are very few specific representations of those who carried out the acts, or detailed information about the victims themselves. In fact, there are only two areas where this can be seen. There is a display board that contains information on the main Khmer Rouge leaders, and there is a display with approximately a few hundred photos of Khmer Rouge foot soldiers, none of whom are identified (a point to which we will return). For the most part, representations of the Khmer Rouge in the museum are ambiguous and play off the collective aesthetic and identity promoted by the Khmer Rouge: dressed in black, often androgynous, and devoid of individual characteristics. The only detailed information on who is responsible for the atrocities is to be found on the board with the Khmer Rouge leaders, and this only includes a very select group of individuals who represent the uppermost ranks of the Khmer Rouge.

The Khmer Rouge are represented at the genocide museum as unified and highly organized. This distorts the chaotic and fragmentary nature of the Khmer Rouge, the limited knowledge many lower-level Khmer Rouge had about the upper levels of the regime's leadership, and the lack of a cohesive and overall policy during the period of Democratic Kampuchea. Most Khmer Rouge had no idea who Pol Pot and other senior "leaders" were between 1975 and 1979, which has significant implications for the widely utilized "only following orders" line of defense. The nature of the atrocities in Cambodia was far from systematic. However, there is a clear and systematic effort within state-endorsed heritage sites to funnel attention to a limited sub-set of personalities who are seen as guilty of the atrocities – a point made by Long and Reeves (2009). This narrative can also be seen in the ECCC, where the Cambodian government has strongly resisted further inquiry beyond the five defendants.

The structure and context of the displays at the museum blur the lines between victims and perpetrators – which can be clearly seen in heritage narratives throughout Cambodia. A stark example of this is the placement of photographs of Khmer Rouge soldiers in the

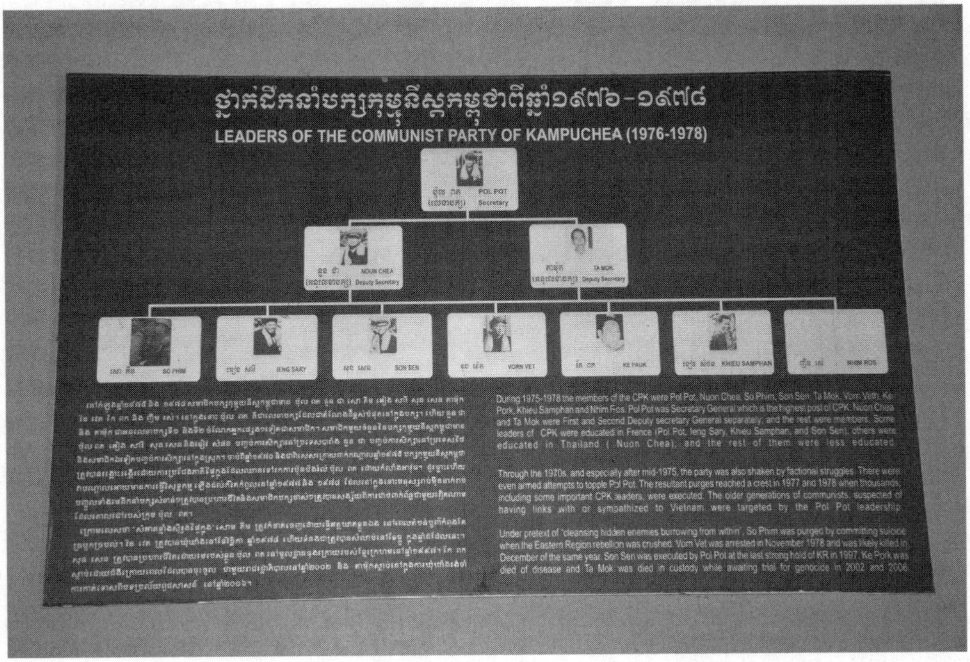

Figure 33.1 Display board in the Tuol Sleng Genocide Museum showing the organizational structure of the Khmer Rouge leadership. Source: photo by Patrick Daly.

exhibit of the "victims" of the Khmer Rouge. The only way to tell that the people in the photos were Khmer Rouge is their hats. Otherwise, the layout, pose, and format of the photos are identical in all regards to the photos of the prisoners. There is no explicit textual mention that clarifies the nature of these people in the photos, and these two displays of Khmer Rouge cadres are the only exhibits in the museum that lack English or French translation of the Khmer text. The obvious juxtaposition of the Khmer Rouge with other prisoners creates a visual appearance that reduces the differences between the two – and can easily leave a visitor with the impression that they are one and the same. The blurred narrative is reinforced by many of the guides, who typically state that the people in the photos were Khmer Rouge, and then go to great lengths to explain that they were killed during many of the internal purges of the regime that occurred.

This narrative excludes mention of the roles that such people might have had before they fell out with the Khmer Rouge, and creates a context in which the majority of people within the Khmer Rouge double as victims. It is typically overlooked that the prison was mainly used for the processing of political prisoners and the weeding out of internal Khmer Rouge "traitors." A significant percentage of people interrogated and tortured at Tuol Sleng, and killed at Choeung Ek, were at one time members of the Khmer Rouge (Williams 2004). The photos displaying many of the "victims" date from 1978, almost three years into the reign of the Khmer Rouge, and close visual inspection raises doubts about whether all those on display had spent the previous three years toiling in sub-human conditions in the labor camps of Democratic Kampuchea. It is likely that visitors to the museum are looking into the eyes of at least some young men

Figure 33.2 Photos of Khmer Rouge soldiers killed by the regime on display amongst photos of civilian victims of the Khmer Rouge in the Tuol Sleng Genocide Museum. Source: photo by Patrick Daly.

Figure 33.3 Photos of victims of the Khmer Rouge on display in the Tuol Sleng Genocide Museum. Source: photo by Patrick Daly.

and women who where Khmer Rouge cadres and responsible for carrying out acts of violence. It is difficult to imagine the key sites representing the victims of the Holocaust blurring the lines between victims and perpetrator – and even more so to have a site where thousands of Nazis were killed memorialized. Little is done to make this explicit at the museum, and the resultant narrative suggests that if at some point the Khmer Rouge turned against a person, then that person has been exonerated – irrespective of what that person might have been involved in prior to the purge.

The final aspect that drives the presentation of heritage narratives in Cambodia is the rationalization of guilt and involvement in atrocities. While this does not feature prominently within the visuals at the museum or at killing field sites, it plays a major role within the scripts recited by guides. It is standard for guides to ask rhetorical questions: "Why kill farmers?" "Why kill babies?" "Why would people do these things?" Visitors are constantly reminded that many of the people who followed the Khmer Rouge were "young," "uneducated," "poor," "from the countryside," "brainwashed," and so on. All of these characterizations serve as excuses for why such acts were carried out, while at the same time neglecting to consider the fact that there were many knowledgeable adults involved in Khmer Rouge atrocities.

It is clear from a number of surveys that the majority of Cambodians want some sort of justice to be done, which includes recognizing all the individuals involved in atrocities, accountability for such actions, and public statements and apologies by all guilty parties (Linton 2004). Many see this as critical to finally enabling a deeply scarred nation to move on from the events of the past. However, for nearly two decades, the main approach used by successive governments in Cambodia has been to bring former Khmer Rouge back into the fold, with amnesties widely given in exchange for demobilization. Senior leaders have made it clear that they do not want truth and reconciliation commissions, wide-scale public accountability, and an expanded set of trials. They claim it is for the good of the nation, to hold the fabric of Cambodia together, and to avoid giving former combatants an excuse to return to conflict. All of this has contributed toward the official heritage narrative that has been largely uncontested in an authoritarian state where public discourse is discouraged and civil society is weak. It is worth questioning how much of the shuttered heritage in Cambodia – which has been at least implicitly endorsed by the international heritage community – is influenced by the many important figures within the current government, including the prime minister, as well as district governors, senior military figures, and members of the economic elite who were involved in the Khmer Rouge. A case can be made that it is firmly in the interests of many who carried out, participated in, and/or are associated with atrocities, and who now occupy positions of power, to bury the past and move on, even if it comes at the expense of the needs of affected persons and victims who still wait for truth, accountability, and justice.

Contested Narratives of Responsibility and Victimhood: Heritage in Post-War Japan

Japan's post-conflict heritage has long been problematic, both within Japan and for Asian countries involved in World War II. The perceived reluctance of the Japanese to accept comprehensive responsibility for atrocities carried out by their soldiers has been a source of contention for China and Korea, amongst others. A close look at narrative construction and post-war heritage exposes a range of widely divergent and often heated opinions within Japan. The resultant heritage is an imperfect compromise that typically fails to satisfy all parties in Japan, let alone other international parties. However, these narratives have allowed Japan space to recover from the war and become a major economic power, raising questions about the practical utility of selective heritage. Drawing on secondary sources, we explore how Japan's post-conflict heritage has been selectively crafted as part of a complex negotiation between several key stakeholders in post-World War II Japan. One key stakeholder group consists of Japanese nationalists and conservatives, who continue to downplay Japan's role as an aggressor and focus on the nobility of Japanese soldiers. The nationalist narrative presents Japan as having legitimate reasons for going to war that include liberating "Asians" from Western imperialism and has a strong basis in emperor-worship and state Shintoism (Jeans 2005). Alternative post-conflict narratives acknowledge Japan's war crimes and atrocities, but also highlight the importance of peace and stress that Japan is a changed nation. Central to the post-war identity and recovery of Japan has been a perspective shared by both sides of the political spectrum that, regardless of the circumstances, Japan was the victim of the most destructive acts of violence in human history: the dropping of atomic bombs. All these elements are stitched into Japan's heritage landscape. However, this complicated set of narratives has failed to facilitate reconciliation between Japan and international parties such as the Chinese and Koreans, who continue to request full accountability and responsibility from Japan.

Japan's Yasukuni shrine and Yushukan Museum venerate war dead, and are perceived by some as applauding Japanese militarism (Kingston 2007). The Yasukuni shrine is significant for many Japanese nationalists because it recognizes those who fought for the emperor. Many Japanese conservatives argue that an acceptance of blame for the war would empty the sacrifices made by Japan's war dead and their families of their significance. Although Japan has officially apologized for atrocities carried out, the wording of the resolution renders the issue of responsibility and accountability ambiguous, as evidenced by its reference to "colonial rule and acts of aggression in the modern world." This has been regarded by Asian victims as an "attempt to mitigate Japan's actions and spread blame in a way that deflects attention away from widespread atrocities committed by the Imperial armed forces" (Kingston 2007: 299).

The Yushukan Museum, renovated in 2002, expresses the idea that Japan fought the war to liberate Asian territory, with the exhibits showing no signs of acknowledgement or contrition for the atrocities committed during the conflict (Higashi 2005). Kingston argues that the Yushukan Museum further reinforces the image of the Yasukuni shrine as a symbol of Japan's "failure to come to terms with its war history and the futility of attempting to assert a one sided, exculpatory narrative" (Kingston 2007: 302). We interpret this not as a failure to come to terms but rather a manifestation of the strategic crafting of narrative that focuses almost exclusively upon Japanese stakeholders. The narrative that developed in Japan reflects internal conflicts about the extent of responsibility Japan should accept for the war. It also reflects the use of heritage to facilitate healing and recovery for Japanese stakeholders. The ambivalence of the narratives contributed in part to Japan's successful post-war recovery and maintaining vestiges of national pride and identity.

The Hiroshima Peace Memorial is a post-conflict heritage site that preserves the legacy of the first atomic bomb used on human targets. The Genbaku Dome was the only structure left standing in Hiroshima after the atomic bombing of the city, and it serves as a "stark and powerful symbol of the most destructive force ever created by mankind" (UNESCO 1996). Further, the heritage site "expresses the hope for world peace and the ultimate elimination of all nuclear weapons":

> Firstly, the Hiroshima Peace Memorial, Genbaku Dome, stands as a permanent witness to the terrible disaster that occurred when the atomic bomb was used as a weapon for the first time in the history of mankind. Secondly, the Dome itself is the only building in existence that can convey directly a physical image of the tragic situation immediately after the bombing. Thirdly, the Dome has become a universal monument for all mankind, symbolizing the hope for perpetual peace and the ultimate elimination of all nuclear weapons on earth. (UNESCO 1996)

During the nomination process for World Heritage designation, the Genbaku Dome drew strong responses from other parties involved in World War II. The omission of the historical context of World War II in representing the atomic bombing of Hiroshima has been noted in dissenting opinions offered by the United States and China over the site's inscription as a UNESCO World Heritage site, as seen in the statements below:

> The United States is concerned about the lack of historical perspective in the nomination of Genbaku Dome. The events antecedent to the United States' use of atomic weapons to end World War II are key to understanding the tragedy of Hiroshima. Any examination of the period leading up to 1945 should be placed in the appropriate historical context.

The official Chinese rebuttal takes this even further:

> During the Second World War, it was the other Asian countries and peoples who suffered the greatest loss in life and property. But today there are still few people trying to deny this fact of history. As such being the case, if Hiroshima nomination is approved to be included on the World Heritage List, even though on an exceptional basis, it may be utilized for harmful purpose by these few people. This will, of course, not be conducive to the safeguarding of world peace and security. For this reason China has reservations on the approval of this nomination. (UNESCO 1996)

The dominant narrative surrounding the Hiroshima Peace memorial is that Japan's unique experience as the sole victim of the dropping of atomic bombs endows it with a moral responsibility to advocate for the elimination of nuclear weapons. With a focus on the devastation of the atomic bomb, the exhibit does not situate the event historically, and downplays Japan's role as an aggressive colonizer that committed atrocities. Emphasizing the "evil of the atomic bomb" and the injury done to Japan highlights the importance and significance of this atrocity over others, in an "imagined hierarchy of state-sponsored evil" including atrocities carried out by Japan such as the Sook Ching massacre in Singapore, the Nanjing massacre in China, and the mass rape of Korean "comfort women" (Giamo 2003). Giamo argues that by foregrounding the destruction caused by the atomic bomb, and rendering everything that preceded the act as abstract or insignificant, "the peace memorial severs historical consciousness from the Pacific War and of the question of responsibility from the last acts themselves" (Giamo 2003: 704).

Interestingly, Ian Buruma (1994) argues that Hiroshima fills a similar symbolic niche in Japan as Auschwitz does in Germany – a singular element of the conflict that stands above all else, and casts a long problematic shadow that has profoundly shaped post-war identity. However, whereas Auschwitz resonates with shame and guilt in Germany, and directly implicates them in one of the most notorious crimes ever perpetrated, Hiroshima is an appalling act that happened *to* the Japanese. This underlies the narrative of victimhood that has strongly influenced identity and heritage in Japan, and which raises the ire of people who suffered at the hands of the Japanese. Partly in response to criticisms about war denial, the Nagasaki Atomic Bomb Museum, opened in 1996, tries to situate Nagasaki's experience as a victim of an atomic bomb within a context of the tragedy of a wider war. In doing so, the museum's representation of the conflict "decisively challenges the imperialist ambitions of the wartime Japanese government and exposes aspects of the brutality of the Japanese army in Manchuria and elsewhere" (Duffy 1997: 50).

Since the 1990s – perhaps stimulated by the fiftieth anniversary of the ending of the war – there has been a notable increase of more explicit public statements from Japan taking responsibility for atrocities, and offering apologies and regrets for suffering caused. This has been accompanied with the expansion of peace museums and memorials, and the incorporation of more detailed historical context within existing sites (Jeans 2005). It also, somewhat ironically, runs parallel to the intense discussion in Japan about repealing or revising Article 9 in the Japanese Constitution, which limits Japan's military strength and forbids the launching of an offensive war. This debate has focused on emergent threats in the region such as China and North Korea, and questions about Japan's ability and obligations to participate in international military operations and peace-keeping missions.

The immediate dynamics of post-war Japan were shaped by a number of factors, most importantly the direct stewardship of the United States. While a number of

Japanese military personnel and government officials were tried for war crimes and punished, there were great pressures to maintain stability in Japan. General Douglas MacArthur, who governed Japan during the first phase of the American occupation, allowed many government officials to remain in positions of influence, including the emperor. He, and many others, advocated helping Japan recover quickly, and it was in their interests to downplay the image of the war-mongering Japanese – as depicted so casually and widely during the war years to shape American perceptions.

Consequently, little effort was made to demand full accountability, especially for atrocities carried out in China – which became the "enemy" after 1949, just as Japan became a firm American ally. It was also very useful for both people within the Japanese establishment who wanted to maintain their economic and social positions, as well as for their American benefactors, to present Japan as a newly pacified nation – one that had learned the lesson of the atomic bombs. Driven by cold war necessities, the Americans did not dwell on issues of guilt and accountability, largely preferring to close the case on the war and look forward, which suited many within Japan, for whom defeat was a major source of shame and who suffered significant trauma and loss of life. There was never a major push to parade the Japanese as vanquished foes; rather, there was an imperative to show a "reformed" partner. This directly contrasts with the post-war process in the European theatre, where Nazi guilt was undisputed, and Germany made major steps to accept full responsibility for the crimes they carried out. The dynamic of the first two decades after the war set the tone for much of Japan's post-war heritage.

Conclusion

This chapter highlights some of the tensions inherent within the construction and management of heritage in post-conflict situations. There are cases where stakeholders push for ambiguity, actively reposition their roles within the conflict, or shape narratives of guilt and responsibility to suit a range of agendas. In Cambodia, powerful forces calling for stability and economic development have limited truth and accountability. This has led to a superficial national reconciliation and elimination of armed conflict. However, this has arguably limited the abilities of some stakeholders to find justice, heal, and move on from wounds that not only continue to fester, but are being passed on to subsequent generations. It has also played into the strategic interests of some within the Cambodian power elite.

Meanwhile, the situation in Japan has been reduced to a simple story of Japanese denial – but one that fails to engage with the complexities of Japanese perspectives on the subject. The Japanese have long struggled to find a balance that will satisfy all internal stakeholders, as well as non-Japanese affected by the war. The fact that almost 70 years after the ending of the conflict, war heritage sites enrage stakeholders speaks to the challenges of managing post-conflict heritage. This raises a number of important and difficult questions. Is accountability a fair price to pay for stability? Does ending the conflict and bringing former combatants into the national fold outweigh the moral needs of justice? Would full transparency facilitate reconciliation and recovery, or would it ignite, exacerbate, and perpetuate hatred and distrust? And what role should heritage play within this?

Given the complexity of needs in post-conflict situations, in particular establishing a balance between the need for moral justice and the political needs of peace and stability, there are a number of issues when managing post-conflict heritage. UNESCO has a specific mandate to promote peace through education, science, and culture – which includes heritage. In most cases, UNESCO has played a more conservative role regarding heritage, with its main initiatives focusing upon the conservation and preservation of different forms of heritage. However, as can be seen in cases such as the Old Bridge in Mostar, Bosnia (see Connor, this volume) and the Genbaku Dome, there are cases where UNESCO has endorsed and even driven narratives that have favored peace over accountability and justice, focused on forgetting rather than remembering. Heritage practitioners need to be more critical of using heritage as an instrument of conflict resolution and peace-building. As we have demonstrated, there is great potential for heritage to become a tool for supporting political reconciliation and stability. However, it often comes at the expense of victims of conflict and can undermine justice.

Notes

1 The literature on post-conflict studies, peace processes, reconciliation, justice, and so on is extensive. Because of the size limits of this chapter, we only provide a brief summary of aspects that are most relevant to our discussion about heritage.

2 One of the authors has visited the Tuol Sleng Genocide Museum at least once a year since 2006 to evaluate Khmer Rouge heritage sites related to tourism and the ECCC.

References

Ball, H. (1999) *Prosecuting War Crimes and Genocide: The Twentieth-Century Experience.* Omaha: University Press of Kansas.

Bass, G. (2002) *Stay the Hand of Vengeance: The Politics of War Crimes Tribunals.* Princeton: Princeton University Press.

Basu, P. (2008) Confronting the Past? Negotiating a Heritage of Conflict in Sierra Leone. *Journal of Material Culture*, 13 (2), 233–247.

Berdal, M. (2009) *Building Peace after War.* Abingdon: Routledge.

Bloomfield, D., Barnes, T., and Huyse, L. (2003) *Reconciliation after Violent Conflict: A Handbook.* Stockholm: International Institute for Democracy and Electoral Assistance.

Buckley-Zistel, S. (2006) Remembering to Forget: Chosen Amnesia as a Strategy For Local Coexistence in Post-Genocide Rwanda. *Africa*, 76 (2), 131–150.

Buckley-Zistel, S. (2009) Nation, Narration, Unification? The Politics of History Teaching after the Rwandan Genocide. *Journal of Genocide Research*, 11 (1), 31–53.

Buruma, I. (1994) *The Wages of Guilt: Memories of War in Germany and Japan.* New York: Farrar, Straus, and Giroux.

Chandler, D. (1991) *The Tragedy of Cambodian History: Politics, War, and Revolution since 1945.* New Haven: Yale University Press.

Ciorciari, J. (2011) Cambodia's Trek toward Reconciliation. *Peace Review*, 23, 438–446.

Daly, P., and Rahmayati, Y. (2012) Cultural Heritage and Community Recovery in Post-Tsunami Aceh. In P. Daly *et al.* (eds), *From the Ground Up: Perspectives on Post-Tsunami and Post-Conflict Aceh, Indonesia.* Singapore: Institute for Southeast Asian Studies Press, pp. 57–78.

Duffy, T. (1997) The Peace Museums in Japan. *Museum International*, 49 (4), 49–54.

Giamo, B. (2003) The Myth of the Vanquished: The Hiroshima Peace Memorial Museum. *American Quarterly*, 55 (4), 703–728.

Giblin, J. (2013) Post-Conflict Heritage: Symbolic Healing and Cultural Renewal. *International Journal of Heritage Studies*, 20 (5), 500–518.

Higashi, J. (2005) The Two Faces of War Memorials in Japan. Available at: http://falstadsenteret.no/ic_memo/2005_two_faces_japan.pdf (accessed February 27, 2014).

Hilker, L. (2011) Young Rwandans' Narratives of the Past (and Present). In S. Straus and L. Waldorf (eds), *Remaking Rwanda: State Building and Human Rights after Mass Violence*. Madison: University of Wisconsin Press, pp. 316–330.

Jeans, R. (2005) Victims or Victimizers? Museums, Textbooks, and the War Debate in Contemporary Japan. *Journal of Military History*, 69 (1), 149–195.

Kiernan, B. (2008) *The Pol Pot Regime: Race, Power, and Genocide in Cambodia under the Khmer Rouge, 1975–79*, 3rd edn. New Haven: Yale University Press.

Kingston, J. (2007) Awkward Talisman: War Memory Reconciliation and Yasukuni. *East Asia*, 24 (3), 295–318.

Kugelmass, J. (1995) Bloody Memories: Encountering the Past in Contemporary Poland. *Cultural Anthropology*, 10 (3), 279–301.

Lehrer, E. (2010) Can There Be a Conciliatory Heritage? *International Journal of Heritage Studies*, 16 (4/5), 269–288.

Linton, S. (2004) *Reconciliation in Cambodia*. Phnom Penh: Documentation Center of Cambodia.

Logan, W., and Reeves, K. (eds) (2009) *Places of Pain and Shame: Dealing With "Difficult Heritage."* London: Routledge.

Long, C., and Reeves, K. (2009) "Dig a Hole and Bury the Past in It": Reconciliation and the Heritage of Genocide in Cambodia. In W. Logan and K. Reeves (eds), *Places of Pain and Shame: Dealing with "Difficult Heritage."* London: Routledge, pp. 68–81.

MacDonald, S. (2009) *Difficult Heritage: Negotiating the Nazi Past in Nuremberg and Beyond*. New York: Routledge.

McDowell, S. (2008) Selling Conflict Heritage through Tourism in Peacetime Northern Ireland: Transforming Conflict or Exacerbating Difference? *International Journal of Heritage Studies*, 14 (5), 405–421.

McEvoy, J. (2011) Managing Culture in Post-Conflict Societies. *Contemporary Social Science: Journal of the Academy of Social Science*, 6 (1), 55–71.

Meierhenrich, J. (2011) Topographies of Remembering and Forgetting: The Transformation of *lieux de memoire* in Rwanda. In S. Straus and L. Waldorf (eds), *Remaking Rwanda: State Building and Human Rights after Mass Violence*. Madison: University of Wisconsin Press, pp. 283–296.

Meskell, L. (1998) (ed.) *Archaeology Under Fire: Nationalism, Politics and Heritage in the Eastern Mediterranean and Middle East*. London: Routledge.

Meskell, L., and Scheermeyer, C. (2008) Heritage as Therapy: Set Pieces from the New South Africa. *Journal of Material Culture*, 13 (2), 153–173.

Rowlands, M. (2008) Civilization, Violence and Heritage Healing in Liberia. *Journal of Material Culture*, 13 (2), 135–152.

Thomson, S. (2011) Re-education for Reconciliation: Participant Observations on *ingando*. In S. Straus and L. Waldorf (eds), *Remaking Rwanda: State Building and Human Rights after Mass Violence*. Madison: University of Wisconsin Press, pp. 331–342.

Tunbridge, J., and Ashworth, G. (1996) *Dissonant Heritage: The Management of the Past as a Resource in Conflict*. Chichester: Wiley.

UNESCO (1996) Hiroshima Peace Memorial (Genbaku Dome). World Heritage List entry. Available at: http://whc.unesco.org/en/list/775 (accessed November 16, 2013).

Viejo-Rose, D. (2011) *Reconstructing Spain: Cultural Heritage and Memory after Civil War*. Brighton: Sussex Academic Press.

Williams, P. (2004) Witnessing Genocide: Vigilance and Remembrance at Tuol Sleng and Choeung Ek. *Holocaust and Genocide Studies*, 18 (2), 234–254.

Williams, P. (2008) *Memorial Museums: The Global Rush to Commemorate Atrocities*. London: Bloomsbury Academic.

Winter, T. (2006) *Post Conflict Heritage, Postcolonial Tourism: Politics and Development at Angkor*. London: Routledge.

Winter, T. (2014) Post-Conflict Heritage in Asia: Shifting Geographies of Aid. In P. Basu and W. Modest (eds), *Museums, Heritage and International Development*. London: Routledge, pp. 295–309.

Wood, T. (2006) Touring Memories of the Khmer Rouge. In L. Ollier and T. Winter (eds), *Expressions of Cambodia: The Politics of Tradition, Identity and Change*. London: Routledge, pp. 181–192.

CHAPTER 34

Achieving Dialogue through Transnational World Heritage Nomination: The Case of the Silk Roads

Ona Vileikis

Serial transnational World Heritage nominations are an innovative approach to protecting and recognizing a number of cultural heritage sites under the umbrella of one property of Outstanding Universal Value. As stated in the operational guidelines for the Convention Concerning the Protection of the World Cultural and Natural Heritage (1972), or as it more commonly known, the World Heritage Convention, in the case of transnational nominations, the property includes component parts, such as monuments, groups of monuments, or archaeological sites, located in two or more states that may not be contiguous (UNESCO 2013: para. 138). Although the operational guidelines propose that the property represents a single instance of Outstanding Universal Value and requires a single main management system, each component part requires a specific approach based on its own characteristics. Thus, new challenges arise for the preparation of nomination dossiers and the management of these types of properties.

In contrast to a single-site nomination, the amount of data to be handled in serial transnational nominations is usually greater, and might be present in various formats and languages. Moreover, different policies and heritage management procedures might exist in each country, and even within the same country, especially in federal systems. From policy-makers to community groups, another challenge is the large number of stakeholders to be involved in the nomination and management of such a World Heritage property. All these aspects provide a breeding ground for a variety of conflicts

A Companion to Heritage Studies, First Edition. Edited by William Logan, Máiréad Nic Craith, and Ullrich Kockel.
© 2016 John Wiley & Sons, Inc. Published 2016 by John Wiley & Sons, Inc.

regarding site management. Aside from procedural conflicts, even conflicts of value may sometimes arise based on different cultural traditions (Martin and Gendre 2010; UNESCO 2013: paras. 96–119).

What options are open to us to help us better document and manage serial transnational heritage? One option is to use technology-based tools such as information management systems that aid in heritage data management and presentation, and serve as an information tool for the interested public. Following UNESCO and the Advisory Bodies' recommendations about the use of digital technology, the application of information management systems in cultural heritage in the long term is a cost-effective tool to easily use, store, share, manage, and monitor properties (UNESCO *et al.* 2011). Another option lies with the improved interpretation and implementation of internationally recognized charters and conventions for cultural heritage and conservation standards that aim to guide stakeholders and site managers protect heritage sites. Among these charters, the World Heritage Convention (1972), the Venice Charter (ICASHB 1964), and the Burra Charter (Australia ICOMOS 2013) are some of the most important ones. Finally, the active participation of multiple stakeholders can be achieved by involving them in expert discussion panels, policy development, and all steps of the process leading to inscription, from the preparation of the Tentative Lists, nomination dossier, and management systems, to daily site management and monitoring (Rössler 2012; UNESCO 2013: para. 12). As such, preparing the nomination of and subsequently managing a serial transnational property can start a dialogue at various (inter)national levels – political, professional, stakeholder, and public.

In this chapter, the aforementioned challenges of serial transnational World Heritage nominations will be discussed, and further ideas will be presented to tackle them. Throughout the chapter, the Central Asian Silk Roads serial transnational World Heritage nomination will be used as a case study.

A Dynamic World Heritage Convention

Since its inception, the World Heritage Convention (1972) has been perceived as a dynamic instrument for international collaboration, and the protection and safeguarding of heritage of outstanding value around the world in all its diversity. In 2014, the World Heritage List included 1007 properties, of which 779 were cultural, 197 natural, and 31 mixed (UNESCO 2014a). As stated in the convention itself, "Each State Party to this Convention recognizes that the duty of ensuring the identification, protection, conservation, presentation and transmission to future generations of the cultural and natural heritage referred to in Articles 1 and 2 and situated on its territory, belongs primarily to that State."[1] Therefore, each State Party should take effective measures to achieve the protection, conservation, and presentation of its heritage, among them "to adopt a general policy which aims to give the cultural and natural heritage a function in the life of the community and to integrate the protection of that heritage into comprehensive planning programmes."[2] In this respect, the World Heritage Convention has certainly led to developments, bringing in new strategies and concepts aimed at international dialogue and cooperation, and the concepts of cultural routes and serial heritage.

In 1994, the World Heritage Committee adopted the Global Strategy for a Representative, Balanced and Credible World Heritage List (UNESCO 1995). It aimed to improve the implementation of the World Heritage Convention (1972) and decrease imbalances on the World Heritage List with its traditionally more Eurocentric but increasingly more Sino-centric focus. States Parties were encouraged to become part of the World Heritage Convention, to submit their Tentative Lists as stated in Article 11 of the convention, and to prepare nominations mainly in less-represented or underrepresented regions and heritage categories, for example, Cultural Routes in the Asia Pacific Region (ICOMOS 2004). Up till now, this goal has not been entirely achieved. For instance, of the 191 States Parties that have ratified the World Heritage Convention, 30 still do not have a World Heritage property in their territory, and most of the properties inscribed are situated in industrialized countries in Europe, as well as China.

At the time of the adoption of the Global Strategy for a Representative, Balanced and Credible World Heritage List in 1994, the concept of Cultural Routes was proposed during an experts' group meeting in Madrid, Spain, and later, in 1995, discussed in Berlin, Germany, during a World Heritage Committee session. In 1998, the ICOMOS International Scientific Committee on Cultural Routes was created for the further development of the idea of Cultural Routes, a concept later included in the 2005 edition of the operational guidelines as Heritage Routes (UNESCO 2005, Annex 3: 21–24). Heritage Routes are based on the dynamics of movement and the idea of dialogue and exchange among countries or regions, with continuity in space and time and multidimensional characteristics. This concept recognizes heritage as part of its surrounding (UNESCO 2013, Annex 3: 24.ii). Some examples of cultural routes that are included on the World Heritage List are the Route of Santiago de Compostela in Spain (1993), the Routes of Santiago de Compostela in France (1998), the Camino Real de Tierra Adentro in Mexico (2011), and the recently listed Qhapaq Ñan Andean Road System in South America, and the Silk Roads: The Routes Network of Chang'an-Tianshan Corridor (2014).

Furthermore, contributing to the Global Strategy for a Representative, Balanced and Credible World Heritage List and enhancing the credibility of the World Heritage Convention (1972), serial transnational nominations have become a positive mechanism for encouraging cohesion and interaction between Member States of the World Heritage community. The concept of a series of sites has been included in the World Heritage Convention's operational guidelines since the 1980s. This type of property comprises more than one component part, and some involve a diverse geography and a large variety of heritage typologies, from ancient archeological sites to heritage routes. The challenges and opportunities of serial sites have been discussed on a number of occasions by the World Heritage Committee, such as in Quebec (2008) and Seville (2009), and during expert meetings in Vilm, Germany (2008, 2009) and in Ittingen, Switzerland (2010). As a result, recommendations have been made to enhance the support of the World Heritage Centre and the Advisory Bodies, especially on the policies and procedures related to nomination and management, and amendments to the World Heritage Convention operational guidelines were proposed to better define the concept of serial nominations. These suggestions were included in the 2011 revision of the guidelines, together with a specific Tentative List Submission Format for serial transnational nominations (UNESCO 2011, Annex: 2b), a confirmation of the dynamism of the World Heritage Convention.

Starting in 1983 with the Jesuit Missions of the Guaranís (Argentina, Brazil), there are currently 11 cultural serial transnational properties on the World Heritage List. More are being prepared and evaluated, such as the Viking Age Sites in Northern

Europe, the Great Spas of Europe, and other corridors of the Silk Roads (Martin and Gendre 2010; UNESCO 2014b).

After more than 40 years of conservation and protection of cultural and natural heritage, the World Heritage Convention (1972) is the international heritage treaty ratified by most countries, and a powerful instrument for fostering sustainable development and cooperation beyond national borders. As Kishore Rao, director of the World Heritage Centre, stated on the occasion of the fortieth anniversary of the World Heritage Convention: "Through the World Heritage programme, the local communities value and protect their heritage and offer it to the world for appreciation. This helps in fostering intercultural dialogue, better understanding and mutual respect."[3] Therefore, the process of serial transnational nominations is instructive and in line with the spirit of the convention. It creates networks and exchange between experts, responsible authorities, and institutions. It builds regional pride, raises national awareness, and encourages nations to share in the conservation of their shared heritage. However, these initiatives come with considerable challenges, and a need for innovative conservation and management strategies.

Transnational Nominations: A Challenge

Preparing World Heritage nominations is a costly and time-consuming exercise. They require proper methodologies and tools for the harmonization of documentation and management procedures (UNESCO *et al.* 2011). These tasks are even more challenging in the case of serial transnational nominations. The main issues and challenges found for this type of property are related to the organization of documentation and the management framework; that is, the first steps towards the sustainable management of cultural heritage and the mitigation of inappropriate change.

Documentation

"Good documentation tells the complete story of an object" (Moore 2001: 1). Indeed, both heritage documentation and inventories are essential tools for the management of cultural heritage. They provide the background for local, state, and national listing, and with it legal protection to mitigate change. Informed decisions are taken with the most accurate and complete data available.

Whereas early efforts were focused on listing sites, over the past decade the World Heritage Committee has shifted its attention towards the improvement of management and the establishment of systematic monitoring and reporting mechanisms to protect a site's recognized Outstanding Universal Value (UNESCO 2002, 2004). In order to achieve this, the requirements of the nomination dossier – as the baseline information source for the management, monitoring, and assessment of the state of conservation – have been updated. Information has now to be more accurate and complete. For example, maps with clearly delineated boundaries and buffer zones should be provided, as well as a statement of Outstanding Universal Value, and established management and monitoring procedures for the property.

In serial transnational nominations, different inventorying and policy procedures might exist. Also, relevant information might be presented in various formats and languages.

This can be illustrated with the example of the Belfries of Belgium and France, a World Heritage serial transnational property comprised of 56 component parts.

The Belfries of Belgium and France count with three different heritage inventories, and no active common platform for management or monitoring exists. The Service du Patrimoine, under France's Direction Générale des Patrimoines, is supported by the Association des Biens Français du Patrimoine Mondial, an agency seeking to improve the quality of the protection and promotion of World Heritage-listed buildings. In Belgium, each region with belfries listed has its own heritage agency: in Wallonia, the Département du Patrimoine, and in Flanders, the Onroerend Erfgoed. Each body is responsible for the inventory, protection, conservation, valorization of the cultural immovable heritage, as well as for policy implementation in their region. Unlike Belgium, since their inscription, the belfries in France are coordinated by the Association Beffrois et Patrimoine, and are organized under the Belfry Cities Network. Both bodies are in charge of management and interpretation at a regional and local level.

Between 2008 and 2015, for the second periodic reporting cycle, the responsible agencies have successfully worked together. However, while the periodic reporting exercise has provided a ground for regional cooperation and promotion of coordination at a transnational level for the implementation of the World Heritage Convention (1972), the process of data analysis and reporting has been difficult, as up until now neither a specific nomination nor a periodic reporting format exists for serial transnational properties. Despite, the large number of component parts, in the case of periodic reporting, these properties have to report as one.

Greater complexity of serial properties requires data repositories to serve as the basis for recording and actively protecting, managing, and monitoring heritage places in order to maintain the values of the property, as well as to integrate information at a transnational level. A new trend is the use of geospatial content management systems (GeoCMS), online databases linked to a geographic information system (GIS), which makes certain management processes more user-friendly and efficient. As shown below, their application in cultural heritage, such as the Silk Roads Cultural Heritage Resource Information System (CHRIS) for the preparation of the Silk Roads transnational nomination, has shown that these systems positively change the way of managing and sharing common cultural heritage as they help to identify, assess, manage, and monitor cultural resources, and establish priorities for future actions. However, the application of these systems always needs to be accompanied by adequate heritage-related legislation, institutional frameworks and resources, and a proper site management system (Vileikis *et al.* 2012a, 2014).

Management

One of the main concerns of the World Heritage Committee and its Advisory Bodies is the proper management of properties on the World Heritage List. As the World Heritage Convention's operational guidelines state, "Each nominated property should have an appropriate management plan or other documented management system which must specify how the Outstanding Universal Value of a property should be preserved, preferably through participatory means" (UNESCO 2013: para. 108). As heritage is subject to threats, a proper management framework reduces the risk of loss of the attributed values shaping a property's Outstanding Universal Value. However, States Parties often consider that legal protection and control can replace a management system, a mistaken belief since the long-term implications of this cannot be foreseen. For instance, heritage is nowadays used as a tourism brand and to provide economic well-being. However, controlling massive tourism is a challenge. Without adequate human and technical resources, and proper site planning and management, tourism can damage properties, and repairs can be costly, if not impossible. In the case of serial properties, coordinated management is crucial (UNESCO 2013: para. 114).

Differences in political systems, administrative and legal frameworks, and professional and capacity-building, frequently present obstacles both at the nomination stage and afterwards when a property is under shared management. Therefore, from the outset of the process, there is need for a management system that includes the meaningful involvement of all players or stakeholders, is flexible enough to manage change, and which plays an active role in sustainable development. First, the difference between the scope of the management system at transnational and site-specific levels should be clarified. Both are necessary for protection, but have different actors with different responsibilities.

On the one hand, a management system can serve as an umbrella, coordinating the serial property as a whole, identifying potential changes of the sites' Outstanding Universal Value, and monitoring and reporting the effective implementation of the World Heritage Convention (1972). This management mechanism usually defines the common aims, objectives, and overarching management strategies, and sets up international collaboration. However, one of many challenges is to keep the management system described in the nomination dossier operating in practice after the nomination.

On the other hand, the management system should ensure the protection of its component parts. National authorities are responsible for the regular management and conservation strategies of their sites, the allocation of resources, and the successful implementation of the national legal and institutional framework. At a regional or local level, the active participation of NGOs or other types of associations could also be instrumental.

The Silk Roads: A Shared Heritage

As the former director-general of UNESCO, Frederic Mayor, has noted, "Since time immemorial, the movement of peoples and intercultural exchanges have played a crucial role in the evolution and transformation of human civilization" (Mayor 1997: 3). For more than two millennia, the Silk Roads, a network of routes linking Europe and Asia, has been one outstanding example. Different languages, cultures, traditions, objects, and religions and beliefs traveled with their human bearers on long journeys across deserts, steppe, mountain ranges, and tracts of sea and lakes, and this exchange is still happening today (Asimov and Bosworth 1998). The Silk Roads' Outstanding Universal Value reflects all heritage dimensions manifested in different typologies. The trade along this route produced not just a dazzling exchange of goods and wealth across boundaries, but also contributed to the dynamic development of towns, settlements, and knowledge, as well as the infrastructure that facilitated trade and transportation.

The Silk Roads are a historical network of pathways covering thousands of kilometers spread over the Eurasian continent (Whitfield 2007), with the road from Xi'an to

Antioch covering 7000 kilometers (Bergman 1939). From the second century BCE to the sixteenth century AD, aside from its well established economic value and its main product – silk – the Silk Roads also saw the exchange of other relevant values by land and sea, and part of its resultant legacy includes art, knowledge, and traditions, as well as propagated religions and beliefs. As Elisseeff remarks, the records and logbooks of countless travelers described "all there was to be seen, temples or palaces; all there was to be heard, songs and instrumental music; all that could be collected, stones, and plants; and all that provided solace, whether inns or stopping-places, markets or caravanserai, monasteries or sanctuaries" (Elisseeff 2000: 3).

Along its roads one can find a vast diversity of landscapes. Additionally, many regions contributed with their own architectural and urban solutions, based not just on their geography but on the needs and type of exchange of the cultures that once were settled there. There is a series of oases starting in Xi'an, China, and following the Gansu Corridor, a 1000 kilometer narrow passage connecting the northern roads of Tian Shan. One of the main oasis cities at the start of this corridor as one travels west to east is Dunhuang, with nearby Buddhist cave sites such as the Mogao Caves, a World Heritage property since 1987. Today, along the Gansu Corridor one can find archaeological sites of transportation, defense facilities such as Shihao and Souyang, cities and towns like Luoyang, and religious sites, such as the Kizil cave temple or the Subash Buddhist ruins, all of them located in China.

After crossing the Taklamakan Desert, these routes lead to the oases, steppe, and mountain passes of Central Asia. In the Zhetysu northern region, there are archeological remains of sites that once served as cities or palaces. Examples are the sites of Krasnaya Rechka in Kyrgyzstan, or Akyrtas, Aktobe, and Talgar in Kazakhstan. A large part of the Central Asian region is bordered by the Amu Darya and Syr Darya rivers, and the Aral Sea. Within this region, main hubs could develop, such as Samarkand, Shakhrisyabz, Bukhara, and Ichan-Kala in Uzbekistan, the four of which are listed World Heritage cities. Furthermore, along the ancient Sogdian road, going from the ancient town of Penjikent in Tajikistan, passing through Uzbekistan towards Merv in Turkmenistan, there are also religious complexes such as Chor-Bakr, landmarks like Vobkent Minaret, and archaeological sites like Poykent (Baipakov *et al.* 2011). The aforementioned sites are just some examples of the large number of heritage places along the Silk Roads. In fact, the Old World Trade Routes database counts 2971 places. It is an online archive that geographically and chronologically references the trade routes of Eurasia and Africa during the period 4000 BC to circa AD 1820 (Ciolek 1999).

Without doubt, the Silk Roads are a historical manifestation of dialogue and the enrichment of Eurasian civilizations. Yet Central Asia is one of the underrepresented regions on the World Heritage List. Within the five countries of Kazakhstan, Kyrgyzstan, Tajikistan, Turkmenistan, and Uzbekistan, there are eleven single cultural World Heritage properties listed, mainly falling into the categories of historic cities and archeological sites. Uzbekistan was the first to inscribe a property, Itchan Kala (1990), but it was not until 2010 that Tajikistan inscribed its first and only cultural property (UNESCO 2013). Thus, as a follow up to the Global Strategy for a Representative, Balanced and Credible World Heritage List, ICOMOS and the Asia-Pacific Section of the World Heritage Centre have been closely collaborating with the Asian States Parties in reviewing their national Tentative Lists, giving special attention to the transnational Silk Roads nomination.

Toward the Silk Roads Nomination

Over the last two decades there has been growing interest in China and in the Central Asian countries that lie along the route of the Silk Roads in developing their heritage and linking it to the tourism sector of their economies. Although still in its infancy in the Central Asian countries, heritage sites are slowly developing and being made accessible. With this has come an increasing interest in the Silk Roads, an example of transnational heritage that is already well known in large parts of the world. Today, the preparation of the nomination is bringing together experts and stakeholders with different interests and levels of influence as an example of a transnational partnership that reveals much about the benefits and challenges of this form of inscription.

In 1988, UNESCO launched the Integral Study of the Silk Roads: Roads of Dialogue. It was a ten-year project with the purpose of carrying out field studies to investigate scientific, technological, and cultural exchange between East and West, encouraging research at international and national levels, and promoting the concept of shared heritage. As a result, five expeditions took place: the Desert Route (1990), the Maritime Route (1990–1991), the Steppe Route (1991), the Nomadic Route (1992) and the Buddhist Route (1995). Together with the development of seminars and research programs, the opening of research centers and the dissemination of numerous publications demonstrated both the historic and ongoing importance of the Silk Roads. This initiative served as the basis to what would later turn into a series of sub-regional workshops and training sessions for the preservation of culture and identity, and the adoption of geopolitical decisions toward the preparation of the Silk Roads World Heritage nomination (see Lawton 1997).

The concept of the Silk Roads was proposed as a potential theme for a serial transnational World Heritage nomination in the Asian region by Kazakhstan, Kyrgyzstan, Tajikistan, Turkmenistan, Uzbekistan, and China as a result of the action plans developed in 2003. After a series of consultation meetings in 2005 and 2006, the first Silk Roads concept paper was drafted during the Dushanbe Silk Roads meeting in 2007. This paper was later updated and in 2009 adopted in Almaty together with the draft of the statement of Outstanding Universal Value for the Silk Roads (see Lin, Peshkov, and Turekulova 2013).

The World Heritage Centre, in close collaboration with States Parties, and with the support of ICOMOS, has explored a strategic and methodological approach for the preparation of the nomination. By 2010, twelve States Parties had joined the Silk Roads project and submitted a bibliography and literature, in addition to updating their national Tentative Lists to facilitate the preparation of the ICOMOS Silk Roads Thematic Study. This study was mainly aimed at providing comparative data and analysis of the sites, as well as profiling the distribution and distinctiveness of Silk Roads sites (Williams 2014).

As part of the nomination strategy, and in line with UNESCO recommendations (Martin and Gendre 2010) and the Silk Roads concept paper (see Lin, Peshkov, and Turekulova 2013: 42–50), the Silk Roads Thematic Study identified 54 main corridors. As defined by the study, corridors are specific paths or roads between nodes including a buffer to capture a broader area of landscapes and sites that might not be major nodes. Some examples of nodes are minarets at the intersection of roads, and major urban centers such as Samarkand, Amul, and Burana. Most of the corridors still represent very long routes (600 to 1400 kilometers in length), and at this scale it is problematic to achieve ideal management and coordination at the transnational level. However, it is anticipated that this approach will become more manageable in the future, as the concept of transnational cooperation becomes better understood and implementation mechanisms are developed. One example is the Silk Roads: The Routes Network of Chang'an-Tianshan Corridor of Kazakhstan, Kyrgyzstan, and China, the first corridor listed under the umbrella of the Silk Roads serial transnational World Heritage nomination during the 2014 World Heritage Committee Meeting in Qatar.

International support has been allocated and research has been conducted into the development of appropriate methodologies for documentation and management, these to be included in the nomination dossier and for the future monitoring of the sites. Three main projects supported the serial transnational nomination. At an initial stage, 2007 to 2011, the UNESCO Norway Funds-in-Trust project supported sub-regional meetings in Central Asia and a national meeting of each participating country. From 2010 to 2013, the UNESCO Japanese Funds-in-Trust project provided capacity-building and the promotion of technology transfer, and set basic frameworks in the field of the documentation of cultural heritage. Simultaneously, the Silk Roads Cultural Heritage Resource Information System, a project funded by the Belgian Science Policy Office and developed by a Belgian consortium headed by the Raymond Lemaire International Centre for Conservation at the University of Leuven, developed an information management system for the preparation of the nomination dossier, together with capacity building in Central Asia and academic research on monitoring serial transnational nominations.

The Silk Roads Cultural Heritage Resource Information System

In order to prepare the nomination dossier in Central Asia, an information management system was developed under the framework of the Silk Roads Cultural Heritage Resource Information System project – hereafter simply Silk Roads CHRIS (Vileikis *et al.* 2012b, 2014). It complies with the requirements of the nomination and the periodic reporting formats (UNESCO 2013, Annexes 5, 7) and was tailor-made to the overall Silk Roads nomination following the nomination strategy agreed among the States Parties.

The Silk Roads CHRIS is a geospatial content management system (GeoCMS) with online access restricted to the users. The data model has been developed to store information at two scales: corridor (property), and component part (sites and monuments). It is divided into two sections, the nomination dossier and the monitoring tool. The GeoCMS allows a variety of digital media and electronic texts to be managed, searched, and published. It is implemented as a user-friendly web application. The administrator of the web GeoCMS has access to tools for uploading geographical information so that the users can view, navigate, and perform basic spatial analyses. The system uses background maps, such as predefined Google maps or prepared raster data with better accuracy, that is, any type of digital image represented by reducible and enlargeable grids, such as satellite images and aerial photographs. WorldView-2 satellite images of the sites with a resolution of 0.5 meters were acquired and added to the system to improve the maps, indicating the boundaries of the nominated area and buffer zones.

The Silk Roads CHRIS works with open standards with respect to data models and formats, including metadata and spatial web services. The use of dropdown menus with data linked to a gazetteer with typologies of the Silk Roads, or metadata for images and a bibliographic repository added by States Parties, allows for precise querying and provides the possibility to link these items to the dossier. It empowers States Parties to add and share all relevant information in the layout and structure of the nomination dossier and the monitoring tool. This information together with geographical data can be reviewed, edited, and printed out as in pdf format. By 2013, a significant amount of data was added by the States Parties, such as 323 images and 2.2 gigabytes of input data for only one corridor.

The system was introduced to the Central Asian States Parties based on their requirements, and feedback was given to improve the specifications of the system. As a result, States Parties were trained in the use of the system, and were given continuous on-site as well as online support. Moreover, training sessions were conducted in data collection, heritage documentation and recording, as well as values, condition, and risk assessments for the preparation of the information. After several field campaigns in Uzbekistan, testing and training has also been carried out in monitoring, a tool already implemented in the Silk Roads CHRIS and ready to be used by the States Parties (Vileikis *et al.* 2014) (see Figure 34.1).

The Silk Roads CHRIS is now fully operational and hosted in Central Asia. The States Parties acknowledged the importance of this tool as they could accurately compile their information and upload it onto a continuously updated nomination dossier. The system was commended for its user-friendliness; no IT or GIS skills are required, and it is comprehensible to most Central Asian users as it uses both Russian and English, and more languages could be added as required.

The more accurate and systematic the documented baseline information, the easier it will be for the relevant authorities to take decisions towards effective management and protection of the values for which sites are nominated. They could also carry out more efficient monitoring, state of conservation inspections and periodic reporting as requested by the World Heritage Committee. Throughout the preparation of the nomination dossier, the dossier submission phase, and monitoring, the Silk Roads CHRIS has been successfully used as a supporting tool. This documentation tool, together with a proper management system and national regulations, will help to ensure the protection of the property.

Figure 34.1 Training in the use of the Silk Roads Cultural Heritage Resource Information System and architectural heritage recording, Chor Bakr, Uzbekistan. Source: photo by Ona Vileikis.

The Management System Approach

The series of sub-regional meetings already mentioned led to the creation of a management structure at different management levels: Silk Roads Cultural Route, Corridor, State Party, and local/regional level. This division allows for an identification of the responsible bodies, and helps to set up appropriate coordination. Its composition is as follows.

First, the overall management system of the Silk Roads is headed by an overarching intergovernmental coordinating committee (see Figure 34.2). It is composed of one policy-maker and one expert or academic representing each of the twelve involved States Parties, and its chair rotates among the States Parties every two years. The committee is supported by the Secretariat of the ICOMOS International Conservation Centre in Xi'an, and a working group. The Secretariat facilitates the sharing of information among the countries during the nomination and management processes. With the increase in the amount of information and accessibility of digital technology, it has been shown that the Secretariat's website and has become a useful platform, providing access to the Secretariat's content management system and links to other databases, websites, and projects related to the Silk Roads such as the Silk Roads CHRIS. The main task of the working group is to maintain easy contact and facilitate day-to-day dialogue for the preparation of the nomination dossier and future management. Additionally, a regional facilitator was designated to assist in the exchange of training and knowledge within the Central Asian region.

Second, each established corridor has its own transnational coordination. At this scale, a memorandum of understanding should be signed between the different nominating States Parties, one for each corridor. The memorandum includes an action plan and time frame for the preparation of the nomination. Each corridor has an advisory committee with working groups. The advisory committee is represented in the coordinating committee at political and academic levels. It is in charge of the overall management of the corridor, and reports during meetings of the coordinating committee. It sets up action plans and time frames during the nomination phase, and

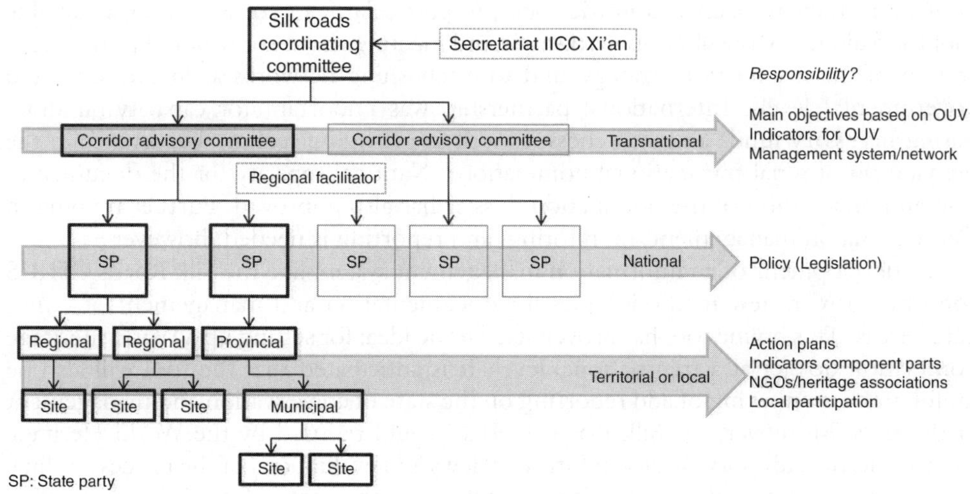

Figure 34.2 The Silk Roads management system. Source: figure by Ona Vileikis.

later establishes the overall specifications for the management plans to protect the Outstanding Universal Value at the level of component parts. It also serves as the interface of the international network. During the nomination, work between advisory committees and experts was essential. Additionally, several training courses in geophysics and archeological documentation provided by the Japanese Funds-in-Trust were carried out at a sub-regional level.

At the national level, the development of the nomination led to discussion about the revision of laws to achieve the desired standards of preservation of cultural heritage. In Uzbekistan, possibilities are currently being discussed at the senate level to adapt the cultural heritage management system to respond to World Heritage requirements; that is, taking UNESCO as a new statutory body for the heritage list, legalizing buffer zones under a special decree, and introducing new management structures leading to the creation of the site manager position for each World Heritage property. As a result, a new decree for the creation of a World Heritage unit has been approved (see GoU 2014).

The national management system has identified what is unique to each site or to the whole system. Different management levels were necessary to designate responsibilities among the authorities and for a better coordination. In the future, monitoring and reporting as well as the role of community participation in decision-making will be emerging topics for the Silk Roads.

The Way Forward

Documentation is the first major step towards effective management and monitoring of the sites. With the increasing number of listed World Heritage properties, data also increases. Digital technology, such as GeoCMS, offers new user-friendly solutions for managing large datasets at a transnational level. The use of this technology also allows for the application of monitoring tools such as remote sensing to track physical changes to properties.

The Silk Roads experience has shown that States Parties can welcome transnational cooperation regarding the protection, promotion, management, and transmission of heritage in their respective countries, and, in particular, can consider it as a valuable tool for dialogue. Consultation workshops and meetings have contributed to the preparation of the nomination strategy, and to establishing networks at institutional and governmental levels. International partnership was important for capacity-building, raising necessary funds and awareness, as well as providing technical assistance in the preparation of serial transnational nominations. National capacity for the documentation and preparation of the nomination dossier has also improved. Further training in Central Asia on management, monitoring, and reporting is needed, however.

The development of an information management system like the Silk Roads CHRIS contributed with new methodologies for documentation and management of nominated areas. This online tool has proven itself to be ideal for setting up a World Heritage nomination dossier at a transnational level. It is anticipated that the tool will also be useful in the monitoring of and reporting on the state of conservation and management of the sites. Moreover, the Silk Roads CHRIS could be used by the World Heritage Centre and the Advisory Bodies in future reviews and evaluations of the process or final nomination dossier, and could also be linked to the state-of-conservation online platform of the World Heritage Centre.

Transparent collaboration and the sharing of information, practices, and expertise in the safeguarding of common cultural heritage is a step toward strengthening transnational dialogue among countries. This can be achieved, especially through serial transnational nominations, as shown by the Silk Roads nomination experience, which is proving to have been successful in achieving a more representative and balanced natural and cultural addition to the World Heritage List.

Acknowledgements

The author would like to acknowledge the support of the Central Asian States Parties, the Belgian Science Policy Office, UNESCO's World Heritage Centre, UNESCO offices in Almaty and Tashkent, the International Institute for Central Asian Studies, and the UNESCO National Commissions in Central Asia. In addition, the author would like to thank Koen Van Balen (Raymond Lemaire International Centre for Conservation, University of Leuven), Tim Williams (Institute of Archaeology, University College London), and Mario Santana Quintero (Carleton University) for their continuous advice.

Notes

1 World Heritage Convention (1972), art. 4.
2 World Heritage Convention (1972), art. 5a.
3 Kishore Rao, director of the World Heritage Centre, 2012. Available at: http://whc.unesco.org/en/40years/ (accessed February 27, 2015).

References

Legislation

Convention Concerning the Protection of the World Cultural and Natural Heritage (World Heritage Convention) (UNESCO, 1972). Available at: http://whc.unesco.org/archive/convention-en.pdf (accessed March 19, 2015).

GoU (Government of Uzbekistan) (2014) Decree No. 200 from 21.07.2014 of the Cabinet of Ministers on Additional Measures to Enhance Protection and Utilization of Tangible Cultural and Archaeological Heritage. Available at: http://www.lex.uz/pages/getpage.aspx?lact_id=2432524 (accessed August 25, 2014).

Other Works

Asimov, M.S., and Bosworth, C.E. (eds) (1998) *History of Civilizations of Central Asia,* Vol. 4: *The Age of Achievement:* AD *750 to the End of the Fifteenth Century,* Part 1: *The Historical, Social and Economic Setting.* Paris: UNESCO.

Australia ICOMOS (2013) Charter for Places of Cultural Significance (Burra Charter), revised version. Available at: http://australia.icomos.org/wp-content/uploads/The-Burra-Charter-2013-Adopted-31.10.2013.pdf (accessed June 29, 2014).

Baipakov, K.M., *et al.* (2011) *Prominent Archaeological Sites of Central Asia on the Great Silk Road.* Samarkand: International Institute for Central Asian Studies.

Bergman, F. (1939) *Archaeological Researches in Sinkiang, Especially the Lop-Nor Region.* Stockholm: Bokförlags aktiebolaget Thule.

Ciolek, T.M. (1999) Old World Trade Routes Project. Available at: www.ciolek.com/owtrad.html (accessed June 3, 2014).

Elisseeff, V. (2000) Approaches Old and New to the Silk Roads. In V. Elisseeff (ed.), *The Silk Road: Highways of Culture and Commerce*. New York: Berghahn Books, pp. 1–26.

ICASHB (1964) (International Congress of Architects and Specialists of Historic Buildings) (1964) International Charter for the Conservation and Restoration of Monuments and Sites (Venice Charter). Available at: http://www.icomos.org/charters/venice_e.pdf (accessed March 9, 2015).

ICOMOS (2004) The World Heritage List: Filling the Gaps – An Action Plan for the Future. Available at: http://whc.unesco.org/document/102409 (accessed February 27, 2015).

Lawton, J. (ed.) (1997) *Integral Study of the Silk Roads: Roads of Dialogue*. Paris: UNESCO.

Lin, R., Peshkov, Y., and Turekulova, N. (eds) (2013) *Central Asian Serial Nominations: Central Asian Silk Roads*. Paris: UNESCO.

Martin, O., and Gendre, S. (eds) (2010) UNESCO World Heritage: Serial Properties and Nominations. Presentation at the international expert meeting World Heritage and Serial Properties and Nominations, Ittingen, Switzerland, February 25–27.

Mayor, F. (1997) Preface of the Director-General. In J. Lawton (ed.), *Integral Study of the Silk Roads: Roads of Dialogue*. Paris: UNESCO, p. 3.

Moore, M. (2001) Conservation Documentation and the Implications of Digitisation. *Journal of Conservation and Museum Studies*, 7, 1–19.

Rössler, M. (2012) Partners in Site Management. A Shift in Focus: Heritage and Community Involvement. In M.-T. Albert, M. Richon, M.J. Viñals, and A. Witcomb (eds), *Community Development through World Heritage*. World Heritage Papers 31. Paris: UNESCO, pp. 27–30. Available at: http://whc.unesco.org/documents/publi_wh_papers_31_en.pdf (accessed February 27, 2015).

UNESCO (1995) Report of the 18th Session of the World Heritage Committee (Phuket, Thailand, 12–17 December 1994). Document WHC-94/CONF.003/16. Available at: http://whc.unesco.org/archive/repcom94.htm#global (accessed May 25, 2013).

UNESCO (2002) Monitoring World Heritage. World Heritage Papers 10. Available at: http://whc.unesco.org/documents/publi_wh_papers_10_en.pdf (accessed November 2, 2010).

UNESCO (2004) Decisions, World Heritage Committee, Seventh Extraordinary Session – Paris. Document WHC-04/7 EXT.COM/17. Available at: http://whc.unesco.org/en/decisions/40 (accessed May 13, 2013).

UNESCO (2005) Operational Guidelines for the Implementation of the World Heritage Convention. Document WHC. 05/2 2. Available at: http://whc.unesco.org/archive/opguide05-en.pdf (accessed February 27, 2015).

UNESCO (2011) Operational Guidelines for the Implementation of the World Heritage Convention. Document WHC.11/01. Available at: http://whc.unesco.org/archive/opguide11-en.pdf (accessed October 2, 2013).

UNESCO (2013) Operational Guidelines for the Implementation of the World Heritage Convention. Document WHC.13/01 July 2013. Available at: http://whc.unesco.org/archive/opguide13-en.pdf (accessed October 2, 2013).

UNESCO (2014a) World Heritage Tentative List. Available at: http://whc.unesco.org/en/tentativelists (accessed July 28, 2014).

UNESCO (2014b) World Heritage Centre – World Heritage List. Available at: http://whc.unesco.org/en/list (accessed June 25, 2014).

UNESCO, ICCROM, ICOMOS, and IUCN (2011) Preparing World Heritage Nominations, 2nd edn. Available at: http://whc.unesco.org/document/116069 (accessed February 27, 2015).

Vileikis, O., Cesaro, G., Santana Quintero, M., Van Balen, K., Paolini, A., and Vafadari, A. (2012a) Documentation in World Heritage Conservation: Towards Managing and Mitigating Change – The Case Studies of Petra and the Silk Roads. *Journal of Cultural Heritage Management and Sustainable Development*, 2 (2), 130–152.

Vileikis, O., Dumont, B., Tigny, V., Van Balen, K., Serruys, E., and De Maeyer, P. (2014) The Silk Roads Cultural Heritage Resource Information System: For World Heritage Monitoring and Preservation. *International Journal of Heritage in the Digital Era*, 3 (2), 375–392.

Vileikis, O., Serruys, E., Dumont, B., Van Balen, K., Santana Quintero, M., De Maeyer, P., and Tigny, V. (2012b) Information Management Systems for Monitoring and Documenting World Heritage: The Silk Roads CHRIS. *International Archives of the Photogrammetry, Remote Sensing and Spatial Information Sciences*, 22, 203–208.

Whitfield, S. (2007) Was There a Silk Road? *Asian Medicine*, 3, 201–213.

Williams, T. (2014) The Silk Roads: An ICOMOS Thematic Study. Working Paper. Charenton-le-Pont: ICOMOS. Available at: http://openarchive.icomos.org/1487/1/ICOMOS_WHThematicStudy_SilkRoads_final_lv_201406.pdf (accessed February 27, 2015).

CHAPTER 35

World Heritage: Alternative Futures

Britta Rudolff and Kristal Buckley

Introduction

In 2009, the General Assembly of States Parties to the 1972 Convention for the Protection of the World Cultural and Natural Heritage (commonly known as the World Heritage Convention) established an open-ended working group to debate, reflect on, and strategize for the future of the convention. Since that time, an array of scenarios for alternative directions has been discussed.

At its fortieth anniversary celebration in Kyoto in 2012, the World Heritage Convention was referred to by many speakers as having reached a crossroads, a juncture at which a decisive path toward its future sustainability, credibility, and long-term viability needs to be selected (Vujicic-Lugassy 2013). Lengthy lists of challenges and gaps highlighted the shortcomings of the World Heritage Convention after four decades of implementation, and these now feature equally in contemporary discourses alongside those that refer to the convention's enormous success and flagship status within UNESCO.

While the World Heritage Convention's popularity seems likely to increase, along with pressure for new World Heritage listings, the original intent of its authors – mutual support for conservation and international cooperation towards this end – seems to have shifted out of focus. In a time of growing utilization rather than implementation of the convention, its credibility is critically at stake.

A Companion to Heritage Studies, First Edition. Edited by William Logan, Máiréad Nic Craith, and Ullrich Kockel.
© 2016 John Wiley & Sons, Inc. Published 2016 by John Wiley & Sons, Inc.

To remain successful and acknowledged as an international standard-setting instrument for heritage protection, the World Heritage Convention (1972) will need to redefine its implementation strategies, first and foremost by ensuring that its own standards are respected. Will these strategies be characterized by an increased focus on rigorous and professional approaches that many call for, but which are often perceived as elitist or Eurocentric? Or will it succeed in developing innovative twenty-first-century strategic approaches and heritage conceptions which ensure its long-term credibility and sustainability?

Considering the Future

Throughout the forty years' life of the World Heritage Convention (1972), the future has seemed variously promising and/or of concern to participants in and observers of its implementation. This has been a matter of reflection at regular intervals over this period, often initiated by celebration of each decade of the convention's existence.

The tenth anniversary of the World Heritage Convention occurred only a short time after the first inscriptions on the World Heritage List were made in 1978, based on the relatively succinct first versions of the convention's operational guidelines. Yet even at this early stage, many of the recognizable components of today's system were in place, and a large number of properties had been inscribed (see Anon. 1983). There was already some concern about the difficulties involved in selecting properties for the World Heritage List, ensuring credible expert evaluations, workload pressures, and recognition of the challenges of comparative analysis for cultural properties (Slatyer 1983; LeBlanc 1984). Some "alternative" ideas that are raised by some observers today, such as closing the World Heritage List to ensure its exclusivity, were raised at this time (Linstrum 1984). The concept of Outstanding Universal Value had been made operational through the drafting of the ten inscription criteria (four for nature and six for culture), as well as the application of the concepts of "authenticity" and "integrity" (Cameron and Rössler 2013).

By the early 1990s, the twentieth anniversary of the convention marked significant changes that shaped the way the system works today (Pressouyre 1996; von Droste 2011; Cameron and Rössler 2013). These included the recognition of cultural landscapes (including associative cultural landscapes), and stronger strategic reactions to concerns about the imbalance (or lack of "representativity") of the World Heritage List. As a result, the Global Strategy for a Representative, Balanced and Credible World Heritage List (hereafter, the Global Strategy) was adopted by the World Heritage Committee in 1994 (UNESCO 1994; Labadi 2013). Also in the early 1990s, the World Heritage Centre was established within UNESCO, and reactive monitoring processes were developed to support the conservation imperative of the World Heritage Convention (von Droste 2011).

The thirtieth anniversary of the convention occurred after the turn of the millennium, giving added weight to the mood of reflection and recognition that the goals and challenges were not the same as those of the 1960s and 1970s, when the World Heritage Convention was conceived (Labadi 2007b; Strasser 2002). A review of the processes of the convention occurred at this time, culminating in major changes to the convention's operational guidelines adopted in 2005 (UNESCO 2005).

The celebration of the fortieth anniversary of the convention in 2012 was characterized by heightened concerns about the future. As already noted, a process of reflection on the future of the World Heritage Convention (1972) was initiated by the World Heritage Committee in 2008, and formally established by the General Conference of States Parties in 2009 (UNESCO 2009c). An open-ended working group discussed in great detail visions of and opportunities for the convention's future. The strategic output of this process was a strategic plan to guide the implementation of the World Heritage Convention for the next 10 years (UNESCO 2011b).

At the same time, an evaluation of the effectiveness of the Global Strategy was conducted as part of an external audit, which was reported to the World Heritage Committee in 2011 (UNESCO 2011a). Many serious obstacles to achieving the aims of the Global Strategy – over almost 20 years of implementation – were identified by the auditors. But there were some positive outcomes. These included the increased number of States Parties to the World Heritage Convention (1972), an increased percentage of States Parties with properties on the World Heritage List, and better guidance to support inscription of historic cities, cultural landscapes, and cultural routes. In contrast, there was poor progress in increasing the proportion of natural heritage properties and properties from outside of Europe and North America on the World Heritage List. The audit noted that the most marked increase in nominations was from the Asia-Pacific region, with corresponding decreases for Africa and the Arab states (in relative terms). Concern was expressed regarding the apparent poor effectiveness of preparatory assistance in ensuring successful nominations, and the trend towards extremely rarefied explanations of Outstanding Universal Value, with the conclusion that nationalistic drivers were more prominent in nominations and inscriptions than at the outset of the Global Strategy (UNESCO 2011a).

> While, during the first years of the implementation of the [World Heritage] Convention properties described as iconic were inscribed, the refining of the categories has led to the inscription on the tentative lists of sites where the outstanding universal value is only perceptible to hyper-specialists. Moreover, due to the prestige of the [World Heritage] List and the economic interests at stake, States Parties insist upon the nomination of properties that, in the opinion of the Advisory Bodies, do not appear to respond to global recognition but more to a national or regional recognition. (UNESCO 2011a: para. 18)

Responding to these trends and concerns, Rao (2010) advocated the "upstreaming" of World Heritage processes, whereby the World Heritage Committee's Advisory Bodies – in particular the International Council on Monuments and Sites (ICOMOS) and the International Union for the Conservation of Nature (IUCN) – could work in partnership with States Parties on their Tentative Lists and on the justification of Outstanding Universal Value of proposed properties so that there would be fewer cases where the Advisory Bodies recommended against inscription. In 2009, a meeting was held in Phuket, Thailand, oriented around this possibility (UNESCO 2009a). In 2011, the World Heritage Committee launched a pilot program for such upstream processes, which is still underway (UNESCO 2011c).

"Upstreaming" enjoys a high degree of support as an idea, and might continue to develop and better address the problem of "failed" or "flawed" nominations – seen by some, such as Rao (2010), as the major point where the World Heritage Committee's decisions have been increasingly "politicized." However, it cannot address the other issues that equally seem to threaten a more confident future for the World Heritage Convention (1972). These include the now-extreme situation of overloaded workloads relative to financial, human, and time resources for all institutions that make up the system (von Droste 2011). This situation is due in part to the large and rapidly growing size of the World Heritage List, and the growing number and complexity of the pressures on the conservation of more than 1000 World Heritage properties (Meskell 2014; Bandarin 2013). Furthermore, the continuing predominance of certain themes and geo-cultural representations on the World Heritage List is accompanied by the contested character of World Heritage designation and protective mechanisms in many parts of the world, particularly where the rights and interests of local communities and indigenous peoples have not been respected (Disko and Tugendhat 2013; Logan 2012; Oviedo and Puschkarsky 2012).

Reacting to continuing concern about the impact of current trends of "politicization," the director-general of UNESCO hosted a session at the organization's headquarters in Paris in 2012, entitled "The World Heritage Convention: Thinking Ahead." Each of the Advisory Bodies offered proposals for improving the system, and there was a free flow of opinions from over 40 national delegations (ICOMOS 2012; ICCROM 2012; IUCN 2012). The report presented by the director-general about the session stressed the interests of all participants in enhanced dialogue, transparency, and cooperation, more capacity-building, and more technical support for conservation actions – all within a dramatically more constrained financial context (UNESCO 2013c). This desire to have "more-with-less" is not difficult to understand, but despite the good intentions of all participants, it does not provide a clear direction or road map for the future (or even the present).

Today, the World Heritage Convention (1972) is often referred to as the "flagship" of UNESCO (Bokova 2012), and its most successful instrument. This alludes to the near-universal participation of the Member States of UNESCO, the profile and status of the World Heritage List, the proliferation of its ideas into national institutions throughout the world, and the obvious and continuing enthusiasm for active engagement by Member States in its activities (see Cameron 1992; Cameron and Rössler 2013; Francioni and Lenzerini 2008).

Given these notions of "success," it is perhaps surprising to note that many perceptions of the future are currently pessimistic – contrasting sharply with the descriptions of earlier optimistic times, and the sense of shared vision (Cameron and Rössler 2013). In part this is a case of seeing World Heritage as a potential "victim of its own success" (Bandarin 2007: 20; see also Francioni and Lenzerini 2008: 410), but also reflects an awareness of shifting values and priorities. These include a reduced respect for scientific expertise, a determination to redress perceptions in imbalances in cultural diversity and geo-cultural representation, and overt attempts to translate international recognition to national prestige and tangible economic benefits.

As we now look to the next milestone – the half-century of World Heritage – the appetite for new nominations to the World Heritage List continues unabated, the resources of the system stretched ever tighter, and there is little capacity for introducing the innovations that have been often discussed. This particular combination of factors – in addition to the "success" of the World Heritage Convention – underpins a mood of pessimism, or at least uncertainty about the future.

Actors within this system express concerns about the potential loss of the achievements of the past 40 years, made in relation to the "spirit" and original intentions for the World Heritage Convention (1972). These include increasing losses of credibility due to changes in decision-making, potentially reducing the prestige of the World Heritage List and its valuable "brand." There are concerns about reduced claims to excellence and high standards in heritage conservation promoted by World Heritage. Finally, there are also concerns about the loss of a focus on intercultural dialogue and internationalism, as the World Heritage Convention increasingly becomes a tool for promoting nationalist goals, shaping and shaped by the processes of globalization.

Alternative Futures

Over the last ten years there has been an increasing interest among heritage studies scholars in the operation of the World Heritage system and its impacts. For example, Smith has famously tagged UNESCO, ICOMOS, and the World Heritage system as the primary means of promulgation of an "Authorized Heritage Discourse" (Smith 2006). Other scholars have started to populate the back rows of World Heritage Committee sessions, providing a separate stream of commentary and ethnographic analysis (Meskell 2011, 2012, 2013b, 2014; Brumann 2012; Schmitt 2009), and others have contributed numerous detailed commentaries and case studies.

In contrast, it seems that the critique from natural heritage commentators has focused less on the fundamental framing of the World Heritage system, and more on its outcomes for nature conservation. These urge the maintenance of high standards, identify gaps, advance governance and management approaches that better incorporate community engagement and traditional ecological knowledge, raise concerns about pressures such as climate change, and advocate holistic concepts of nature and culture (see Figgis *et al.* 2012; Brown, Mitchell, and Beresford 2005; Dudley 2011).

Against the general context of criticism, overload, and pessimism, what does it mean to consider alternative futures? Certainly it is not a matter of looking for small incremental changes to the World Heritage Convention's operational guidelines that are already contemplated. It is also more than the processes of change that are already on the table, such as "upstream" assistance to States Parties and capacity-building.

There is a growing literature that frames the possibilities for change very widely, including alternative modes of governance, financing, and decision-making (see Bertacchini, Saccone, and Santagata 2011; Frey and Steiner 2011; Elliott and Schmutz 2012). While these are important and interesting contributions to the broader dialogue, in our view they do not provide alternatives that are realistic. In particular, proposed solutions that would take key processes out of the hands of States Parties seem unlikely, since this is the central premise of the drafting of the World Heritage Convention (Francioni and Lenzerini 2008: 404).

In our consideration of alternative futures, we have discounted ideas that would require rewriting or amending the World Heritage Convention (1972), since their likelihood seems remote. This might seem a significant constraint on the spectrum of possibilities; however, despite the fixed points created by the convention text, and the inevitability that it will seem increasingly outmoded as it ages, substantial evolution in the ideas and methods has been and continues to be possible via the frequent changes to the convention's operational guidelines. These include broader and more complex interpretations of key concepts, as well as changing notions of good practice in the management and protection of heritage properties (including traditional management).

We therefore focus on possibilities for future enhancements in relation to the intended purposes of the World Heritage Convention, while also pushing for the further evolution of heritage concepts and mechanisms. Based on this, we have identified six inter-related problems where focused reform could deliver significant, alternative, and better futures for the World Heritage system. These are: (1) the problem of Eurocentrism; (2) the problem of inflation and overload; (3) the reduction of credibility; (4) the problem of inclusion; (5) the nature/culture divide; and (6) the problem of conservation. The remainder of this chapter will briefly outline these problems, and some ways in which they might be addressed.

Eurocentrism and Global Balance

Accusations of elitism and Eurocentrism in both the text and implementation of the World Heritage Convention (1972) are not a recent phenomenon, and were raised as early as in the late 1980s and early 1990s (UNESCO 1988, 1994). However, they became much more vocalized around the turn of the millennium, with lobbying for UNESCO's Convention for the Safeguarding of the Intangible Cultural Heritage (2003), or as it commonly known, the Intangible Heritage Convention. This new convention was promoted to become the desired antidote, a non-Eurocentric convention, a convention for the South (Matsuura 2001: 1), or "a corrective to the World Heritage List" (Kurin 2004: 69). The continuous criticism of the World Heritage Convention as elitist and Eurocentric in the drafting process of the Intangible Heritage Convention reinforced this idea (Kono 2004: 41).

The perception of these two aspects, elitism and Eurocentrism, rested predominantly on the definition of cultural heritage in the World Heritage Convention (1972). It also reflected the apparent imbalance of the World Heritage List, with approximately half of its inscribed sites located in Europe and North America. While as early as 1988 the Global Strategy process was created to address the regional and other imbalances on the World Heritage List, "in the light of the … unsatisfactory representation of several regions and themes, the [World Heritage] Committee decided to conduct a 'Global Study' described as 'a retrospective and prospective global reflection on the Convention'" (UNESCO 1988), the definition of cultural heritage is part of the World Heritage Convention text and cannot be revised. It is debatable whether the definition of monuments, groups of buildings, and sites as included in Article 1 of the convention is indeed Eurocentric in a strict sense, or rather a child of its time reflecting a global conception of heritage – or "cultural property" as it was predominantly called at the time – influenced by some Western scholarly debates and approaches.

The founders of the World Heritage Convention (1972), as well as those who accompanied it during the earliest years, seem to suggest that while the definition was certainly based on Western scholarly heritage conceptions, it was the consensus of an intergovernmental process and a global heritage conception at the time. In fact, North American influences largely determined the definition, in that it remained closely tied to the draft text drawn up by Russell Train, with its North American conception of shared characteristics between natural and cultural heritage (Batisse 2005), as well as the very term "heritage," which was previously unheard of in the European cultural and in particular natural heritage contexts (Rudolff 2010a). In the early 1990s, when the issue of Eurocentrism was first debated at a UNESCO expert meeting, the definitions were considered as limited by the heritage conceptions at the time the World Heritage Convention was drafted, rather than being continuously limited by European dominance in the convention's implementation. Both international (UNESCO 1982) and European conceptions of heritage had in the meantime evolved far beyond the focus on monuments, buildings, and sites, taking in "cultural groupings that were complex and multidimensional and demonstrated in spatial terms the social structures, ways of life, beliefs, [and] systems of knowledge" (UNESCO 1994: 2–3).

A solution to Eurocentric tendencies in the definition of heritage was first developed in 1994 as part of the Global Strategy, aimed at creating a global balance among representations on the World Heritage List and the reinterpretation of heritage definitions. While the concept of cultural heritage has been somewhat broadened by the inclusion of cultural landscapes and cultural routes, thus widening potential global participation in the World Heritage Convention (1972), unfortunately the Global Strategy cannot be considered equally successful. Inspired and guided by the UN standard concept of equitable geographical balance (Thakur 1999), this endeavor has been translated into a desire for equally balanced heritage appreciation, that is, a comparable amount of World Heritage properties per country, or at least region or regional group (UNESCO 2000). This ambition has become the stumbling block of World Heritage listing activities (Rudolff 2010b), and the World Heritage system's inability to respond to the growing disparity has in the eyes of the UNESCO external auditor further reduced the credibility of the system and its decision-making bodies (UNESCO 2011a).

Inflation and Credibility

Credibility, balance, and representativeness were the anticipated aims of the Global Strategy, and remain desired goals for the development of the World Heritage system into the future. While not all the specific measures designed under the Global Strategy have achieved this aim, a number of them have made positive contributions, such as thematic studies on underrepresented themes, and capacity building initiatives to support the development of Tentative Lists. However, the limitations on nominations per year – currently 2 per State Party and 45 in total – continues to be ineffective (UNESCO 2011a). It cannot be proven at this point that these measures have increased the representation of under- or non-represented regions and themes, but apparently they managed to slow down the general inflation of the World Heritage List, and probably an increase in the North/South divide (Rudolff 2010a).

Alternative visions for the Global Strategy have been formulated in various ways, challenging the restrictions imposed on nomination numbers, but also more generally the conception of ideal global representation as being geographically or culture/nature balanced. Suggestions include a wide range of options, including the idea of closing the list in the future (Anon. 2009), not inscribing new sites on an annual basis (UNESCO 2011a), and a moratorium on inscriptions by World Heritage Committee members and states with sites on the List of World Heritage in Danger (DFAE 2011). Other ideas include the proposal that each overrepresented State Party should first support a nomination project from an underrepresented region (UNESCO 2004: 173), or even more rigorous restrictions in line with the Cairns-Suzhou decision, further reducing the annual submission limit for nominations.[1]

In strategic planning processes, goal-oriented projects like the Global Strategy would usually be commenced with the formulation of a vision, objectives, and indicators to analyze the strategy's success in the course of implementation. However, it seems that states have very different ideas and conceptions as to the aims of the Global Strategy (see Turtinen 2011: 1), and it entirely lacks an agreed vision, and in particular, shared ideas as to how a perfect, credible, balanced, and representative World Heritage List should appear. Turtinen, on behalf of the Swedish delegation to the World Heritage Committee, observed that "the strategy needs to be clearly defined as a first step … [and] an adequate monitoring mechanism with appropriate indicators … should be developed" (Turtinen 2011: 2).

We agree that a discussion on aims and indicators of the Global Strategy might be a promising start for the definition of relevant studies and solutions, at least with regard to the concepts of balance and representativeness. This view is also supported by the external auditor's report:

> The evaluation of the Global Strategy presented at each session is based on an inadequate mechanism that reduces the notions of credibility, representativity and balance to a series of simplified statistical tables on numbers and regions of World Heritage properties. This tool is not based on scientific criteria, contributing to a drift towards a more political rather than heritage approach to the Convention. (UNESCO 2011a: para. 7)

While a credible list was initially understood to be one that reflects some undefined kind of balance, the term "credible" has more recently been interpreted in relation to processes of establishing and maintaining the World Heritage List – in particular the perceived politicization of World Heritage Committee decisions, as well as the condition of sites on the World Heritage List in terms of visitor infrastructure, conservation, and management. Two former chairpersons of the World Heritage Committee observed in a shared letter to all States Parties that debates of the committee are becoming "less and less technical and … more and more political. We see this trend as maybe the most threatening to the future of the [World Heritage] Convention" (Lacoeuilhe and Marciolionyte 2008).

It is our observation that this trend has increased since these remarks were made, a view apparently also shared by the director-general of UNESCO, Irina Bokova, in her opening remarks to the thirty-sixth session of the World Heritage Committee in St Petersburg:

> In recent years, some developments within the inscription process have weakened the principles of scientific excellence and impartiality that are at the heart of the [World Heritage] Convention … The credibility of the inscription process must be absolute at all stages of the proceedings – from the work of the advisory bodies to the final decision by the States Parties, who hold the primary responsibility in this regard. Today, criticism is growing, and I am deeply concerned. (Bokova 2012)

The politicization of decisions of the World Heritage Committee has also been criticized more openly by heritage professionals, and in press coverage, especially since 2012, when World Heritage Committee sessions began to be live-streamed via the internet (Tourtellot 2012; Tammik 2011). Several aspects have been analyzed to illustrate this politicization, including the increasing divergence of committee decisions from the recommendation of its Advisory Bodies (Meskell 2013b), the increased inscription of properties located in the territory of states serving on the committee at the time of their inscription, and the increased representation of states by their diplomatic corps rather than by heritage professionals, which are said to have more ambitions to boost their careers by ensuring listing regardless of professional concerns (Steiner and Frey 2012: 28).

We consider that apart from whether World Heritage Committee discourses are led by professional or political actors, it is of concern that the committee increasingly abandons the guidelines and procedures it has itself established, inscribing sites on the World Heritage List prematurely, and overruling all previously established benchmarks for such action.

Credibility of the World Heritage Convention (1972) would be best illustrated by a World Heritage List that includes a wide and global representation of the cultural histories and evolutionary phenomena – regardless of nation-state boundaries and geopolitical alliances – in sites effectively managed and adequately conserved. However, at present the World Heritage system does not encourage global representation, effective management, and conservation by means of its rules and regulations. It might be time to review these rules – both those applied and those increasingly abandoned – in view of not only more satisfactory World Heritage listing procedures, but also better conditions and visitor experiences at World Heritage sites.

There is much opportunity to seek inspiration within UNESCO and to learn from the context of other heritage conventions and instruments, which have at times succeeded in better addressing some of the challenges at hand. For example, the Intangible Heritage Convention (2003) has paid early attention to capacity-building for inventorying and nomination preparation (UNESCO 2011d). Despite the fact that the Intangible Heritage Convention equally fails to illustrate an equitable geographical balance in its three listing initiatives, this phenomenon is much more rarely traced to a lack of capacity or financial resources for the preparation of nomination files, the cost of which continuously increases in the World Heritage context (ICCROM 2012). The reason is a far more simplified nomination format with word limits, such as 25,000 words for candidatures to the representative list (UNESCO 2014a), and comprehensive guidelines on how the questions are to be filled out (UNESCO 2014b).

In our view, a careful review with the aim of simplifying the current nomination format of the World Heritage Convention (1972) could not only assist increased numbers of nominations from underrepresented regions with limited financial and human resources, but also relieve some of the resource constraints of the Advisory Bodies in the process of evaluating the nominations, allowing for additional dialogue during these processes. We consider that it would be of particular advantage to divide the nomination process into two consecutive phases, as proposed by ICOMOS (2012). According to this proposal, the first phase would be dedicated to a review of Tentative List entries to confirm whether the sites merit the requirements of Outstanding Universal Value. Only sites for which Outstanding Universal Value was confirmed would then be retained on the Tentative Lists, and be moved forward for the preparation of complete nomination dossiers (ICOMOS 2012).

The Convention on the Protection and Promotion of the Diversity of Cultural Expressions (2005) also provides perspectives that might be worth exploring. In its attempt to integrate different worldviews and conceptions of culture, heritage, and diversity, this convention highlights its objective, "to encourage dialogue among cultures with a view to ensuring wider and balanced cultural exchanges in the world."[2] It has also created operational guidelines on several essential articles which integrate open language and allow for the interpretation of terms in different cultural contexts (UNESCO 2009b). We suggest that during the envisaged review of the operational guidelines for the World Heritage Convention, including the criteria for the establishment of Outstanding Universal Value, as decided by the World Heritage Committee at its thirty-eighth session (UNESCO 2014c), the approach of the Convention on the Protection and Promotion of the Diversity of Cultural Expressions might be an inspiring example, permitting a simplified text for the criteria that leaves space for different interpretations within different worldviews and cultural contexts, and would allow for a broader sense of inclusion in World Heritage activities.

Inclusion and Rights

Issues of inclusion and exclusion are one source of tension in the implementation of the World Heritage Convention (1972) today. These include questions about who makes key decisions in implementation processes, which value systems and heritage concepts are used, who is informed about the processes, who consents, and who benefits from World Heritage listing and management activities. Mapping knowledge flows is therefore closely aligned to the degree of agency that each of the key actors in the systems can exercise – including States Parties, the World Heritage Committee and the World Heritage Centre, but also cultural groups, communities, NGOs and civil societies.

In 2007, the fifth "C" (community) was added to the four "Cs" (conservation, credibility, communication, and capacity-building) that had formed the World Heritage Committee's strategic objectives since the Budapest Declaration of 2002 (UNESCO 2002, 2007). Since then, the role of communities has been very prominent in the rhetoric of the World Heritage system, but ensuring that these ideas are consistently implemented has been less certain.

Inclusion issues largely relate to the centrality of States Parties in the implementation of the World Heritage Convention (Francioni and Lenzerini 2008: 404–9; Logan 2013). Member States are the decision-makers, nominators of properties to the World Heritage List, and are responsible for commitments to conservation made when properties are inscribed. It should therefore not be surprising that nominations will advance themes, national characteristics, and identities that are consistent with the circumstances of national priorities and international prestige, rather than an "objective" reflection of the natural and cultural heritage within each state's borders, based on prioritizing among larger anthropological perspectives (Labadi 2007a). In other words, issues of inclusion begin at the point where the visibility of some cultures in the World Heritage List is problematic, due to the inability of colonized and minority cultures to directly assert their identities through the valorization – and in some cases, the economic opportunities – afforded by World Heritage listing.

On the other hand, not all peoples seek or welcome World Heritage recognition of their cultural and natural heritage, but find themselves on the World Heritage List nevertheless. In such situations, the problems of inclusion and transparency center on issues of consent, self-determination, and political power. These are especially clearly drawn in relation to the rights and interests of indigenous peoples, particularly in "settler" and postcolonial nations. Although the definition and recognition of indigeneity is contentious in many parts of the world, there are World Heritage properties in every region where the role of local communities is central to the maintenance of cultural values and especially Outstanding Universal Value.

The World Heritage Committee has acknowledged the importance of the involvement of indigenous peoples, and in 2000/2001 a proposal to establish the World Heritage Indigenous Peoples Council of Experts (WHIPCOE) was considered (UNESCO 2001). This proposal had a short life, and was not implemented due to an inability to reach consensus on how such a body would be resourced and how it would relate to the existing structures. In general, there seemed to be a rejection of further mechanisms to involve non-state players (Logan 2013; Meskell 2013a; Cameron and Rössler 2012). However, since the adoption of the United Nations Declaration of the Rights of Indigenous Peoples (United Nations 2007), and its underscoring of the need for free prior and informed consent, the pressure to create new and more effective mechanisms for the involvement and respect for the rights of indigenous peoples has re-emerged (Te Heuheu, Kawharu, and Tuheiava 2012). In 2012, an expert meeting was held as part of the program to mark the fortieth anniversary of the World Heritage Convention, and again outlined the perspectives of indigenous peoples whose lands and waters are included in World Heritage properties (Disko and Tungendhat 2013). A call for action and a series of recommendations for changes to the World Heritage Convention's operational guidelines were developed and presented to the World Heritage Committee, although there is no indication that even these moderate and pragmatic proposals will be implemented in the near future.

Whether or not the World Heritage Committee chooses to act on these proposals, one attempt to work around these blocks has been the joint work by the three Advisory Bodies titled "Our Common Dignity" (Sinding-Larsen 2014; ICOMOS 2011). This has focused on awareness-raising among members of the Advisory Bodies, the discussion of case studies, and enhancements to their working methods in order to better reflect rights-based approaches. While some of this reflection has concerned the rights-based claims and concerns of indigenous peoples, as discussed already, it has a far broader application, and the joint work of the Advisory Bodies is currently looking at the enabling factors that can improve rights-based outcomes across a broad spectrum of contexts (Shaheed 2011, 2013; Assi 2012; Logan 2012; Larsen 2012). It is possible that the framing of rights discourses might be an obstacle to these efforts, since States Parties could be reluctant to join in dialogue on these terms. The tensions between individual and collective rights, and the take-up of the language of rights to include potentially conflicting outcomes (such as the "right to develop"), are further reasons why work on rights-based approaches cannot fully address the problems of inclusion alone.

Supporting Conservation

Much of the attention and analysis of the World Heritage system continues to focus on the contents of the World Heritage List (balance, representation, and themes), and the fairness and transparency of the processes involved in building the list. However, in our view, the future credibility and success of the implementation of the World Heritage Convention will depend significantly on how, and how well, inscribed properties are conserved and protected in the long-term.

Because of the large size of the World Heritage List, it is not possible to gain an overview of the state of conservation of all the properties inscribed for their cultural values. Over the past 20 years, the systems for monitoring – particularly reactive monitoring and periodic reporting – have been progressively elaborated. However, the ability of the system to effectively monitor and directly assist with the conservation of cultural and natural heritage is already under significant pressure due to work overload, the sheer scale of the task, and the varying orientations of States Parties in relation to sharing problems with the global community. It is therefore common that States Parties and site managers perceive these processes as onerous and punitive, rather than supportive.

Several strands of potential change have been identified in order to improve the conservation outcomes of properties on the World Heritage List. Some of them relate to issues concerning the partial closure or "slowing down" of the listing machinery to free more time and resources for conservation actions (an issue we have already discussed). Others point to the present-day reluctance of the World Heritage Committee to utilize existing mechanisms such as the List of World Heritage in Danger, noting that there are few mechanisms in the system that provide positive incentives (Meskell 2014; IUCN 2012). Discussing the removal of the Galapagos Islands from this list in 2010, it was reported that "Ecuador felt that to stay on the [list] was a slight," and concluded that "the hard fact is that danger listings, as well as inscribing sites in the first place, are getting infected by politics" (Anon. 2010).

Finding new incentives has so far been only tentatively successful. The 2011 World Heritage Committee decision to showcase examples of best practice was one attempt to remedy this imbalance (Vigan in the Philippines was recognized for its sustainable management), and the World Heritage Capacity Building Programme has likewise developed a number of case studies around the idea of sharing best practices in World Heritage management (UNESCO 2012). Some of the other proposals that have been made are likely to be politically unpalatable or legally impractical, such as the more frequent inspection and delisting of properties that do not continue to meet the desired standards of conservation (Cleere 2011: 181).

As the IUCN has shown in its work on developing the Outlook program for natural World Heritage (IUCN 2014), a big part of the solution to this problem will lie in finding better monitoring arrangements, but without increasing the "policing" and "judging" character of the roles of the Advisory Bodies. In our view, the call for "upstream" collaboration between the Advisory Bodies and communities, site managers, and government authorities to reduce the number of unsuccessful nominations should be complemented by a much stronger focus on "downstream" cooperation along the same lines, building on the existing practice of inviting advisory missions of the Advisory Bodies when help is needed.

At the present, one of the strongest emerging issues of implementation is to resolve – or at least ameliorate – the often artificial divide between nature and culture. While it is commonly understood that the conceptual dichotomy of nature and culture can be traced back to the Greek philosophers (e.g. Aristotle 1996), and that it is an artifact of the West that has persevered into the modern era (Brockwell, O'Connor, and Byrne 2013; Buckley and Badman 2014), the dichotomy has nevertheless been replicated in many non-Western contexts in the twentieth century. Given the prevalence of the Aristotelian dichotomy within modernity, it was a surprising – and initially not fully intended – move forward that the World Heritage Convention (1972), after merging three different draft texts for natural heritage by IUCN, cultural heritage by UNESCO and ICOMOS, and a combined World Heritage Trust approach drafted by the United States, integrated the categories culture and nature in one convention (Battise 2005).

However, what may have seemed innovative in the 1970s still remains a basis for division in the implementation of the World Heritage Convention. A number of States Parties have started to challenge the divide, and have conceptualized nominations which challenge the underlying division of culture and nature, and their expression in established criteria. Recently, nominations were prepared that might have been classically considered as mixed sites or cultural landscapes, but which highlighted neither the natural nor cultural qualities, but rather the relationship between them in their justification of Outstanding Universal Value.[3] These nominations emphasized the relationships between the people and the land, and in particular their mutual inter-dependence in a larger system which gives and sustains life beyond the categories of culture and nature. In our view, these challenges are more than overdue, and have already initiated intense discussions which point at the need to review existing processes and integrate a wider range of worldviews (as discussed earlier).

Finally, it is easily recognized that much of the pressure concerning the conservation of World Heritage properties comes from development contexts and challenges. Obviously, World Heritage properties do not exist in isolation from their physical, social, and economic contexts, and treating conservation as something that only takes place "inside" a designated property can only go so far (Galla 2012).

It is in this context that the efforts of UNESCO to promote culture as a fourth "pillar" of sustainability, and a key element of the post-2015 international development agenda, are relevant (Bandarin 2013; Hayashi, Boccardi, and Al Hassan 2013; UNESCO 2013b). The question is how much influence heritage conservation activities can play in relation to poverty alleviation, gender equality, and sustainable development. There are many high-level aspirational statements about the economic benefits of heritage conservation, and the links to cultural identity and community identity are easily appreciated. However, too often the flow of benefits in relation to tourism and development does not reach local communities. Evidence of concrete and measurable contributions of heritage conservation to the Millennium Development Goals and sustainability – likely to be required when arguing for the essential role of culture in sustainable development – is difficult to obtain. It may be worthwhile seeing if the World Heritage Convention and site-specific data collected over four decades can provide convincing examples to promote the future role of heritage in the global agenda of the United Nations.

Concluding Remarks

This chapter provides a very brief overview of the issues that will determine the future of the World Heritage Convention (1972) – including the likely and unlikely futures, and conventional and alternative futures. In concluding, we must note that this is a personal and specifically located perspective. We locate ourselves as cultural heritage practitioners, teachers, and scholars, trained and employed in Western academic institutions, with direct experience as actors inside key components of the World Heritage system – including, at various times, national delegations, Advisory Body delegations, and the World Heritage Committee.

We know and readily acknowledge that our perspectives on the present – and possible futures – are significantly informed by these roles and experiences. We are well acquainted with the current condition of pessimism that informs much of the discussion about the future; keenly, even painfully aware of the adverse outcomes that can occur, due in part to the problems of perceived Eurocentrism, overload, inflation, exclusion, and the complex pressures that counter our efforts and good intentions. Paradoxically, like many others we work alongside, we also remain more or less committed to the possibilities that continued implementation of the World Heritage Convention can bring.

Our perspectives and experiences allow us to be cautious about predicting the future for World Heritage. The work of Cameron and Rössler (2013) and others has demonstrated the wonderment of the "pioneers" of the system as they reflect on the World Heritage system today, and the many aspects that they did not even imagine. Working in the twenty-first century, our time of intensive engagement with the World Heritage Convention takes place after the valorized work of these pioneers, at a time when the future seems mostly insecure and unpredictable. We also note that several of the ongoing developments of the World Heritage Convention are influenced by processes of cultural diplomacy rather than advances in the heritage profession.

These are important and fascinating times, as many heritage studies scholars have discovered. It is hard to foresee how our contemporaries might look back on this time and reflect on today's trends and events with hindsight. As the World Heritage Convention sets out for turning 50, the most important thing that consideration of alternative futures can do is to direct and stimulate the energy and commitment needed for those working in the present to continue, to keep working toward the shared goals established by the World Heritage Convention, to strive, to improve, and to innovate. The present is challenging, important, and endlessly engaging, and the future – as is always the case – will take care of itself.

Notes

1 The Cairns-Suzhou Decision refers to decisions taken by the World Heritage Committee in 2000 and 2004 which limit the number of new nominations that each State Party is allowed to submit per year. These decisions were taken in order to ensure a manageable workload for the World Heritage Committee, the Advisory Bodies, and the World Heritage Centre, but also aimed to assist in improving the representativeness of the World Heritage List.

2 Cultural Diversity Convention (2005), art. 1.c.

3 The most widely discussed recent example has been the Canadian nomination of Pimachiowin Aki, which was deferred by the World Heritage Committee at its thirty-seventh session in 2013 (see UNESCO 2013d). However, there are other nominations that have also demonstrated this issue. The specific issues for nominating and evaluating mixed properties is the subject of current work by the World Heritage Committee; see e.g. UNESCO (2014d).

References

Legislation

Convention Concerning the Protection of the World Cultural and Natural Heritage (World Heritage Convention) (UNESCO, 1972). Available at: http://whc.unesco.org/archive/convention-en.pdf (accessed March 19, 2015).

Convention for the Safeguarding of the Intangible Cultural Heritage (Intangible Heritage Convention) (UNESCO, 2003). Available at: http://unesdoc.unesco.org/images/0013/001325/132540e.pdf (accessed March 19, 2015).

Convention on the Protection and Promotion of the Diversity of Cultural Expressions (Cultural Diversity Convention) (UNESCO, 2005). Available at: http://unesdoc.unesco.org/images/0014/001429/142919e.pdf (accessed March 19, 2015).

United Nations (2007) Declaration on the Rights of Indigenous Peoples (UNDRIP). Document A/RES/61/295. Available at: http://www.un-documents.net/a61r295.htm (accessed March 19, 2015).

Other Works

Anon. (1983) How the World Heritage Convention Works. *Ambio*, 12 (3/4), 140–145.

Anon. (2009) The Limits of Soft Cultural Power. *Economist*, September 10. Available at: http://www.economist.com/node/14428543 (accessed March 21, 2015).

Anon. (2010) UNESCO's World Heritage Sites: A Danger List In Danger. *Economist*, August 26. Available at: http://www.economist.com/node/16891951 (accessed March 21, 2015).

Aristotle (1996) *Physics*, trans. R. Waterfield. Oxford: Oxford University Press.

Assi, E. (2012) World Heritage Sites, Human Rights and Cultural Heritage in Palestine. *International Journal of Heritage Studies*, 18 (3), 316–323.

Bandarin, F. (2007) Introduction: Present and Future Challenge of the World Heritage Convention. In S. Labadi (ed.), *World Heritage: Challenges for the Millennium*. Paris: UNESCO, pp. 18–23.

Bandarin, F. (2013). The World Heritage Convention in the post-2015 International Development Agenda. In V. Vujicic-Lugassy (ed.), *Celebrating 40 years of the World Heritage Convention*. Paris: UNESCO, pp. 110–113.

Batisse, M. (2005) Nature and Culture: Recollections of a (Conventional) Marriage. In M. Batisse and G. Bolla (eds), *The Invention of World Heritage*, Vol. 2. Paris: Association des Anciens Fonctionaires de l'UNESCO, pp. 13–42.

Bertacchini, E., Saccone, D., and Santagata, W. (2011) Embracing Diversity, Correcting Inequalities: Towards a New Governance for the UNESCO World Heritage Convention. *International Journal of Cultural Policy*, 17 (3), 278–288.

Bokova, I. (2012) Address by Ms Irina Bokova, UNESCO Director-General, on the Occasion of the Opening of the 36th Session of the World Heritage Committee. Document DG/2012/096. Available at: http://unesdoc.unesco.org/images/0021/002167/216700e.pdf (accessed March 21, 2015).

Brockwell, S., O'Connor, S., and Byrne, D. (eds) (2013) *Transcending the Culture–Nature Divide in Cultural Heritage: Views from the Asia-Pacific Region*. Canberra: Australian National University Press.

Brown, J., Mitchell, N., and Beresford, B. (eds) (2005) *The Protected Landscape Approach: Linking Nature, Culture and Community*. Gland: IUCN.

Brumann, C. (2012) Multilateral Ethnography: Entering the World Heritage Arena. Working Paper No. 136. Halle: Max Planck Institute for Social Anthropology.

Buckley, K., and Badman, T. (2014) Nature+Culture and World Heritage: Why It Matters. In C. Cameron and J. Hermann (eds), *Exploring the Cultural Value of Nature: A World Heritage Context*. Conference proceedings. Montreal: University of Montreal, pp. 105–121. Available at: http://www.patrimoinebati.umontreal.ca/documents/Proceedings_2014_FINAL.pdf, (accessed April 12, 2015).

Cameron, C. (1992) The Strengths and Weaknesses of the World Heritage Convention. *Nature and Resources*, 28 (3), 1–11.

Cameron, C., and Rössler, M. (2012) World Heritage and Indigenous Peoples: The Evolution of an Important Relationship. *World Heritage Review*, 62, 44–48.

Cameron, C., and Rössler, M. (2013) *Many Voices, One Vision: The Early Years of the World Heritage Convention*. Farnham: Ashgate.

Cleere, H. (2011) The 1972 UNESCO World Heritage Convention: A Success or a Failure? *Heritage and Society*, 4 (2), 173–186.

DFAE (Département fédéral des affaires étrangères) (2011) *Evaluation de la Stratégie globale: Commentaires de la Suisse.* Bern: DFAE.

Disko, S., and Tugendhat, H. (eds) (2013) Report on the International Expert Workshop on the World Heritage Convention and Indigenous Peoples, 20–21 September 2012, Copenhagen, Denmark. Copenhagen: IWGIA. Available at: http://whc.unesco.org/en/events/906/ (accessed April 11, 2015)

Dudley, N. (2011) *Authenticity in Nature: Making Choices about the Naturalness of Ecosystems.* London: Earthscan.

Elliott, M.A., and Schmutz, V. (2012) World Heritage: Constructing a Universal Cultural Order. *Poetics*, 40, 256–277.

Figgis, P., Leverington, A., Mackay, R., Maclean, A., and Valentine, P. (eds) (2012) *Keeping the Outstanding Exceptional: The Future of World Heritage in Australia.* Sydney: Australian Committee for IUCN. Available at: https://portals.iucn.org/library/efiles/edocs/2013-026.pdf (accessed March 21, 2015).

Francioni, F., and Lenzerini, F. (2008) *The 1972 World Heritage Convention: A Commentary.* Oxford: Oxford University Press.

Frey, B.S., and Steiner, L. (2011) World Heritage List: Does It Make Sense? *International Journal of Cultural Policy*, 17 (5), 555–573.

Galla, A. (ed) (2012) *World Heritage: Benefits beyond Borders.* Cambridge: Cambridge University Press/UNESCO.

Hayashi, N., Boccardi, G., and Al Hassan, N. (2013) Culture in the Post-2015 Sustainable Development Agenda: Why Culture is Key to Sustainable Development. Paper presented at the International Conference "Culture: Key to Sustainable Development," Hangzhou, China, May 14–17.

ICCROM (2012) Present and Specific Challenges Confronting the 1972 World Heritage Convention. Briefing Paper. Rome: ICCROM.

ICOMOS (2011) Our Common Dignity: Rights-Based Approaches to Heritage Management. Resolution 17GA 2011/30. Available at: http://www.international.icomos.org/Paris2011/GA_2011_Resolutions_EN_finaldistr_20120109.pdf (accessed May 25, 2015).

ICOMOS (2012) The World Heritage Convention: Thinking Ahead. Briefing paper. Paris: ICOMOS.

IUCN (2012) A Future for World Heritage: Challenges and Responses to Assure the Credibility of the World Heritage Convention. Available at: http://cmsdata.iucn.org/downloads/a_future_for_world_heritage__iucn_non_paper_september_2012.pdf (accessed April 13, 2015).

IUCN (2014) IUCN World Heritage Outlook. Available at: http://www.worldheritageoutlook.iucn.org/ (accessed March 21, 2015).

Kono, T. (2004) The Basic Principles of the Convention for Safeguarding of Intangible Heritage: A Comparative Analysis with the Convention for Protection of World Natural and Cultural Heritage and Japanese Law. In Okinawa International Forum (ed.), *Utaki in Okinawa and Sacred Spaces in Asia: Community Development and Cultural Heritage.* Tokyo: Japan Foundation, pp. 37–43.

Kurin, R. (2004) Safeguarding Intangible Cultural Heritage in the 2003 UNESCO Convention: A Critical Appraisal. *Museum International*, 56 (1/2), 66–77.

Labadi, S. (2007a) Representations of the Nation and Cultural Diversity in Discourses on World Heritage. *Journal of Social Archaeology*, 7, 147–170.

Labadi, S. (ed.) (2007b) *World Heritage: Challenges for the Millennium.* Paris: UNESCO. Available at: http://whc.unesco.org/documents/publi_millennium_en.pdf (accessed March 21, 2015).

Labadi, S. (2013) *UNESCO, Cultural Heritage, and Outstanding Universal Value.* Walnut Creek, CA: AltaMira Press.

Lacoeuilhe, V., and Marciolionyte, I. (2008) Letter of October 8. Submitted to the Workshop to Reflect on the Future of the World Heritage Convention, February 25–27, 2009. Paris: UNESCO.

Larsen, P.B. (2012) Advisory Body Evaluations of World Heritage Nominations in Relation to Community and Rights Concerns. Report. Available at: http://www.icomos.no/cms/icontent/filer/whrba/15_2013_0722_A_F_Peter_BL_DiscnPaper.pdf (accessed March 23, 2015).

LeBlanc, F. (1984) An Inside View of the Convention. *Momentum*, special issue, pp. 17–32.

Linstrum, D. (1984) An Alternative Approach? An Interview with Anne Raidl. *Momentum*, special issue, pp. 50–55.

Logan, W. (2012) Cultural Diversity, Cultural Heritage and Human Rights: Towards Heritage Management as Human Rights-Based Cultural Practice. *International Journal of Heritage Studies*, 18 (3), 231–244.

Logan, W. (2013) Australia, Indigenous Peoples and World Heritage from Kakadu to Cape York: State Party Behavior under the World Heritage Convention. *Journal of Social Archaeology*, 13 (2), 153–176.

Matsuura, K. (2001) Address on the Occasion of the Ceremony for the Proclamation of Masterpieces of the Oral and Intangible Heritage of Humanity. UNESCO document DG/2001/52. Available at: http://unesdoc.unesco.org/images/0012/001225/122595E.pdf (accessed March 21, 2015).

Meskell, L. (2011) From Paris to Pontdrift: UNESCO Meetings, Mapungubwe and Mining. *South African Archaeological Bulletin*, 66 (194), 149–156.

Meskell, L. (2012) The Rush to Inscribe: Reflections on the 35th Session of the World Heritage Committee, UNESCO Paris, 2011. *Journal of Field Archaeology*, 37 (2), 145–151.

Meskell, L. (2013a) UNESCO and the Fate of the World Heritage Indigenous Peoples Council of Experts (WHIPCOE). *International Journal of Cultural Property*, 20, 1–20.

Meskell, L. (2013b) UNESCO's World Heritage Convention at 40: Challenging the Economic and Political Order of International Heritage Conservation. *Current Anthropology*, 54 (4), 483–494.

Meskell, L. (2014) States of Conservation: Protection, Politics, and Pacting within UNESCO's World Heritage Committee. *Anthropological Quarterly*, 87 (1), 217–244.

Oviedo, G., and Puschkarsky, T. (2012) World Heritage and Rights-Based Approaches to Nature Conservation. *International Journal of Heritage Studies*, 18 (3), 285–296.

Pressouyre, L. (1996) *The World Heritage Convention, Twenty Years Later*. Paris: UNESCO. Available at: http://whc.unesco.org/en/documents/127674 (accessed March 21, 2015).

Rao, K. (2010) A New Paradigm for the Identification, Nomination and Inscription of Properties on the World Heritage List. *International Journal of Heritage Studies*, 16 (3), 161–172.

Rudolff, B. (2010a) *Intangible and Tangible Heritage: A Topology of Culture in Contexts of Faith*. Bonn: Scientia Bonnensis.

Rudolff, B. (2010b) Local Identity on the Global Stage: On the Challenges of Representing Diversity. In M.-T. Albert and D. Offenhaeusser (eds), *World Heritage and Cultural Diversity: Challenges for University Education*, Frankfurt am Main: IKO, pp. 104–112.

Schmitt, T. (2009) Global Culture Governance. Decision Making about World Heritage between Politics and Science. *Erdkunde*, 63 (2), 103–121.

Shaheed, F. (2011) Report of the Independent Expert in the Field of Cultural Rights. UNGA document A/HRC/17/38. Available at: http://daccess-dds-ny.un.org/doc/UNDOC/GEN/G11/122/04/PDF/G1112204.pdf?OpenElement (accessed April 11, 2015).

Shaheed, F. (2013) Report of the Special Rapporteur in the Field of Cultural Rights. UNGA document A/68/296. Available at: http://daccess-dds-ny.un.org/doc/UNDOC/GEN/N13/422/91/PDF/N1342291.pdf?OpenElement (accessed April 11, 2015).

Sinding-Larsen, A. (ed.) (2014) *World Heritage and Rights-Based Approaches: Report from Workshop in Oslo, 1–3 April 2014*. Oslo: Norge ICOMOS. Available at: http://cmsdata.iucn.org/downloads/world_heritage_and_rights_based_approaches_2014_oslo_report.pdf (accessed March 21, 2015).

Slatyer, R.O. (1983) The Origin and Evolution of the World Heritage Committee. *Ambio*, 12 (3/4), 138–140.

Smith, L. (2006) *Uses of Heritage*. London: Routledge.

Steiner, L., and Frey, B.S. (2012) Correcting the Imbalance of the World Heritage List: Did the UNESCO Strategy Work? *Journal of International Organization Studies*, 3 (1), 25–61.

Strasser, P. (2002) Putting Reform into Action – Thirty Years of the World Heritage Convention: How to Reform a Convention without Changing Its Regulations. *International Journal of Cultural Property*, 11, 215–266.

Tammik, O. (2011) Delegates Warn Against Politicization of UNESCO World Heritage Committee. *News.err.ee*, October 26. Available at: http://news.err.ee/v/Culture/f890c9f5-c587-482b-9af3-1aa7a29621d8 (accessed March 21, 2015).

Te Heuheu, T., Kawharu, M., and Tuheiava, R.A. (2012) World Heritage and Indigeneity. *World Heritage Review* 62 (February), 8–17. Available at: http://whc.unesco.org/en/review/62/ (accessed April 11, 2015).

Thakur, R. (ed.) (1999) What is Equitable Geographic Representation in the Twenty-First Century? Report of a Seminar Held by the International Peace Academy and the United Nations University. New York: United Nations University. Available at: http://archive.unu.edu/unupress/equitable.pdf (accessed March 21, 2015).

Tourtellot, J. (2012) Archaeologists Blast Hasty World Heritage Listings. *National Geographic Newswatch*, April 18. Available at: http://voices.nationalgeographic.com/2012/04/18/archaeologists-blast-hasty-world-heritage-listings/ (accessed March 21, 2015).

Turntinen, J. (2011) Letter of July 8. Response to Circular Letter CL/WHC-11/15: Independent Evaluation by the UNESCO External Auditor of the Global Strategy and the PACT Initiative. 2011. Paris: UNESCO.

UNESCO (1982) Mexico City Declaration on Cultural Policies. Declaration adopted by the UNESCO World Conference on Cultural Policies, Mexico City, July 26 to August 6. Available at: http://portal.unesco.org/culture/en/files/12762/11295421661mexico_en.pdf/mexico_en.pdf (accessed March 21, 2015).

UNESCO (1988) Progress Report, Synthesis and Action Plan on the Global Strategy for a Representative and Credible World Heritage List. Document WHC.98/CONF.203/12. Available at: http://whc.unesco.org/en/documents/1551 (accessed March 23, 2015).

UNESCO (1994) Expert Meeting on the "Global Strategy" and thematic studies for a representative World Heritage List. Document WHC–94/CONF.003/INF.6. Available at: http://whc.unesco.org/archive/global94.htm (accessed March 21, 2015).

UNESCO (2000) Report of the Working Group on the Representativity of the World Heritage List. Document WHC.00/CONF 204/INF.08. Available at: http://whc.unesco.org/en/documents/311 (accessed March 21, 2015).

UNESCO (2001) World Heritage Committee, Twenty-Fifth Session: Progress Report on the Proposed World Heritage Indigenous Peoples Council of Experts (WHIPCOE). Document WHC–2001/CONF.208/13. Available at: whc.unesco.org/document/9475 (accessed March 21, 2015).

UNESCO (2002) Budapest Declaration on World Heritage. *Document CONF* 202 9. Available at: http://whc.unesco.org/en/decisions/1217 (accessed February 5, 2015).

UNESCO (2004) Summary Record of the 28th session of the World Heritage Committee (Suzhou, China). Document WHC–04/28.COM/INF.26. Available at: http://whc.unesco.org/en/documents/5308 (accessed March 23, 2015).

UNESCO (2005) Operational Guidelines for the Implementation of the World Heritage Convention. Available at: http://whc.unesco.org/archive/opguide05-en.pdf (accessed March 23, 2015).

UNESCO (2007) Evaluation of the Results of the Implementation of the Committee's Strategic Objectives: Proposal for a "Fifth C" to Be Added to the Strategic Objectives. Document WHC-07/31.COM/13B. Available at: http://whc.unesco.org/en/decisions/5197/ (accessed March 23, 2015).

UNESCO (2009a) Report of the Expert Meeting on Upstream Processes to Nominations: Creative Approaches in the Nomination Process. Report of expert meeting, Phuket, Thailand, April 27–29. Available at: http://whc.unesco.org/en/events/673 (accessed March 23, 2015).

UNESCO (2009b) Articles 7, 8 and 17 of the Convention on the Protection and Promotion of the diversity of Cultural Expressions: Operational Guidelines. Available at: http://en.unesco.org/creativity/convention/2005-convention/operational-guidelines (accessed March 23, 2015).

UNESCO (2009c) Reflection on the Future of the World Heritage Convention. Document WHC–09/33.COM/14. Available at: http://whc.unesco.org/archive/2009/whc09-33com-14Ae.pdf (accessed March 23, 2015).

UNESCO (2011a) Independent Evaluation by the UNESCO External Auditor, Vol. 1: Implementation of the Global Strategy for a Credible, Balanced and Representative World Heritage List. Document WHC11/35.COM/INF9A. Available at: http://whc.unesco.org/archive/2011/whc11-35com-INF9Ae.pdf (accessed March 23, 2015).

UNESCO (2011b) World Heritage Strategic Action Plan. Document WHC11/18.GA/11. Available at: http://whc.unesco.org/en/documents/115441 (accessed March 23, 2015).

UNESCO (2011c) Reflection concerning the upstream process. Document WHC 11/35.COM/12C. Available at: http://whc.unesco.org/en/documents/106685 (accessed March 23, 2015).

UNESCO (2011d) Identifying and Inventorying Intangible Cultural Heritage. Brochure. Available at: http://www.unesco.org/culture/ich/doc/src/01856-EN.pdf (accessed March 23, 2015).

UNESCO (2012) Sharing Best Practices in World Heritage Management. World Heritage Capacity Building Strategy. Web page available at: http://whc.unesco.org/en/recognition-of-best-practices/ (accessed February 5, 2015).

UNESCO (2013a) Operational Guidelines for the Implementation of the World Heritage Convention. Available at: http://whc.unesco.org/archive/opguide13-en.pdf (accessed March 23, 2015).

UNESCO (2013b) The Hangzhou Declaration: Placing Culture at the Heart of Sustainable Development Policies. Available at: http://www.unesco.org/new/fileadmin/MULTIMEDIA/HQ/CLT/images/FinalHangzhouDeclaration20130517.pdf (accessed March 23, 2015).

UNESCO (2013c) Summary and Follow-Up of the Director-General's Meeting on "The World Heritage Convention: Thinking Ahead." Document WHC–13/37.COM/5C. Available at: http://whc.unesco.org/en/documents/122817 (accessed March 23, 2015).

UNESCO (2013d) Decisions Adopted by the World Heritage Committee at its 37th Session (Phnom Penh, 2013). Document WHC-13/37.COM/20. Available at: http://whc.unesco.org/archive/2013/whc13-37com-20-en.pdf (accessed March 23, 2015).

UNESCO (2014a) ICH-02 Form for Nominations to the Representative List of the Intangible Cultural Heritage of Humanity. Available at: http://www.unesco.org/culture/ich/index.php?lg=en&pg=00184 (accessed March 23, 2015).

UNESCO (2014b) ICH-02 Form: Instructions for Nominations to the Representative List of the Intangible Cultural Heritage of Humanity. Available at: http://www.unesco.org/culture/ich/index.php?lg=en&pg=00184 (accessed March 23, 2015).

UNESCO (2014c) Decisions Adopted by the World Heritage Committee at its 38th Session (Doha, 2014). Document WHC–14/38.COM/16. Available at: http://whc.unesco.org/archive/2014/whc14-38com-16en.pdf (accessed March 23, 2015).

UNESCO (2014d) Reflections on Processes for Mixed Nominations. Document WHC-14/38.COM/9B. Available at: http://whc.unesco.org/archive/2014/whc14-38com-9B-en.pdf (accessed March 23, 2015).

von Droste, B. (2011) From the Seven Wonders of the Ancient World to the 1,000 World Heritage Places Today. *Journal of Cultural Heritage Management and Sustainable Development*, 1 (1), 26–41.

Vujicic-Lugassy, V. (ed.) (2013) *Celebrating 40 years of the World Heritage Convention: Proceedings, Closing Event of the Celebration of the 40th Anniversary, November 2012 / Kyoto, Japan*. Available at: http://whc.unesco.org/en/news/1077/ (accessed March 23, 2015).

CHAPTER 36

Challenges for International Cultural Heritage Law

Ana Filipa Vrdoljak

Introduction

Daily media reports in January 2014 of the systematic shelling of historic religious and cultural monuments and sites, the targeting of civilian populations, and leveling of entire neighborhoods during the civil war in Syria led to renewed public outcry and international condemnation. These acts are reminiscent of those perpetrated by the combatants during the wars that raged following the break-up of Yugoslavia two decades earlier. They replicate strategies engaged in by participants in civil conflicts across time and around the globe. Since the nineteenth century, international law, and more particularly international humanitarian law, has addressed, condemned, and prohibited such acts. After the Cold War and in response to the atrocities perpetrated during the Yugoslav wars, the international community expressed its commitment to holding individuals to account by establishing international criminal tribunals. Their jurisprudence and related international developments enriched international humanitarian law and international criminal law. Yet, in the decades since, there has been a waning in the resolve and solidarity of the international community in this aim. While these events and responses have a broad resonance in international law generally, they are also emblematic of the challenges faced by legal efforts to protect and promote cultural heritage globally.

The period from the shelling of Dubrovnik, Sarajevo, and Mostar in the 1990s to the bombardment of Homs and Aleppo in the 2010s witnessed a significant expansion

A Companion to Heritage Studies, First Edition. Edited by William Logan, Máiréad Nic Craith, and Ullrich Kockel.
© 2016 John Wiley & Sons, Inc. Published 2016 by John Wiley & Sons, Inc.

in interventionist activities by the international community, and then their gradual contraction in this new century. The factors that fostered the cosmopolitan drive during this brief period had a positive impact on the protection of cultural heritage during armed conflict and peacetime. They also put into stark relief the perpetual challenges facing the legal protection of cultural heritage at the international level, which forms the core of this chapter. In the first part, I consider how the international community is conceived and acts in these circumstances. I explore the notion of the cultural heritage of humanity that underlies such international cooperation, with particular reference to the use of the Convention Concerning the Protection of the World Cultural and Natural Heritage (World Heritage Convention) (1972), in conflicts from Yugoslavia to Mali. In the second part, I examine how individuals (and groups) are conceptualized under international human rights law, particularly cultural rights and the right to access culture, and responsibilities of perpetrators under international humanitarian law and international criminal law. In essence, this structure serves to illustrate how the state, which continues to define and dominate international law, remains a central actor in hindering and promoting the protection of cultural heritage within and beyond its territory.

The International Community, Common Heritage, and International Cooperation

In the first part of the chapter I take a macro viewpoint, looking outward from the state. But as it will become clear, the two themes of what constitutes cultural heritage and how it is to be legally protected reflect and complement changes evolving at the micro level, which I examine in the second part of the chapter, which focuses on the individual. The challenges that plague the protection of cultural heritage at the international level today characterize the persistent limitations of international law generally. Indeed, it is a telling case study for international law and the ongoing privileging of the state and national interests in its articulation and implementation. Yet, there is a clear transition from earlier understandings of a society of states to the present-day idea of the "international community," which is exemplified in the evolving meaning of the "cultural heritage of humankind" and international cooperation over the last century and a half.

The earliest attempts to codify international law principles in the modern period occurred in the nineteenth century with efforts to set down the laws of war between states. The unencumbered ability to engage in war was viewed as a prerogative of the state. These initiatives to humanize the impact of war on civilians were extended into an international concern to limit its effects on cultural property. The regulations annexed to the Convention with Respect to the Laws and Customs of War on Land (1899), or Hague II, and the Convention Respecting the Laws and Customs of War on Land (1907), or Hague IV, both reference the need to protect movable and immovable heritage during armed conflict and belligerent occupation.[1] Hague II and Hague IV were recognized as customary international law, that is, binding even on non-States Parties to the conventions by the International Military Tribunal at Nuremberg in 1945. The prohibitions contained in these early multilateral treaties have been reaffirmed by subsequent instruments finalized following later conflicts that caused large-scale loss of life and destruction of cultural heritage, including UNESCO's specialist Convention for the Protection of Cultural Property in the Event of Armed

Conflict (1954), known as the Hague Convention, along with Protocol to the Hague Convention (1954) and the Second Protocol to the Hague Convention (1999). Three characteristics mark out the movement of the protection of cultural heritage as being beyond the preserve of the state, namely, the articulation of an international community per se, the notion of the "cultural heritage of mankind" as a common good, and international cooperation in the protection and preservation of this common good.

The conceptualization of an international community to oversee the protection of cultural heritage could only occur with the ceding of authority and sovereignty of states through their signing of relevant treaties. Yet, even the World Heritage Convention (1972), which has the highest take-up rate of all contemporary international instruments covering the protection of cultural property, that is, 190 States Parties of the 193 current Member States of the United Nations (as at March 2014) cannot claim to represent the international community in this field (Francioni 2008: 5). Under treaty law, the obligations under the World Heritage Convention are not obligations owed to the world at large, but rather are owed to the other States Parties to the convention (O'Keefe 2004: 189). However, the UN Security Council has taken the protection of sites listed under the World Heritage Convention beyond these narrow contractual strictures. This occurred with Security Council Resolution 1483 of 22 May 2003 (UNSC 2003: para. 7) concerning the dispersal of cultural objects during the Iraq conflict and occupation, which bound all UN Member States even if they were not signatories to the Hague Convention (1954), the Protocol to the Hague Convention (1954), or the UNESCO Convention on the Means of Prohibiting and Preventing the Illicit Import, Export and Transfer of Ownership of Cultural Property (UNESCO Convention) (1970). Similarly, the European Union has called on its Member States to prevent the transfer and facilitate the return of cultural objects removed from Syria since the start of the civil war in 2011 (European Union 2013: art. 3; see also Ki-moon, Bokova, and Brahimi 2014).

While efforts to define an international community beyond the territorial boundaries of states have been slow, there has been movement the other way; that is, the interjection of the international community into the affairs of a state in respect of cultural heritage in danger on the territory of the state. Starting with the Nuremberg Tribunal judgment in the mid twentieth century (IMT 1947), and progressing to the jurisprudence of the ad hoc International Criminal Tribunal for the Former Yugoslavia (ICTY)[2] and recent referral by Mali to the prosecutor at the International Criminal Court (ICC) (Coulibaly 2012), there has been a gradual (but sporadic) expansion of the protection of cultural heritage under international humanitarian law beyond inter-state armed conflicts to civil conflicts. Indeed, the UN secretary general called on the Security Council in 2012 to impose sanctions on the perpetrators of attacks on religious and cultural sites in Timbuktu that are designated as "part of the indivisible heritage of humanity" (Ki-moon 2012a: 1). This move reinforces the transition from a society of states which defined international law-making and the protection of cultural heritage with it until the mid twentieth century, to an international community driven by common core values to which all states are answerable, even for acts perpetrated by them on their own territory. So, for instance, the cultural landscape and archeological sites of the Bamiyan Valley in Afghanistan were inscribed on the World Heritage List and the List of World Heritage in Danger in 2003 because of the importance of the statues of the Buddha as representations of the Gandharan School of Buddhist art in Central Asia, but also as testimony to the destruction of the monuments by the Taliban in 2001, an event "which shook the world" (UNESCO 2003b).

However, it is important to note the limitations of these examples. Nuremberg has often been criticized as victor's justice, the ICTY covered conflicts arising from the dismantling of a federated state, and the Malian referral was undertaken by the government against rebel forces. These limitations are multiplied in respect of damage and destruction perpetrated within a state during peacetime. Perhaps the most celebrated recent example is the destruction of the monumental Bamiyan Buddhas, where the international community could do little more than condemn this act of destruction through a UNESCO Declaration Concerning the Intentional Destruction of Cultural Heritage (Intentional Destruction Declaration) (UNESCO 2003a) and in various UN fora.

The key concept grounding a notion of international community is the "cultural heritage of humanity." This idea has permeated the earliest articulations of protection of cultural heritage in modern international law, and is consistently referenced in contemporary instruments in the field.[3] For example, the Convention on the Protection of the Underwater Heritage (Underwater Heritage Convention) (2001) recognizes such heritage as "an integral part of the cultural heritage of humanity and a particularly important element in the history of peoples, nations, and their relations with each other concerning their common heritage."[4]

This concept draws upon a principle in international law that covers outer space, the seas, and Antarctica, but it is distinguishable from how it is generally applied. The "common heritage of mankind" is understood as a common good to be enjoyed by all peoples and across generations, and is informed by related international environmental law principles. Accordingly, in its judgment concerning the shelling of Dubrovnik in 1991, the ICTY found that the accused, Miodrag Jokic, had perpetrated war crimes, as he had deliberately targeted a World Heritage listed site that was of "outstanding universal value."[5] Likewise, when investigating the referral by Mali, the ICC prosecutor found that the destruction of the World Heritage listed mausoleums in Timbuktu in early 2012 was prima facie a war crime as the acts involved sites and objects whose "value transcends geographical boundaries, and which are unique in character and are intimately associated with the history and culture of the people" (ICCP 2013: 31). The joint UN-UNESCO statement on Syria in March 2014 concluded with a plea that, "Now is the time to stop the destruction, build peace and protect our common heritage" (Ki-moon, Bokova, and Brahimi 2014: 1).

Yet, communities, particularly indigenous peoples, resist the application of the broader international law concept of "common heritage of humankind" to cultural heritage because it is viewed as yet another manifestation of removing their agency in respect of their own cultural heritage. It is important to note that when the phrase is used in respect of cultural heritage, it is invariably accompanied by the phrase "since each people makes its contribution to the culture of the world."[6] In nineteenth-century treaties, cultural heritage was protected as a common good because of its importance to the advancement of knowledge, the arts, and sciences for all humanity. By the mid twentieth century, there was recognition of its relationship to the relevant community for whom it is significant for their collective identity and development, and its importance as a manifestation of cultural diversity. This shift is reflected in the resurgent recognition of the importance of access to cultural heritage for the enjoyment of human rights, especially cultural rights, of individuals and members of groups like minorities and indigenous peoples (Shaheed 2011). While the protection of cultural heritage during armed conflict and belligerent occupation has expanded little to cover intangible heritage, the increasing cross-fertilization of international humanitarian law and human rights law enables a broader interpretation of existing legal protections that cover cultural rights and intangible heritage (Vrdoljak 2008: 250). That said, the promotion of cultural diversity in the protection of cultural heritage is not tolerated where it violates the human rights of members of vulnerable groups, such as women, people with disabilities, children, and so forth (Shaheed 2012). As explained below, this qualifier is contained in recent international instruments for the protection of cultural heritage and the promotion of cultural diversity.

The idea of an international community is further elaborated in the protection of cultural heritage in international law through the obligation concerning international cooperation. The Declaration on the Principles of International Cultural Co-operation adopted by UNESCO's General Conference in 1966 acknowledged that "each culture has a dignity and value which must be respected and preserved," and "in their rich variety and diversity, and their reciprocal influences they exert on one another, all cultures form part of the common heritage belonging to all mankind" (UNESCO 1966: art. 1.1.3). The declaration adds little by way of explicit content concerning international cooperation. Specialist cultural heritage instruments also reference this obligation. The Hague Convention (1954) covering protection during armed conflict begins: "it is important that this heritage should receive international protection; ... Being of the opinion that such protection cannot be effective unless both national and international measures have been taken to organize it in time of peace."[7] The World Heritage Convention (1972), which covers protection during war and peacetime, states:

> Considering that, in view of the magnitude and gravity of the new dangers threatening them, it is incumbent on the international community as a whole to participate in the protection of the cultural and natural heritage of outstanding universal value, organized on a permanent basis and in accordance with scientific methods.[8]

These instruments, and those that followed that referred to an obligation of international cooperation, do provide the obligation of international cooperation with content as it relates to the relevant treaty.[9] Some instruments are more firmly entrenched in an understanding of international cooperation as being contractual between states, and more particularly States Parties to the relevant convention.[10] Others arguably move beyond this narrow understanding of the international community to encapsulate obligations upon an entity beyond its States Parties.[11] In its purest form, this is exemplified in the application of the obligation on neutral or third-party states, that is, states that are not bound because of existing treaty obligations or customary international law. Examples include the restitution processes which occurred following World War II,[12] and the obligation contained in Security Council Resolution 1483 (UNSC 2003). This development intrinsically arises from the notion that if the protection of cultural heritage at the international level is ground in its importance to all humanity, and this is a "value especially protected by the international community," then all states have an "interest in [its] protection."[13] These examples, however, are rare.

International cooperation is vital for the enforcement of legal obligations concerning cultural heritage against individuals and between states. Under the World Heritage Convention (1972), international protection of "world cultural heritage" is defined as "a system of international co-operation and assistance designed to support States Parties ... in their efforts to conserve and identify that heritage."[14] The convention requires States Parties to assist in the identification, protection, conservation, and presentation of World Heritage wherever it is located (provided assistance is requested from the state on whose territory the site is located), and not to take deliberate measures which may directly or indirectly damage sites on the territory of other States Parties.[15] Invariably, multilateral treaties covering cultural heritage promote this rationale of assistance in protection and conservation among the contracting states. The UNESCO Intentional Destruction Declaration urged cooperation in respect of the exchange of information concerning possible risks of intentional destruction, consultation in respect of actual or impeding acts of destructions, and assistance for educational programs and capacity-building for prevention and repression (UNESCO 2003a: art. 8). Similarly, Security Council Resolution 2139 of 2014 on Syria called on all parties to the conflict to "save [its] rich societal mosaic and cultural heritage, and take appropriate steps to ensure the protection of Syria's World Heritage Sites" (UNSC 2014: preamble). This stance is proactive.

More often, however, the request for cooperation is reactive, and hence the call for repression. So, for instance, Security Council Resolution 1483 of 2003 on Iraq called on all UN Member States to prohibit the trade in, and facilitate the safe return of, cultural objects illicitly removed from Iraqi territory during the conflict and occupation (UNSC 2003: para. 7). It also called on the cooperation of relevant international organizations like UNESCO and INTERPOL, which emphasizes that the international community is not the sum of states. Likewise, the request by Malian authorities for the ICC prosecutor to investigate and prosecute rebels responsible for the destruction of ancient mausoleums and looting of manuscripts on its territory (Coulibaly 2012; Ki-moon 2012b; African Union 2012; ICCP 2013). Both a State Party and the UN Security Council can refer acts against cultural property which amount to war crimes, crimes against humanity, or genocide for investigation and prosecution by the International Criminal Court.[16] As explained below, examples of individuals or groups of individuals being held to account for such acts are isolated. Usually, a state sanctions an investigation and prosecution of acts that have occurred on its own territory, especially when it relates to the treatment of anti-government or opposition forces or a deposed regime. While the international community may condemn such acts within states, it remains reluctant to breach the sovereignty and territorial integrity of states. Similarly, while international instruments concluded after the 1990s extend universal jurisdiction to international crimes involving cultural property,[17] there are no examples of a state invoking jurisdiction on this basis for such crimes to date.

Individuals, Groups, and Human Rights

The increasing recognition of the individual in international law since the mid twentieth century has not only whittled down the pervasiveness of the state; it has profoundly shaped the interpretation and implementation of rights and obligations as they related to cultural heritage. Human rights law norms have been a driving force in reconfiguring what constitutes cultural heritage in international law and how it is to be protected. In opening up the field, it has also laid bare the competing and conflicting interests involved. This second part highlights how the themes explored in respect of the international community are mirrored at the micro level concerning developments relating to the individual. It provides an overview of how the definition of cultural heritage has altered, and how those with rights to cultural heritage have moved beyond state interests alone. As will be shown, this development is most overtly defined with claims to access to cultural heritage as part of cultural human rights. Finally, there is a brief explanation of how in international law it is the individual as perpetrator rather than the state or group that is held criminally responsible for acts against cultural heritage.

While the Universal Declaration of Human Rights adopted by the UN General Assembly in 1948 contains several rights that encompass cultural rights broadly understood, the dedicated provision covering cultural rights is limited in its scope. For example, it recognizes the right of everyone to freely "participate in the cultural life of the community" (United Nations 1948: art. 27). This provision has undergone fundamental changes in recent years with human rights bodies adopting a more expansive interpretation of what constitutes "culture" and by going beyond individuals as the only right-holders of this human right. The changes mirror those described above in respect of the protection of cultural heritage under international humanitarian law. This human right was originally interpreted as the right of individuals to participation in national cultural life, with culture confined to so-called "high" culture, such as museums, libraries, and theatres (Donders 2002: 139). In recent decades, it has been redefined as a right of a person as an individual, in association with others or within a community, to "participate in the culture of their choice" (UNCESCR 2009: para. 55). Article 15 of the International Covenant on Economic, Social and Cultural Rights (1966), which transforms Article 27 of the Universal Declaration of Human Rights into treaty law, required States Parties to remove obstacles that restrict access to one's own culture or other cultures "without discrimination and without consideration for frontiers on any kind" (UNCESR 2009: para. 55.d). Likewise, recent multilateral instruments adopted under the auspices of the UN specialist agency on culture, UNESCO, have not only promoted the importance of cultural diversity for humanity – as in the Universal Declaration on Cultural Diversity (UNESCO 2001) and the Convention on the Protection and Promotion of the Diversity of Cultural Expressions (Cultural Diversity Convention) (2005) – but also recognized other stakeholders beyond states, including individuals, communities (such as minorities and indigenous peoples), and the international community.[18] UN human rights bodies have advised that cultural diversity and protection for the long-term viability of cultural groups is important for the community itself and the entire society (UNHRC 1994). Accordingly, the United Nations and its agencies have explicitly condemned forced assimilation policies and practices as "illegal" (United Nations 1992: art. 1.1), while noting that a measure of integration is necessary for a state to "respect and ensure human rights to every person within its territory without discrimination" (United Nations 2005: 6). The prohibition against forced assimilation relates to the acts of states and non-state actors.

Similarly, the definition of culture and cultural heritage has altered with the interpretation of the right to cultural life. This is reaffirmed by the UN Committee on Economic, Social and Cultural Rights (UNCESCR) which has emphasized the need to move away from "the material aspects of culture (such as museums, libraries, theatres, cinemas, monuments and heritage sites)" and embrace "proactive measures that also promote effective access by all to intangible cultural goods (such as language, knowledge and traditions)" (UNCESCR 2009: 17). The UNCESCR has noted that, "Culture shapes and mirrors the values of well-being and the economic, social and political life of individuals, groups of individuals and communities" (UNCESCR 2009: para. 13). The transformation in the definition of culture entails an emphasis on its "living" or evolving nature; that is, "transmitted from generation to generation" (Shaheed 2011: 4).

This development in human rights law has been complemented by the evolution of multilateral agreements covering the protection of cultural heritage. Prior to the 1990s and UNESCO's Recommendation on Participation by the People at Large in Cultural Life and Their Contribution to It (UNESCO 1976), treaties such as the Hague Convention (1954), the UNESCO Convention (1970), and the World Heritage Convention (1972) covered tangible heritage. In the intervening years, multilateral agreements have been concluded on intangible heritage and cultural diversity, such as the Convention for the Safeguarding of the Intangible Cultural Heritage (Intangible Heritage Convention) (2003) and the Cultural Diversity Convention (2005). Indeed, the World Heritage Convention, through its 1992 set of operational guidelines (UNESCO 1992), became the first multilateral instrument to recognize cultural landscapes, a mode of protecting the intangible as well as the tangible aspects of a protected site. For example, a site may be listed as an "associative cultural landscape" on the World Heritage List because of its "powerful religious, artistic or cultural associations of the natural element rather than material cultural evidence, which may be insignificant or even absent" (UNESCO 2008 Annex). Similarly, the scope of the Intentional Destruction Declaration explicitly covers "cultural heritage including cultural heritage linked to a natural site" (UNESCO 2003a: art. 2). Recent cultural heritage agreements also refer to "future generations,"[19] "present and future generations" (UNESCO 2001: art. 1) , and "succeeding generations" (UNESCO 2003a: art. 1).

The recognition of a more holistic understanding of cultural heritage and broader range of stakeholders laid bare the inherently conflicting claims to it and its interpretation. Contestation may involve competing claims, including: between an individual (asserting the right to property) and the state (promoting its right to protect national cultural patrimony) seeking to prevent the sale of a privately owned artwork on the international art market;[20] between the state (and the international community) and a group, as in the case of the destruction of the mausoleums and looting of manuscripts in Mali;[21] between two states, such as the decades-long conflict between Thailand and Cambodia concerning the temple of Preah Vihear;[22] between a state and the international community, as occurred with the destruction of the Buddhas of Bamiyan by the then government of Afghanistan; and between an individual asserting the right to participate in one's culture and the community asserting the right to determine membership of the group (UNHRC 1981).

Contemporary instruments covering cultural heritage and diversity make clear that neither the state nor groups can invoke culture or religion to derogate from human rights norms. The UNESCO Universal Declaration on Cultural Diversity explicitly provides that promotion and protection of cultural diversity cannot be used to justify violations of existing human rights norms (UNESCO 2001: art. 4).[23] Likewise, human rights instruments stipulate that the exercise and enjoyment of cultural rights cannot violate others' human rights (see UNESCO 1976: preamble; UNCESCR 2009). The UNCESCR has indicated in respect of the right to participate in cultural life that "no one may invoke cultural diversity to infringe upon human rights guaranteed by international law, nor to limit their scope" (UNCESCR 2009: 6). So, for example, the UNCESCR has found that it is mandatory for States Parties to ensure equality between men and women in respect of the right to participate in cultural life by eliminating "institutional and legal obstacles as well as those based on negative practices, including those attributed to customs and traditions" (UNCESCR 2009: 7). Yet, States Parties to a range of human rights treaties – in particular, the Convention on the Elimination of all forms of Discrimination against Women (1979) and the Convention on the Rights of the Child (1989) – have invoked religion or culture to limit their obligations under these instruments (Donders 2013: 205). The right to participate in cultural life is further elaborated by the fact that it is defined as a freedom that rests with the individual. In its most stark form this is manifested as the right to leave the group. The UNCESCR has noted that "[t]he decision by a person whether or not to exercise the right take part in cultural life individually, or in association with others, is a cultural choice and, as such, should be recognized, respected and protected on the basis of equality" (UNCESCR 2009: 2).

The intersection of human rights law and legal protection of cultural heritage has become overt in deliberations around the right to access cultural heritage. As noted earlier, multilateral instruments concerning the protection of cultural heritage contain an inherent bias toward states. Indeed, even in those instances where other stakeholders are acknowledged and referenced in these treaties, it is a state which decides to sign up to the instrument's obligations, and its implementation must come from the relevant State Party. Nonetheless, reflecting the increasing influence of human rights law jurisprudence on the interpretation of existing cultural heritage instruments and vice versa, the rights (and obligations) of states as they relate to cultural heritage even in long-established instruments are being redefined. So, for instance, the UNESCO Convention (1970) is often referenced as a strikingly state-centric treaty. Yet, in the decades since the end of the Cold War, UN human rights bodies and the UNESCO Intergovernmental Committee for Promoting the Return of Cultural Property to its Countries of Origin or its Restitution in case of Illicit Appropriation (ICPRCP) have emphasized the obligation of States Parties to ensure that vulnerable groups (particularly minorities and indigenous peoples) within their territory do not suffer cultural loss as a consequence of illicit trade, and that it facilitate the return of objects if they are removed (Vrdoljak 2012). This shift is exemplified by the diplomatic efforts of the United States (and NGOs) on behalf of the Hopi, a Native American indigenous community whose lands lie within US territory, to prevent the public auction in Paris in 2013 of ceremonial masks created by them (Mashberg 2013).

Perhaps the most significant (but also limited) movement indicative of this shift and synergy between human rights law and cultural heritage law is the overt recognition of a right to participate in the protection of cultural heritage. For example, the Intangible Heritage Convention (2003) provides that, "Within the framework of its safeguarding activities of the intangible cultural heritage, each State Party shall endeavor to ensure the widest possible participation of communities, groups and, where appropriate, individuals that create, maintain and transmit such heritage, and to involve them actively in its management."[24] Yet, this provision is substantially narrower than that proposed in earlier drafts. The convention has been criticized not only for reducing the role to non-state actors, but for also emphasizing the role of the state through the inclusion of a system of listing heritage that attracts protection under the treaty. Nonetheless, the significance of this development or its ripple effect on other pre-existing instruments in the field of cultural heritage law should not be underestimated. While the World Heritage Convention (1972) does not contain such a provision, its operational guidelines were amended to recognize a "partnership approach to nomination, management and monitoring" of World Heritage sites by "individuals and other stakeholders, especially local communities, governmental, non-governmental and private organizations and owners" as providing a "significant contribution to the protection ... and the implementation of the Convention" (UNESCO 2008: 10).

The fullest example of this approach is the Council of Europe's Framework Convention on the Value of Cultural Heritage for Society (2005), known as the Faro Convention, which recognizes the right of individuals and communities to participate in the protection of cultural heritage.[25] This agreement provides a "framework of reference for heritage policies ... and underpin[s] existing Council of Europe instruments concerning more specific aspects of cultural heritage" (CoE 2005: 1). Drawing inspiration from the Council of Europe's Convention on Access to Information, Public Participation in Decision-Making and Access to Justice in Environmental Matters (1998), which was developed and adopted in respect of environmental law matters, the Faro Convention embraces a multi-stakeholder and shared-responsibility approach to cultural heritage, and extends standing to NGOs.[26] Human rights jurisprudence, including that of the International Court of Justice, suggests that the interpretation of these principles as they have developed to protect the environment can inform their application in cases of the protection of cultural heritage.[27]

Yet, this development comes with a caveat. As noted earlier, there are often multiple (and competing) stakeholders for the protection of cultural heritage, and it is therefore not surprising that, in her report on access to cultural heritage, the UN special rapporteur on cultural rights noted that "varying degrees of access and enjoyment may be recognized, taking into consideration the diverse interests of individuals and groups according to their relationship with specific cultural heritage" (Shaheed 2011: 1). She notes a general call by a State Party for participation is insufficient. Rather, states, and courts which may be required to decide cases involving competing claims, must be alive to this diversity of interests (Shaheed 2011: 1).

Significantly, and in contrast to the limited form of rights recognized under international cultural heritage law flowing to non-state actors, it is only individuals that attract criminal sanctions for violations of international humanitarian law and international criminal law. Despite unsuccessful efforts to hold high-ranking officials criminally responsible for acts perpetrated against cultural property during World War I, the first successful prosecution by the international community occurred before the International Military Tribunal (IMT) at Nuremberg (IMT 1947: 237), and subsequent related proceedings. The IMT judgment observed that: "Crimes against international law are committed by men, not by abstract entities, and only by punishing individuals who commit such crimes can the provisions of international law be enforced" (IMT 1947: 221). The criminal responsibility of individuals in this field has been reaffirmed in recent decades through the work of the International Criminal Tribunal for the Former Yugoslavia and the International Criminal Court (Vrdoljak 2008: 280). The international community has, however, persistently refused to recognize the criminal responsibility of states (Crawford 2002: 37, 243–44). Indeed, when asked to revisit this point in the case of genocide in Bosnia Herzegovina with respect to the destruction of cultural property, the International Court of Justice affirmed this position.[28] Conversely, it is important to note that non-state actors are increasingly called upon to act consistently with treaty obligations for the protection of cultural heritage that explicitly relate to States Parties. For instance, the joint UN-UNESCO statement on Syria calls on "all countries and professional bodies involved in customs, trade and the art market, as well as individuals and tourists" not to engage in the illicit transfer of cultural objects and "adhere to the UNESCO 1970 Convention" (Ki-moon, Bokova, and Brahimi 2014) – that is, the UNESCO Convention (1970).

Conclusion

More than half of the multilateral instruments that make up the contemporary international legal framework for the protection of cultural heritage were adopted in the decades after the end of the Cold War. These later treaties have profoundly broadened the definition of what is being protected and the range of stakeholders attracting rights and obligations. Protection is no longer confined to tangible cultural heritage. And those recognized as subjects in international law have moved beyond states. States remain the dominant actors, but their role is being significantly redefined. This growth in the articulation of international cultural heritage law has exposed existing concerns and attracted new challenges. The proliferation of specialist instruments has not always been met by uniformity of purpose. Rather than succumb to the ever-increasing temptation to adopt another specialist convention, either through UNESCO or other UN fora and thereby potentially limit existing protection, there is a clear need to better understand how these instruments operate together. Perhaps what is required is a framework instrument, like the Council of Europe's Faro Convention (2005), which provides an overarching set of principles inspired by developments in human rights and environmental law, by which all its existing international cultural heritage treaties must be interpreted. This approach would enhance the promotion of cultural heritage in a more holistic fashion, and enable the effective participation of the international community, communities, groups, and individuals in its protection. This path would provide a coherent and consistent approach, and reinforce the direction embraced by recent treaties.

Notes

1 For the relevant regulations for Hague II, see *American Journal of International Law*, 1, suppl. (1907), p. 129; for Hague IV, *American Journal of International Law*, 2, suppl. (1908), p. 90.
2 See *Prosecutor v. Dusko Tadic* (1995), pp. 66–70.
3 See the preambles to the Hague Convention (1954), World Heritage Convention (1972), Intangible Heritage Convention (2003), and Cultural Diversity Convention (2005).
4 Underwater Heritage Convention (2001), preamble.
5 *Prosecutor v. Miodrag Jokic* (2004), p. 46.
6 See the preambles to the Hague Convention (1954), Intangible Heritage Convention (2003), and Cultural Diversity Convention (2005).
7 Hague Convention (1954), preamble.
8 World Heritage Convention (1972), preamble.
9 See Underwater Heritage Convention (2001), preamble; Intangible Heritage Convention (2003), preamble and art. 6; Cultural Diversity Convention (2005), art. 1.1.
10 See the UNESCO Convention (1970) and the Underwater Heritage Convention (2001).
11 See World Heritage Convention (1972) and Intangible Heritage Convention (2003).

12 See the Agreement Between the United States, the United Kingdom and France in Respect of the Control of Looted Works of Art (1946), *Department of State Bulletin*, 25 (1951), p. 340.
13 *Legality of the Threat or Use of Nuclear Weapons* (1996), p. 226.
14 World Heritage Convention (1972), art. 7.
15 World Heritage Convention (1972), art. 6.
16 Rome Statute (1998), arts. 13, 14.
17 See Second Protocol to the Hague Convention (1999), art.16; UNESCO (2003a: art. 8.2).
18 The Hague Convention (1954) refers to "peoples" and "all mankind"; the UNESCO Convention (1970) makes reference to "nations"; the World Heritage Convention (1972) refers to "nations" and "mankind as a whole"; the Cultural Diversity Convention (2005) refers to "groups," "societies," "humanity," "citizens," "civil society," "minorities," "indigenous peoples," "persons," and the "private sector"; the Underwater Heritage Convention (2001) references "humanity," "peoples," "nations," "international organizations, scientific institutions, professional organizations, archaeologists, divers, other interested parties, and the public at large"; the Intangible Heritage Convention (2003) mentions "communities, in particular indigenous communities, groups," "humanity," and "individuals"; the Intentional Destruction Declaration (UNESCO 2003a) refers to the "cultural identity of communities, groups and individuals"; and the Cultural Diversity Convention (2005) refers to "humanity," "communities, peoples and nations," "peoples and societies," "minorities and indigenous peoples," "women," and "individuals, groups or societies."
19 World Heritage Convention (1972), art. 4.
20 See *Beyeler v. Italy* (2000).
21 See *D.H. and Others v. the Czech Republic* (2007).
22 *Request for Interpretation of the Judgment of 15 June 1962 in the Case Concerning the Temple of Preah Vihear* (*Cambodia v. Thailand*) (2013).
23 See also the Intangible Heritage Convention (2003), art. 2.1; Cultural Diversity Convention (2005), art. 2.1.
24 Intangible Heritage Convention (2003), art. 15.
25 Faro Convention (2005), art. 12.
26 Faro Convention (2005), art. 11.
27 *Pulp Mills on the River Uruguay* (*Argentina v. Uruguay*) (2010), para. 210.
28 *Application of the Convention on the Prevention and Punishment of the Crime of Genocide* (*Bosnia and Herzegovina v. Serbia and Montenegro*) (1996), p. 47.

References

Legislation

Agreement between the United States, the United Kingdom and France in Respect of the Control of Looted Works of Art (1946). Reprinted in *Department of State Bulletin*, 25 (1951), 340.

Convention Concerning the Protection of the World Cultural and Natural Heritage (World Heritage Convention) (UNESCO, 1972). Available at: http://whc.unesco.org/archive/convention-en.pdf (accessed March 19, 2015).

Convention for the Protection of Cultural Property in the Event of Armed Conflict (Hague Convention) (UNESCO, 1954). Available at: http://unesdoc.unesco.org/images/0008/000824/082464mb.pdf (accessed March 19, 2015).

Convention for the Safeguarding of the Intangible Cultural Heritage (Intangible Heritage Convention) (UNESCO, 2003). Available at: http://unesdoc.unesco.org/images/0013/001325/132540e.pdf (accessed March 19, 2015).

Convention on Access to Information, Public Participation in Decision-Making and Access to Justice in Environmental Matters (Aarhus Convention) (Council of Europe, 1998). Available at: http://www.unece.org/fileadmin/DAM/env/pp/documents/cep43e.pdf (accessed March 19, 2015).

Convention on the Elimination of all forms of Discrimination against Women (United Nations, 1979). Available at: http://www.ohchr.org/Documents/ProfessionalInterest/cedaw.pdf (accessed March 19, 2015).

Convention on the Means of Prohibiting and Preventing the Illicit Import, Export and Transfer of Ownership of Cultural Property (UNESCO Convention) (UNESCO, 1970). Available at: http://unesdoc.unesco.org/images/0013/001333/133378mo.pdf (accessed March 19, 2015).

Convention on the Protection and Promotion of the Diversity of Cultural Expressions (Cultural Diversity Convention) (UNESCO, 2005). Available at: http://unesdoc.unesco.org/images/0014/001429/142919e.pdf (accessed March 19, 2015).

Convention on the Protection of the Underwater Cultural Heritage (Underwater Heritage Convention) (UNESCO, 2001). Available at: http://unesdoc.unesco.org/images/0012/001246/124687e.pdf#page=56 (accessed March 19, 2015).

Convention on the Rights of the Child (United Nations, 1989). Available at: http://www.ohchr.org/Documents/ProfessionalInterest/crc.pdf (accessed March 19, 2015).

Convention Regarding the Laws and Customs of Land Warfare (Hague IV) (1907). Reprinted in *American Journal of International Law*, 2, suppl. (1908), 90–117.

Convention with Respect to the Laws and Customs of War on Land (Hague II) (1899). Reprinted in *American Journal of International Law*, 1 suppl. (1907), 129–159.

Framework Convention on the Value of Cultural Heritage for Society (Faro Convention) (Council of Europe, 2005). Available at: http://conventions.coe.int/Treaty/en/Treaties/Html/199.htm (accessed March 19, 2015).

International Covenant on Economic, Social and Cultural Rights (United Nations, 1966). Available at: http://www.ohchr.org/Documents/ProfessionalInterest/cescr.pdf (accessed March 19, 2015).

Protocol to the Hague Convention of 1954 (UNESCO, 1954). Available at: http://unesdoc.unesco.org/images/0008/000824/082464mb.pdf#page=66 (accessed March 19, 2015).

Rome Statute of the International Criminal Court (ICC, 1998). Available at: http://www.icc-cpi.int/nr/rdonlyres/ea9aeff7-5752-4f84-be94-0a655eb30e16/0/rome_statute_english.pdf (accessed March 19, 2015).

Second Protocol to the Hague Convention of 1954 (UNESCO, 1999). Available at: http://unesdoc.unesco.org/images/0013/001306/130696eo.pdf (accessed March 19, 2015).

Case Law

Application of the Convention on the Prevention and Punishment of the Crime of Genocide (*Bosnia and Herzegovina v. Serbia and Montenegro*) (1996), International Court of Justice. Judgment of July 11. Available at: http://www.icj-cij.org/docket/index.php?p1=3&p2=3&k=f4&case=91&code=bhy&p3=4 (accessed March 7, 2015).

Beyeler v. Italy (2000), European Court of Human Rights. Application No. 33202/96, Grand Chamber Judgment, January 5. Available at: http://hudoc.echr.coe.int/sites/eng/pages/search.aspx?i=001-58832#{%22itemid%22:[%22001-58832%22]}(accessed March 7, 2015).

D.H. and Others v. the Czech Republic (2007), European Court of Human Rights. Application No. 57325/00, Grand Chamber Judgment, November 13. Available at: http://hudoc.echr.coe.int/sites/eng/pages/search.aspx?i=001-83256#{%22itemid%22:[%22001-83256%22] (accessed March 7, 2015).

Legality of the Threat or Use of Nuclear Weapons (1996), International Court of Justice. Advisory Opinion of July 8. Available at: http://www.icj-cij.org/docket/index.php?p1=3&p2=4&k=e1&p3=4&case=95 (accessed March 7, 2015).

Prosecutor v. Dusko Tadic (1995), International Criminal Tribunal for the Former Yugoslavia. No. IT-94-1-A, Appeals Chamber, October 2. Available at: http://www.icty.org/x/cases/tadic/acdec/en/51002.htm (accessed March 7, 2015).

Prosecutor v. Miodrag Jokic (2004), International Criminal Tribunal for the Former Yugoslavia. Judgment, No. IT-01-42/I-S, ICTY Trial Chamber I, March 23. Available at: http://www.icty.org/case/miodrag_jokic/4#tdec (accessed March 7, 2015).

Pulp Mills on the River Uruguay (*Argentina v. Uruguay*) (2010), International Court of Justice. Judgment of April 20. Available at: http://www.icj-cij.org/docket/index.php?p1=3&p2=3&k=88&case=135&code=au&p3=4 (accessed March 7, 2015).

Request for Interpretation of the Judgment of 15 June 1962 in the Case Concerning the Temple of Preah Vihear (*Cambodia v. Thailand*) (2013), International Court of Justice. Judgment of November 11. Available at: http://www.icj-cij.org/docket/index.php?p1=3&p2=3&k=89&case=151&code=ct2&p3=4 (accessed March 7, 2015).

Other Works

African Union (2012) Solemn Declaration on the Situation in Mali. Statement from the 19th Ordinary Session of the Assembly of Heads of State and Government of the African Union, Addis Ababa, Ethiopia, July 15-16. Available at: http://www.au.int/en/content/19th-ordinary-session-assembly-heads-state-and-government-african-union-addis-ababa-ethiopia (accessed March 7, 2015).

CoE (Council of Europe) (2005) Explanatory Report for the Framework Convention on the Value of Cultural Heritage for Society. Available at: http://conventions.coe.int/treaty/en/reports/html/199.htm (accessed March 7, 2015).

Coulibaly, M. (2012) Referral under Article 14 ICC Statute from Malian Minister for Justice to ICC Prosecutor, 13 July 2012. Available at: http://www.icc-cpi.int/NR/rdonlyres/A245A47F-BFD1-45B6-891C-3BCB5B173F57/0/ReferralLetterMali130712.pdf (accessed January 30, 2014).

Crawford, J. (2002) *International Law Commission's Articles on State Responsibility: Introduction, Text and Commentaries.* Cambridge: Cambridge University Press.

Donders, Y. (2002) *Towards a Right to Cultural Identity?* Antwerp: Intersentia.

Donders, Y. (2013) Cultural Pluralism in International Human Rights Law: The Role of Reservations. In A.F. Vrdoljak (ed.), *The Cultural Dimensions of Human Rights.* Oxford: Oxford University Press, pp. 205–239.

European Union (2013) Council Decision 2013/760/CFSP of 13 December 2013 Amending Decision 2013/255/CFSP Concerning Restrictive Measures against Syria, O.J. L 335/50 of 14.12.2013. Available at: http://eur-lex.europa.eu/legal-content/EN/TXT/HTML/?uri=CELEX:32013D0760&from=EN (accessed March 7, 2015).

Francioni, F. (2008) Introduction. In F. Francioni and F. Lenzerini (eds), *The 1972 World Heritage Convention: A Commentary.* Oxford: Oxford University Press, pp. 5–8.

ICCP (International Criminal Court Prosecutor) (2013) Situation in Mali. Article 53(1), Report, 16 January 2013.

IMT (International Military Tribunal) (Nuremberg) (1947) Judgment and Sentences, October 1, 1946. *American Journal of International Law*, 41 (1), 172–333.

Ki-moon, B. (2012a) Secretary-General's Remarks to the Security Council on Mali. Speech delivered at the UN Security Council, New York, August 8. Available at: http://www.un.org/sg/statements/index.asp?nid=6232 (accessed January 30, 2014).

Ki-moon, B. (2012b) Report of the Secretary-General on the Situation in Mali, UN document S/2012/894 (28 November 2012). Available at: http://www.un.org/en/ga/search/view_doc.asp?symbol=S/2012/894 (accessed March 7, 2015).

Ki-moon, B., Bokova, I., and Brahimi, L. (2014) Joint Statement on Syria. Available at: http://www.unesco.org/new/fileadmin/MULTIMEDIA/HQ/CLT/pdf/12_March_2014_SG_Bokova_Brahimi_signed_Joint_press_on_Syria.pdf (accessed January 30, 2014).

Mashberg, T. (2013) Auction of Hopi Masks Proceeds after Judge's Ruling. *New York Times*, April 12. Available at http://artsbeat.blogs.nytimes.com/2013/04/12/french-judge-rules-that-auction-of-hopi-masks-can-proceed/?_r=0 (accessed March 8, 2015).

O'Keefe, R. (2004) World Cultural Heritage: Obligations to the International Community as a Whole? *International and Comparative Law Quarterly*, 53, 189–210.

Shaheed, F. (2011) Access to Cultural Heritage. Report of the independent expert in the field of cultural rights. UN document A/HRC/17/38 (21 March 2011). Available at: http://daccess-ods.un.org/TMP/9947426.31912231.html (accessed March 7, 2015).

Shaheed, F. (2012) The Enjoyment of Cultural Rights by Women on an Equal Basis with Men. Report of the special rapporteur in the field of cultural rights. UN document A/67/287. Available at: http://daccess-ods.un.org/TMP/4079464.9720192.html (accessed March 7, 2015).

UNCESCR (2009) General Comment No.21: Right of Everyone to Take Part in Cultural Life. Document E/C.12/GC/21. Available at: www2.ohchr.org/english/bodies/cescr/docs/gc/E-C-12-GC-21.doc (accessed March 7, 2015).

UNESCO (1966) Declaration of Principles of International Cultural Co-operation. Available at: http://portal.unesco.org/en/ev.php-URL_ID=13147&URL_DO=DO_TOPIC&URL_SECTION=201.html (accessed March 7, 2015).

UNESCO (1976) Recommendation on Participation by the People at Large in Cultural Life and Their Contribution to It. Available at: http://portal.unesco.org/en/ev.php-URL_ID=13097&URL_DO=DO_TOPIC&URL_SECTION=201.html (accessed March 7, 2015).

UNESCO (1992) Operational Guidelines to the World Heritage Convention. Document WHC-92/CONF.002/12. Available at: http://whc.unesco.org/archive/repbur91.htm#opgu (accessed March 7, 2015).

UNESCO (2001) Universal Declaration on Cultural Diversity. Document 31C/Res.24, Annex. Available at: http://portal.unesco.org/en/ev.php-URL_ID=13179&URL_DO=DO_TOPIC&URL_SECTION=201.html (accessed March 7, 2015).

UNESCO (2003a) Declaration Concerning the Intentional Destruction of Cultural Heritage (Intentional Destruction Declaration). Document 32C/Res.39. Available at: http://portal.unesco.org/en/ev.php-URL_ID=17718&URL_DO=DO_TOPIC&URL_SECTION=201.html (accessed March 7, 2015).

UNESCO (2003b) Decision to Inscribe the Cultural Landscape and Archaeological Remains of the Bamiyan Valley, Afghanistan. Document 27 COM 8C.43. Available at: http://whc.unesco.org/en/decisions/628 (accessed March 7, 2015).

UNESCO (2008) Operational Guidelines for the Implementation of the World Heritage Convention. Document WHC.08/01. Available at: whc.unesco.org/archive/opguide08-en.pdf (accessed March 7, 2015).

UNHRC (1981) Lovelace v. Canada Communication No.24/1977. Document A/36/40. Available at: www.ohchr.org/Documents/Publications/SelDec_1_en.pdf (accessed March 7, 2015).

UNHRC (1994) General Comment No. 23: Rights of Minorities (Art. 27). Document HRI/GEN/1/Rev.1, 38. Available at: http://tbinternet.ohchr.org/_layouts/treatybodyexternal/Download.aspx?symbolno=CCPR%2fC%2f21%2fRev.1%2fAdd.5&Lang=en (accessed March 7, 2015).

United Nations (1948) Universal Declaration of Human Rights. UNGA Resolution 217 A (III). Available at: http://www.un.org/en/documents/udhr/ (accessed March 19, 2015).

United Nations (1992) Declaration on the Rights of Persons Belonging to National or Ethnic, Religious and Linguistic Minorities. Document A/RES/47/135. Available at: http://www.un.org/documents/ga/res/47/a47r135.htm (accessed March 7, 2015).

United Nations (2005) Commentary of the Working Group on Minorities to the United Nations Declaration on the Rights of Persons Belonging to National or Ethnic, Religious and Linguistic Minorities. Document E/CN.4/Sub.2/AC.5/2005/2. Available at: http://daccess-ods.un.org/TMP/398036.83757782.html (accessed March 7, 2015).

UNSC (2003) Resolution 1483 of 22 May 2003. Document S/RES/1483. Available at: http://www.un.org/en/ga/search/view_doc.asp?symbol=S/RES/1483%282003%29 (accessed March 7, 2015).

UNSC (2014) Resolution 2139 of 22 February 2014. Document S/RES/2139. Available at: http://www.un.org/en/ga/search/view_doc.asp?symbol=S/RES/2139%282014%29 (accessed March 7, 2015).

Vrdoljak, A.F. (2008) Cultural Heritage in Human Rights and Humanitarian Law. In O. Ben-Naftali (ed.), *International Human Rights and Humanitarian Law*. Oxford: Oxford University Press, pp. 250–304.

Vrdoljak, A.F. (2012) Human Rights and Illicit Traffic in Cultural Objects. In S. Borelli and F. Lenzerini (eds), *Cultural Heritage, Cultural Rights, Cultural Diversity: International Law Perspectives*. Leiden: Martinus Nijhoff, pp. 107–140.

CHAPTER 37

The New Heritage Studies and Education, Training, and Capacity-Building

William Logan and Gamini Wijesuriya

The modern conservation movement that began to influence heritage practice globally from the mid nineteenth century propagated a "one size fits all" approach. It dealt primarily with monuments and sites, which were seen as belonging only to the past, threatened by the actions of nature and human beings, and best understood and interpreted by heritage professionals – the experts – through the application of scientific approaches (Wijesuriya 2010). In this view, the role of the present generation is to act as guardians and to ensure that, in the words of the Venice Charter, monuments and sites are passed on to future generations "in the full richness of their authenticity" (ICASHB 1964: pmbl.). Such authenticity was to be judged in terms of materials, form, design, and setting, thus placing the main focus on fabric and leading to an educational response that focused on the technical.

This way of understanding heritage and going about its conservation has been identified as the Conventional Conservation Approach (Wijesuriya 2010). Since the 1980s, scholars have criticized it as too narrow and fabric-bound, and have sought to focus more on the cultural politics underlying the interpretation and valuation of heritage. Among those developing these criticisms, Laurajane Smith (2006) characterized the conventional approach as Authorised Heritage Discourse. The present volume makes it abundantly clear that it is now necessary to deal with a wide variety of issues, many of which have been discussed in the preceding chapters, and that the range of disciplines relevant to the task has broadened beyond archaeology and architecture to

A Companion to Heritage Studies, First Edition. Edited by William Logan, Máiréad Nic Craith, and Ullrich Kockel.
© 2016 John Wiley & Sons, Inc. Published 2016 by John Wiley & Sons, Inc.

embrace history, geography, anthropology, politics, economics, law, and urban and regional planning.

Over the last three decades, both the community and professional views of what constitutes cultural heritage and its value for contemporary society has broadened in many countries around the world. This widening is seen in the debates about philosophy and practice in the key global organizations – UNESCO, the International Centre for the Study of the Preservation and Restoration of Cultural Property (ICCROM), the International Council on Monuments and Sites (ICOMOS), the International Council of Museums (ICOM), and the International Union for the Conservation of Nature (IUCN) – and is reflected in the programs taught and the research undertaken in educational and training institutions at national and global levels. Several important shifts can be discerned. One of the key drivers of this change has been the UNESCO Convention Concerning the Protection of the World Cultural and Natural Heritage (1972), commonly known as the World Heritage Convention. In addition to its radical thinking in envisaging heritage as both natural and cultural, and bringing them together into a single normative statement and protective system, the World Heritage Convention has become the most powerful and influential international instrument in providing a platform to support the broadening of the concept of heritage and related educational, training, and capacity-building programs.

Moving from a mid-twentieth-century focus on iconic monuments and archeological sites, the criteria adopted for evaluating cultural nominations to the World Heritage List have been widened to encompass values that have enabled the inscription of a wider range of places, such as vernacular building ensembles, historic villages, and designed parks and gardens. In 1993, cultural landscapes and their associative values were added, while the last decade has seen a greater emphasis on the intangible values of places and a debate about broadening the understanding and management of historic cities through the Historic Urban Landscape approach.

Another major trend seen in heritage practice is the move from a narrowly technical or fabric focus to values- and community-based approaches (Askew and Logan 1994: 5; Logan 2010: 39, 2013b: 35; ICCROM 2013). The World Heritage system itself has moved to a values-based approach to managing listed properties, and in periodically revising the Operational Guidelines for Implementing the World Heritage Convention, increased weight has been put on associative values that are to be defined collectively by all stakeholders, including indigenous communities. A number of questions – Whose heritage? In whose interest is a place being inscribed? – have been given higher priority, as, too, has the development of more inclusive heritage registers.

The global debate on heritage and its conservation, both within the World Heritage context and beyond, has also led to a recognition that wide variations exist in the way heritage is understood from one cultural region of the world to another, and that such variation is in fact part of the world's rich and creative cultural diversity. This recognition has led to the evolution of new ideas such as "integrated urban and territorial conservation" and "living heritage" that encourage community-based approaches to managing heritage. These debates were further strengthened through the Nara Document on Authenticity, which had a major impact on heritage conservation theory and practice, concluding as it did that the ways of conserving heritage should be in accord with local ways of understanding heritage.

These matters are taken up in this chapter, where it is argued that much Western knowledge and practice remains indispensable, but that there is a need to fill in the gaps – especially by drawing in other knowledge areas, particularly those developed in the non-Western world, and ethical considerations, including the relationship between heritage practice and human rights. These new areas require new approaches in the preparation of practitioners as well as others engaged in heritage processes. The aim is not, however, just to prepare professional practitioners, but to enable better understanding of heritage issues among policy-makers, the communities whose heritage is being conserved and "safeguarded," and other potential heritage supporters. Different groups with different needs and interests require different pedagogical approaches. A basic distinction is made in the chapter between education and training, with a third approach – capacity-building – being seen as overarching and more potent. The chapter considers the role, actual and potential, of UNESCO and its allied global bodies, as well as universities and schools, and concludes by outlining some key challenges.

Closing the Knowledge Gaps

The Conventional Conservation Approach had both complementary and contradictory impacts on different societies because of its inherited assumptions and gaps (Wijesuriya 2010). Among aspects overlooked at the philosophical level but which are now being addressed were diversity, continuity, and community. Diversity in particular refers to the way different societies view their past and perceive heritage, as well as their approaches to conservation and management. In dealing with heritage, it is inevitable that how different societies perceive their past will have implications for dealing with the remains of the past.

For instance, the linear approach to understanding time in Europe contrasts with the circular way time is perceived by people of the Buddhist and Hindu faiths, and some indigenous communities in the Pacific. Anyon, for example, explains that for Native Americans:

> time is often not the linear concept it is to most Americans ... To the Zunis, the present does not have to look like the past because the past lives on in the everyday actions of the Zuni people. The essential cultural difference is that non-Indians want to see the past to know it, whereas to Indians the present embodies the past and thus they do not necessarily have to see their past to know it. (Anyon 1991: 217)

Matunga, meanwhile, explains the conception of time held by the indigenous Maori community: "The past is viewed as part of the 'living present.' This is at odds with the view that there is a firm line between the past and the present, and which often results in the relinquishing of obligation to the past in favour of the present" (Matunga 1994: 219).

Research done by ICCROM (Wijesuriya 2007, n.d.) suggests that the idea of continuity and change has been ignored within conventional conservation discourse. What we call heritage today is those features created in the past that have continued to survive through periods of great change and have been themselves commonly – perhaps even normally – subject to change. Indeed, what we are engaged in is the process of managing change or, one can even argue, of managing continuity. Despite physical changes, many heritage places continue to perform the original function for which they were created. Change in both tangible and intangible heritage expressions are inevitable phenomena that should be recognized and respected.

With modern heritage discourse transferred to the rest of the world, heritage conservation became part of the official duties of the state and set within established legal and institutional frameworks. Concerns of sub-national communities were either ignored or overlooked, and heritage was defined, conserved, and managed by professionals with the help of a plethora of international doctrines and normative documents. Putting fences around heritage places that separated them from local communities, and removing residents from within heritage sites along with their traditional practices and rituals, were the recurrent components of conservation programs whose single-minded aim was to safeguard material remains.

Recognition of diversity, continuity, and community concerns has forced the heritage sectors to revisit the intangible aspects of heritage in the definition, conservation, and management of heritage. As Stovel suggested in discussing the Nara Document, "respecting cultural diversity requires respect for the particular heritage values associated with the expressions of a cultural group, and careful attention to efforts to define and understand those values" (Stovel 1995: 155). The gradual acceptance of the value-based approach provides an opportunity for expanding the way we perceive heritage and approaches to conservation and management, and to incorporate intangible values more fully into the understanding and safeguarding of the significance of heritage places.

There are also knowledge gaps to be addressed in relation to managerial and technical issues. It is evident that the challenges to heritage are enormous, and the need to work with a large audience is an imperative (Wijesuriya, Thompson, and Young 2013). It is critical that the understanding of existing heritage management systems is expanded in order to find ways to improve their effectiveness, and to contribute to social and environmental reform agendas related to poverty alleviation, sustainability, and climate change. New advances in technical and scientific knowledge should be embraced, and digital technologies in particular should serve all aspects of the heritage conservation process. For these to be added to the heritage conservation toolbox, further widening of training and capacity-building activities at all levels is essential.

Strengthening Ethical Considerations

Under the Conventional Conservation Approach, heritage was identified and interpreted, and conservation interventions were defined by professional experts and bureaucrats mainly through centralized government institutions. The concerns of local communities living in and around heritage monuments and sites were marginalized in such considerations, even though they were frequently the creators and traditional guardians of that heritage. Reflecting the new view that began sweeping through the World Heritage system from the early 1990s, however, Koïchiro Matsuura, the former director-general of UNESCO, made clear that the Conventional Conservation Approach was no longer acceptable: conservation is not an end in itself, he said, and the heritage we are trying to protect must be meaningful for and give meaning to contemporary society if it is to be protected for future generations (Matsuura 1999). A supremely important task for the World Heritage Committee, he concluded, was public awareness-building and education for world heritage conservation:

> This calls for us all to invest in intelligence and knowledge. For without the understanding and support of the public at large, without the respect and daily care by the local communities, which are the true custodians of the world heritage sites, no amount of funds or army of experts will suffice to protect these sites. (Matsuura 1999: 4)

The UNESCO position is that it is imperative that the values and practices of local communities, together with traditional management systems, are fully understood, respected, encouraged, and accommodated in management plans if heritage resources are to be sustained for the future (de Merode, Smeets, and Wastrik 2004: 9). Many countries have introduced better mechanisms for working with indigenous groups, although this is always subject to a degree of government commitment and, as Logan (2013c) has shown in the case of Australia, this can alter sharply with changes in the government in office. Also in Australia, Sullivan, Hall, and Greer (2008) discuss the immense difficulties faced by Aboriginal communities in caring for their heritage – indeed, for asserting their custodianship of it. They explain that difficulties occur even where there are partnerships based on goodwill between Aboriginal people and non-indigenous heritage practitioners.

> The archaeologists and heritage managers tend to dominate discussion and decision-making processes while Aboriginal people often find the "experts" to be puzzling, impractical, and opaque. Their previous experience with researchers and government officials has made Aboriginal people wary, and because of their marginalisation in education, social, and political systems they are often unaware of the legal situation, of the way bureaucracies work, and of available support systems. (Sullivan, Hall, and Greer 2008: 38)

This shift towards a more critical approach to heritage practice encourages scholars and practitioners to consider the human rights implications of conservation interventions, and to devise ways in which local people, including indigenous peoples and ethnic minorities in particular, can be empowered to play a meaningful role in determining how their heritage is identified and managed (Langfield, Logan, and Nic Craith 2010).

This ties in closely with the work being done by Farida Shaheed, the independent expert at the UN Human Rights Commission in Geneva, who focused in 2011 on access to and enjoyment of cultural heritage as a cultural right (Shaheed 2011). It also resonates with efforts by the Advisory Bodies, notably the IUCN and ICOMOS, to move the World Heritage system towards a rights-based approach to site management. Stefan Disko (this volume) outlines efforts to ensure that indigenous groups are accorded the right to free, prior, and informed consent when their cultural heritage is being considered for nomination to the World Heritage List. The same right should, of course, apply to nominations to the lists established under the Convention for the Safeguarding of the Intangible Cultural Heritage (2003), and, indeed, to lists at national and local levels. This new approach has already encouraged a rich stream of research in universities, and a number of books are now available that deal with the links between cultural diversity, heritage, and human rights (e.g. Silverman and Fairchild 2007; Langfield, Logan, and Nic Craith 2010).

Education, Training, and Capacity-Building: "Horses for Courses"

It is clear that for effective safeguarding of cultural heritage, the focus is not "knowledge transfer" to heritage practitioners but "knowledge acquisition" by a wide range of audiences. The need to engage multiple audiences in defining, planning for conservation, and managing has become more than a necessity. To achieve broader heritage goals, it is not enough to focus simply on the preparation of practitioners. There are other key audiences outside of the profession who have or should have a major impact on the heritage process as decision-makers and policy-makers, and as communities and networks. The capacities of these multiple audiences should be strengthened for effective heritage identification, managing, utilizing, and safeguarding. These groups have different needs, interests, and abilities, and different pedagogical approaches are required to strengthen their capacities.

In terms of content, the Conventional Conservation Approach isolated heritage places within tight site boundaries and buffer zones in the conviction that the key problems lay within the site and were related to its fabric. At the same time, the field of heritage conservation as an intellectual and practical endeavor was divided among a small number of disciplines. This did not reflect the reality: pressures of many kinds, including climate change, urban development, tourism, and financial shortcomings, come from outside of heritage boundaries, but often exert a critical impact on heritage management and survival. Accepting the need to deal with such pressures in the preparation of heritage practitioners necessarily means greatly expanding the multidisciplinary character of educational and training programs. Recent pedagogical shifts in the educational field away from the "filling empty vessels" approach towards more learner-focused approaches should be strengthened, especially those that develop reflexivity and independent thinking, and that use new digital interactive technologies. Moreover, if heritage conservation is no longer to be seen simply as a technical issue but recognized as always involving fundamental philosophical and ethical questions, a range of additional skills need to be incorporated into heritage courses in universities such as cultural mapping and conflict-resolution skills. This will be based on improved cross-cultural understanding, the development of mutual respect between teachers and learners, and a realization that the educational process is a two-way flow.

Education and training are two different processes and can involve different agencies, universities focusing more on the former although also providing training, while professional bodies, government departments, and other agencies focus on training (Logan 2010). University education is broad, questioning, liberating, and improving. Of course, there is a necessity to provide such technical expertise, but universities have also to engage students in larger philosophical concerns, inculcate in them an appreciation of ethical responsibility, and encourage critical analysis and debate. University education has breadth and depth of teaching based on research and analysis, and it provides students with opportunities for wider reading, specialization through writing dissertations, engagement in debates, and, especially, time to digest ideas because of the longer length of university programs when compared to training courses. Although only a limited number of university graduates from heritage studies programs enter into practice, they nevertheless form the very core of heritage practitioners. Academics should address the growing needs of heritage in their teaching and research to provide the scientific basis for the emerging conservation issues raised in this volume.

By contrast, training, at least as presently envisaged, is narrower in focus, shorter in program length, and more directed at meeting the specific needs of employers or special interest groups. Such training activities provide platforms for sharing knowledge and experience among trainers and the trainees. In the World Heritage context, the World Heritage Committee first adopted a Global Training Strategy in 2001 (ICCROM 2000), which mainly focused on heritage practitioners in different aspects of World Heritage processes combined with traditional ICCROM training activities. Training programs follow a number of pedagogical approaches as they are highly dependent on factors such as location, duration, cost, availability of resource persons, and available places for fieldwork. However, some of the key common elements are to:

- reflect on the diversity of conservation understandings and techniques;
- engage a wide geographical representation of participants and trainers;
- allow sufficient time and motivation to share experience among participants and resource persons;
- involve a wide array of practitioners as program facilitators;
- link the program, to the extent possible, with real world experience.

The third term – capacity-building – is used in many instances synonymously with training. Indeed, capacity-building may contain aspects of education and training, but the focus extends well beyond practitioners to cover a wider audience that is, or should be, engaged in the heritage conservation process. The United Nations Development Programme has defined capacity as "the ability of individuals, organizations and societies to perform functions, solve problems, and set and achieve objectives in a sustainable manner" (UNDP 2006). This emphasizes the point that capacity-building does not only involve individuals, the conventional audience of education and training. Representing a major move from the training emphasis of its 2001 strategy, in 2011 the World Heritage Committee adopted a new World Heritage Strategy for Capacity Building (UNESCO 2011), which recognizes that since capacity resides in practitioners, institutions, communities and their networks, there are different audiences, and that capacity-building activities will involve different learning areas and a diverse range of pedagogical approaches. In general, however, such activities will all have the common goals of:

- strengthening the knowledge, abilities, skills, and behavior of people with direct responsibilities for heritage conservation and management;
- improving institutional structures and processes through empowering decision-makers and policy-makers;
- introducing a more dynamic relationship between heritage and its context and, in turn, greater reciprocal benefits by a more inclusive approach. This involves engaging communities in order to strengthen their ability to actively participate in the decisions made about their heritage.

It should be noted that capacity building goes beyond the formal activities of the education and training of individuals to include a variety of other methods and tools. For instance, the publication of resource manuals can be considered as a tool designed to strengthen the capacities of policy-makers and communities, as well as practitioners. It is important, too, to note that moving from the education and training of practitioners towards broader capacity-building is not only needed for World Heritage, but also for heritage sectors at national and local levels. We will return to the World Heritage Strategy for Capacity Building in due course.

Institutional Frameworks and Activities: UNESCO and the Advisory Bodies

World Heritage, UNESCO's flagship program, has had considerable influence on heritage discourse and practice, not all of it for the good. On the negative side, it empowered the dominant heritage discourse of the West and enabled experts to impose their views in a more rigorous and official manner. For instance, the charters and other doctrinal texts of ICOMOS, the application of which were voluntary before the advent of the World Heritage Convention (1972), were increasingly imposed through the operation of the nomination, state of conservation, periodic reporting, and other World Heritage processes. On the positive side, however, these processes also opened up avenues for exploring the gaps, particularly in relation to management and technical aspects. Hitherto loosely defined terms like "authenticity" were debated and further clarified through initiatives such as the Nara Document on Authenticity (ICOMOS 1994), and approaches developed at national levels, such as those captured in Australia's Burra Charter (1979, revised 2013; see Australia ICOMOS 2013) were brought into the mainstream of World Heritage management (Logan 2004).

As might be expected given its full name, UNESCO has had long involvement in education, training, and capacity-building in the heritage area. One of UNESCO's earliest endeavors to promote and propagate heritage conservation was the creation by its General Conference in 1956 of the International Centre for the Study of the Preservation and Restoration of Cultural Property (ICCROM). When the World Heritage Convention (1972) was created, specific references to ICCROM were made in the text as an advisory body to help and work with the convention. Its Secretariat was established in 1958, with headquarters in Rome. Its main strength has been in organizing short-term training courses. In its early days, the focus was more on architectural and mural conservation, but from the 1990s onward the focus of training courses has shifted towards management skills, including for World Heritage, with courses available regionally as well as in Rome. Over the last 10 years, ICCROM's training courses have covered:

- heritage impact assessments;
- management planning;
- disaster risk management;
- heritage and sustainable development;
- the conservation of cultural landscapes;
- urban conservation.

Two more modules addressing linkages between nature and culture in managing World Heritage sites and engaging communities have been developed and await implementation. UNESCO initially acted as a major contributor through country programs for awarding scholarships to attend ICCROM training activities, and for higher degree and exchange programs mostly focusing on practitioners. These funding programs have slowly disappeared with a fall in UNESCO's finances and changing priorities, and with the expansion of heritage programs in universities. Since 1974, ICCROM's training directory has listed all academic and other institutions conducting degree and training courses.

In the World Heritage context, while ICCROM has been identified as the priority partner in training, it is expected that the other Advisory Bodies will provide input and support for capacity-building activities in the culture sector. The International Council on Monuments and Sites (ICOMOS), a non-governmental organization founded in 1965 with headquarters in Paris, promotes the application of theory, methodology, and scientific techniques to the conservation of heritage places. Its work is based on the principles of the Venice Charter (ICASHB 1964) and is carried out through its international executive committee, 95 national committees, 27 international scientific committees, and 11,088 individual members. The International Union for the Conservation of Nature (IUCN), an intergovernmental organization based in Gland, Switzerland, has a similar capacity-building role, but focuses on the natural heritage sector. Founded in 1948, it brings together national governments, NGOs, and scientists in a worldwide partnership. Its mission is to influence, encourage, and assist societies throughout the world to conserve the integrity and diversity of nature, and to ensure that any use of natural resources is equitable and ecologically sustainable.

Institutional Frameworks and Activities: The World Heritage Capacity Building Strategy

As mentioned, the World Heritage Capacity Building Strategy (UNESCO 2011) was adopted by the World Heritage Committee at its thirty-fifth session in 2011, replacing the Global Training Strategy of 2001. ICCROM had led the development of the strategy in collaboration with the World Heritage Centre, the IUCN and ICOMOS, and is currently running a program to achieve its objectives. In keeping with the spirit of the World Heritage Convention (1972), the strategy is also meant to serve both cultural and natural heritage sectors.

There were serious reasons emerging from the World Heritage inscription and management processes to motivate the World Heritage Committee and the Advisory Bodies to move from a training to a capacity-building approach. One reason was the critical situation being revealed by the state of conservation monitoring of World Heritage properties. By 2008, the state of conservation reports on sites from all parts of the world showed 122 (77 percent) had major infrastructure issues, and 102 (64 percent) had management issues. Such problems compelled the heritage sector to work more closely with other agencies beyond the boundaries of a heritage place and with a variety of different stakeholders, and bring in new learning areas suited to different audiences and their capacities. Another reason was that the World Heritage Committee had adopted the Budapest Declaration (UNESCO 2002), listing capacity-building as one of its four strategic priorities, the others being credibility, conservation, and communication (UNESCO 2014c). A fifth C – communities – was added at its thirty-first session in Christchurch in 2007, further strengthening the need to move beyond educating and training professionals to a broader program of capacity-building.

In principle, the strategy recognized three areas where capacity resides and their respective audiences: practitioners, institutions and communities, and networks.

The table below identifies these audiences and the related learning areas with which any education or training institution has to cope if it is operating within the World Heritage context.

An international program of activities based on the above principles aimed at strengthening the capacities of all audiences has been prepared and is now being implemented. The development of regional capacity-building strategies and associated programs based on the results of periodic reporting in each of UNESCO's regions is encouraged. These will be different for each region in order to respond to contexts and needs, although a basic methodology is suggested that can be adopted in each region. States Parties are also encouraged to develop national capacity-building strategies capturing the above principles and not limited to working with practitioners. This exercise will allow an individual State Party to better understand specific national and property-based capacity-building needs. The State Party should also investigate what national, regional, and international capacity-building institutions exist that can assist in the development of national and local capacities. This could be useful in enabling the State Party to identify exact human-resource needs in national institutions, not merely in heritage organizations but also in related institutions dealing with tourism, planning, and development. Such national strategies would also be best placed to ensure that there is capacity-building for other relevant stakeholders associated with World Heritage properties, or indeed properties of national and local significance, and in particular at the level of local communities. In certain instances, it may be useful for more than one country to work on a joint strategy.

Table 37.1 Different audiences and learning areas in the heritage sector.

Where capacities reside: target audiences for capacity-building	*Principal learning areas*
Practitioners (including individuals and groups who directly intervene in the conservation and management of World Heritage properties)	Implementation of the Convention (Tentative Lists, nomination, etc.) Conservation and management issues: • planning, implementation, and monitoring • technical and scientific issues • resource utilization and management
Institutions (including State Party heritage organizations, NGOs, the World Heritage Committee, Advisory Bodies, and other institutions that have a responsibility for the enabling environment for management and conservation)	Policy-making for learning areas mentioned above: • legislative issues • institutional frameworks/issues • (governance, decentralization) • financial issues • human resources • knowledge
Communities and Networks (including local communities living on or near properties as well as the larger networks that nurture them)	Reciprocal benefits and linking with sustainable development and communities; stewardship; communication and interpretation

Source: Wijesuriya, Thompson, and Young (2013: 51). © UNESCO, ICCROM, ICOMOS, IUCN.

Institutional Frameworks and Activities: UNESCO, Schools, Universities, and Category 2 Centres

Since the 1990s, UNESCO has made a concerted effort to achieve results at the school level through its World Heritage program (see Logan 2013a). UNESCO's relationship with schools should ideally lead to two complementary sets of activities: the encouragement of young people to join in UNESCO's campaign to safeguard heritage of Outstanding Universal Value; and safeguarding heritage that is of value specifically to young people themselves. Logan (2013a) has found, however, that so far most UNESCO initiatives have related to the former, including a series of international work camps held in various regions as part of a World Heritage Education Programme, and the development in 1998 of the useful World Heritage in Young Hands kit (UNESCO 2014e). Much less attention has been given to listening to what children and youth consider to be the important heritage they would like to see protected (Logan 2013a: 35).

UNESCO's connection with universities has a long and honorable history, dating back to the appointment of the former Oxford scholar, Julian Huxley, as it first director in 1946. As a member of the UNESCO Preparatory Commission, Huxley was highly influential in setting the goals and philosophy of the new global organization (see Huxley 1946). The university connection continued with the regular commissioning of scholars such as Claude Lévi-Strauss to write key reports (Lévi-Strauss 1952; see also Stoczkowski 2008). Nevertheless, despite the fact that the World Heritage Convention (1972) calls on States Parties to "foster the establishment or development of national or regional centers for training in the protection, conservation and presentation of the [*sic*] cultural and natural heritage and to encourage scientific research in this field,"[1] UNESCO was slow in achieving concrete results at the national level. Being an intergovernmental organization, UNESCO treads carefully, working through persuasion rather than directly interfering in the affairs of its sovereign Member States, and none of those that are States Parties to the World Heritage Convention, with the exception of Japan, appeared to have moved to create a national or regional center for heritage education by the turn of the century.

One way UNESCO has sought to influence universities is through the creation of networks. In 1991, UNESCO's General Conference decided to set up a global network with two interlinking components: the UNITWIN program, under which universities agreed to collaborate, usually across the North/South divide; and the appointment of UNESCO chairs (UNESCO 2014d). The aim of both components is to facilitate institutional capacity-building and knowledge and skills transfer through training, research, information sharing, and outreach activities in UNESCO's major program areas of education, the natural sciences, the social and human sciences, culture, and communication and information. There were 660 UNESCO chairs in October 2014 (UNESCO 2014d); of these, 23 were designated to the field of cultural heritage, although several of the earlier ones created in the 1990s appear now to be defunct. There are no chairs in the natural sciences focusing on natural heritage.

Apart from a tenth anniversary meeting held at UNESCO Paris headquarters in November 2002, there has been little linkage between the various UNITWIN programs or the UNESCO chairs in heritage. A number of other networks have tried to fill this gap, but have also been less successful than hoped. The Forum UNESCO: University and Heritage (FUUH) network was established by UNESCO in 1995, initially under the management of the Valencia Polytechnic University in Spain, but now jointly managed by that university and the World Heritage Centre. The FUUH mission is broad, and emphasizes supporting UNESCO's initiatives in favor of cultural and natural heritage protection. The FUUH is an informal network whose main collaborative activity has been a series of international conferences, initially held annually and later biennially, in universities across the world (UNESCO 2013). The main FUUH activity currently seems to be the regular publication of an electronic newsletter disseminated among member universities and other interested parties.

Other networks have been established at a regional level. For instance, in 2001, ICCROM joined forces with UNESCO's Office of the Regional Advisor for Culture in Asia and the Pacific, based in Bangkok, to form the Asian Academy of Heritage Management. This is a network of institutions, mostly universities in the Asia-Pacific region, that offer professional training in the field of cultural heritage management (AAHM 2014). Such training is seen to be critically important, given the region's context of rapid environmental degradation, urban infrastructure development, and mass tourism. Since 2008, the network has become more self-governing, and its principal activity is a major regional conference held every 18 months or two years

Re-emphasizing Skills Training: the Category 2 Centres

There has been a move over the last ten years to give greater emphasis to skills training that is a result of wider problems in the World Heritage system, especially the proliferation of inscribed places with severe management and sustainability issues. There are now 45 properties on the List of World Heritage in Danger, and 150 were subject to close scrutiny in 2014 by the World Heritage Committee (UNESCO 2014a, 2014b). The World Heritage Committee's attempt to contain the problem through its state of conservation and periodic reporting mechanisms is clearly not sufficient, and there is a sense among some in UNESCO's Cultural Sector, as well as in some national chapters of ICOMOS, that there is a need for training more focused on meeting the specific demands of World Heritage sites. The implication is that existing university programs are not providing the necessary skills, and that there is no alternative source of training.

UNESCO, the World Heritage Committee and its Secretariat, the World Heritage Centre, have therefore recently encouraged the development of a new set of Category 2 Centres (C2Cs) in universities and other institutions that will provide training and capacity-building activities related specifically to World Heritage. These centers, while not legally part of UNESCO, are associated with it by way of formal arrangements approved by UNESCO's General Conference. There are now six such centers focusing on World Heritage. Many States Parties are keen to establish a C2C, which is in line with their responsibilities under the World Heritage Convention (1972), but they must guarantee funding, possess staff with sufficient experience, and, perhaps most important, have a genuine commitment to making the C2C function effectively.

University Responses

Initially, education and training providers responded to the global conservation effort spearheaded by UNESCO by creating a series of specialist courses in archaeology and architecture dealing with the technical conservation of monuments, and others focusing on science- and laboratory-based materials conservation, museology, and public history (Logan 2010). During the 1980s and 1990s, other universities moved into the heritage field, and courses were developed that, in relation to heritage places, shifted from technical restoration to focus on broader planning and management issues, often connected to economic development through tourism. The increasingly holistic conception of heritage within the last 20 years has led to a new batch of multidisciplinary "heritage studies" courses drawing together at least heritage places and museum studies, and beginning to focus on intangible heritage and traditional knowledge systems. Indeed, in some countries, such as the United Kingdom, Australia, and, more recently, the United States, heritage studies has emerged as a new interdisciplinary area in its own right, with a strong emphasis on the interconnections between philosophy, theory, and practice. Some universities have chosen to specialize in the study of World Heritage issues, and seven such courses are currently listed on the UNESCO web site (UNESCO n.d.a). Other universities include World Heritage alongside studies that are more focused on heritage at the national and local levels.

The "new heritage studies" takes the position that heritage is not merely a reflection of the world's rich and creative diversity, but is rather the very foundation of the cultural identity of people, and that as a consequence its maintenance is a basic human right (Logan 2013b: 42). It follows that heritage conservation can no longer be seen merely as a technical issue, but one which needs to be seen in an ethical context. This shift is also reflected in teaching and research in a number of university courses, where heritage is understood as being produced through sociopolitical processes reflecting society's power structures. The close link between heritage and identity is recognized, as is the link between official heritage definitions and nation-building, and the misuse of "heritage" in some countries to reinforce the power of political elites and dominant ethnic groups. This means that while there remains a very clear need to produce graduates with practical architectural and archeological conservation expertise, and heritage planning and interpretation skills as required for the more effective management of heritage assets, the social sciences can add skills for analyzing social, political, and economic contexts, and for negotiating heritage conservation outcomes in situations where the identification, evaluation, and interpretation of heritage items is contested between various groups within a community. When talking of World Heritage, this means that conservation should be seen as a tool for attaining the ethical mission set by UNESCO in its Constitution (UNESCO 1945) and other statements.

Following the publication of Laurajane Smith's *Uses of Heritage* (2006), the new heritage studies has taken a more aggressive approach in some universities. Referred to as "critical heritage studies," this approach is useful in highlighting the need for academics and practitioners to question what Smith calls the Authorised Heritage Discourse, and to see heritage as a verb rather than a noun, a process rather than a thing. The movement appears to be picking up momentum, and the global Association of Critical Heritage Studies has been established, with a biennial conference program inaugurated in June 2012 at the University of Gothenburg, Sweden.

Challenges for the Future

The new heritage discourse must capture indispensable areas of Western knowledge, but also other knowledge areas that have been generated in order to address the gaps, particularly in the case of non-Western and more context-dependent approaches to cultural heritage. With regard to indigenous communities, and for that matter all minority groups, especially where they are marginalized within the wider national society, a key challenge for educators, trainers, and capacity-builders is to provide skills that will help bridge communication barriers. It is important to note that many scholars in the Western world seem uncomfortable in acknowledging the "context" of cultural heritage activities, the slow adoption of the values-based approach to conservation and management being perhaps the most concrete expression of this difficulty. This has to change, and the diversity of views and approaches to heritage today need to be presented to different audiences and in a variety of learning environments. This "new" heritage, with its much broader compass, also brings a wide variety of learning areas requiring different skills and methods, as well as approaches for their application, to ensure knowledge acquisition by different audiences.

While reference is conventionally made now to the conservation of cultural heritage as being a multidisciplinary activity requiring a holistic approach, both in management and education, in reality many obstacles make this difficult to achieve. It is regrettable that the definition and management of heritage is divided between UNESCO conventions and programs, as well as in administrative arrangements at the global level and, commonly, at the national level too. Faculty divisions within universities continue to make it difficult to educate students across the range of disciplines needed to practice heritage conservation in a more holistic way, even to deal with natural and cultural values under the World Heritage Convention (1972), let alone working with intangible values, cultural expressions, and heritage representation in museums, or to deal with growing concerns about heritage sustainability, environmental degradation, and the potential impacts of climate change. Innovative course-credit arrangements and collaborative programs between faculties and universities need to be found to overcome these obstacles.

It is quite clear that the growth of the World Heritage system requires new responses, probably including a shift away from serving the political and economic interests of States Parties and towards the original UNESCO mission (Logan 2012: 125–27; Meskell 2013). It is perhaps unfortunate, however, that World Heritage education and training seems to be moving towards a dual system comprising C2Cs and the rest, the former receiving UNESCO patronage and the latter receiving less or no support. This can be seen as running against the advice of the independent external evaluation of UNESCO when it recommended five strategic directions, the fifth being to develop a partnership strategy that included renewing, not scaling down, links with and between institutes, programs, universities, and centers of excellence that can improve UNESCO's performance (UNESCO 2010: 11). The majority of the strongest universities in the heritage field will be outside the "Category 2 family" that is being created. There is a concern that the C2Cs will be perceived as having UNESCO's imprimatur, but may not attain the same standards of teaching and research. This has led to a sense of dismay in some universities.

This is a risky business. It is possible that critical heritage studies will expand in the non-C2C universities, and possibly assume an even more questioning stance towards UNESCO and its World Heritage program than it has to this point. Other institutions may also be affected. The Asian Academy of Heritage Management, for example, will no longer be in line with UNESCO's approach. ICCROM has already begun adjusting. The UNESCO chairs in the cultural heritage field are likely to be brought under the direct control of the World Heritage Centre, if they survive at all. In a carefully managed education system, both of these approaches should coexist so that students and researchers are able to ground theory in an understanding of practice. One of the more hopeful features of the World Heritage Strategy for Capacity Building (UNESCO 2011) is that a key component is working collaboratively with other institutions such as universities and C2Cs.

Meanwhile, we need to remind ourselves that not all efforts need to be directed towards World Heritage; it is very important not to neglect the needs of nationally and locally significant heritage, or, indeed, intangible heritage as well as heritage places and artifact collections in museums and galleries. The overall aim of heritage conservation is, as the World Heritage Convention (1972) so clearly puts it, "to give the cultural and natural heritage a function in the life of the community."[2] This applies to heritage at all levels, and represents the greatest challenge for educators, trainers, and capacity-builders as we move through the twenty-first century.

Notes

1 World Heritage Convention (1972), art. 5.
2 World Heritage Convention (1972), art. 5.

References

Legislation

Convention Concerning the Protection of the World Cultural and Natural Heritage (World Heritage Convention) (UNESCO, 1972). Available at: http://whc.unesco.org/archive/convention-en.pdf (accessed March 19, 2015).

Convention for the Safeguarding of the Intangible Cultural Heritage (Intangible Heritage Convention)(UNESCO,2003).Availableat:http://unesdoc.unesco.org/images/0013/001325/132540e.pdf (accessed March 19, 2015).

Other Works

AAHM (Asian Academy of Heritage Management) (2014) About AAHM. Available at: http://asian-academy.org/about-aahm/ (accessed October 1, 2014).

Anyon, R. (1991) Protecting the Past, Protecting the Present: Cultural Resources and American Indians. In G.S. Smith and J.E. Ehrenhard (eds), *Protecting the Past*. Boca Raton, FL: CRC Press, pp. 215–222.

Askew, M., and Logan, M. (1994) *Cultural Identity and Urban Change in Southeast Asia: Interpretative Essays*. Geelong: Deakin University Press.

Australia ICOMOS (2013) Charter for Places of Cultural Significance (Burra Charter), revised version. Available at: http://australia.icomos.org/wp-content/uploads/The-Burra-Charter-2013-Adopted-31.10.2013.pdf (accessed June 29, 2014).

De Merode, E., Smeets, R., and Westrik, C. (eds) (2004) *Linking Universal and Local Values: Managing a Sustainable Future for World Heritage*. World Heritage Papers 13. Paris: UNESCO World Heritage Centre. Available at: http://whc.unesco.org/documents/publi_wh_papers_13_en.pdf (accessed February 14, 2015).

Huxley, J. (1946) *UNESCO and its Purpose and its Philosophy*. London: Frederick Printing Co.

ICASHB (International Congress of Architects and Specialists of Historic Buildings) (1964) International Charter for the Conservation and Restoration of Monuments and Sites (Venice Charter). Available at: http://www.icomos.org/charters/venice_e.pdf (accessed March 9, 2015).

ICCROM (2000) A Global Training Strategy for Cultural Heritage to Improve Implementation of the World Heritage Convention. Rome: ICCROM. Available at: http://cif.icomos.org/pdf_docs/Documents%20on%20line/ICCROM%20Global%20Training%20Strategy%202000.pdf (accessed September 9, 2014).

ICCROM (2013) Promoting People Centred Approach to Conservation – Living Heritage. Available at: http://www.iccrom.org/priority-areas/living-heritage/ (accessed October 2, 2014).

ICOMOS (1994) Nara Document on Authenticity. Available at: https://www.google.com.au/?gws_rd=ssl#q=Nara+Document+on+authenticity (accessed February 14, 2015).

Langfield, M., Logan, W., and Nic Craith, M. (eds) (2010) *Cultural Diversity, Heritage and Human Rights: Intersections in Theory and Practice.* London: Routledge.

Lévi-Strauss, C. (1952) *Race and History.* Paris: UNESCO.

Logan, W. (2004) Voices from the Periphery: The Burra Charter in Context. *Historic Environment*, 18 (1), 2–8.

Logan, W. (2010) Development of World Heritage Studies in University Education. In D. Offenhausser, W.C. Zimmerli, and M.-T. Albert (eds), *World Heritage and Cultural Diversity.* Frankfurt am Main/Cottbus: IKO Verlag für Interkulturelle Kommunikation/Brandenburg Technical University, pp. 38–43.

Logan, W. (2012) States, Governance and the Politics of Culture: World Heritage in Asia. In P. Daly and T. Winter (eds), *The Routledge Handbook of Heritage in Asia.* London: Routledge, pp. 113–128.

Logan, W. (2013a) Patrimonito Leads the Way: UNESCO and the Cultural Heritage of Children. In K. Darian-Smith and C. Pascoe (eds), *Children, Childhood and Cultural Heritage.* London: Routledge, pp. 21–39.

Logan, W. (2013b) Learning to Engage with Human Rights in Heritage Education. In M.-T. Albert, R. Bernecker, and B. Rudolff (eds), *Understanding Heritage: Perspectives in Heritage Studies.* Frankfurt am Main: IKO Verlag für Interkulturelle Kommunikation, pp. 35–48.

Logan, W. (2013c) Australia, Indigenous Peoples and World Heritage from Kakadu to Cape York: State Party Behaviour under the World Heritage Convention. *Journal of Social Archaeology*, 13 (2), 153–176.

Matsuura, K. (1999) Address by Mr Koïchiro Matsuura, Director-General of the United Nations Educational, Scientific and Cultural Organization (UNESCO) at the Opening of the Twenty-third session of the World Heritage Committee, Marrakech (Morocco), 29 November 1999. Available at: http://unesdoc.unesco.org/images/0011/001182/118260e.pdf (accessed September 29, 2014).

Matunga, H. (1994) Wahi Tapu: Maori Sacred Sites. In D.L. Carmichael, J. Hubert, B. Reeves, *et al.* (eds), *Sacred Sites, Sacred Places.* London: Routledge, pp. 217–226.

Meskell, L. (2013) UNESCO's World Heritage Convention at 40: Challenging the Economic and Political Order of International Heritage Conservation. *Current Anthropology*, 54 (4), 483–494.

Shaheed, F (2011) Report of the Independent Expert in the Field of Cultural Rights, Farida Shaheed. Human Rights Council Seventeenth Session Agenda Item 3. UNHRC document A/HRC/17/38. Available at: http://www.unesco.org/new/fileadmin/MULTIMEDIA/HQ/CLT/images/Report%20of%20Farida%20Shaheed.pdf (accessed February 14, 2015).

Silverman, H., and Fairchild, D.R. (eds) (2007) *Cultural Heritage and Human Rights.* New York: Springer.

Smith, L. (2006) *Uses of Heritage.* London: Routledge.

Stoczkowski, W. (2008) Claude Lévi-Strauss and UNESCO. *UNESCO Courier*, 5 (rev. edn.), 5–9.

Stovel, H. (1995) Cultural Diversity and Ethics of Conservation. In A. Ahoniemi (ed.), *Conservation Training: Needs and Ethics*. Helsinki: ICOMOS Finish National Committee, pp. 153–160,

Sullivan, S., Hall, N., and Greer, S. (2008) Learning to Walk Together and Work Together: Providing a Formative Teaching Experience for Indigenous and Non-Indigenous Heritage Managers. In F.P. McManamon, A. Stout, and J.A. Barnes (eds), *Managing Archaeological Resources: Global Context, National Programs, Local Actions*. Walnut Creek, CA: Left Coast Press, pp. 35–54.

UNDP (2006) UNDP and Capacity Building. Available at: www.jposc.org/documents/workshop_georgia_UNDP_and_CD.ppt (accessed September 30, 2014).

UNESCO (1945) Constitution of the United Nations Educational, Scientific and Cultural Organization. Available at: http://unesdoc.unesco.org/images/0022/002269/226924e.pdf#page=6 (accessed March 19, 2015).

UNESCO (2002) Budapest Declaration on World Heritage. Document WHC-02/CONF202.9. Available at: http://whc.unesco.org/en/decisions/1217/ (accessed February 14, 2015).

UNESCO (2010) Report on the Independent External Evaluation of UNESCO. Executive Board report. Document 185 EX/18 Add. Available at: http://unesdoc.unesco.org/images/0018/001891/189160e.pdf#page=16 (accessed October 4, 2014).

UNESCO (2011) World Heritage Strategy for Capacity Building. Document WHC-11/35.COM/9B. Available at: http://whc.unesco.org/archive/2011/whc11-35com-9Be.pdf (accessed August 27, 2014).

UNESCO (2013) Forum UNESCO: University and Heritage. Available at: http://www.forumunescochair.upv.es/eng/catedra_unesco_upv/seminarios.html (accessed October 1, 2014).

UNESCO (2014a) List of World Heritage in Danger. Available at: http://whc.unesco.org/en/danger/ (accessed September 30, 2014).

UNESCO (2014b) State of Conservation (SOC). Available at: http://whc.unesco.org/pg.cfm?cid=171&l=en&&action=list&soc_start=2014&soc_end=2014&&maxrows=150 (accessed September 30, 2014).

UNESCO (2014c) Partnerships. Available at: http://whc.unesco.org/en/partnerships (accessed September 30, 2014).

UNESCO (2014d) UNITWIN/UNESCO Chairs Program. Available at: http://www.unesco.org/new/fileadmin/MULTIMEDIA/HQ/ED/pdf/listchairs3102014.pdf (accessed October 3, 2014).

UNESCO (2014e) The Kit – World Heritage in Young Hands. Available at: http://whc.unesco.org/en/educationkit/ (accessed September 29, 2014).

UNESCO (n.d.a) World Heritage Convention: Frequently Asked Questions. Available at: http://whc.unesco.org/en/108#education (accessed September 30, 2014).

Wijesuriya, G. (2007) Conserving Living Taonga: The Concept of Continuity. In D. Sully (ed.), *Decolonising Conservation-Caring for Maori Meeting Houses outside New Zealand*. Walnut Creek, CA: Left Coast Press, pp. 59–69.

Wijesuriya, G. (2010) Conservation in Context. In M.S. Falser, W. Lipp, and A. Tomaszewski (eds), *Proceedings of the International Conference on Conservation and Preservation: Interaction between Theory and Practice*. Florence: Edizioni Polistampa, pp. 233–248.

Wijesuriya, G. (n.d.) Living Heritage. In C. Anthomarci and A. Heritage (eds), *Sharing Conservation Decisions*: Rome: ICCROM, forthcoming.

Wijesuriya, G., Thompson, J., and Young, C. (eds) (2013) *Managing Cultural World Heritage*. World Heritage Resource Manual Series. Paris UNESCO. Available at: http://whc.unesco.org/en/managing-cultural-world-heritage/ (accessed October 4, 2014).

Index

A Companion to Heritage Studies, First Edition. Edited by William Logan, Máiréad Nic Craith, and Ullrich Kockel.
© 2016 John Wiley & Sons, Inc. Published 2016 by John Wiley & Sons, Inc.